BESTSELLING BOOK SERIES

Money Manag...
All-in-One For C...
For Dumm...

MW00979014

Tips for Building Your RRSP over Time

✔ **Remember the basic risk/reward rule.** A comfortable increase in your risk level can generate a substantial gain in rewards. Determine your personal risk level, obtain professional advice, then make your decision.

✔ **Diversify, diversify, diversify.** Mix your RRSP investment between bonds (for security) and equity-based mutual funds (for long-term growth). Then diversify within each group.

✔ **Maximize foreign content.** Canada Customs and Revenue Agency's limit is 30 percent of book value, but there are ways to exceed it legally.

✔ **Consider a spousal RRSP.** If you earn substantially more than your spouse, and are likely to build a larger retirement fund, a spousal RRSP balances assets and growth, helps to produce equal retirement incomes, and reduces income-tax levels.

✔ **Set a target for your retirement needs.** Don't underestimate the income you will need to pursue an active, rewarding retirement.

Tips for Reducing Taxes for Your Estate

✔ Leave capital property that has gone up a lot in value to your spouse.

✔ Name your spouse as beneficiary of your RRSPs and RRIFs.

✔ Leave your children or grandchildren cash or property that has not gone up a lot in value.

✔ Use the principal residence exemption to leave your vacation property to your children without triggering a capital gain.

✔ Give away capital property while you're still alive if you have a capital loss to offset any capital gain.

✔ Make sure your will gives your executor power to use your unused RRSP contributions to make a contribution to your spouse's RRSP.

✔ Give your executor enough information to make use of any unused capital losses when you die.

Tips for Small Business Success

✔ **Decide whether small business is right for you.** Before you dash out and start up your own business, stop and think whether you have the right stuff to be an entrepreneur. If you don't, it's better to realize that *before* you sink a lot of time, effort, and money into a business start-up.

✔ **Don't be a loner.** Starting up a business takes a lot of work, so get professional help — at the very least you'll need a lawyer, an accountant, and an insurance agent or broker.

✔ **Pick your product and market carefully.** Do pre-start-up customer research to identify a target market for your product or service, to estimate the size of the market, and to make sure you have the right to use all of your brilliant ideas.

✔ **Budget for your business's first year.** Calculate carefully how much money you'll need to set up your business and run it for the first year. Then think about where you'll get the money you need. You have to be realistic about how much money you'll be able to borrow.

For Dummies: Bestselling Book Series for Beginners

Money Management All-in-One For Canadian For Dummies®

Eight Essential Keys to Successful Mutual Fund Investing

1. The only investments that are suitable for most of your long-term savings are high-quality global stocks and high-quality bonds from stable governments.

2. Pretty well everything that's worth investing in is also easy to explain and understand.

3. The most important things to look for in a mutual fund are low and easy-to-understand annual expenses, top-quality holdings, and a broad mix of investments.

4. The more bells and whistles attached to the fund, or the fancier the concept, the higher the expenses. And that reduces your return.

5. Star fund managers almost invariably go into a slump and either drop back into the pack or even become underperformers.

6. Buy a bond fund.

7. When you're buying funds, ask to see a sample account statement. If you can't understand it, or if they don't have one to show you, then shop elsewhere.

8. Own index funds that mindlessly track the Canadian, U.S., and international stock markets, plus a couple of regular Canadian and global equity funds.

Investing Online: Valuable Canadian Money Management Web Sites

- Canada Savings Bonds — Information about Canada Savings Bonds and online management of existing savings bond accounts: www.cis-pec.gc.ca

- *Canadian MoneySaver* — personal finance advice (subscription-based): www.canadianmoneysaver.ca

- Equifax — researching your credit history: www.equifax.ca

- Globefund.com — Mutual fund research site produced by *The Globe and Mail*: www.globefund.com

- Globeinvestor.com — Investment fund research site produced by *The Globe and Mail*: www.globeinvestor.com

- Industry Canada — Canadian credit card rates (in "Consumer Information" section): www.strategis.ic.gc.ca

- Morningstar Canada — Canadian investment fund research site: www.morningstar.ca

- Webfin.com — Canadian investing and personal finance information resource (mostly free): www.webfin.com

Copyright © 2003 John Wiley & Sons Canada, Ltd. All rights reserved.
Cheat Sheet $2.99 value. Item 3360-2.
For more information about John Wiley & Sons Canada, Ltd. call 1-800-567-4797

For Dummies: Bestselling Book Series for Beginners

Money Management

ALL-IN-ONE

For Canadians

FOR

DUMMIES®

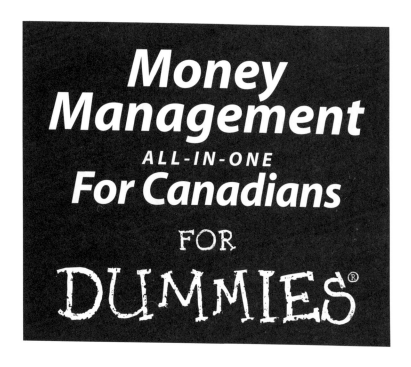

Money Management

ALL-IN-ONE

For Canadians

FOR

DUMMIES®

by Andrew Bell, Andrew Dagys, CMA, Tony Ioannou
with Moira Bayne and Wendy Yano, Margaret Kerr,
JoAnn Kurtz, John Lawrence Reynolds

John Wiley & Sons Canada, Ltd

Money Management All-in-One For Canadians For Dummies®

Published by
John Wiley & Sons Canada, Ltd
22 Worcester Road
Etobicoke, ON M9W 1L1
www.wiley.ca

National Library of Canada Cataloguing in Publication

Money Management All-in-One For Canadians For Dummies / Andrew Bell ...[et al.].

Includes index.

ISBN 0-470-83360-2

1. Finance, Personal. I. Bell, Andrew, 1960-

HG179.M653 2003   332.024   C2003-905468-3

Printed in Canada

1 2 3 4 5 TRI 07 06 05 04 03

Distributed in Canada by John Wiley & Sons Canada, Ltd.

For general information on John Wiley & Sons Canada, Ltd., including all books published by Wiley Publishing, Inc., please call our warehouse, Tel 1-800-567-4797. For reseller information, including discounts and premium sales, please call our sales department, Tel 416-646-7992. For press review copies, author interviews, or other publicity information, please contact our marketing department, Tel: 416-646-4584, Fax 416-236-4448.

For authorization to photocopy items for corporate, personal, or educational use, please contact Cancopy, The Canadian Copyright Licensing Agency, One Yonge Street, Suite 1900, Toronto, ON, M5E 1E5 Tel 416-868-1620 Fax 416-868-1621; www.cancopy.com.

About the Authors

Andrew Dagys is a bestselling author who has written and co-authored several books, *including Investing Online For Canadian For Dummie*s (first and second editions), *The Internet For Canadians For Dummies Starter Kit* (first and second editions), and T*he Financial Planner for 50+*. Andrew contributes columns to *Forever Young, Canadian Living* magazine, and other publications. He has appeared on Canada AM and several CBC broadcasts to offer his opinions on the Canadian and world investment landscape.

An avid investor, Andrew uses the Internet to advantage to identify compelling investment opportunities. His business, The Treetop Group, has helped match some of those opportunities with the financial needs of Canadian clients for years. Andrew also enjoys speaking to business and general audiences on the latest investment trends, and new developments in computer technology that empower Canadians to help meet their personal objectives. He lives in Toronto with his wife, Dawn-Ava, and three children — Brendan, Megan, and Jordan.

Andrew looks forward to your comments, and can be reached at aj-dagys@rogers.com.

Andrew Bell, author of *Mutual Funds For Canadians For Dummies*, was an investment reporter and editor with the *Globe and Mail* for 12 years. He joined Report on Business Television as a reporter in 2001. Bell, an import from Dublin, Ireland, was for 10 years the main compiler of Stars & Dogs in Saturday's *Globe*. The roundup of hot and damp stocks and mutual funds was an invaluable therapeutic aid in relieving his own myriad jealousies, regrets, and resentments. He has also taken to the stage, where he practises a demanding "method" that involves getting the audience and other performers as off balance and upset as possible. He lives in an unfinished and perhaps unfinishable construction project in Cabbagetown, Toronto, with his wife, two children, and very rare brown-and-black tabby cat.

Tony Ioannou, co-author of *Buying and Selling a Home For Canadians For Dummies*, is currently a senior associate with Dexter Associates Realty, and has been interviewed many times in the Vancouver media about the state of the Vancouver real estate market. Tony obtained his real estate licence in 1984, and has consistently been a top producing salesperson with NRS Block Bros., and with Dexter Associates Realty since 1990. In 1990 he obtained his agents (brokers) licence, but continues to enjoy working as a residential real estate sales person primarily on the West Side of Vancouver. He has also worked as a division director for the Real Estate Board of Greater Vancouver. Tony was born and raised in Sydney, Australia, and immigrated with his family to Vancouver in 1973. He completed high school in Vancouver and obtained a Bachelor of Arts degree in Urban Geography from the University of British Columbia. He has lived in Vancouver's Kitsilano neighbourhood for the past 20 years and is an avid mountain biker and golfer.

Moira Bayne, co-author of *Buying and Selling a Home For Canadians For Dummies*, is a writer and editor based in Toronto. She writes on topics as diverse as investing and health care, gardening and home decorating. A passionate do-it-yourselfer, she is committed to convincing other people that they can too.

Wendy Yano, co-author of *Buying and Selling a Home For Canadians For Dummies*, is also a writer and editor, has worked on books ranging from the Lemon-Aid car guides to The Canadian Encyclopedia. Wendy recently bought her first home in Toronto's Riverdale area and obsesses over home renovations and maintenance.

Margaret Kerr and JoAnn Kurtz, co-authors of *Canadian Small Business Kit For Dummies* and *Wills and Estates For Canadians For Dummies Planning Kit*, are lawyers, and they are also both entrepreneurs — and they have the bumps, bruises, and scars to prove it. Occasionally, they find they have a minute of free time here and there, and that's how they came to be the authors of, among other books, *Buying, Owning and Selling a Home in Canada* (now in its second edition); *Canadian Tort Law in a Nutshell* (with Laurence Olivo); and *Make It Legal: What Every Canadian Entrepreneur Needs to Know About the Law.*

John Lawrence Reynolds, author of *RRSPs and RRIFs For Dummies*, is a graduate of McMaster University (English & Psychology) and holds Certified Advertising Agency Practitioner recognition from the Institute of Canadian Advertising. In the mid 1970s, he walked away from an executive position with a major advertising agency to pursue a career in film directing, writing, and photography. Soon he was balancing business and promotional writing with travel assignments—he has sailed the Nile, Rhine, and Amazon rivers, dived off Australia's Great Barrier Reef, hiked through rice paddies in Bali, and stalked perfect dim sum in Hong Kong. John has written and published ten books, including five mystery books—two of them Arthur Ellis award winners for Best Mystery Novel by a Canadian—as well as books on ballroom dancing, gardening, and true crime. His professional writing assignments have included RRSP and pension-related material for a number of leading companies. He has also been a loyal RRSP contributor and investor for over 25 years. John lives in Burlington, Ontario with his wife Judy and two self-indulgent cats.

Publisher's Acknowledgments

We're proud of this book; please send us your comments at canadapt@wiley.com. Some of the people who helped bring this book to market include the following:

Acquisitions and Editorial

Editor: Melanie Rutledge

Substantive and Copy Editor:
Michael Kelly

New Business Development Manager:
Christiane Coté

Production

Publishing Services Director:
Karen Bryan

Project Manager: Elizabeth McCurdy

Project Coordinator: Robert Hickey

Layout and Graphics: Pat Loi

Proofreader: Michael Kelly

Indexer: Belle Wong

John Wiley & Sons Canada, Ltd.

Bill Zerter, Chief Operating Officer

Robert Harris, Publisher, Professional and Trade Division

Publishing and Editorial for Consumer Dummies

Diane Graves Steele, Vice President and Publisher, Consumer Dummies

Joyce Pepple, Acquisitions Director, Consumer Dummies

Kristin A. Cocks, Product Development Director, Consumer Dummies

Michael Spring, Vice President and Publisher, Travel

Suzanne Jannetta, Editorial Director, Travel

Publishing for Technology Dummies

Andy Cummings, Acquisitions Director

Composition Services

Gerry Fahey, Executive Director of Production Serviceds

Debbie Stailey, Director of Composition Services

Contents at a Glance

Table of Contents

Introduction

・・

*W*hen planning for your financial future, you may sometimes feel as if you're navigating a field that's plugged with all sorts of roadblocks and landmines and barbed-wire fences and any number of impediments, all designed to keep you from finding information that you can apply to your specific needs. This book recognizes the challenges that you face in figuring out how your home-buying decision relates to your investment choices, which relates to your estate planning scenarios, which may even relate to a small business opportunity. With *Money Management All-in-One For Canadians For Dummies,* you'll find much of what you're looking for to help you get out of that field of impediments and get into a secure and rewarding financial bunker.

About This Book

Like all *For Dummies* books, *Money Management All-in-One For Canadians For Dummies* is a reference — the kind of book that's most useful if you keep it by your side at all times, especially when making your most important money management and investment decisions. (Though if you make all your most important decisions during a time of contemplation in your shower, you may want to avoid that keep-it-by-your-side bit.)

If you're reading this Introduction at your neighbourhood bookstore — trying to decide whether or not to purchase this book — look around you at the dozens (or hundreds or even thousands, if you're at Chapters) of money management books that you can choose from. With all those options, can one book possibly promise *all* the information you need about money management and investing? In a word, no. But this book does its best to give you *all* the information you need to get you on your way to a successful and rewarding financial future.

Conventions Used in This Book

Because some information in this book really deserves to stand out, you'll find certain conventions that apply to the following situations:

- ✔ Web site addresses appear in `this font`.

- ✔ Terms and phrases that may be unfamiliar to you appear in *italics*. You can then find an appropriate definition of that term or phrase nearby.

- ✔ **Bolded** words or phrases highlight the action parts of numbered steps or keywords in bulleted lists.

- ✔ The occasional sidebar (a shaded grey box) has information that's interesting to know but not necessarily critical to your understanding of a particular money management topic.

Throughout the book, you'll find cross-references to other sections that have information that adds to or supplements the content you're perusing. If that cross-reference directs you to a section in the same Book, you'll read something like, "Check out Chapter 4 for more information." If the cross-reference is to a different Book, look for something like, "Chapter 2 in Book V has more about this topic."

How to Use This Book

Because all *For Dummies* books are designed to be used as references, you never *need* to read one from cover to cover, though you're certainly welcome to do so if inclined. Here are a few suggestions as to how you may choose to read this book:

- ✔ **Go ahead and read it from page one to the index.** Even though it's designed as a reference, that doesn't mean that it hasn't been organized in a logical manner. You'll find basic money management material toward the beginning of the book, with your more advanced information toward the end of the book.

- ✔ **Make copious use of this book's table of contents and index.** Look up the topic you're interested in, find and read the information you need, and then put down the book and put your new-found knowledge to work. As an added bonus, the opening page of each Book here has a brief table of contents for that Book only — look for the page with the cartoon on it.

- ✔ **Use the book as a paperweight to hold all your investment documents in place on a blustery day.** You won't get much money-management advice out of this use, but hopefully, you'll have already made good use of the book in that way.

Foolish Assumptions

The only real assumption made about you — the reader — is that this book makes no assumptions about you. You may be just getting out of school and ready to take on a career, or you may be looking for ways to minimize the hidden costs of managing your estate. No matter your financial acuity, you're sure to find something in this book that will be helpful to you. Of course, some Books are more elementary than others, but even if you're an already savvy investor, you may surprise yourself and find something valuable in Chapter 1 of Book I.

How This Book Is Organized

This book has eight Books devoted to a specific money-management-related topic. You'll find some basic information and advice in just about every Book, but the following outlines what you'll find in each distinct Book:

Book I: Taking Stock of Your Financial Situation

Before trying to take on too much money management advice, you first need to assess your existing financial state. Are you a saver or a spender? What is your money personality? Do you have a good idea about what you *need* versus what you *want?* This Book helps you understand what kind of financial state of affairs you're in today.

Book II: Money Management Basics

The ABCs of money management really begin with the BCDs: budgeting, credit, and debt. If you can get a grasp on these fundamentals, you're off to a good start in getting your financial home in order. This Book helps you make sense of these concerns, all with a wary eye (or two) on how they impact your relationship with the taxman.

Book III: Home Sweet, Home Free

Buying your home may be the single-most critical financial decision you make. No matter how you slice it, purchasing a home takes a great deal of money and even more financial planning. This Book offers advice on what you need to know to help you make the best home-buying decisions.

Book IV: Investment Fundamentals

This Book starts you on the road to developing your own investing strategies. After helping you figure out what investment goals and tactics are most comfortable (and rewarding) to you, this Book gives an overview of the types of investments that are available to you and how to develop an effective diversification strategy around them.

Book V: Making Your Investments Work for You

Whether you've reviewed Book IV to plan your investment strategy or you're comfortable enough with your investment goals that you don't need Book IV, Book V is the place to look for tips and tricks for selecting, buying, and monitoring your investments. This Book helps you know where to look for the best mutual funds, stocks, and bonds, as well as how to keep track of their performance — online and off.

Book VI: Somewhere over the Rainbow: Retirement Planning

Technically another Book for developing your investment strategies, this Book focuses on your post-career needs, RRSP-style. And when you're ready to start making RRSP investment decisions, take advantage of the easy-to-use RRSP planner at the end of this Book.

Book VII: Estate Planning

You *do* have an estate. It may not compare in size and stature to those of Canada's wealthiest, but you *do* have an estate, and you need to make sure you earmark its fruits properly for those whom you love the most. This Book helps you develop an estate strategy that will save your loved ones hassle and tax money after you've gone on to your own great reward.

Book VIII: Taking Care of Business

Are you managing a small or mid-sized business in Canada? Or do you have lofty goals of opening the retail world's "next big thing" on the corner of your neighbourhood's busiest intersection? Or do you simply plan to start a little knitting business from your home, selling baby hats and grandma sweaters on eBay? This Book has the information you need to help you make your start-up business decisions, as well as how to manage your small business once you've, er, started up.

Icons Used in This Book

If you know your *For Dummies* books, you know your *For Dummies* icons, those little margin markers that alert you to particularly enlightening or helpful information. This book uses the following icons:

This icon highlights especially helpful advice that's likely to be right on target with your money management needs.

Stay alert when you spot this icon: The information that it showcases is offered to help you avoid particularly damaging money management decisions.

Don't worry if you're not too alert around this icon. The information you'll find next to it is sure to be interesting or even entertaining, but it's not likely to be essential or critical to your money management plans.

Every topic has little tidbits of information that are useful to keep in mind for any scenario. This icon helps you, er, remember them.

Yes, this book is a whopping 800-plus-pages long. But you won't find the answer to every question that you may have about your money management needs. This icon indicates some suggestions of where you may want to look for additional information.

Where to Go from Here

To your chequebook, your financial software, your calculator, or even your abacus. With this book (and those tools), you can start working on your money management goals immediately.

Book I
Taking Stock of Your Financial Situation

The 5th Wave   By Rich Tennant

"WE TOOK A GAMBLE AND INVESTED ALL OUR MONEY IN A RACE HORSE. THEN IT RAN AWAY."

In this book . . .

The opening section of any good book (or any bad book, for that matter) will probably give you an overview of the subject matter that the book covers. This book is slightly different. This opening Book gives you an overview of a topic with which you're probably pretty familiar: you. However, you may not feel as familiar as you want to be with your financial personality. This Book helps you find out what kind of money manager and investor you are so that you can maximize any money management and investment decisions you make based on your review of the rest of this book.

In this Book, you'll discover loads of tools, such as tables and question lists, to help you find your inner money manager. You can also work though the process of establishing specific goals for your financial future, and figure out what your spending and saving habits may be, especially when determining what you really need to buy versus what you really want to buy.

Here are the contents of Book I at a glance:

Chapter 1

Your Financial Snapshot

In This Chapter

▶ Taking stock of your net worth

▶ Evaluating your spending habits

▶ Recognizing your money personality

*W*hether you're in Montreal, Medicine Hat, or Mozambique, just about every map you come across will likely have a "You Are Here" arrow. Why? Because you can't get to where you want to be if you don't know where you are. Your financial snapshot is a tool to help you map out and reach your financial goals, and it's useless unless you know where you are now and where you want to go. Determine your current financial situation by taking a thorough survey of your financial status. This chapter shows you how.

This chapter also helps you understand why it's important to consider your financial future. Survey after survey, in both Canada and the U.S., show that it's crucial to get a financial snapshot of your current situation as a starting point to mapping out and achieving your financial goals.

In 2003, more than half of Canadians (and Americans) considered financial planning to be more important to them than in 2002. Financial planning experts generally agree that the growing importance of financial planning for Canadians is mainly because more people now realize that those who plan well tend to accumulate less personal debt, as well as save more than those who fail to plan their financial futures.

Recent surveys have also found that more Canadians are adjusting their financial plans than in earlier periods. Revisiting your financial plan is another key theme of this book. When your personal circumstances and goals change, your financial plans need to change accordingly to be effective.

The work you can do in this part of the book is just that — work. It involves calculators, research, phone calls, and coffees. But the end result will help you reach your personal goals by arming you with more financial resources and freedom. With finances firmly under control, you're much better poised to meet your retirement objectives — complete access to health care, lots of travel, and time for leisure! Failing to map out your financial condition can lead to scenarios best left to your imagination.

Figuring Out What You're Worth

When it comes to placing value in what you have, worth is much more than how much cash you have been able to stash away, whether in the form of salary, savings, chequing accounts, and so on. Determining your worth is an exercise that can include any number of decisions about any number of things that have value. Did you inherit a really ugly — but valuable (to someone else!) — vase from Uncle Ted? Save your memories, sell the vase, and factor the proceeds into your worth assessment.

Knowing your financial worth at any given point in time tells you where you stand relative to your goals. This information provides you with a reality check that may cause you to more fully turn on your income tap, and put a bigger plug in your expenses drain. If you have a large enough sink, you will have saved lots of cash for your future goals.

This section discusses some of the most common financial elements to include when figuring out what you're worth. Table 1-1 later in this section gives you a chance to do a quick calculation of your own net worth.

Determining your income

How much money do you take home after federal, provincial, and municipal taxes? The answer to that question depends on how you earn income.

The usual suspect: your paycheque

How much is deducted from your paycheque for pension, unemployment insurance, and health benefits deductions? That net pay figure doesn't reflect your worth; rather, it gives you an idea of the money that you have coming in on a regular basis. From that pool of steady income, you can build on those items of value that reflect your worth, whether they're material items such as a home or jewellery or investment items such as stocks or insurance policies.

Business income and the taxman

You can generate income from other sources as well. If you're a full-time entrepreneur or operate a part-time moonlighting business, you know that your business exists to try to make money. Even when it doesn't succeed at first in generating positive cash flow, you can still get a bit of income from your business — with a little help from the taxman.

Book I

Taking
Stock of
Your
Financial
Situation

Making business expenses work for you

Before you attempt to write off your expenses to generate cash income from a tax refund, consider the ability of your business to show a profit and whether your business had profits or losses in the past. CCRA will be more likely to allow deductions where profitability has been demonstrated in the past; you're showing them that your business plan can work.

Financing your business may also help your case with CCRA. If you financed your business, it's one more way of telling CCRA that you are operating in a business-minded manner.

You can deduct reasonable business expenses for tax purposes. If those expenses happen to exceed your business income, voilà, you may generate some cash flow in the form of a tax refund. In fact, the Canada Customs and Revenue Agency (CCRA) now has to go a bit easier on you in this regard, thanks to two recent landmark cases resolved by the Supreme Court of Canada.

The court ruled that CCRA should not look for a "reasonable expectation of profit (REOP)" but should instead look at whether your business activity is "undertaken in pursuit of profit." In other words, CCRA has to consider whether you had an "intention to profit" from your business that is operated in a "sufficiently commercial manner." This is an easier set of tests to pass than the old REOP test. The new intention-based rules give you more of a fighting chance to deduct business expenses and even to get a tax refund for your efforts. Here, the taxman may be able to pay you!

Income from property

Thousands of Canadians own real estate properties that they rent out for income. Even more Canadians own investment property such as stocks, mutual funds, and income trusts that generate dividend and distribution income. When determining your income for the purpose of helping you calculate your net worth, don't forget to factor in the positive impact of income you get from your rental property, vacation property, or investments. Some of the most successful wealth-builders in Canada have used a multiple stream of income strategy to achieve financial independence. The majority of Canadian millionaires have an array of salary, rental, investment, and capital-gain income streams. Diversify your income if you can.

Unexpected windfalls

Don't forget to include temporary, part-time, or seasonal income, which you may want to treat as "found money," putting it directly into your savings or investment plan. With the benefits of compound interest, such investments may mean much to your future. You can find a detailed discussion of compounding (interest that is paid on interest already earned) in Chapter 1 of Book IV so that you truly understand the benefits of forgoing small pleasures now for giant rewards.

Tracking your savings

How much money do you have in a bank, trust, or credit union savings account(s)? Do you have a money market account? Guaranteed investment certificates (GICs)? For the purposes of figuring out your financial worth, your savings list includes liquid assets, or assets that you can readily turn into cash.

If you find that you have too many accounts in too many places, try consolidating them into fewer accounts. By consolidating, you can save fees, make tracking your assets easier, and make more money with accounts that pay higher interest.

Factoring in other assets

Other assets refer to those items — material or otherwise — that are less liquid than the ready-cash-at-hand savings accounts that you have. By evaluating these assets carefully, you may find that you can make them serve your purposes better by liquidating them (converting them into cash) and transferring their value to a more liquid asset.

While far from conclusive, your other assets may include stocks; bonds; mutual funds; retirement funds; insurance; real estate; and other investments, such as vehicles (land, water, or air!), jewellery, cash value of insurance policies, and collectibles (such as stamps or antiques).

Table 1-1	Your Net Worth	
Type of Asset	*Asset*	*Value*
Cash	Chequing account(s)	_____
	Savings account(s)	_____
	Money market account(s)	_____
	GICs	_____
	Other	_____
Stocks, bonds, and mutual funds	Stocks	_____
	Bonds	_____
	Mutual funds	_____
	Commodities	_____
	Securities	_____

Type of Asset	Asset	Value
	Options	_____
	Other	_____
Retirement funds	RRSP(s) or RRIF(s)	_____
	Company pension plan	_____
	Profit-sharing plan	_____
	Other	_____
Real estate	Equity in main residence	_____
	Equity in vacation home(s)	_____
	Equity in co-owned property	_____
	Equity in rental property	_____
	Other	_____
Insurance	Annuities, surrender value of	_____
	Life insurance, cash value of	_____
Personal Property	Airplane	_____
	Antiques	_____
	Art (paintings, sculptures, etc.)	_____
	Automobile	_____
	Boat	_____
	Camper	_____
	Collectibles (stamps, coins, etc.)	_____
	Gold and/or silver	_____
	Furniture, appliances, and so on	_____
	Jewellery	_____
	Recreational vehicle	_____
Other	_____	_____
	_____	_____
	_____	_____
Total **My net worth as of**	_____	_____

Figuring Out What You Spend

In your financial life, you may spend (or pay bills) until you have no more money. Then you wait for your next paycheque and start the process all over again. That approach may have worked (although not all that well) back in the days when you were collecting an allowance from Mom and Dad. It may have worked even in university — at least you wouldn't freeze. As time goes on, though, this "system" becomes less and less sound.

This section helps you figure out where you are currently spending your money so that you can lay the groundwork for wiser, more informed decisions about your spending.

Keeping a spending diary

Keeping a spending diary helps you determine how you're spending your money on a day-to-day basis. For your diary, use a small notebook that fits in your pocket or purse. Carry it everywhere. Attach a pen or pencil to it so that you have no excuse for not writing down every purchase you make. Every day. Every cent. Keep your spending diary for at least a month.

On each new page, write the day and date. Record all your purchases, whether you spent cash, used a credit card, or added to a tab. At the end of each day, total your expenses. (To make this exercise even more useful, divide your weekly after-tax income by seven, write that amount on each day's page and, at the end of the day, figure out whether you spent more than you made that day.)

Try one of these three ways to keep your diary:

- ✔ **Basic:** Create just two columns — one for the amount and one for a description.

- ✔ **Detailed:** Decide how many categories you want, and then draw and label your columns (you'll probably want to use two facing pages). Categories may include groceries, restaurant meals, snacks, transportation, clothing, and telephone calls.

- ✔ **Obsessive:** Draw fewer columns for wider categories, such as food, transportation, utilities, clothes, and miscellaneous. Write a key in the front or back of your notebook so that you can keep track of the items within each category. For example, under food you could use G for groceries, R for restaurant meals, S for snacks, and so on, as shown in Table 1-2.

Book I

Taking
Stock of
Your
Financial
Situation

If your miscellaneous column adds up too fast, you probably need more categories. And if you find that you're altering your spending habits as you keep your diary, don't write your totals until the end of the month.

Table 1-2	Sample Daily Spending Diary	
Food	*Transportation*	*Miscellaneous*
R $10.50	B $5.25	N $2.75
S $2.50	F $39.48	C $39.00
G $33.88		

You, of course, will want to create your own key based on your lifestyle. In the sample table above, for example, B may stand for bus fare, F for fuel, N for newspapers, and C for a very expensive cup of coffee (or clothing, if you're into that).

Using other tools to track your spending

Your bank and credit card statements can help you keep a handle on your spending. Rather than just checking to make sure that the amounts are correct, use these records to find out how much money you spend in each category that you use in your spending diary.

Using the information that you've gathered, you can use pencil and paper to create a financial worksheet. If you have a home computer, financial software has become so inexpensive and so easy to use that you may choose that way to keep track of your spending and savings habits.

The time you invest now to gather your information and understand your financial fingerprint pays off in easier tracking and decision making later. You've already made the decisions about your money; now you just have to apply them.

Reviewing your bank records

Every month, your bank, credit union, or other financial institution sends you a list of how much you put into your accounts and how much you spent out of them. Bank records are a good place to use different-coloured highlighters to put your expenditures in categories: To start, try green for savings and red for impulse purchases.

Your banking can be smoother if you have a computer and Internet access so that you can use online banking. Most banks have set up systems where you can see current and even past records online. You can find out whether a specific cheque has cleared. You can check your current balance. You can check your records when it's convenient for you rather than waiting for the post office to deliver your statement. (Some banks, in fact, are now eliminating paper statements altogether.)

In addition, you can make your financial tracking life easier by using your computer to set up automatic payments for such expenses as

- ✔ Mortgage
- ✔ Utilities
- ✔ Telephone
- ✔ Credit cards
- ✔ Savings

The easier you make it to keep track of your finances, the more likely you are to do it.

Monitoring your credit card statements

Those handy reports — or devastating reminders of how much you've spent and how much you owe, depending on your perspective — that you get every month recording your credit card activity also help you draw your financial map. Signing on the dotted line to make a purchase is so easy that many people do so much more often than they should. Again, using highlighters, mark each purchase to be tallied in a specific category.

Using financial management software

Computers can do many things for you. Luckily, keeping track of your money is one of them! Programs such as Quicken and Microsoft Money are inexpensive yet flexible. These programs do the basics, such as keeping track of your cheque record and balancing your chequebook. But that's just the beginning.

Like the paper worksheet in Table 1-3, later in this chapter, financial management software creates a budget for you according to your specifications. Even better than automatically calculating totals as you enter amounts, the software enables you to move items from category to category. (For example, you may want to move restaurant meals from a Food category to a Personal category — your choice.) This software enables you to be as specific or as imprecise as you want. You can create categories down to the nth degree, not only monitoring how much you spend in groceries but also how much of that you spend for meat, cereal, cookies, and ice cream — or whatever your idea of the four basic food groups may be.

Book I

Taking
Stock of
Your
Financial
Situation

Flexibility allows you to reorganize your budget so that it gives you the information you want. Once you've set up a budget, you aren't stuck with it. And as your situation changes, you can customize your budget to reflect your new reality.

With your software package, you can compare your forecasted spending with your actual spending in any category, know when expenses are due with the use of a financial calendar, monitor your loan payments, manage your investments, and create reports and graphs to show how you're progressing toward your goals.

Don't put off budgeting because you don't have a computer. Software is nice, but not necessary. On the other hand, don't avoid using a computer for budgeting simply because you're intimidated by them. You likely have a friend or family member who is comfortable with computers. (And you can get help from any number of *For Dummies* books that can help you through any computer issues you have.)

Evaluating where your money goes

With your spending diary in hand, you have the information you need to set up your budget. Knowing where money goes can help you keep it from going!

Table 1-3 is a budgeting worksheet that shows you what your history of spending looks like. Using the last six months of bank and credit card records, figure your expenses in each category. For items that fluctuate, such as food, add up your six-month total (SMT). Then double that amount to get your yearly cost. Divide your SMT by 2 for your quarterly cost for that item. Divide your SMT by 6 to determine your monthly cost. Divide your SMT by 26 to calculate your weekly cost. Prepare to be shocked at how much you're spending in some categories.

Table 1-3	Budgeting Worksheet		
Expenses	*Weekly*	*Monthly*	*Yearly*
Housing			
Rent or mortgage	_____	_____	_____
Condo association dues	_____	_____	_____
Maintenance	_____	_____	_____
Property taxes	_____	_____	_____
Insurance	_____	_____	_____

(continued)

Table 1-3 *(continued)*

Expenses	Weekly	Monthly	Yearly
Furniture and appliances			
Other housing expenses			
Utilities			
Gas			
Telephone			
Water			
Electricity			
Other utilities expenses			
Food			
Groceries			
Eating out			
Other food expenses			
Transportation			
Automobile lease/payment 1			
Automobile lease/payment 2			
Licensing			
Insurance			
Maintenance			
Gasoline			
Taxis and public transportation			
Parking/tolls			
Other transportation expenses			
Health			
Doctor(s)			
Dentist(s)			
Eye care			
Prescriptions			

Expenses	Weekly	Monthly	Yearly
Insurance	_____	_____	_____
Other health expenses	_____	_____	_____
Education			
Tuition/school fees	_____	_____	_____
Books and supplies	_____	_____	_____
School activities	_____	_____	_____
Other education expenses	_____	_____	_____
Personal			
Clothing, shoes	_____	_____	_____
Haircuts	_____	_____	_____
Cosmetics	_____	_____	_____
Pet care	_____	_____	_____
Childcare	_____	_____	_____
Child support (you pay out)	_____	_____	_____
Allowances	_____	_____	_____
Gifts	_____	_____	_____
Donations	_____	_____	_____
Membership dues	_____	_____	_____
Books and magazine and newspaper subscriptions	_____	_____	_____
Laundry/dry cleaning	_____	_____	_____
Hobbies	_____	_____	_____
Vacations	_____	_____	_____
Entertainment	_____	_____	_____
Other personal expenses	_____	_____	_____
Investments			
Savings accounts	_____	_____	_____
RRSP(s)	_____	_____	_____

(continued)

Book I

Taking Stock of Your Financial Situation

Table 1-3 *(continued)*

Expenses	Weekly	Monthly	Yearly
Mutual funds	_____	_____	_____
Bonds	_____	_____	_____
Other investment expenses	_____	_____	_____
Credit and loan			
Credit card 1	_____	_____	_____
Credit card 2	_____	_____	_____
Credit card 3	_____	_____	_____
Department store card	_____	_____	_____
Gasoline card	_____	_____	_____
Student loan	_____	_____	_____
Other credit and loan expenses	_____	_____	_____
Total Expenses	_____	_____	_____

Income	Weekly	Monthly	Yearly
Wages, total	_____	_____	_____
Gratuities	_____	_____	_____
Royalties	_____	_____	_____
Dividends and interest	_____	_____	_____
Trust fund	_____	_____	_____
Pension	_____	_____	_____
CPP and EI	_____	_____	_____
Child support paid to you	_____	_____	_____
Gifts	_____	_____	_____
Total Income	_____	_____	_____

With Table 1-3, you can know how much you're spending in each category. After you create a budget based on what you want to spend in each category and adjust your spending habits accordingly, you'll be able to tell when you overspend or underspend in a category. Neither situation is cause for despair or jubilation as long as your long-term expenditures stay within your personal range. If you consistently overspend, you may need to cut costs, or you may have underestimated your costs initially. On the other hand, if you consistently underspend your allowance in any category, you may be able to lower that budget item and reallocate the difference.

Identifying Your Money Personality

The best-laid plans are worthless if you can't follow them. To find the best plans for you, and to help you stick to your budget, you need to understand how you feel about money and how you react to money matters. This section describes a few of the most common money personality types.

You need to understand not only your own money personality, but that of your spouse or partner as well. (As you teach your children about budgeting and saving, you'll need to identify their money personalities, too.) Once you recognize your money personality type, you can identify what habits you need to keep or change to reach your financial goals.

Saving for a rainy day

If your money personality is closest to a saver, you have trouble spending money even when doing so is in your best interests.

You may think that a saver wouldn't have any changes to make. But you can actually save to the point of hurting yourself. When going out of your way to save a few dollars or cents creates extra effort or inconvenience for you (or for your family or friends), you've likely "spent" where you could have "saved." For example, if you hire a cube van to move a few heavy items, and rush to return it before a deadline so that you can save a few dollars or get back a deposit, you may cause yourself and those who are helping you to have a few aches and pains (literal and figurative).

Spending like there's no tomorrow

If you're a spender, your immediate reaction to available cash (or even available credit) is to figure out what you can buy with it. Sometimes you spend because you can't resist salespeople. Spenders use credit if they don't have cash, with no concern for the long-term consequences of that debt.

A spender has more problems to overcome than the obvious. The attitude that any money available is available only to spend, rather than to put in savings, is its own problem. But it's not unbeatable. If you learn to stop, evaluate, consider alternatives, and make a decision instead of reacting to the desire to spend (or giving in to a sales pitch), you'll have a more secure financial future. Millions of aging North Americans are only now realizing that their savings are inadequate relative to their future goals. The good news is that many of these people have also begun to shift gears to spend less, save more, and retire well!

Spending on a whim

If you're an impulse buyer, your spending habits are a little different from plain old spenders. When you see something you like, you buy it without evaluating the purchase in terms of your long-range goals. Impulse buyers react to one or two types of items (whereas spenders buy everything!).

An impulse buyer is similar to a spender. But an impulse buyer doesn't even have to "find" money available for spending. Just seeing something to buy is enough to bring out the wallet or credit card. The desirable habit to cultivate is the same as that for a spender. If you figure how many hours of after-tax income would be needed to buy an item, you can stop much of your impulse buying in its tracks. If you have a working sound system, for example, is it really worth hundreds of work hours to replace it with a new one?

Taking your time on a purchase

The last category is the cautious buyer. If this is your money personality, you are a serious comparison shopper who may waste more time making a decision than the item is worth.

Cautious buyers may waste both time and money. But time is money. Not only may a cautious buyer spend too much time gathering information about various features and comparing prices, but there's also the cost of phone calls and driving around. Even worse, a cautious buyer may not enjoy a purchase after making it if he or she sees the item on sale later. If you're a cautious buyer, use those good comparison-buying skills, but learn when enough information is enough to make a decision, and ignore any information that you gather after the purchase.

If you have a lot of trouble making a buying decision, you may not need to buy that item at all.

Chapter 2

Setting Financial Goals

· ·

In This Chapter

▶ Learning how to set realistic money management goals

▶ Establishing your financial priorities

▶ Selecting the best money management strategies for accomplishing your goals

· ·

*W*ith a picture of your net worth and your savings rate, as discussed in Chapter 1, you're in a great position to take appropriate action with your money. Managing your money is a skill to be learned, just like learning to play softball or learning a new word processing program. As with any other skill, money management takes practice, realistic expectations, and the example and advice of those who have "been there and done that." This chapter is about setting realistic expectations for your personal finances, translating those goals into realistic actions in a proactive way.

Your path to financial security and economic success starts with this chapter. Here you can find out what it takes to become a skilled money manager and appreciate the rewards that good money management brings to your financial situation. Just do it, as Nike wisely implores. If you really want to get into this role, feel free to dress up in fancy Bay Street power threads and call yourself a money manager, even if it is only your money that you're managing!

What Are Your Goals: Then and Now

Graduating from high school or university may have been your most important goal in the past. Or maybe your biggest goal was to land a new job or get back on your feet after a divorce. Perhaps you've achieved those goals and haven't really given much thought to what comes next. Perhaps you have a vague sense that you want to pay off your debts, start a family, put your children through college, or start your own business. None of these or any other goals will happen unless you make them happen.

Achieving financial success isn't a matter of luck. Financial success requires attention, discipline, and sound money management.

Setting financial goals is something like going grocery shopping. You go to the store with a sense of what you need or want to buy. But the number of choices, sales, and attractive displays may cause you to get sidetracked.

You're starting with the desire to manage your money successfully so that you can achieve your financial goals. But it's easy to get distracted. Just as a shopping list helps a shopper stay focused, a money-management list can help you get off to a good start. Take a minute to check off the items on the following money management "shopping list" that seem important to you. This shopping list can help you figure out your financial goals:

- ✔ Spend less than I make
- ✔ Make good consumer choices, and get good value-for-money spent
- ✔ Establish a good credit rating
- ✔ Curb my spending appetite
- ✔ Save some money every time I get paid
- ✔ Spend enough time on money management
- ✔ Take personal responsibility for managing my money
- ✔ Work out a budget
- ✔ Balance my chequebook
- ✔ Know where to get good financial advice
- ✔ Distinguish between short-term and long-term financial goals
- ✔ Keep good records
- ✔ Use banking services
- ✔ Pay my bills and taxes on time

How many items apply to you? Chances are that you think you need to do all these things. And you do. But you don't need to do everything at once. What you need to do first are the basics. The basic approach to managing your money starts with knowing your financial goals.

In general, your goal is probably financial security. Almost everyone wants financial security. The trouble comes in defining just what financial security means to you. Start right now and complete this sentence:

I will be financially secure when I _____

_____ .

You may define financial security as being able to retire at age 65 without worrying about having enough money to live the rest of your life the way you want to. Or you may define financial security as being able to retire at age 50. The definition is up to you.

To get started on the road to financial security, begin to think in terms of the next five years. What can you do in the next five years that will help you accomplish your long-range goal of financial security?

Book I

Taking
Stock of
Your
Financial
Situation

Determining Your Goals: A Five-Year Plan

Sound money management is achieved through simple, realistic goals. Once you have determined your personal financial goals, it is important to classify those goals as short-term or long-term. Making this distinction is important because it provides your financial strategy with direction. When you have your short-term, mid-term, and long-term goals clearly in mind, your goals become like building blocks. You can more easily defer some of the things you hope to accomplish in the short run because you know that with a longer time frame, those things will happen.

To help sort out your goals, ask yourself where you want to be financially in five years. In Table 2-1, indicate which of the following goals are important for you to accomplish within the next five years. On a scale of 1 to 5, 5 is very important and 1 isn't very important.

Table 2-1	Five-Year-Goal Worksheet				
Goal	*[1]*	*[2]*	*[3]*	*[4]*	*[5]*
Reduce debt	[ ]	[ ]	[ ]	[ ]	[ ]
Save money	[ ]	[ ]	[ ]	[ ]	[ ]
Buy a car	[ ]	[ ]	[ ]	[ ]	[ ]
Buy a home	[ ]	[ ]	[ ]	[ ]	[ ]
Start an investment program	[ ]	[ ]	[ ]	[ ]	[ ]
Reduce income taxes	[ ]	[ ]	[ ]	[ ]	[ ]
Buy life insurance	[ ]	[ ]	[ ]	[ ]	[ ]
Take an expensive vacation	[ ]	[ ]	[ ]	[ ]	[ ]
Put kids through university	[ ]	[ ]	[ ]	[ ]	[ ]
Other _____	[ ]	[ ]	[ ]	[ ]	[ ]
Other _____	[ ]	[ ]	[ ]	[ ]	[ ]

Look at the items that you checked in the "5" column. Do you think that it's realistic to try to accomplish all your 5s in the next five years? What do you think you can do in one year? The answers to these questions will help you focus on the important aspects of managing your money.

Setting Priorities

It's easy to want it all — a nice place to live, clothes with logos and labels, a great car, meals at romantic restaurants, vacations, and so on. The list expands so easily. The fact is that you have limited resources. You must work with what you have — not with what you want to have, and not with what you think you will get next month or next year.

All managers wish for more resources to accomplish their goals. All managers wish that they had more time, more money, more people, and more experience. But effective managers are resourceful and use what they have to get the best results. They prove their skills by accomplishing tasks with discipline and motivation — skills that you can develop when you approach money management with the commitment to making do with the money you have.

Managing your money to accomplish your goals

Take another look at your five-year-goal worksheet in Table 2-1. If you selected debt reduction as a very important goal, you'll probably decide on money strategies that will make that goal happen. If you selected both reducing your debts and buying a great car, your money strategies will have to be different. In fact, you may realize that your resources don't allow you to do both at the same time. One objective will have to take priority over the other.

From Table 2-1, select the three items that you identified as most important to your short-term and long-term financial goals. Now rank those three objectives in their order of importance, as shown in Table 2-2.

Table 2-2	Ranking My Priorities		
Priorities	*Short-term*	*Mid-term*	*Long-term*
1.			
2.			
3.			

Do you think that you need or want to make any adjustments to your worksheet? Chapter 3 examines the difference between money needs and money wants in greater detail. For now, stick with what you think you need to accomplish short-term and long-term.

Book I

Taking
Stock of
Your
Financial
Situation

Now estimate the percentage of your income that you'll probably have to allocate to each of your top three priorities. Does common sense tell you that these percentages are realistic? Pay attention to your common sense; it can become your best friend.

Write down what you know or expect your annual income will be this year before and after taxes and deductions.

Your gross income is your earnings before taxes and deductions get taken out of your paycheque. Your net income is your take-home pay — your earnings after all taxes and deductions. Your net income may seem like a lot of money, or it may seem like a pathetically small amount. In either case, as the manager of your money, you start with this amount.

Managing your time

Like the old adage says, "Time is money." Deadlines are a fact of both personal and professional life. As the manager of your money, you will struggle with many of the same constraints that business managers experience. On the one hand, you'll wish that you had more time to accomplish your goals; on the other, you'll wish that you could see and enjoy the results of your work sooner.

To become a successful money manager, you have to become a successful time manager as well.

Everybody has the same 24 hours in each of the 7 days of the week. Yet some people just seem to get more done than others do. Why? Because they have clear goals, good time management skills, commitment, and discipline. You, too, can put time management and money management skills to work in order to accomplish your financial goals.

Do a quick review of your typical week. Estimate the time you spend working, sleeping, eating, travelling, reading, watching television, shopping, dating, interacting with family, and playing. Which activity takes the most of your time? Is that activity really the top priority in your life? Setting your work aside for a moment, how much time have you set aside for the things that will help you achieve your financial goals? What time do you have for managing your money so that your priorities can become a reality?

Take the initiative to set aside half an hour every week (a weekend afternoon may be good, but find a time that works best for you) to develop your skills as an effective manager of your money and time. Time is one of your most valuable resources.

You can spend that half-hour doing any number of things. Consider the following:

- Make a list of your goals for the week.
- Review your out-of-pocket expenses against your budget.
- Read an article on personal finance.
- Call your financial adviser, trusted friend, or parent and ask for advice about a purchase or financial decision that you expect to make in the coming week.
- Evaluate your money management skills during the past week and give yourself a grade. Target one area for improvement.
- Evaluate your time management skills during the past week and give yourself a grade. Target one area for improvement.
- Set aside $5 to $25 in an envelope for a special occasion.
- Identify at least one thing that you believe you accomplished as a money and time manager during the past week.
- Start a weekly journal and enter a short list of your goals and accomplishments for the week.
- Compare your goals for the week against the priorities that you set for yourself on the worksheet earlier in this chapter. Make adjustments.

Forming Strategies for Success

Some experts think that setting financial goals is the easy part of money management. The hard part is making it happen. The plans you make to accomplish your goals are called strategies. The thing about strategies is that you can change them.

Your plans or strategies for successful money management can change if you find that they aren't accomplishing their purpose. Just as a business manager has to make adjustments to respond to one problem or challenge after another, you can become skilful in making adjustments to manage your money more effectively.

Although many strategies are available to you as a money manager, at least two guidelines can help you evaluate the success of a strategy:

   ✔ Be flexible but focused.

   ✔ Learn to live on less.

Be flexible but focused

As a money manager, you want to develop a balance between keeping your goals clearly in mind and responding creatively and constructively to changing circumstances and unforeseen situations. No one can anticipate every circumstance in life. Just when you think that you can save a little more during one month, the car needs a repair that you didn't count on. Or perhaps you see an ad in the paper for an item that you really need. Although you hadn't planned to make the purchase now, you think that, by doing so, you would save money in the long run.

One of the best qualities of successful managers is good judgment. This is especially true of good money managers. Good judgment relates to common sense. Good judgment and common sense are not part of the school curriculum; you learn these in your life experiences.

Learning from your mistakes can be costly, but it's usually effective. Don't be afraid to change and try something else if one of your money management strategies isn't working.

Often, you learn good judgment by the example of others you know and respect. Encourage others to share their stories with you. From their stories about the decisions they've made, you'll learn about the good sense to be flexible. You'll learn the balance of keeping your eye on your goals while making adjustments for setbacks or unexpected difficulties.

Find the level of risk you're comfortable with. If you don't have family responsibilities, then taking greater risks may be easier. Taking the risk of changing jobs is easier if you're single than if you provide for a family. Some people find investing in a speculative stock easier than others. Know yourself and your financial obligations.

Know that your goals may change as your circumstances change. Be flexible and replace goals that no longer suit your needs and wants. Your strategies may change because of proven successes and failures. Be flexible and make the necessary adjustments. If this approach sounds too vague to be useful now, test it out by asking someone whose judgment seems sound and whose decisions you respect. Ask that person, "Am I being too rigid about (name a goal, strategy, or specific circumstance)?" Or ask, "How can I be more flexible about (name the specific situation)?"

Learn to live on less

The single most important skill you can develop as a money manager is to live beneath your means. You've probably heard this guideline — the key to your financial freedom — expressed in many different ways: Live on less. Put something away from every paycheque. Save for a rainy day. All too many people avoid heeding this important advice.

In the section, "Managing your money to accomplish your goals," earlier in this chapter, you may have written down your net annual income. Try to imagine living on 90 percent of that income. Calculate how much you would need to save every month and every year to live on 90 percent of your net income. Think of a business manager who suddenly finds out that that the budget for a particular project has been cut by 25 percent. The project still must be completed on time and with the same quality standards. As your own money manager, you can appreciate the flexibility and commitment to your goal that such adjustments require.

If your ultimate goal is to attain financial security, chances are that you won't be able to accomplish that goal on your income alone. The ticket to financial security is to save some of your money. If you don't manage to save some of your money on a regular basis, you won't have money to invest. Investment is a reliable way to accomplish the ultimate goal of financial security. The way to save money regularly is to live beneath your means. Investing allows your money to grow, so if you don't invest some of your money, you can't achieve financial security. The logic is simple and compelling. (See Books IV and V for more details on investing.)

Put aside for the moment the wish to own that boat or fancy car. Now is the time to face reality and develop the skills that you need to manage your money well enough to accomplish your financial goals.

Write this down!

Chapter 3 focuses on making good choices about spending. Before you make those choices, however, you need to take the time to nail down some strategies:

- **Review your five-year plan.** On a blank sheet of paper, write down what you consider to be your most important long-term goal. This is what you hope to accomplish in about five years. Label that Goal A.

- **Look ahead a few years.** Write down what you consider to be your most important financial goal for the next two to five years. This is your mid-term goal. Label that Goal B.

- **Focus on this year's achievement.** Write down your most important financial goal for this year. This is your short-term goal. Label that Goal C.

✔ **Re-evaluate your long-term goals.** Take another look at your five-year-goal worksheet in Table 2-1. After each item, write A, B, or C if the item relates to any of your specific financial goals.

✔ **Summarize your strategies.** Make a chart that lists your short-term goal and the money management strategies that will help you accomplish that goal. Do the same for your mid-term goal and related strategies, and your long-term goal and strategies.

✔ **Track your progress.** Put your chart of A, B, and C goals and strategies on the refrigerator door so that you're reminded of them every day.

Think now about the annual increase that you can realistically expect if you stay with the same job for the next five years. These increases may seem large or small to you. In a way, the size of the increases doesn't matter. What does matter is that you accept the realities of your situation and manage your money accordingly.

If you postpone major expenditures (such as the purchase of a new car or an expensive vacation) now in order to accomplish your most important objectives, will you realistically be able to afford those expenses later, given the revenue you expect? Begin to think of adjustments that you need or want to make in your expectations.

Chapter 3

Distinguishing Needs and Wants

In This Chapter

▶ Distinguishing your financial needs from your economic wants

▶ Recognizing the range of choices within the categories of needs and wants

▶ Making choices that relate directly to your financial goals

*O*ne of the responsibilities of being an effective money manager is to look at your financial situation objectively. Your objective eye lets you step back from the transactions that you have conducted in the past and encourages you to look at the bigger picture of your financial situation. In practice, of course, this self-assessment process is easier said than done. But to help you stay disciplined, this chapter provides some guidance to help you fully consider what your needs and wants really are.

Look at the habits and attitudes that you have developed up to now towards managing, spending, and saving your money. Have you made good choices thus far? As your own money manager, you want to make good choices for your hard-earned money. Making good choices involves distinguishing what you need now, and in the longer term, from what you only wish you had now.

What I Really Need Is . . .

Just what are the necessities of life? And how do these necessities change over time? Certainly, what you thought you needed at age 5 (a bike, a grilled cheese sandwich) would not be on your list of perceived needs when you are 15 (designer shoes, wheels, a new video game, a meal at the mall) or 25 (a new suit, a trip to Hawaii, money to pay the rent or mortgage, a romantic dinner on the town).

Start with the basics: You need housing, food, clothing, and some form of transportation to get to and from your job and other important places. But the range of choices you have to address those basic needs is staggering. Your cost, in terms of both money and opportunity costs, will vary greatly depending on your financial goals and the choices you make.

An *opportunity cost* is something you have to give up in order to pursue a particular decision. For example, if you decide to work late one evening, your opportunity cost involves giving up dinner with your family. If you decide to go to graduate school, your opportunity cost involves forgoing a higher standard of living in the immediate future in hopes of bettering your opportunities later in life.

Housing

Your housing choices may include living at home, renting an apartment, sharing an apartment or home with roommates, or buying your own place. For example, plug in some numbers for each of these options:

- ✔ If you rent a studio or one-bedroom apartment, your rent may run $500 a month.

- ✔ If you share an apartment or home with other roommates, your fair share may be $350 a month.

- ✔ If you buy your own house or condo, you may have to save $5,000 to $10,000 for a down payment, and your monthly mortgage may be $1,200 a month.

- ✔ If you take in a roommate or boarder to share your housing costs, or you take a smaller apartment or buy a smaller house, you can reduce your housing costs.

Your choice of housing depends on what you think you can afford as well as what you perceive the opportunity costs to be. Use Table 3-1 to apply the opportunity-cost concept to each housing choice, using figures that seem realistic for each choice listed.

Your perception of the benefit(s) derived from each choice is just as important as the opportunity cost. By adding a fourth column to Table 3-1, you can identify what you think the benefit(s) for each choice are.

What did you identify as the opportunity costs for sharing housing with roommates? Chances are, you mentioned a loss of independence. The opportunity costs associated with the other choices may involve settling for less in terms of the other major expenses in your life. For example, if you choose to rent a fancy apartment, you may have less to spend on a car. The choices you make for the basics depend on what you consider important in order to achieve the goals that you identified in Chapter 2.

Table 3-1	Monthly Housing Costs and Benefits		
Choice	*Money Cost*	*Opportunity Cost*	*Benefits*
Rent an apartment			
Share housing with roommate(s)			
Buy a condo or house			
Take in boarder			
Downsize housing			
Other _____			

Food

Do you have any idea how much you spend on food each week or month? Are you counting fast-food stops and going to restaurants? Although food is certainly a necessity, you probably shouldn't count restaurant food as a necessity. Dining in a restaurant is usually considered entertainment. Eating out is something you want or enjoy more than something you need.

Use Table 3-2 before making decisions about the money you spend on food. Identify the opportunity costs and benefits for each of your options.

Table 3-2	Monthly Food Costs and Benefits		
Food Choices	*% of Total Expenses*	*Opportunity Cost*	*Benefits*
Breakfast out			
Lunch out			
Dinner out			
Weekly groceries			
Other _____			

Sorting out your food choices and weighing the opportunity costs and benefits will help you make better money management decisions. You can discover how unwise it is to spend 40 percent of your net income on food when you also need to include in your budget costs for transportation and clothing. And you haven't even introduced all those things that you want and are tempted to consider necessities — such as monthly cable, cellphone, and Internet access fees.

Transportation

In the category of transportation, too, you have a wide range of choices. Take a look at the choices you've made in the past to get a better idea of your money management patterns. Then fill in Table 3-3.

Table 3-3	Monthly Transportation Costs and Benefits		
Transportation	*% of Total Expenses*	*Opportunity Cost*	*Benefits*
Car purchase payments			
Car lease payments			
Gasoline			
Insurance			
Maintenance, repairs, etc.			
Public transportation			
Other _____			

You already know that owning or leasing a vehicle is the most expensive form of transportation. And within the arena of owning a vehicle — car, minivan, sport utility vehicle, or motorcycle — many choices test your money management skills. You may want the best, but you soon find that you can't afford all that you want. This is where the critical skill of distinguishing between your economic needs and wants is crucial.

You may decide that you need a car. The car you choose can range from a top-of-the-line model with payments of $700 a month for five years to a clunker for less than $1,000 total (all before factoring in repair costs). Your choice relates to your financial goals and the economic means, or income, at your disposal.

Clothing

Clothing costs are perhaps harder to deal with. People generally don't spend a fixed amount on clothes each month. However, a major clothing purchase, such as a coat, could cause a big bubble in a monthly budget without good money management skills.

The choice in clothing is enormous. You have a sliding scale from designer labels to resale shops. You may love to shop for clothes, or you may hate it. Try to separate your love (or hate) for clothes shopping from the opportunity costs and benefits-specific clothes items.

Try to review your clothing costs for the last year. Begin by recalling major purchases. Estimate the number of times you go into a clothing store every week or month. Guess at how much you spend each time you make a purchase. The money you spend on clothes is probably greater than you think.

Adding it up

Using Tables 3-1, 3-2, and 3-3, tally the amounts that you currently spend each month on the basics — housing, food, transportation, and clothing. Begin to think about the adjustments you want to make in any of those categories in order to accommodate greater spending (or savings) for any of your necessities. For instance, if buying a home is one of your priorities, then you can anticipate paying a greater amount for the "necessity" of housing. A greater commitment to your housing expense may well require spending less in another area of your budget.

What I Really Want Is . . .

One of the biggest differences between being an adult and being an adolescent is the amount of money you have available for "discretionary" spending. When you were a teenager, chances are that your parents paid for your housing, food, and transportation. The money you earned, you spent — unless your parents insisted, or trained you in money management skills, to save some.

So fast food, CDs, DVDs, video games, movies, "fashionable" clothing, and entertainment tickets often become the "necessities" of adolescents. Any survey of teenagers will likely indicate that their top expenses will be for entertainment, clothing, and music, not necessarily in that order. But for adults, these items fall into the category known as discretionary spending.

Understanding discretionary spending

Thinking of all the things you want outside the basic necessities as "extras" may be hard to do, but in the world of personal finance, that's reality. Take this opportunity for a reality check so that you can recognize the distinction between what you need (necessities) and what you want ("extras").

As your own money manager, you may wish that you had more money available for discretionary spending. And you may be appalled at which goods and services are commonly relegated to the category of "extras." Look over the following checklist of items that you may consider as ordinary parts of living. Indicate whether you think an item is a basic need (N) or a discretionary want (W).

Table 3-4	Allocating Needs and Wants	
_____ Stockpot		_____ Pet
_____ Manicure		_____ Beer
_____ Down comforter		_____ Books
_____ Television		_____ Movie tickets
_____ Internet access		_____ Bread
_____ Vacation in Florida		_____ Videos
_____ Washing machine		_____ Stove
_____ Dishwasher		_____ Wallet
_____ Haircut		_____ Acupuncture
_____ Cologne		_____ Sweater

Count up your Ns and Ws. The list of wants should be far greater than the list of needs. Your needs list may include the haircut, bread, and sweater. Some people would argue that a wallet is a necessity; others may disagree. Still, only about 25 percent of these items can be considered real necessities.

The "extras" in your life far exceed your needs. One of the most difficult skills you have to learn as a money manager is how to say no to yourself.

Recognizing the influence of advertising (if you sell it, we will come)

One of the reasons you may have a hard time distinguishing between economic needs and wants is that advertising does such a good job. You're bombarded with advertising on the radio, on television, on the Internet, in the print media, and on billboards and buses.

The purpose of advertising is to promote goods and services so that the prospective customer psychologically transforms a want into a need. Companies spend a lot of money to create a look, feel, and message that works on your emotions. Companies test their products and marketing strategies on focus groups and use the feedback to develop even stronger messages for their targeted audience.

One of your jobs as an adult is to liberate yourself from the persuasions of advertising. One way to do so is simply to ask yourself: "Do I really need this (whatever it is)?" Once you identify something as a want rather than a need, you gain control over the choice of whether to buy something.

Making Good Choices

Making good decisions about your hard-earned money is a skill that you can learn while playing the game of DICE. No, you're not going to gamble with your money; DICE is an acronym for

✔ **D**istinguish between needs and wants

✔ **I**dentify the opportunity costs and benefits associated with each of your choices

✔ **C**hoose an item based on your priorities, not on impulse

✔ **E**njoy your well-chosen purchase as a gift to yourself

In the beginning, you may make some unwise choices. But as you gain experience as a money manager, your judgment will improve if you use the DICE approach.

Distinguish between needs and wants

As you can read in the section "All I Really Want Is . . . ," get in the habit of distinguishing between what you need and what you want. Society encourages you to think that things you wish for are really things you need. Make a declaration of independence and start making those judgments for yourself.

Your needs relate to the list of goals that you developed for yourself in Chapter 2. Which of the following do you consider needs as opposed to wants?

____ Housing   ____ Food   ____ Transportation

____ Taxes   ____ Insurance   ____ Savings

____ Clothing   ____ Utilities   ____ Self-improvement

Chances are that you consider all these categories essential to your financial success and your economic goals. Financial success is a result of the proper ordering of needs and wants, and allocating personal resources accordingly. For example, food is an essential item in every budget. Good money managers curtail the amount of money they spend on this item in order to save for other priorities.

What would you add to your list of essentials? Try limiting your list of essentials to ten items. These will become your priority list for later use.

Remember that within each category in your list of essentials, you have a multitude of choices. But limit the range to three: basic, middle of the road, and luxury. After each of your essential items, identify whether you want the basic, middle, or luxury choice to help you accomplish your financial goals.

Identify the opportunity costs and benefits

When you make decisions about spending your money to provide for the essentials on your list, remember the worksheets on housing, food, and transportation (Tables 2-1, 2-2, and 2-3) that helped you identify your options. For each option, you can name the opportunity cost — what you will give up to pursue a given option — and the benefit — what you will gain when you select that option.

All these steps may seem clumsy at first, but soon they'll become habit, and you'll find yourself gaining both speed and confidence in identifying the relative benefits and costs of the choices that you have. Weighing the relative costs and benefits enhances your skills as a money manager.

Choose what's best for you

Knowing what's best can seem difficult or confusing. That's why having your list of priorities close at hand is worthwhile. In Chapter 2, you have the opportunity to write down long-term Goal A, two- to five-year Goal B, and one-year Goal C. Here, make a list of your ten most essential economic needs. Next to each category on this list, write B for Basic, M for Middle of the Road, or L for Luxury to indicate what you think you will be able to afford. Add this list to the refrigerator.

Refer to these lists whenever you must make a decision about your essential economic needs. Obviously, choosing what's best for you involves selecting the option that's most in line with your stated goals.

Only you know your financial goals and economic priorities. Only you can make money management decisions that will help you achieve your personal goals.

Evaluate your choices

Book I

Taking
Stock of
Your
Financial
Situation

The way to continue making good money choices is to review your choices in terms of how they further your financial goals. Learn to reward positive behaviour. Learn from the mistakes of poor choices as well. Both kinds of choices can develop your skills as a money manager.

Following are a few ways to reward yourself for sound money management:

✔ Pat yourself on the back by doing something you enjoy — take a walk, enjoy a hot bath, spend some time in your garden, or sign up for an inexpensive art, cooking, or dance class.

✔ Share the good news — tell a friend or family member about your choice and why it feels good in terms of your priorities.

✔ Make a donation to a charitable organization or cause that you support. Keep receipts of these donations so that if you itemize on your tax return, you can take a deduction.

✔ Follow the DICE approach for another major purchase and feel good about how much better you are becoming at making wise choices.

Chapter 4

Saving Smartly

• •

In This Chapter

▶ Understanding the role of savings in your financial security

▶ Motivating yourself with the benefits of a savings plan

▶ Using less of your resources now to accomplish your long-term goals

• •

*E*very so often you may hear about an unexpected and generous bequest of some humble benefactor to a hospital or university. The article indicates that the benefactor was a teacher or janitor making a modest amount of money. Somehow, over the years, the individual amassed a great fortune. The story usually indicates that the person just lived frugally and saved a lot. The moral of those stories is that it isn't how much you earn, but how much you save, that makes the difference between financial success and just getting along. In fact, this is also a moral to a *Frugal Living For Dummies* story, and another resource that can help you save for your future.

If you didn't develop the habit of saving money as a child, and you're tired of living from paycheque to paycheque, this chapter can help you find ways to save. This chapter also explains the benefits of savings, gives you tips on how to save, and shows you what to do with savings after they accumulate.

To discover the variety of investment vehicles in which to place your savings, check out Book IV.

The Benefits of Saving

Why save at all? Because your savings protect you from emergencies such as major car repairs or even the loss of a job. Your savings also allow you to make those major purchases, like car or home, that are so important to you. You can also convert your savings to investments that enable your money to grow.

Without savings, you live with financial anxiety. Emergencies are a fact of life — not a surprise that strikes out of the blue. Your savings should include an emergency fund to deal with the "unexpected" disasters such as car repairs,

Savings plans on the job

If you're lucky enough to work for a company that will help you contribute to your RRSPs, be sure and take advantage of that on-the-job perk. They calculate the percentage you authorize and deduct it right off your gross pay, and in many circumstances, match it with a contribution of their own. This type of investment, just like your regular RRSP, decreases your taxable income and helps grow your retirement savings. So it's a win-win opportunity not to be missed.

a plumbing snafu, or a leaky roof. This emergency fund should be left alone and not used for investment purposes.

You have two other reasons to save your money. The first is to make major purchases, such as a house, car, or post-secondary education. The second is to make sound investments. Financial experts agree that the way to financial security and a comfortable retirement is to invest money so that it will grow. The money you spend will not grow for you. The money you earn will not grow substantially unless you make sound investments. You will have no money to invest, unless you save.

Savings are the key to financial security. Without savings, you will not have money to invest so that your money grows in value and your financial future becomes more comfortable. You can save money in many ways — whether it's by joining a savings plan at work or by creating your own regular savings habits. The important thing is to start saving something.

Tips for Saving Money

The following tips can help you save the money you need to make your financial goals become realities. Remember that if you don't save, you won't be able to afford the things you want, and you won't have a secure financial future.

Set up a separate savings account

Establishing a separate account for your savings is important because doing so enables you to watch your savings grow and see milestones. Don't let your savings "mingle" with your regular chequing account, because spending it would be too easy. If you keep your savings separate, it is more secure. You also earn a greater rate of interest on your savings account than you would if you left the money in your chequing account.

Book I

Taking
Stock of
Your
Financial
Situation

A separate savings account may help you avoid monthly charges on your chequing account. Many banks waive the monthly chequing fee if you also have a savings account with them.

The first bill you pay out of your paycheque — whether you actually write a cheque or you have the amount automatically deducted — should be the savings amount you're committed to living without.

If you're employed, you can automate your savings process by arranging for automatic deductions. For example, you can typically have as little as $50 taken from each paycheque and transferred automatically to your savings account or money market account. You can also have money automatically deducted and put into an RRSP program or other type of investment.

Learn to live on less

Take a look at your net income. Whatever it is, reduce it (on paper!) by 10 percent. Then take that 90 percent figure as the amount you have to work with for your personal budget. What do you do with the 10 percent that you "no longer have"? Put it in your savings account.

If taking 10 percent off your net income seems too drastic, then try this approach: When you next review your budget and pay your bills, write a cheque for 1 percent of your take-home pay and deposit it in your separate savings account. The second month, take 2 percent off the top of your take-home pay and put it in savings. Increase the amount by 1 percent each month. By the end of one year, you'll be saving 12 percent of your net income.

Avoid credit cards

Leave your credit cards behind. Impulse purchases are tempting when you carry plastic. These impulse buys add up, and they basically destroy your budget and erode your commitment to responsible money management.

When you pay by cash or cheque, you significantly reduce the amount you spend. As an added benefit, you avoid the outrageous credit card interest rates that compound in the blink of an eye.

Try to limit yourself to one or, at most, two credit cards. Consider the card as an emergency backup, not a constant companion. Don't be lulled into thinking that you need a credit card to establish your credit rating; you don't.

Reduce your taxes

Contributing to an RRSP may reduce your take-home pay, but it also reduces your tax liability. In other words, you are taxed based on the money remaining after your contributions are deducted from your gross income. The best way for Canadians to reduce the taxes they pay, RRSPs are an important part of any plan for financial security. Start your RRSP as soon as you can and contribute monthly rather than being part of the mad rush at the end of February. It is easy to arrange with your bank to contribute each month a set amount into your plan. The earlier you start building your fund, the more it will be worth when you retire. Charitable donations also reduce taxable income.

Canada Customs and Revenue Agency has many free publications about tax planning that can help you reduce your taxes — you can order them online at www.ccra-adrc.gc.ca. Or check out *Tax Tips For Canadians For Dummies* (published by John Wiley & Sons Canada) for expert tips and advice.

Save all "found" money

Consider all "found" or extra money as direct contributions to your savings plan. Found money can consist of monetary gifts, dividends, or interest income. Without delay, deposit this money in your special savings account and smile. Don't let yourself feel deprived that you're being denied a splurge. Instead, concentrate on the fact that you'll have the pleasure of seeing a long-term goal come true. A small, immediate pleasure is a small price to pay for a greater sense of accomplishment.

The longer you let gift money sit around at home, the less likely it is that you'll save it.

After you pay a debt, save the same amount

What a great sense of relief you get when you pay off your car, your student loans, or an instalment loan! When you finish writing that last cheque, put down your pen and smile. But next month, when you go to pay your bills, write a cheque for the same amount (or even half the amount) and put it into your special savings account.

Remember that you learned to live with that debt as part of your fixed expenses. After the loan or debt is paid off, you can continue to do without that money.

Book I

Taking
Stock of
Your
Financial
Situation

Do your research

Most libraries have a good collection of books and materials on personal finances. Many also engage speakers who are experts in various aspects of finance and investing. Lots of people have good ideas about saving money. You can benefit from their experience and suggestions.

Even if you walk away with only one good idea per book, that idea will keep you growing as a money manager. And once you have accumulated some money in your savings account, you'll want direction about investing your hard-saved money. (See also Books IV and V for information about investing.)

Use a piggy bank

When you were a child, you may have been encouraged to make contributions to a piggy bank. Get a "piggy bank" for yourself now. A large jar, or something you can see through, is best. At the end of every day, empty the change from your wallet or pants pocket and put it in the piggy bank. Next to the piggy bank, keep a notebook; in it, record the amount of change you put into the bank. At the end of every week, tally the amount that you have contributed to the piggy bank.

If you can, set up a matching strategy for your piggy bank savings. When you tally the week's collection at the end of the week, add the same amount all at once to the jar. You can double your savings in a pretty painless way. You can plan to take this money to the bank when your piggy bank is full to the brim or on a special occasion, whatever suits your personality.

Use the Internet for research

You can find many Web sites devoted to managing personal finances. *Canadian MoneySaver*, in addition to publishing its print magazine, has a Web site (www.canadianmoneysaver.ca) from which you can access a library of articles from past and current issues (for an annual subscription fee of $22.95). You also receive investment advice from scores of financial advisors, including financial planners, tax gurus, portfolio managers, investment advisers, lawyers, and others. This site also has helpful links to other specialized financial Web sites.

Once online, also check out www.webfin.com, a Canadian Web site devoted to financial matters where the content is mostly free. SmartMoney.com (www.smartmoney.com) and Bankrate.com (www.bankrate.com) are U.S.-based Web resources, but most of the money management principles that they publish can be applied by Canadians as well. Again, much of their content is free!

Try not to nickel-and-dime your coin contributions. You may be surprised how little you'll miss those loonies and toonies hanging around in your pocket or change purse.

Set up a buddy system

Saving money doesn't have to feel like drudgery, and it doesn't have to make you a miser. A little motivation from a friend can help. Think about finding a "money buddy" to help you save money regularly. Your money buddy can be someone from work, a relative, or a neighbour whom you know or suspect is also trying to save money.

Invite your money buddy to share a sack lunch with you one day a week, or if lunch isn't convenient, make it a phone call. Compare notes on your progress and offer each other encouragement. Swap ideas for saving money that you may have come across in an article or a conversation.

Chapter 5

Spending Wisely

• •

• •

Reducing your expenses may sound like a negative experience. Think of all the things you'll have to do without! When you finish this chapter, however, you'll feel the delight of having your spending under control. A bonus is the disappearance of stress from not knowing how you're going to pay your bills and plan for your future. Because you'll have made spending decisions before you even leave your home, and because you'll know that sticking to those decisions will help you meet your goals, you won't spend time and energy on every spending decision.

If your best planning still finds "more month than money," the solution is to increase your income. Like you never thought of that, right? The difference is that in the past, your "plan" consisted of dreaming "if only I made more money." Here, you'll learn how to figure the amount you need, how to determine whether your need is short-term or long-term, and exactly where you can find your personal pot of gold.

Finding Alternatives to Spending

Chapter 1 suggests ways to monitor your spending, such as using various coloured highlighters to categorize your purchases as they appear on your bank and credit card statements, or using computer software to track your finances. No matter your method, you should categorize your spending so that you can create your own wise spending pattern.

As you categorize your spending, you can change your categories or even add and subtract categories. One important note to remember is that your system shouldn't frustrate you to the point that you stop your efforts to control your spending. Your financial health is important, so make it easy.

Spend, rent, or borrow?

When the lawn is as high as an elephant's eye, do you go out and buy a lawn mower? Doing so would seem logical ... except that your lawn takes only half an hour to mow. Once a week. Maximum.

Does your neighbour have the hugest, most magnificent maple tree in the province — with piles of autumn leaves in the yard to go with it? Raking all those leaves is a big job — for one month out of 12. Is that month of activity really worth the purchase of a leaf blower?

Chapter 1 includes a table in which you can start to list everything you own. If you've completed that table, expand that list by adding things that you forgot and then writing down what each item cost and how often you use it. (And check out Chapter 4 for more about distinguishing between needs and wants.) Until you decided to get control of your spending, you probably thought that you needed each of these things because you actually use them. Listing how much they cost and how often you use them gives you a whole new perspective.

Remember that the cost of insuring, maintaining, and storing rarely used items is an ongoing expense, even on appliances that are paid for. Make sure to factor these costs into your list.

For each item that you own but rarely use, you have four choices:

- ✔ Keep it and use it until it wears out.
- ✔ Sell the item and then rent or borrow a replacement only when you have a need for it.
- ✔ Sell the item and then pay someone to perform that chore with his or her own equipment.
- ✔ Find a lower-cost alternative to the item.

After you pick one of these four choices, put a new cost on each item in your list. How much money could you free up by renting, borrowing, or co-owning?

Now that you have this information, how will you use it? The choices you have tell you not only what to do with your current appliances, but also how to handle future needs. For example, when the leaf blower can't huff and puff anymore, you have four choices:

Book I

Taking
Stock of
Your
Financial
Situation

- ✔ Replace it.
- ✔ Rent a leaf blower only when the leaves come a-tumbling down.
- ✔ Make arrangements to borrow someone else's leaf blower when the need arises.
- ✔ Use a rake.

Whether you're renting, borrowing, or co-owning, make sure that your "partners" share your attitude on maintenance, cleanup, storage, and general care of tools and appliances.

Spend or barter?

With the proper incentive, anyone can make a deal. You may say that you don't know how to barter, but return for a minute to your childhood, and you'll see that you've always had the skill. Remember the words, "But Mom, if you buy me this toy, I'll eat all my vegetables for a week"?

Even in the grown-up world, you have negotiating skills — and bartering is negotiating. Maybe you want your washing machine fixed, your lawn mowed, or your eavestroughs cleaned out. All you need to do is find something that you can do for someone else in return for the service you need. For example, you help a friend with his resumé and, in exchange, he helps build you some bookshelves.

You have skills to trade, too. Think about the things you can do that other people want done for them. Make a list of all the skills you use at work or in pursuing your hobbies — designing Web sites, filling out tax returns, hanging wallpaper, taking photographs, and so on. Remember that personal skills (for example, closet reorganizing) and thinking skills (for example, planning a vacation) are tradable, too.

Using a fresh piece of paper (or a new computer file), start a list of all your skills. Keep this list with you. As you go about your life, you'll think of more and more skills to add to this list. You may want to divide the list into things you're willing to do, things you'll do if you have to, and things you don't ever want to do again.

Consider bartering clubs, which may facilitate this part of your money management. To find a bartering club, look in your local Yellow Pages, search the Internet, ask a librarian, or check with neighbourhood organizations, professional and trade associations, service organizations, alumni associations, and churches.

Every club has its own rules, but, like any other organization, someone has to pay the organization's costs. These include accounting, mail costs, promotion fees, and so on. If you're interested in joining a bartering club, you need to know the following information:

- ✔ Is there a fee to join? An annual fee?
- ✔ What fees are assessed on barters?
- ✔ Who belongs now? (Get a list.)
- ✔ Are the club membership and services growing or shrinking?
- ✔ How long has the club been in existence?
- ✔ Can you drop your membership whenever you want, as long as you "pay" whatever outstanding "debt" is in your account?

Find out as much as you can about a club before you join. If other members aren't reliable, are so fussy that they'll always complain about your contribution, or live so far away that they can't fulfill your needs, don't join.

Making Over Your Lifestyle

Giving your lifestyle a make-over is not the same as lowering your standard of living or depriving yourself. In fact, it can be quite the opposite. The emphasis here is on style. As the preceding sections on sharing and bartering demonstrate, a lifestyle make-over involves an attitude shift that will help you get the most for your dollar. The following sections will help you reach your financial goals.

Use coupons rather than pay full price

The art of saving money by using coupons is a consumer industry in itself. Whether you've never used coupons or you use them and want to get more from your efforts, the tips in this section can help you meet your goals.

"Couponing" is a skill for which reading carefully really pays off. First, you have to find coupons. Check newspapers and newspaper inserts, the packaging of items you've already bought, the back of your supermarket receipts, and coupon trade boxes inside stores, to name a few sources. Before buying a product that you know you want, check out company Web sites for coupons and other promotional items. This approach works especially well for food and pharmaceutical items.

Don't buy something just because you have a coupon for it. If you won't use the product for a while, you have to store it; if it's something you don't like, you'll never use it.

Keep up with the Joneses, but get better deals

Organizations to which you belong, such as Costco or Price Club, can come to your aid with special deals. Because these organizations buy in bulk, they often get a lower rate and can pass those savings along to you.

If you're planning a car trip and a gasoline credit card offers hotel discounts, this may be the time to obtain that card. If you have trouble with overspending on credit cards, you can close out your account as soon as the trip is over.

Remember that you don't have to spend a lot to have fun

When you first determined to get your financial house in order, you probably thought that entertainment was going to go by the wayside. Even with cable, television is a pretty poor long-term amusement. Luckily, you have many other options.

- ✔ **Support — and enjoy — the arts.** If the theatre, the opera, live music, and so on are your passion, you can enjoy them without breaking your budget. Many of these events use volunteer ushers. You usher; you attend for free. The downside is that you may have to see the same play ten times — and you can't walk out on a stinker. In the long run, however, you'll have a good time without spending a lot of money. And because you have to wear a uniform, you don't have to buy expensive going-to-the-theatre clothes!

- ✔ **Cruise for deals.** Some travel agencies sell off cruises and other deals at very good prices to people who can fill vacancies at the last minute. You can buy into these deals at 50 percent or less of the listed price. Sometimes you have to become a member of a travel group's club in order to be notified of an opening. Will you use or save enough to make membership fees worthwhile? These discounted offers are great, especially for retirees and self-employed people, whose schedules are more flexible.

✔ **Browse for can't-beat airfare.** Nearly all the major airlines offer last-minute airfare deals that allow you to take off on spur-of-the-moment weekend trips. You have to sign up to receive these e-mail updates, and they often include special rates on car rentals and hotel rates in the destinations to which the special fares apply. Check out individual airline Web sites, or go to www.expedia.ca, an online discount travel agency that does trip searching and booking for you. Expedia's offerings include last-minute deals.

Spend less and enjoy life more

Look for your own opportunities to reduce your expenses without reducing your quality of life. Instead of always looking to your wallet to pay for entertainment, use the creative skills that you've been developing. Knowledgeable, reliable people are in demand everywhere.

✔ Does your child's class need a chaperone for a school trip? Volunteer for the job.

✔ If you can't devote the time to be a regular usher at a theatre, offer a skill or time in trade for attending a dress rehearsal.

✔ If you like sports, find out what personnel are needed to put on an event. Could you be an assistant coach for a children's soccer or baseball league? Can you help organize a local tennis tournament?

✔ Can you speak a second language? Offer a friend language lessons in exchange for her teaching you to play guitar.

Living on Less

If you went to the store to buy one size and brand of bread and could pay either $2 or $2.50 for it, which would you choose? Sounds like a dumb question, doesn't it? Yet every day, people make the wrong decision.

Here are some ways to live on less without sacrificing quality of life:

✔ **Dig for deep discounts:** Shop at discount stores instead of convenience stores, and buy the same items for less. Head to the library or browse the Internet for a local or area-wide directory of discount and outlet stores.

✔ **Brown-bag it:** Take your lunch to work instead of buying it; you'll have a healthier lunch and save money, too.

✔ **Telecommute, if you can:** Negotiate with your employer to work at home. You can save restaurant, travel, car wear-and-tear, and clothing expenses.

Negotiate who is going to pay for the equipment, telephone lines, and other expenses. If those expenses are your responsibility, you may be spending instead of saving money.

✔ **Analyze your purchase decisions:** Understand your real goal before you make a purchase. If you want to lose weight, you can do so for free by walking in the park or by taking advantage of the company gym. Either one is cheaper than signing a contract at an exercise facility.

✔ **Consider the "previously owned":** A used car is "new" to you. Not only do you pay less, but your insurance costs are less than on a new car, your depreciation is slower, and you don't have to dread that first ding in the door.

✔ **Always use a shopping list:** Just as the lines on the highway keep you driving in the lane, a shopping list keeps you from giving in to temptation. Even if you decide to purchase something not on your list, you will have considered and weighed the purchase.

Book I

Taking
Stock of
Your
Financial
Situation

Hanging On to Your "Found" Money

The fastest way to undo all your hard work is to think of your money as a tradeoff between spending on one item and spending on another. Yes, you can take advantage of the savings that come from buying in quantity — if you've figured for waste, storage costs, and the other possible expenses of having a large quantity of one item on hand.

If you release yourself from always worrying about money by reducing your expenses, you may feel "rich" because you at last have cash in your pocket. That "found" money should go first toward debt reduction (as Chapter 3 in Book II discusses in depth) and then to savings (see Chapter 4 in this Book).

Does paying off debts and then putting money toward savings mean that you don't get to enjoy the fruits of your labour? Of course not. You get to enjoy being free from worry, seeing your debts disappear, and watching your savings grow.

While you're paying off debts and starting a savings program with your "found" money, don't even think about the credit available on your credit cards. Using that credit means more debt, which is exactly what you don't want.

Earning Additional Income

If all your money-saving, coupon-cutting, and planning still leaves you short of achieving your goals, look for ways to earn more income.

- ✔ **Getting a raise would be nice — and it's even possible!** Contact trade associations, your alumni association, and unions, and do research at the library or on the Internet, to find out what others doing your job are earning. If you find that your wage is lower than average, take your research to your boss and ask for a raise.

- ✔ **Take an inventory of your skills.** Look for skills that you use at work, but maybe aren't appreciated by your boss and aren't being recognized in your paycheque. Bosses don't have to think about what's going right — so they don't! You need to remind your boss about your accomplishments. If you can prove that you're underpaid, negotiate a raise.

- ✔ **Allow your hobbies to earn you extra money.** For example, if you know how to work with wood, you can sell the furniture that you build or help people build things for a fee. You may have to do a little research to see how much you should charge customers, but hobbies still are a good source of income that's a pleasure to earn.

You not only need to survey your knowledge and skills to see where you might earn extra income, but you also must decide how much you want to earn and what it will cost you to do so. Remember to calculate material and tool expenditures as well as time expenditures. Will you recoup your investment? Will you have enough income to write off those expenditures on your income taxes as business expenses?

Think about whether you want to take on any extra work for a short, medium, or long period of time.

- ✔ **Short-term need:** If you want to do extra work only long enough to pay off your credit card or other debt, you may want to look for seasonal work or register with a temporary-employment agency. Because you won't be working extra for a long time (you get to define "long"), you'll probably have the energy to work longer hours, work more days per week, commute a little farther, and so on.

- ✔ **Mid-term need:** If this extra job is going to go on for a while because you need the extra income for a longer period, such as while your child grows up, you don't want to commit yourself to so many hours, so much travel, or so many days per week that you don't have a life. That's a quick way to burn out. Not only will you fail to reach your goals, you'll be discouraged and may even think that you can't reach your goals or that budgeting doesn't work.

> ✔ **Long-term need:** To earn extra income for a long-term need, such as retirement, consider the same things that you did for a mid-term need. Recognize that the decisions you make will affect your lifestyle for a long time.

If you're going to be forced to spend more time at work, have more commuting costs, have wasted "dead" time (blocks of time between jobs that are long enough to be annoying but short enough that you can't really use them for naps, grocery shopping, or whatever), it may be time to consider cutting back on your lifestyle. Moving to less expensive housing, sharing housing, seeking sales, bartering more aggressively, and so on, will allow you to make more life-enhancing decisions sooner.

For mid-term or long-term extra income needs, consider trading some of the income for cutting back on your lifestyle. The tips in this chapter can help you make your money go further so that you can enjoy your life and still get out of debt and start a savings program.

Book I

Taking
Stock of
Your
Financial
Situation

Book II
Money Management Basics

The 5th Wave   By Rich Tennant

"I can always tell when Philip is working on family finances. A 'cursor' appears on both sides of the computer screen."

In this book . . .

When it comes to basics, this Book delivers the BCDs. (You can find what you need to know about the A's — all about you — in Book I.) B is for budget — creating one that's reasonable and achievable, and developing a record-keeping strategy that will help you keep track of your budget. C is for credit — establishing good credit, and keeping it in good shape, will go a long way to keeping your money management portfolio intact. D is for debt — discovering which debt is good debt and which debt you should avoid (or pay down, if you're already too, too familiar with your debt).

Finally, this Book helps you understand your money management basics in the context of the big C: the CCRA. The Canada Customs and Revenue Agency will accept your involuntary donations year after year. In this Book, you can find out what that all means, and its impact on your financial future.

Here are the contents of Book II at a glance:

Chapter 1

Getting Credit (Where Credit Is Due)

In This Chapter

▶ The pros and cons of credit

▶ Determining acceptable levels of credit debt

▶ Discovering the pros and cons of paying cash versus using credit

*Y*ou may remember your first credit card as a badge of adulthood. At university campuses from Vancouver to Halifax, students are enticed by offers of credit cards. You may get mail from banks almost weekly offering pre-approved credit and competitive rates. If you don't have a bad credit history, banks should be more than willing to extend you some credit.

Getting a credit card is one thing. Using it effectively is another story altogether. And that's the story of this chapter.

The Pros and Cons of Credit

Securing credit is like applying for a loan: You ask a financial institution to lend or "rent" you the use of its money. For the use of the money, you can expect to pay "extra" money. The terms of your agreement specify the rate of interest — the extra money you pay in order to pay back your debt to the institution that issued the credit card.

The benefits of establishing credit are significant. They include the following:

✔ The ability to make major purchases when you don't have immediate cash for the item(s)

✔ A sense of security that you can handle an unexpected emergency by using credit

✔ The convenience of shopping without carrying a lot of cash

✔ Monthly itemized credit statements that enable you to track your purchases

    ✔ Worldwide acceptance

Establishing credit is a double-edged sword. With its benefits come some major disadvantages, including the following:

    ✔ Easily available credit can make spending second nature.

    ✔ If you can't pay off your credit balances on time, you affect your credit rating.

    ✔ You can fall into the trap of paying off some of the credit debt instead of paying the whole amount.

    ✔ When you add credit expenses to the stated price, you end up paying more than you expected.

For many Canadians, over-aggressive use of available credit can result in a debt load that is very difficult to sustain.

Establishing Credit for the First Time

When you're fresh out of college, starting over after a divorce, or emerging from bad debt or bankruptcy, your thoughts turn to establishing or re-establishing credit. Here are some tips for establishing credit and getting off to a good start in managing credit debt:

    ✔ Open a chequing account and a savings account at a local bank or credit union. Keep your balance at the acceptable minimum level, and never overdraw your account.

    ✔ Make an appointment with your personal banker to apply for a bank credit card. Come prepared with a statement of your personal assets and liabilities and your monthly budget.

    ✔ Apply for a charge account at a local store. Shop at this store and charge your items. Pay your bills promptly — these cards usually have obscenely high interest rates.

    ✔ Ask a parent or mentor to co-sign for a credit card issued in your name. With this arrangement, you have personal responsibility for payments, and your credit history will be reported in your name. The co-signer agrees to take on the liability for credit payments on an account if you can't pay.

    ✔ Keep trying. You may be rejected for one credit card and then be granted another, especially after you establish your creditworthiness by opening bank accounts and successfully using bank cards and store charge cards.

Deciding on an Acceptable Level of Credit

When the credit card offers start coming, they seem to compete with each other by raising the level of credit that they will extend to you. You may get a small thrill when you receive a letter from a credit card company telling you that you're prequalified for a line of credit that boggles your mind.

These days, companies are offering $10,000, $25,000, and even up to $100,000 lines of credit. This is absurd! Why would anyone want that much credit card debt? You may be flattered to think that someone would extend you a line of credit for large amounts of money, and you may be tempted to say, "You never know when that money would come in handy." Don't give in to temptation too easily — you need to think seriously about the level of credit debt that your income can tolerate. Just because a lender is willing to extend that line of credit doesn't mean you have to use it. Still, the temptation to do so is great, and many fall into the trap of using their line of credit to the maximum.

Imagine Mr. and Mrs. Conservative — the couple who pay cash for everything and don't owe anyone money. Their debts are paid. Their cars and house are paid for. Their children went to college and are now buying houses of their own. Yes, they borrowed money, but only to buy their home, and then they paid off the mortgage ahead of time.

Now, imagine Mr. and Mrs. Bigspender — the couple you like to be with because they always pick up the tab for dinner. They talk about the expensive vacations they take. They live in a large home and drive expensive cars. They're up to their eyeballs in debt. They have no clue about how to change their spending and debt habits. Who's really having all the fun!

Your own comfort with credit card debt is likely to be somewhere in the middle. The following tables can help you figure out what your level of debt should be.

First, use Table 1-1 to identify the amount of debt you currently carry. The first two lines of the table are examples; fill in your own debts in the remaining lines. (Feel free to add lines if you need to.)Most financial advisers recommend a personal debt limit of between 10 and 20 percent of your net income, maximum. To figure out your personal debt ratio, use Table 1-2.

Table 1-2 helps you determine the level of credit that's acceptable to you with your net income. If your debt margin is too close for comfort, sit down right now and write down three ways that you can reduce your monthly credit-instalment payments. If your debt margin is comfortably less than your monthly credit obligations, don't rush out to buy things on credit. Instead, congratulate yourself on your frugality and revisit your savings plan (see Chapter 4 in Book I).

Book II

Money Management Basics

Table 1-1	Monitoring Your Debts and Monthly Payments			
Creditor's Name	*Loan*	*Total Due*	*Monthly*	*Maturity Payment*
Main St. Bank	Car	$5,040	$140	36 months
VISA		$1,000	$120	10 months
Total debt				
Total monthly payments				

Table 1-2	Determining Your Debt Ratio	
Your monthly net income		
To accommodate debt of 20 percent, divide your net income by 5.		
To accommodate debt of 15 percent, divide your net income by 6.7.		
To accommodate debt of 10 percent, divide your net income by 10.		
Your monthly debt obligations (see the "Total monthly payments" line in Table 1-1)		
Calculate your debt margin (the ratio of debt to net income) by subtracting your monthly debt obligations from whichever level of debt you're comfortable with		
Figure out your personal debt ratio by dividing your monthly debt obligations by your monthly net income		

Avoiding the Credit Card Trap with the Two-Card System

Many financial advisers will tell you never to take your credit cards out of the house. As soon as you do, their easy availability makes frivolous purchases easier and more tempting.

For many people, the stack of plastic in their wallets gives them a sense of security and pleasure. The greater the number of credit cards, however, the greater the danger of overspending. To avoid costly credit card abuse, consider the two-card system, described in the following sections.

Finding a good card

Selecting a credit card that works best for you is often as difficult as establishing credit in the first place. You have so many choices — most financial institutions offer co-branded Visa or MasterCard cards. In general, though, credit cards vary in at least four aspects:

- **Annual fees:** Some cards charge an annual fee ranging from $25 to $75. Some cards waive the annual fee for first-time customers but charge the fee in subsequent years after the customer has become accustomed to using the card. But other cards do not charge an annual fee. Look for these cards.

- **Interest rates:** Rates vary, generally ranging from 8.5 percent to 20 percent. It pays to shop around and compare interest rates.

- **Grace periods:** Some cards begin to charge interest from the date of each purchase; others begin to charge interest from the date of expected payment. Again, shop around to find a card that offers a longer grace period. In fact, you should reject outright those cards that charge immediate interest from the date of purchase.

- **Co-branding:** More and more credit cards are partnering with airlines, gasoline companies, and financial institutions to give customers incentives to use their cards. Some cards give frequent flyer miles on a particular airline for the dollar value of purchases made with the card. Others offer free gasoline or discounts on purchases. This type of card may be advantageous to you, but weigh the interest rates and annual fees against the benefits.

Using the two-card system

After you compare cards, select two that serve your needs and refuse or cancel all the rest. Determine to use one card with the lower interest rate for large purchases, because you probably cannot pay off the balance in one month, and the other, with the higher interest rate, for smaller purchases, because you will pay off this balance each month.

The two-card system works best when you know that you'll be making a major purchase. Perhaps you know that you need a refrigerator or you want a better sound system. These are big-ticket items, and you probably don't have ready cash available for the purchase.

Become familiar with the timing of the billing for your large credit card purchases and time your major purchases accordingly. For example, if you make a purchase immediately after the billing date and you have a grace period of 25 to 30 days, you have, in effect, free credit for almost two months. If you buy that refrigerator on February 2, the day after your billing date, the purchase will not appear on your bill until March 1. You often have 30 days to pay without interest. If you pay the entire bill on April 1, you will not have paid any interest for that purchase.

If a finance charge is calculated on the average daily balance with newly purchased items included, finance charges are immediately added to your bill, and it's better to pay the bill as soon as you get it, because the charges add up daily.

Use the second credit card for your smaller purchases. Pay the amount due on this credit card in full each month. Limit your spending to accommodate those purchases that you can pay off entirely and those larger purchases that you can manage while still maintaining the comfortable debt ratio that you identified earlier in this chapter.

Understanding the Cost of Credit

Credit costs you money. For example, if you use your credit card to buy a $120 watch as a Christmas gift, here's how the costs add up: First, add in the provincial sales tax (PST) and goods and services tax (GST). Then add in the finance charge. This charge, in its common usage, means the combination of the interest rate and any transaction fee the credit company adds to single or cumulative transactions. If your finance charge is 19.2 percent and you pay $10 a month for a year to pay for the watch, your watch costs $120, plus PST and GST, plus about $15 in credit charges. All of a sudden, that watch seems a lot more expensive.

If you leave part of your bill unpaid, the creditor will charge you interest. The creditor also assesses a transaction charge for the service of extending credit to you. The entire finance charge is taken from your payment, and your debt is reduced only by what's left over. For example, if you make a partial payment of $50 and the finance charge is $10, your debt is reduced not by $50 but by $40. Partial payments reduce your debt very slowly.

Recognize signs of trouble

The more you buy on credit, the more you pay to reduce your debt. You know that you're in credit trouble if you recognize any of the following warning signs:

- You find yourself charging more and more and paying with cash less and less.

- You let some bills slide and postpone payment for a month.

- You make partial payments instead of paying the entire bill.

- Your debt-to-net-income ratio exceeds 20 percent.

- You take out new credit cards to cover additional purchases after you max out the cards that you're currently using.

Book II

Money Management Basics

Cut credit costs

Only you can control what you buy on credit. Credit cards that get out of control cost you money and delay your ability to invest in your financial future. Try the following tips to reduce your credit costs:

- Shop for a low-cost or free credit card.

- Don't pay extra annual fees for premier cards that offer gold or platinum benefits unless you really need the extra benefits that they offer. Don't pay for services that you will not use, no matter how neatly packaged the offer.

- Use your credit cards only for necessary purchases. Don't charge for items such as toys, liquor, or vacations. If you can't pay cash, you don't need them at the moment.

- If you're making a major purchase on a credit card, select a card that charges a lower interest rate.

- Review your credit card statements carefully each month. Attend to mistakes or questions about your bill promptly.

- Pay the entire bill on every credit card every month.

- Reduce the amount of credit available to you. Cancel credit cards that you don't need.

- Consolidate your credit card debt so that you pay interest charges on only one card.

- Pay off outstanding credit card balances before taking on further debt. Re-evaluate the amount of debt that you're willing to carry in relation to the amount of money you want to save.

- Pay off the credit cards with the highest interest rates first.

Chapter 2

Getting Into Debt

. . . .

In This Chapter

▶ Defining credit, debt, and expenses

▶ Figuring out how much you owe

▶ Determining how you got into debt

▶ Setting your priorities

▶ Looking at the resources or assets you have for reducing your debt

. . . .

Knowing the different types of debts and expenses that drain the money out of your pocket every month can help you prioritize your payments and identify places to cut back. This knowledge also helps you assess how effective your choices are likely to be; some of the available options may or may not help, depending on the type of debt you have.

Understanding Debts and Expenses

Debt is anything owed. Debt can be very short term, like ordering a meal in a restaurant and having to pay for it before you leave, or long-term, like buying a house with a 30-year mortgage. Whatever you have to pay is a debt. But to understand debt's impact on your financial future, you need to understand credit. This book deals only with personal credit, which has two aspects: having funds put at your disposal (loan, cash advance); and time given for payment of goods and services sold on trust (credit cards, instalment plans). Both involve the promise of future repayment, usually with interest.

Credit

The way you get credit is by establishing creditworthiness, which is a measure of your reliability to repay a loan. Lenders consider three factors in determining creditworthiness:

- **Capacity:** The measure of your ability to repay; refers primarily to your income.
- **Capital:** The value of what you own, including property, investments, and savings.
- **Character:** Generally regarded as the most important factor. To determine this, lenders rely on reports of your credit history.

Credit bureaus collect information on the borrowing and repayment patterns of all consumers. They put everything about you that may affect repayment — including the name of your employer, income, mortgage, outstanding bills, legal problems, available credit — into this history. Credit reports that are sent to potential lenders, and which can be requested by employers when you apply for jobs, are based on your credit history.

The reason credit histories suffer so badly when you don't pay your bills is that credit is not merely a convenience, it is a legal contract built on a foundation of trust. In failing to pay bills, you are both breaking the law and betraying trust. Most consumers don't think of credit this way — but creditors do. You may want to think about how you view credit, because it affects how you use it.

You can research your credit history on your own. You can purchase a copy of your up-to-date credit history from companies such as Equifax (www.equifax.ca) — the same resources that creditors use to evaluate your credit history.

Debt

The "Assessing Your Situation" section later in this chapter provides guidelines to help you determine whether your debt is enough to worry about. However, any debt is too much if you're not completely comfortable with it. If you can't easily pay all your bills every month, or if you carry a balance on any of your credit cards, you're already wading into the bog. If you don't do something to change your direction, you'll be in over your head before you know it.

Debts are broken down into a variety of categories. Understanding and identifying these categories can help you prioritize your payments and identify places to cut back. All debts are either secured or unsecured.

Secured loans

A *secured loan* is a loan backed by collateral — something of value that you own — and pledge to a lender to insure payment. You make a promise, usually in the form of a printed security agreement, stating that the creditor, or person or company you owe money to, can take a specified item of your property if you fail to pay back the loan.

Often, the item pledged is the one being purchased. The pledged item can also be an item that you already own. If you stop paying for any reason, the pledged item goes to the creditor.

Book II

Money Management Basics

The most common items purchased by a secured loan are:

- ✔ Houses and condos
- ✔ Motor vehicles (cars, trucks, and motorcycles)
- ✔ Major appliances (refrigerators and washing machines)
- ✔ Furniture
- ✔ Expensive jewellery

Generally speaking, secured loans are high priorities in your debt repayment plan, especially if the loans are for a home or transportation. You may be willing to have someone repossess a diamond necklace, but you certainly don't want anyone foreclosing on your mortgage and repossessing your home.

Unsecured loans

An *unsecured loan* is a loan not backed by collateral — anything you own that can be taken by the lender if you can't pay the debt. The majority of debt in Canada is in the form of unsecured loans — primarily credit cards — but this category also includes student and personal loans, and dental bills. (*Personal loans* are unsecured loans that you take out to pay for specific expenditures, such as a vacation, a wedding, or a major appliance.) The lender grants you credit based on your creditworthiness or, in some cases, on the creditworthiness of a co-signer (someone who agrees to repay the loan if you are unable to.)

Because unsecured loans are riskier for lenders, most of these loans have higher interest rates than secured loans do. Due to high interest rates, particularly on credit cards, these loans can represent the biggest drain on your finances.

The face of Canadian debt

Debt certainly has various forms, and Canadians are no strangers to credit. Following is the most recent snapshot (1999) that Statistics Canada (www.statcan.ca) took of Canadians' appetite for debt:

Nature of debt	Average $ debt per family unit	Median $ debt per family unit	Debt for Canada (in $million)
Mortgages	$82,800	$69,000	$355,094
Line of credit	$13,500	$5,000	$26,281
Credit card and instalment debt*	$3,000	$1,800	$14,251
Student loans	$10,400	$7,300	$14,877
Vehicle loans	$11,200	$9,000	$29,089
Other debt	$9,300	$4,000	$18,485

Includes traditional (e.g. VISA, American Express), retail, gas, and other credit cards. Instalment debt is the total amount owing on deferred payment or instalment plans where the purchased item is to be paid for over a period of time.

Expenses

Expense is spending or cost — just another form of debt, really. But expense is traditionally short-term, like food costs or the phone bill. (Of course, putting expenses on a credit card makes them part of your "real" debts, with the increased possibility of added interest payments.)

Many sources use the terms expense and debt interchangeably, so understand that whichever term is used, it always ends up meaning that money is going out.

Essential expenses

Some expenses must be paid, either because of the law or because you still need someplace to live, even if you're broke. These essential expenses are divided into two categories: essential fixed expenses and essential variable expenses.

Essential fixed expenses do not vary from month to month. You may see annual increases in some categories, but you can often anticipate these expenses and plan for them.

Essential fixed expenses include the following:

- ✔ Rent or mortgage payments
- ✔ Car payments
- ✔ Insurance (auto, health, life)
- ✔ Alimony/child support

Essential variable expenses differ from month to month, but they often offer you a greater opportunity to cut costs, either by finding less expensive alternatives or by cutting back on use. Essential variable expenses include the following:

- ✔ Food
- ✔ Utilities (water, gas, electricity)
- ✔ Phone
- ✔ Gasoline or other transportation costs
- ✔ Health care expenses

Book II

Money
Management
Basics

There are other payments that are not normally included under essential expenses — primarily debt repayment — because these payments are not considered part of an "ideal" budget. They include payments on secured loans (other than home equity or improvement loans and mortgage), unsecured loans, student loans, personal loans, and instalment payment plans.

Because your goal is to be debt-free and have a beautifully unblemished credit report, you want to keep repaying your debts.

Another essential expense is taxes. Most of the time, adequate taxes are deducted from your paycheque. But if you find at the end of the year that you owe taxes, the expense can add to your debt burden. Of course, if you're self-employed, the expense may become a problem even before the end of the tax year. Either way, you need to keep a few things in mind when you're trying to prioritize your payments:

- ✔ Paying taxes is always and unequivocally essential, if for no other reason than that the Canada Customs and Revenue Agency (CCRA) can hurt you worse than almost anyone else.
- ✔ That said, know that CCRA wants to help you pay your taxes. CCRA offers a number of useful taxpayer information publications, and can refer you to free tax services. Also, CCRA can help you put together a payment schedule for paying your taxes.

Nonessential expenses

Just about everything that's not listed in the "Essential expenses" section is nonessential. Some services, conveniences, and luxuries have become such a normal part of everyday life that you may think they're essential, but they're not.

Popular nonessentials include:

- Cable TV
- Lawn services
- Cleaning services
- Magazine subscriptions (unless they're business related)
- Cigarettes and alcohol
- Restaurant meals
- Movies (especially full-priced ones)
- Club memberships

Borderline/debatable expenses

Just as one person's meat is another person's poison, so, too, one person's nonessential expense can be another person's necessity. Because no one else possesses precisely the same combination of characteristics, needs, priorities, and circumstances that you do, some expenses — perhaps many — require careful consideration. It's important to be honest with yourself about what you really need, and what you are simply accustomed to or find convenient.

An expense is considered borderline or debatable when, due to circumstances or life situation, it cannot easily be dropped into either the essential or the nonessential category. Borderline expenses may be nonessential in themselves, but you may be nearly finished paying for something with no hope of regaining your investment. They may be debts owed to people you can talk into waiting a little while longer for repayment. Also, some essential expenses (such as a phone) have extra features (such as three-way calling) that are nonessential in most cases.

Following are examples of expenses that may be borderline or debatable:

- If you're young and healthy, permanent life insurance is debatable. Consider term life insurance until you're out of debt.
- Health club membership may be debatable. If you just signed up and owe thousands, dump the membership. If you paid a huge, nonrefundable initiation fee several years ago and pay only a small monthly or annual

maintenance fee now, the membership is probably worth keeping — especially if you use the health club as a low-cost alternative to costlier activities.

✔ Health and auto insurance may be essential, but low deductibles aren't. Find out whether you can lower your payments by having a higher deductible. However, make sure to budget for extra savings to cover the higher deductible.

✔ Clothes are less debatable than you may think. For most people (other than growing children), clothes don't need to be replaced that often. Consider sticking with what you have for a couple of years unless something disintegrates or you have to go on a job interview and you don't have anything appropriate to wear.

Book II

Money Management Basics

Identifying your expense types

To identify how your expenses and debts can be categorized, write down everything on which you spend money. Include as much detail as possible in your list, making the list as long as necessary.

Although big purchases obviously cause greater debt, the little, unplanned things — the ones you hardly even notice — are often the ones that undercut your best intentions. For example, snacking out of vending machines combined with stopping for gourmet coffee on the way to work each day can add up to nearly $1,000 a year.

Using the following codes, identify the status of each expense item on your list:

✔ S = Secured loan

✔ U = Unsecured loan

✔ EF = Essential fixed expense

✔ EV = Essential variable expense

✔ N = Nonessential expense

✔ R = Expense that can be reduced

✔ C = Expense that can be cut entirely

✔ ? = Need to research whether this expense can be reduced or cut

Note: You don't see a code for borderline/debatable items because items are borderline only until you decide which category they belong in. Making that decision is one of the things you need to accomplish in this exercise.

Table 2-1 gives you an idea of how your worksheet may look.

Table 2-1	Items on Which You Spend Money
Item	*Category*
Mortgage	S, EF, ?
Food	EV, R
Phone, general	EV, R
Phone, extras	_____
Entertainment	_____
Magazines	_____
Gasoline	_____
Health club	_____
Beverages purchased at office	_____
Car payment	_____
Life insurance	_____
Personal loan(s)	_____
Cigarettes	_____
Cable TV	_____

Continue to add lines, making the list as long as necessary. You want to account for everything on which you spend money.

This chart is not a contract. Expenses do not need to remain static. As circumstances change, you can add or delete items or change the status of an item. If a job change makes it necessary for you to have a pager, for example, you can simply move that expense from the nonessential to the essential category.

For the next few days, you may want to keep a notebook and jot down items that you didn't think to add to your expense list. (Those items could include the toll you always pay on the way to work, the laundry money you always toss in a jar so that you'll have it when you need it, or the drink that you have with friends every Friday night.) The more aware you are of where your money goes, the easier it will be to keep your expenses under control.

By the time you're through with this worksheet, you should have a pretty good idea of where your money is going, what you must include in your budget, and where you can cut back.

You can reduce most expenses if you put your mind to it. The more you reduce expenses, the more quickly you can improve your credit history.

Assessing Your Situation

One thing that's true for everyone is that, in order to plan how to get somewhere, you have to know where you're starting. That's why you need to start by assessing your financial situation.

How you got into debt is particularly significant because the work you need to do and the changes you want to make will be different if, for example, your debts were caused by job loss as opposed to uncontrolled spending. Determining your priorities will help you later in the budgeting and rebuilding process.

Book II

Money
Management
Basics

Figuring out how much you owe

You can set your repayment priorities later. Right now, you need to figure out where you stand in the negative column.

Total debt

Use Table 2-2 to record all your debts. Total up your debts by type, and then calculate your grand total. This final number represents your total outstanding debt. If an item in the sample worksheet doesn't apply to you, skip it; also feel free to add or delete items so that the worksheet accurately reflects your debt. Also, add the percentage interest rate being charged for each credit card and loan next to the amount due.

Table 2-2	Calculating Your Total Debt	
Home Debt	*Amount Due*	*Annual Interest Rate*
Mortgage	$_____	_____
Home equity loan	$_____	_____
Furniture on instalment plan	$_____	_____
Appliances on instalment plan	$_____	_____
Past-due utility bills	$_____	_____
Total home debt	$_____	

(continued)

Table 2-2 *(continued)*

Auto Debt	Amount Due	Annual Interest Rate
Loan/ car 1	$_____	_____
Loan/ car 2	$_____	_____
Total auto debt	$_____	

Credit Card Debt	Amount Due	Annual Interest Rate
MasterCard	$_____	_____
Visa	$_____	_____
Other	$_____	_____

(Add as many other lines as necessary)

	Amount Due	Annual Interest Rate
Total credit card debt	$_____	

Miscellaneous Debt	Amount Due	Annual Interest Rate
Health care bills	$_____	_____
Personal loans	$_____	_____
Student loans	$_____	_____
Other loans	$_____	_____
Total miscellaneous debt	$_____	

Outstanding Taxes	Amount Due	Annual Interest Rate
Federal	$_____	_____
Provincial	$_____	_____
Municipal	$_____	_____
Other	$_____	_____
Total tax debt	$_____	
Total all debts	$_____	

Notice that you didn't have to include regular expenses such as utilities (unless they're past due), food, and fuel. That's because, even though these expenses arise regularly, they really aren't part of your debt (unless you charge them). However, they do have an impact on how much money is available to go toward your debts. So don't get rid of any information that you have on these expenses, because you'll need it when you do your budget. (See Chapter 3.)

Rent and lease payments were also excluded because they are not debt in the same sense that a loan is, though you are legally obligated to pay both, even if you give up the apartment or car. Also, alimony and child support were not included. Although these are all debt obligations, if you owe them, and have to be part of your calculations, they are not things that you can pay off early or reduce.

Debt as percentage of income

To determine how serious your debt is, you need to determine how much of your monthly net income (that's income after taxes — your actual take-home pay) is going toward paying debt. To do so, follow these steps:

1. Add up your monthly debt obligations, including rent or mortgage payment, lease or car loan payments, other loan payments, credit card payments, alimony, and child support.

2. Divide the total by the amount of your monthly income after taxes. Unlike the total debt amount that you calculated earlier, for this calculation consider only the monthly payments you make.

For example, imagine that you have a mortgage payment of $800, an automobile loan payment of $300, a credit card payment of $100, a student loan payment of $200, an instalment loan payment of $100, and take-home pay of $4,500.

Here's how this monthly debt obligation translates into debt as percentage of income:

$800 + $300 + $100 + $200 + $100 = $1,500 in monthly debt obligations

$1,500 ÷ $4,500 = 33.3 percent

In other words, 33.3 percent of the monthly net income ($4,500) goes toward paying off debt.

If your debt obligations are 25 percent or less of your take-home pay, you're in reasonable shape. If they're between 25 and 35 percent, you should be concerned and begin thinking about how you can try to get closer to 25 percent. If they're over 35 percent, you're headed for serious trouble or may already be there — you must move quickly and decisively to reduce debt.

The 33.3 percent in the sample formula, therefore, is not yet catastrophic but is well into the "time to get serious about debt" range.

On a card or piece of notepaper, write your current percentage, then write next to it the percentage to aim for (25 percent or less). Write today's date on the card, and write down how long you think it will take you to achieve your goals. (Don't worry, you can always revise this estimate as you progress.) Place it somewhere you can see it regularly, to help you keep your goal in mind.

Book II

**Money
Management
Basics**

How did you get into debt?

It's possible that you played no part in the accumulation of debt — you may have inherited it from others or acquired it as a result of circumstances beyond your control, such as a serious illness or a natural disaster. In that case, you simply need to address the mechanics of paying bills and rebuilding credit. With the disciplines of a few money-saving and debt-retiring strategies, you may find yourself in a stronger position than before your debts accrued.

Most people, however, have a pattern of debt — a series of behaviours that get them into the hole. The more uncertain you are of how you got into trouble, the more likely it is that you'll need to change some of your behaviours.

This important exercise will help you determine how you got into debt. You need to be really honest with yourself for this to work. If you've run up thousands of dollars in credit card debt, don't call it "bad luck." Get a sheet of paper and start to write down behaviours or triggers that get you into trouble. Don't judge yourself or your debts as you write. No one else needs to see this list. Simply write down everything that's fuelling your debt.

To get started on your list, answer the following questions:

✔ Why did you take on your first significant debt load?

✔ How do you feel about debt?

✔ How does spending money make you feel?

✔ Do you ever "binge shop"? If so, what sorts of things trigger the binges?

✔ What reaction do you have to advertisements for items that you want but can't afford?

✔ Do you believe that paying the minimum amount on your credit card will get the balance paid off?

✔ Are you ever surprised by how high a bill is?

✔ Do you forget about money that you've spent?

✔ Do you balance your chequing account regularly?

✔ Do you have any expensive hobbies or habits?

✔ Do you feel competitive with or threatened by those around you?

✔ How often do you eat out?

✔ When you eat out with friends, do you collect cash from others, charge the meal, and then buy something else with the cash instead of paying down your credit card debt?

✔ Do you plan your purchases or do you buy on impulse?

Review your list on how much you owe. The information may give you even more ideas about how you got into debt. Add any discoveries to your list of trouble behaviours and triggers.

As you write, more ideas may come to you. Record everything that crosses your mind regarding your spending habits, whether it's a feeling that you must pamper yourself to deal with stress, a hope that you can overcome your sense of dissatisfaction with life, or a belief that you need to impress someone.

A journal can be particularly helpful in identifying emotion-triggered spending, as well as in tracking your progress and recording what you learn, both about the process and about yourself.

As you continue through the rest of this book, add to your list any new information that you discover about yourself. Knowing why you spend and what your triggers are can help you figure out how to stop uncontrolled spending.

Book II

Money Management Basics

Determining your priorities

Obviously, one major priority is to get out of debt. At this point, however, you need to think about what your priorities in life are; how they relate to or may be affected by debt; and how they fit into the process of getting out of debt.

For this exercise, think about your real priorities — the things that matter deeply to you. You need to account for considerations like family and beliefs first and foremost, no matter what type of debt you're facing.

Later, when you start to create your budget, you can prioritize your "wish list" — the things that you would like but that aren't really vital in the greater scheme of things — in order to identify expenses that you can reduce or cut. But right now, think about the priorities that will help you determine what kind of path you will take.

Here are some questions to answer as you think about your priorities:

- ✔ Where does your family fit into the picture?
- ✔ Is taking a second job an option (financially, emotionally)?
- ✔ Is giving to charity or religious organizations important to you?
- ✔ For your own peace of mind, how quickly do you want to be out of debt? What are you willing to sacrifice to get there?

> ✔ What things that are important to you are affected by your debt, or may be affected by it if you do not remedy it? (This may include anything from not being able to join friends for dinner to having to postpone starting a family or losing your house.)
>
> ✔ What goals do you have that may be attainable once you're out of debt? (This could be anything from educating children to enjoying a comfortable retirement.)

As you think about your priorities, jot down the things that matter most to you — the things that will have an impact on how and why you want to get out of debt.

If you have young children or aging parents, you may not view a second job as an option. In this case, you're making family a priority and accepting the possibility of a slightly longer repayment period. The debts aren't going anywhere, but the people are, so this is a good choice.

Getting out of debt is about making your life better, not worse.

Looking at your resources and assets

In evaluating the resources and assets you have for getting yourself out of debt, consider not only your income but also any capital available, including savings, investments, and property. This exercise has two steps:

1. **Calculate your monthly income.**

   You'll use this figure later to work out your budget. Because income can change over time, the wisest approach is simply to figure out what you're taking in at the present time.

2. **Determine any additional funds that may be available to you.**

   If you need to make dramatic changes in your debt profile, also consider potential sources of money.

Set up your calculations something like Table 2-3, with the various real or potential sources of funds separated.

Table 2-3	Calculating Your Total Assets
Income (after Taxes)	*Amount*
Primary wages	$_____
Secondary wages (second job/secondary wage earner)	$_____
Alimony/child support	$_____
Government support	$_____
Other income	$_____
Total income	**$_____**
Easily Accessible Money	*Amount*
Savings	$_____
Investments	$_____
Total easily accessible money	**$_____**
Less Accessible Money	*Amount*
Home equity	$_____
Car equity	$_____
Boat equity	$_____
Other (such as equity in a vacation home or undeveloped property)	$_____
Cash-value insurance	$_____
Total less accessible money	**$_____**
Other Possible (Though Less Desirable) Sources of Money	*Amount*
RRSPs	$_____
Total other sources of money	**$_____**

Reviewing your assets helps you determine where your money is, which, in turn, helps you with both the budgeting process and improving your debt picture (see Chapter 3).

Chapter 3

Getting Out of Debt

● ●

In This Chapter

▶ Creating a budget that manages your debt

▶ Keeping up with your minimum payments

▶ Paying down your debts

▶ Looking at ways to find more money in your budget

▶ Deciding whether bankruptcy is appropriate for you

● ●

*I*n Chapter 2, you determined where you are in terms of your debt — your starting point. You also began to think about where you're going. Now it's time to plan the "trip." This process includes setting specific goals, determining how long the journey should take, and creating a "map" to help you get there.

Putting Together a Budget

This map is your budget, which helps you do two things: plan your spending and track your progress. A budget may seem restrictive at first, but it frees you from the worry of not knowing how you're doing financially. A budget can give you greater control and keep you on the road to your destination — freedom from debt. Budgets are great vehicles to help you get where you want to be, but they require a special fuel — your commitment!

Determining and refining your debt repayment goals

Setting goals takes effort and commitment. You'll need to think carefully about where you want to be financially, as well as what future plans you have that may be affected by your finances. You'll also need to be reasonable, and not set yourself impossible goals. Take this seriously, but don't panic about it — you can modify your goals as time goes by.

The following sections discuss the key elements that you will need to consider to create goals that are both attainable and motivating.

Be positive

Your goal should not be something negative, such as "to spend less money." Staying motivated by a negative goal is difficult. Charting your progress is also difficult — when have you cut enough? To be effective, your goal needs to be an accomplishment, not a sacrifice.

Instead, your goal should be something like "to enjoy the freedom of carrying a debt load of only 25 percent of my take-home pay." That goal is positive and quantifiable. Other possibilities may be "to pick up the mail without being nervous," "to feel that I am in control of my finances," or "to get to a point where I can start investing so that more money is coming in than going out." These goals aren't as easily quantifiable as the percentage-of-take-home-pay goal, but the point is to find something that keeps you motivated and excited about the process.

Take your plans into account

In a way, you've already established one goal: to be out of debt. Although this is your primary goal, you may want to consider other, secondary goals, which will be made possible by your success with your primary goal.

Depending on where you are in life, your plans may be to have children, put children through university, buy a house, or enjoy a secure retirement. All these goals will benefit — and some are only possible — if you get your finances under control. The nearer in time your plans lie, the more quickly you want to eliminate your debt and begin saving. For example, if you want to buy a house in five years, you may be willing to work harder to pay off your credit cards so that you can get a mortgage. And you may even want to give yourself an extra year or two to save up for furniture so that you don't get into too much debt again.

Over time, your lifestyle, earning power, and attitudes may change, so review your goals regularly to make sure that they still reflect your plans.

Establish a time frame

The general structure of goal-setting is to establish immediate goals, intermediate goals, and long-term goals.

- **Immediate goals** are goals that you expect to accomplish in the next few weeks, such as finishing your budget, getting started on paying debts, and making necessary adjustments to your spending.

- **Intermediate goals** are goals that need to be set at regular intervals every six months, for example. At these intervals, you can review your accomplishments and reassess your direction. But as always, these should also be specific goals, such as "credit card X will be paid off by this date."

✔ **Long-term goals** are the goals that take you to the end of your debt problems and beyond. These goals may include getting to a point where you have no credit card debt, followed by having your debt in the 25 percent range, possibly followed by paying off your mortgage and/or building future wealth.

You can always adjust the dates if you don't accomplish everything you planned by a given date — or if you're paying off debts faster than you expected. These time goals aren't carved in stone but rather are goalposts — you try to get the ball between the posts, but it doesn't always happen. However, without goalposts, you'll never know whether you scored.

 Make sure to allow yourself a realistic amount of time to get out of debt. You probably didn't get into debt overnight, and you certainly won't get out of debt overnight. Different factors can contribute to getting out of debt in more time or less, including your level of income and your level of commitment to the process.

Write down your goals

You probably have plenty of good reasons for writing down anything that's important:

✔ You tend to remember information better if you take the time to write it down.

✔ You're more likely to believe something that you see written out. Seeing it on paper makes it real, concrete, and tangible.

✔ You have something to look at, which makes it harder to forget or ignore that you've made a decision.

✔ You have proof that you've already accomplished an important task. Goal-setting is a major step in the process of getting out of debt, and once you've set the goal, you can start getting excited about the destination.

Write out your positive, long-term goal statement at the top of a sheet of paper. Beneath it, write out the dates you've set for attaining your short-term, intermediate, and long-term goals.

If you haven't already started a file or three-ring binder for the project of getting out of debt, now is a good time to do so. Place your sheet of written goals in the front of the binder or file. This way, you have everything you need in one place: goals, worksheets, and any other information you collect.

In addition to the sheet of paper listing your goals that you put in your file or binder, you can write out your positive, long-term goal statement on a 3 x 5–inch card and post it where you'll see it regularly, such as on the bathroom mirror.

For this reminder note, you can rephrase the statement in a less formal way. For example, instead of "In five years, I want to have my debt to 25 percent of my take-home pay," you may write it as "In five years, if I stick with this, I can be free!" Write whatever gets you the most excited about this process. You can then rewrite the note every time you reach an intermediate goal ("Just four more years!"). Updating your note helps keep you out of the "Are we there yet?" syndrome that accompanies many long-term projects.

Creating a budget

Creating your budget is your "road map" for getting out of debt. No single perfect form fits everyone's needs and circumstances, but you do need to consider some basic elements if your budget is going to work. An effective budget needs to be:

- ✔ **Realistic:** Forcing numbers to work out on paper isn't hard, but these numbers need to work in real life.

    Even if you need to watch every penny at this point, don't make the numbers so low that you have no hope of succeeding. If, as you go along, you find ways of cutting costs further, you can always change an entry.

- ✔ **Concise yet comprehensive:** You don't want your budget to have so much detail that you spend your whole life keeping it updated, but you do want to include all the expenses that you can identify or predict.

    You often can group several expenses into one category. Although you may need to track expenses more precisely from day to day (you may even want to carry a notebook in which to record them), you can consolidate some items in the budget (for example, coffee from the gourmet shop, candy from the office vending machine, and a quart of milk picked up on the way home can all be part of the food budget). See Chapter 1 in Book I for more tips about figuring out what you spend.

- ✔ **Flexible:** Feel free to improve the format of the budget as you continue to work with it. Add more lines if necessary, or delete lines. Change your spending estimates as needed, too. You may find that you guessed too low, or you may discover ways to save money that enable you to lower an amount.

    If your financial situation changes — you get married, find a new job, relocate, or have a new mouth to feed — you may want to draw up a new budget.

- ✔ **Open to all concerned, garnering everyone's cooperation and commitment:** Anyone in the household who contributes to income and/or expenditures needs to be involved in the budget discussions. In particular, those who contribute to the household income need to get in on the planning stages, budget creation, and review process. They need to "buy in" to the project for it to work.

Small children may not need to be included in the planning, but they should know that "something is happening," because the budget will affect them, too. If they feel that they're part of the project, they may be more understanding when you can't buy things for them. In fact, small children can get excited about being involved and may want to contribute by saving their allowance, collecting pop bottles, or finding other ways to contribute to the family's success.

To establish your budget, you first want to create a master copy of the budget worksheet (see Table 3-1) with no numbers filled in. You may want to include a few blank lines in each category on the master, in case you need to add other items later. Then photocopy this master document to create budget worksheets to work on.

Book II

Money Management Basics

A dozen copies (one for each month) is a good start, because you'll want to work within a budget for at least a year. Even if you can get yourself to that magic 25 percent figure in less time, you should live on a budget for a year to help create a budget mindset that keeps you from falling back into the hole you just climbed out of. Some people live on a budget their entire lives because it's the only way they keep themselves out of trouble. You may not have to do so, but if it helps, it's an option.

Your worksheet also needs to be well organized and easy to read and keep updated. If working with the budget and calculating totals becomes difficult, you'll give up. This process is serious, so make the effort to create a document that's easy to work with.

Although you'll personalize this worksheet to meet your own needs, some categories need to be a part of everyone's budget. Also, some organizational options may make the budget easier for you to manage. Be sure to do the following:

✔ Include a space after each item for estimated expense, for actual expense, and for the difference between estimated and actual.

✔ Divide the budget worksheet into essential and nonessential expenses (see Chapter 2). You may wish to further divide essential expenses into fixed and variable; doing so makes it easier to see where you may need to make changes to the budget or to your spending. (Chapter 2 helps you create a list of debts and expenses that can help you accomplish this. Just check the category you indicated for each item.)

✔ After the total for the expense section, list your sources of income and total them.

✔ The final entry on the budget is the calculation of money remaining. Subtract your total expenses from your total income to determine what remains. The remainder is called your discretionary income.

Table 3-1 gives you an idea of what your budget might look like. Feel free to alter the format to meet your own needs, but be sure to include enough information to make the budget effective. And don't forget any debatable items that may not be listed below. Also, if you have regular legal or accounting expenses, don't forget to include them.

Table 3-1	Budget Worksheet for (Month) _____		
Expense	*Estimated*	*Actual*	*Difference*
Essential Fixed Expenses			
Rent/mortgage	$	$	$
Housing association fees	$	$	$
Car payment	$	$	$
Car insurance	$	$	$
Life insurance	$	$	$
Homeowner's/renter's insurance	$	$	$
Property taxes	$	$	$
Alimony/child support	$	$	$
	$	$	$
	$	$	$
Essential Variable Expenses			
Home maintenance	$	$	$
Food	$	$	$
Electricity	$	$	$
Gas (utility)	$	$	$
Water	$	$	$
Phone	$	$	$
Gasoline (auto)	$	$	$
Auto maintenance/repairs	$	$	$
Public transportation	$	$	$
Health care expenses	$	$	$
Child care	$	$	$

Expense	Estimated	Actual	Difference
Charitable donations	$	$	$
Household goods (cleaning supplies, cooking utensils, etc.)			
	$	$	$
Savings	$	$	$
	$	$	$
	$	$	$
Fixed Loan Payments			
Student loan	$	$	$
Personal loan	$	$	$
Instalment loan 1	$	$	$
	$	$	$
	$	$	$
Credit Card Payments			
MasterCard 1	$	$	$
MasterCard 2	$	$	$
Visa 1	$	$	$
Visa 2	$	$	$
Department store cards	$	$	$
Gasoline cards	$	$	$
Other cards	$	$	$
Charge Cards (cards that must be paid off each month)			
American Express (regular)	$	$	$
Diner's Club	$	$	$
Nonessential Expenses			
Barber/beautician	$	$	$
Magazine/newspaper subscriptions	$	$	$
Gifts	$	$	$
Charitable donations	$	$	$

Book II

Money Management Basics

(continued)

Table 3-1 *(continued)*

Expense	Estimated	Actual	Difference
Cable TV	$	$	$
Club dues	$	$	$
Sports	$	$	$
Lessons/camp	$	$	$
Dining out	$	$	$
Movies	$	$	$
Hobbies	$	$	$
Cigarettes	$	$	$
Alcoholic beverages	$	$	$
Domestic help	$	$	$
Lawn services	$	$	$
	$	$	$
	$	$	$
Total Monthly Expenses	**$**	**$**	**$**
Monthly Income			
Take-home pay (after taxes)	$	$	$
Interest income	$	$	$
Alimony/child support paid to you	$	$	$
Other	$	$	$
	$	$	$
	$	$	$
Total Monthly Income	**$**	**$**	**$**
Total Money Remaining			
Total Monthly Income			$
Total Monthly Expenses			− $
Total Money Remaining			= $

Notice that on the sample budget, no blank lines appear under the loan and credit card categories. The simple reason is that you should not be adding items to these categories. If all goes as planned, you'll be eliminating debt categories, not adding them.

You can use the blank lines under the other expense or income categories for seasonal expenses or annual bills, such as auto licences, vacations, holiday gift purchases, bonuses, and tax preparation services.

If you're self-employed, don't forget to list estimated quarterly taxes under Essential Fixed Expenses.

After you create your own budget worksheet and make copies of the blank form, plug in figures. You'll know some numbers immediately, especially the fixed expenses. (Chapter 2 has worksheets that you can create to record your income and assets and where you spend your money, which will help you prepare your budget.) Be as accurate and realistic as possible when filling in amounts.

For utility prices, you can phone your local utility companies. They often can tell you precisely what your average monthly costs have been. Utility companies may also offer a payment plan where you pay the average of your annual bills every month rather than dealing with seasonal dips and rises. Averaged payments can make the budgeting process much easier.

All these figures go in the Estimated column, since it's what you're predicting your costs will be or what you think you'll be able to put toward paying off your debts. (*Note:* For the fixed, essential expenses, for most of the year, the Estimated column will match the Actual column, but they are still included because it will be easier when you total the columns.) Work in pencil so that you can erase entries if necessary. Put down the minimum payment amounts for all credit cards, unless you regularly set and pay a higher amount.

Finally, with all the items in the Estimated column filled in, total your expenses and income, and then figure your remaining money.

Evaluating your budget

If your Total Money Remaining figure is zero or negative, you have to revise your budget. First, examine your nonessential expenses. Which ones can be reduced? Which ones can be eliminated? Keep working until you can't think of anything else to reduce. Be honest with yourself about what you can and can't give up or reduce. You really don't need a $65 haircut or cable TV, for example. To succeed, however, don't focus on what you're giving up, focus on what you're gaining: eventual economic freedom.

If you do have money remaining, you can use it to help get yourself out of debt faster, as explained in the upcoming section, "Using Your Budget to Get Ahead of Your Debt." If cutting or reducing nonessentials isn't enough to get you into a positive situation, you may need to start examining your essential expenses. Check out "Moving Money to Improve Your Debt Picture," later in this chapter, to discover how to "find" more money in your budget.

Staying up-to-date

Setting up your budget is just the beginning of your move to financial freedom. Keeping your budget going takes less work than setting it up, but it requires more commitment.

As the month progresses and bills come in, fill in the Actual column for each item and calculate the difference between the estimated amount and the actual amount, noting whether the difference is positive or negative.

Set aside time every month to total the preceding month's worksheet and to review (and update if necessary) your budget for the coming month. You can make seasonal adjustments in order to anticipate times when spending may be higher, or fine-tune entries as you get better at living according to a budget.

Stay up-to-date by making a commitment to the following:

- **Regularity:** Only by being systematic and updating your records regularly can you get a good picture of your spending patterns. Being consistent helps you know where your money is going and how you're progressing. Also, if you fall behind, catching up may appear to be a discouragingly difficult task.

- **Accuracy:** You don't have to worry about every penny, but you should try to be as accurate as possible in recording amounts. Carrying a notebook can help you because you may not remember the pop machine, coffee cart, or vending machine — the types of expenses that can add $2 or $3 to each day's expense total.

- **Honesty:** If you're anything less than honest when figuring your budget, you're only hurting yourself. If you record less than what you spend, not only will you never have accurate records, you may never succeed in getting out of debt. Knowing your true financial picture is the only way to make a budget work.

Using Your Budget to Get Ahead of Your Debt

When you have a budget in hand, along with a picture of your debt situation, you can strategize about how best to tackle your debt. This section tells you how to get started, giving you strategies for reducing your debt and preventing yourself from getting even further into debt.

Using your discretionary income to pay off high-interest debts first

Discretionary income is the money you have left after you've paid all the bills you have to pay — the Total Money Remaining figure at the end of your budget worksheet earlier in this chapter. This money is the income that you use at your discretion for "extras," from treats to investing — unless you're in debt.

The budget that you created includes items that may normally fall into the discretionary income category (movies, dining out, and so on) simply because at this stage, you have to plan all your expenses. Depending on your level of debt, you may not have much discretionary income after all the items on your budget are accounted for. If you do have some money to spare, you can use it to help get yourself out of debt faster. This process helps cut down on one of the worst drains of money there is — interest payments.

The single most devastating expense you have is the interest on credit cards. Most people don't realize how much they pay in interest or how much difference even the smallest changes can make. Here's an example:

> Say you have a credit card that has a balance of $1,500. If the annual interest is 21 percent (a fairly standard rate) and you make the minimum payment of 3 percent of the balance each month, repaying the total will take you more than 14 years, and you will have paid more than $1,800 in interest (for a total of $3,300).

> If you pay just $5 over the minimum payment per month, you'll save more than $600 on interest and cut more than five years off the repayment time. If you pay $10 more per month, you'll cut nearly $900 and eight years off the interest and time that making only the minimum payment hits you with.

Those numbers show a pretty dramatic difference. And these figures are based on the assumption that you don't spend any more after you run up the initial $1,500. If you keep adding purchases, they all figure into the interest rate.

To keep your creditors at bay, you must continue to make the minimum payment due on each card on which you owe. After you account for those expenses, any discretionary income that you have left in your budget (the amount in the Total Money Remaining column back in Table 3-1) should go toward paying off the credit cards that have the highest interest rates.

If you planned your budget with more than the minimum payment going to each card with an outstanding balance, redo it so that you're paying the minimum on the cards with lower interest rates and putting the rest of your "extra" money toward paying off the highest cards. Follow these steps:

1. After you create your budget and plug in the minimum payment for each credit card, take as much of your discretionary income as possible and use it to pay down the credit card charging the highest interest.

   If you wrote the interest rates on your debt worksheet in Chapter 2, you'll be able to tell at a glance which credit card you need to target.

2. After you've paid off the credit card with the highest rate, put your discretionary income toward the credit card with the next highest rate.

3. Continue this process until you've paid off all your credit cards, continuing to take the card with the highest interest and put as much discretionary income as possible toward that debt.

Discretionary income is, as its name implies, money that you can use at your discretion. Occasionally, you may want to reserve a little more discretionary income to celebrate the holidays or enjoy a much-needed weekend away. However, until you're getting cozy with that 25 percent debt figure, you want to plow as much of your discretionary income as possible into paying off high-interest debts.

Think of paying off high-interest debts as saving your future buying power, because that's precisely what it is. Nothing eats into your financial potential like a high interest rate.

Cut up your credit cards

Here comes the hard part: As soon as you've paid off the balance on a credit card, cut up the card and close the account with a quick phone call to the credit card company.

You may not be able to take the scissors to every credit card you have (because it's nearly impossible to transact business these days without at least one major credit card), but do so with the majority of your cards. Plan to keep one or two of the major cards (Visa, MasterCard, or American Express) and get rid of everything else.

In fact, you probably should cut up all but the chosen two cards as soon as you start working on eliminating your debt. (Cutting up a card doesn't mean that you erase the balance, of course, but it does prevent you from making additional purchases on the card.) Whatever you do, don't charge anything while you're still carrying a balance; it just makes the interest worse and the repayment time longer.

If you must have a charge card (which is possible if you have children, need a card for emergencies, or travel for business), consider getting a new card with no balance. Use this card only when you can't use cash or a cheque, and charge only an amount that you can pay off completely when the bill arrives. Because your goal is never again to carry a balance on a credit card, you absolutely do not want to start running up another balance.

Forget your savings for the time being

While you're seriously in debt is the only time in your life that anyone will tell you that your nest egg is a bad idea. If you have any money in a savings account, close the account and put the money toward paying off your high-interest credit cards. Why earn 1 or 2 percent interest on a savings account when you're paying 18 to 21 percent interest on your credit cards?

Liquidate any other assets you have, such as GICs, stocks, bonds, mutual funds, and even collectibles, and use that money to pay down your high-interest debts as well. Nothing can earn you enough to make it worth keeping in the face of debt on a credit card that charges a 21 percent interest rate.

There are only two exceptions to the "throw everything at your credit cards" plan:

- ✔ Hang onto enough money to cover one month's expenses (if possible), because emergencies do arise. If you can't scrape together a month's worth, at least save enough to buy food and gas.

- ✔ As long as you can still make the minimum payments on all your debts, don't cash in your RRSPs. The tax hit would probably be worse than the interest on your credit cards. Also, jeopardizing your future simply to avoid interest payments is not a wise tradeoff.

  If you're facing foreclosure, however, that's another matter. Go ahead and liquidate all your assets, including retirement accounts; you don't want to lose your home.

Book II

Money Management Basics

Paying down other debts

If you stick to your budget, you will free yourself of credit card debt. At that point, you may still have other debts to deal with, such as auto loans, student loans, and a mortgage loan. Even if you're close to that 25 percent debt figure, you may still want to rid yourself of debt entirely.

The way to do so is simply to follow the same procedure for high-interest debt, described earlier in this chapter: Continue to choose the debt with the highest interest and put as much of your discretionary income as possible toward that debt. As you pay off debts, remember to update your budget and reallocate your resources. Also make sure not to neglect other debts while you focus on the highest-interest one; you don't want to lose your car or your home by failing to make your monthly payments.

Some types of loans, such as mortgages, assess a prepayment penalty if you pay off the loan early. Make sure to read the fine print on your loan agreement before you end up costing yourself more than you're saving!

Moving Money to Improve Your Debt Picture

One thing you can do to get a slightly faster start along the path to reaching your final goal of being debt-free is to move your money to where it can do the most good. This tactic includes everything from finding ways to lower your interest payments to locating and plugging the "leaks" in your budget that let money get away from you. This section shows you how to do all that and more.

Finding cheaper debt

In addition to paying off your high-interest debts (see the preceding section for more information about this important debt reduction strategy), you may also be able to find lower-interest debts to help you get out of debt faster. The following are some sources of cheaper debt.

Lower-interest credit cards

How often do you get offers for credit cards with really low interest rates? Probably almost daily. If you've never taken advantage of these low rates (or you took advantage of them and just ran up more debt), it may be time for you to look at these offers again.

Of course, these reduced rates are usually for a limited time only, so check the offer to make sure that the post–hot deal interest rate isn't higher than what you're paying now. But if the rate is the same or lower than what you're currently paying, you'll come out ahead even if you can't pay off the whole thing during the trial period.

In addition, some credit cards have a regular interest rate that's lower than the rate on the majority of cards. If you don't have a brochure for a great deal on a new credit card, you can research some of the better rates available by going online.

Here are a couple of Web sites for finding good rates on credit cards, as well as rates on other things that may interest you. Remember, if you don't have a computer or aren't currently on the Internet, most libraries offer free Internet access — so you don't need to spend a dime to view these sites.

Book II

Money Management Basics

- ✔ `www.strategis.ic.gc.ca`: The federal government department Industry Canada's Web site lists which credit cards offer the lowest rates, as well as other useful tips, in its "Consumer Information" section.

- ✔ `www.webfin.com`: Get information on mortgages, car loans, the best credit card deals, and lots of other personal finance info.

After you transfer balances from the higher-interest to the lower-interest cards, cut up the old cards, mail them back to the banks or other organizations that issued them, and close the accounts. The only potential exception is an emergency backup card with a zero balance. Otherwise, do "plastic surgery" and get rid of as many cards as possible.

Don't just throw them out. You need to mail the cut-up cards back to the banks or issuing organizations to get the accounts closed and off your credit report.

Credit union loans

If you belong to a credit union, find out what types of loans are available. You may be able to get a personal loan at a rate far lower than what you're paying in credit card interest. If you've been a member in good standing for some time, you could even get a loan at a rate lower than what a bank would offer.

Mortgage refinancing

Refinancing a mortgage is advantageous because not only can it free up money for your current difficulties, it can also lower your payments for the duration of the mortgage. This strategy helps you inch your monthly debt obligation closer to that desirable 25 percent figure by enabling you to use more money per month to pay down higher-interest debts.

You can start by talking to your bank. For the best mortgage rates, however, you need to shop around. Personal finance Web sites also give mortgage rate information. And the Canadian Mortgage Housing Corporation (CMHC), the Crown corporation that insures more than a third of all mortgages in Canada, can help a lot in this particular area of finance.

Also, if refinancing your mortgage would free up enough money to help you, doing so is a much better deal than taking out a home equity loan (see the following section), because home equity loans carry interest rates that are a couple of points higher than the current mortgage rate.

Even if you think you'll need a home equity loan too, refinance your mortgage before you consider the loan. You may be surprised at how much you save, and you may decide against the loan. Plus, it's harder to renegotiate your original mortgage once you have a second mortgage on the house.

Considering home equity loans

If you've been in your home for a few years, you may have built up considerable equity. Using that equity can help get you out of debt, but some potential dangers are involved. Also, always remember that a home equity loan (formerly known as a second mortgage) is sort of like "unbuying" your house, and you have to buy it back again.

Think about these pros and cons if you're considering a home equity loan:

- ✔ **Pro:** If you negotiate a good rate, the interest rates can be considerably lower than those on many other forms of debt, especially credit cards.

- ✔ **Con:** If you haven't curtailed your bad spending practices and haven't stuck to a budget, you're putting your home in jeopardy. Unless you've already demonstrated both a willingness and an ability to spend only what is necessary, don't put your home at risk. If you think that not having much to spend is a drag, think of what a drag it would be to be homeless and not have anything to spend.

If you decide that you're ready for a home equity loan and feel certain that you're not risking more than you want to lose, go ahead and get the loan. But get only as much as you need to cover your debts. Don't get anything extra.

Refuse to give in to the temptation to buy something else with money that you may see as being there for the spending. It's not. You have to pay it back. A home equity loan is a less expensive debt than a credit card, but it's not "found money." It's plain-old debt in a different disguise.

If, on the other hand, your total available equity doesn't cover all your debts — well, I think you know what to do by now. Pay off those credit cards, the highest ones first. If you can pay down all your credit cards, decide what your next costliest debts are (perhaps a car payment or an instalment loan for a large appliance). Your best bet after paying off credit cards is probably to pay off items that can be repossessed.

"Finding" more money

You can look in a number of places for extra money — not all of them easy, but all worth considering.

The first thing to do is to review your nonessential expenses (discussed in Chapter 2). Scrutinize anything not related to your survival — think digital TV, those weekly facials, those super-deluxe gourmet coffees that you pick up on the way to work each morning. Then cut out those items that you can live without.

You may even want to review your essential expenses and decide whether you can get by with spending less. For example, you could move into a less expensive apartment and save money each month, or you could buy food and other essentials in bulk to cut your costs.

You may think that these small things won't make much of a difference, but consider this: If you have a 30-year mortgage of $100,000 at 8 percent, adding just $1 per day to your payment can save you $27,000 in interest and cut four years off the duration of the loan. These changes may look small, but they can have a huge impact in the long run.

The following sections list some specific places to look for money. For other ways (increasing deductibles on insurance, finding cheaper sources of clothes, and so on), see the section on borderline/debatable expenses in Chapter 2. When you get into the swing of things, you'll probably think of other areas in which you can cut back or other projects that you can do to save or earn money.

Reducing essential variable expenses

Learning to reduce essential variable expenses is one way that most people, even those who are not in debt, try to cut down on their monthly expenses. Getting good at this is useful even after you reach your goals.

- ✔ **Reduce your taxes:** Well, at least temporarily. If you normally get a refund from your income taxes, revisit your TD 1 form. This is the form your employer uses to determine the correct amount of tax to be withheld from your pay cheques. Carefully go through the form to ensure you are claiming all the exemptions you are entitled to. You may not get a refund next year, but your take-home pay will increase.

- ✔ **Get out the scissors:** Start using coupons and shopping for bargains. (However, don't drive miles and miles to save 2 cents on milk, because you will burn more in gas than you will save.)

- ✔ **Eat up:** Never go to the grocery store hungry, because you'll tend to buy more than you intended.

- ✔ **Avoid brands:** Buy generic food and over-the-counter drugs.

- ✔ **Shop around for insurance rates:** Change automobile insurance companies, or raise your deductible, to get a lower monthly premium.

- ✔ **Layers, layers, layers:** Wear a sweater instead of turning up the heat, or open the windows instead of running the air conditioner. A few degrees of difference in temperature can make a significant difference in your heating and cooling bills.

- ✔ **Do it yourself:** Learn to do minor repairs and home maintenance jobs yourself.

- ✔ **If it's broke, fix it:** Repair or mend items rather than replacing them.

- ✔ **Use your feet:** Walk (or carpool or take public transportation) when possible to save money on gasoline.

Changing your (expensive) habits

Your habits can have a huge impact on the outflow of money. Consider these examples:

- ✔ **If you smoke, quit.** A two-pack-a-day habit, at $3 a pack, translates into $2,190 per year.

- ✔ **Stop drinking.** As with smoking, what seems like a negligible amount of money adds up swiftly.

- ✔ **"Borrow" some savings.** Head to the public library rather than purchasing books at a bookstore. In addition to books, you can check out videos, cassette tapes, and CDs for free.

- ✔ **Take your lunch to work.** Dining even in an inexpensive restaurant can add a couple of dollars a day to your budget. Bring your own coffee, too, unless your company supplies it for free.

- ✔ **Adjust your movie-going habits.** Go to movies only during matinee hours or after they hit the discount theatres. You can also rent videos or borrow them from the library and have a family movie night at home.

Finding miscellaneous money

You can look for, or earn, more money in a variety of other places:

- ✔ **Switch to an interest-bearing chequing account.** Even if you don't earn much in interest, any money you earn helps your situation.

- ✔ **Stop paying for chequing.** Look for a chequing account that requires a lower minimum balance for free chequing. If you switch from a bank that has a $1,500 minimum to one with a $1,000 minimum, you can instantly apply the $500 to paying off debts.

- ✔ **Hold a garage sale.** If you have items that are more valuable than the usual garage sale stuff, try selling them through the newspaper, by posting a note on the bulletin board at work, or on the Internet.

- ✔ **Get a part-time job.**

- ✔ **Tutor or consult in a field in which you excel.**

- ✔ **If you're doing good work, ask for a raise.**

- ✔ **Rethink vacation.** Find out whether you can get vacation pay instead of taking time off. You don't want to do this with all your vacation time because even folks who are broke need time off, but doing it for part of your vacation may help you along.

- ✔ **Rent out a spare room.**

- ✔ **Barter.** Find a friend or acquaintance who will babysit your kids in return for your mowing their lawn, or vice versa. Find someone who will fix your car in exchange for your cooking dinner, or who'll lend you videos in exchange for books, or who'll drive you to work if you teach him or her how to use a computer. You get the idea. The possibilities are almost limitless.

Book II

Money
Management
Basics

Cutting to the quick

If you've cut back everything else and you still can't make ends meet, you may have to do something about your essential expenses. Consider the following ideas:

- ✔ **If you have two cars, sell one.** Take public transportation or carpool. If you must have two cars, see whether can you downgrade — get a vehicle with lower payments.

- ✔ **Revisit your housing situation.** If your financial situation is really bad, consider selling your house and buying either a smaller house or a condo. Remember, it's better to sell your home than to have it taken away, because then you have nothing. This suggestion applies only if you have cut all nonessential expenses and still can't make your monthly payments.

- ✔ **Adjust your alimony payments.** If you're paying alimony or child support to a former spouse who is doing better than you are financially, you may be able to apply for a reduction in those payments.

Some of these measures may seem drastic, but they're not nearly as drastic, or as potentially damaging, as bankruptcy (which you can learn more about in the next section). The measures in this section may inconvenience you, but they're not designed to destroy your credit history or ruin your life, as bankruptcy can.

Talking to your family

As a last resort, turn to your family for financial assistance. Do you have relatives who could lend you money to pay off your debts? Consider promising them a return on investment. For example, you could pay them 5 percent interest on the loan and still save a vast amount of money if the interest on your debts is high.

Of course, it's vital that you pay back these loans. Because you have an insider's view of what it's like to be strapped for cash, you certainly don't want to put anyone you care about in a similar position. Besides, it's almost impossible to overstate how important it is for your self-esteem, your sense of accomplishment, and the success of your long-term goals that you pay back all debts, including (and maybe especially) those owed to family.

Filing for Bankruptcy Protection

If you say "debt" most people immediately think "bankruptcy." There is certainly an epidemic of personal bankruptcy in Canada today. But bankruptcy is not an easy solution. It can seriously disrupt your life, it ruins your credit history, and it's possible it won't get rid of most of your debts. Make sure you know all the facts before you consider this option.

Your best bet — avoid bankruptcy

If a chronic gambler deserts his wife and leaves her with a hefty mortgage, $90,000 in credit card debt, and six children, she might want to consider bankruptcy. For almost everyone else, bankruptcy is probably a bad choice. Here's why:

- You can lose much of your personal property. (The court sells the property to pay your creditors. If you're going to lose everything anyway, why not sell it yourself? You'll probably get a better price for it, and you won't have a bankruptcy ruining your credit report.)

✔ The blot remains on your credit record for six or seven years, so you probably won't be able to take out loans, get credit cards, or do anything else that requires a review of your credit record.

✔ If a friend or relative co-signed a loan, they are not protected by your bankruptcy and will have to repay your debts.

✔ Bankruptcy takes away the safety net of security that credit can supply your family.

✔ Bankruptcy hurts innocent people who trusted you to repay. It has a major impact on merchants and lenders and can, in the long run, mean job loss or business closure.

✔ You aren't likely to learn the necessary lessons to keep you from repeating your folly. In fact, 50 percent of the people who file bankruptcy file it again later in their lives because they have changed no patterns and learned no new skills.

✔ You expose your financial lifestyle to the public. Your bankruptcy petition, schedules, and payment plan are public documents, available to the public.

✔ Any job that involves being bonded (bank teller, jewellery clerk) may be in jeopardy.

✔ Bankruptcy is humiliating. It seriously undercuts your self-esteem and makes it difficult for you to make positive changes in your life.

Many of these points apply only if your filing is successful, which is not necessarily guaranteed. If you fail to follow any of the necessary steps, such as showing up for the creditors' meeting, answering the court's questions honestly and completely, or producing the necessary and verifiable books and records, the case can be dismissed. If this happens, you still owe everything you did before you started, and you're out whatever you've spent so far on bankruptcy proceedings.

Today, too many people are filing for bankruptcy to escape debt that is merely inconvenient. The courts are getting stricter, and are looking more closely at all cases. Judges are on the lookout for people who are simply trying to get out of paying their bills, as opposed to those who are truly suffering hardship. If a judge determines that you have enough income to cover the monthly payments for your debts, and especially if you have any discretionary income left after making those payments, it's likely that your bankruptcy case will be thrown out of court.

Book II

Money Management Basics

How bad is it?

Canadians have taken on a lot of debt, as noted in Chapter 2. When the economy slows down, jobs are lost. When people lose their jobs, they often lose the means to pay down their debts. If debts cannot be further deferred or restructured, bankruptcy becomes a likely next step.

In Canada, the fairly recent consumer (non-commercial) bankruptcy landscape looked as follows:

- 2003: 83,000 bankruptcies estimated
- 2002: 78,210

- 2001: 79,398
- 2000: 75,088
- 1999: 72,994
- 1998: 75,459

As the stock market ended its bull run in 2000, and as the economy began to sputter, it's not surprising to see the number of bankruptcies edge up. It seems that regardless of the state of the Canadian economy, bankruptcies happen.

Understanding dischargeable and nondischargeable debts

Not all debts go away when you file for bankruptcy. Most unsecured debts are dischargeable, which means that you are no longer legally required to repay them. However, some unsecured debts are nondischargeable — that is, you still have to repay them even after filing for bankruptcy. For secured debts, you surrender the property that you used as collateral, or pay the debt if you want to retain the collateral.

Which type of debt you have determines whether you have anything to gain from declaring bankruptcy.

- **Dischargeable debts** include, but are not limited to, credit card purchases, rent, and health care bills.
- **Nondischargeable debts** include, but are not limited to, student loans, alimony or child support, any debt or liability arising out of fraud or embezzlement, debts incurred as a result of criminal acts, and eve-of-bankruptcy spending sprees (or any substantial purchases close to the time of filing).

In addition, after you file for bankruptcy, your creditors have 45 days to object. If they file a suit, it's possible that a discharge will be denied for the debt in question.

However, you can't really guess what the judge will decide about your creditors' suits (unless you know that one of your creditors is in worse shape financially than you are), but you should be able to identify your dischargeable debts. If that's what most of your debts are, then bankruptcy can help reduce your debt burden — but don't forget, that doesn't mean it makes your problems go away.

Alternatives to bankruptcy

Bankruptcy is a drastic move with serious long-term consequences. Here are other options to consider first:

Book II

Money
Management
Basics

- ✔ **Talk to your creditors:** Hard as it may sound, you can call up your creditors and explain why you haven't made your payments. Ask for lower payments over a longer time frame. They may allow it.

- ✔ **Credit counselling:** Credit counselling services differ from province to province, but all of them can give sound advice on creating a budget and sticking to it.

- ✔ **Consolidation order:** If you live in British Columbia, Alberta, Saskatchewan, Nova Scotia, or P.E.I., you can apply for a consolidation order, which defines the amount and the times that you have to make payments to the court. The court will then pay your creditors. (In Quebec a similar option is called a voluntary deposit.) With a consolidation order you can pay off your debts over three years and you're free from wage garnishees and harassment from creditors. Plus, you get to keep your stuff.

- ✔ **Consumer proposal:** Under the Bankruptcy and Insolvency Act, you may make a proposal to your creditors to reduce the amount of your debts, extend the time to repay the debt, or provide some combination of both. (More on this later in the next section.)

If none of these methods solves your debt problem, then you may want to consider bankruptcy.

The consumer proposal

As a last measure before declaring outright bankruptcy, you can make a consumer proposal to your creditors that you pay less each month over a longer period of time, or pay a certain percentage of what you owe. The main benefit is that your unsecured creditors cannot take legal steps to recover debts from you — such as seizing property or garnisheeing wages. You can make a consumer proposal if your debts total less than $75,000, not including a home mortgage.

The procedure begins when you seek the help of an administrator, who may be a trustee or someone appointed by the Superintendent of Bankruptcy. He or she will assess your finances, and give you advice about what kind of proposal may be best for you and your creditors. You'll have to sign the required forms, and the administrator will send the proposal — along with a report that lists your assets, debts, and creditors — to the Official Receiver, as well as to each of your creditors. The creditors then have 45 days to decide whether to accept or reject your proposal.

If your creditors accept it, your consumer proposal determines the amount and time periods by which you'll clear yourself of debt. If they reject it, then just about the only option left is bankruptcy.

It will cost you money to make a consumer proposal: you have to pay a filing fee to the Superintendent of Bankruptcy, and the administrator will expect to be paid. The fees for administrators, however, are determined by law, and you can check them out at the Superintendent of Bankruptcy's Web site, at `osb-bsf.ic.gc.ca`.

Starting bankruptcy proceedings

Bankruptcy is a legal process outlined in the Bankruptcy and Insolvency Act of Canada. Because you can't pay your debts, you assign all of your assets, except those exempt by law, to a licensed trustee in bankruptcy. This process relieves you of most debts, and legal proceedings against you by creditors should, in most cases, stop.

Finding a trustee

In bankruptcy proceedings, a trustee is someone licensed by the federal Superintendent of Bankruptcy to represent your creditors and act as an officer of the court. But the trustee can also be your best friend, giving you information and advice about the bankruptcy process, and making sure that your rights, as well as the rights of the creditors, are respected.

Trustees in bankruptcy are usually listed in the telephone book under "Bankruptcy" or "Trustee," or in the provincial government section. If you can't find a trustee, contact the nearest office of the Superintendent of Bankruptcy at Industry Canada.

Besides the trustee, the other major participant in a bankruptcy is the inspector. Inspectors are appointed by your creditors to represent them before the trustee, and are expected to assist and/or supervise the trustee during bankruptcy proceedings.

Surrendering your property

When you declare bankruptcy, your property is given to the trustee, who sells it and distributes the money among your creditors. Your unsecured creditors will not be able to take legal steps to recover their debts from you. Also, all property used as collateral for secured debts returns to your creditors. (If you want to keep it, you must pay for it.)

As with a consumer proposal, first you have to meet with a trustee who will assess your financial situation and explain your options. If you decide to go through with the bankruptcy, the trustee will ask you to surrender your credit cards, and will help you complete several forms you'll have to sign. You're considered bankrupt only when the trustee files these forms with the Official Receiver.

You have to sign at least two forms. One is an "assignment"; the other is your "statement of affairs." In the assignment, you state that you are handing over all of your property to the trustee for the benefit of your creditors. In the statement of affairs, you list your assets, liabilities, income, and expenses. As well, you have to answer several questions about your family, employment, and disposition of assets.

Although the trustee prepares the forms for you, you are responsible for making sure that they are accurate. Review them carefully before you sign. Keep copies of notices and all other documents the trustee sends to you.

Usually, a meeting of creditors isn't necessary once you've filed the forms and declared bankruptcy. But sometimes the creditors or the Official Receiver may request one. If a meeting of creditors is called, you must attend. You may also be required to go to the Official Receiver's office to answer questions about your financial affairs under oath.

If all goes according to plan, and this is the first time you've declared bankruptcy, your debts will be discharged automatically after nine months. That means you're relieved of most of your debts.

Great, huh? Well, not quite, because most of your worldly possessions have been sold to pay off whatever outstanding debts can be paid. On the other hand, bankruptcy is designed specifically not to leave you destitute. By law, you will be allowed to keep certain possessions that the government deems necessary for your survival and well-being: food, clothing, a portion of home equity, medical and dental aids — that sort of thing. What you are allowed to keep differs widely from province to province, so be sure to check with your trustee about what you'll be left with when the ink dries on your bankruptcy forms.

You can now begin the process of rebuilding your life, with no credit, little property, a seriously damaged credit history, and still carrying any nondischargeable debts that are outstanding.

Determining whether bankruptcy is for you

Before you go to the trouble and expense of beginning the proceedings, appraise your situation and determine if you have anything to gain from filing bankruptcy. Gather your debt worksheets and your budget, then ask yourself the following questions and think about what your answers may mean when you're considering bankruptcy. Be precise and realistic, because the trustee and court officials will be.

✔ **Do you have any discretionary income left after you make the minimum payments on all bills and cover all essential expenses?**

If your answer is yes, forget bankruptcy. More than likely, your application will be dismissed.

If your answer is no, go on to the next question.

✔ **Would a trustee be likely to view any items in your budget as nonessential?**

If your answer is yes, you have two options: Eliminate the item yourself and put the money toward your bills, or, if the item is important to you, avoid bankruptcy so that you can retain your option of spending that money.

If your answer is no, go on to the next question.

✔ **Are you behind on payments of secured debts, such as mortgage and car payments?**

If your answer is yes, contact the creditors and try to make arrangements to catch up on payments.

If your answer is no, continue to pay your bills and budget carefully; you're probably not a good candidate for bankruptcy.

✔ **Compare all the debts on your debt worksheet to the list of nondischargeable debts earlier in this chapter. Is a considerable portion of your debt nondischargeable?**

If your answer is yes, you have little to gain from filing for bankruptcy.

If your answer is no, go on to the next question.

✔ **Do you have property that you could sell (that is, without liens or other impediments) that would probably be taken from you if you filed for bankruptcy?**

If your answer is yes, you may want to sell It yourself, apply the money toward your bills, and keep your credit record clean.

> If your answer is no — that is, either you have no property that could be taken away or there are liens on the property, so it couldn't be sold — bankruptcy may be an option.
>
> ✔ **Did a friend or relative co-sign any of the loans that the bankruptcy would affect?**
>
> If your answer is yes, talk to that individual to find out if he or she is able to repay, because the debt will become that person's if you file for bankruptcy. If your friend or relative can repay, perhaps he or she can do so without having you file, and then you can repay that individual in time.
>
> If your answer is no, continue looking into bankruptcy if you feel that it's necessary.

Pretty much all the other considerations are personal or emotional. Are you comfortable with having officials establish your budget? Are you comfortable with the thought of having this mark against your credit history for years and being unable to get loans, credit cards, and so on? Do you lack the discipline to carry out a repayment plan without the threat of legal intervention? Are you willing to give up much of your property to creditors? Will you be able to recover emotionally from the process? Indeed, the bankruptcy process is about as much fun as a root canal.

Book II

Money Management Basics

Chapter 4

Budgeting and Recordkeeping

· ·

In This Chapter

▶ Categorizing your spending into essentials and non-essentials

▶ Controlling your impulse spending

▶ Dealing with emergency expenses

▶ Finding out how to make using a budget a habit

▶ Saving time and frustration by getting organized

· ·

*I*n Chapters 2 and 3, you gathered and organized information so that you can create a realistic and workable budget. In this chapter, you use the information that you collected, making changes and fine-tuning so that your tools will work for you.

Determining Your Essential Expenses: What You Need

Essential fixed expenses are those obligations that you must pay regularly — usually monthly. Essential fixed expenses are the same month after month.

Although charitable contributions are not considered by most people to be essential expenses, you can put those items in the essential category if you want to pay them regularly, and if they are important to you.

Essential variable expenses are due every month, but the amounts vary from month to month: food, gas, electricity, long-distance telephone expenses, and so on. In this category, you prorate (average) regular expenses to a monthly cost. Do so by figuring your yearly cost and dividing by 12 (if you're using a monthly budget) or 52 (if you're using a weekly budget).

Essential fixed expenses include:

- ✔ Insurance that you pay quarterly, semiannually, or annually
- ✔ Mortgage payment or rent
- ✔ Automobile payment
- ✔ Student loan payment

Essential variable expenses include:

- ✔ Groceries
- ✔ Utilities (gas, electricity, water, and so on)
- ✔ Public transit fares
- ✔ Gasoline
- ✔ Auto repairs and maintenance
- ✔ Health care and pharmaceuticals
- ✔ Haircuts, toiletries, and other personal care items
- ✔ Education and professional development costs (for your children or yourself)
- ✔ Savings for retirement
- ✔ Savings for large expenses, such as furniture, appliances, and replacement automobiles

As you update your budget, you'll remove items such as student loans as you pay them off.

Determining Your Nonessential Expenses: What You Want

After you pay your essential expenses, what you have left is your discretionary income. From that, you pay your nonessential expenses (and put the rest in savings and investments).

Nonessential expenses include the following:

- ✔ Books, magazines, and newspaper subscriptions
- ✔ Restaurant meals

    ✔ Movies and concerts

    ✔ Gifts

    ✔ Vacations

    ✔ Hobbies

Chapter 1 of Book I lists various money personalities. These personalities identify how you feel about money and spending. Recognizing your money personality — and the money personalities of family members — helps you make better decisions about the money that you've identified as nonessential spending.

In creating your budget, you're looking toward the future. You want to determine which items that you listed as fixed expenses really should be considered nonessential. You may be shocked at the total of these items, but don't be discouraged.

The whole point of a budget is to have a plan for your money before you spend it. Without a budget, you can leave the house with $200 in cash, come back five hours later, and be able to account for only half that amount. With a budget, you'll never do that again. More importantly, you will be able to make firm spending decisions based on criteria that you have already set for yourself.

Book II

Money Management Basics

Recognizing and Avoiding Hidden Expenses

Hidden expenses are those sneaky money-eaters that lurk everywhere. Knowing what and where they are and how much they cost helps you cut them by avoiding the items to which they are attached. This section identifies these hidden costs.

Bank machine, bank, and credit card fees

Hidden costs can quickly transfer your money from your pocket to an institution's profit statement. Be careful of the following:

    ✔ Annual fees

    ✔ Below-minimum use and below-minimum balance fees

    ✔ High interest rates

✔ Late-payment penalties

✔ Independent ATMs (automated teller machines) not affiliated with any financial institution that charge fees of up to $3 for cash withdrawals.

✔ Per-use fees

Read all "change of terms" inserts that you receive from banks, credit unions, credit card companies, and the like. The information that they contain may be a wake-up call to change how and where you do business.

Not knowing what fees you're liable for with your money-handling institutions is the same as using a credit card without knowing what rate of interest you're paying. If you don't carry a balance on your credit card, the interest rate is irrelevant. If you don't incur fees from your bank and so on, you don't care what that rate is, either. But you need to know what and how much they are so that you know what to do to avoid them.

Gratuities and delivery charges

The more services you use in your lifestyle, the more you'll pay in gratuities and delivery charges. Having meals or groceries delivered is convenient and may save you time, but in addition to paying for what you eat, you pay delivery costs and a tip to the delivery person — neither of which you can have for dessert.

Catalogue and Internet shopping can save a lot of time, along with parking and car-use costs. An add-on cost, however, may be shipping charges (often unrecoverable if you return the item). You may need to pay insurance costs as well to protect against the item getting lost or damaged in transit. Plus, when you buy something in a store, you can inspect it before you take it home. And you can watch for sales.

This doesn't mean that you should always shop in stores; it just means that you need to know and compare the costs of various ways of taking care of your needs. If you use the time you save to earn more income, for example, the convenience may be worth the cost.

Sales, luxury, and utility taxes

Not all items are taxed at the same rate. Basic groceries, for example, are not taxed anywhere in Canada, but "snacks" (basically anything that can be eaten in one sitting) are, in some jurisdictions.

Governments have determined some items as luxury items. Liquor is a common example. In some places, the tax on a soft drink is lower than the tax on a beer — even though you drink either one. The choices you make in what may seem to be the same category can lower these hidden costs. Read your receipts carefully. These days, most cash registers put added taxes, such as those for liquor, next to the item purchased so that you can readily see how much you're paying for items for which substitutes may be available.

Choosing one item over another may not save you a ton of money, but making saving decisions over and over can help put you on the path to financial security.

Book II

Money
Management
Basics

Factoring in Emergency Expenses

You don't want to panic every time the refrigerator breaks down or the dog eats spoiled food and has to go to the vet. The budget you'll create later in this chapter reflects that emergencies do happen, so you'll have the savings put aside to pay for such contingencies.

You can move some items from the emergency category to a "savings for replacement" category by keeping track of those budget items. For example, one of the biggest money-eaters in the emergency category can be your automobile, especially if it isn't maintained properly and regularly.

Table 4-1 can help you keep track of your car's care and feeding. List all repairs, regular service (whether done at a service station or by you), and tire purchases. Review your car's service manual to be certain that you're following the manufacturer's recommendations.

When deciding which auto parts to buy, the existence of a warranty and its terms can be deciding factors. Keeping track of the life of the warranty helps you get your dollar's worth. If a shop wants to add chargeable parts or labour to those covered by the warranty, ask to see what needs to be replaced and why.

Some warranties are prorated (the cost for wear and tear is deducted), and others offer replacements (you get a new tire or other part). Knowing what you're buying makes comparisons easier.

Keep similar records on major appliances and furniture. Table 4-2 shows you what information you need to plan replacement purchases.

Table 4-1 **Automobile Maintenance: Major Repairs**

Date	Odometer Reading	Repair Description	Repair Warranty	Cost	Date Last Done

Table 4-2 **Major Purchases/Replacement Needs**

Item	Date Purchased	Warranty Length	Expected Life	Purchase Price	Replacement Cost	Expected Replacement Date
Central air conditioner						
Clothes dryer						

Item	Date Purchased	Warranty Length	Expected Life	Purchase Price	Replacement Cost	Expected Replacement Date
Clothes washer						
Computer equipment						
Dishwasher						
Furnace						
Garage door opener						
Lawn mower						
Microwave						
Refrigerator						
Sofa						
Stereo						
Stove						
Sump pump						
Television						
Vacuum cleaner						
Water heater						
Other						
Other						
Other						

Now that you have an idea of how much money you need to keep in an account to be able to pay cash for these items as you need them, you can put these amounts in your budget. You may choose to save up the money for these items in your emergency fund, but we suggest that you set up a household expenses fund to cover them.

Taking Taxes into Account

Most people have their taxes deducted from their paycheques and don't need to deal with them separately until they file their tax returns. As your investment plans bring in more dividends and income, or you take on another job that doesn't deduct taxes — for example, a freelance or contract job — be sure to review your tax withholdings and adjust them as needed. Doing so prevents a big tax bill at the end of the year; you avoid penalties, too.

If, however, you're getting refunds — especially large refunds (you get to define large for yourself) — you need to make adjustments so that the taxes you pay throughout the year better reflect your liability. A refund is not "found money." It is money that you loaned to the government without earning interest on it. You wouldn't put your money in a zero-percent-interest savings account, so don't loan the government money at zero interest.

Some reasons that you may be getting a refund:

- ✔ You haven't claimed the number of deductions to which you're entitled. Be sure to adjust your deductions as your family situation changes.

- ✔ You deliberately paid additional taxes because you expected to earn outside income from which tax deductions would not be taken; then you didn't earn that income.

- ✔ Your employer is deducting too much according to the number of dependants you're claiming, or you haven't updated your deductions as your circumstances have changed.

- ✔ You worked overtime. The tax table assumes that you were making that income every week, resulting in too much tax being withheld.

Paying Yourself First

Paying yourself first is one of the best money management decisions you can make. Simply put, paying yourself first means that you put money into a savings program to meet your short-term, mid-term, and long-term goals (see Chapter 2 in Book I) before you pay anything else — including your rent or mortgage! If you're living from paycheque to paycheque, you may think that you can't do this. But determining where you spend your money shows you how you can pay yourself first and gain many benefits.

One thing you discovered when you tracked how you spent your money in the past is that emergencies always get paid somehow. If an insurance payment came due, you scrimped on restaurant meals or entertainment so that you had enough money to pay that important bill before your insurance was cancelled.

If you can "find" the money when you absolutely must have it, then you can live on less than you've been spending. The obvious conclusion is that you can put money aside for savings if you respect yourself enough to pay yourself first.

Chapter 5 in Book I goes into detail about lowering your expenses. For now, it's enough to identify the money that you didn't need to spend. Put that money in the savings category of your budget. When the insurance payment came due, for example, you told yourself that you didn't have money to spend on restaurant meals or movies. Isn't your future at least as important as paying for your insurance?

You'll find that when you have savings (and you will), the lowered stress, greater stability, feeling of financial security, and general well-being you enjoy are worth much more than the time and effort you invest in creating and maintaining your budget.

Book II

Money Management Basics

Setting Up a Basic Budget

Discovering and dealing with your spending personality type gives you hints on how to change your habits to create a realistic budget and keep it up to date. This section shows you how to set up a budget that reflects the reality of your current financial life.

Table 4-3 is a sample budget to show you what your budget may look like. Using the information from your spending diary, insert the values for what you paid in each category last month in the Last Month Actual column. After you determine what you should be spending in each category, put those amounts in the This Month Budget column. At the end of another month, put the amount that you actually spent in each category in the This Month Actual column.

This budget leaves you space in the Over/Under column to compare each item's real value with its real cost. When you compile your budget, you want to be able to compare real versus projected values on a monthly, quarterly, and yearly basis.

Note that these categories are not the same as those in Table 2-2. You'll determine which categories you need to include, so we want to show you how budget worksheets can vary. Choose categories that reflect your situation.

Table 4-3	My Monthly Budget			
Expense	*Last Month Actual*	*This Month Budget*	*This Month Actual*	*Over/ Under*
Housing and Utilities				
Mortgage or rent	$	$	$	$
Homeowners' or condo assn. fees	$	$	$	$
Electricity	$	$	$	$
Gas	$	$	$	$
Water	$	$	$	$
Telephone	$	$	$	$
Home maintenance	$	$	$	$
Subtotal, Housing and Utilities	**$**	**$**	**$**	**$**
Food				
Groceries	$	$	$	$
Restaurant meals	$	$	$	$
Subtotal, Food	**$**	**$**	**$**	**$**
Clothing and Shoes				
Adult 1	$	$	$	$
Adult 2	$	$	$	$
Child 1	$	$	$	$
Child 2	$	$	$	$
Subtotal, Clothing and Shoes	**$**	**$**	**$**	**$**
Insurance				
Auto	$	$	$	$
Health	$	$	$	$
Homeowner's/Renter's	$	$	$	$
Life	$	$	$	$
Other	$	$	$	$
Subtotal, Insurance	**$**	**$**	**$**	**$**

Expense	Last Month Actual	This Month Budget	This Month Actual	Over/ Under
Health care				
Dentist	$	$	$	$
Doctor	$	$	$	$
Optometrist	$	$	$	$
Other practitioner	$	$	$	$
Eyeglasses, contact lenses	$	$	$	$
Prescriptions	$	$	$	$
Other	$	$	$	$
Subtotal, Health care	**$**	**$**	**$**	**$**
Auto				
Gasoline	$	$	$	$
Maintenance	$	$	$	$
Payment	$	$	$	$
Tolls	$	$	$	$
Taxis and public transportation	$	$	$	$
Subtotal, Auto	**$**	**$**	**$**	**$**
Personal				
Charitable contributions	$	$	$	$
Child Care	$	$	$	$
Cosmetics	$	$	$	$
Entertainment	$	$	$	$
Haircuts	$	$	$	$
Magazines/newspapers	$	$	$	$
Membership dues	$	$	$	$
Vacations	$	$	$	$
Other	$	$	$	$
Subtotal, Personal	**$**	**$**	**$**	**$**

Book II

Money Management Basics

(continued)

Table 4-3 *(continued)*

Expense	Last Month Actual	This Month Budget	This Month Actual	Over/ Under
Savings and Investments				
Savings/Money market account	$	$	$	$
Education fund	$	$	$	$
Mutual fund	$	$	$	$
New car fund	$	$	$	$
New home fund	$	$	$	$
Retirement fund	$	$	$	$
Emergency savings account	$	$	$	$
Other	$	$	$	$
Subtotal, Savings and Investments	$	$	$	$
Taxes				
Federal income tax	$	$	$	$
Provincial income tax	$	$	$	$
CPP/EI	$	$	$	$
Property tax	$	$	$	$
Subtotal, Taxes	$	$	$	$
TOTAL EXPENSES	$	$	$	$
Income				
Gross wages 1	$	$	$	$
Gross wages 2	$	$	$	$
Interest income	$	$	$	$
Alimony/Child support paid to you	$	$	$	$
Other	$	$	$	$
TOTAL INCOME	$	$	$	$
Difference between income and expenses (put shortages in parentheses)	$	$	$	$

Often, your mortgage, property taxes, and insurance are lumped together in one payment. Don't "charge" yourself twice if you pay these expenses as part of your mortgage payments.

Make sure to account for all your expenses, but put them in any category that makes your budget work for you. For example, you may want to put your homeowner's or renter's insurance under Housing and Utilities rather than under Insurance. Moving items to other categories will reflect how you spend your money; your budget will reflect how you want to allocate your resources. Also, as you recognize new items, add them to your budget.

Sticking to Your Budget: Be Disciplined

Realizing that you need a budget, gathering your information, and putting that information into a usable form are giant strides toward securing your financial future. This chapter shows you how to build on the foundation that you established by creating a budget.

You have many good habits that took time to cultivate. Sometimes it's hard to remember them because once you have a good habit, you don't really think about it until you start to lose that good habit. Give yourself credit for developing habits such as the following:

- ✔ I brush my teeth every day.
- ✔ I change the oil in my car regularly.
- ✔ I send birthday cards to my friends and family.
- ✔ I get to work on time.

In the interest of appreciating that you can learn budgeting habits, too, check off in the following list those good habits that you've already picked up:

- ✔ I pay my bills on time.
- ✔ I balance my chequebook.
- ✔ I compare prices when I shop.
- ✔ I verify the charges on my credit card statement.

None of these habits, by themselves, will make your life either wonderful or awful. But adding good habits on top of good habits improves your life immensely.

You can't just fling your old bad habits out the window. To learn to be an effective budgeter, you must coax yourself into developing good habits. Check off the following activities that you can accomplish:

Book II

Money
Management
Basics

- ✔ Recognize how budgeting benefits me
- ✔ Notice changes in my spending habits and decide whether the changes are good or bad
- ✔ Revise my budget when my circumstances change
- ✔ Seek help when I need more information
- ✔ Set aside time every week to review my budget
- ✔ Write down changes that I want to make instead of keeping them in my head

Failing to use and revise your budget has many drawbacks:

- ✔ You miss out on the many benefits that budgeting brings to your financial life, such as the ability to make reasoned decisions rather than react to situations.
- ✔ You waste the time that you already spent collecting data.
- ✔ Your stress level rises.
- ✔ You don't feel good about yourself.

Reining In Your Impulse Spending

If, every time you return from the store, you have more items than you intended to purchase, you're not entirely at fault. Store managers have studied consumers for years. Stores purposely use floor plans that tempt you to buy things you didn't know you wanted and expose you to as many buying opportunities as possible. For example, why is milk, probably the most-purchased item in any supermarket, at the back of the store? Those wily store managers know that if you have to look at long aisles of tempting items going to and from picking up your milk, your shopping cart will very likely end up with more than milk in it.

Don't confuse good buys with impulse purchases. If you find a half-price sale on something your family uses and you can use it all before it spoils, that's a good buying decision, unless it means that you can't pay another bill and will have to pay a penalty on that bill.

Recognizing your triggers

Previously, you may not have thought of your purchases as being "triggered." But if the milk scenario seems familiar to you, then you have your own triggers. Common triggers are

- ✔ **Fatigue:** You work hard; you deserve a treat.

- ✔ **Hunger:** You don't have the energy to make a decision, so you treat yourself to junk food rather than a nutritious meal.

- ✔ **Overwork:** You've worked hard, so you feel that you deserve a treat.

- ✔ **Money in your pocket:** You have the cash to pay for it, so why not have a treat?

- ✔ **Depression:** You try to make yourself feel better by buying yourself a treat.

- ✔ **Elation:** You think that nothing can go wrong when you feel so good, so you have a treat.

- ✔ **Celebration:** You or your friend/sister/brother/college roommate deserves a nice present to celebrate a birthday/anniversary/new job.

- ✔ **Competition:** You have to give the nicest gift, or at least one that's as nice as so-and-so's.

- ✔ **The desire to impress someone:** You think, "Wait until so-and-so sees this!"

Assuring your long-term financial health is the best "treat" you can give yourself at any time!

You probably know the kinds of things you're most likely to purchase on a whim. Go to that area of your house and write down those things that you've purchased so that you can see how much money you've wasted by not making thoughtful decisions.

For example, are tools your weakness? Do you find it impossible to pass by a hardware store? Then take your survey in your workshop, garage, or tool shed. Or do you love buying yourself clothes? Then go to your closet. See the jacket you bought because the colour was beautiful? Of course, you have nothing that goes with it. How many items were on sale but don't really work well with the rest of your wardrobe?

Write down every item that falls into the impulse-spending category. You don't need to go through every door or find every impulse purchase, but do write down all the impulse buys that you find in plain sight.

You'll use the list that you make in the next section. If you're part of a couple or you're doing this exercise with your children, everyone should be reassured before you start this survey that its only purpose is to gather information.

If you use your survey to find fault with your or others' purchases, you'll quickly defeat the purpose and discourage helpful suggestions.

Before you go on, write an estimated cost next to each item. Then put a plus sign (+) next to anything you think you have used as much as you should have for the price. For example, you may have used your snow blower every time it snowed, but that means that it has cost you $87 for each five-minute snow-removal job — no + there. And don't forget the cost to insure that expensive piece of equipment.

Now put an asterisk (*) next to each item for which you could have purchased a reasonable substitute at a lower cost. We're not talking about something that arbitrarily went on sale, but something for which a small investment of time would have resulted in paying a much lower price. Next to the asterisk, write the price you think that you could have paid for a reasonable substitute. (Don't put garage-sale or second-hand-sale prices here — you have no guarantee that you would have found a substitute.)

Don't ignore small impulse purchases. Although you may not have included those items on this list, you purchase them more often, so they add up quickly.

Stopping yourself from making a purchase

Now that you recognize what makes you indulge in impulse spending and what the payoff can be when you make informed purchases based on your financial goals, you can control your triggers. You can do so by making conscious decisions before the temptation to buy reaches out to grab you.

Setting your "stop" triggers doesn't mean that you never get to treat yourself. If the supermarket is your downfall, for example, give yourself a set amount to spend any way you like. After a few trips to the store during which you can't decide what one treat you want, you'll find that you don't want any of them all that much!

If your impulse triggers go off in the hardware store or another type of store that sells big-ticket items, again give yourself a "treat budget." If you don't have enough money to buy what you want today, you can save up your treat allowance until you have enough money in that "account." But you don't get to buy now and pay with your future allowance!

Rounding Up Your Support Team

All kinds of people and organizations are around to help you meet your goals. In the case of people, you need to know why they want to help you, how much time and energy they can offer, and what their individual money personalities are. You may want to review the section on identifying money personalities at the end of Chapter 1 in Book I before you assign helping roles to your support team.

Spouse/significant other

The best way to work as a team with your spouse or significant other is to agree on your goals and the prioritization of those goals. You may have to compromise on individual goals in order to reach your goals as a couple or family.

Often, one partner is a better money manager than the other. That partner may be better at resisting temptation, computing amounts, dividing long-term goals into mid-term and short-term goals, setting priorities, budget balancing, and so on. Or one partner may be better at some activities while the other handles the remaining tasks.

The secret to a good partnership is agreeing to goals and how you're going to reach those goals. Then each partner does the best job possible for his or her responsibilities. In spite of the word partner, you may decide to give one person more authority than the other — as long as you both agree on who should have more authority when it comes to financial matters, and you remember that financial security, not "being in charge," is your goal. As time goes on and changes need to be made, use the same negotiating and compromise that brought you as far as you are to help you set up a new system.

Children

If you have children, you certainly want to involve them in learning how to handle money. Keeping children involved in the budgeting process also helps them learn the financial lessons that they need to know at each stage in their lives.

For example, when Charles' children started getting allowances, he deducted 10 percent from each child's allowance. Needless to say, the first few deductions caused much upset. The lesson was that adults don't get to keep all they earn because they must pay taxes. Just as adults get police and fire protection and roads to drive on from their taxes, the children got a place to live, meals, and vacations from their "taxes."

When the children's dog got sick, they had to use part of their savings to help pay the veterinarian's bill. They learned what savings were for and how they could meet goals by saving today.

No child is too young to participate in the family budget. But the younger a child is, the shorter-term the goal must be to fit with young children's shortened attention span and patience. If your children are not part of your "budgeting board of directors," everyone gets cheated. They not only miss out on important lessons, but their feelings and wishes are not reflected in two strategic parts of family life: budgeting and buying decisions.

Parents

Your parents have lived longer and met and survived more financial challenges than you have. Their individual and collective money personalities are important as to what kinds of help they can provide and what kinds of help you want from them.

If your parents can handle requests for loans and advice in a businesslike manner (and if you'll respond with an equally businesslike attitude), you can ask for loans and advice. If they have the attitude that whoever pays gets to make the rules, they'll probably want more control and expect answers to more questions than you're willing to give them. If you're desperate for their help, one of the compromises you may have to live with is that you must live with their money personalities.

Just as you would negotiate the conditions of a new job before you accept it, you must negotiate the terms of your parents' involvement in your financial life before you agree to open that scary door.

Friends

Friends have many of the same pluses and minuses that parents do, except you aren't required to keep them forever. One of the benefits of friends' involvement in helping you reach your goals is that you can restrict them to just one area of your financial decision-making. You may think you know your friends well, but when money enters the picture, personalities can clash. If a friend gives you a loan, draw up a written agreement on the amount of the loan, when it is to be repaid, and how much interest is to be paid. If your friend suddenly decides that the loan gives permission to tell you how to run your business or your life or your child's life, diplomatically remind your "friend" of the contract.

Still, you may identify friends from whom you'd like advice on your finances. You can invite those friends into your financial circle based on your ability to work with the strengths and weaknesses of each person's money personality. If someone is a closer friend to one marriage partner than the other, the two of you must discuss and negotiate that factor as well. As you set financial priorities, your good relations with your partner must take precedence over getting advice or help from a friend.

Professional and free services

Professional sources can help you gather information, set goals, set priorities, or stay on your financial path. You can use these sources from the start, use them once in a while, or even discard them from your financial life once their purpose has been served.

Accountants do much more than fill out tax returns. They can help you set goals, remind you of factors that you have forgotten or ignored, use their backgrounds with a variety of people's problems and solutions to help you pick the best of both, start you on a good financial plan no matter what your age or income, help you revise your plans and goals as you get older, and — the part you'll probably enjoy the most — help you reduce the taxes you pay.

Book II

Money Management Basics

Depending on your accountant's practice, you may also be able to get information about estate planning, insurance practices, housing, health care, and scholarships.

Your employer, union, or trade organization may have an EAP (Employee Assistance Program). The services that an EAP offers vary from provider to provider. Although some services may not be strictly financial, getting free or low-cost services in any area of concern will positively impact your financial situation and your ability to reach your goals.

Some EAPs offer budgeting, savings, tax, and estate planning services, either individually or in groups. The programs may also offer substance abuse help, family or individual counselling, workshops on buying and maintaining a home, and credit counselling. Whatever the topic, if you need information about it and don't pay for it, you've eliminated that budget expense while still learning what you need to know.

Your church or temple, community groups, credit bureaus, libraries, schools, financial institutions, and associations (such as Masons, Eastern Star, Rotary, and alumni groups) may offer budgeting and savings programs, either free or at a low cost. Look in local newspapers and newsletters for ads announcing such programs. Your local library or social service agency may also keep track of such listings.

The program offerings from these groups may also include:

- ✔ Avoiding repair costs through regular maintenance
- ✔ Building (or rebuilding) a good credit rating
- ✔ Buying the right amount of insurance for you
- ✔ Evaluating banking services
- ✔ Handling credit wisely
- ✔ Avoiding the hidden costs of holiday shopping

✔ Learning about programs that help pay for education, health care, housing, and utilities

✔ Managing money

✔ Purchasing your first home

✔ Surviving a layoff or divorce

Many suppliers of such services offer customized programs.

Dealing with Emergency Expenses

Unexpected expenses can severely disrupt your financial status. The three situations that usually get people in financial trouble are:

✔ Health care emergencies

✔ Vehicle repair and replacement

✔ Expensive appliances that wear out

Those expenses are the reason you have an emergency expense fund. (If you don't, go back to Chapter 3 and revise your budget!) If your fund isn't large enough, however, you can take short-term actions to avoid ending up in a spiral of debt:

✔ If your income is low, ask the local government and social services agency if low- or no-interest loans are available for these types of emergencies. Religious organizations also may have such funds.

✔ Ask your credit card companies and other creditors to let you skip a payment without penalty. They'll still add an interest charge, which raises your total debt, but the tactic frees up immediate money so that you can take care of the emergency.

✔ Pawn some possessions. Pawning is really a secured loan — you get cash in exchange for an item of value. If you pay back the loan (with interest, of course) by the deadline, you can retrieve your item.

✔ If you have a medical emergency, ask your health care provider about available services that would offset expenses for you, such as free or low-cost housing while your loved one is in the hospital and free or low-cost meals.

✔ If your problem is with your car and you have a good relationship with a garage, try to negotiate a time-payment plan at low or no interest (rather than the higher rate that you would be paying on your credit card).

✔ Take out a home-equity loan or second mortgage. These are not the best choices, however, because the rate of interest on them tends to be high.

Also, read the fine print. On some of those loans, you could lose your house if you miss one loan payment. Make sure, too, that you have the right to pay the loan off early to cut the interest expense.

✔ If you belong to a social or service organization, find out whether it has a formal or informal system for helping members. For example, a student from Norway who came to study in Canada discovered that because of a miscommunication, he had arrived two weeks before his housing was available. He was a member of Mensa, so he called the local contact. Someone in the local group put him up, rent-free, for the two weeks — and gave him a tour of the local area, topped off with a Labour Day picnic.

Be creative. This is another situation in which knowing the financial (and other) personalities of your family members and friends helps. Either the boldest family member or friend, or the one with the strongest "saver" personality, will be the best negotiator for these perks.

Paying for an emergency by credit card may get you in debt at a high interest rate. If you must use a credit card, be sure to choose the one with the lowest interest rate. Now may be the time to take advantage of a low-introductory-rate card that has been offered to you — but do so only if you can pay off the balance before the end of the introductory rate expires, or if the regular rate is reasonable.

Book II

Money Management Basics

Organizing Your Records

Your role as a money manager will not seem so burdensome if you know that you have what you need to succeed. Why begin a weekly or monthly money management session with a sense of frustration because you can't find the information you want or need? Make it easy for yourself and use the information in this chapter to support your money managing efforts.

Getting organized is at least half the battle in developing money management skills. If you just take the time, purchase a few supplies, and follow the simple steps identified in this section, you're well on your way as a successful money manager. Make an appointment to meet with yourself every week — a short, half-hour meeting will do. Then move into a monthly appointment where you allow an hour.

Getting started really doesn't take much. You need the following supplies to organize your financial records. If you don't have them, make a shopping list and go to the store:

✔ **Pens, pencils, paper, paper clips, and manila folders:** Tabbed folders let you see your records at a glance.

✔ **A file container:** You can use a cardboard box, a plastic crate, or a regular filing cabinet — whatever matches your budget.

✔ **Envelopes and postage stamps:** A box of business envelopes makes your financial correspondence and payments easier. Have a supply of stamps on hand, too, so that you can be sure to make your payments on time.

✔ **An appointment book or notebook:** Record your business appointments and any expenditures that you can't track with receipts.

✔ **Software:** If you have a computer, software programs such as Quicken and Microsoft Money can help you organize and track financial information.

Creating folders for keeping your financial records

Label a folder (include the year on the label) for each of the following items that applies to your financial situation. Put your folders in alphabetical order in your file container. Add additional folders as your situation calls for them.

✔ Registered Retirement Savings Plan (RRSP)

✔ Automobile — Insurance and loan

✔ Automobile — Maintenance

✔ Bank accounts

✔ Charitable contributions

✔ Credit cards

✔ Educational records

✔ Health insurance

✔ Home — Improvements

✔ Home — Insurance

✔ Home — Maintenance

✔ Home — Mortgage

✔ Income tax — Federal

✔ Income tax — Provincial

✔ Insurance — Life and disability

✔ Loan (specify type)

✔ Mutual funds

✔ Property tax bills

✔ Real estate investment

✔ Stocks

✔ Warranties

✔ Will and/or trust

Consolidate all the information you have and add it to each folder that pertains to that file. Record essential information on the cover of each folder. Identify the name, address, phone number, and number for each account, policy, or whatever. Collecting this information takes a little time but makes contacts and record-keeping much easier over the course of the year. Table 4-5 shows an example of what you may need for your insurance file. Fill in the information and staple them to the inside cover of the relevant folder. Some forms can do double duty.

Book II

Money Management Basics

Table 4-4	Tracking Insurance

Insurance (automobile, health, home, life, and disability):

Insurance company/ Financial institution _____

_____

Address _____

_____

Phone _____

Name of representative _____

Phone if different from above _____

Claim number _____

Policy number _____

Payments _____

_____

Communication Log	Date	Name	Results

These basic forms illustrate the kind of essential information for each of your folders. When you have information at your fingertips, you put it to better and more frequent use.

Keeping personal records

You'll also benefit from keeping personal information in one place. So while you're organizing, set up a personal file with the following information:

- ✓ **Social Insurance Number(s):** Include your Social Insurance Number, as well as your spouse's, your childrens', your parents', and your siblings'.

- ✓ **Contact information:** List the names and addresses of each of your adult children and your parents. Include work-contact information when available.

- ✓ **Birth certificates:** Collect original birth certificates for each member of your family and keep them in this folder.

- ✓ **Marriage certificate/divorce decree:** Include your marriage certificate and/or divorce documents in your folder.

- ✓ **Personal will:** No matter what your age, make sure that you have an up-to-date will. If you already have a will, take another look at it to see whether you need to make adjustments. If you don't have a will, make getting one a priority.

- ✓ **Living will:** You can ask your doctor to draw up a statement for a living will or pick up a form to fill out. Share this information with your family and keep a copy in your personal folder.

Staying organized

Now that you've started the process of organizing your financial records, you want to stay on track. That means visiting your folders often, updating your financial information regularly, and maybe even scheduling a monthly appointment with yourself to help you stay organized and on track.

Chapter 5

Planning for the Inevitable: Taxes

In This Chapter

▶ Understanding income taxes

▶ Being aware of "hidden" taxes

▶ Amassing and organizing your tax records

▶ Staying out of tax trouble

Some taxes are paid out every day. In provinces and territories that levy PST, Provincial Sales Tax, a sales tax is added to the majority of purchases you make. The federal government adds GST, Goods and Services Tax, to many items we buy. The gasoline you buy includes taxes added on by federal and provincial governments. Receipts should show the breakdowns, so have a look next time you buy.

Planning for Income Taxes

Income taxes have become so complex that most Canadians need help figuring out what they owe and how to report their income. Ignorance only compounds tax problems. You can't claim that you don't know the tax requirements and expect your tax debt to be forgiven. Books and pamphlets are written in abundance on this subject. Even the Canada Customs and Revenue Agency (CCRA) has developed and made available free publications to help you understand tax matters.

Staying informed

Purchase a tax preparation guide every year. These guides keep you informed and more than pay for themselves in the form of taxes saved. Even if you choose to have a professional prepare your taxes, the current tax guide enables you to ask informed questions.

You have to be informed about CCRA requirements. To help you do so, CCRA offers a wide variety of free publications that you can order by calling 800-829-3676. Or you can download publications and forms from the CCRA Web site (`www.ccra-adrc.gc.ca`), or pick up information at your local library and bookstore. The Certified General Accountants of Canada publishes an annual basic tax guide that you can download for free at `www.cga-canada.org`.

Getting organized

Whether you do your taxes yourself or turn the task over to a professional, you need the proper records. More than half the time spent on preparing income taxes is related to keeping and organizing records and studying the rules and procedures for filing. If you keep good records, you have completed more than half the battle!

Set up a separate file drawer or box that can accommodate folders. At the beginning of each calendar year, buy manila folders and label them with the year and any of the following categories that apply to your situation. (No matter what time of year you're reading this, organize your folders for the current year now.) Then save your receipts and other information in the appropriate folders.

- ✔ **Income documents:** Your employer and financial institutions are required to send you income and interest information in January of each year. Your T-4 form tells you and CCRA how much money you earned and how much was withheld.

- ✔ **Forms:** These forms report money you receive from freelance assignments, interest payments from banks, and stock dividends.

- ✔ **RRSPs:** A Registered Retirement Savings Plan is an account that you set aside for retirement by using pretax dollars. You can subtract the amount you contribute to your RRSP from your taxable income.

  Interest on personal loans, credit charges, and car loans is not tax-deductible.

- ✔ **Deductions — Charity:** You can deduct from your income tax contributions that you made to charitable and not-for-profit organizations. Some limitations apply, but save your receipts.

- ✔ **Moving expenses:** Many expenses connected with changes in the location of your employment can reduce your gross income if you move farther than 40 kilometres.

✔ **Home expenses:** Save all records and receipts connected with maintaining and improving your home. Part of those costs may be deductible if you have a home business office in your house.

✔ **Deductions — Work:** The cost of certain tools, uniforms, memberships, training programs, mileage, and books can be tax-deductible if they're related to improvement and on-the-job training.

Deciding whether to itemize

Whether or not you do your own taxes, you have to decide whether claiming the standard deduction or itemizing your deductions will work better for you.

A tax adviser can review your tax situation and recommend whether itemizing your deductions would be more beneficial. Generally, if your tax situation is fairly simple, claiming the standard deduction is easier. If, however, you have had outstanding medical expenses, have purchased a home, or have made some other significant change in your life, itemizing deductions may be in your best interest.

If the total value of your itemized deductions exceeds the value of the standardized deduction, it's better to itemize your deductions and file the more detailed tax return. Take the time to complete the tax worksheets found in tax guidebooks and software. These worksheets can help you decide whether to itemize.

Getting the records you need

You use the same records to complete all your forms. See the section "Getting organized" for a list of these items. You file provincial income taxes simultaneously with your federal forms. Figures for adjusted gross income relate to the deductions for federal and provincial taxes. You receive income tax forms in the mail, or you can pick them up at post offices, public libraries, and tax preparation offices.

Knowing what gets taxed

Provinces, counties, and municipalities have the right to secure funding through taxation. And they're very good at identifying additional sources of revenue. Typically, provinces add their own taxes to the following:

Book II

**Money
Management
Basics**

✔ **Alcoholic beverage tax:** The range varies for various types of alcohol, but 10 percent is about the average. Beer, for example, is usually taxed at a lower rate than liquor that contains 20 percent or more alcohol. This kind of tax is sometimes referred to as a "sin" tax.

✔ **Fuel tax:** All fuels used on public highways are subject to tax.

✔ **Motor vehicle registration tax:** A vehicle tax is imposed on automobiles, trucks, buses, tractors, motorcycles, semi trailers, and trailers for the privilege of using a motor vehicle in the province.

✔ **Tobacco tax:** Both the federal and provincial governments impose a cigarette tax in an effort to reduce cigarette consumption. In addition, a tax is imposed on other tobacco products, such as cigars and chewing tobacco. The rates vary.

✔ **Insurance tax:** Out-of-province companies and foreign companies doing insurance business within a province are subject to additional taxes for the privilege of doing business in that province. Basically, though, the taxes that any company — even in-province — pays for the privilege of doing business in a province are passed on to the consumer of its goods or services.

✔ **Public utilities tax:** Suppliers of electricity, light, gas, and telecommunications within provinces are subject to various fees, taxes, and surcharges.

✔ **Real estate transfer tax:** Many municipalities charge a fee for buying and selling real estate, including your home. This tax is paid when the deed is recorded with the municipality.

Reducing How Much Tax You Pay

Although you can't spend all your time and energy looking for ways to avoid taxes, you can do some simple things to avoid paying more than you have to. Consider the following:

✔ **Contribute to an RRSP:** This is the best way for all Canadians to reduce their taxable income. This is the most-used method of reducing the tax you pay, and you might want to consider taking out a short-term loan to make your contribution. You can pay off the loan with the increased return you'll receive and beef up your plan in the process. Speak to your banker about how this works and be sure to meet your loan commitments. Invest early, invest often, and end up with more money for yourself at the end of the day.

✔ **Keep good records:** Pay close attention to the section in Chapter 4 about organizing your financial records. Good tax planning really pays off. Believe it or not, if you know where you're at, you are more likely to file your return on time and accurately right off the bat.

✔ **Know when to get help:** Tax professionals can help you file a return that optimizes your deductions. Remember that they aren't miracle workers though. If you feel like you're in over your head, seek their advice and, though you'll pay for it, you're likely to stress less and keep more in your wallet.

✔ **Spend less:** You have to pay a sales tax on whatever you buy, but if you don't buy the most expensive items available, you don't pay the maximum taxes. If, for example, you buy a luxury Oriental rug that costs $5,000, you'll pay a tax of, say, 8 percent. So a $5,000 rug actually costs you $5,400 with the sales tax. But if you buy a rug that costs $500, at the same sales tax rate, your rug costs only $540. Don't forget the GST; that will add to you initial cost as well.

✔ **Buy store brands:** Many items, such as diapers, kitty litter, pain relievers, and water, to name a few — whether premium or house brands — accomplish the same thing when used properly. Why pay a premium price for a disposable item and pay the additional tax that goes with it?

✔ **Shop catalogues:** When you buy an item from a catalogue, you may not have to pay the provincial sales tax on that item. That's the good news; the bad news, however, is that you pay a shipping and handling charge that often exceeds what you would pay in tax. Be careful purchasing from U.S.-based companies — you have to factor in not only shipping but also exchange and possibly even customs charges.

✔ **Barter:** As an individual, you may be able to trade one of your skills or services to another person with a complementary skill or service. And if you can barter your plumbing skills for a friend's electrical skills, you can also avoid a cash transaction that requires a retail sales tax.

✔ **Take advantage of coupons, discounts, and bargains:** If you have the time and inclination, you can buy just about everything you need to purchase at a cheaper price somewhere.

Book II

Money Management Basics

Avoiding Tax Trouble

No one wants to hassle with CCRA. Certain flags on a tax return increase your chances of being subject to a CCRA examination, or audit. If you keep good records and file on time, you stand a good chance of steering clear of an audit. But you do need to consider the clues that CCRA looks for.

Staying alert to audits

CCRA generally considers the following situations red flags:

- ✔ Claiming more than 35 percent of adjusted gross income on itemized deductions
- ✔ Claiming persons other than children, grandchildren, or parents as dependents
- ✔ Claiming large deductions for travel and entertainment not in proportion to income
- ✔ Taking office-in-home deductions while employed elsewhere
- ✔ Clues to unreported income, such as an unusually low income in the restaurant business
- ✔ Underreporting tip income from businesses that receive gratuities
- ✔ Claiming high interest deductions
- ✔ Claiming bad debts
- ✔ Taking large depreciation and maintenance deductions for rental property
- ✔ Claiming high business use of a car in a business that traditionally doesn't have high car use
- ✔ Claiming disproportionate charitable donations

You have no cause for panic when you're audited if you have calculated your taxes fairly and kept good records. And not all audits result in additional tax charges and penalties. If you are audited, you're responsible for substantiating your claims with sufficient records. In some cases, CCRA may simply request additional documentation or an explanation.

You have rights as a taxpayer, and CCRA is required to inform you of these rights before an audit. You can ask for more time to produce the required documentation and ask to stop the CCRA interview to consult with a tax adviser. You can bring an adviser or witness with you, and you can tape the interview. You also can appeal the audit findings. By keeping comprehensive records and filing honest returns you should avoid this altogether.

Doing the right thing

The complexities of tax law and tax reporting are daunting. Here are some tips for doing the right thing:

✔ **Be honest and fair.** Attempts to defraud the government by purposely giving false or incomplete information about a significant tax issue are punishable.

✔ **Keep meticulous records.**

✔ **Order and use CCRA documents and assistance.** Filing forms and general guides are widely available. Look for them at your local Canada Post outlet, library, or tax preparation office, or check out the CCRA Web site at www.ccra.adrc.gc.ca.

✔ **Pay for competence if you want someone to prepare your tax returns.** Tax preparers who are certified and sign your tax forms are generally more reliable than someone who has made a hobby of preparing tax forms. Go with the professionals; tax codes are complicated and you need the expertise of those who are informed with the current requirements. Ask your friends, family, or lawyer for tax preparer recommendations.

✔ **Use electronic filing.** The benefits of electronic filing are many: CCRA confirms receipt of your return, so you don't have to wonder about mail delays. Electronic filing is more accurate because it eliminates data entry errors at CCRA. And if you're expecting a tax refund, you'll likely get it quicker.

Book II

Money Management Basics

Book III
Home Sweet, Home Free

The 5th Wave   By Rich Tennant

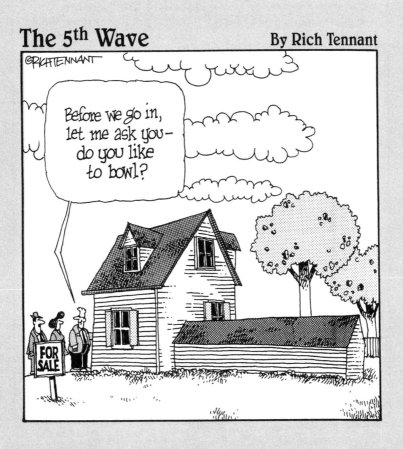

In this book . . .

*B*uying or selling a home is an incredibly enormous undertaking, not recommended for the faint of heart, the short of memory, or the big of debt. These are the biggest financial and lifestyle choices you'll ever make, so choose wisely.

However, armed with information in this book, you can calmly face the real estate world and find out how it works. You'll learn what fixed-rate, open-term mortgages are. You'll use the word chattel in everyday conversation. And, most important, you'll discover what your priorities are, and how to match them with a home — a home of your own.

Buying a new home or leaving an old and cherished one involves a lot of decisions and considerations. This book outlines them all, setting you on the path to your new life, wherever that may be.

Here are the contents of Book III at a glance:

Chapter 1

Deciding to Buy

. . . .

In This Chapter

▶ Deciding that you're ready to buy

▶ Owning versus renting

▶ Learning about common homeowning concerns

▶ Investigating your finances

▶ Understanding mortgages

▶ Checking out your mortgage options

▶ Insuring your mortgage

▶ Choosing a mortgage lender

. . . .

Dorothy said it best: There's no place like home. You may be a jet-setting entrepreneur or a stay-at-home parent, but it's a pretty safe bet that where you live is your most cherished space. You need a place to wind down, to relax, and to rejuvenate. Whether you own or rent (or mooch off your parents), the place you call home is the foundation of your life.

We all want our homes to be perfect — even though our definitions of perfect change over time. Maybe as a teenager, your perfect bedroom was all black with huge speakers in every corner of the room. Twenty years, three children, two dogs, and a father-in-law later, your idea of perfect is an ensuite bathroom with good water pressure, a Jacuzzi, and a lock on the door. We all need a living space that can adapt to our changing needs and wants, and, of course, what better way to have that living space than to own it?

The idea of owning a home can be scary: Your water pipes could freeze and break, your basement could flood, your electrical system could need a complete overhaul. People can put thousands of dollars into their homes for renovations, thousands more for emergency repairs, and then there's daily upkeep, seasonal maintenance, taxes. . . . But ask homeowners if it's worth it, and they'll nod their heads vigorously and show you their Zen rock garden, the self-designed workshop in the basement, and the "Elvis room" with white and gold sequined walls, blue suede curtains, and pink Cadillac couch.

Even though owning your home can dictate how much money you have for other things and leave you constantly worrying about finances, researching and planning will help you stay in control. You can and should decide how much home you can afford, and that's why the first three chapters of this Book is geared toward getting you the home you want — at a price that doesn't leave you eating macaroni and cheese three times a day for the next 20 years. After all, you want your home to complement your lifestyle, not overrun it. You want enough money left over to create that "Elvis room" you've dreamed of.

Should You Buy Right Now?

Although you may think researching real estate markets and waiting for the right time to buy are the only ways to get a good deal, your personal situation is what should really determine your decision to buy. Are you able to pay your mortgage, utilities, taxes, insurance, and whatever maintenance comes up, not only for the next year, but also for the next 5, or 25? (We show you how to get a picture of your financial situation in "Getting Up Close and Personal with Your Finances," later in this chapter.)

Are you willing to remain in the same place for the next five years? Considering the closing costs involved whether you're a seller or a buyer — you should set aside about three thousand dollars for closing-day costs such as legal and insurance fees, appraisals and surveys, taxes, and other little oddities — you should be prepared to keep your home for at least a few years. It's a good idea to avoid selling your home quickly, because chances are you would have to sell at a lower price. So even if the market is at an all-time low and interest rates are way down, buying a home could be a huge mistake if you're in the middle of a career change or planning a move to Luxembourg in a year.

Maintaining a house requires a big commitment — of money and time. Each season presents a list of chores to maintain your home's integrity and efficiency. Overlooking the overflowing eaves or the leaky roof may lead to significant water damage; neglecting your furnace could cause hundreds of dollars in repairs to it and your frozen home. There are many situations in which a little neglect can transform into expensive repairs and sometimes irreversible damage, resulting in huge losses when it's time to sell. If you don't budget the time and money for regular upkeep, be prepared to invest more time and money down the line.

Renting versus buying

Owning your home instead of renting almost always makes more sense in the long run, especially if you settle in one area. The biggest advantage of owning over renting is that your monthly payments are an investment (and they'll eventually cease!). The most common complaint about buying a home is having to pay the mortgage, and more specifically, the interest on the mortgage. You can live with your parents until you've made enough money to buy a home outright, but your parents may not want to live with you for that long!

Renting your home instead of owning it does have advantages, and there are times in your life when owning isn't the best option for you. One of the biggest reasons to buy a home is for stability, but if you like your flexible lifestyle, this may be a burden to you. Owning a home is a serious commitment, and if your priorities aren't geared to making regular mortgage payments, or having a permanent address, it may be better to rent.

If you're in one of the following situations you should probably wait a while to buy a home:

- ✔ **Having financial woes:** Although you can leap into home ownership with as little as a 5 percent down payment in some cases, you still have to come up with that 5 percent. And you'll have to be prepared to make those regular mortgage payments for what may seem like an eternity, not to mention all the other costs of being a homeowner. Getting a mortgage may also be tricky if you're saddled with other loans and have significant debts.

- ✔ **Living in transition:** You haven't decided to live in one place. Saddling yourself with a chunk of property and debt if you think you're really going to want to spend the next year island-hopping around Greece is not the best move.

- ✔ **Lacking job security:** If you end up relocating for employment, you may have to get rid of your home in a hurry. If you don't have a reliable or steady source of income, lenders may not be willing to authorize a mortgage because you can't guarantee you'll have more work in the coming years.

- ✔ **Space uncertainty:** Although you can't really predict having triplets, there's no sense in buying a two-bedroom bungalow if you're pretty sure that your brother-in-law's family of seven and their three dogs will move in with you for an unspecified amount of time. Unless this is your way of ensuring they can't live with you, you may find you have to change houses sooner than you'd like. If you are considering setting up a home office or starting a home-based business in the future, make sure you have a spare bedroom or room in the basement to expand.

Book III

Home Sweet, Home Free

✔ **Facing a bad housing market:** Generally speaking, you should focus on your own situation rather than the real estate market. But there may be a time when interest rates skyrocket and yet homes sell for twice as much as their listing prices — in these circumstances, it's probably better to wait until the market cools down to buy a home. If a monthly cost analysis shows that buying a home would be 20 to 30 percent more than renting a comparable home, think twice about buying.

✔ **Waiting for the gravy train:** You and your friend are starting a new biotech company that will revolutionize the health care industry, and you need some start-up capital. You decide to invest all your savings in the company instead of real estate. If your company takes off, you may be able to buy an estate in the south of France instead of a bungalow in the suburbs.

Considering common homeowning concerns

You may be skeptical about the complications of buying a home. There are many different kinds of homes and ownership of homes, however, so you don't have to let your hatred of shovelling snow stop you from owning. The following are the most common reservations about home owning:

✔ **Unexpected costs:** One of the main arguments for renting is that you know what your monthly costs are, and they don't change. When you own a house, and the furnace breaks down, you have to fix it. But consider that when you rent, your landlord may not get around to fixing things right away, or he may be in Florida for the holidays and you may be stuck in the cold for a while. Although living in the same building as your landlord may guarantee some things are fixed in a hurry, your concern about a missing screen on your bedroom window may not be her priority. And maybe she likes the house at 18°C during the winter and 30°C in the summer. Sometimes paying the money to get things fixed is worth the hassle, but if you pay for a repair in your rented home, you may never see that money again.

So, though the responsibility for repairs in your home will fall on your own shoulders, the main point is that you have the control. And with a mortgage you know from the beginning how much you'll be paying each month for the length of your mortgage; with renting, it's hard to get that guarantee.

✔ **Extra work:** Don't like doing lawn work, shovelling snow, fixing leaks? Your partner or child refuses to do your dirty work for you? Instead of renting to avoid such chores, you may prefer to buy a condominium where someone else takes care of the maintenance. If you buy an apartment-style condo, you won't even have a sidewalk to worry about!

Keep in mind that once you move into a new home, you'll have new rates for some monthly expenses like utilities (heating, hydro, water). You may be taking on new costs such as property taxes and home and garden maintenance. New homeowners should also prepare for the worst by ensuring they have a reserve fund for emergency repairs. Make sure you have enough monthly income left over after your mortgage payments to cover these costs, as well.

Anticipating the typical costs for a new homeowner

Okay, so you want a better idea of exactly what kind of costs a new home-owner faces? Here goes.

- ✔ **Maintenance:** You may have a high-maintenance relationship or a low-maintenance relationship with the home you buy. Be sure your finances can handle the costs of regular repairs. Also, keep an emergency fund for unexpected repairs, and contribute to it on a regular basis. If you dip into it to help pay your way to Tahiti, that's your call, but be aware that your basement could be flooded when you return, and then you may not have the cash to pay the plumber.

- ✔ **Insurance:** You will need proof of fire and extended coverage insurance before you can finalize the purchase of your new home, since the property itself is the *only* security against the loan. If your new home burns down . . . well, you understand. Insurance costs vary, depending on your deductible, the value of your home and its contents, and the type of coverage you get, as well as each insurer's rates. Shop around for an affordable policy that covers you for replacement of your personal property and grants you a living allowance if your home is destroyed. A policy with public liability insurance is also a good idea, as it protects you if someone is harmed on your property.

- ✔ **Utilities:** When you buy a home, you assume all the heating, cooling, water, and electricity bills for the property. If you live in the colder, draftier parts of this country, you already know that heat is the most important utility there is. And if you've ever rented a house and paid the hydro bill separately for electric heat, you've already been walloped by one of the biggest bills you've ever experienced. If the house you're buying is new, you'll probably pay less for utilities because of better insulation and construction quality. If you're buying a resale home, ask the owners for copies of their utility bills so that you can figure out average heating costs.

Book III

Home Sweet, Home Free

- **Taxes:** Property taxes are calculated based on your home's assessed value and the local tax rates. Unfortunately, property tax rates can fluctuate yearly, and they vary from region to region. Most real estate listings will state the amount of the previous year's taxes for the property being sold. When you're looking at new homes, find out from the selling or buying agent, or the owners, what the previous year's taxes were. If you need a high-ratio mortgage to buy a new home, your lender may insist that property tax instalments be added to your monthly mortgage payments. (See "High-ratio mortgage insurance," later in this chapter for more details.)

- **Condo fees:** The great thing about living in a condo is that someone else looks after all the pesky maintenance and landscaping stuff. The flip side is you have to pay for it in your condo fees. In addition to your mortgage payments, condo fees alone can cost as much as rent in a decent apartment.

Understanding the market

The housing market fluctuates, experiencing both strong and weak periods. History has shown, however, that the market will rise in the long run. So don't focus too much on waiting for the "right time" to buy. It's nearly impossible to predict how the market will go, and if you wait around forever for the market to be perfect you'll waste tonnes of potential investment money on rent! Generally speaking, after you've bought your first home you'll continue to own it for years to come, and its value will increase. It's your personal situation that really should matter, because that will determine whether you have to sell the home in a hurry, and whether you can really afford to buy in the first place.

Having said all this, chances are you still want to know how the market works, because there are periods when it's best to be a buyer (and conversely, times when it's best to be a seller). You can see what the current market is like by checking out the prices in the local paper and asking your real estate agent how the current market compares to the past 12 months. Your agent can tell you how homes have been selling in the past year, what the *median sales price* was (the median sales price is the actual middle price between the highest and lowest selling prices, not the average price), and sometimes even how long homes were on the market, the types of homes sold, and their neighbourhoods. You can also check out local or national listings on the Internet. The MLS (Multiple Listing Service), a trademark and service of the Canadian Real Estate Association, can be accessed online at www.mls.ca. It's another gateway to lots of information on homes for sale in Canada.

A good overall economy will naturally produce a stronger market with more people looking to buy. Chances are, of course, there will be more sellers, because with more money, owners may decide to "trade up" and buy bigger homes. A strong economy also produces more construction and housing developments, opening up the market to more new homes.

To understand the housing market, there are a couple of terms and effects that you should know about.

- ✔ **Buyer's market:** Ideally you'll want to buy when many sellers want to sell but few buyers are looking to buy. Homes take longer to sell and so buyers can take more time to make decisions. To sell a home in this market, the seller will have to list at a really good price, and sometimes even offer other incentives, such as secondary financing (financing options are discussed later in this chapter).

- ✔ **Seller's market:** The opposite of a buyer's market is a seller's market. Few homes are on the market, but buyers are plentiful, which results in fast home sales at prices close to, or even above, the listing prices. Some homes will sell even before they're listed. Because of the rise in sales, a lot of owners may sell their homes themselves. In a seller's market, buyers have less negotiating power, less time to decide, and may even find themselves in a bidding war for homes. So if you're buying in a seller's market, be prepared to make quick decisions. Have all your homework done and your financing arranged.

- ✔ **Seasonal influences:** Winter in Canada is notorious for being cold and unpleasant everywhere but the south coast of B.C. People don't like to venture out much, unless it's for necessities such as groceries and hockey games (and skiing). Besides, who wants to look for a home when they're busy buying Christmas presents? Frostbite aside, the winter months also tend to be slower for the real estate market because people with children don't like to move during the school year. A lot of homes won't be on the market simply because sellers know their homes look best in the summer with the flowers, the leaves, and the sunshine. This means, of course, that the homes on the market at this time of year probably have to be sold urgently, and so you may find a good bargain. You may just have to deal with uncomfortable temperatures on moving day! The exceptions to this rule of seasonality are Toronto, Vancouver, and Calgary. For the past few years, these local real estate markets have experienced no significant seasonal slowdowns.

- ✔ **Interest rates:** If you need a mortgage to purchase your home (lucky you, if you don't!), you'll find that interest rates make a big difference in how much home you can afford. When interest rates are high, fewer buyers tend to be in the market for a new home. You can see the logic: A 6.5 percent interest rate on a $200,000 mortgage loan will cost you approximately $13,000 in interest in one year, while the same $200,000 loan at a 10 percent interest rate will cost you about $20,000 interest! Different types of mortgages can increase or decrease your interest rate from what banks consider the current standard.

Book III

Home Sweet, Home Free

Getting Up Close and Personal with Your Finances

Although it can be depressing to examine your meagre income next to your substantial expenses, you'll be even more depressed if you can't make your mortgage payments on your new home. In assessing what size mortgage you're eligible for, your lender (usually a bank) takes into account only those debts you *have* to pay. The really expensive food you buy for your 16 cats or the trips to Aruba you take every other month to work on your tan are not accounted for. If you don't want to find yourself with hungry rebellious felines, then you should examine your real monthly expenses to calculate how much of your income you can realistically put toward your mortgage payments. Take a look at Table 1-1: Once you've deducted your total monthly expenses from your total monthly income, the remaining amount is what you can afford to pay toward your mortgage each month.

However, before you even think about mortgage costs, you need to have a lump sum amount in your bank to make the down payment on a new home. Your down payment can amount to as little as 5 percent of the purchase price of the home you want to buy. And one more thing: In addition to the down payment, you need another chunk of money (a few thousand dollars) to pay the closing costs on a new home.

Table 1-1	Monthly Budget Worksheet	
	Income	*Monthly Amount*
Net income after taxes	_____	_____
-Partner's net income after taxes	_____	_____
-Other income: investments, gifts, annuity, trust fund, pension, etc.	_____	_____
Total Income	_____	_____
	Expenses	*Monthly Amount*
Investments		
RRSP	_____	_____
Education funds	_____	_____
Other	_____	_____
Debts		
Credit cards	_____	_____

	Expenses	Monthly Amount
Lines of credit	_____	_____
Student loans	_____	_____
Other loans/debt	_____	_____
Transportation		
Auto loan or lease payments	_____	_____
Insurance	_____	_____
Registration	_____	_____
Repairs/maintenance	_____	_____
Fuel	_____	_____
Parking	_____	_____
Public transit	_____	_____
Household Costs		
Groceries	_____	_____
Utilities		
Hydro/electricity	_____	_____
Water	_____	_____
Gas	_____	_____
Home insurance	_____	_____
Telephone	_____	_____
Cable television	_____	_____
Internet	_____	_____
Health		
Medication	_____	_____
Glasses/contacts	_____	_____
Dental/orthodontics	_____	_____
Therapist	_____	_____
Special needs items	_____	_____

Book III

Home Sweet, Home Free

(Continued)

Table 1-1 (Continued)

	Expenses	Monthly Amount
Miscellaneous		
Life insurance	_____	_____
Education		
Tuition fees	_____	_____
Books/supplies	_____	_____
Daycare	_____	_____
Entertainment	_____	_____
Restaurant meals	_____	_____
Vacation	_____	_____
Clothing/accessories	_____	_____
Recreation/sports equipment	_____	_____
Membership fees	_____	_____
Pets	_____	_____
Gifts	_____	_____
Other	_____	_____
Total Expenses	_____	_____

Understanding the Types of Mortgages

Mortgages break down into two types based on the amount of the down payment and therefore the amount of risk the lender is assuming by advancing you the money.

Conventional mortgages

A *conventional mortgage* covers not more than 75 percent of the purchase price of the house or the appraised value, whichever is lower. (See Chapter 2 for more information on home appraisals.) So if you want to buy a $200,000 house, you need a $50,000 down payment (25 percent of purchase price) if you're applying for a conventional mortgage.

High-ratio mortgages

High-ratio mortgages account for between 75 and 95 percent of the purchase price of a house or condominium, or the property's appraised value, whichever is lower. So you can still buy your $200,000 home, even if you have only a $10,000 down payment (just 5 percent of the purchase price). However, if you are taking out a *variable rate mortgage* (see a discussion on variable mortgages later in this chapter), you may be restricted to at least a 10 percent down payment. Your lender can advise you on the minimum down payment you will need for your chosen type of mortgage when you go through the pre-approval process.

Either the Canada Mortgage and Housing Corporation (CMHC) or GE Capital Mortgage Insurance Company (Canada) must insure high-ratio mortgages. This insurance protects the lender if you default on your mortgage payments. An insurance premium ranging from 0.5 percent to 3.75 percent of the mortgage amount, pre-determined by a sliding scale, will be added to your mortgage. Be prepared to pay an extra .25 percent insurance premium if you are taking out a variable rate mortgage. There's more about mortgage insurance later in this chapter, and of course your lender or mortgage broker can answer all your questions, too.

High-ratio mortgages are available for properties with a purchase price up to $300,000, depending on where you live in Canada. In parts of British Columbia and Ontario, both CMHC and GE Capital will provide high-ratio mortgages for a purchase price up to $300,000. In most other parts of the country, the ceiling price is $250,000. However, there are parts of the country, including much of Quebec and many rural areas of other provinces, where high-ratio mortgages are limited to a purchase price of $175,000. A full list of the high-ratio mortgage limits, plus a wealth of other mortgage and real estate information and online tools, can be accessed at the CMHC Web site, at www.cmhc-schl.gc.ca, and the GE Capital Web site at www.gemortgage.ca.

Book III

Home Sweet, Home Free

Mortgage Basics and Jargon 101

One cool thing about getting a mortgage (unlike a computer, for example) is that every element has a clear purpose. Once you sit down with a pen and paper and calculator, or simply open your spreadsheet program on your computer and start plugging in numbers, it all starts to make sense really, really quickly. There are five chief elements to every mortgage:

- **Mortgage principal:** the amount of the loan
- **Interest:** the amount you pay for borrowing the money
- **Blended payments:** regular payments made toward the principal and the interest

✔ **Amortization period:** the period of time over which the calculation of the size of the required payments is based

✔ **Mortgage term:** the time period over which you agree to make payments to your lender under certain conditions — for example, at a specific interest rate

Mortgage principal

The total amount of the loan you get is called the *principal.* So if you need to borrow $150,000 to buy a house, then your principal is $150,000. The principal will become smaller and smaller as you pay off the loan.

Interest

Interest is the money you pay a lender in addition to repaying the principal of your loan — a sort of compensation so your lender profits from giving you a loan. The *interest rate,* calculated as a percentage of the principal, determines how much interest you pay the lender at each scheduled payment — the cost of borrowing the money.

People like to buy houses when interest rates are low because they can either buy a more expensive house than if the rates were higher, or they can pay off the mortgage more quickly. For example, at a 5 percent interest rate, a $100,000 principal would cost you approximately $5,000 in interest each year. At a 7 percent interest rate, you would pay approximately $7,000 in interest in a year on a principal amount of $100,000. That's a difference of approximately $2,000 a year that would go to paying off your principal in the low-interest-rate scenario rather than being gobbled up by interest.

Each lender will have subtle differences in how much extra money you may put against the principal (pre-payment options), with different payment schedules offered, and most importantly, they will give you a discount on the posted rates if and when you convert into a longer, fixed rate. Don't hesitate to try to negotiate a good discount. In general, the longer the term of the mortgage, the more room there is for you to negotiate. Do your research before you commit to a mortgage — you have lots of options out there.

The way your lender adds up the interest you owe has a big impact on the amount of interest you pay over the life of the mortgage. If interest is *compounded daily* (added to your balance owing every day), you will pay more over the lifetime of the mortgage than if interest is compounded semi-annually. Most mortgages are compounded semi-annually, but your lender may offer you other options.

Fixed rate mortgage

Because interest rates rise and fall, some times are better than others for taking out a mortgage. To give yourself some stability, you can choose a *fixed rate mortgage* that allows you to lock in at a specific interest rate for a certain period of time (*mortgage term*). If interest rates are rising, you may want to lock in at a fixed rate so that you know what your monthly costs will be over the term of your mortgage. Once a mortgage term expires, you can renegotiate your interest rate and the length of time (term) that you will make payments at the new rate. As you shop for mortgages, you can see that each lender specifies a certain interest rate for a certain term: Under most market conditions, the lower the fixed interest rate, the shorter the time period you can lock in to pay that rate. However, a longer-term, fixed rate mortgage allows you to put a dent in your principal before facing the possibility of an increase in your monthly payments. Take a look in the financial pages of the newspaper and you'll see a chart of mortgage rates that will look something like Table 1-2. The six-month to five-year options you see are all fixed rate. Many financial institutions offer terms that exceed five years, but Table 1-2 reflects the most common options out there.

Fixed rate mortgages are offered with a variety of options, so make sure you talk to several lenders to see who offers you the most competitive interest rates and terms.

Book III

Home
Sweet,
Home Free

Table 1-2		Mortgage Rates					
Banks	*Variable Rate*	*6-month*	*1-year*	*2-year*	*3-year*	*4-year*	*5-year*
Banks "R" Us	6.5	7.5	7.9	8.1	8.3	8.4	8.5
Mr. Bank	6.45	7.45	7.5	7.75	7.8	8.9	8.0
Mortgage Trust	6.75	7.5	7.45	7.7	7.9	8.05	7.95

Variable rate mortgage

Canadian banks report that up to half of all mortgage applicants now take out *variable rate mortgages.* A variable rate mortgage is a closed mortgage (usually set up with a one- to six-year fixed term) where the interest rate fluctuates with the market. If the borrower (that's you) sees that interest rates are starting to rise, you can usually lock into a fixed rate for the balance of the mortgage term. The first option you see in Table 1-2 is a variable rate mortgage.

However, not all variable mortgages are created equal. If you want to lock into a fixed rate for the balance of the mortgage term, some banks may charge a penalty to lock in the mortgage, or dictate that you must lock in for at least another three years, no matter how much time is left on the original mortgage term. Other banks may be totally flexible and allow you to lock into a fixed rate any time during the original mortgage term with no penalty and no requirements to extend the mortgage. It pays to shop around and to negotiate the best terms possible.

The interest rates of variable rate mortgages will vary from lender to lender, but most will be offered in some relation to *prime rate,* which is the interest rate that banks charge their most creditworthy borrowers (that is, the big corporate clients). Rates for variable mortgages will usually vary from half a percentage point below prime to half a percentage point above prime. The borrower should also make sure that he or she is comparing the same prime rate — most lenders will list a variable rate mortgage at one-half to three-quarters a percentage point above the well-recognized and respected Bank of Canada prime rate, while another bank will offer a rate one-quarter of a percentage point below "Bank of Bumpf" prime. This may be an elevated prime rate, which of course means their rate is no bargain at all. Again, and it can't be emphasized enough, you should negotiate the best mortgage terms and conditions you can.

Another factor to consider is a *teaser rate* — an initial low rate for the first few months (sometimes up to the first year!) that entices borrowers with a snappy slogan such as "1 percent mortgage now available!" However, after the initial teaser period expires, the mortgage will revert to a rate that fluctuates in relation to the prime rate that the bank is offering. You have to make sure that the mortgage still makes sense once the teaser rate is calculated into the rate of the mortgage. If the teaser is only for three months of a five-year term and the balance of 57 months is at a relatively high rate, the "1 percent mortgage" is actually a rip-off. In this case, you would be better off getting a variable rate mortgage with a competitive rate in relation to prime, with no penalty or restrictions to lock in if rates jump during the term of the mortgage.

Variable rates are not for everyone — you'll need to keep track of interest rates to make sure you lock in your mortgage rate before interest rates rise. There is a bit of a gamble involved, but the payoff can be a lower interest rate if you're prepared to watch interest rates and monitor when to lock them in.

If you use a mortgage broker, or know your bank manager very well, he or she may call or e-mail you to let you know that a jump in mortgage rates is rearing its head. If you know you'll be getting that call (that is, if the bank manager is your beloved aunt, who owes you a debt of gratitude ever since you rescued her cat from that tree), it lowers the risk of taking a variable mortgage. You should also recognize that rates fluctuate and any rise in rates may be temporary, so you may want to think carefully before locking in your variable rate mortgage. Stay on top of economic news to help you make sound decisions; see Chapter 4 in Book V for advice on where to look.

Also, find out about escape options. If you pay out this mortgage early (before the third anniversary), what penalty will be charged?

You may want to consider a *convertible mortgage.* Convertible mortgages are typically six-month or one-year fixed terms where the interest rate is fixed but you may lock into a longer term (typically a three-year term or longer) at any time without penalty.

Blended payments

Mortgages are set up so that you get a huge chunk of cash to buy your home and then you repay the money in regularly scheduled payments. In effect, each mortgage payment you make is split: One portion goes toward paying off the principal and the other portion goes toward paying off the interest. Hence, *blended payments.*

Every time your lender compounds the interest that you owe on your loan, your monthly blended payment changes. As you pay down your principal, the actual amount of your payment does not change but the portion of the payment that goes toward the principal increases and the amount that goes toward interest slowly decreases.

If your mortgage is $100,000 (with an 8 percent interest rate compounded semi-annually) to be paid over a period of 25 years, your monthly payments will be approximately $772. Table 1-3 illustrates this.

Book III

Home
Sweet,
Home Free

Table 1-3	Breakdown of Blended Payments			
Timeline	Your Monthly Payment	Principal	Interest	Principal Balance
1 month	$772	$105	$667	$99,895
6 months	$772	$109	$663	$99,358
1 year	$772	$113	$659	$98,691
5 years	$772	$156	$616	$92,274
10 years	$772	$232	$540	$80,763
20 years	$772	$515	$257	$38,065

You can see that as you pay down the principal, the distribution of your payments changes. Gradually, you begin paying more money toward the principal than toward the interest you owe to your lender.

TIP

The more frequently you make mortgage payments, the faster you pay down your principal, which means that the more quickly you eliminate your mortgage, the less interest you pay. Payment schedules can be arranged monthly, semi-monthly, biweekly (every two weeks), or weekly. Arrange with your lender to make payments as often as you can reasonably manage. If you can make weekly payments rather than monthly ones, you'll save thousands of dollars over the lifetime of the loan. Table 1-4 illustrates how making more frequent payments can really whittle down the time it takes to repay a mortgage. If you can, it's usually a great idea to accelerate your mortgage payments. It's amazing how much quicker it is to extinguish your mortgage with aggressive pay downs!

Table 1-4	Mortgage Payment Frequency Comparison	
Calculations for a 25-year $200,000 mortgage at 8 percent interest, compounded semi-annually		
Payment Options	*Monthly Payments*	*Years to Repay Mortgage*
Monthly	$1,526	25
Biweekly	$763	20
Weekly	$382	19.8

Amortization period

The *amortization period* of your mortgage is the length of time on which the calculation of your monthly payments is based. The advantage of a longer amortization is that the monthly payments are smaller and therefore more manageable. The disadvantage is that the longer the amortization, the longer you carry a principal and therefore the more you pay in interest. And interest really adds up. You can see in Table 1-5 that the total interest on a 25-year amortization is almost double what you'd pay for a 15-year amortization.

Table 1-5	Amortization Payment Comparison		
Calculations for a $150,000 mortgage at 8.5 percent, compounded semi-annually			
Amortization	*Monthly Payments*	*Total Paid*	*Total Interest*
15 years	$1,464	$265,000	$115,000
20 years	$1,288	$310,000	$160,000
25 years	$1,193	$360,000	$210,000

Mortgage term

A *mortgage term* is the specific length of time you and your lender agree the mortgage will be subject to certain negotiated conditions, such as a certain interest rate. Terms range from 6 months to 10 years, but occasionally a lender will offer a 15- or 25-year term.

At the end of the term, you generally have the option to pay off your mortgage in full, or to renegotiate terms and conditions. If interest rates are ridiculously high, you will probably want to negotiate a shorter term, and then arrange a longer term once rates are more favourable. If interest rates are deliciously low, lock in for the longest term you can negotiate. At the end of your mortgage term, you can also transfer your mortgage to another lender who may offer you a better rate, at no cost to you. It's at this point when you'll typically have lots of negotiating power. Negotiate whenever you can!

Mortgage-a-rama: All the Nifty Options

Depending on how much of a down payment you can make, you will be eligible for either a conventional or a high-ratio mortgage. If you can bankroll a conventional mortgage, then you have at least 25 percent of the money needed to buy a new home. If your savings amount to between 5 and 24 percent of the home's price, then you can only qualify for a high-ratio mortgage. Either way, you still have a number of mortgage options to choose from.

Book III

Home Sweet, Home Free

Before you sign on the proverbial dotted line, you need to know your mortgage payment options. There are open mortgages, closed mortgages, and mortgages that offer something in between. Whichever option you choose affects how much money you pay over the lifetime of the loan and the flexibility of the terms. Some mortgages allow you to pay off your principal in lump sums as you wish and prepay your principal without any penalties. Other mortgages allow you to prepay only once a year on the anniversary date of the mortgage, or there may be no possibility of prepayment at all.

✔ **Open mortgages are flexible.** If you have an *open mortgage,* you can pay it off in full or in part at any time with no penalty. By chipping away at your principal early, you can save crazy amounts of money in interest. Of course, every penny you save in interest is a penny that doesn't get into your lender's anxious little hands. That's why the average fixed interest rate quoted for an open mortgage is 0.4 to 0.6 percent higher than a closed mortgage for the same term (a specified period of time). The majority of open mortgages with a fixed interest rate are available only for a short term. Most variable rate mortgages have a fixed five-year term, but may be open after three years, and as you can see in Table 1-2, variable rate mortgages are usually offered at a lower rate.

An open mortgage is a good choice if you're going to move again soon, if interest rates are expected to plummet, or if you're expecting a huge cash windfall once oil is discovered in the scrubland you bought near Medicine Hat. This kind of mortgage is good for the short term when rates are high, and it can usually be converted to a closed mortgage any time.

✔ **Closed mortgages are more stable.** The advantage of signing on to a *closed mortgage* for a term is that you will typically get lower interest rates and you will be able to budget for fixed, regular payments. The downside is that if you need to move before your term is up, or if you have extra cash, such as an income tax refund, which you'd like to put toward paying off a large portion of your principal, you may pay a penalty for this privilege. Most closed mortgages will give the borrower the ability to prepay 10 to 20 percent of the outstanding balance without penalty, often on the anniversary date of the mortgage. In some cases, there may be restrictive conditions that prevent you from getting out of the mortgage altogether — even if you sell your home. Read the fine print before you sign!

Different financial institutions offer a range of mortgages involving different degrees of flexibility for prepayment. Even most closed mortgages have some prepayment options. You can make specified maximum prepayments, usually between 10 and 20 percent, once a year either on any payment date or on the anniversary date of the mortgage, and in some cases you can increase each payment. You're charged a penalty if you pay down more.

Portable mortgages

If your mortgage is *portable,* you can take it with you to your new house. When you get ready to move, you'll be glad you asked about this option, especially if you negotiated great terms or if interest rates have gone up since you locked in to your current mortgage. Even if you're buying a more expensive house, it's still to your advantage. For example, if you have a $200,000 mortgage at 6 percent interest, and you're in the third year of a five-year term, you can take the mortgage with you to the $375,000 house you want to buy. You will need an additional $50,000 loan to be added to your principal. If the going rate on new loans is 8.5 percent interest for a three-year mortgage to match the remaining three years of your five-year term, you'll need to negotiate a blended rate on the new amount. The blended mortgage payment will be composed of two parts: your initial payment toward your $200,000 mortgage plus the second payment toward the additional $50,000 mortgage. Remember that your payment will be the result of "blending" two mortgage rates, and of course, your monthly payment itself will consist of interest and principal components.

Both conventional mortgages and high-ratio mortgages can be portable. However, if you have a portable high-ratio mortgage, the one element you can't transfer to a new property is the CMHC insurance premium required on all high-ratio mortgages. That insurance is property-specific, so you'll have to pay it again at your new digs.

Assumable mortgages

When you're buying a house, in addition to contacting financial institutions about mortgages, you may want to ask the sellers if they would allow you to take over their mortgage as part of the price you pay for the house. This option is quick and it saves you the usual costs of mortgage arrangements like appraisals and legal fees. It may also save you money in interest payments if the seller's mortgage rate is lower than what is currently available on the market. Do check the remaining term on the mortgage and discuss this option with your real estate agent or your real estate lawyer.

Having an *assumable mortgage* on your home means that when you want to sell it, you can have a qualified buyer assume the mortgage. This is a great incentive if you have good terms and conditions, and it saves the buyer time to find financing and money to set it up. Again, most mortgages are assumable as long as the buyer can qualify for the mortgage amount.

You can still expect to go through some financial examination even if you're assuming the seller's mortgage. The lender will want to ensure that you meet the mortgage requirements. See "The information game: What your lender wants from you" later in this chapter for more on supplying personal and financial information to your lender.

Vendor (seller) take-back mortgages (VTB)

In some cases, if the sellers are anxious to move, if the market is really sluggish, or if they're looking for a good investment once they get their equity out of the house, sellers may offer to lend you the money for your mortgage. This is called a *vendor take-back mortgage*. The sellers may offer you lower rates than big financial institutions will, and they won't require the appraisals, inspections, survey fees, and financing fees you would expect to pay a traditional lender. You will, however, want to have your lawyer draw up the papers to guarantee that everything is in order. Some people will sell buyers a mortgage and then pass it on to a mortgage broker to handle instead of dealing with it personally.

Book III

Home Sweet, Home Free

Builder/developer interest rate buy-down

If you're in the market for a new home, you may find builders and developers willing to offer mortgages with an *interest rate buy-down*. This may take the form of a vendor take-back mortgage where the builder/developer will lend you the money, or more commonly, the builder may buy down the interest rate of the mortgage you are getting from a bank — usually by 2 or 3 percent. This explains those newspaper ads for projects and subdivisions for sale with 3 percent mortgages.

The goal of the interest rate buy-down is to sell real estate. The buy-down will help a buyer who is having trouble qualifying for a mortgage at current rates, or allow a buyer to qualify for a larger mortgage and therefore buy a more expensive property in the development. Keep in mind, however, that these mortgages are typically not renewable. This means that once the term is up, your mortgage rate, and therefore your monthly payments, is likely to climb significantly.

Once that mortgage term is up, you need to negotiate new terms, and find a new lender — usually a bank. Naturally, your lender will do an appraisal of your property. You're expecting this. What you're perhaps not expecting is that your new lender may appraise your one- or two-year-old house at thousands less than the price you paid for it. Here's why this happens: Builders want to offer reduced interest rates as an incentive to buyers. However, they're still protecting their bottom lines, so to compensate for offering lower interest, they incorporate the cost of the *buy-down* into the price of the house itself. This means you pay a larger principal on the builder's inflated price of the house. Hey, builders have to eat too!

The solution? Arrange a mortgage with a financial institution and ask the builder or developer to buy down the interest with your lender. This way, you can take advantage of the deal on the interest rate and you still have the option to renew your mortgage with your lender at the end of the term. Another option is to take your mortgage at market rates and ask the builder to lower the selling price accordingly.

"Can I have a mortgage with that, please?" Like car dealers, sellers can really sweeten the deal by helping you put the financing in place — an option that could save you a lot of money. This is the case with the last three mortgage options addressed: assumable mortgages, vendor take-back mortgages, and builder/developer interest rate buy-down. But buyer beware: Read the fine print and consult with your agent or lawyer before accepting any seller's mortgage offer — it may just be too good to be true.

Mortgage Insurance

As you already know, mortgages are a big deal. If you have a high-ratio mortgage, your lender will require *mortgage loan insurance* from the Canada Mortgage and Housing Corporation (CMHC). A private sector company, GE Capital Mortgage Insurance Company (Canada), also offers mortgage insurance at the same rates as the CMHC, but offers a couple of competitive differences. For example, GE Capital may consider up to 50 percent of the rent from an unauthorized suite as income, while the CMHC will not consider any revenue from an unauthorized suite. Mortgage insurance covers your lender in case you default on your payments. You may also choose to purchase mortgage life insurance. This way, if something happens to you, your mortgage payments will be made by the insurance company and not be a burden on your family (see "Mortgage life insurance" later in this chapter).

High-ratio mortgage insurance

If you have a down payment of less than 25 percent of the purchase price of your house, then you're eligible for a high-ratio mortgage. However, lenders will require that you have mortgage insurance so their risk is protected. The high-ratio insurance is arranged by the lender.

How to qualify for high-ratio mortgage insurance

Many buyers have high-ratio mortgage insurance coverage through the Canada Mortgage and Housing Corporation. The only alternative is GE Capital Mortgage Insurance Company (Canada), and both institutions have four standard eligibility requirements:

- ✔ The home you're buying will be your principal residence.

- ✔ The home you're buying is in Canada.

- ✔ Your *gross debt service ratio* is not more than approximately 30 percent. The ratio is the percentage of gross annual or gross monthly income needed to cover all housing-related costs (including principal and interest on the mortgage; property taxes; 50 percent of condo fees, if applicable; and hydro, water, and heating). So, the total you spend on housing must not be more than approximately 30 percent of your gross (pre-tax) household income.

- ✔ Your *total debt service ratio,* which includes all the factors in your gross debt service ratio plus any car loans, student loans, and credit card debt, is not more than 40 percent of your gross (pre-tax) household income.

Investors buying an investment property that will not be their principal residence can also get a high-ratio mortgage, but the insurance premium will be higher, up to 5 percent of the mortgage amount.

What high-ratio mortgage insurance will cost you

Two fees are connected with mortgage insurance: the premium and the underwriting fee. The premium for high-ratio mortgage insurance is typically 0.5 to 3.75 percent of the mortgage amount, determined by a sliding scale. If you're taking out a variable rate mortgage, be prepared to pay an additional 0.25 percent insurance fee. The underwriting fee is the cost associated with underwriting your mortgage insurance application. Fees vary based on the work involved in underwriting your mortgage. You can expect to pay between $75 and $165 for underwriting costs.

Mortgage life insurance

Mortgage life insurance guarantees your mortgage will be paid in full if you die. Some lenders offer this insurance and will add the premium to your mortgage payments. It's still a good idea to shop around through an insurance broker for the best rates, though. You may want to get insurance coverage for all parties responsible for the mortgage (for example, if your home is in your name and your spouse's, both of you should be insured).

The lender may offer insurance where they will pay off the balance of your mortgage upon your death. This is commonly referred to as *declining balance insurance*. However, you may also want to consider *regular term insurance*. The premiums should be comparable to declining balance insurance, but this policy covers you for the full amount of your mortgage should you pass away — not just the outstanding balance.

Who Ya Gonna Call?

Mortgages are a good business. That's why so many institutions besides banks have got in on the show. This is good for you because if you don't find the terms and conditions you want in one place, you can shop around. And once you've decided whom you want to do business with, then you can haggle for the options you want.

You do not need to have an account with an institution to qualify for a mortgage there. And there is no reason to limit yourself to banks and trust companies in your mortgage hunt. Credit unions, caisses populaires, and pension funds also supply mortgages, and many don't require that you be a member in order to be eligible. You can also look to insurance companies, finance companies, and private lenders.

Mortgage brokers can also be a useful resource. Mortgage brokers are not affiliated with any particular institution; they can match you with the lender who gives the best terms and rates for your situation. In addition to banks, trust companies, pension funds, and private lenders, mortgage brokers can access real estate syndicates and foreign banks. The lender typically pays mortgage brokers a finder's fee (a percentage of your mortgage). However, if your credit history is particularly spotty you may be asked to pay a fee to the mortgage broker and/or lender. Keep in mind, though, that the mortgage broker industry is loosely regulated in Canada, exposing you to some measure of financial risk. Review any draft mortgage broker agreement with your lawyer.

The information game: What your lender wants from you

Once you've become intimate with your financial life and the worldof mortgages, it's time to cozy up to your lender — often known as "the bank." Basically, your lender needs two things from you — detailed personal information and paperwork. Don't take the probing questions personally. Everyone goes through the same process, whether it's Elizabeth R., Queen of England, or Gaia Sandalfoot, just off the commune.

Tell us about yourself

Prospective lenders will want to know all about you. They'll ask about your financial status and employment as well as your personal information and history. Expect questions like these:

- ✔ **What is your age, marital status, number of dependants? Where do you work? What is your position? How long have you been with the company? What is your employment history?** Unless you're self-employed, you will probably need a letter from your employer confirming your position with the company. If you are self-employed, you should bring your tax assessments (not your tax returns) from the past two years to confirm your earnings.

- ✔ **What is your gross (pre-tax) family income?** You may need proof of income like a T-4 slip or, if you're self-employed, personal income tax returns. You will also be asked to show proof of other sources of income from pensions and rental property.

- ✔ **What do you currently spend on housing? If you're a homeowner, what is the current market value of your house?** You may have to provide copies of your rental lease agreement for the apartment or suite you're renting or a copy of your current mortgage.

Book III

Home Sweet, Home Free

✔ **Do you have funds for a down payment?** The lender wants to ensure that your down payment is your own money (and not a loan), so you will probably have to show, through bank records, that your down payment was accumulative or in your bank account for at least three months. If the down payment is a gift from dear old Aunt Bibi, then you'll need a letter from her confirming that the money is not a loan. You'll also be required to demonstrate that the money has been deposited to your account. You also may have to provide current banking information.

✔ **What assets do you have and what is the value of each one?** You can include vehicles, properties, and investments.

✔ **What liabilities do you have?** You can include credit card balances, car loans, student loans, and lines of credit.

Lenders will also ask your consent to do a credit check. A credit check may give you a good or bad credit rating depending on your financial history. We recommend you contact a credit-reporting agency, such as Equifax Canada or your local credit bureau, to obtain a copy of your credit report. (You can also do this online at www.equifax.ca.) Examine it in detail. If you find inaccurate or outdated information in the report, you can have those items corrected or removed to make your credit rating as glowing as it can possibly be.

Let's have it in writing please: The paperwork

Most banks can pre-approve your mortgage over the phone. You may have to fax them the required paperwork, and in return, they will fax you a written confirmation outlining the terms of your mortgage pre-approval. Often you will not meet your banker until you receive the seller's acceptance of your offer to purchase their home, and you're ready to seal the deal by finalizing all the financing.

Getting all the papers together for a mortgage is just the beginning of a long paper shuffle you will be doing until you finally get the keys to your new home. Be prepared with the following documents when you meet with your lender:

✔ Copy of a recent appraisal for the home you're buying (if requested — the bank may already have ordered it for you)

✔ Copy of the property listing

✔ Copy of the Agreement of Purchase and Sale (for a resale house)

✔ Plans and cost estimates if you're buying a new house (construction loans only)

✔ Certificate for well water and septic system (if applicable)

✔ Condominium financial statements (if applicable)

✔ Survey certificate

Trading places: Questioning your lender

Just because you're the one requesting money doesn't mean you can't ask questions. Lenders profit from your business, so don't be afraid to bring up your concerns. You should expect to be answered directly in a courteous manner and you should reply to your lender's questions in kind. Keep a list, and have paper with you to use in meetings or on the telephone so that you can be sure to cover all the bases.

Stay cool and calm as you chat with prospective lenders. Remember, you're shopping for a mortgage, not begging for one. Keep this list handy to be sure you ask the right questions:

✔ **What is your name, title, and phone number?** Start with the basics.

✔ **Is all my information kept confidential?** A reputable mortgage lender will not share your information indiscriminately.

✔ **What mortgage types and terms do you have available? Do you have any that are specifically designed for my situation?** Many major banks have special offers for first-time homebuyers, for example.

✔ **What are your current mortgage rates?** Compare the rate offered on closed mortgages to the rate offered for open mortgages. An open mortgage gives you more flexibility and can save you money, but usually has a higher interest rate than a closed mortgage, as explained earlier in this chapter.

✔ **How are you making your mortgages competitive with other lending institutions? Are any discounts or cash-back options available?** Some lenders lower their interest rate a bit if you ask nicely or show them lower rates from the competition; other lenders offer you a percentage off your mortgage up front — usually between 1 and 3 percent as a cash-back program — to help you with your closing costs.

✔ **What mortgage fees do you charge? Is there a mortgage application fee?** Make sure you know what kind of costs your lender expects you to cover.

✔ **Do you pre-approve mortgages? Is there a fee for this?** Most institutions do not charge a pre-approval application fee.

✔ **How long will it take to process my loan request? Once it is approved, how long should I allow before I close the deal?** When you set your closing dates for the purchase of a new home, the schedule for your transfer of funds is crucial. Know what to expect.

✔ **How is the interest compounded?** Most lenders compound interest semi-annually (every six months). Ask if your lender offers any other compounding options that may save you money.

✔ **Can I convert from a variable to a fixed rate mortgage?** As explained earlier in this chapter, if you choose a variable rate mortgage (VRM), you're vulnerable to fluctuations in the current interest rate. When interest rates rise you pay higher mortgage payments; when rates fall you pay less. You want the option to convert your VRM to a fixed rate mortgage if interest begins to climb significantly.

✔ **What are my payment options?** As detailed earlier in this chapter, to save yourself a lot of money in the long run, you should make payments as often as you can — weekly is best.

✔ **Can I pay off the mortgage early? Is there a penalty for this? Can I pay down some of the principal without penalty? How much a year?** You also want to have the option to make an extra lump sum payment toward your mortgage principal, at least once or twice a year to help you save on the interest.

✔ **Is mortgage life insurance available with your mortgages? Will it cover both my partner and me?** You want to protect your family members in case something happens to you. But check the cost. A separate insurer may offer lower insurance premiums for the same coverage.

✔ **If my credit rating is not acceptable at this point, what can I do to improve it? Or what options do I have?** Be prepared: Any lender who offers mortgages will check your credit rating.

Chapter 2

Discovering Your Perfect Home

. . . .

In This Chapter

▶ Finding the right agent

▶ Knowing all about your appraiser

▶ Locating a good real estate lawyer

▶ Knowing what you want in a home

▶ Finding home listings, local information, and professional help online

▶ Uncovering homes for sale

▶ Comparing the homes you see and picking a winner

. . . .

Close your eyes (okay, don't really close your eyes 'til you've finished reading the rest of these instructions), lean back, put your feet up, and picture your ideal home. Maybe it's a century-old Victorian manor with turrets and a coach house. Maybe it's a modernist square, with kilometres of skylights and orderly gardens. Maybe it's a condo with a view of the park, a huge balcony, on-site tennis court, and bowling alley. Got a good picture of it? Excellent. Take a mental snapshot — that's probably the only way you're going to see that home.

Yes, most of us have to settle a bit. But if you're old enough to buy a house, you're probably familiar with the fine art of compromise by now. This section will help you prioritize what you need, what you want, and what you'd be really lucky to find. Once you've figured that out, you'll find advice on where to look and what to look for, as well as tips on discriminating between real and imagined benefits, obvious and not-so-obvious drawbacks.

Selecting Your Home-Buying Team

You're taking a really big step when you decide to purchase a house. Fortunately, lots of experienced people are around to help. Do yourself a favour and pick a good team. Don't be afraid to ask a lot of questions and shop around until you find professionals you have confidence in and you can relate to. In this chapter, you'll find tips to help you locate the three key players on your home-buying team: your real estate agent, your appraiser, and your lawyer.

Your agent

Lots of real estate agents will want to work with you. Make sure you find one you want to work with. You will rely on your agent for information and advice about your specific situation. Your agent deals with the sellers, negotiates for you, and advises you throughout the process. Try to find someone who speaks your language . . . literally and figuratively.

When you apply this scenario to buying a home, your helper is your real estate agent, and the action hero is the agent's broker (you'll find more about brokers a little later in this section). In brief, what you're looking for in an agent is someone who has the following:

- ✔ **Knowledge:** Your agent must be familiar with the neighbourhoods you like and the style and price range of house you are looking for.

- ✔ **Experience:** Your agent should be someone who has worked with clients like you before, who knows how to help you buy the house you want for a fair price, and who can anticipate problems before they come up.

- ✔ **Time:** Your agent must be willing to spend time to give you the support and direction you need . . . when you need it.

- ✔ **Contacts:** Your agent should have colleagues and advisors to call in when you need financial advice or assistance, legal work, appraisals, and so on.

- ✔ **Ethics:** Your agent should always have your best interests in mind.

- ✔ **Established broker/office manager:** Your agent relies on the back-up of a respected and well-connected broker who is often also the office manager. If a serious problem arises, you'll rely on this indispensable person too.

- ✔ **Web skills:** Your agent should be able to search listings on the Internet and be readily available via e-mail. See "Home Shopping Online," later in this chapter for more on the Web.

Understanding your relationship with your agent and the broker/manager

You thought you had your work cut out for you just understanding the relationships you already have in your life. Well, the relationships among you, your agent, and the agent's broker can be no less confusing. But help is on the way! In this section, you discover the ins and outs of what an agent and a broker do, and then a bit about the different types of agents out there.

- ✔ **Real estate agent (also sometimes referred to as salesperson or sales associate):** Subcontracted by broker to work on behalf of buyer or seller or, very rarely, both.

- ✔ **Broker or broker/nominee:** Legal "agent" who works on behalf of the buyer or seller or both; usually manages and oversees daily operations of a brokerage company.

When you decide to work with a real estate agent, you are effectively engaging the services of the agent's broker as well, regardless of whether you meet that individual. The broker is the person you can turn to if things go terribly, terribly wrong and your agent can't manage the situation. A skilled broker is able to call in favours if bureaucratic roadblocks or procedural questions arise or if your home purchase spirals into one of the rare legal disputes that can happen when closing a real estate deal. As mentioned earlier, the broker is the action hero with all the tools and influential friends to stay one step ahead of the game and save the day.

Note: Some real estate agents also have the qualifications to legally call themselves brokers, but they tend to use the more commonly understood term of *agent* or even *salesperson.* In many provinces, a broker's licence (called an agent's licence in B.C.) requires additional training and testing and a licence designation beyond that of a salesperson. With this extra education, an individual can own a brokerage or run an office (be the "nominee" for the office) and ensure that the salespeople and all of the office's trust accounts adhere to the requirements of the provincial Real Estate Act.

A broker or brokerage company, and by extension a real estate agent, may be a seller's agent or a buyer's agent. In some cases, real estate agents working for the same broker will represent both the seller and the buyer in a deal. Although each party has its own real estate agent, since both agents work for the same broker or legal agent, the situation is referred to as *dual agency.* The agent that you are working with to find a home may show you a property that is listed with his or her office. If you buy that property, you will have to agree to enter into a limited dual agency agreement.

Another term you'll encounter is *realtor.* This is a trademark of the Canadian Real Estate Association (CREA). Only brokers and real estate agents who are CREA members may use this term to describe themselves professionally. Extensive training and continuing education are required. Realtors are required to follow a very strict Code of Ethics, and Standards of Business Practice, designed to protect *your* best interests.

The rules and regulations governing agency relationships vary a bit from province to province. Ask your local real estate board or your provincial real estate councils for specifics. In general, agency relationships break down as follows.

Seller's agent

When real estate agents are *seller's agents* they owe full loyalty to the seller and must give them all information and take every action to obtain the highest price and best conditions of sale for the sellers. Don't expect the seller's agent to tip you off to the fact that a seller is anxious to move and would probably accept $10,000 less than the asking price. And if you meet a seller's agent at an open house, be discreet. If you say that you're going to put in a bid on the home at $10,000 less than the asking price, but you're willing to pay full price in order to get into the neighbourhood, the seller's agent is legally obliged to disclose that information to the seller. Remember the one point in your favour: The seller's agent also has a legal obligation to tell you, the buyer, if he knows of any serious problems with the home being sold. Expect honest, complete answers to your inquiries.

Buyer's agent

Surprise, surprise — a *buyer's agent* works in the best interest of the buyer. Even though your buyer's agent's commission is paid out of the seller's proceeds from the sale, her legal and ethical duties are to you. Your buyer's agent should keep your personal and financial information confidential. If the sellers let slip that they are going through a messy divorce and want to sell the house as soon as possible, your buyer's agent will share this information with you. Likewise, if your agent finds out the sellers are willing to accept a lower price. Your buyer's agent helps you determine how much you can spend on a new home and how much is reasonable to offer on the homes you are considering. A buyer's agent negotiates the best deal possible on the buyer's behalf, ideally the lowest price and best conditions for you, the buyer.

Dual agency

If both the buyer's and the seller's agents work for the same broker or brokerage company, this is called *dual agency.* One company is brokering a deal between two parties, and it legally represents both sides. This situation can open up a number of conflict-of-interest concerns.

To head off any problems, the broker is legally obliged to tell you and the seller that she is representing you both. Ask the broker to explain clearly what the implications are for the sale negotiations. You will be asked to accept the dual agency situation in writing. If you're unsure what to do, contact your local real estate board for clarification. Although both agents may work out of different offices and not know each other, if they work for the same company they must also acknowledge in writing that they are in a dual agency situation.

Choosing an agent

When you choose a real estate agent, look for someone who will work hard for you. Someone who asks questions to clarify what you need and what you want is way ahead of someone who tries to *tell* you the same information.

The best agent will be curious about you, your family, your finances, and your future plans. Someone who asks questions and listens to your answers will serve you far better than someone who takes charge and tells you what you want. Your agent should respect your time and independence; a good agent will provide you with all the information you need, and give you room to make your own decisions. The best client-agent relationship usually results when the agent and buyer have similar temperaments in terms of enthusiasm, sense of humour, and energy level.

It is very important that you select an agent who works primarily in the community or area where you want to live. Real estate agents should possess an in-depth knowledge of neighbourhoods, selling prices, schools, property taxes and utility rates, local amenities, and civic issues.

Choose a full-time agent over one who works part time. The real estate market changes constantly and part-time agents just won't be able to keep up with new listings and market activity. A full-time agent not only stays more in touch with the market, but also is more familiar with the paperwork involved.

Be sure your agent is familiar with the use of the *Multiple Listing Service (MLS),* a trademark of the Canadian Real Estate Association. Most agents have access to MLS. This credible and complete database of all currently listed properties makes it easy for agents to run a search for properties that fall into your price range and offer the amenities you are looking for.

Book III

Home Sweet, Home Free

The Web can be a great help in your search for an agent. First, you can access real estate Web sites to find someone who's right for you; look through the agency's home listings online to find the person representing homes that are similar to your own. Then, when sizing up prospective agents, look for one who is Internet savvy. He or she can access MLS listings on the Web and e-mail them to you, saving you many phone messages, trips to the agent's office, and fruitless home visits. The upcoming section, "Home Shopping Online," has more information on using the Internet. Browsing home listings online, sometimes including a virtual reality tour, is one of the great uses of the Internet!

Taking referrals into account

If possible, use an agent recommended by a friend, relative, business associate, or someone else you trust. If the agent provided good service to that person, chances are that you'll get good service too.

Speaking to a head broker at a major real estate company may be extremely helpful. Even if you're moving cross-country, chances are the broker will have a list of contacts for agents working in particular areas, as well as agents who deal with particular types of properties. Search the Internet too: www.mls.ca is an excellent site that is linked to all real estate boards across Canada and can help you get a feel for prices and neighbourhoods anywhere in the country. Through this site, you may also find an agent active in an area you want to check out. Another popular site is Homestore Canada, www.homestore.ca, where you can browse home listings; access online calculators; and get tips about moving, home decorating, renovating, and more.

Once you have the names of a few agents, arrange to meet with them. Ask each of them to bring a record of all the houses they've listed and sold in the past year. This way you can verify what kind of homes, neighbourhoods, and price ranges are most familiar to each agent. You will also figure out quickly whether you get along with the agent. Remember that an agent with good people skills will not only be nicer to work with; he will represent you well to sellers and will be an effective negotiator when the time comes to make an offer.

Asking the right questions, making the right choices

You can ask these questions when you're interviewing prospective agents:

- ✔ **How long have you been an agent? Do you work full time?** The longer your agent has been in the business, the more you benefit from the wide range of experience.

- ✔ **What professional designation do you have? Are you continuing your education?** A dedicated professional strives to update skills and knowledge. To stay current, your agent should have completed at least one course in the previous year.

- ✔ **Who do you represent?** Some agents work on behalf of buyers and some prefer to work on behalf of sellers.

- ✔ **How many clients do you have right now, and will you have the time to work with me?** A good agent has an established client list and will be working with a number of buyers and sellers at any time.

- ✔ **Do you have access to the Multiple Listing Service (MLS)?** Knowledge of the MLS is an essential tool in the home search process.

- ✔ **How many agents work in your office?** An active and vibrant office is typically up to date on market activity and aware of new listings as they come onto the market.

✔ **Does your office have an active and attentive manager/broker?** You need to know you have someone to turn to if you and your agent need help with a particularly complicated or unusual circumstance.

✔ **Will any responsibilities in my home search be delegated to someone else?** You want to know that you're going to receive the agent's personal attention.

✔ **What neighbourhoods/types of homes do you specialize in?** You probably already know the kinds of properties you're interested in and you want your agent to be an expert in that particular field.

✔ **What price range do you deal in primarily?** You have a budget and you need an agent who's skilled at working within that money range.

✔ **How many people have you helped buy a home in the past year?** You want an active agent who's successful in the current real estate market.

✔ **How many people have you helped sell a home in the past year?** It never hurts to know the stats on your agent, but the best agent for you doesn't necessarily have the hugest number of sales.

✔ **Can you refer me to real estate lawyers, mortgage brokers, inspectors, or appraisers if I need their services?** Any agent with some experience will have a few contacts that you can capitalize on.

✔ **Do you have a list of client testimonials that I could look at?** Read over what former clients have to say about your agent. If your agent doesn't have testimonials to read, contact former clients about their experiences.

Suppose you haven't chosen an agent and you go to an open house and absolutely love the house, what do you do? Remember that the agent holding the open house works for the seller. If you are comfortable with that agent, you can ask her to represent you, and enter into a limited dual agency agreement. However, if you are not comfortable with the agent or the concept of a dual agency relationship, you can scramble and find another agent to work with you as your buying agent. You do not have to work with the agent holding the open house unless you want to.

It doesn't matter who you talk to — the agent; your Uncle Wayne, who referred you to the agent; the senior broker where the agent works; or the agent's most recent clients — don't be shy, and don't let things slip because you don't want to offend anyone. No question is too silly and all questions are relevant. After all, you are trusting your real estate agent to help you make the biggest single investment of your life.

Making your agent work for you

Explain your home-buying requirements to your agent. Bring along your list of household and neighbourhood priorities (see the section, "Knowing What You Want in a Home," later in this chapter). Once the agent knows your needs,

Book III

Home Sweet, Home Free

tastes, and budget, the fun really starts — you go on tour. Your agent will show you around various homes and neighbourhoods until you decide you've found the one you want. When you're ready, your agent will present your offer to the sellers. In most cases, your real estate agent will help you negotiate the sale terms and conditions and close the deal for you. To facilitate the whole sale process your agent should give you referrals (if you need them) to other professionals, including real estate lawyers, appraisers, financial advisors, lenders, contractors, and inspectors. (There should be more than one of each to ensure favouritism isn't a factor.)

A good agent will be adaptable and creative in order to meet your needs. If you can't visit a house in person, you may be able to arrange for an online "virtual" tour, or if you're planning a cross-country move, your agent may be able to provide a video tour of some homes.

Your agent helps you best if you are straightforward. If you decide to work with more than one agent, let them both know and tell them why. Since most agents are connected to the MLS system they will all be trying to show you the same listed houses that fit your price, location, and style specifications. The more agents you work with in one area, the more likely you are to get poor service. It's probably better to work with one agent whom you trust and who has the time to help you and the personality to make it work than with several semi-committed agents.

Most real estate agents are hard-working, responsible professionals who do everything they can on your behalf. It will probably be really obvious to you if your agent doesn't fall into this category, but just in case, here is a handy list of warning signs that point to poor agents:

- ✔ They never point out any problems with the houses they show you.

- ✔ They swear up and down that the foundation isn't crumbling, even though your two-year-old has kicked loose some masonry.

- ✔ They show you only houses that are being listed by their company.

- ✔ They show you only mansions when you are in the market for a semi-detached.

- ✔ They make you feel pressured or bullied.

- ✔ If your real estate agent is (a) too busy, (b) too pushy, (c) too clueless, end the relationship!

You're in the driver's seat — your agent is supposed to be guiding you into a great deal, not over the edge of a cliff. If you signed a brochure (an acknowledgement of the buyer-agency relationship, not a contract) it doesn't bind you to that agent forever. Call the local and provincial real estate board for advice on your particular situation. If you signed a buyer's contract with the agent that stipulated that you would pay a finder's fee to the agent if he finds you a house (as opposed to the usual sharing of commission paid by the seller), make sure that contract has a termination date or a release clause if you want to terminate that agreement.

Don't commit to anything that you don't feel comfortable with. You want to buy a house, and you want the process to be as pleasant and hassle-free as possible.

Your lawyer

Once you have signed the offer, your lawyer or notary handles the final mortgage and closing paperwork. Your lawyer furnishes the following important services:

- **Title search:** Checks that the sellers of the home are the registered owners of the property; checks that any claims registered against the property (any debts or liens for example) are cleared before the title is transferred to you.

- **Conveyancing:** Prepares and reviews all documents needed to transfer the ownership of the new home and ensures you get valid title (the deed) to the property.

- **Application of title insurance:** Gets insurance that protects you and the lender in the event of any problems with the title or zoning of the property.

- **Survey review:** Confirms that the survey is accurate and valid.

- **Assessment of builder commitments:** Reviews the specification lists and contractual obligations if you're purchasing a newly built home to ensure that the builder provides everything you're entitled to receive.

- **Inspection review:** Checks for a complete inspection if you are purchasing a new house, and makes sure that your new house has a valid occupancy permit from the local city or municipality.

- **Tax investigation:** Finds out whether any municipal taxes are owing if you're buying a resale home, or determines if you or your builder is responsible for paying GST if you're buying a newly built home.

- **Land transfer tax:** Calculates the amount of the land transfer tax that you must pay (if applicable in your province).

- **Fees payable to seller:** Tallies the *adjustments* (the amounts you owe the seller to compensate for prepaid utility bills, property taxes, and other service fees paid in advance).

- **Mortgage paperwork:** Draws up your mortgage documentation if the bank allows your lawyer to do this, which is usually the case (there are rare cases where the bank will want their lawyer to draft the mortgage documents).

Book III

Home Sweet, Home Free

Where your lawyer earns her stripes (and your cash): Managing the contract

The *contract of purchase and sale* (sometimes called the *agreement of purchase and sale*) is the legal document you use to make an offer to purchase a home, and you need to be sure it's drawn up correctly. (See Chapter 3 for more information on the contract of purchase and sale and adding conditions, or *subject to* clauses.) If your real estate agent has many years of experience drawing up home purchase offers, you may feel confident that she can write an offer and present it to the sellers without a lawyer's scrutiny. Don't take chances. Ask your agent to add a subject clause to the offer that gives your lawyer a chance to review the agreement of purchase and sale after the sellers have accepted your offer, but before all the conditions of sale (the *subject to* clauses) are removed. You will likely have to stipulate a short 24- or 48-hour time period for the legal review or the seller's agent will object to this condition.

Remember that the agreement of purchase and sale is a legally binding contract. A lawyer may be able to give you valuable input before you sign your agreement. Damage control is often less effective, and more costly and time-consuming than prevention. Yes, everyone makes mistakes. But if it's your *lawyer's* mistake, at least your lawyer is insured, which in turn protects you.

If you're buying a newly built home, you'll use your builder's agreement of purchase and sale, and it will be quite different from the standard form found in your province or region. No two builders' contracts are alike; they tend to be lengthy documents and often contain details that favour the builder. Have your lawyer or notary advise you which clauses to remove before you sign, and which to clarify with the builder/seller.

Where to find a lawyer or notary

The corporate lawyer who you went to public school with in grade 3 is probably not the best legal counsel to use when you're buying a home. Look for someone who specializes in real estate law. In most of Canada, you'll need a lawyer; in Quebec, you'll hire a notary. Friends, neighbours, or relatives who have recently bought or sold a home are a good source of recommendations. Your real estate agent, broker, or lender will also have contacts among local lawyers or notaries and should be able to give you the names of several real estate specialists to choose from. You can also find legal associations on the Internet.

Find someone who speaks your language. As you interview lawyers and notaries, pay attention to how open they are to your questions and how clear their answers are. If they make their fee structures sound complicated, they may not be able to adequately explain the ins and outs of your agreement of purchase and sale or other legal documents involved in the purchase of your home. Choose a lawyer you can understand and who has the patience to explain terms adequately.

Don't base your final choice of lawyer or notary only on *price.* More experienced lawyers will often charge higher rates but get more done in less time, saving you money in the long run. Also, keep in mind that you are hiring a lawyer to give you peace of mind. A competent lawyer or notary should be able to explain every step of the transaction to you in clear and simple language regardless of whether the firm occupies a flashy corporate office tower or a modest street-level suite.

Before you hire a real estate lawyer, make sure you know a bit about what you're getting into. Consider the following sections as guidelines for the questions you ask.

Local real estate experience

Laws regarding rent control, condominium conversion, and zoning are regional. A local real estate lawyer or notary will be up to date on all regional laws and probably have good connections with the enforcing bodies. These two questions are key:

- ✔ How many years have you specialized in real estate law?
- ✔ How long have you worked in this region or city?

Fees and disbursements

You probably already know that a lawyer's fees can be positively heart-stopping. Since you can't skip the cost of a lawyer (though your heart's probably skipped several beats by now!), you'd better know how much you should budget to cover legal expenses. Start by making these inquiries — and write down the answers:

- ✔ How do you structure your fees?
- ✔ Do you provide free estimates of cost?
- ✔ If I opt for a flat fee, what services are included?
- ✔ Under what foreseeable circumstances may I require additional services?
- ✔ When and how will you let me know if the fees go above the amount estimated?
- ✔ How much would you recommend I budget for disbursements?
- ✔ What taxes are applicable to the fees?

When you're searching for a lawyer, ask the ones you interview for references. Take the names and telephone numbers of some recent clients (if possible). If you found lawyers' or notaries' names using the phone book or a professional association, asking for references is especially important. Call the lawyer's references and see what they have to say.

Book III

Home Sweet, Home Free

Reference checks

For those of you who feel nervous about speaking to complete strangers as you're checking references, keep this list handy. Try asking a lawyer's former clients the following:

- ✔ Were you satisfied with your lawyer's services?

- ✔ Did you find any surprises in the final bill for your lawyer's services and disbursements?

- ✔ Did you feel your lawyer adequately explained to you the implications of all the decisions you made and documents you signed?

- ✔ Is there anything else about this professional or the services provided that I should know?

Your appraiser

Your mortgage lender will probably insist that their appraiser conduct the assessment of the home you're buying. If this is the case, you have no say in the choice of the appraiser. But chances are the lender's appraiser is both qualified and experienced. After all, a financial institution depends on the appraiser's expertise to decide whether to lend out hundreds of thousands of dollars.

What is an appraisal?

An *appraisal* is an evaluation of a home's worth. When you pay a professional for an appraisal of your house, you get an unbiased, informed assessment. The appraiser looks at the property and makes an assessment based on the home's size, features, amenities, condition, and recent sales of comparable homes in the neighbourhood.

Appraisal reports must contain the purpose of the appraisal, the legal description or identification of the property examined, a listing of *encumbrances* (any financial charges owing against the property), and an analysis of the best use of the property.

The most common method of appraisal is the *CMA*, which is short for *comparative market analysis* (although sometimes it stands for *competitive market analysis* or *current market analysis*). To determine a property's CMA, the appraiser compares the home you're considering buying to other homes in the same neighbourhood that are comparable in size, features, and amenities.

Two less common methods for determining a home's worth are *replacement cost* or *rental income approach.* The replacement cost appraisal approach involves figuring out how much it would cost to rebuild exactly the home in exactly that spot. But because building costs are not always square with market value (for example, a house across the street from a nuclear power plant is not going to sell for what it would cost to rebuild), the replacement cost approach is less common. But using a replacement cost approach may be more useful if you're trying to appraise a home in a rural area where there are no other neighbourhood homes to provide a comparison. A rental income approach is useful only if the home under consideration has rental units. The rental income approach makes a comparative evaluation, like a CMA as outlined above, but it also takes into account the extra income that will be generated by the rental units within a home.

In most circumstances, a comparative market analysis (CMA) is the best way to evaluate what you should actually consider paying for a home. Before you make an offer on a home, your agent should prepare an overview of the market for you — essentially a CMA to help you determine fair market value. If you are not using an agent, then an appraiser is necessary.

What will the appraiser look for?

The appraiser scours the house and the neighbourhood. In particular, appraisers look at the following:

- ✔ **Size, age, and condition of the house:** Does the home need repairs now or in the near future? Have upgrades, refinishing, or renovation work been put into the home recently? (This part of the appraisal tends to focus on kitchens and bathrooms.)

- ✔ **Operating systems:** Do the heating, air conditioning, plumbing, and electrical systems all function properly?

- ✔ **Amenities:** What kind of luxury features does the home possess, such as a pool, wine cellar, hot tub, solarium, or four-car garage?

- ✔ **Neighbourhood characteristics and immediate surroundings:** What does the yard back onto? Which way do the windows face? Are schools, shopping, and transit services nearby? Is the home within what's considered a safe neighbourhood?

- ✔ **Special or unique features of the home:** Is it a designated heritage home, or is it situated on a ravine lot with a stunning view?

Book III

Home
Sweet,
Home Free

Appraisers are required to do only a visual inspection, but they may probe further. This means the appraisal process can vary in length, from a quick walk-through to a few hours' inspection. If you are requesting a *very* small mortgage or have great assets and collateral securing your mortgage, the appraiser may even do a *drive-by appraisal,* a quick confirmation that the home is still standing and appears to be of fair value.

What should I look for in an appraiser?

Certification is what you look for in an appraiser, plain and simple. An independent appraiser should have an AACI (Accredited Appraiser Canadian Institute) or CRA (Canadian Residential Appraiser) designation. Make sure you ask to see your appraiser's credentials.

Reputation is also key — it's always best to work with someone you can trust. Ask any friends who've bought homes recently for their suggestions or contact the *Appraisal Institute of Canada* (www.aicanada.ca) for a list of certified independent appraisers in your area.

How much should I expect to pay?

You can expect to pay anywhere from $200 to $500 for an appraiser's services. You may be able to work out an agreement with your mortgage lender to pick up the appraisal cost. Ask your agent about writing into your offer to purchase that it is (1) subject to financing, but also (2) subject to the buyer (you) receiving a satisfactory appraisal. (See Chapter 3 for details on adding conditions to your offer.) This will help you make sure that your house "appraises out" — you don't want to carry a mortgage on what you thought was a $500,000 home when it's appraised at only $375,000. The price of an appraisal varies depending on how difficult a job it is for the appraiser. If there have been many recent sales in your neighbourhood and the home doesn't have scores of out-of-the-ordinary features, it will be a straightforward assessment and a cheaper assessment.

Knowing What You Want in a Home

So many elements make up a home that often it's hard to decide which ones are most important to us. You may take many things for granted when you have them (like huge closets!) but don't forget to make a record of those (sometimes) small items that make all the difference in your satisfaction with where you live. Remember to think seasonally, too. It's hard to remember in July that you need enough backyard space for a homemade ice rink, but come December when your four-year-old daughter needs to practise her speed skating six times a day, what are you going to do?

Part of knowing what you want is knowing what you don't want. "I don't want to mow grass" is a good start, for example. Or, "I don't want a basement where my shoulders hit the ceiling." There are things we don't like about our current home and other people's homes, whether it's the lack of water pressure, the windows not opening wide enough, or the lack of street parking. By identifying your pet peeves, you can zero in on what you're looking for.

Being pragmatic about your wishes

We all know what we'd like in our ideal home. The features of your dream home provide a good starting point for your search; most of us judge potential homes with our standards of perfection in mind.

Try to keep your mind focused on your home-buying needs. You shouldn't let your emotions overrule practicalities. Even though you really want the home with the incredibly landscaped backyard, reminding yourself that the rest of the house just doesn't meet your basic needs will help you to over-look the cosmetics.

If you're a first-time buyer, remember you are just that — buying for the first time. Chances are good that you'll sell your home in five to ten years, and trade up to a bigger one. So don't worry if you can't buy your absolute dream home in the perfect neighbourhood right now. Instead of trying to buy a home with seven bedrooms for the twelve kids you plan to raise, realize that you can live comfortably right now with a four-bedroom home with a fenced-in backyard at a reasonable price. You may not like the idea of buying a smaller "starter home," but it puts you in a better position to buy a bigger home down the road without sacrificing vacations, evenings out, and hockey lessons to your mortgage. What you can afford will probably never match your ideal, but with a little bit of flexibility, you can find a home that suits you until child number eight comes along.

Book III

Home Sweet, Home Free

Making the list

Since you're probably going to be making compromises, it's important to keep focused on your basic needs, and not give them up too quickly, while being aware of where you can be flexible. Here are some of the things you'll need to consider:

- ✔ **Location:** Perhaps the most obvious factor . . . where do you want to live? Once you have been pre-approved for a mortgage, you'll have a good idea what you can afford, which may determine where you will end up living. But within your price range, you will have a lot of options based on the type of home you are looking for.

- ✔ **Type of home:** What type of home would best suit your needs? If you have a habit of falling down the stairs and breaking your toes, you may think about buying a bungalow or an apartment-style condo. Or, perhaps you were thinking about a detached home, what with the "talented" family of violinists and all. If your tastes run to modern architecture, you won't want to look at century-old Victorian-style homes.

- **Exterior:** What do you need outside? Is there enough room for the Great Dane to do laps? Do you need fencing around your yard to keep the kids in? Do you need a sunny yard to garden in, or are you more of a herbicidal maniac? Like to throw summer parties? Then you'll probably want that sunny yard bricked in or covered with a large deck. Or maybe you need a lot of pavement on which to park your three cars, two motorcycles, and RV.

- **Kitchen:** What do you need in a kitchen? If you have a big family, you probably want an eat-in area and an automatic dishwasher. If you're a professional cook, counter space and large appliances may be your priority. The presence of appliances may not be the deciding factor, but room to install them is.

- **Bathrooms:** How many do you need? If you're looking for anything with more than one storey, bathroom location is important, too. Is there one on the ground floor, or do you have to send your guests up to the one between your kids' rooms? If you like to take long, relaxing bubble baths on Sundays, you won't be interested in a home with only stand-up showers.

- **Bedrooms:** How many bedrooms are you looking for? Do you need an extra one for a home office or frequent house guests? If you're just starting out and you may be having children in the not-so-distant future, count them in when calculating your needs. If your children are finally off to college and moving out, you may want fewer bedrooms.

- **Other considerations:** How small is *too* small for your bedroom? For your kitchen? Will stairs be a problem for anyone in your household, now or in the future? Do you need a finished basement for your home office, your home theatre, or your kids' playroom?

Use Table 2-1 to organize the features you need or want in a new home. Complete the chart by considering what is absolutely essential to your needs and what you would really like to have (but that you *could* live without). For some items in the chart, such as a dishwasher or a fireplace, it's a simple yes/no proposition. A fireplace may be "nice to have," but is it really "essential"? You decide.

Choosing features in a home isn't all sunshine and roses. You may think you want a corner lot with a big yard, but have you bargained for the snow shovelling, leaf raking, and lawn mowing that goes with it? How about the settling foundation and structural decay of your dream Victorian mansion? This is not to say that you should change your mind about what you want, but when you set your priorities, think about the drawbacks of maintenance and repair that go along with the benefits of home owning.

Can you afford to be picky? You should be picky if you don't like where the washroom is, or the stairs in the middle of the living room. Don't be picky if you don't like the doorknobs. Even central air you can install later for less than, say, tearing down a wall or two to open up the dining room. Make concessions on small things you can fix or change yourself later.

Table 2-1	Home Priority List	
Feature	*Essential Need*	*Nice to Have*
Type of Home		
Detached, semi, etc.	_____	_____
Victorian, modern, etc.	_____	_____
Number of storeys	_____	_____
Interior		
Size (m2 or ft2)	_____	_____
Number of rooms	_____	_____
Living Room		
Size (m2 or ft2)	_____	_____
Open concept/separate dining room	_____	_____
Fireplace	_____	_____
Flooring	_____	_____
Ceiling height	_____	_____
Kitchen		
Size (m2 or ft2)	_____	_____
Condition	_____	_____
Eat-in area	_____	_____
Fridge	_____	_____
Stove (gas?)	_____	_____
Dishwasher	_____	_____
Large kitchen cupboards	_____	_____
Accessible kitchen cupboards	_____	_____
Countertops	_____	_____
Flooring	_____	_____
Bedrooms		
Number	_____	_____
Walkout to balcony	_____	_____

Book III

Home
Sweet,
Home Free

(Continued)

Table 2-1 (*continued*)

Feature	Essential Need	Nice to Have
Closet in each room		
Flooring		
Main Bedroom		
Size (m2 or ft2)		
Ensuite bathroom		
Walk-in closet, south-facing window, fireplace, or other special feature		
Flooring		
Bathroom		
Number of bathrooms		
Size (m2 or ft2)		
Location(s)		
Shower/tub/Jacuzzi		
Flooring		
Sunroom/Den/Home Office		
Size (m2 or ft2)		
Location		
Flooring		
Family Room		
Size (m2 or ft2)		
Location		
Flooring		
Hallways		
Width (m or ft.)		
Linen closet		
Coat closet near main entrance		
Flooring		

Feature	Essential Need	Nice to Have
Basement		
Size (m2 or ft2)	_____	_____
Finished	_____	_____
Basement/in-law apartment	_____	_____
Washer/dryer	_____	_____
Freezer	_____	_____
Heating (oil, gas, etc.)	_____	_____
Flooring	_____	_____
Other		
CAC (central air conditioning)	_____	_____
Central vacuum	_____	_____
Finished attic	_____	_____
Property will accommodate expansion	_____	_____
Water view	_____	_____
Security system	_____	_____
New windows	_____	_____
Sliding glass doors	_____	_____
Natural light	_____	_____
Exterior		
Frontage (size and direction facing)	_____	_____
Brick/siding/wood	_____	_____
Roofing material (slate, cedar shake, asphalt shingles)	_____	_____
Parking		
Garage	_____	_____
Carport	_____	_____
Space	_____	_____
Private/shared driveway	_____	_____

Book III

Home Sweet, Home Free

(Continued)

Table 2-1 (*continued*)

Feature	Essential Need	Nice to Have
Street parking	_____	_____
Yard		
Size of lot (m2 or ft2)	_____	_____
Shed	_____	_____
Deck/patio/porches	_____	_____
Fence enclosure	_____	_____
Swimming pool	_____	_____
Established landscaping	_____	_____
Landscaping/garden space	_____	_____
Sunlight	_____	_____

Home Shopping Online

The Internet is a great place to start looking for a home in the hypothetical world, before you're ready to tackle the home tours and real estate agent relations in real life. Browsing home listings on the Web gives you an idea of what's available in the region you're looking at and the price range you can expect to pay. Plus, it lets you stay on top of new homes as they're listed, without trawling the neighbourhood for signs on the lawn.

Smart start: The MLS listings

The Multiple Service Listing (MLS) Web site, www.mls.ca, is a great place to start your home hunt. Brought to you by the Canadian Real Estate Association, the MLS site lets you search for homes across Canada by linking you to local real estate board Web sites.

How does it work? Easy. From the MLS homepage, you can choose the province you're looking for, and after that the city, town, or region. From there, you're led to a screen that asks you to specify the type of property you're interested in. Haven't decided between a condo or a townhouse? Not a problem — you can select more than one at the same time. You can then specify a price range, number of bedrooms and bathrooms, and even view. (Try to avoid "oceanfront" if you're looking in the Prairies.)

Homestore Canada's (`www.homestore.ca`) search feature works much the same way, but lets you access only selected MLS listings. In other words, some, but not all, brokers choose to post their properties on the Homestore Canada Web site. Those who do so tend to use the site as an additional advertising medium. However, Homestore Canada's additional features make this a must-visit site that's loaded with useful information for home buyers. It's a great educational site for anything to do with homes.

Once you're into your MLS hunt, it's easy to think you'll remember a certain home or listing, but you'll forget it once you've gone through 20 more listings and your eyes have glazed over. Each home listed in MLS has its own MLS number, which is the locator used by real estate agents and Internet surfers like yourself to find the home. Think of it as the home's barcode. Take this number down on a piece of paper, along with a little info to help you remember it, such as "Brick two-bedroom $175,000." If you want to find it again easily, return to the MLS homepage, where you can simply type the number in and be directed to the listing.

After you set your preferences, MLS shows you those properties that match your needs. You'll see a brief description of each home, a price, a photo if one is available, and the name and contact information of the real estate agent. Click the listing, and you may be led to the full MLS listing for the home, which will include such details as lot size and dimensions of rooms, as well as additional photos, if they're available. The information in the MLS listings is standardized and extremely thorough; data on each home are listed on a form with most of the vital stats you'll need.

Book III

Home Sweet, Home Free

Does your dream home simply *have* to be at the base of Mount Snowytop, or on the shores of scenic Lake Blackfly? No need to search through a pile of listings in the general area that may not meet your needs. Click the MLS Web site's "Community Keyword Search" button, which lets you search listings by community, geographical landmark, or attraction.

The independents: eBay and private sellers

So where do you go for privately listed homes on the Web? One of your first stops, if you haven't been already, is eBay's Canadian page, `www.ebay.ca`. In case you've been trapped under a large piece of furniture for the past eight years, eBay is *the* pre-eminent online auction site, where you can bid for just about anything you can pay money for, from antique paperweights to cars and real estate. There's no stuffy auctioneer heading up this marketplace — auctions happen directly between the bidder(s) and the seller, with eBay acting as a virtual "auctioneer."

But here's the thing about real estate on eBay that's a little different from those 1960s Surfer Barbie and Ken dolls or the stacks of old stamps: You don't actually bid on or purchase real estate on eBay. That's right — the prices are indications of the seller's asking price, and the listings, rather than being actual auctions, are more like advertisements, where the seller gets to list the home with some details and contact information, and you can follow up via e-mail, phone, and the like. So, unlike that $1.99 DVD of *Blazing Saddles,* you can't log on to eBay and end up with a home purchase 20 minutes later.

eBay's real estate offerings (click on the Real Estate category to get there) are divided into sections, such as "residential," "commercial," "land," or "timeshares for sale." So far, these private listings aren't as numerous as what you would find through MLS, but you may be able to find a diamond in the rough with repeated visits. But how do you know who this seller is, anyway, aside from the ever-so-helpful "Joe Shmoe Homes, Inc." seller name? eBay regulates all of its members through a feedback system, where members can leave positive or negative comments on both buyers and sellers. With one click you can access that feedback record, and quickly get a very good sense of whether this person's above board.

Even if you're looking at Canadian properties, on ebay.ca it's probable that some of the prices you see are in U.S. currency — which makes a significant difference in the selling price. Look for the "C" or "US" preceding the asking price.

But the wide world of eBay need not be your only stop when looking for plum private sales. A number of smaller, classified-ad-type Web sites also list homes on the Web. Most of these are regional by province, and can best be found by typing something like "Quebec private sale homes." Some, such as Quebec's Télé-Annonces (www.teleannonces.ca), list a combination of real estate agent–drepresented and private sales.

Home Shopping Offline

If you already have a list of priorities that clearly outlines the features you need and want in a home, and you've done some neighbourhood research, you probably have a good idea of what and where you want to buy. Now you can focus your attention on the real estate market.

Using your agent

Be open to the expert guidance your real estate agent has to offer. If you hired an agent, let that person match you with a new home. Agents spend hours every day looking at homes, and they have years of real estate experience. A good agent who's in touch with the market may even know about sale properties before they're officially put on the market. (Look for advice on finding an agent earlier in this chapter.)

Give your agent as much information as you can about what you're looking for, but be open to his advice. If you feel your agent's not listening to you or not providing you with good service, talk about the situation. If you're not able to clear up the problem, you may need to find a different agent.

If you only want to live on one particular block, or in one specific apartment building, you can ask your agent to send out letters to people living there to find out whether they're considering moving. You may be able to find a property before it hits the market.

Watching the neighbourhood

Frequent the neighbourhoods you're interested in. Look for new "For Sale" signs and jot down the address, listing agent's name and phone number, or private seller's number. Talk to your agent about booking a time to see the home, or make your own appointment if you don't have an agent. Spending some time in the area gives you a better impression of the number of homes for sale, and your chances of finding a home there. If there appears to be little turnover, you may have to search in a different location. Make a note of any streets in the area that you definitely do *not* want to live on (such as the street where backyards face the abandoned sugar refinery) so that you and your agent don't waste time booking appointments to see homes there.

Book III

**Home
Sweet,
Home Free**

Monitoring MLS listings

The *Multiple Listing Service (MLS)* is a very useful home search tool. The MLS database contains listings of all homes for sale that are represented by a selling agent. A typical MLS listing gives you a great deal of detail about a given home, including the number and size of rooms, lot size, interior dimensions (square metres or square feet), approximate property taxes, and additional information — details such as "renovated kitchen" or "professionally landscaped." You can search MLS listings online at www.mls.ca.

Figure 2-1 shows a sample home listing. Note that a listing contains many important details, which can save you, the buyer, wasted trips to see inappropriate homes. The distance to shopping and transit is given, as is information about plumbing, heating, and sewers. You should be alert to the fact that the MLS listing information available online is not as detailed as the MLS information you'll get in print through an agent or broker. In the online MLS world, withholding the name and address of vendors is done to protect their privacy. It also compels prospective clients to call an agent to get the exact location and other particulars of a listed house.

OFFERED FOR SALE

4080 SUNSET STREET, VANCOUVER

Area:	**Vancouver West**	**Price:**	**$499,900**
Sub Area:	**Point Grey**	**Status:**	**Active**
Lot Size:	**68' x 120'**	**Title:**	**Freehold**
Taxes:	$3,849 (2003)	Zoning:	RS – 1
Age:	38	Bedrooms:	3
Basement:	None	Bathrooms:	2 full (1 en-suite)

Construction:	Frame	Possession:	T.B.A.
Foundation:	Concrete Slab	Clear Title:	Yes
Exterior:	Wood Siding	Mortgage:	Treat as Clear Title
Roof:	Wood Shingle	Sewer:	Municipal
Fuel/Heating:	Natural Gas/Forced Air	Water Supply:	Municipal
Fireplace:	1	Fireplace Fuel:	Wood
Vendor Interest:	Freehold	Remodelling:	Completely

Amenities:	Wheelchair Access, Workshop, Extra Parking Avail
Equipment Included:	Fridge, Stove, Dishwasher, Washer, Dryer, Window Coverings, Security System, Built-in Vacuum
Site Influence:	Central Location, Recreation Near, Transit Near, Shopping Near
Parking:	2 (Covered) Double Carport

Floor Area:	1,850 sq ft	Unfinished Floor Area: none	
Rooms:	Living Room: 18' x 16'	Dining Room:	12' x 10'
	Master Bed: 15' x 12'	Bedroom:	12' x 10'
	Bedroom: 11' x 10'	Kitchen:	10' x 10'
	Eating Area: 10' x 7'	Foyer:	10' x 6'

Comments: Totally renovated 8 years ago, this immaculate rancher features gleaming hardwood floors, luxurious en-suite with Jacuzzi, all in an unbeatable location — a must see!

Listing Broker:	Dexter Associates Realty List date: February 11, 2003
Listing Agent:	Tony Ioannou (604) 228-9339 E-mail: ioannou@direct.ca

Figure 2-1:
This sample listing resembles a typical MLS listing.

Hearing the word (of mouth) on the street

The more people who know you're buying, the more people will suggest properties to you. Friends may have friends in the area who are thinking of selling. If you talk to people in the neighbourhood you're considering, you may get leads from strangers, too. Neighbours may know who's outgrowing their home or who's retiring to Florida next winter. Don't underestimate the value of word-of-mouth networking.

Don't get so caught up in getting a bargain that you lose sight of what you're buying. If your cousin's neighbour's daughter-in-law's brother is trying to sell a home to you, make sure it's the house you want before you even think about shaking his hand. Don't forget you're trying to buy a home, not make a deal. Never ever engage in oral agreements even if the price seems right. You need a written agreement and the opportunity to do some in-depth investigation before you negotiate the price and terms of sale. An objective assessment of the property value and a professional home inspection must be carried out to ensure you make the right purchase decision.

Reading the news

Most cities have free weekly real estate magazines and newspapers that can usually be picked up at real estate offices, street boxes, and convenience stores. These weeklies contain a selection of local residential listings. However, they often promote various real estate agents as much as they promote the listings. In most cases, the real estate weeklies do not present all the homes on the market; they print just the listings of the companies that advertise within them. Some of the weeklies will also rotate ads so that a house will appear every second week. In some areas, two or three real estate weeklies are published, and you would have to read them all to see everything on the market. Be aware that the printed listings are several days old by the time you see them, which may hurt your chances of buying any of the listed homes within the magazine or paper.

The classified sections of local newspapers also have real estate information worth examining — you should watch for open houses. Often the advertisements have keywords to clue you in on the property. "Reduced" or "motivated seller" may be good bargains. Terms such as "TLC needed," "fixer-upper," or "handyman special" send strong cautionary signals.

Book III

Home Sweet, Home Free

Going to open houses

Often sellers host open houses when they first put their homes on the market, giving you a great opportunity to check them out. You can talk to the seller's agent in person. Find out why the sellers want to sell, and how motivated they are to sell. If you don't like the idea of having other people looking at the home at the same time as you, remember that you can always make an appointment to see the home again privately. Pay attention to what other potential buyers have to say; they may notice something about the home that you've missed, or have done some productive snooping where you were too shy to look. Listen to their potential plans for the home; they may give you some good ideas.

Don't misrepresent yourself to the seller's agent. If you're working with an agent of your own, be up front about it when talking to the seller's agent at the open house. When an agent spends time and effort on your behalf and then finds out you're working with someone else, you can expect an angry reaction. Don't jeopardize your situation by being dishonest; you may face difficult sale negotiations if the seller's agent is unhappy with you.

In a hot real estate market, you'll find that many properties sell without ever hosting an open house. A home may be listed on MLS and a few days later the selling agent holds an open house to give other agents an opportunity to view the home, but a public open house just isn't necessary.

Comparison Home Shopping

To help you organize your thoughts as you look at various homes, use the comparison chart in Table 2-2 to record information about the homes you see. Make a copy of the chart and take it with you when you go to an open house or on a private home tour. Recording all the details makes it easier for you to keep track of the potential benefits or drawbacks you observe about each home.

Table 2-2   Home Comparisons

	Home 1	Home 2	Home 3	Home 4
General Info				
Address				
Type/style of home				
Dimensions (m² or ft²)				
Age of home				
Size of lot (m² or ft²)				
Facilities (applicable to condominiums)				
Asking price				
Property taxes				
Fees (applicable to condominiums)				
Financial reserve fund (applicable to condominiums)				
Overall condition				
Exterior				
Frontage				
Siding				
Condition				
Eaves				

(Continued)

Book III

Home
Sweet,
Home Free

Table 2-2 (Continued)

	Home 1	Home 2	Home 3	Home 4
Roof				
Material				
Age				
Parking				
Driveway				
Garage				
Number of parking spots (applicable to condominiums)				
Yard				
Condition				
Size				
Landscaping				
Porch				
Deck/patio				
Shed				
Fencing				
Swimming pool				
Special features				
Utilities				
Heating				

	Home 1	Home 2	Home 3	Home 4
Type				
Average annual cost				
Electrical service				
Amps				
Type/age of wiring				
Water				
Municipal/well				
Hot water tank				
Sewers/septic				
Central air conditioning				
Living Room				
Size				
Condition				
Flooring				
Windows				
Dining Room				
Size				
Condition				
Flooring				

(Continued)

Book III

Home Sweet, Home Free

Table 2-2 (Continued)

	Home 1	Home 2	Home 3	Home 4
Windows				
Kitchen				
Size				
Condition				
Eat-in area				
Flooring				
Windows				
Appliances				
Stove/oven				
Electric/gas				
Condition				
Fridge				
Freezer				
Age/condition				
Washer				
Dryer				
Dishwasher				
Freezer				
Microwave				

	Home 1	Home 2	Home 3	Home 4
Attic				
Condition				
Insulated				
Bathrooms				
Number of bathrooms				
Size				
Ground floor bathroom				
Basement				
Finished				
Size				
Flooring				
Windows				
Separate entrance				
Bedrooms				
Number of bedrooms				
Main bedroom				
Size				
Condition				
Flooring				
Closet				

(Continued)

Book III

Home
Sweet,
Home Free

Table 2-2 (Continued)

	Home 1	Home 2	Home 3	Home 4
Ensuite bathroom				
Other features				
Bedroom 2				
Size				
Condition				
Closet				
Bedroom 3				
Size				
Condition				
Closet				
Family Room				
Size				
Condition				
Sun Room/Office/Den				
Size				
Condition				
Other Features				
Central vacuum				
Light fixtures				
Fireplace				

	Home 1	Home 2	Home 3	Home 4
Coat closet				
Linen closet				
Security system				
Soundproofing (applicable to condominiums or townhouses)				
Balcony				
High ceilings				
Kitchen pantry				
Jacuzzi/hot tub				
Sliding glass doors				
Neighbourhood				
Overall				
Police/fire station nearby				
Public transportation available				
Parks				
Schools				
Shopping				
Distance from workplace				
Traffic				
Nuisances				

(Continued)

Book III

Home Sweet, Home Free

Table 2-2 (Continued)

Other Comments	Home 1	Home 2	Home 3	Home 4

Chapter 3

Getting the House You Want

. . . .

In This Chapter

▶ Writing it all down — making your offer to purchase

▶ Setting out terms and conditions

▶ Going through your contract of purchase and sale

▶ Getting what you pay for: Professional home inspections

▶ Staking out your territory: Land surveys

▶ Insuring your newly built home: New home warranties

. . . .

*I*t's finally here — that Mecca you've been searching for — your ideal gem of a home. Your goal is to successfully negotiate a deal to buy the wondrous abode. Look in this chapter for advice on making an offer to purchase a home and how to write the best possible terms into your sale contract, as well as make sure that you do the things necessary to be certain your home is all it's cracked up to be. You can also find out what the conditions (*subject to* clauses) in your agreement mean — and why you want them, anyway.

Yes, it's boring and complicated, but paperwork is a huge part of buying a home, so you'd better read this chapter. Offers, contracts, inspections, surveys, closings, even warranties . . . it's all here for the learning. Then there is the active process of negotiating the terms and conditions you want and closing the deal — when and how you want.

Soon enough you can go back to loafing around watching TV, or tooling around on your bike, or driving your kids all over town, or whatever it is you liked to fill your time with back before you decided to buy a new home. Here's what you need to know to make your purchase and get yourself the home you want.

The Contract of Purchase and Sale

The contract of purchase and sale sets the groundwork for negotiation, so it should specify the parties involved, the property, as well as the elements on your "want list." Standard forms exist (though they vary slightly from region to region), and most people freely cross out the terms that don't apply and add in their own. You and your agent will modify the contract to reflect your requirements and add conditions and requirements that are in your best interest. See Figure 3-1 for a standard contract of purchase and sale for use in the province of Ontario. Because much of the contract's legalese can be daunting, the main parts of the contract are described in plain language. Also, your lawyer or agent will be more than happy to go through it with you and answer any questions you may have.

Go through any contract you sign very carefully. Determine your needs and wants for each item. Write them down if it helps. The common advice for every decision also applies here: Be realistic. If you don't want to go above your offer price, be flexible on other terms.

Knowing who's who and what's what in your contract

The terminology and organization of contracts may vary from region to region, but five elements are basic to every contract of purchase and sale:

- **Vendor:** The *vendor* is the seller (or sellers). The seller's full legal name, exactly as it is shown on the current title deed to the house, is written into the contract.

- **Purchaser:** The purchaser is you, the buyer. Write in your legal name, exactly as it is shown on your personal identification documents and exactly as it should be shown on the deed. If you and a partner are making a joint purchase, add both full names. Joint purchases can take two forms: *joint tenancy* and *tenancy in common.* The differences between the two are significant. Joint tenancy allows for the "right of survivorship" from one spouse to the other when one dies. Tenancy in common allows for one spouse's interest in the house to go to that spouse's heirs, not automatically to the other spouse.

- **Subject property:** *Subject property* refers to the street address and an exact legal description of the property you are buying. This may also include the lot size, a general description of the home (semi-detached, single family dwelling with a mutual drive, or other), the specific lot and plan number, and any *easements.* An easement is a specified area of a property that is acquired by another property owner for her benefit. For example, your neighbour's driveway may cross the corner of your property. Since it's her driveway, even though it's technically on your property, she has the right to use that part of your property to park her car. These types of "mutual driveways" are commonplace in older residential neighbourhoods. This "right of passage" is registered on your title.

✔ **Purchase price:** The *purchase price* is the price you're initially willing to pay. This price will probably change throughout the negotiation; it's typical to see it go up and down repeatedly. When setting your offer price, keep in mind the additional closing costs you'll be incurring, such as land transfer tax, realty taxes, fuel and water rates, legal fees, and insurance costs. Also allow yourself room to negotiate up. If it's a seller's market (more people are looking to buy than there are homes for sale), you may want to make a higher initial offer right off.

✔ **Deposit:** Your *deposit* is not only part of your down payment but also an indication to the seller of your interest in the house and a sign that you are negotiating in good faith. The initial deposit may be relatively low, but the total deposit may be much more. At least 5 to 10 percent of the purchase price is often considered a fair amount for a total deposit, but there are no hard and fast rules.

List the amount of the deposit that is accompanying your offer and specify that it will be applied to the purchase price of the house on the closing (or completion) of the sale. Normally, the deposit will be held in trust by your agent in a trust account until the completion of the sale. You may want to write in that any interest that accrues while the funds are in trust accrues to the buyer, and will be paid after completion of the sale. Note that if you back out of an offer once it has been accepted and all the terms and conditions have been met, you will most likely have to forfeit your deposit to the vendor and will likely open yourself up to other legal action. If you want to try and get out of the deal, you should consult a lawyer and be prepared for bad news.

Reading all about terms and conditions (subject to clauses)

Most contracts have a blank space where you can write in the specific terms and conditions of your offer. This is where you build as much safety into your offer as you need. Conditions are typically worded as *subject to* clauses (I will buy the house, *subject to* financing, *subject to* inspection, *subject to* selling my current house, or some other condition). Basically you are saying, in legal terms, I will buy your house if particular conditions are met, such as the following examples:

✔ **Subject to financing:** You will buy the home if you're able to arrange a suitable mortgage. (Note that some buyers specify the maximum interest rate, the payment schedule, and the monthly payment amount they can consider.)

✔ **Subject to selling my present home:** You will buy the seller's home if you can sell the home you currently own (within a set period of time, such as 60 to 90 days).

Book III

Home
Sweet,
Home Free

OREA Ontario Real Estate Association

AGREEMENT OF PURCHASE AND SALE
(FOR USE IN THE PROVINCE OF ONTARIO)

REALTOR®

BUYER,.., agrees to purchase from
(Full legal names of all Buyers)

SELLER,.., the following
(Full legal names of all Sellers)

REAL PROPERTY:
Address...fronting on the.......................side of...
in the..
and having a frontage of...more or less by a depth of..more or less and legally described as
....
....(Legal description of land including easements not described elsewhere)...................................(the "property").

PURCHASE PRICE: ....Dollars (CDN$)................................
DEPOSIT:
Buyer submits (....................................)...Dollars (CDN$)................................
(Herewith/Upon acceptance)

by negotiable cheque payable to...to be held in trust without interest pending completion or
other termination of this Agreement and to be credited toward the Purchase Price on completion. Buyer agrees to pay the balance as follows:

SCHEDULE(S)...attached hereto form(s) part of this Agreement.

1. **CHATTELS INCLUDED:**...
....

2. **FIXTURES EXCLUDED:**..
....

3. **RENTAL ITEMS:** The following equipment is rented and **not** included in the Purchase Price. The Buyer agrees to assume the rental contract(s), if assumable:
....

4. **IRREVOCABILITY:** This Offer shall be irrevocable by...until.................p.m. on the..........................day of..........................., 20..........,
(Seller/Buyer)
after which time, if not accepted, this Offer shall be null and void and the deposit shall be returned to the Buyer in full without interest.

5. **COMPLETION DATE:** This Agreement shall be completed by no later than 6:00 p.m. on the.........................day of..................................., 20............
Upon completion, vacant possession of the property shall be given to the Buyer unless otherwise provided for in this Agreement.

6. **NOTICES:** Seller hereby appoints the Listing Broker as Agent for the purpose of giving and receiving notices pursuant to this Agreement. **Only if the Co-operating Broker represents the interests of the Buyer in this transaction,** the Buyer hereby appoints the Co-operating Broker as Agent for the purpose of giving and receiving notices pursuant to this Agreement. Any notice relating hereto or provided for herein shall be in writing. This offer, any counter offer, notice of acceptance thereof, or any notice shall be deemed given and received, when hand delivered to the address for service provided in the Acknowledgement below, or where a facsimile number is provided herein, when transmitted electronically to that facsimile number.

FAX No..(For delivery of notices to Seller)   FAX No. ....(For delivery of notices to Buyer)

7. **GST:** If this transaction is subject to Goods and Services Tax (G.S.T.), then such tax shall be..the Purchase Price.
(included in/in addition to)
If this transaction is not subject to G.S.T., Seller agrees to certify on or before closing, that the transaction is not subject to G.S.T.

8. **TITLE SEARCH:** Buyer shall be allowed until 6:00 p.m. on the ....day of...................................., 20...................., (Requisition Date) to examine the title to the property at his own expense and until the earlier of: (i) thirty days from the later of the Requisition Date or the date on which the conditions in this Agreement are fulfilled or otherwise waived or; (ii) five days prior to completion, to satisfy himself that there are no outstanding work orders or deficiency notices affecting the property, that its present use (..) may be lawfully continued and that the principal building may be insured against risk of fire. Seller hereby consents to the municipality or other governmental agencies releasing to Buyer details of all outstanding work orders affecting the property, and Seller agrees to execute and deliver such further authorizations in this regard as Buyer may reasonably require.

9. **FUTURE USE:** Seller and Buyer agree that there is no representation or warranty of any kind that the future intended use of the property by Buyer is or will be lawful except as may be specifically provided for in this Agreement.

10. **TITLE:** Provided that the title to the property is good and free from all registered restrictions, charges, liens, and encumbrances except as otherwise specifically provided in this Agreement and save and except for (a) any registered restrictions or covenants that run with the land providing that such are complied with; (b) any registered municipal agreements and registered agreements with publicly regulated utilities providing such have been complied with, or security has been posted to ensure compliance and completion, as evidenced by a letter from the relevant municipality or regulated utility; (c) any minor easements for the supply of domestic utility or telephone services to the property or adjacent properties; and (d) any easements for drainage, storm or sanitary sewers, public utility lines, telephone lines, cable television lines or other services which do not materially affect the present use of the property. If within the specified times referred to in paragraph 8 any valid objection to title or to any outstanding work order or deficiency notice, or to the fact that said present use may not lawfully be continued, or that the principal building may not be insured against risk of fire is made in writing to Seller and which Seller is unable or unwilling to remove, remedy or satisfy or obtain insurance save and except against risk of fire in favour of the Buyer and any mortgagee, (with all related costs at the expense of the Seller), and which Buyer will not waive, this Agreement not withstanding any intermediate acts or negotiations in respect of such objections, shall be at an end and all monies paid shall be returned without interest or deduction and Seller, Listing Broker and Co-operating Broker shall not be liable for any costs or damages. Save as to any valid objection so made by such day and except for any objection going to the root of the title, Buyer shall be conclusively deemed to have accepted Seller's title to the property.

11. **CLOSING ARRANGEMENTS:** Where each of the Seller and Buyer retain a lawyer to complete the Agreement of Purchase and Sale of the Property, and where the transaction will be completed by electronic registration pursuant to Part III of the Land Registration Reform Act, R.S.O. 1990, Chapter L4 and the Electronic Registration Act, S.O. 1991, Chapter 44, and any amendments thereto, the Seller and Buyer acknowledge and agree that the exchange of closing funds, non-registrable documents and other items (the "Requisite Deliveries") and the release thereof to the Seller and Buyer will (a) not occur at the same time as the registration of the transfer/deed (and any other documents intended to be registered in connection with the completion of this transaction) and (b) be subject to conditions whereby the lawyer(s) receiving any of the Requisite Deliveries will be required to hold same in trust and not release same except in accordance with the terms of a document registration agreement between the said lawyers, the form of which is as recommended from time to time by the Law Society of Upper Canada. Unless otherwise agreed to by the lawyers, such exchange of the Requisite Deliveries will occur in the applicable Land Titles Office or such other location agreeable to both lawyers.

Figure 3-1:
A contract
of purchase
and sale
from
Ontario.

INITIALS OF BUYER(S): ( )   **INITIALS OF SELLER(S):** ( )

OREA Standard Form: Do not alter when printing or reproducing the standard pre-set portion.   Form No. 100   01/2003   Page 1 of 2

12. **DOCUMENTS AND DISCHARGE:** Buyer shall not call for the production of any title deed, abstract, survey or other evidence of title to the property except such as are in the possession or control of Seller. If requested by Buyer, Seller will deliver any sketch or survey of the property within Seller's control to Buyer as soon as possible and prior to the Requisition Date. If a discharge of any Charge/Mortgage held by a corporation incorporated pursuant to the Trust And Loan Companies Act (Canada), Chartered Bank, Trust Company, Credit Union, Caisse Populaire or Insurance Company and which is not to be assumed by Buyer on completion, is not available in registrable form on completion, Buyer agrees to accept Seller's lawyer's personal undertaking to obtain, out of the closing funds, a discharge in registrable form and to register same, or cause same to be registered, on title within a reasonable period of time after completion, provided that on or before completion Seller shall provide to Buyer a mortgage statement prepared by the mortgagee setting out the balance required to obtain the discharge, and, where a real-time electronic cleared funds transfer system is not being used, a direction executed by Seller directing payment to the mortgagee of the amount required to obtain the discharge out of the balance due on completion.
13. **INSPECTION:** Buyer acknowledges having had the opportunity to inspect the property and understands that upon acceptance of this Offer there shall be a binding agreement of purchase and sale between Buyer and Seller.
14. **INSURANCE:** All buildings on the property and all other things being purchased shall be and remain until completion at the risk of Seller. Pending completion, Seller shall hold all insurance policies, if any, and the proceeds thereof in trust for the parties as their interests may appear and in the event of substantial damage, Buyer may either terminate this Agreement and have all monies paid returned without interest or deduction or else take the proceeds of any insurance and complete the purchase. No insurance shall be transferred on completion. If Seller is taking back a Charge/Mortgage, or Buyer is assuming a Charge/Mortgage, Buyer shall supply Seller with reasonable evidence of adequate insurance to protect Seller's or other mortgagee's interest on completion.
15. **PLANNING ACT:** This Agreement shall be effective to create an interest in the property only if Seller complies with the subdivision control provisions of the Planning Act by completion and Seller covenants to proceed diligently at his expense to obtain any necessary consent by completion.
16. **DOCUMENT PREPARATION:** The Transfer/Deed shall, save for the Land Transfer Tax Affidavit, be prepared in registrable form at the expense of Seller, and any Charge/Mortgage to be given back by the Buyer to Seller at the expense of the Buyer. If requested by Buyer, Seller covenants that the Transfer/Deed to be delivered on completion shall contain the statements contemplated by Section 50(22) of the Planning Act, R.S.O.1990.
17. **RESIDENCY:** Buyer shall be credited towards the Purchase Price with the amount, if any, necessary for Buyer to pay to the Minister of National Revenue to satisfy Buyer's liability in respect of tax payable by Seller under the non-residency provisions of the Income Tax Act by reason of this sale. Buyer shall not claim such credit if Seller delivers on completion the prescribed certificate or a statutory declaration that Seller is not then a non-resident of Canada.
18. **ADJUSTMENTS:** Any rents, mortgage interest, realty taxes including local improvement rates and unmetered public or private utility charges and unmetered cost of fuel, as applicable, shall be apportioned and allowed to the day of completion, the day of completion itself to be apportioned to Buyer.
19. **TIME LIMITS:** Time shall in all respects be of the essence hereof provided that the time for doing or completing of any matter provided for herein may be extended or abridged by an agreement in writing signed by Seller and Buyer or by their respective lawyers who may be specifically authorized in that regard.
20. **TENDER:** Any tender of documents or money hereunder may be made upon Seller or Buyer or their respective lawyers on the day set for completion. Money may be tendered by bank draft or cheque certified by a Chartered Bank, Trust Company, Province of Ontario Savings Office, Credit Union or Caisse Populaire.
21. **FAMILY LAW ACT:** Seller warrants that spousal consent is not necessary to this transaction under the provisions of the Family Law Act, R.S.O.1990 unless Seller's spouse has executed the consent hereinafter provided.
22. **UFFI:** Seller represents and warrants to Buyer that during the time Seller has owned the property, Seller has not caused any building on the property to be insulated with insulation containing ureaformaldehyde, and that to the best of Seller's knowledge no building on the property contains or has ever contained insulation that contains ureaformaldehyde. This warranty shall survive and not merge on the completion of this transaction, and if the building is part of a multiple unit building, this warranty shall only apply to that part of the building which is the subject of this transaction.
23. **CONSUMER REPORTS: The Buyer is hereby notified that a consumer report containing credit and/or personal information may be referred to in connection with this transaction.**
24. **AGENCY:** It is understood that the brokers involved in the transaction represent the parties as set out in the Confirmation of Representation below.
25. **AGREEMENT IN WRITING:** If there is conflict or discrepancy between any provision added to this Agreement (including any Schedule attached hereto) and any provision in the standard pre-set portion hereof, the added provision shall supersede the standard pre-set provision to the extent of such conflict or discrepancy. This Agreement including any Schedule attached hereto, shall constitute the entire Agreement between Buyer and Seller. There is no representation, warranty, collateral agreement or condition, which affects this Agreement other than as expressed herein. For the purposes of this Agreement, Seller means vendor and Buyer means purchaser. This Agreement shall be read with all changes of gender or number required by the context.
26. **SUCCESSORS AND ASSIGNS:** The heirs, executors, administrators, successors and assigns of the undersigned are bound by the terms herein.

DATED at..this.............................. day of..., 20............. .
SIGNED, SEALED AND DELIVERED in the presence of: IN WITNESS whereof I have hereunto set my hand and seal:

(Witness) .... (Buyer) .... (Seal) ● DATE................

(Witness) .... (Buyer) .... (Seal) ● DATE................

I, the Undersigned Seller, agree to the above Offer. I hereby irrevocably instruct my lawyer to pay directly to the Listing Broker the unpaid balance of the commission together with applicable Goods and Services Tax (and any other taxes as may hereafter be applicable), from the proceeds of the sale prior to any payment to the undersigned on completion, as advised by the Listing Broker to my lawyer.

DATED at..this.............................. day of..., 20............. .
SIGNED, SEALED AND DELIVERED in the presence of: IN WITNESS whereof I have hereunto set my hand and seal:

(Witness) .... (Seller) .... (Seal) ● DATE................

(Witness) .... (Seller) .... (Seal) ● DATE................

SPOUSAL CONSENT: The Undersigned Spouse of the Seller hereby consents to the disposition evidenced herein pursuant to the provisions of the Family Law Act, R.S.O.1990, and hereby agrees with the Buyer that he/she will execute all necessary or incidental documents to give full force and effect to the sale evidenced herein.

(Witness) .... (Spouse) .... (Seal) ● DATE................

CONFIRMATION OF EXECUTION: Notwithstanding anything contained herein to the contrary, I confirm this Agreement with all changes both typed and written was finally executed by all parties at............a.m./p.m. this..........day of..., 20............. . ... (Signature of Seller or Buyer)

CONFIRMATION OF REPRESENTATION

I hereby acknowledge and confirm the Listing Broker represents the interests of the ....in this transaction.
(Seller/Seller and the Buyer)

Signature of Listing Broker or authorized representative
Name of Listing Broker:..
(............) Tel. No. F AX No.

I hereby acknowledge and confirm the Co-operating Broker represents the interests of the ....in this transaction.
(Seller/Buyer)

Signature of Co-operating Broker or authorized representative
Name of Co-operating Broker:..
(............) Tel. No. F AX No.

ACKNOWLEDGEMENT

I acknowledge receipt of my signed copy of this accepted Agreement of Purchase and Sale and I authorize the Agent to forward a copy to my lawyer.

(Seller) ....DATE................
(Seller) ....DATE................
Address for Service:.. Tel. No.(............)
Seller's Lawyer:..
Address:..
(............) Tel. No. (............) FAX No.

I acknowledge receipt of my signed copy of this accepted Agreement of Purchase and Sale and I authorize the Agent to forward a copy to my lawyer.

(Buyer) ....DATE................
(Buyer) ....DATE................
Address for Service:.. Tel. No.(............)
Buyer's Lawyer:..
Address:..
(............) Tel. No. (............) FAX No.

FOR OFFICE USE ONLY **COMMISSION TRUST AGREEMENT**

To: Co-operating Broker shown on the foregoing Agreement of Purchase and Sale:
In consideration for the Co-operating Broker procuring the foregoing Agreement of Purchase and Sale, I hereby declare that all moneys received or receivable by me in connection with the Transaction as contemplated in the MLS Rules and Regulations of my Real Estate Board shall be receivable and held in trust. This agreement shall constitute a Commission Trust Agreement as defined in the MLS Rules and shall be subject to and governed by the MLS Rules pertaining to Commission Trust.

DATED as of the date and time of the acceptance of the foregoing Agreement of Purchase and Sale. Acknowledged by:

Signature of Listing Broker or authorized representative   Signature of Co-operating Broker or authorized representative

Page 2 of 2

- ✔ **Subject to the home's repair:** You will purchase the home if the seller fixes the leaky roof or other substandard feature.

- ✔ **Subject to legal review:** You will purchase the home provided that your lawyer reviews and approves the contract (usually within a specified amount of time, such as 24 to 48 hours).

- ✔ **Subject to inspection:** You will buy the home if it passes a professional building inspection.

- ✔ **Subject to survey:** You will purchase the home if a land survey is conducted or a legal, up-to-date land survey is provided, showing that the home does not violate any easements or rights-of-way, and showing the location of any buildings, such as a garage, on the property.

Specific requirements can also be written in the same area as your conditions, such as the stated requirement that the seller agrees to remove the abandoned car from the garage prior to the completion date. The contract may not have enough space to add all your terms and conditions; if so, they can be written up on *schedule forms,* which are attached to the main body of the contract. Schedule forms (or *addenda* or *appendices* in some provinces) are extra forms that allow you to write as many terms and conditions as are necessary on additional pages that form part of the contract. Make sure that all the schedules you attach are listed on the contract. Keep in mind that when you start negotiating, you and the seller may end up adding or removing conditions. For example, if the vendor will not fix the roof, then you may agree to remove that condition, but try to deduct the estimated cost of that repair from your offered price.

Don't overdo on the conditions. It's definitely a good idea to write a thorough, detailed offer. But make sure you keep your conditions from piling up. Be reasonable. Don't write into your offer that you have the right to inspect the property seven times before the closing date — a couple of times should suffice.

Once you and the seller sign off on all the terms and conditions of your purchase offer, your conditions will (hopefully!) be met and you can then add the paperwork (addendums or waivers, if necessary) to confirm, for example, that the roof has been repaired, that you have secured a mortgage, that you have sold your current house, and so on. Once all the conditions are removed, you enter into a binding agreement to purchase.

Scheduling the deal

Timing of the sale — which includes scheduling the *completion date,* the *possession date,* and the *adjustment date* — is handled differently in different parts of Canada. Your agent will be able to tell you what to expect and help negotiate dates that will work for you.

As a basic guideline, be aware of the following important deadlines:

- ✔ **Irrevocability/Time allowed for acceptance:** *Irrevocability,* or *the time allowed for acceptance,* is a deadline written into your terms and conditions — for example, 48 hours — for the seller to respond to the offer, or counteroffer. If you hear nothing after 48 hours, it means the seller has refused your offer. You can, however, make another offer after that point. You may also revoke your offer any time up until it is accepted.

- ✔ **Viewed date:** The *viewed date,* a specific date on which you viewed the house, confirms that the property and everything included in the sale will be in the same condition that they were in when you toured the home and observed them on that particular date. The viewed date is written into the contract.

- ✔ **Completion date:** The *completion date* (also known as the closing date) is the date when the money (via certified cheque, bank draft, cash, or lawyer's/notary's trust cheque) will be delivered. Note that the seller is entitled to his proceeds *on* the completion date. Therefore, all bank waiting periods should have been cleared in order to make the money readily available to the seller. To avoid difficulties, you should deposit the money or hand over a cheque at least two days before the completion date. Because of the legal transfer of funds, the completion date is also the date by which all documents need to be registered, signed, and acknowledged as legally binding.

- ✔ **Possession date:** The *possession date* is when the property is vacant for you to move in. You will not be able to move in to (take possession of) the property before the seller has received your payment. Usually, possession takes effect at noon on the day specified in the contract. Under some circumstances, however, you may take possession on the completion date.

- ✔ **Adjustment date:** On the *adjustment date,* you, the buyer, assume all tax rates, local improvement assessments, and utility charges related to your new property. Any bills that have been prepaid will be pro-rated and your portion will be charged to you. The adjustment date is usually the same as the possession date.

Book III

Home Sweet, Home Free

Many contracts of purchase and sale are signed without absolutely definite closing and possession dates in mind. Unless you're adamant that you must close on February 29 or on your astrologically chosen day, letting the sellers know that you would like to close in approximately 30 or 60 days (or however many you're thinking) is recommended to give the sellers some flexibility. You and the sellers will probably agree on some arbitrary date to write into the contract — to change at a later date, if necessary. Once your offer is accepted, though, it's a good idea to agree on a final set of dates early on, so that you can start to finalize things with your lawyer, lender, and home insurance agent. Your real estate agent or lawyer can draw up an amendment or waiver to your contract to change the date if both parties agree to the change.

In some provinces, such as British Columbia, the closing date and the possession date are usually two separate dates, allowing for the money the buyer
gives to the seller to be processed before the buyer gets possession of the
home. In other provinces, such as Ontario, the possession and completion
dates are usually the same, so that you have possession of the home as soon
as you are legally responsible for it. Because you use a lawyer's trust cheque
or a bank draft, the seller doesn't worry about the cheque bouncing. If your
possession and completion dates are the same, you may find yourself waiting
impatiently while your lawyer goes down to city hall or the Land Titles Office
with the seller's lawyer to change the title to your name — you probably
won't get the keys until mid-afternoon of the closing day. So don't hire your
movers for 9 a.m. on the day of closing, because they'll just spend hours waiting around to get into your new home.

When not to close: Don't close on a Friday if possible, or at the end of the
month. These are busy days at the Land Titles Office and you don't want a
problem to hold up the closing until the following Monday.

Should it stay or should it go?

The following three parts of the contract let you and the seller agree on what
items of the house will stay for you to enjoy, and what items leave with the
seller's moving truck:

- **Chattels:** *Chattels* are items that are not structurally part of the house
  and can be removed, but you may want to include them in the sale.
  Commonly purchased chattels include major appliances such as the
  fridge and stove, but you can include those drapes the sellers said
  they'd leave, or the unique works of art that make the "Elvis room" so
  magical.

- **Fixtures:** *Fixtures* are things that are affixed to the house, such as light
  fixtures, overhead fans, and built-in bookcases. Unless otherwise noted,
  fixtures are included in the purchase price of the home. If a crystal chandelier in the dining room makes your jaw drop, be prepared for the seller
  to stipulate that it be excluded from the sale. If you don't want to let the
  chandelier go, be prepared to raise your offer to make sure it becomes
  yours.

- **Rental items:** *Rental items* are things that the sellers rented, such as hot
  water heaters or propane tanks and security systems. They are not
  included in the house's purchase price unless you and the seller agree
  that they are. The contract should note that the buyer will assume the
  lease and all lease obligations for the propane tanks or security system.
  If the seller has not provided copies of the rental or lease documents
  prior to your making your offer, make your offer subject to your receiving
  and approving the lease agreements as necessary.

Make sure that the seller doesn't bash the head off that Elvis bust you love before you move in, or steal the most valuable crystal teardrops from the chandelier. When you're writing up your contract's conditions, include a phrase such as "the property and all included items will be in substantially the same condition as when viewed by the buyer at the date of inspection." If you have any concerns that the seller may remove a fixture, try to inspect the house again just before the completion date.

Signing it all away

The signatures of both parties — all sellers and all buyers — are usually required on each page of the contract. These signatures should be witnessed where necessary. In some provinces, it may be sufficient to initial some of the pages. Your agent or lawyer will tell you where to sign and where to initial. If any changes are made during the negotiations, the buyer and the seller must initial the change to show that it's been accepted.

The sellers must indicate their country of residency in the contract, some-where near their signature. If the sellers are residents of Canada, there is no problem. However, if the sellers are not Canadian residents, your lawyer will want to make arrangements to ensure the sellers have paid all taxes due (or alternatively, that taxes due are withheld from the proceeds of the sale). Otherwise, there is a possibility that the taxman from the Canada Customs and Revenue Agency could come knocking on your door looking for taxes payable from the long-gone sellers. Make sure the "residency" box or line is completed on the contract.

Book III

Home Sweet, Home Free

The Ins and Outs of Inspections

This can't be stressed enough: Make sure your offer is subject to an inspec-tion. Don't become part of one of many dreadful horror stories that could have been avoided with a simple home inspection; it's wise to have a profes-sional inspector examine the home. Some sellers have inspections done before they put their homes on the market (a pre-inspection), but as a buyer you should have your own professional home inspection done. Occasionally, lenders require an inspection before approving a mortgage, so unless you're Mr. or Mrs. Moneybuckets and have the cash in your back pocket, getting financing may be your main motivation for getting an inspection. The same goes for condominiums. In the Vancouver market, for example, a lender may request a copy of an inspection report if she's unsure about a particular building's soundness, before giving final approval for the mortgage.

Include a *subject to inspection* clause in your contract of purchase and sale to purchase any home. In effect, this clause acts as a safety mechanism: It releases a buyer from the obligation to purchase a home if an inspector finds major faults in the building.

Once the seller accepts your offer, have the house inspected as soon as possible. If the inspector finds any problems, you'll want as much time as possible to resolve them and make decisions. Even if the home is sound, the inspector will be able to share a lot of good information about your new house with you and tip you off to anything that you'll want to keep an eye on.

Your inspector will look at the structural elements of the home, including the basement, the roof, and the heating, plumbing, and electrical systems. She usually goes systematically through the home and gives you a full, written report when she's finished. A good inspector will also make recommendations on what should be improved (for example, install GFCI outlets and a vent in the bathroom, or add a handrail to the basement stairs).

If any problems are uncovered — and this can be anything from a leaky faucet to a leaky basement — it's decision time. One option is to *collapse* (cancel) your offer, since the condition of a positive inspection was not met. Your other option is to write in a new condition that will require the seller to fix the leaky basement and any other problem areas. You are now renegotiating the contract, and adding new conditions requires consent from both the seller and the buyer. If the seller refuses to accept a new conditional clause, your next option is to propose a price reduction to cover the costs you will incur to fix the problem. If you and the seller can't reach an agreement, you can collapse the offer and look for another house. Keep in mind that the seller is under no obligation to renegotiate. In fact, she may have priced the house acknowledging there was work to be done, and in her mind she has already discounted the price to cover the repairs.

Inspection costs can vary greatly if you're buying a very large or unusual property. In most cases, however, you'll find inspectors charge a fee in the range of $300 to $800. A typical building inspection will take at least two or three hours. On completion, you should receive a full, written inspection report that's signed and dated by the inspector.

In the event you are buying a larger, custom-built house (lucky you!) or a multi-family property, you may want to have a more comprehensive inspection conducted to inspect and analyze complex systems within the house. In this case, you may want to pay extra for a *comprehensive inspection* that will produce a *technical audit* report. This type of inspection typically takes 20 person hours or more to perform and includes disassembly and disruption of the home's systems and components. You will need to get the owner's permission before conducting a technical audit because the inspector will be dismantling key components of the owner's home. If you're interested in a technical audit, check to make sure that your inspector is capable of performing this type of inspection, and get a price estimate before proceeding.

Inspecting a newly built home

Even if you're buying a newly built home, you should have an inspection done before you accept the home. You can make this part of your pre-completion inspection, before the completion of the sale. In new construction contracts, there is usually a provision for a pre-completion *deficiency inspection* of the property. You can write into your contract that a professional building inspector will accompany you when you are doing your deficiency inspection. Before you agree to the terms of the sale contract, talk to your lawyer to ensure that you are entitled to a deficiency inspection.

If you don't know enough about construction to recognize potential problems or faulty work, you should bring along a professional home inspector. After the visual inspection is completed, you will be asked to sign a *certificate of completion* (sometimes also referred to as a *certificate of completion and possession*), stating that everything you paid for is complete. You can have the certificate drawn up by your lawyer and a representative of the builder, although many provincial New Home Warranty Program–registered builders will already have professionally prepared documents for this purpose. Any apparent omissions or defects discovered during your inspection should be noted on the certificate of completion, since this certificate is registered at your local NHWP office. Filing the certificate is necessary for your warranty coverage to commence. (You can find more on New Home Warranty Programs later in this chapter.)

Your inspector should double-check that the materials the builders used are the same as what you requested or expected, that new appliances are properly installed, and that fittings and equipment are located as specified. Look at many of the same things you would investigate if you bought a resale home: Make sure the *gradient,* the angles of the land around the foundation, will direct water away from the house and look for any signs of leaking in the basement and from the roof. Check the metal flashings around windows and the chimney to make sure they are properly caulked, and check to make sure all the toilets flush properly. You wouldn't believe what gets thrown down the toilet during the construction process! Look into whether your province has a New Home Warranty Program.

Anticipating the inspection

A professional inspector knows what to look for to ensure that a resale home is up to snuff — that it meets modern requirements and has a sound structure. An average inspection should take at least two or three hours, depending on the size of the home. A good inspector will have you accompany him and will encourage lots of questions. Sometimes the inspector will start when you're not in the home — there's not much for you to do when the inspector is poking through the attic. You should definitely be present for the last hour or two of the inspection so that the inspector can go over the good, the bad, and the ugly with you.

An inspection is a visual walk-through to report on the elements of the home. It's not meant to be a picky this-doorknob-won't-turn-fully kind of examination, but an overall report of whether the home is sound. Of course, there are no guarantees, since a home may have problems even the inspector can't find. If the sewer system (which belongs to the city) under your new house is about to collapse, causing the bottom to literally fall out of your home, there's no way an inspector can anticipate that.

The inspector completes most of the inspection report while touring the property, so the report is usually organized into locations starting with the site itself, and working through the exterior and interior of the house. Your inspection report should cover all categories of concern relevant to each part of the house and property, including structural, exterior, interior, plumbing, electrical, and heating and ventilation components. The following sections include a rough list of the kinds of problems an inspection report will alert you to.

Home exterior

Your inspector will examine the following exterior components of the house:

- **Roof surface:** The roof should be in at least *visibly* good condition. An unacceptably aged roof surface will be obvious, but in the early stages roof degeneration can be quite subtle, and virtually invisible to the untrained eye. A roof surface in poor condition can mean water leakage, poor insulation, and in extreme cases even lead to roof collapse.

- **Eaves:** The eaves should be in good condition, with no holes and minimal rust. Eaves in poor condition mean rain and snow will not drain appropriately and this can cause serious difficulties if water accumulates on your roof or near your home's foundation.

- **Chimney(s):** The chimney(s) should be free from cracks or loose sections in the masonry, and should have a chimney cap. Chimneys in poor shape could cause ventilation problems.

- **Chimney flue(s):** The chimney flue is the exhaust vent over the fireplace. An unused fireplace can quickly have its flue blocked by debris or even a bird nest or two. Flues that are not in good condition may signal a malfunctioning or improperly maintained chimney.

- **Windows:** The windows should not show any signs of wood or water damage. Damaged windows will be sure indications of water and air penetration into the interior of the home.

✔ **Siding/exterior walls:** Whether brick or siding, the house's exterior walls should be free of cracks, gaps, or signs of water damage. These will be possible indications of damage to *interior* materials, rotting, or moulds inside walls. Watch out!

✔ **Gradient:** The gradient, or slope of the ground, should be properly angled away from the home. An incorrect gradient will allow water drainage into the basement or foundation, causing water damage, rotting, or even fungus growth.

✔ **Foundation:** The house's foundation should be free of cracks, bulges, or deformities. These abnormalities could indicate an extremely serious structural problem. Also, termite tubes or other signs of infestation will manifest themselves in this area.

✔ **Septic system/cesspool:** Septic tanks and cesspools should be tested for possible leaching. You can request a dye test if the inspector does not plan to run one.

Basic home interior

This is what you can expect your inspector to check for on the inside:

✔ **Flooding/leaks:** The inspector will note these and other visible signs of water damage inside the home. The inspector will also be able to tell you if any waterproofing measures, a *sump pump,* or other additions have been installed. A sump pump is an electric pump installed in a recess in the basement (or occasionally outside the house) that will kick into action if the level of water in the drainage system starts to rise. The pump will mechanically aid the gravitational flow of the water away from the house. Waterproofing a home is extremely expensive, and this makes it important for buyers to be aware of measures already in place.

✔ **Insulation/ventilation:** This becomes problematic if the home leaks or doesn't allow moisture to evaporate, putting pretty much all of the major structural components at risk. Excessive moisture can cause rotting, rust, electrical shorts, and fungal growth. Furthermore, good insulation and ventilation will keep heating and cooling costs to a minimum.

✔ **Other unsafe components:** This is largely dependent on the age of the house. For example, paint may be old enough to contain lead; there may be missing railings on staircases; or there could be *urea formaldehyde foam insulation (UFFI)* throughout the home (see the nearby sidebar, "Alienated by UFFI," for information on UFFI). Building materials change over the years and so do safety standards. A qualified inspector will have up-to-date information and will recognize potentially dangerous components.

Book III

Home Sweet, Home Free

Alienated by UFFI

No, we're not talking about Martians; insulation is the topic of discussion here. *UFFI,* or *urea formaldehyde foam insulation,* was a popular insulation in the mid-1970s. Unfortunately, when the UFFI foam ingredients were not mixed properly, the resulting insulation released quantities of formaldehyde gas in homes, causing long-term adverse health effects for some people. UFFI was banned in Canada in 1980. However, UFFI may still be in some homes today: The government gave out three times more grants for manufacturing UFFI insulation than the number of rebates that have been applied for to replace it.

If the UFFI in a home was installed properly, it should not break down or pose a risk to you. The Canada Mortgage and Housing Corporation (CMHC) will now insure UFFI-equipped homes. As a safeguard, you may still want to include a clause in your offer to purchase contract, stating that the seller warrants that the home is not insulated with UFFI. Most sellers will be able to disclose that, to the best of their knowledge, they are or are not aware of any UFFI in their home.

Interior systems/mechanics

Your inspector examines these systems:

- **Plumbing:** Plumbing systems and pipes may no longer be up to scratch. The inspector will be on the lookout for rust and leaking or water stains that warrant further examination. Checking water pressure and the condition of drains and pipes is also part of the job.

- **Heating:** Heating systems may be outdated or inefficient. For example, the valve that controls the flow of hot water into radiators can rust away, leaving you with no way to turn down the heat in that individual unit. Other problems may be unsafe exhaust venting or chimneys that are blocked. The inspector looks for all of these problems, as well as for indications that the furnace, including the motor and burners, is functioning properly.

- **Electrical:** Electrical systems may be potential fire hazards or simply not dependable. Wiring always warrants extra attention. Your inspector should check any exposed wiring and its condition. If your home or condominium was built in the 1970s, it may have aluminum wiring that is not reliable. With aluminum wires, electricity can actually flow away from the screws used to hold the wiring in place at the back of an electrical outlet. Air pockets may form between the wires and the screws, letting electricity arc between them, ultimately burning the wire away and deadening the outlet. Your inspector checks for signs of brittle, loose, and otherwise unreliable wiring, and also for problems such as reverse polarity outlets and two-prong convenience outlets.

Once you get the inspector's full report, you'll be able to evaluate whether the home in question is as good as it looks. The inspection report should list any substandard or failing elements, and the inspector should make suggestions regarding necessary repairs and how those jobs should be prioritized. Your inspector may also be able to furnish some rough estimates of the repair costs.

A good inspector won't offer to do home repairs for you — it would be a huge conflict of interest. Your inspector should not recommend contractors to do the repairs unless they are very specialized repairs that require highly skilled trades. Your inspector is hired to investigate your home — not to give work to his buddies in the building trades.

Choosing a good inspector

Find a licensed inspector with a good reputation and membership in the *Canadian Association of Home and Property Inspectors (CAHPI)*. The CAHPI maintains minimum standards for home inspectors regarding education and professional conduct. If you know any people who have recently bought (or possibly sold) their home, ask if they had an inspection and if they were happy with the inspector. If not, there are a number of resources to try. Ask your real estate agent, friends, relatives, or people in the neighbourhood if they can recommend some good inspectors, or call your provincial or regional association of home inspectors. You can also access CAHPI on the Web at www.cahi.ca. (The association was formerly known as the Canadian Association of Home Inspectors, if you're curious about the missing P in the Web address.) Your local CAHPI office can provide the names of home inspectors in good standing who work in your neighbourhood. If you still haven't found anyone, check the Internet (some real estate board sites have links to real estate lawyers, inspectors, or appraisers) and as a last resort look in the phone book (the "eeny meeny miney moe" method). Find out whether the people you call are members of an association of home inspectors, have an office you can visit (rather than only a cell phone number), and have a current business licence.

Book III

Home Sweet, Home Free

You Are the Owner of All You Survey

Once upon a time, kings and queens built their castles on hills because they could rule over all they could see. In today's smaller kingdoms, you can rule over all you survey. It's a surprising fact that many of Canada's home buyers don't bother to get an updated land survey before closing the deal — especially when you consider that your lender will probably want to see a copy before agreeing to finance the purchase, and your lawyer will draw up your deed using information from the survey. The sellers may have a survey of the property and the bank may accept a recent survey, but if there is any uncertainty, a new survey will be required. No surveys are required for condominiums.

Land surveys are also known as building location certificates, mortgage certificates, surveyor's certificates, real property reports, plot plans, and certificates of non-encroachment.

Understanding why you need a survey

A land survey is a legal map of a property's boundaries. In the best-case scenario, the seller will have provided you with an up-to-date survey that's perfectly legal — in other words, one that's copyrighted and valid only if the original is signed and sealed. If the survey the seller hands you is old, unsealed, or otherwise fishy in any way, get your own done. When it's performed by a professional who is familiar with your region, a land survey clarifies the following issues:

- ✔ It informs you of zoning, building, or land commission restraints. This means that you'll be able to know whether that swimming pool you plan to build (not to mention the solarium that the previous owner built) is legal.

- ✔ It gives you certified, accurate measurements of the property and the exact location of the house, garden shed, garage, and any other buildings on it.

- ✔ It lets you know of environmental or contamination problems on your site, such as whether your well draws on runoff from a nearby major road, or whether the site is in an area proven to contain dangerous levels of lead in the soil.

- ✔ It states who may review the survey. A land survey, contrary to popular belief, is not a public document.

If no up-to-date survey is available, be sure to write *subject to survey* into your offer — this will allow enough time for a proper and thorough survey to be done. A slipshod, cheap, hurried survey won't do you any good if a boundary dispute comes up, or if you decide to subdivide, build an addition, or re-mortgage.

Finding a professional surveyor

Like finding a good doctor or mechanic, the first step in the hunt for a professional surveyor is to ask around. Ask the previous owners of the home for the company they used — or if your lender has requested a survey, they will often recommend one.

They may provide you with an excellent surveyor who is familiar with your locality — and all the environmental, archaeological, and regulatory quirks that might go along with it. Your agent, banker, or lawyer may also be able to recommend a surveyor.

Failing this approach, hit the Yellow Pages. You may also be able to surf the Net for a good surveyor. Many provincial land surveyors' associations have Web sites, complete with member lists and other helpful information. Look for long-established companies, or those that are members of your provincial land surveyors association. Call three of them, describing the job you need done, and be ready to supply them with a legal description of the property as well as the civic address. Record how each company proposes to do the job and approximately how much they would charge to do it. Finally, ask to see samples of their work. Compare the companies' methods, estimates, and samples, and you'll find the surveyor who is right for you.

Does This Come with a Warranty?

A $30 clock radio comes with a warranty, but what about your house? If you're buying a newly built home, you may be covered by something called a *New Home Warranty*. But it's nothing like the piece of paper that came with your new coffee maker. A New Home Warranty is actually a type of third-party insurance. And it may or may not come with your home, depending on whether or not your builder has bought into a plan.

Book III

Home Sweet, Home Free

Complicated? Well, yes. Basically, a New Home Warranty is insurance for your builder while the home is being built. Then, once the *certificate of completion* has been transferred over to you, it becomes a kind of consumer warranty. Unlike homeowner's insurance, the builder rather than the home buyer buys the policy. Of course, just because you don't buy it doesn't mean you won't end up paying for it: The builder will likely tack the cost of the warranty on to the purchase price.

Legislation concerning New Home Warranties varies across the country, and not all provinces require them. In other words, not all homes come with them, and not all homes are covered in the same way. You'll have to ask your builder whether your home is protected by one. Your builder should be able to provide you with a registration, enrolment, or membership number for the warranty plan. That way, you can check with the issuer of the warranty to ensure that everything is in order.

If you do have a warranty for your house, keep it. Keep all documentation and policy information, registration confirmation, and contact numbers somewhere safe, where you can access them if you ever need to.

Note that in order to be covered under a province's *New Home Warranty Program (NHWP),* you may have to pay a registration fee, although generally the builder pays all associated fees. Pay attention to the timing and schedule of the warranty. Some coverage is good for only one year after you take possession of the house, and coverage of different problems may expire at different times. If you do have any problems or questions, you should call your provincial NHWP office. They can answer your questions and give you a list of builders that are registered with them as members of the NHWP. Some provincial NHWP offices provide ratings of the local registered builders based on track record for both creating and solving problems. Others supply you with a list of criteria that builders have to meet in order to be registered members. Either way, you get the security of knowing you're choosing a builder that has been evaluated on a regular basis and meets high standards for quality and service. The NHWP should be listed in your local phone book, or your provincial government's Consumer Affairs ministry can direct you to the warranty program specific to your province.

Knowing what's covered

So what does your New Home Warranty cover? The details vary across the country. Most include protection for some (but not necessarily all) the following, with different items covered for different lengths of time:

- ✔ Settling cracks in drywall (usually for the first year or two);
- ✔ Defects in workmanship and materials;
- ✔ Water penetration;
- ✔ Violations of building and safety codes;
- ✔ Structural defects; and
- ✔ Down payment protection.

Timelines on the coverage also vary from sea to shining sea, so you'll have to check your specific policy for the details. It's important to know what you are covered for as well as what you're *not* covered for.

With a warranty, you're in the driver's seat

A warranty can come in handy when things go wrong. If your "unobstructed view of the lake" is seen through a gaping hole in the wall, you'll want to have that certificate to turn to. In the best of worlds, you let your builder know of the problem and he builds you a new bay window where you can relax and enjoy the vista. In the worst of worlds, he may argue that the hole isn't really a hole, but a great alternative to a cat door. Without another person there to arbitrate — except for the courts — things can get ugly pretty quickly.

In the event that you and your builder disagree over needed repairs, or what exactly qualifies as a defect, a New Home Warranty can come in handy. Because a New Home Warranty is backed up by a third party, someone else can step in to settle disputes, keeping both your interests and the builder's interests in mind.

You may want to think twice about your purchase if your builder isn't making a warranty part of the bargain. If you're buying a condo, make sure that you get a warranty for the unit and that the condominium board has a separate warranty that covers the common elements.

Put it in writing

Verbal agreements don't usually hold much clout. If you notice any defects and wish to make a claim, you *must* put the complaint in writing to your builder and keep a copy for your records. You should also send a copy to the issuer of the warranty to keep on file in case of a dispute. Photographs are also a good way to document problems. Many builders will give you a form to fill out; otherwise, organize your concerns room by room and include as much detail as possible about the nature of the problem. These documents should always include the plan number, lot number, and address of the residence in question. Oh, and of course, you have to file before the end of the warranty period.

When things go awry

Your warranty should outline a "reasonable time frame" in which builders should fix any problems that have been brought to their attention. "Reasonable," unfortunately, can mean a lot of things. One plan, for instance, gives builders up to a year to rectify defects. So if the light fixture in your bathroom doesn't work, you may be sitting in the dark for a long, long time. Getting your brother to rewire may not be a good idea: Most plans won't automatically reimburse you if you go ahead and get someone else to do the work, and some repairs may void the warranty altogether.

Book III

Home Sweet, Home Free

Chapter 4

Deciding to Sell

· ·

· ·

Decisions, decisions, decisions . . . Should you stay or should you go? Should you buy, then sell, or vice versa? Can you afford to move? Can you find something better or more suitable than what you have?

If you're thinking about putting your home on the market, this is the chapter for you. Just like buyers using Chapter 2, you won't find pat answers to these questions here, but you *will* find help on how to answer them yourself.

Few decisions have a bigger impact on your life — at every level — than deciding to sell your house. In fact, moving is one of the three most stressful life events (after death and divorce). A major change is scary, but as our lives develop, change may be necessary and even welcome. How much change you're ready for is up to you. You may decide you don't really need to move — you need to tear down some walls and finally renovate that bathroom.

This chapter can help you sort your priorities so that you can be sure that you really do want to sell your home and that you know what you want to gain from the sale. Taking the time to consider how selling your home affects your life helps you avoid costly and unnecessary mistakes, and ensures that you'll be satisfied with your choices. Thinking it through and deciding what you really need gives you incredible peace of mind.

Good Reasons to Stay Put

Examine your lists of likes, dislikes, needs, wants, and priorities (we provide guidelines for such a list in Chapter 2). Pay particular attention to the physical features you want or need in a home and your financial status and goals. Both of these considerations may be reasons for you to stay in your current home.

✔ **Renovating is a viable option:** If you're after more space, a new look, modernization, or greater efficiency, renovating your home may be the wisest course of action. If you live in a great neighbourhood, consider building an addition. Renovations may be a steal compared to the transaction costs of selling, and they may also add to the resale value of your house. See Chapter 6 for more details on which home renovation projects add the most value when you do decide to sell your house. If you want to move because your house needs some costly repairs, investigate your options carefully. You may end up paying for the repairs anyway when your house doesn't sell because of them, or when the buyers insist on deducting the repair cost from the price they will pay for the house. Buyers often overestimate the cost of repairs in order to protect themselves from the worst-case scenario.

Consider taking out a *home equity loan* to cover the costs of renovations. Home equity loans, also known as *second mortgages,* and *home equity lines of credit,* give you access to the equity you have in your home.

✔ **Your finances are shaky:** If you are already having trouble living within your means, it may be wise to delay buying your dream home until you've paid off your credit cards or student loan and devised a realistic plan to reach your financial goals. Even if you are thinking about moving to a less-expensive house, keep in mind that you will incur plenty of one-time expenses when you sell your house, buy a new one, and move. This means you have to be looking for accommodation in a range several thousand dollars below what you initially thought you could afford. If you can possibly get your debts under control while staying in your current home, your financial and emotional state will be that much better off.

Nothing is more stressful than trying to move when you are strapped for cash, except perhaps trying to move when you are strapped for cash *and* time.

Good Reasons to Sell

Even if you love your home, there are times when it just won't be able to adapt to your ever-changing needs. Because you can't always build what you need or make the neighbourhood exactly how and where you'd like it, it's often best to find a new place to call home. If any of the following conditions describe your situation, you're probably ready to sell.

✔ **The location of your home is unsuitable.** If you have a job offer in a great location with good long-term employment potential, or if you are ready to retire and look forward to the security and low maintenance of a retirement community, selling your house makes a lot of sense. (And if you're relocating for professional reasons, you may get a tax break on all of your moving expenses.)

✔ **Your house is too small or too big.** If you and your family need more space and you don't want to renovate, or you can't get a building permit to put an extension on the back of the house, moving is probably your best bet. On the flip side, if the last of your six kids has finally moved out of your seven-bedroom home, it may be time to downsize — before any of them decide to move back!

✔ **Life throws you a curve ball.** After a traumatic event like a divorce or the death of a family member, you may simply want to leave bad memories behind. Take the time to review your financial situation and personal goals so that you make a move that is right for you.

✔ **Life is fine — but the neighbourhood isn't.** Maybe your life hasn't changed a bit, but somehow the neighbourhood has changed around you in ways you're not happy about. If you find yourself with the best house on the street — or the worst — it's a good time to move. If every other bungalow in your formerly sleepy neighbourhood has been replaced by a monster home, next time a real estate agent calls you, it's time to say, "Yes, as a matter of fact, I am interested in selling!"

Book III

Home Sweet, Home Free

Timing: Sell First and Then Buy, or Vice Versa?

Not a gambler? Even for people who enjoy moving from home to home, timing the move is really tricky. On the one hand, you could find yourself with no house, having sold your home and not found a new one of the appropriate size, style, or location. On the other hand, you could find yourself with no money as you carry two houses. You can avoid these pitfalls by basing your timing decisions on current real estate market trends, and your own needs and priorities.

Riding the real estate cycle

Real estate goes through cycles. It's a *seller's market* when there are a lot of buyers and not many homes available. This is also called a *hot market* because homes tend to sell more quickly and for a higher price. In a hot market, you may nail down the house you want — the tough part in this case — and then sell your house.

It's a *buyer's market* or a *slow market* when there are more homes listed for sale than there are buyers shopping for new homes. Prices tend to be lower and homes take longer to sell in a buyer's market. If the market is slow but there are lots of houses you can see yourself happy in, sell your house first — the hard part in a slow market — and then pick your next house from among your favourites.

Although trying to sell your home in a buyer's market means you may have to drop your asking price, chances are the next house you buy will also be at a reduced price, since market conditions tend to be similar within a particular city or region. Unfortunately, if you're moving cross-country, you can't count on being so lucky.

Real estate also goes through predictable highs and lows over the course of a year. Spring is usually a peak transaction time anywhere in Canada. If you need to sell your house quickly during a slower time of the year, drop your price closer to actual market value, or even a smidgen below actual market value. On the other hand, if you want to get the best price possible, put your house on the market at the beginning of the peak season. Market activity varies with geography too, so talk to a local agent to find out what the trends are in your area. Price is an important marketing tool, so you want to get it right the first time. The section, "Pricing Your House to Sell," later in this chapter, gives you the lowdown on pricing do's and don'ts.

Meeting your needs

Your needs form another important variable in the buying and selling equation. Do you need to sell your home quickly? Do you want a certain price, and if so, are you willing to wait for it? Do you want to be in your next home by a particular date?

If you want to get your kids moved into a new house before the beginning of the school year, you may decide to buy that perfect house in the new neighbourhood before you have sold your current house. The way to avoid hanging on to two houses is to price your current home to sell. For example, if you have to sell and are facing the prospect of owning two homes in six weeks' time (carrying both would probably cost you an extra $2,000 to $3,000 per month), drop your asking price by a couple of thousand dollars. Accepting an offer — albeit below your original asking price — meets two important needs: your kids start the new school year off on the right track and you have only one home to carry — much more manageable. Examine your financial situation and determine your personal priorities early. But as a rule, it is almost always better to sell before you buy.

Anticipating how much you can get for your house

If you're going to sell your home, naturally you want to recoup the money you spent buying it and fixing it up, and you're thinking about how much money you *need* in order to buy your next home. Unfortunately, these factors don't determine the resale value of your home.

The cold, hard truth is that *buyers* determine the actual market value for your house through what they offer to *pay* for it. If all the similar houses in your neighbourhood sell in a certain price range, buyers will likely offer a similar price for your home. Surveying the asking prices and recent sale prices of comparable homes in your neighbourhood gives you a basic idea of what price you can expect to get (the upcoming section, "Pricing Your House to Sell," has the details). In effect, timing is everything — being aware of the real estate market's trends makes you better prepared to get the price you really want or need.

If you are working with a real estate agent or broker, ask for a *comparative market analysis (CMA),* a report used to determine a home's market value. Your home is "ranked" next to similar homes in your neighbourhood based on details like size, condition, desirable features, and listing and sale prices. If you are selling on your own, you would be wise to get a professional appraisal to determine the actual market value of your home. (See the "Pricing Your House to Sell" section, later in this chapter, for more on comparative market analyses.)

Although it's not exactly a scientific approach, try talking to your neighbours to get an idea of what your home is worth. It's a safe bet that everyone on your street will also give you opinions on how much more your house could sell for with its renovated kitchen or the new hardwood floors.

Your house gets the most exposure to the buying market in its first few weeks of listing. The closer your house is priced to its actual market value, the more quickly it will sell. If you price your home too high and scare off buyers in the beginning, you may have to go through a few price reductions in order to sell. It makes much more sense to price your house realistically from the get-go — you'll sell it months earlier.

Knowing what you can spend on your next house

Figuring out how much you can afford on your next house is a long but relatively simple equation. It involves solely the basic math of addition and subtraction. You need to total your cash in-flow and out-flow, then subtract the expenses from the income. The tricky part is taking inventory of all your sources of income and expenditure, and the exact amounts associated with each.

Careful calculations help you be realistic about what you can afford. Once you know how much you can spend, you need to investigate whether it really will get you the kind of house you want, while maintaining your standard of living and allowing you to save for long-term financial goals.

Never assume *anything* when investigating what you will get for your money. The perfect home may not be in the perfect neighbourhood. The perfect neighbourhood may have listings in your price range only for properties half the size you need. You may have to make sacrifices to make improvements, so you need to know what your priorities are. Even if you can make a decent profit on the sale of your current home, there's no guarantee you'll be better off if you sell.

The safety net: Conditional subject-to-sale offers

One way to synchronize buying and selling is to find a house you like, make an offer conditional on the sale of your current house, and once the conditional offer is accepted, *then* put your house on the market. If the condition (selling your house) is not met by the expiry date in the clause, then the offer you made for the other house becomes null and void if you and the seller don't extend the *subject-to-sale* clause's time frame.

By writing a subject-to-sale condition into your purchase offer, you don't have to buy the house you want until you've sold the house you are living in — giving you the peace of mind and the financial security that comes with not owning two homes *and* not being homeless.

You should be keenly aware of the fact that a subject-to-sale conditional offer is less attractive to a home seller, and therefore puts the buyer in a weak negotiating position. Since most sellers don't want to delay the sale of their home, they often are willing to accept a "clean" offer for less money. If the seller receives such an offer and is considering it, they will usually invoke the *time clause,* the amount of time the first buyer has to either remove all the conditions from their offer — including the subject-to-sale condition — or withdraw their offer altogether. Now it's time to hustle. If you really want that house, you need to remove your subject-to-sale clause and firm up your offer, even though the competitive offer may be several thousand dollars less. Some sellers won't even look at offers made subject to the sale of the buyers' current house, as they don't believe the buyers are serious. Ask your real estate agent how conditional offers are received in your local market.

Here's how it works. You write into your offer a subject-to-sale clause that essentially states, "This offer is subject to the sale of the buyers' current residence located at [address], on or before [expiry date of clause]. However, if another acceptable offer is received, the sellers will notify the buyers in writing and give the buyers 48 hours [24 or 72 hours is also common] to remove the subject-to-sale condition as well as all other conditions from the offer or the offer will be considered null and void." The *expiry date* of the clause indicates the amount of time you have to sell your house from the time the offer is accepted and therefore to remove the condition and make your offer firm, or withdraw your offer if the condition was not met. This date is usually negotiated to fall between four and six weeks after the offer is accepted and it can be extended if both parties agree.

Don't confuse the expiry date of the clause with the completion date of the offer itself. The *completion date* specifies the date you will close the deal if all the specified conditions are met. It is the day you become the legal owner of the property.

The *time clause,* which is negotiable, identifies how long you have to remove the subject-to-sale condition or withdraw your offer should the seller receive another acceptable offer before the expiry date on your clause. You see, even after the sellers accept your conditional purchase offer, they will still actively market their home, looking for a "clean offer" — an offer without conditions. If the seller receives another acceptable offer, they will *invoke the time clause* and notify you in writing that you have 24/48/72 hours (or whatever was written into the clause) to make a decision. At this point you can remove the conditions and commit to buying the house — whether or not you have sold your own — or you can withdraw the offer.

If you've really found your dream home and your conditional offer has been accepted, you don't want your subject-to-sale clause to expire or the time clause to be invoked before you sell your current property. You must price your house to sell, which means being very realistic about its market value. The closer your house is listed to market value, the more quickly you will receive good offers.

For most people, it makes sense to put your house on the market *while* you look for your next home. This gives you a good sense of what buyers are willing to pay for your house, and saves you from inflating the amount you think you can spend on your next home. If offers come rushing in, you can always accept the best, subject to the purchase of your next house.

Some buyers won't accept a seller's proposed counteroffer, especially if the counteroffer is conditional on the sellers' purchase of their next home. If you find yourself in this position, you have to decide what you're willing to risk. If you sell before you've found a new home, you risk becoming homeless — at least temporarily. On the other hand, if you reject the buyer's offer because you can't include the condition of buying your next house, you may wait a long time before receiving another one, depending on the market conditions and your pricing strategy.

If you have a lot of money, you could just buy your dream home and *then* put your current house on the market. Through *bridge financing* you can use the equity in your first property to finance the purchase of the next. It's the riskiest option financially, but it guarantees that you get the house you absolutely want.

Buying time with the closing dates

Getting the paperwork right is the next step in making a smooth transition. Once you've found a buyer for your current home and a new house to move into, you'll need to schedule each *closing date,* the day you transfer ownership of a property and finalize the sale. Ideally, both the sale of your current home and the purchase of your new one should close one right after the other. This affords you the most security financially — and emotionally. If it simply can't be done, the next best option is to try to extend the closing date on your purchase so that it follows the closing date of your home's sale. See Chapter 6 for details on negotiating deadlines that will work for you.

Try to avoid the last day of the month or year as a closing date. These times are particularly busy for the agencies that will be registering and filing paperwork for the transfer of ownership, termination of insurance, and the like, not to mention movers.

Pricing Your House to Sell

It's common sense that if you price something too high, it won't sell. This is especially true for big-ticket items like houses. Potential buyers are skittish to begin with at the prospect of having to make such a big decision. If your price tag is too high, you'll scare them off right away. The key is finding the balance between reeling in the buyers at the start and getting your home's true value in the end (after negotiation, of course).

Knowing how much your home is worth

The best way to find out how much your home is worth is to ask a professional. You can hire a professional appraiser to give you an *appraisal,* or you can ask your real estate agent to give you a *comparative market analysis (CMA),* sometimes also referred to as a *current market analysis* or a *competitive market analysis.* A sample CMA is shown in Figure 4-1.

COMPARATIVE MARKET ANALYSIS

COMPARABLE ('02) HOMES RECENTLY SOLD

Address	Age	Lot Size	Floor Area	Bdrms	Bthrms	Bsmt	Listed Date & Price	Selling Date & Price	Ass. Value ('02)
312 Main St.	55	33 x 120	2000	3	3	Full	Dec./02 $430,000	Feb. 20/03 $425,000	$419,987
2525 Ontario St.	48	33 x 120	1956	3	2	Part	Nov./02 $425,000	March 3/03 $410,000	$405,700
4323 E. 21st	51	33 x 120	1830	3	2	Full	Sept/02 $420,500	Feb 5/03 $405,000	$410,050

COMPARABLE HOMES FOR SALE NOW

Address	Age	Lot Size	Floor Area	Bdrms	Bthrms	Bsmt	Listed Date & Price	Ass. Value ('02)
3737 E. 25th	63	33 x 112	1860	3	3	Full	Dec. 15/02 $409,000	$386,510
461 Main	47	33 x 122	1750	3	2	Full	Jan 19/03 $419,000	$392,100
518 Manitoba	45	33 x 120	1905	4	2	Part	Jan 25/03 $439,000	$398,000
2431 Main	55	35 x 115	2000	3	3	Full	Feb 5/03 $440,000	$405,205

YOUR HOME

Address	Age	Lot Size	Floor Area	Bdrms	Bthrms	Bsmt	Recommended List Range	Recommended Sale Range
495 Main	51	33 x 120	1850	3	2	Full	$439,000/$449,000	$425,000/$435,000

MARKET VALUE DEFINED: ... the price expected when a reasonable time is allowed to find a purchaser when both seller and prospective buyer are fully informed.

LISTING PRICE: ... the price asked for a property, as set by the vendor. The vendor is urged to take into account information supplied and market conditions.

Sales Representative: _Shelon Walker_

Figure 4-1: Your real estate agent should give you a comparative market analysis that looks something like this. It will let you see what similar houses in your neighbourhood are selling for so that you can determine your home's fair market value (FMV).

Book III

Home Sweet, Home Free

As far as assessing the market value of your house, appraisals and CMAs are essentially the same. Both consider all the factors influencing the worth of your property (such as location, square footage, general condition of the home, and amenities). They research the recent sale prices and current asking prices of similar homes in your area, compare the finer details, and adjust up or down to determine your home's *fair market value (FMV)*. If your home has, say, an attached double garage, then it may be worth a little bit more than someone else's down the street that, like yours, is a three-bedroom two-storey with four baths and a finished basement, but comes with only a carport.

Most real estate agents will prepare a CMA for you free of charge. You will always have to pay an appraiser. If you're selling without an agent, you should definitely hire an independent appraiser. The legal system, as well as most financial institutions, recognizes only appraisals prepared by certified professional appraisers.

Your buyer can put a *clause* (a condition) into the offer stipulating that it is subject to the home's sale price being confirmed by an independent appraisal. If your buyer's appraisal reveals they have offered more than your home is worth, your buyer may retract the offer, or your buyer's mortgage lender may refuse to finance the purchase.

Avoiding the three most common pricing mistakes

Yes, it's your home and you can ask whatever price you'd like for it, but remember to proceed with caution. Your selling price heavily influences your likelihood of selling success; it can determine whether your home is snapped up by eager buyers or languishes in the classifieds for months. Here are three pricing mistakes that sellers often make.

Trying to make a hefty profit

The reasoning for setting a high price goes something like this: "If someone buys it for the high price, great, I made some money. If I have to drop the price a little to sell, then I haven't really lost anything because I still got a fair price." The problem is, it doesn't work that way. Your home gets the most attention for the first few weeks it's on the market. If you set the price too high, you run the risk of buyers bypassing your home due to its high price. If your home isn't fairly priced for those crucial first few weeks, it may become stale by the time you do lower the price. Buyers see your listing and think, "If it's been on the market for this long and they have to keep lowering the price, there must be *something* wrong with it." They may then turn around and purchase something else by the time you lower your price.

Furthermore, if the initial asking price is too high, the buyer won't feel that there is competition for the home — and this means they won't be in any hurry to make an offer. Either way, by the time you do lower the asking price, agents (and their buyers) have lost interest in your home and you may have to sell for less than you would have gotten had you priced your house realistically in the beginning.

The only real circumstance where you can be "optimistic" in your asking price is in an overheated seller's market where there are few, if any, homes that directly compete with yours. In this dream-come-true scenario, you can ask a higher price than your CMA would otherwise indicate. Better yet, you may get offers from competing buyers, driving the price higher than what recent sales would indicate your house is worth.

Setting the sale price based on your needs

Many sellers have a new location (or even a new house) in mind and know how much money they need to make on the sale of their current home in order to purchase a new one. Other sellers may be planning to "trade down" as a way to make money they can then invest for retirement. Frankly, buyers don't care about your needs. Buyers have their own needs to worry about, one of which is paying fair market value for their new house. If you keep the sale price too high because you "need the money," you simply won't be able to sell your home.

Setting the sale price based on how much you have "put into" your home

Thirty thousand dollars' worth of renovations does not necessarily equal an extra thirty thousand dollars on the sale price of your home. Some improvements to your home will increase its value, others will not (for example, kitchens and bathrooms are often the best places for renovations that add to the resale value of a home). Cosmetic improvements, such as fresh paint, are always good investments. Although they will not increase the value of your home by a significant margin, basic home touch-ups are relatively cheap and extremely important for making a good first impression on buyers. A good agent will know what counts and what doesn't, and so will most buyers — you can also check out Chapter 6 to find out which renovations are most valuable for sellers.

Book III

Home Sweet, Home Free

Estimating the Costs of Selling

On the surface, the economics of selling your home seem pretty simple. You sell your home and, hopefully, you make enough money to cover the purchase of another one. If the sale price of your current home is greater than what you pay for your new home, "I save money" appears to be the logical conclusion. Unfortunately, a few steps in the middle of the process may shrink your profits from the sale. With proper planning, you can accurately estimate the proceeds of the sale to find out for sure. This section takes you through the expenses you are responsible for as the seller.

After you have investigated the anticipated market value of your home and each of the selling costs described here, then you've already done the hard part. Just fill in Table 4-1 to determine the net proceeds you'll realize from selling your home. Start with your home's estimated sale price and subtract whichever associated costs apply. What you're left with are the net proceeds from the sale.

Table 4-1	Calculating the Net Proceeds from the Sale
Item	**Amount**
Estimated sale price	
– Agent's commission	
– Legal fees	
– Repairs or renovations	
– Discharge of your mortgage	
– Property taxes and prepaid utilities +/–	
– Moving costs	
– Survey fees (if applicable)	
– Appraisal fees (if applicable)	
– Location-specific expenses (if applicable) (termite inspection, well water inspection)	
– GST (if not already included)	
Net proceeds from sale =	

Agent's commission

Unless you have time and energy to burn, chances are you'll hire an agent to help with the sale of your home. Your agent receives a commission when you sell — usually a percentage of the sale price — as does your buyer's agent. And guess what, you are responsible for both! A typical total commission expense may be between 4 and 6 percent of the selling price, but rates are negotiable. If you decide to sell privately, you will probably still deal with buyers who are using an agent, so you may get stuck with some commission fees no matter what.

Legal fees

The sale of a home requires complex legal documentation. You may need a lawyer to draw up or check over all paperwork and documents. Depending on the amount of work to be done, your legal fees will vary. Talk to several lawyers to get an idea of how much your case may cost, but budget at least $500 to $1,000, including *conveyance* (the transfer of the title to the property), and more if you need documents to be drafted by the lawyer.

Repairs or renovations

Most homes will *not* require major renovations to ensure a sale. If you've kept your home in good shape or if your home is relatively new, you may need to do only minor repairs. First impressions go a long way — no matter how new your home is, pay attention to cosmetic details (chipped paint, leaky faucets, loose doorknobs, and so on). The better your home looks, the quicker it will sell.

Your buyer will have a building inspector evaluate your home (for plumbing and structural problems, and so on) to find out what improvements (if any!) are necessary. Whatever repairs are needed may be deducted from the selling price, likely with a margin of error that will benefit your buyer. In some circumstances you may wish to have your home inspected first if you suspect there is a serious problem, or if you live in an area where properties, often condos, are commonly listed as having a "positive inspection" available to potential buyers. Other people use their inspections as a marketing tool to demonstrate how "good" their homes are and thereby to get top dollar for them. If you're selling a condominium and the building has a *positive engineering report,* you have an excellent selling point — use it. A glowing inspection report from a reputable agency provides an incentive to potential buyers. However, if the inspection reveals any serious liabilities, you are legally obligated to disclose that information to potential buyers.

There is no right answer to whether or not you should absorb the cost of the building inspection. You may be wasting your money since the buyers will probably have their own inspection done anyway, but you could see some benefits at the negotiating table. Seek the advice of your agent (if you have one). If you choose to have your home inspected, remember to include the inspection fees when totalling the cost of repairs and renovations.

Book III

Home
Sweet,
Home Free

Discharge of your mortgage

If you don't have a mortgage, give yourself a pat on the back and skip ahead to the next point; otherwise, read on! Most lenders have a few options available for handling your mortgage when you sell, depending on the specifics of your current mortgage agreement. You may be allowed to take your mortgage with you to your new home, you may be able to let the buyer assume it, or you may be able to pay it off early. (Find out about the options in the section, "Dealing with Your Current Mortgage," later in this chapter.)

Lenders often charge legal and/or penalty fees when you choose one of these options. Check your mortgage agreement to see what is permitted and talk to your lender to find out what fees you may incur. Fees are sometimes negotiable. If you have been a loyal client of your lender for many years, you may be able to "talk down" a prepayment penalty, but don't hold your breath. Many lenders have a policy against renegotiating. Whatever arrangements you make with your lender, be sure to get a copy *in writing.*

Property taxes and prepaid utilities

The day you usually pay your property taxes is not likely to coincide with the day you sell your home (if Fate loves you that much, skip ahead to the next point). In the sale contract, there will be an *adjustment date* (the day the buyer assumes all responsibility for paying property taxes, and so on). Usually the adjustment date is the same day as the *possession date,* or the day you hand the buyer the keys. In effect, your buyer may owe you a refund on a portion of your annual property tax (or you may owe the buyer some money if you don't prepay your property taxes). Likewise, any prepaid utilities, condo fees, or assessments need to be reviewed. Your lawyer can work out exactly how much is owed to whom and adjust the taxes as part of the conveyance or statement of adjustment. (The *statement of adjustment* shows the net result for the vendor [seller] or purchaser of the home, taking into account the purchase price, deposit, real estate commissions, legal fees, property purchase tax, property taxes, and all other adjustments.)

Moving costs

Obviously, how much it costs to move depends on how much stuff you are moving, how far you are moving it, and what moving company you hire. Other factors may enter into the tally, including the time of year and any "special care" items you may be moving (such as your baby grand piano). Do your research. Find out exactly how much stuff you've accumulated over the years and how much it's really going to cost to get it to your new home. An extra few hours assessing the contents of your basement and garage, plus a phone call or four, are a lot less hassle than under-budgeting your moving costs by several thousand dollars, or finding out too late that your one-bedroom home has three bedrooms' worth of memorabilia (two-thirds of which will not fit into the moving truck).

Survey fees

Some banks require a survey in order to approve a mortgage on a house. (There are no surveys required for condos; most condo buildings have a building or strata plan that shares the square footage of the unit in lieu of a survey.) Usually, this cost is absorbed by the buyer (as you probably already know), but it's not uncommon for sellers to have an existing survey certificate from when they purchased the house. If no alterations or additions have been made to the property, it may still be acceptable to the bank. The fee for having a survey done depends on the size and particularities of your property (be warned, it could cost over $1,000).

Appraisal fees

You need to know the value of your home before you set the selling price. If you're not using an agent, you may want to hire a professional appraiser for an expert opinion of how much your home is worth. (Your buyers will still have a second appraisal done — their mortgage lender may require it, or they may simply want to be certain they are getting a good deal.) If you are using a reputable and experienced agent, you may not bother with a pre-listing appraisal.

Don't confuse an inspection with an appraisal. An inspection reveals any major structural or systems-related problems with your home that will need to be fixed before you sell; an appraisal investigates what the market value of your home is. The appraiser may take into account if there are any of those problems that the inspector looks for, but he is really only interested in the dollar value on the bottom line.

Location-specific expenses

Some geographic regions come with their own unique set of housing issues. As a seller, you may be responsible for extra costs associated with your particular region.

Book III

Home Sweet, Home Free

Believe it or not, there are termite hot spots in Canada. If you know you live in a hot spot, you may want to have a termite inspection performed. Insects and other pest problems may be part of a standard home inspection. If you live in a region notorious for pest infestations, you may have to pay for a separate inspection. It is possible in some cases to get a termite warranty. If you have one, and keep it active, it may cover the cost of the inspection.

As a rural dweller, you may want to have the well water tested or a modern filtration system installed. As a resident of Nova Scotia, you may want to have the results of a recent ground test for radon handy for showings. Maybe you live on a fault line or maybe you live on a flood plain. Wherever you live, be aware of the extra expenses you will incur due to your location.

GST

Regardless of whether the sale of your home is GST-exempt, this tax applies to most services you will use in selling your home. So expect that real estate agents, lawyers, appraisers, building inspectors, surveyors, and anyone else you hire to help sell your home will charge GST on top of their service fees.

Selling your home is an expensive endeavour. Unfortunately, money is not the only currency associated with selling. You're also going to spend time — lots of it. No one can supply you with the numbers in discussing all the expenses you will encounter when selling your home; you need to figure them out for yourself. This is because each situation is different and each requires investigation, which will eat up many hours. The old saying that "time is money" certainly applies when it comes to selling your home. Many aspects of home selling can't be done on your own, and there are many other tasks that you must take on yourself. Anything you pass off to someone else will cost you money; anything you don't will cost you time.

Dealing with Your Current Mortgage

What happens to your current mortgage if you decide to sell your home? You have three choices:

- ✔ Pay off your mortgage.
- ✔ Let your buyer take over your mortgage along with your home.
- ✔ Take your mortgage with you to your new home.

When your parents were buying their first house they probably had to beg and pray for a mortgage. Times have changed. Today's mortgage market is buyer-driven. Instead of crawling into the bank on your hands and knees and pleading for your mortgage, you can stand tall and ask potential lenders, "What can *you* do for *me*?" Here are a couple of items the lender may offer you:

- ✔ A .5 to 1 full percentage point reduction off the current interest rate if you're looking for a new *first* mortgage on a property (it doesn't matter how many mortgages you've had in the past on other properties — only the home you are looking to buy is in question here).

- ✔ A legal package that allows you to use the lender's lawyers, at a discount, for the *conveyance* of the title and preparation of the mortgage documents. The "conveyance" of title is the transfer of ownership, the registration of the new owners, and the registration of the mortgage, at the appropriate Land Titles Office.

You may find even more competitive terms offered in the near future, as our southern neighbours continue to make competitive inroads into the Canadian mortgage market. Before you make any final decisions, *shop around and negotiate.* Money is a commodity, and some lenders will charge you a higher price to use their money than others will.

Paying off your mortgage early

If you've owned your home for a long time, you may have built up substantial *equity.* Equity is the difference between the value of your property and the outstanding debts against it — for example, if your home is worth $250,000 and you have paid off all but $12,000 of your mortgage, you have accumulated $238,000 worth of equity in your home. If you have only a small portion of your mortgage to pay off, you may consider *discharging* it (paying it off early).

Most lenders offer financing plans to help you discharge your mortgage faster while avoiding high penalty fees. A financing plan may allow you to do one of the following to help discharge your mortgage more quickly:

- ✔ Increase the amount of your mortgage payments.

- ✔ Make mortgage payments more often.

- ✔ Exercise prepayment options (*prepayment* means that you can pay a certain amount of the principal each month or each year in addition to your regular payments, or a percentage of the principal can be paid down each time you renew your mortgage terms).

Using any of the above options decreases the length of time it takes to pay off your mortgage. (We discuss mortgages in detail in Chapter 1.)

If you're a long-range planner and you're considering selling your home in the next five years, talk to your lender to see about renegotiating your terms. You may be able to modify your payment schedule or negotiate a mortgage renewal that permits you to discharge your mortgage as soon as possible, without paying a *penalty fee* (you pay this fee to your lender as compensation for paying off your mortgage early).

If you want to pay off your mortgage with a single cheque you will likely pay a penalty fee. The amount of a penalty fee is usually equal to either three months' interest or an *interest rate differential,* and the bank will charge you the higher of the two. If interest rates have gone down since you signed on to your mortgage, your lender stands to lose a portion of the interest money when you pay off the loan early. For example, if you're making payments on your existing mortgage at a 10 percent interest rate and the current rate is now 7 percent, your lender will charge you for the 3 percent difference. Because the lender can only charge the current 7 percent rate on any loans it currently negotiates, the rate differential penalty accounts for the reduced profit your lender will make on new loans, as compared to your original loan.

Some financial institutions may negotiate the mortgage penalty fees if your buyer also takes out a mortgage with them, or if you use the same lender for your next mortgage, but don't hold your breath. Whatever arrangement you make with your lender, get a copy *in writing.*

Letting your buyer take over your mortgage

If you're trying to sweeten the deal for a potential buyer, and your mortgage rate is lower than the current rate, consider taking advantage of the assumability option. Basically, you allow your buyer to assume your mortgage at its existing rate when he purchases your home. Assumability is often restricted to fixed rate mortgages. (See Chapter 1 for a discussion of fixed rate and other types of mortgages.)

It's rare to assume a seller's mortgage, however. Generally, if circumstances make your mortgage look attractive to a buyer, it's probably a mortgage you want to hang on to, rather than approaching a lender for a new mortgage at the higher current interest rate. The only scenarios that truly warrant considering the assumability option occur (1) when you've got a great mortgage and your highest priority is selling *fast* (and you can afford not to take that great mortgage with you), or (2) if you're in a tough buyer's market and the incentive of a below-market mortgage rate will help you sell your home.

Here's how the assumability option works. Your buyer must meet your lender's credit requirements before your lender approves the mortgage transfer from you to your buyer. There may also be fees (which could be hefty) for the legal work and paper shuffling required. Fortunately, because most lenders now require your buyer to meet their credit and income standards, you no longer risk taking financial responsibility if your buyer fails to pay the mortgage in the future, as was the case in the past in some provinces.

If your buyer assumes your mortgage, you benefit in three ways:

- ✔ An assumable mortgage is a marketing tool; it may be just the enticement a buyer needs — the lure of a lower interest rate.

- ✔ Because your lender is already familiar with your home, the home appraisal requirement may be waived, saving the buyer a few hundred dollars, and by doing that your house may be more enticing to the buyer.

- ✔ If the buyer assumes your mortgage, you're no longer responsible for the discharge penalty fees, which saves you even more money.

Do not take it for granted that you will be absolved of all responsibility if the new owner defaults on mortgage payments! Make absolutely sure to indemnify yourself — get it *in writing* — that you have no further financial obligations with regard to the mortgage once your buyer assumes it, and that you are *fully discharged* from the mortgage.

Book III

Home Sweet, Home Free

Taking your mortgage with you to your new home

Most mortgage agreements have a *portability* option that allows you to apply your current mortgage to a new home if you decide to sell. "Porting" your mortgage may be your best alternative if there's too much still owing on your mortgage for you to consider paying it off immediately, and if your existing mortgage rate is lower than the current rate.

Often, only fixed rate mortgages are portable. If your new home requires extra financing, you can usually borrow additional funds at the current rate — your new mortgage rate will be a blend of your mortgage's existing interest rate and the current interest rate. For example, if you have three years left on a five-year mortgage term, you may be able to borrow the extra money at the current three-year rate. (So the additional $20,000 you borrow to finance your new home will fit into your existing mortgage at the current three-year rate.) The additional mortgage you just took out to finance your new home has the same expiry date as your original mortgage. When the time comes to renew them, you renew them as one mortgage.

Porting mortgages has become quite common due to the low interest rates of recent years, but choosing what's best for you always depends on your unique financial situation and how much risk you are willing to take. If you've taken to following the rise and fall of mortgage rates religiously in the past few years, you may feel confident in allowing your buyer to assume your current mortgage so that you can take out a new variable-rate or short-term open mortgage on your new home. (See Chapter 1 for details on variable rates and open and closed mortgages.) If you can stand the headache of renegotiating your mortgage every six months, you'll probably end up saving money in the long run.

If you're not a risk-taker and can't be bothered to scour the financial section of the newspaper every morning for the latest trends in mortgage rates, it's worth the bit of extra money you may pay to port your fixed rate mortgage, just for the peace of mind.

If you're wondering about the benefits of porting your existing mortgage to a new home, you can check out the financial consequences online. Surf the Internet — find a Canadian online mortgage calculator (try www.canadamortgages.com) and pretend you're going to port your existing mortgage and borrow a bit more at the current rate. The calculator will determine your new blended interest rate, and tell you what your payments will be. You can simply multiply your monthly payments by the number of months in the mortgage term to get the total amount that you will pay if you port your mortgage.

Use the mortgage calculator a second time to figure out the total amount you would pay on a new mortgage at whatever the current interest rate happens to be. If the total amount payable for a new mortgage is less than you would pay by keeping your current mortgage with a new blended interest rate, then you stand to save if you pay off the current mortgage rather than porting it to your new home. Just be sure that the savings you will make with the new mortgage are greater than the penalty fee you'll be charged for paying off your current mortgage early.

Reversing your mortgage

If you need extra income to help maintain your current standard of living after you retire, or if you need extra income for personal care expenses, you may want a *reverse mortgage*. A reverse mortgage is an agreement between you and a lender that allows you to "tap into" the equity built up in your home. You can do this in a few different ways: Your lender may give you a lump-sum payment, send you monthly payments, offer a line of credit, or some combination of these options.

There are some standard restrictions on who can enter into a reverse mortgage agreement — usually, you must be at least 62 years old and have no outstanding debts against your home. However, you do not need to meet credit or income requirements to be eligible for a reverse mortgage. In Canada, reverse mortgages are offered through the Canadian Home Income Plan (www.reversemortgage.org/canadian.htm).

The amount of money that you can access ranges from 10 to 48 percent of the value of your home. The total funds you can access is determined by:

- ✔ The value of your home
- ✔ Your age
- ✔ Current interest rates
- ✔ The type of reverse mortgage you choose

Unlike a conventional mortgage, a reverse mortgage does not have to be repaid right away — repayment starts when your home ceases to be your principal residence (a home is no longer considered a principal residence if the borrower moves elsewhere, dies, or sells the home). When you do begin to repay the mortgage, you are responsible for the borrowed principal plus interest and any other legal or administrative fees associated with the agreement.

The amount that you must repay for a reverse mortgage *cannot* exceed the value of your home, and you *cannot* be forced to sell your home to repay the mortgage if you still reside there. When lenders determine the amount a borrower can receive, they're betting that the home will not depreciate significantly and that the borrower will not reside there so long that payout exceeds the value of the home.

Repayment can be made by you, your family, or your estate, and need not involve the sale of your home. If you do decide to sell your home, whatever profit you make over the market value of your home is yours (or your family's, or estate's) to keep. Should the sale generate less than the value of the reverse mortgage on your home, it is usually the responsibility of a third party, such as an insurance provider, to make up the difference.

Although not many homeowners have taken out reverse mortgages, the popularity of this option is growing. If you feel it's important to pass down your home to children or grandchildren, you may not want to experiment with a reverse mortgage.

Book III

Home Sweet, Home Free

Many seniors consider a reverse mortgage because they cannot pay all the bills required to maintain their home. Seniors should investigate whether or not they can *defer* their property taxes, which would mean one less hefty bill to pay each year, and may allow them to postpone or eliminate the need for a reverse mortgage. If property taxes are deferred, they are generally repaid when the homeowner moves out of the property, or when the home is sold. Consider this tax-deferral option first before opting for an often restrictive reverse mortgage!

Chapter 5

Preparing Yourself and Your House to Sell

*T*his chapter contains the most "for sale by owner" information, since it not only outlines the steps in putting your home on the market, but also contains lots of useful information for everyone. From choosing an agent (if you want one) and a lawyer, to getting an appraisal or inspection, as well as all the contracts, statements, and steps in between, this chapter gets you from the decision to sell to the point where you're ready to talk to potential buyers.

If you're a really take-charge kind of person with some time on your hands, you may be considering selling your home privately. Wait just a minute, though! You need to know what's in store for you in the home-selling process. Read this chapter to be sure you're making the right decisions, whether you want a real estate agent to handle your sale or you're determined to do it yourself. An experienced lawyer who specializes in real estate will ensure everything goes smoothly, whether or not you are using an agent. If you want to sell your home on your own, you will rely on a real estate lawyer to draft and review all your documentation. Either way, make sure you have the right kind of help to secure your home's sale.

Identifying the Right Real Estate Agent

Most people approach the task of selling their homes as a team sport. Make things easy for yourself by picking the best players to back you up. The most important positions on your selling team are your real estate agent and your real estate lawyer. Choose both individuals with care. In this section, you discover the ins and outs of finding the best agent. You can find the same for lawyers a little later on. Another potential member of your selling team is your real estate agent's broker. See Chapter 2 for more on the relationship among you, your agent, and her broker.

Real estate agents, also known as *salespeople* or *registrants* in some provinces, can use the term *realtor* provided that they are registered members of their local real estate boards or associations. This means they are licensed professionals and are legally bound to protect and promote your interests as they would their own.

Picking the perfect real estate agent for you is partially luck and partially knowing what to look for. You should interview several candidates before you make a decision.

What to look for in your agent

The best real estate agents score high on the list of qualities below. Keep these in mind when you're asking more targeted questions during your interview (you can find a list for that as well, in the very next section). Your agent should:

- **Be a full-time professional.** When you sell your property, you hand over a sizable amount of money to your real estate agent — probably anywhere between 2.5 and 6 percent of the price, and up to 10 percent on recreational properties. A good agent earns a commission by giving you good advice, promoting your property, skilfully closing the deal, and taking care of the details. To do the job right, you need a full-time professional. A big part of selling a house is being in contact with many buyers and understanding what they respond to. Don't settle for anything less than a dedicated, full-time real estate agent.

- **Charge a reasonable commission rate.** Find out what commission the agent charges on a sale. Is the agent's commission rate in keeping with the average you have been quoted? A range of commissions is charged across the country and commissions are calculated differently in different areas. In Toronto, a seller may pay a 5 to 6 percent commission. By comparison, in Vancouver, many companies charge a 7 percent commission on the first $100,000 of a sale and 2.5 percent on the balance. Recreational properties are usually more difficult to sell than conventional homes, so commissions may be as high as 10 percent of the sale price.

The agent willing to accept the lowest commission isn't necessarily going to do the best job of selling your home. Often a company that charges a lower commission requires the owner to pay for all advertising (including occasionally buying a sign from the agent!), as well as doing all their own showings and even hosting the open houses. Sometimes a company quotes a low commission to secure a listing, and after the house has been on the market for a month or so, recommends that you pay a higher commission for more services. Suddenly the commission looks pretty much like all the other quotes you found. Also make sure that the commission quoted allows for commission to be paid to a buyer's agent. Make sure the total commission quoted is all you will be paying — you don't want any surprises.

✔ **Inform you how she handles holdover clauses as they apply to commission.** In some rare cases, you may still owe your agent the commission even if your home doesn't sell while you have it listed with her agency. Your agent can use a *holdover clause* to claim a commission even if your home's sale happens after the listing expires. An average holdover period may last 60 to 90 days from the expiration of the contract. Occasionally, a buyer who made an unacceptable offer on your house while it was listed may approach you again once the listing has expired, this time with an acceptable offer. Depending on the timing of the offer and the wording of the listing contract, you may still have to pay your agent the commission. Check the fine print of the listing contract to see if there is a holdover period, and ask your agent if her company has ever enforced the holdover period.

Book III

Home Sweet, Home Free

If a real estate agent doesn't negotiate a fair and equitable commission for himself, will he negotiate a good price for your house when dealing with buyers? If you're looking for a good deal overall, the commission may not be the best place to cut corners.

✔ **Quote a reasonable listing price for your home.** Beware the agent who quotes the highest listing price. He is likely trying to tempt you with false promises to get you as a client. When you interview real estate agents, ask them not only what listing price they would assign your house but also how they determine this price. You'll quickly sense how knowledgeable the agent is about houses in your neighbourhood, as well as the real estate market in your price range. Take a look at Chapter 4 to find out how you can get a pretty good idea of what's reasonable — and why pricing your home too high initially is a big mistake.

✔ **Have a good track record.** Ask the agent how many years she's been working as a real estate agent. Ask for references — get the names and numbers of at least three people whose homes she's sold in the past year or two. Call the references your agent provides. If the people you speak to have mixed feelings about the way the sale was handled, find out what went wrong and how, looking back, they would have prevented it. Hindsight is always 20/20. What questions will they ask real estate agents next time they are preparing to sell?

✔ **Have a stellar local record.** If you're selling a starter home in the suburbs, the best real estate agent in the neighbouring city isn't the right choice for you. You want an agent who works full time in your area. Your agent's networking and connections are, in fact, the most valuable marketing tool available to you. The more local agents (and therefore buyers) that your agent works with, the larger the pool of potential buyers for your home.

Working with your local real estate star, you'll see that the agent knows your neighbourhood inside and out. A well-versed local agent knows what homebuyers are after, and how to showcase your neighbourhood and community. Chances are good that the agent has an idea how to sell your house from the moment she pulls up to the curb.

✔ **Sell houses like yours.** The agent who sold the largest number of local monster homes last month is not the best candidate to sell your starter home. Hire an agent who lists and *sells* lots of other starter homes — someone who's constantly working with people in the market for a home like yours, and who understands which buyers will be interested.

✔ **Make selling your home a priority.** Be alert to signs that the real estate agent won't have time to personally work on marketing your house. Some top-selling agents just have too many listings to personally take care of your property. Their assistants take care of the legwork, attend open houses, schedule showings. You don't want to find out partway through the process that the agent you so carefully selected has delegated your listing to an assistant.

But a busy agent is busy for a reason. If your real estate agent has many listings, that means many phone calls to sell other homes. If your agent is in demand, he's probably a good one.

Similarly, you don't want to list your house with an agent whom you'll never see again until the listing is ready to expire and they swing by to renew the contract. If the agent is planning an extended vacation in the near future, or heads off to the cottage on weekends, don't use that agent! Sometimes selling your house takes longer than you think it will, even when the price is right. For all the work you are doing to keep your property looking its best, you don't want to let buyers slip through your fingers while your agent is cavorting with the locals in Bora-Bora.

✔ **Be Web-proficient.** The Internet is a great research tool and is radically and rapidly changing how the worldwide real estate market works. An agent who has been inspired to be proficient on the Web is an agent who can adapt and innovate along with the times.

✔ **Have specific ideas for marketing your home.** You can even request a written marketing plan from each of the real estate agents you interview. The marketing plan should include the listing price for your home, a list of comparable properties on the market, recommendations for making your home more marketable, plans to advertise and promote the property, and details on how the agent intends to manage open houses.

✔ **Be enthusiastic about the prospect of working with you to sell your home — from start to finish!**

Build a list of real estate agents to interview. Once you've decided to sell your house, you'll start to notice "For Sale" signs and "Sold" signs posted on people's lawns. Take a walk around the neighbourhood and write down the names and phone numbers of the agents who have the most signs up. The more "Sold" signs the better. Presto! You have a list of agents who are clearly active in your neighbourhood and skilled at closing deals. Interview them. Talk to people you know who have bought and sold houses recently. Add to your list the names and numbers of local real estate agents who come with good recommendations.

What to ask your agent

Once you've got a healthy list of agents to interview, consider some of the following questions that will quickly narrow it down.

✔ Are you a full-time real estate agent?

✔ How long have you been in the business?

✔ What area do you work in primarily?

✔ Do you use the Internet as a sales tool?

✔ Do you have a Web site?

✔ Do you have access to real estate portals such as www.mls.ca?

✔ Do you take colour digital photographs of homes to post online?

✔ Do you typically sell houses in any specific price range?

✔ What asking price would you recommend for our house?

✔ How did you determine the asking price for our house?

✔ What specific ideas do you have for marketing our house?

✔ Would you be present at all showings of our house?

✔ Do you use lock boxes? If so, how do you log visits?

✔ How many local homes in our price range did you sell last year?

✔ Can I get the names and numbers of three people whose homes you sold in the past two years?

✔ How will you keep me informed once my home goes on the market?

Don't Let Your House Come Back to Haunt You — Hire a Good Real Estate Lawyer

In case you're wondering whether you need a real estate lawyer to help with the sale of your home, the answer is yes. Emphatically, YES! There's a reason law school takes *years* to get through — because laws are complex and sophisticated. No matter how smart you are, you need a professional. Period. Your lawyer performs a number of necessary tasks to cement your home's sale, tasks that you don't have the knowledge or resources to accomplish — unless maybe you're a lawyer yourself.

You risk losing hundreds of thousands of dollars if you try to put the sale through yourself and get it wrong. If you can spare hundreds of thousands of dollars and you really want to represent yourself, you can go ahead and gamble — it's legal. But for 99 percent of homesellers, selling their homes without a lawyer's involvement simply isn't worth the risk.

At the very least, you require a lawyer (or a notary public, especially in Quebec) to handle the change of ownership for your home, even if you're selling the home privately. Don't forget, a real estate lawyer has liability insurance as a safeguard in case any problems arise with transferring the title for your home.

Picking the right real estate lawyer

Recommendations from friends, family, and business associates give you the best place to start your search for a top-notch real estate lawyer. Often banks work with real estate lawyers, and your local bank manager may be able to give you the names of some of the lawyers they use.

Your provincial law society also has names of local real estate lawyers — get a list of names and telephone numbers so that you can make further inquiries. When you call the lawyers on your list, ask them to estimate how much work will be required for your particular circumstances, and what the approximate costs will be.

Cost out lawyer's fees

When you call your lawyer to make an appointment, ask how much it will cost (as if you need to be reminded), what approximate amount you will have to bring into the lawyer's office, and the preferred method of payment. Make sure that you specifically ask for the *"all in"* cost, which will include all your legal fees, any applicable taxes and adjustments for property taxes, and other pro-rated fees.

Lawyers charge a flat fee, usually around $300 to $500, but that's not the total cost of their legal services. You also pay disbursements and taxes. *Disbursements* are any fees that your lawyer encounters while working for you. (Disbursement fees can include, for example, courier fees, registration fees, long distance phone calls, reproduction costs for documents, and any other costs your lawyer pays on your behalf.) And, of course, you're responsible for the tax on any goods or services provided. An average "all in" cost for the straightforward sale of a residential property with a single mortgage, which can be discharged using the proceeds of sale, may be about $1,000, give or take a few hundred dollars. The cost varies, however, depending on the complexity of your case.

You should also ask what your lawyer's rates are, in the event that something goes wrong and you need extra services. Most of the time, extra services can be obtained on an hourly-rate basis.

Know when to contact your lawyer

Most home sellers go to their lawyers *after* they have signed the sale contract. For simple, straightforward sales done through a real estate agent, you can safely wait to see your lawyer until you have the accepted conditional offer in hand. If you're selling privately or if yours is a complicated sale, ideally your lawyer reviews the conditions of sale prior to you signing any agreement of purchase and sale.

If you're selling through an agent, a typical scenario may run something like this: Your agent comes over to your home at 7:00 p.m. with the buyer's offer. The buyers will pay the price you want, but there are a few *conditions* (see Chapter 3 for a discussion of conditions). Your agent thinks the conditions are typical and shouldn't evolve into any problems, but you would like a second opinion from your lawyer. You need to make up your mind quickly and want to jump on that great price. Unfortunately, your lawyer closed up shop at 5:00 p.m. So you write in a clause making the contract or agreement of purchase and sale subject to your lawyer's approval within 24 hours and you go ahead and sign. If you have an experienced and reputable agent, there shouldn't be any problems with this strategy.

In a private sale, the prudent course is to review the conditions of the offer with your lawyer before signing anything. Because you don't have a real estate agent to review the conditions of the sale agreement, you take a significant risk if you accept the offer unadvised. Most buyers' offers are not made and sealed in a slam-dunk time frame. At a minimum, the *subject to lawyer's review* clause allows you to sign the contract and still have a safety hatch in the event that your lawyer subsequently discovers problems. Provincial real estate associations across Canada have standard forms for their contracts of purchase and sale, which have been created by lawyers. If your buyer uses one of the appropriate standard provincial forms such as the Ontario Real Estate Association's document (shown in Chapter 3), chances are that your lawyer will not uncover any problems with the paperwork involved. However, the content of the offer may still need to be reviewed. If you fear your home's

Book III

Home Sweet, Home Free

sale is going to get complicated, talk to your agent to get an idea of the *likely* conditions before you see any buyers' offers. Your agent can help you compile a list of possible scenarios to present to your lawyer for an expert legal opinion. Armed with the advice of your agent and your lawyer, you're as ready as you'll ever be to evaluate an offer that comes in late on a Saturday night.

Definitely make the offer subject to review by your lawyer if your buyer stipulates conditions that your agent views as strange, or you have a rental unit on your property and the tenants will remain once the new owners take possession. If your lawyer is also your brother, and he's willing to get out of bed at one in the morning to come over and review the offer on the spot — by all means, take advantage of your connections. It's always better to have a professional opinion. But if the timing doesn't allow for a trip to your lawyer's office and you are selling a fully residential property with a real estate agent, you have one mortgage, you are using a standard contract, and there are no unusual encumbrances or conditions, don't be afraid to go ahead and sign — that is, if you're happy with the offer.

Preparing to visit your lawyer

Give your lawyer all the necessary information right off the bat. When you call to make an appointment, ask what documentation you should bring. Your lawyer will probably ask for the following:

- ✔ Legible copy of the accepted offer
- ✔ Latest property tax bill
- ✔ Utility bills for the past year
- ✔ All mortgage information, or your mortgage discharge statement if you no longer have a mortgage, or if you intend to discharge your mortgage with the proceeds of your home's sale
- ✔ Any transfer or conveyance documents from when you purchased the home (if you still have a copy)
- ✔ Documentation for any chattels (any items you agree to leave in the house for the new owners) that are to be included in the sale and that have their own title or lease, such as a leased security system
- ✔ Any additional information relevant to the condition of your property or the title (ownership) of your property

You may be able to fax or e-mail these documents, saving yourself a trip to the lawyer's office.

Taking care of business — what your real estate lawyer does for you

Once your real estate lawyer has all the relevant information, things get cracking. The role of your lawyer and the role of your buyer's lawyer are not set in stone. Although there are some tasks commonly relegated to the buyer's or the seller's lawyer, if you would like to arrange with your buyer to do things differently, there's nothing to stop you from doing so. As the seller, your lawyer's traditional role involves the following tasks:

- ✔ Reviewing the sale contract

- ✔ Ensuring that the titles and documentation for any chattels that are included in the sale are in order

- ✔ Reviewing your mortgage information and performing or verifying calculations

- ✔ Reviewing your property tax bills

- ✔ Pro-rating to the adjustment date any annual utility costs, condominium fees, and municipality fees

- ✔ Determining if any refunds are owed to either you or your buyer, and the amount of these refunds

- ✔ Preparing a statement of adjustments

- ✔ Preparing the transfer deed

Book III

Home Sweet, Home Free

TIP

Performing a title search and verifying that there are no encumbrances (or other adverse conditions) against the property are typically the domain of the buyer's lawyer.

Choosing to Go It Alone

If you decide to sell your home without a real estate agent, your greatest asset is recognizing what you know and what you don't, what you can do yourself and what you should delegate.

Realize that selling a home privately is an "extreme" sport. In between answering the phone, scheduling appointments, verifying potential buyers' identities, confirming their qualifications with financial institutions, and showing off your home, you need to maintain a perfectly groomed house and lawn. You may also be trying to raise a family and hold down a job at the same time. Your lawyer is indispensable when it comes to arranging a title search, negotiating with buyers, and reviewing legal contracts. Fair warning: This is a time-intensive undertaking.

And the stakes are high. Selling your home is a business transaction and a legal transaction — involving your largest single investment. When it comes to marketing your home, negotiating with sellers, and dealing with contracts, you have to make a lot of decisions and do a lot of work that most people rely on their agents to do.

Be realistic and prepared to deal with all the complexities of making a private sale. This section helps you determine your limits so that you know which aspects of home-selling you can handle, and how to find a lawyer or agent to take care of the home-selling processes that you can't handle.

Saving the commission

The big reason people like the idea of selling their homes privately is the money savings they anticipate. By selling privately, you will not pay a *commission* (percentage of the sale amount that goes to the agent who made the sale). Commissions vary across Canada and from agent to agent, but they tally in the thousands. (For details on commissions, see Chapter 4.) In Toronto, for example, where many sellers may pay approximately a 5 percent rate of commission, a $250,000 house generates approximately a $15,000 commission for the agents involved — and don't forget the additional 7 percent GST payable on the total gross commission.

Selling your home yourself will probably cost less than a tenth of what you will pay if you hire a real estate agent to make the sale. However, if your buyer has an agent, then your savings won't be as great because the buyer's real estate agent will want a commission to assist in the sale.

If you want to sell your home yourself to save commission on the sale, you have to work hard. The closer you can match a real estate agent's professionalism, realistic pricing for the current market, and focus on getting the property sold, the more savings you make.

Working out the costs of selling it yourself

You're probably visualizing what you can do with all that commission money you save by selling your home yourself. Well, take those dollar signs out of your eyes! Here are the expensive and troublesome realities you face if you plan to sell your home privately:

- **You may have to lower the asking price for your home.** If a buyer is considering two identical properties with the same asking price, one being sold by the owner, one by an agent, unless you can offer your buyer a better price, chances are he'll take advantage of the expertise and facilitation provided by a real estate agent.

✔ **You incur the cost and hassle of advertising that your home is "for sale."** You will actually have to sell your house before you cash in on your saved commission. In order to reach buyers, you need to drop a significant amount of money on advertising since you won't have access to the Multiple Listing Service (MLS) and all the contacts an agent would provide. The cost of advertising in local and regional newspapers quickly adds up. Visit sites such as www.privatelist.com where you can advertise online and get lots of information on selling privately.

✔ **You are responsible for researching and accurately determining the right price for your home.** Pricing your home is very important. (See Chapter 4 regarding comparative market analysis and potential pitfalls when setting the price for your home.) If you hire an appraiser to assess the current market value of your home, expect to pay between $150 and $300 for this service. A real estate agent may offer you a *comparative market analysis (CMA)* free of charge to try to get you to list with them. A CMA states what your home is worth (its *fair market value,* or *FMV*) based on comparisons to similar homes currently for sale and recently sold in your area.

✔ **Selling your house on your own is not going to fit neatly into a schedule.** You must be very accessible — by phone, by pager, or online if you're going to sell your home privately. Expect prospective buyers to knock at your door at all times of day and night . . . regardless of how large the words "By Appointment Only" appear on the "For Sale" sign in front of your house. You will have to accommodate the needs of prospective buyers' schedules in order to show the home, and if you have a family, you also face juggling their schedules. When you sell privately, you don't have the luxury of a real estate agent who organizes and administrates the showings of your home.

✔ **The legalities involved in selling a home are considerable.** You may not be aware of special legal considerations when selling your home and you could risk being held liable by the buyers. An experienced agent is on the lookout for any possible legal issues — after all, her commission and her reputation are at stake if something goes wrong with the sale of your home. And if she by chance overlooks a legality, she has errors and omissions insurance to cover her — you don't! (See Chapter 2 regarding an agent's roles and responsibilities.)

✔ **Emotions may cloud your judgment.** You need to be professional and objective during negotiations with your buyer. Your personal attachment to the property may prevent you from being an effective negotiator. If you don't have experience at a bargaining table, you're probably not the best person to haggle with a potential buyer's experienced and well-informed real estate agent.

Book III

Home Sweet, Home Free

✔ **Real estate agents will see your "private sale" advertisements in the newspaper and they'll be calling you, too.** Like any ambitious business people, real estate agents look to expand their business, and they're in touch with the market. When your house appears available, agents will solicit you, hoping that you're tired of dealing with the headaches of trying to sell your home yourself and will hire them instead. Many will even tell you that they have a client in tow interested in seeing your house.

Listing Contracts

If your home is going to sell, buyers have to know about it. Marketing your home involves listing it either on your own or through an agent. If you are listing through an agent, you will need to fill out and sign a listing contract. The listing contract gives authorization to one or more agencies to sell your home, and specifies how much you will pay for their services. The contract is a legally binding agreement that places obligations on both you and your chosen real estate agency. You have a few options for listing your home.

Selecting your listing type

When choosing the kind of listing that's right for you, consider all the variables. What are the general market conditions? How well are other homes of the same size, price, and location selling? Do you have the time to be searching for buyers on your own? What is your top priority? Once you know what your needs are, and you know the market conditions for homes like yours, you are in a good position to decide on your listing strategy. And when you have a listing strategy squared away, you'll need to know what to expect when it comes to signing the listing contract.

There are three kinds of listings: MLS (or multiple) listings, open listings, and exclusive listings. MLS listings are the most common.

✔ *Multiple Listing Service (MLS)* **listings authorize your selling agent to work with other agencies' salespeople.** An MLS listing markets your home across Canada, reaching a huge network of real estate agents. Your agent is free to cooperate with all other agencies and gives them all full cooperation and access to your home's listing. The MLS system, along with the local real estate boards that maintain it, has very specific requirements regarding cooperation between real estate agents. MLS listings are often in the best interest of the seller, as they can give your home maximum exposure to the market. The listing contract and the MLS data indicate what portion of the total commission is payable to the buyer's agent — that is, the agent who brings along a ready and willing buyer for the property.

✔ An *open listing* **authorizes one or more agent(s) to sell your home while protecting your right to sell it yourself.** Open listings are rarely if ever used in residential real estate, but are frequently found in commercial real estate where properties or businesses are made available without being actively listed through an agent. The owner may sell the property without an agent or entertain offers that come through any agent. You, the seller, don't have to deal personally with any of the agents who are working on your behalf, and if you find a buyer, you are not obligated to pay any commission fees. Often the buyer will pay the buyer's agent a "finder's fee" for locating the property, and the seller does not have to pay commission. (The buyer's agent will have an agency relationship with the buyer, but the seller has no agency representation.)

✔ An *exclusive listing* **authorizes an agency to market your home for a specified period of time.** Exclusive listings are rare. Generally, exclusive listing contracts don't allow you to sell your home yourself during the listing period, and often involve a *reduced* commission fee, which is a benefit to you. By bypassing the MLS system, an exclusive listing means your agent's not under any obligation to show your property to other agents. Your listing agent has more control over the marketing of your home. Usually the listing agent cooperates with other real estate agents, but the listing *broker* calls the shots. (See Chapter 2 for an explanation of the role of a real estate broker.) As an exclusive listing, the property does not appear on the MLS system (see Chapter 2 for details of the MLS system) and does not get the exposure provided by the MLS database. Most sellers, however, want the extra exposure and agent cooperation guaranteed by the MLS system, and therefore sign an MLS listing.

Most people who really want to sell list their homes via the MLS system, as it gives their homes maximum exposure on the market. Because of this, many buyer's agents do not consider open or exclusive listings to be serious efforts to sell the property.

Book III

Home Sweet, Home Free

Creating your listing strategy

Deciding on your listing type depends on your needs. If you need to sell quickly, take an MLS listing — your home will get maximum market exposure. If you want the best possible price for your home, the surest way to get the right bid is to advertise to as many people as possible that your home is for sale. An MLS listing ensures that your home quickly reaches the right network of real estate agents.

The Canadian Real Estate Association's MLS Web site allows access to nearly all the MLS listings in Canada, through its links to local real estate boards across the country: www.mls.ca. In addition to the Internet, MLS listings also appear printed in your local real estate agent's catalogue. Keep in mind, though, that this printed catalogue has a bit more detail (per listing) than its online counterpart. For example, the printed version lists the property's address; the online version does not. This difference enables you to drive by the property by yourself for an advance peek. The online version's limited information is designed to protect the privacy of homeowners from the public domain — and to ensure that you talk to a real estate agent!

In some areas, versions of the MLS catalogue may be available from your local real estate board as a free newspaper.

Detailing your listing contract

A *listing contract* is a legal document that must be signed by both you and your agent, usually via standard forms that are supplied by your local real estate board. All the particulars about your home appear on the listing contract; it also states under what conditions you are willing to sell, and you and your agent's obligations. Make sure you obtain a copy of your listing contract and that you put it somewhere safe (not the same safe place you put that spare house key you haven't been able to find in five years).

If it makes you more comfortable, or if you are concerned or confused about something in your contract, you can have your lawyer review it before you sign. Remember that although you are listing with an individual salesperson, the listing contract is with the salesperson's *agency.* (So if Suzanne Smith, your real estate agent, works for Sell That House Realty, your listing contract is with Sell That House, not with Suzanne.)

A listing contract deals with three sets of issues:

- **The exact details of the property for sale:** Your home's lot specification, size, building materials, heating and air conditioning systems, number and descriptions of rooms, and other details are presented in the listing contract. Any extra items (movable things, such as appliances or furniture) or chattels included in the sale are also shown on the listing contract. (The contract also specifies if any items are *excluded* from the sale of the home; for example, the chandelier in the dining room or the hot tub.)

- **The financial particulars relating to your home:** The listing contract establishes the asking price for your home, and may disclose information concerning your mortgage (such as balance, payment schedule, maturity date), property taxes, and any legal claims on your property.

- **The precise terms of employment for your agent(s):** Your listing contract specifies who's allowed to market your home and in what manner, as well as stating the time period your home can be marketed by the agent, and what you will pay the agent for marketing your home.

Multiple Listing Service (MLS) listings all come with a standard disclosure statement so that you can reveal all your deep dark secrets — just kidding! Disclosure statements are discussed in detail in the next section.

Your listing contract does *not* obligate you to accept any offers on your home, even if the buyer fully meets the conditions of sale stipulated in the contract. A listing contract creates an agency relationship among you, the seller, and your selling agent. Throughout the selling process, your real estate agent acts in your best interest to sell the home, without misleading or making any misrepresentations to potential buyers. Turn to Chapter 2 for more information on agency relationships.

Disclosure Statements

When you sign the listing contract, you will likely be required to fill out a *disclosure statement,* also known as a *property condition disclosure statement.* The disclosure statement is a legal document in which you describe your property and all other items included in the sale to the best of your knowledge. On making an offer, buyers see your disclosure statement and they must sign it to acknowledge it has been received. For MLS listings in Canada, disclosure is usually mandatory; for *most* exclusive listings, disclosure is recommended.

Basically, the disclosure statement informs the buyer and your agent about the condition of your home, and protects you and your agent from any litigation in the event that a buyer discovers some dreadful problem with your property that you were not aware of. By providing detailed information on the condition of your home, you ensure that your agent accurately represents your property to potential buyers. You *are* responsible, however, if deliberately concealed information about your property comes to light after you have signed and submitted the disclosure statement.

Book III

Home Sweet, Home Free

Who sees my disclosure statement?

Disclosure statements are designed for the benefit of all parties in the transaction. The sellers disclose what they know about the property, and the buyer receives the disclosure statement, often using it as a starting point for a professional home inspection. Both the buyer's and seller's agents refer to the disclosure statement while viewing your home and they may point to any disclosed deficiencies when negotiating the contract.

The disclosure statement puts the onus of accuracy on you, the seller, and any misrepresentation is potentially dangerous. As the seller, you must disclose everything you know about your home, and you're obligated to disclose anything that *you should have been reasonably expected to know*. For example, if there's a minor water leak in your basement that appears only once a year under heavy rains, you should disclose that there's potentially a problem with the drain tile or foundation. The buyers will inevitably find small problems you try to hide.

By signing a legal document that states you have disclosed all knowledge of the condition of your property, should a buyer pursue legal action after becoming aware of some previously undisclosed information, *you* (the seller) are responsible for any concealment — usually *not* your agent. You are only liable, however, if you *intentionally* conceal information. If you don't disclose information because you aren't aware of the issue, it's simply a case of bad luck for your buyer. Your agent would be liable if *she* fraudulently misrepresented any details that are contrary to the information represented by the seller.

Bear in mind that most buyers will do a building inspection, and by doing so, the buyer assumes some responsibility for the condition of the house. The buyers will do their due diligence as they inspect and investigate the house. If the sellers have completed a disclosure statement to the best of their ability, and a problem surfaces that the seller was unaware of and the home inspector missed, the buyer's dispute will likely be with the home inspector and not the seller.

In many areas, the seller may have the option to simply draw a line through the disclosure statement and state on the disclosure form that "the seller makes no representations regarding the subject property, and the buyer is to do their own due diligence." This may occur where the seller lives out of town and has not seen the property she is selling for a couple of years. When a buyer gets a disclosure statement that has not been completely filled out, the buyer will be extra diligent in doing a home inspection, and may also be leery of a seller who is not willing to make any written representation about the condition of the property.

What do I need to disclose?

The disclosure statement deals with all aspects of your property. It asks you about both land and structures. A typical disclosure statement deals with three categories:

General information

This section is geared toward the land areas surrounding your property. You include information about the following, if applicable:

✔ **Public systems:** Is your home connected to public water and sewage systems, and are you aware of problems with either of these systems?

✔ **Rental units:** Do you have rental units, and are they authorized?

✔ **Encroachments, easements, and rights-of-way:** Are there any that aren't registered in your title?

✔ **Ownership issues:** For example, have you received any notices of claims on the property?

Structural information

Here you disclose information specific to your home itself. It may include any or all of the following:

✔ **Insulation and ventilation:** What kind of insulation and ventilation do you have, and are there any problems with it?

✔ **Electrical, plumbing, heating/cooling systems:** Again, are there any problems you are aware of?

✔ **Structural damage:** Is there any flooding, fire, or wind damage to your home?

✔ **Pests:** Have you had any insect or rodent infestations?

✔ **Inspections:** Has your home passed a full inspection? Do fireplaces, security systems, and safety devices meet local standards?

Book III

Home Sweet, Home Free

Additional information

This section provides blank space for any extra information that is relevant to the condition of your property, or for explanations of any problems or conditions that have previously been mentioned, or repaired in the past.

If you are selling your condominium, you need to include information about current restrictions (regarding pets, children, rentals, or use of the condominium unit) and any future restrictions you are aware of (for example, new bylaws or proposals). You also need to disclose information about anticipated repairs or major construction projects planned for the building.

It won't help you to be dishonest when filling out the disclosure statement. Even though your buyer will be relying on the word of your agent, he will also read the sale contract carefully — and you're legally obligated to disclose any known adverse conditions in the disclosure statement that forms part of the sale contract. If you lure an unwitting buyer into making an offer by misrepresenting your property in the disclosure statement, you look foolish when the buyer does his inspection and shows you to be ignorant at best, or a liar at worst. You don't want to lose a ready, willing, and able buyer because you didn't disclose all the necessary facts on the disclosure statement. And you definitely don't want to face a legal battle if your buyer later sues you for not properly disclosing the condition of your home.

Chapter 6

Sealing the Deal

*W*hen the curtain rises on your market-ready home, you need to be prepared. Think of this chapter as your coaching and cheerleading team to help you transform your home into an open house. You'll also find pointers on how to handle buyers once you've wowed them into making offers. And finally, you work your way through sale contracts and negotiations, right up to when you pass the keys on to the new owners.

Making Your House Shine

Now that you're sure about selling your old place and finding a new place to call home, you'll start to notice a big change in your attitude. Your *home* — the place where you relaxed, slept, worked, ate, raised kids, and cuddled pets — will slowly become a commodity, a *house*. And if you get top dollar for this house, you'll be in a better position to buy a great new home.

Undertaking home improvements

One of the most common selling mistakes is to make major renovations before a sale. Pouring thousands of dollars into renovations does not result in an equivalent increase in the market value of your home. Some renovations are "good" and others are "bad" in terms of a return on your investment, and you need to know which is which before jumping in with both feet. Renovations that would have fallen into the good category or the bad category will, if poorly executed, fall into the "ugly" category *and* knock money off your sale price.

Improvements that save your buyer money as the new owner of your home do increase the value of your home to some degree. For example, making your home more energy efficient means your buyer saves on heating and cooling costs. However, this renovation will probably not return more than 30 to 50 percent on your investment. In fact, there are few, if any, renovations for which you will get back all of what you put in. Here are some guidelines as you spruce up your home to sell it:

- ✔ **Inexpensive cosmetic improvements, such as repainting, are always your best bet.** Select colours from a neutral, conservative palette to repaint your house inside and out. This will make your house look brighter, larger, and well maintained. Statistics show that when you sell your house, you will recoup at least 60 to 65 percent of the money you spent on painting.

- ✔ **If interior or exterior structures of your home need improvement to make it saleable, then larger renovations may be worth the time, money, and hassle.** For example, if you neglected to add an extra bathroom to go with those two extra bedrooms you built back in 1995, and your daughters have grown up having to run across the house when nature calls, then it makes sense to add one now. As a general rule, kitchens and bathrooms are good places for renovations. Upgraded features of kitchens and bathrooms make good selling points, and on average, home sellers get about 65 to 75 percent back on the money they put into modernizing.

But if you'll never make back the money you spend, why would you even consider renovations? The fact is, if buyers recognize your home needs work, they'll factor into their offering price a large margin of error for the cost of renovations. You can either sell your home "as is," which means the buyers will pay a lower price and undertake renovations and improvements themselves, or you can undertake some good renovations yourself before you sell. Although you may never get a 100 percent return on the money you spend renovating, you may lose less than if you were forced to drop the sale price into the "as is" category.

If your timeline for selling your home is a few years down the road, you may want to make a major addition to your home. That way, you get to enjoy the new features, plus they'll add value to your home when you eventually sell. But if you're looking to sell *immediately,* leave well enough alone — it's just a bad idea.

Sometimes renovations are simply not warranted. Even though your 50-year-old bungalow could badly do with fixing up, it may not be worthwhile if you notice that all the houses that have sold on your street have been torn down to build spanking brand-new monster homes. If people are buying into the neighbourhood for the land, rather than the house that sits on the land, don't waste effort and money on what will become demolition debris.

If you're thinking about renovating, you should talk to your real estate agent. If you aren't using an agent, a good place to go for information is the Canada Mortgage and Housing Corporation (CMHC) or the Canadian Home Builder's Association. Both organizations offer many products dealing with home renovations, and have plenty of free information available on their Web sites (www.cmhc-schl.gc.ca and www.chba.ca). Also check out Homestore Canada's offerings (www.homestore.ca).

Creating curb appeal

Making a good first impression is crucial to selling your home. Potential buyers don't walk up your driveway blindfolded; their first view of your property is from the street. Your home has to look good outside as well — this is often called *curb appeal.* You never know who's going to drive by your front yard, so consider it part of the marketing strategy.

A big "For Sale" sign in front can go a long way to getting your home noticed, but you want to make sure the next reaction will be "And it looks great!" You have to draw buyers in before you can dazzle them with the built-in cabinetry and the lakeside glass walls that offer the stunning panoramic view of your private shoreline. Getting the right kind of attention requires a plan of attack.

Pay attention to special areas that may need improvement, such as dirty backyard pools and rusting swing-sets. Take the time to look around and tidy carefully, and don't just shove all the clutter into the garage and close the door. If a buyer decides he wants to take a peek to make sure both his mini-van *and* SUV will fit inside, it doesn't look good — and that could cost you a sale.

If you are planning to have an inspection or appraisal performed, now is the time to do it. As part of the spiffing-up process, you'll want to make any repairs suggested by your inspector or appraiser.

Book III

Home Sweet, Home Free

Pretty on the outside

In case you're wondering where to begin, here's a checklist of tasks to help enhance the exterior of your home and yard:

- Clean out the garage, and move any large, infrequently used items into storage elsewhere.

- Clean windows, shutters, eaves, doors, and mailboxes.

- Replace damaged window or door screens.

- Do any necessary repairs and touch up paint.

- Get out the gardening gloves: trim hedges, trees, and shrubs; rake leaves; mow the lawn; weed gardens; tend to flowers.

- Clean oil marks and stains off the driveway.

- Ensure the garage door opener is working properly.

- Clear and clean paths, patios, and patio furniture.

- Make sure your house number is visible from the street.

- Do last-minute dusting and tidying to get rid of any clutter that's accumulated over the past week.

- Pick up all junk mail regularly.

Alluring interiors

So, your home positively sparkles outside in the sunshine — great. But once a buyer moves beyond the exterior, you need to back up that great first impression with something even better inside. Just clean and tidy is fine for the outside, but inside your home there are two extra qualities you must be concerned about: neutrality and ambience.

A garage sale is a great way to get rid of closet clutter. It not only improves the look of your house for showings, but also will make moving that much easier. Now you finally have an excuse to get rid of those extra 12 toasters you got as wedding gifts.

It's not enough to be organized and spotless. Buyers who are touring your home need to be able to see themselves living in it, and that means you have to erase, as much as possible, your personality from the interior. A neutral setting lets buyers start to think seriously about your house as "my new home," and this is the first step toward an offer. Once you've visibly neutralized your house, you need to take care of all the other senses that create ambience — the smells, sounds, and feels that will make your home comfortable and inviting. Use the list in the sidebar "An inviting inside" to make sure you've covered all your bases.

If you plan to repaint, or if you are replacing countertops or fixtures, choose light, neutral colours. Painting is better than wallpaper — it is much easier for a buyer who does not share your design sense to repaint than to strip wallpaper. Light, neutral paint will make rooms brighter and feel larger, and will remove some of your personality from the decor. Simple cosmetic improvements are relatively inexpensive and make a big difference to the appearance of your home.

Be prepared to show at any time of day or night, and on short notice. Keep things clean, and have a contingency plan for your family and pets in case you get an unexpected call from your agent.

An inviting inside

Hardly know where to begin? Take a look at this list and plan to perfect your home's interior appeal:

✔ Hold a garage sale.

✔ Make renovations that you were planning on (see the beginning of this chapter for information on "good" and "bad" renovations).

✔ Repaint or touch up paint, and repair cracking plaster.

✔ Fix leaky faucets, wobbly doorknobs, loose cupboard handles, and squeaky hinges or floorboards.

✔ Clean draperies and upholstery; shampoo carpeting.

✔ Move excess furniture and belongings (especially toys) into storage — buyers will have an easier time walking around and the rooms will appear larger.

✔ Get rid of any unwelcome visitors (like those cute little squirrels that live in your chimney and the family of raccoons in the crawl space) — call an animal removal service, if you must.

✔ Wash inside windows, walls, panelling, and any other surface that may have smudges or fingerprints.

✔ Put away all small appliances and clean any large appliances that are included in the sale.

✔ Lock away jewellery and valuables.

✔ Add comforting touches such as candles or flowers; light the fireplace (if you have one and it isn't August).

✔ Have fresh towels in bathrooms.

✔ Be aware of odours (especially those you may have become accustomed to, such as cigarette smoke or pets) and take counter-measures (try baking bread or putting a few drops of vanilla in a warm oven just before a showing).

✔ Weather permitting, open windows to let in as much fresh air as possible.

✔ Place any inspection reports, records, or information sheets outlining the features of your home in plain view, with enough copies that buyers can take one with them.

Book III

Home Sweet, Home Free

Going to Market

So your home sparkles inside and out and you're ready to get the word out that you want to sell. From the sign on your front lawn to your open house, your marketing techniques are a key part of the home-selling process. Although you may be able to advertise a garage sale with a flyer posted at the end of your street, selling your home will take a bit more effort. To sell your home with the least amount of hassle — and for the highest price — you need to have a marketing plan.

The more professional you are about your advertising, the more trusting your buyer is likely to be. If selling with the help of a real estate agent, you'll automatically benefit from the image and credibility of the company your agent works for, and their marketing expertise.

If selling your house on your own, take a page from the real estate agent's book: A coordinated effort is better than a haphazard one. An agent will explore all avenues for sale and *act* like a salesperson. You should, too. Make the most of the resources available to you, type any information sheets instead of handwriting them, use professional signage, and be polite to buyers.

Your basic "For Sale" sign

If you have a yard, posting a "For Sale" sign in it is one of the best ways to attract buyers. If they're interested in your neighbourhood, buyers will tour the area looking for potential homes. Don't let them miss yours. Your sign should be prominently displayed (perpendicular to the road) and list a number where your real estate agent or you, the homeowner, can be reached. If it's a corner lot, maximize your exposure by putting a sign facing each road, providing local bylaws allow more than one sign.

Consider yourself warned: Unless you put the words "Shown by Appointment Only," your buyers may come knocking at any time of the day or night. In fact, they may come knocking at any time, regardless.

If you're selling on your own, give yourself an edge by investing in a quality "For Sale" sign. On the Internet, check out www.privatelist.com — a Web site for private home sellers — for information about spiffy signs and other issues related to selling privately. You can also look up signs in your Yellow Pages and call local shops for quotes. The sign should say "Private Sale" or "For Sale by Owner" and include a phone number or pager number where you can be reached easily.

Advertise, advertise, advertise

The purpose of placing an advertisement is to get people to phone and book an appointment. You want to give the basic information — such as number of bedrooms, general location, kind of house (bungalow, split-level), and key selling features. Make sure you include the price, which will encourage only serious buyers to call. A good ad will tempt, but not give it all away: After all, you want to entice buyers to actually come by and see your home.

Listing in the newspaper

If you're selling with the help of an agent, you won't have to take care of writing and placing ads in local newspapers and real estate weeklies. However, you can help out your agent by identifying the key selling features of your home. Make a list of the top five or ten reasons you bought the place, and your agent will incorporate these key factors in the ads if they help increase your home's appeal.

Weekend ads generally have a greater readership, but the best coverage is achieved by taking out both a weekend and a daily ad.

Check out the competition. How can you make your house stand out in comparison? Buyers read through real estate advertisements with their own criteria in mind, so put front and centre the amenities that will capture the attention of your target market. Your home's proximity to great schools, its waterfront location, the award-winning design, or an unbeatable view deserves mention in your print advertisements.

If you're selling privately, use the words "Private Sale" or "For Sale by Owner" in your ad. The potential to get a good deal through shared savings on the commission is an excellent selling feature. If you are willing to cooperate with buyers' real estate agents, put "courtesy to agents" or "will cooperate with agents" in your ad. Some buyers will not deal directly with a seller and would prefer to have their agent contact you to coordinate a showing. Some agents will call with prospective buyers for your house; others will be interested in listing your house. Whether or not you decide to use an agent's assistance in selling your home, take the time to talk with them. An agent can offer you great advice on competitively pricing your home, and potentially assist in the sale of your home.

Many real estate agents will be pleased to work with you. If an agent brings you a buyer and you can negotiate a commission fee, you may just have a deal. And since the point here is getting your house sold, it's definitely worth considering.

Book III

Home Sweet, Home Free

Real estate agents are a home seller's number one marketing tool since they're constantly in touch with potential buyers and other agents. The majority of home sales are completed through agent-to-agent contact, not by advertisements or "For Sale" signs.

Reaching beyond your local newspaper

Where else should you advertise? Specialty real estate publications are the most targeted, but you should also advertise regularly in the newspapers, particularly the issues that run the most house listings. You may also want to advertise in national or city-specific papers, as some buyers may be relocating.

Buying a home is a serious business, so you will be wise to treat it as such. Buyers will be wary of giveaways, gimmicks, or anything else that smells of double-dealing. In any advertising, be flattering but sincere when you describe your home. In the end, your home will speak for itself.

In this Web-savvy time, realize that many homebuyers let their fingers do the surfing when they're looking into new homes. Advertising your house on the Internet is a great way to maximize your house's exposure. If you're dealing with a selling agent, ask her whether she'll be listing your home on the company Web site, or even better, the MLS site at www.mls.ca. You can find more about listing on the Net in Chapter 2.

When people phone you, ask them how they heard about your house, so that when it comes time to review your progress, you can stop advertising that isn't producing any results. Advertising will cost money, but missed buyers will cost you more.

Sexy feature sheets

A *feature sheet* is the classy, showy older sister to the newspaper ad. It includes the same basic information — kind of house, number of bedrooms and bathrooms, approximate square footage, neighbourhood, price, and contact telephone number — but it also uses colour and strong design elements to make an impressive pitch for your house.

Selling with the help of an agent? If so, chances are your agent will prepare the feature sheet for you. If you're selling privately, here are some suggestions for making up your own feature sheet:

 ✓ **Attend some open houses and ask for their feature sheets.** If you see a well-designed form, model your own in the same manner. Of course, you can't use any copyrighted text or illustrations, so don't plagiarize, but do take note of what information is specifically outlined and how it's presented most effectively.

✔ **Put a great photograph of your house looking its very best on your feature sheet.** If you don't already have the right shot, hire a photographer or get a talented friend to take photos using a wide-angle lens and a film type that allows for multiple prints. You may even want to use pictures of your house at different times of the year, so that prospective buyers can see how cozy your home looks with a dusting of snow and how magnificent the gardens are in the summertime.

✔ **Ensure the pages of the feature sheet are detailed, but also readable.** Don't feel you have to fill the page completely — white space allows people to focus on the important elements of your feature sheet without feeling overwhelmed, and leaves room for note-taking. Stick to a standard, easy-to-read font for the text and a simple, bold headline. If the elements of good typography are beyond you, ask a design-savvy friend to help you, or look for a professional you can pay to create the feature sheet for you.

If you have a scanner and a colour printer, you can create your own brochure. If you don't, waltz down to the nearest photocopy place; many copy shops now have computer, scanner, and quality colour photocopying facilities. Sometimes this creates a more professional-looking product.

Keep a stack of feature sheets handy to give to prospective buyers who visit. It provides a good reference when they are comparing homes and gives them a reminder of all the features your house offers. The feature sheet is a marketing tool that will keep selling your house even while you're on the golf greens or taking a nap.

Book III

Home Sweet, Home Free

Showing off: The open house

The open house is your home's big day. The basic idea is that your home is open for showing on certain designated days (usually during the weekend). An open house may cut down on the number of private showings you have to give, thereby reducing the disruption to your daily life. Also, many buyers feel more comfortable and leisurely being "one of the crowd," rather than touring on their own.

Some people feel the open house serves to introduce the agent to the buying public in general, as opposed to specific buyers for your house. This may be partly true, but in the end, the more people who see your home, the more chance there is that someone will fall in love with it. Your home should be at its best on the day of the open house, so follow the preparation tips earlier in this chapter. If you haven't already overhauled your home, before the open house is the time to do it.

If you're selling privately, announce the times and dates of your open houses in the classifieds, and post an "Open House" sticker on your "For Sale" sign with the appropriate hours showing. Buyers who happen to drive by and see the notice will think it's their lucky day. Make sure everyone who comes to the open house gets a copy of your feature sheet. Plan ahead so that you don't book an open house on a long weekend — it will probably be a waste of time. If you're not selling privately, you can rely on your agent to take care of all the organizational details of your open house.

All your neighbours — and your neighbours' friends — may troop through your house. Maybe they *are* just being nosy, but remember that word of mouth can be a great marketing tool, too. So let them talk. Give them a reason to talk! The more people who know about your fabulous home, the more potential buyers you may attract.

Whatever you do at the open house, here are three basic rules to observe:

- ✔ **Don't negotiate the price verbally.** Be firm that you will seriously consider all *written* offers.
- ✔ **Don't give a particular reason why you are selling your home.** A good standard response is, "We've enjoyed this house, but it's time to move on."
- ✔ **Don't indicate you are under time pressure to leave.** This gives potential buyers an edge when negotiating.

Recipe for a Successful Contract of Purchase and Sale

Sale contracts are a bit like pancakes. Basic pancakes need flour, eggs, and milk, but beyond that you can add blueberries, bananas, cinnamon, maple syrup, and anything else you like, whether it's in the batter itself or on top. There's no set recipe for great pancakes, but there are some common ingredients. The same goes for real estate sale contracts. The bulk of the recipe will depend on the particulars of your situation. Since no one can tell you exactly what your recipe should be, here you'll find the sorts of things that will be of particular concern to you, the seller, in some key areas. After all, when you cook with quality ingredients, you're much more likely to end up satisfied.

A dash of offer

The offer to purchase is prepared by the buyer's agent, and will usually resemble the copy of the Ontario Real Estate Association's contract of purchase and sale, which appears in Chapter 3. The "Offer to Purchase" section has a threefold function. First, it identifies the parties involved in the transaction: you (the *vendor*), your buyer (the *purchaser*), and your real estate agent (usually referred to as the *agent*). If your home is owned jointly by you and another party (perhaps your spouse or partner), both owners will be identified in the vendor section. Second, the offer will identify the home as it is registered with the local land registry office, the lot and plan numbers, and sometimes the approximate dimensions of the lot. All this information is taken from the listing contract or from the title search that either the buyer or seller (or their agents) has obtained. Last, the offer will set out the major financial details — usually consisting of the offered price and amount of deposit.

Every offer has some common elements. Make sure that all this information (some of which are discussed in greater detail in the upcoming sections) is supplied in the buyers' written offer:

- The name and address of the buyers
- The amount of the initial deposit accompanying the offer, or payable on acceptance of the offer
- The civic and legal address of the property being sold
- The amount of the buyers' initial offer
- Subjects and terms and conditions of the offer
- Items included and excluded from the sale
- Completion, possession, and adjustment dates
- Time that the offer is open for acceptance
- The buyers' signatures (witnessed where necessary)

Book III

Home Sweet, Home Free

Name and address of buyers

The buyers supply their names and addresses, so you know whom you are dealing with. If the offer is made in a company name, you will need to know the position the buyer holds in the company, and whether or not the buyer has signing authority on behalf of the company.

You should also be very careful if the buyer's name is followed by *"and/or nominee."* The buyer may intend to assign the contract to a third party (maybe the daughter who's graduating from medical school in the spring, maybe the money-laundering subsidiary of Crooked Mile Inc.), and ideally the buyer should specify who that third party (or nominee) is on the contract. If the name of the third party is not specified in writing, it *may* create ambiguity in the contract and possibly make the contract unenforceable. Your agent or lawyer can explain the proper way to assign the contract and deal with any potential problems.

Initial deposit and deposits in general

A deposit is an initial amount of money to confirm that the buyers are serious about their offer to purchase your home. A deposit that accompanies your buyers' offer forms part of the down payment when the sale is completed. We recommend that the deposit be made by certified cheque or bank draft. Indeed, in some parts of Canada, the deposit *must* be presented in this fashion.

There's no standard figure for the deposit, but from the seller's perspective, the bigger the better. If the deposit is substantial (a reasonable and substantial deposit is about 5 to 6 percent of the purchase price, depending on price range), it's less likely your buyer will consider walking away before the sale is completed. If you're buying another house based on the sale of your current home, the deposit gives you assurance that your buyer is committed to the purchase of your current home. You do not want to commit to buying a new house unless you feel secure that your buyer's offer is sincere and the sale of your home will be completed on schedule.

Initially, the offer may be presented with a small deposit ($500 or $1,000) that the buyers will increase when all their conditions are removed from the contract. If the buyers don't make a sincere effort to satisfy and remove their conditions, thereby collapsing their offer, they risk forfeiting their deposit. So, by making a small deposit the buyers risk losing less money if they change their minds about buying your home.

The buyers' deposit can be placed in an interest-bearing trust account, so that at least the buyers will earn interest on their money until the completion of the sale.

Civic and legal address of the subject property

Your home's address is included to make sure you are selling the right property. While it's not that much of an issue in towns and cities, if you are selling vacant land you should always check legal descriptions at the land registry office, especially where there may not be a street number and address. If you're unsure about your home's legal description, check your property tax notices or contact the land registry office in your area. You can find a listing in the Blue Pages of your telephone book.

Price of the initial offer

The price is your starting point for negotiations, and probably the first thing you'll want to look at when the offer comes in. If the initial price the buyers offer is at least reasonable, you can probably negotiate an acceptable price for you and the buyer. In an ideal world, the initial offer will be at exactly the price you asked for or better, and you can skip to the part where you negotiate the other terms of your sale contract. If the offer isn't everything you hoped for, see our negotiating tips later in this chapter.

A handful of covenants, a sprinkle of conditions

One of the most important parts of the agreement is the "conditions" of the sale. If you're thinking, "Of greater concern than the price?" the answer is yes. The financial details contained in the "Offer to Purchase" portion of the sale contract are easily and quickly verified. The conditions of sale may be much more complex and can be treacherous if you don't review them carefully.

In Chapter 3 of this book, you'll find a discussion of the various *subject to* clauses that are common in contracts of purchase and sale. Most subject to clauses require the buyers to do some work to satisfy the subjects, such as the buyers approving an inspection report or obtaining a mortgage. These subjects, or conditions, will be noted in the body of the contract and, in essence, the buyers are saying that they will buy your house if it passes an inspection and if the buyers can get their mortgage. There may also be subject to clauses or conditions of the contract that require the sellers to do some work. These clauses may require that you remove the junked car in the garage or repair a loose handrail by a specific time, and before the buyers will commit to buy the house.

Remember that all terms and conditions included in an offer to purchase for your home are negotiable; both parties (you and your buyer) must agree to them. You'll almost never see an offer that doesn't contain any subject to clauses. Sometimes, in a very active market where there are competing offers, the buyer will keep the subject to clauses to a minimum to make the offer as attractive as possible to the seller. Even with a plethora of competing offers, you'll usually find a quick *subject to inspection* clause inserted in the offer. You can choose to reject one or all the subject to clauses the buyer has attached to the offer, but if you do, you risk losing the offer altogether. Use good judgment; if you think the buyer's requests are reasonable, then accept them and let the buyer go about fulfilling the conditions. If one or two of them seem completely ridiculous, talk to your agent about making a *counteroffer* that excludes the conditions that you find unacceptable. Of course, if you're selling privately, you have to take care of this yourself, but do consult your lawyer for help so that you can state your terms clearly in a counteroffer.

Assuming that you do accept a few of the buyers' conditions specified in the subject to clauses of their offer, you must confirm that the items have been addressed. In effect, you're saying that yes, the buyer has arranged his mortgage or approved the inspection report in accordance with subject to clauses in your contract. You and the buyer must acknowledge that these conditions have been met so that they can be removed from the offer.

Procedures vary from province to province for removing subject to clauses from an offer. In Nova Scotia, for example, clauses are typically worded so that if no written notice from the buyer to the contrary is received by the seller, the seller can assume the buyer is satisfied. In most provinces, a standard form is attached to the offer stating that X, Y, or Z condition has been satis-fied; in Ontario you attach a *waiver;* in Saskatchewan, you attach a *condition removal form.* In British Columbia, subjects to clauses are removed using a separate *amendment.* Subject to removal documents are usually prepared by the agents on the applicable standard forms. Standard contracts and add-on forms are suitable for about 99.9 percent of home sales and are mandatory in some provinces. These standard forms are supplied by the real estate agent. If you're not using an agent, your lawyer will have these forms available.

The upcoming sections go over some of the most common subject to clauses so that you have an idea of what your buyers may include in their offer.

Subject to financing

This is the condition that the buyers include in the offer basically as a safeguard until they obtain proper mortgage financing. In some cases, the buyers' financing can require that the home be appraised at an equivalent or greater value than the purchase price. With mortgage pre-approval offered by most lenders, many of today's buyers come to the negotiating table with the security of financial backing. Even if they have a pre-approved mortgage, most buyers should make their offer subject to financing for a short period (a couple of days) to allow the lender to do an appraisal and confirm that the accepted offer is fair market value. If the buyers do not have a pre-approved mortgage, five to seven business days should be adequate for a bank to arrange a new first mortgage. Like all subject to clauses, the *subject to financing* clause must include a date by which it must be removed. A commonly worded subject to financing clause reads like this:

> "Subject to new first mortgage being made available to the buyer by _____, in the amount of $_____ at an interest rate not to exceed ____% per annum calculated semi-annually, not in advance, with a ____ year amortization period, ____ year term and repayable in blended pay-ments of approximately $_____ per month including principal and inter-est (plus 1/12 of the annual taxes, if required by the mortgagee). This condition is for the sole benefit of the buyer."

Subject to financing clauses require the buyers to make a true effort to arrange the required financing. They're not permitted to just sit at home and say, "We couldn't get it." If you think that a buyer did not make a good-faith effort to get financing, and can prove it, you may be in a position to refuse to return the initial deposit if the offer falls apart because this condition has not been met. This is where lawyers get involved, but keep in mind that a clearly worded subject to financing clause and a true concerted effort by the buyer will eliminate the need for lawyers and disputes related to financing subjects.

Subject to inspection

Most offers these days have a *subject to inspection* clause, the condition that the home passes a full inspection. No matter how well you have maintained your home, be prepared to have an inspection conducted by the buyer. If you had your home inspected prior to listing, you shouldn't have any surprises with your buyer's inspection. If your home is relatively new and it passed an inspection before you purchased it, and you have not seen any evidence of problems, you probably don't need to worry about an inspection turning up anything significant. If you own an older home in which the major operating systems and structural components have not been updated or replaced in decades, this condition may become an issue. Even if your home seems to be running smoothly, you may be in for some unpleasant surprises come inspection time. Typically, the clause will read something like this:

> "Subject to the buyer, at their own expense, receiving and being satisfied with an inspection report from a certified building inspector of their choice on or before _____. This condition is for the sole benefit of the buyer."

The main reason against having your own pre-listing inspection is that, should it reveal any problems, you are legally obligated to disclose that information. Disclose everything in writing to avoid future problems.

Subject to sale

Buyers often make an offer conditional on the sale of their previous home prior to an agreed-on date. Perhaps your buyer doesn't expect to have any problems selling his home, but is simply playing it safe. But perhaps he's in a position to make only a conditional offer because he thinks he'll encounter difficulties in unloading his own property, and he has to sell his home to be able to buy your house. We discuss in Chapter 4 why buying before you sell is dangerous. It's your call whether you should accept an offer with this sort of condition. If you are confident in your buyer's ability to sell his previous home, or if you feel you are not in a position to be rejecting reasonably priced offers (conditional or otherwise), then accepting may be the best course. But if you are in a seller's dream market (such as downtown Toronto)

Book III

Home Sweet, Home Free

and you have no doubt that another, unconditional offer will be forthcoming, you may wish to hold out for the better offer. Talk to your agent about market conditions in your area and how they should influence your perception of a "good" offer. The sale clause could be written as follows:

> "Subject to the buyer entering into an unconditional agreement to sell the buyer's property at 123 Main Street, Anywhere, Saskatchewan, by _____. This condition is for the sole benefit of the buyer.
>
> However, the seller may, upon receipt of another acceptable offer, deliver a written notice to the buyer or the buyer's agent [enter name of the buyer's agent and company name] requiring the buyer to remove all conditions from the contract within 12/24/48/72 hours [choose one] of the delivery of the notice. Should the buyer fail to remove all conditions before the expiry of the notice period, the contract will terminate, and all deposit monies will be returned in accordance with the Real Estate Act."

The portion of this clause starting with "However" is known as the *time clause*. This clause is extremely important if you think that you may receive other offers while this buyer is trying to sell his home. The length of the notice period is negotiable and can be as short as 12 hours, but this puts a lot of pressure on the buyer and you will find that many buyers won't agree to this. If you are in a seller's market, you'll want to keep the notice period as short as possible, since this will allow you to deal with a back-up offer relatively quickly, if one comes in. From the buyers' point of view, the longer the notice period, the longer they'll have to arrange interim or bridge financing. And the longer they'll have to consider all their options, and the longer they'll have to sell their house.

If you need to invoke the time clause, you may want to get confirmation that the notice was actually delivered at a certain time. Although technically this is not necessary to make the notice valid and enforceable, it helps keep everyone clear on the process. The delivery can be witnessed by someone, or the buyer or the buyer's agent can sign a copy of the notice to acknowledge they have received it. At this point, there is no negotiating and you are just waiting to see who will buy your home. The notice to invoke the time clause will look like this:

> "This notice constitutes written notice from the seller to the buyer requiring the removal of all conditions (or condition) from this contract within (24/48/72) hours or this contract will terminate at the end of the (24/48/72) hour period and the deposit will be returned to the buyer. This time clause will start running on delivery of this notice to the buyer or [the buyer's real estate agency] which will be at _____o'clock a.m./p.m. on (date), 200_. Therefore, the [24/48/72] hours will terminate at _____ o'clock a.m./p.m. on [date], 200_."

In some provinces, you may have to exclude Sundays and statutory holidays from the time clause. In this case, the clause will read "24/48/72 hours excluding Sundays and statutory holidays." Your agent or lawyer will know local provincial regulations.

Escape clauses

Another category of subject to clauses depends on a third party or requires the approval of one party to the contract. These *third party subject clauses* are often called *escape clauses* or *whim and fancy clauses,* because either party can simply withhold approval and walk away from the contract.

One of the most obvious escape clauses is *subject to a relative or friend reviewing the contract.* This is very ambiguous and hard to enforce, and you should do everything you can to avoid such a condition. Another escape clause would be *subject to the buyer obtaining financial advice.* The buyer should have received financial advice before writing the contract — this is an extremely obvious escape hatch.

You or your agent should recognize escape clauses and try to keep them to a minimum, and where they are necessary keep the time frame as short as possible. Generally, a contract with an escape clause is unenforceable until the subject is removed.

Clauses introduced by the seller

Few vendors are concerned with what happens to the property once it has been sold. However, there may be some cases where the vendor would like to place restrictions or obligations on the new owners of the property. For example, if your home is just this side of being designated a Canadian heritage site, you may want to stipulate in the contract of purchase and sale that the new owners respect the home's historical significance. Such a clause would state that the new owners were forbidden to undertake any major additions or renovations to the original structure other than restorative projects to preserve the character and historical importance of the building. However, most covenants of this sort come with the land and are not the prerogative of the seller to introduce.

If your property has municipal or provincial conditions restricting the use of the property, they should be clearly outlined in the contract to protect you from any future actions by the buyer. If you are not in an unusual position like the one mentioned above, and there were no restrictions or obligations placed on you when you bought the property, you should not attempt to introduce these sorts of clauses.

Book III

Home Sweet, Home Free

Subject to seller's purchase

Another clause that you as a seller may need to include is a *subject to purchase* clause. This condition stipulates that the buyer's offer to purchase will be accepted only if the seller's offer to purchase another home is in turn accepted. Such a clause would be written into the contract of purchase and sale as follows:

> "Subject to the seller entering into an unconditional agreement to purchase the property at _____ by _____.
> This condition is for the sole benefit of the seller."

Subject to purchase clauses are not very common, so it is always a good idea to let the buyer know the seller's plans in advance so that the buyer won't be surprised to see a seller's condition added to the contract.

What's included — fixtures and chattels

Anything that is fixed to the structure of your home (known as a *fixture*) is assumed to be included in the purchase price unless otherwise stated. Anything movable — appliances, furniture, and the like, known as *chattels* — is assumed to be excluded from the sale. Nonetheless, in some provinces, appliances are typically included in the sale price. Find out early in the process what the conventions are for your area. Now is the time to exclude from the sale anything the buyers may think they will be getting, whether it's your fabulous new and astonishingly silent dishwasher, or your great-grandmother's antique chandelier.

The contract of purchase and sale will list exactly what is, and what is not, included in the sale. How would you like to buy a home in Moose Jaw, and take possession in February only to discover the furnace had been ripped out of the basement? These kinds of events are not common, but they have been known to happen. Clearly this section of the contract is of greater importance to the purchaser — the one likely to get the short end of the stick. But you need to do a quick review of this section as well, just to ensure that everything you want to take with you will be yours come moving day.

Time frame of the offer

The time frame of the offer is one of the most important elements of your contract of purchase and sale. This element states that the offer is valid only for a certain length of time. If this length of time expires before the offer is accepted, the offer is null and void and the deposit is returned to the purchaser unless both parties agree to extend the time for acceptance.

The *completion date* is the date on which the buyers pay their money and have the house registered in their name. The *possession date* is the date the buyers assume possession of the property. If all conditions have not been met by the *subject removal date,* the offer can be withdrawn and the transaction terminated.

Pay extremely close attention to these dates. Most contracts hold the vendor responsible for the property until the completion date. If a fire ravages your home the day before the completion date, it's *your* problem. From 12:01 a.m. on the completion date, the property and all included items will be at the risk of the buyer. The buyer will actually have insurance on the house hours before the house is registered in his name.

Arrange to have your insurance policies terminated on the closing date and not before. If possible, avoid the last day of a month or year as a closing date. These are busy days for banks, creditors, insurance providers, and most administrative staff that will be involved in processing the new information generated by the sale. This means you are at an increased risk of otherwise avoidable delays in registering the sale of your home.

If you have rental units

The contract of purchase and sale becomes considerably more complex if your home has rental units and your buyer intends to continue renting out these parts of your property. This aspect is typically a larger headache for the buyer than for the seller. However, if you have tenants at the time of sale, be prepared for some extra hassle. For example, if you live in Ontario, you will have to sign a statement to the effect that you are charging a legal rent. If it turns out you are not charging a legal rent, you're not only in trouble with your tenants, but also with your buyer and your provincial rent-control authority. The possible obstacles are far too case-specific to deal with here — so all you'll find here is some general advice.

If you have a rental unit and are selling to a buyer who intends to continue the tradition, speak to your agent or lawyer about the legal and contractual consequences *before* signing the contract of purchase and sale. If you are getting close to an agreement on price and you want to keep negotiating, you can go ahead and accept the offer, but make it subject to consulting with your lawyer if you have concerns. In many parts of the country, a copy of the rental agreement may become an addendum or schedule to the contract. If the buyer wants to terminate the tenancy, the buyer will request in the contract that the seller give legal and binding termination notice to the tenants in accordance with the provincial tenancy legislation.

Book III

Home Sweet, Home Free

A pinch of acceptance

This final section of the contract is quite simple. Once the contract has been negotiated to your and the buyer's satisfaction, all that remains is to sign on the dotted line (as well as filling in the appropriate dates and seals), and accept the offer subject to the terms and conditions outlined. You must make sure that both parties have initialled any changes made to the contract and that all signatures have been witnessed where necessary.

Controlling the Negotiating Process

In reality, the first step you'll take as a seller in the negotiating process is setting the asking price for your home. (See Chapter 4 for more on setting the price.) Whether or not you're using a real estate agent, your asking price lays the groundwork for the selling process. It can affect how many offers you receive, and it's the springboard from which you'll dive into the deep and murky waters of conditions, terms, and clauses.

Only consider written offers

Don't negotiate until you get a written offer. And don't sign *anything* until you've consulted with your real estate agent or your real estate lawyer (or notary public, if you live in Quebec). You need a professional to make sure the contract is legally binding and the terms and conditions represent you properly. This is tricky stuff. If you have even a signature in the wrong spot, the contract may be null and void.

Don't dismiss early offers. Houses often generate the best offers earliest in the process when they're fresh on the market — and you never know when, or if, the next serious offer will come. Remember that an offer represents an opening bid to start negotiations. Both the buyer and the seller want the same thing: the best possible price and terms of sale. Each party can make certain concessions and certain gains.

The offer may seem to be overly detailed and specific, but to ensure you have a binding contract with no misunderstandings, every detail should be written into your purchase agreement. It may seem silly to include little things like remote garage door openers in the contract, but it's those little things that can drive you crazy if they're not clearly specified in writing.

When you get an offer, your options are to accept it, reject it, or "sign it back," that is, return it to the buyer with a counteroffer proposing a different price or different terms. Review the offer with respect to each of the following considerations.

How low will you go?

First and foremost, we're all interested in the prices we pay for our purchases. Your home is not just a purchase, though; it's an investment — and if you've cared well for your home, you should hopefully be able to make a profit when it comes time to sell the place. Determining what your home is worth in the current housing market takes a bit of analysis. Chapter 4 has detailed information on estimating a realistic sale price for your home. But once you've figured out your listing price, you also need to decide what is the lowest offer you'll accept.

Remember that the initial offer is the buyer's starting point, just as the list price is your initial bargaining position.

Entertain any and every offer you receive. Don't reject anything out of hand, unless your lawyer or real estate agent strongly advises you to do so; make a few changes to the agreement and counter your buyer's offered price. If a buyer is interested enough to write up the paperwork, you have a better-than-decent chance of negotiating a price you're willing to accept.

Remember that negotiating requires give and take. If you don't give buyers an idea of your flexibility, they won't take the time or effort to pursue an agreement. A buyer may be truly interested in getting your house, but put in an offer that cuts $25,000 off the asking price. Don't tear it up; he may be following the "you can't blame a guy for trying" philosophy. The response to your counteroffer may surprise you by being, "Yeah, okay."

"Only if you promise to . . .": Negotiating the subject to clauses

Subject to clauses are a buyer's safety-hatch — a way to escape the contract of purchase and sale if something goes wrong. If a buyer needs to sell his home before he can afford to buy yours, he may make his offer *subject to sale,* meaning that his offer to buy your home will be confirmed only once he's been able to secure the sale of his own current residence. (See "A handful of covenants, a sprinkle of conditions," earlier in this chapter for details.) Three of the most common clauses on an offer to purchase are *subject to financing, subject to inspection,* and *subject to sale.*

- ✔ **Subject to financing clauses** don't offer much room for negotiation. A buyer can't remove this subject clause during the offer/counteroffer process, unless perhaps she has a lot of equity and doesn't really need a mortgage, or requires a small and easy-to-get fast mortgage. Remember, if the buyer didn't need a mortgage, she likely wouldn't have made the offer subject to financing in the first place. You can try to negotiate a shorter time limit for the buyer to arrange her mortgage, however. Often too, a buyer will have a pre-approved mortgage — it's usually only a matter of an appraisal to have the mortgage finalized. If this is the case, then allowing the buyer this clause may put you in a better position to negotiate other things.

- ✔ **Subject to inspection clauses** are commonly included in a buyer's offer to purchase a home. Since it should take no more than two or three days to arrange an inspection, this is an easy clause to negotiate. As with the subject to financing clause, though, you can try to negotiate a shorter time period for the inspection's completion to speed things up. Most inspectors can deliver a copy of the inspection report at the end of the inspection.

✔ **Subject to sale clauses** can be negotiated with regard to the length of time you give your buyer to sell his current home. Any buyer who already owns a home probably can't afford to carry the expense of two homes at once. You have to be reasonable here. No matter how anxious you are to move, allow the buyer a decent amount of time to list and sell his home. Usually four to six weeks is considered fair, and (depending on how badly you want to sell to this particular buyer) you can agree to extend the time period if he can't meet the original deadline.

In conjunction with the subject to sale clause, also include a time clause to keep your options open. If you're waiting for your buyer to secure financing or sell her residence, your time clause can release you to pursue another offer that arrives in the meantime.

The time clause gives the first buyer a specified time period to remove all the subject to conditions from the contract and close the sale. If the first buyer can't remove all the subjects in time, your time clause releases you from the contract and allows you to pursue other offers. See the section, "Subject to sale," earlier in this chapter for more about the time clause.

If you extend the subject to sale clause, you'll probably have to extend the completion and possession dates stated on the contract of purchase and sale. Whatever dates you choose, they'll probably change once your buyer has a buyer for his own house. Your closing date for the sale may depend on your buyer's yet-to-be-negotiated closing dates on the sale of his house.

If you've found a house you really want to purchase after selling your own, you can try to add a *subject to purchase* clause that makes your home's sale conditional on whether you can still get the house you want. But be prepared: your buyer may not be happy with this condition and may not accept its inclusion in the contract. These clauses are not at all common, but in some situations it can give you peace of mind that you won't be homeless if your dream house was snatched up before you had a chance to sell.

If you're selling a condominium, you may encounter a *subject to viewing condominium bylaws and financial statements* clause. In many provinces, the law requires that a condominium corporation provide the buyer with full information on the condo complex and its regulations. Your buyer must acknowledge in writing that the information's been received and approved. There aren't too many negotiating points here, except for the time frame and how far back into the building's history the buyer would like to go.

Expect some regional differences and extra information to be required in different parts of the country. For example, around Vancouver (where there are a number of leaky condominiums), the buyer may ask for any engineering reports or building envelope studies that are available, and the seller must provide the information to the buyer.

In most provinces, once a subject to condition in the contract of purchase and sale has been met, it's formally removed from the contract with a written *waiver, amendment,* or *condition removal form.* These legal documents are usually signed by both parties (the buyer and the seller) to confirm that a condition has been fulfilled and is no longer part of the offer.

"I never liked those drapes anyway": Including appliances and household decor

Anything permanently attached to the property is considered to be part of the package. So any built-in cabinets, built-in appliances, or wall decorations — legally considered *fixtures* — are things you'll be leaving behind for the next owners. Anything portable (*chattels*), on the other hand, is yours to keep, if you want it. Under this logic, the drapes are still yours, but the tracks they hang from aren't; Grandma Bertha's bedside lamp comes with you to your new home, but the beautiful chandelier in the entrance hall belongs to the new owners.

Anything portable that you *do* want to leave behind (the drapes, the refrigerator, the pool-cleaning accessories you won't need in your new condo) must be written into the contract specifically and listed item by item. Something else to keep in mind, though: Anything you *don't* want to leave behind is best removed before showing the house at all. If you can't do that, be sure to make it clear to everyone who walks through the door that those items are not part of the deal. You don't want prospective buyers to fall in love with an antique light fixture that you would never consider parting with, and make an offer that turns on whether or not it's included in the sale. And build *everything* (exceptions and inclusions) into the property section of the contract. If you include a built-in vacuum system, make sure you also include the attachments and powerhead for the system.

Book III

Home Sweet, Home Free

 Even if you plan to include portable items in the sale of your home, do it at the last minute. If the portable items are listed in the contract right from the start, they don't seem like bonuses when you're negotiating, since potential buyers will try to talk down your price anyway. If you wait until *after* the buyers try to talk you down, "throwing the drapes in" or including the washer and dryer may appease them as much as lowering the price.

 Don't include any leased items as part of the sale. Many companies lease security systems and water filtration systems, and if they're left with the house, the buyer will be charged. The last thing the buyer wants is to get a rental bill for a security system she thought she'd bought outright with the house. Specify in writing that the buyer agrees to assume the lease on the security system if there is a lease.

Buyers may also specify that certain items be *removed* as a condition of the offer. Some people just don't want the brown and gold linoleum and faux-wood panelling greeting them on moving day. Some buyers make big requests. For example, you may receive an offer $5,000 below your asking price and with the condition that you remove the shag carpeting. Part of your negotiations will include figuring out the buyers' priorities. Are they just looking for any excuse to cut the price? Are they willing to budge on the rug? As a concession, you may agree to remove the rug but cut less off the price. Or you could try dropping your price and leaving the rug with the property. Your agent or lawyer won't recommend any substantial changes to your home before closing — just in case your home doesn't close for some reason — but, hey, if your buyers insist that if you remove all the tacky light fixtures, and they will agree with the price of your counteroffer, you can probably agree to remove those lights.

The closing date

After having spent a couple of hours reviewing the price, the subjects, and all the inclusions and exclusions, the dates may seem relatively minor. Give yourself a breather from the contract and then refocus. The dates will be the most important factor when moving time comes around. If you can negotiate a sensible and relaxed set of dates now, your move will be much easier at a time when stress will be at an all-time high. Again, if you can get ideal dates scheduled, you may drop a little bit off the price in return for the buyer's flexibility.

The *closing date* (or *completion date*) is the day when the money changes hands and the title is conveyed to the buyer. The *possession date* is the day you receive (or give) the keys to the other party. The *adjustment date* is the day that property taxes, condominium fees, and any other annual municipal fees and utility bills are adjusted to. These last two dates should be one and the same: you get the keys, you start paying the bills.

Ideally, give yourself a one- or two-day overlap where you have the keys for your new house as well as the keys for the house you've sold. The following would be a perfect scenario, starting on a hypothetical Monday:

- **Monday:** Completion date on your present house.

- **Tuesday:** Completion date on the house you're buying.

- **Wednesday:** This is the adjustment date for the house you're buying. You get the keys for the house you're buying at 12 noon (usual time of key transfer) unless you negotiated an earlier time.

- **Thursday:** This is the adjustment date for the buyers of your house. You give the keys to the buyers of your old house at 12 noon.

This scenario gives you a chance to have a relaxing move, and still go back to clean up your old house Thursday morning before you give the keys to the buyers of your old home. The downside is that the buyers pay their money on Monday but don't get their keys until Thursday noon. This is fairly common in some provinces, and for the right price, the buyers will accept the dates once they have negotiated with you on all the terms of the agreement. In other provinces, such as Ontario, it's common to have the closing date and the possession date as the same day. If this is the case, it may be worth arranging interim/bridge financing to close the house you are buying a couple of days before your present home's closing date so that you don't have to store all your possessions, especially if something is delayed.

Discuss with your real estate agent or your lawyer how many days you'll need for the closing. If you're working with a real estate agent, you may still want one or two days to run the contract by a lawyer. In some provinces, legal documents can't be signed on Sundays or statutory holidays.

The *transfer of title* officially closes the contract when you file the paperwork at the land registry office. These offices are typically open weekdays from 9:00 a.m. to 3:00 p.m. No matter how pressed for time you are, don't even try to officially close two contracts on the same day. Leave at least one day to close the sale of your current house and transfer money before you go back down to the Land Registry Office and close the purchase of your next house.

Mulling Over Multiple Offers

If you're lucky enough to be selling your home in a red-hot seller's market, you may get competing offers on your home. This embarrassment of riches has to be treated carefully to ensure you get the offer you want in place without selling the house to two different people.

Keep the following practices in mind to ensure everything goes smoothly:

- ✔ **Keep everyone informed.** If more than one group is interested in your home, it's in your best interest to make sure everyone is kept up to date once offers are starting to be written. In the ideal scenario for the seller, the buyers enter into a bidding contest and pay up to, or over, the asking price.

- ✔ **Act in good faith.** Many buyers will not compete with another group when making an offer. Remember that what's good for the seller is not always good for the buyer. If a seller tries to get cute and delay one offer hoping to get a second competitive offer, both potential buyers may cancel their offers.

Imagine that Ken and Sue have listed their fabulous heritage house for sale. It's a hot seller's market, meaning buyers outnumber sellers, and the low inventory of homes means Ken and Sue should get close to their $499,000 asking price.

Buyers A, B, and C all see the house the first day it's listed for sale, and all come to the same conclusion: The house is gorgeous, the house is well priced, and they want it.

Ken, Sue, and their agent get together to review the offers. Buyers A were the first to notify the listing agent that they had an offer, so their offer is presented first, followed by the offers from B and C. Before making changes to any offer, Ken and Sue discuss all three offers with their agent and decide which offer has the most potential. Buyer C offered $475,000, which was all he could afford. Both A and B offered the full price of $499,000 with similar terms and conditions.

Ken and Sue decide to deal with offers A and B. A's offer is $499,000 and subject only to inspection. The dates are perfect and the $50,000 deposit is attractive. B's offer is $499,000, but it's subject to financing (with B stretching to afford the price) and inspection, with a $25,000 deposit.

Ken and Sue have a couple of options: They can choose to accept one offer as is, or with minor changes that both parties agree to, and hope that the conditions go through and the contract is fulfilled. Or, they can reject both offers as presented and ask A and B to present better offers and hope for an even more advantageous offer. In the end, Ken and Sue decide to accept A's offer. But they actually have a third option: Accept B's offer as a *back-up offer.*

Considering Back-Up Offers

In some provinces, a second offer can be accepted as a back-up offer, subject to the collapse of the first offer. Your agent or lawyer will advise you what is acceptable in your province. The offer would be worded something like the following:

> "This is a back-up offer only and is subject to the seller being released by the buyer from all obligations under the previously accepted Contract of Purchase and Sale by _____, 200_. This condition is for the benefit of the seller."

Looking at Ken and Sue's situation again, they could accept B's offer as a back-up offer subject to A's offer collapsing. B has nothing to lose by being a back-up offer for a couple of days while A has an inspection done. Should A not be thrilled by the inspection, then B would have their chance to purchase the house, subject to their own inspection and financing. If A buys the house, then B's offer would not proceed and B would get the deposit money returned to them.

The other common situation for a back-up offer is when the buyer has added a subject to sale clause to the offer and a second offer comes in, subject to the collapse of the first offer. In this scenario, the first offer should have a time clause in it, giving the buyer 24, 48, or 72 hours (or whatever was negotiated) to remove all subjects from the contract. Once the sellers have a second acceptable offer, the sellers give written notice to the first offer to remove all subjects within the prescribed time frame, or step aside so that the back-up offer will be the offer in effect. An example invoking the time clause can be found in the "Subject to sale" section earlier in this chapter.

In the best of both worlds, the sellers want to sell at their listing price and the buyers want to buy at their originally offered price. Negotiating is what falls in between.

Book III

Home Sweet, Home Free

Book IV

Investment Fundamentals

The 5th Wave   By Rich Tennant

I told Julian to take our money to Rappenship's and put it into a good company.

You want to mail your life savings to Procter & Gamble?!

RAPPENSHIP BROKERAGE

Nick's NEWS

WRAP'N SHIP

In this book . . .

Successful investing begins with a pragmatic evaluation of your long-term investment goals. Every year
will not be an up year; nor will every year be a down year.
Bear and bull markets may arrive or depart at any time.
Your goal as an investor is not to anticipate the up or
down years, but to create reasonable expectations about
how you want your investments to perform.

After creating your expectations, you can work with the
rest of this Book to determine which investments are best
for you — from stocks to bonds to mutual funds — and
which investment vehicles (such as RRSPs) to house
them in.

Here are the contents of Book IV at a glance:

Chapter 1

Setting Realistic Goals and Expectations

- -

In This Chapter

▶ Understanding risk and reward

▶ Writing down your goals

▶ Understanding the importance of compound interest

▶ Determining how much you need to invest to reach your goals

- -

*I*n this chapter, you can focus on the starting points of thoughtful investing. You can also find out why you need to determine your goals and get started on your investment plan as early as possible.

Understanding Risk and Reward

What has drawn you to investing? Maybe it's the hope that the raging stock market of the 1990s will return. Or maybe you're enticed by the idea that you can put your money to work for you by investing it.

Although the benefits of investing are often made clear in success story after success story in advertisements, magazines, newspapers, and online Web sites devoted to investing, it's important to remember that there is no gain without potential pain. That means that when you invest your money, you can lose part or all of it.

Actually, rewards and risks are usually closely related. The greater an investment's potential for reward, the greater the potential for risk and actual loss. The high-flying stock that earned a 100 percent return last month is probably the very same stock that will tumble (and tumble hard) in the months and years ahead. The same goes for bonds, mutual funds, and, potentially, real estate.

You must take on some risk in order to reap the benefits of investing. That's the bad news. The good news is that sometimes, over time, a decent investment may bounce back and make investors whole again.

What's the best you can hope for?

The best you can hope to achieve with an investment depends on the nature of the investment. Some investments — such as savings accounts and Guaranteed Investment Certificates (GICs) — offer stable, secure returns. Other investments — such as stocks, bonds, and mutual funds — depend entirely on market conditions. A return is an investment's performance over time. It's easy to calculate the best-case scenario with vehicles such as savings accounts, Canada Savings Bonds (CSBs) and GICs. On the other hand, you can never predict with total accuracy what kind of return you will get with more volatile investments such as stocks, mutual funds, and corporate bonds.

You can, however, see how these investments have performed in the past. Recent history has many investors believing that the markets can only go up. If you look at returns on some stock investments, you can understand why.

For example, according to the May 2003 issue of *Canadian Business,* one of the top-performing mid-cap stocks on the Toronto Stock Exchange (TSX) for the three-year period ending March 2003 was a company called Ultra Petroleum Corporation. It racked up a staggering three-year return of over 1400 percent. If you were lucky enough to invest $1,000 in March 2000, the beginning of a bear market at that, your money would have been worth over $15,000 three years later. That's probably close to the best three-year return any investor can ever hope for — and then some.

The best-performing stock mutual funds saw mostly dismal returns — between 1 percent and 7.5 percent. Most had negative returns over this bear market period. On the other hand, long-term Government of Canada bonds brought in about a 14 percent return.

When evaluating what you can expect from investments such as stocks, bonds, and mutual funds, a broad historical perspective is helpful. Long-term government bonds have fluctuated considerably since the 1950s, when total returns were as low as 2 percent and 3 percent annually. In the 1980s, those total returns skyrocketed to more than 47 percent. But overall, the average annual return for long-term government bonds from 1950 to the present is a more conservative 6.5 percent.

T-bills, which are short-term debt issues (more on T-bills in Chapter 4), returned about 6.5 percent average in the same period, while corporate bonds were slightly better at about 7.6 percent. Equities (stocks) have yielded the highest average annual return — about 11 percent, but have also tended to be more volatile. For investors who can't tolerate the risk of losing their initial principal (something that is possible even with bonds), safer investments with lower returns might ultimately be the better choice.

What's the worst-case scenario?

You've heard about the best you can hope for, now what about the worst? One of the worst performers on the TSX over the last three years cost investors a frightening 96 percent. In other words, $1,000 would have been worth just $40 by the end of the year, barely enough to cover the commission on a stock trade. Not surprisingly, this performance came from the technology sector, and several of this company's other technology brethren were not far off from this level of despair!

You can lose all of your money in an investment if a company declares bankruptcy.

What's a realistic course?

The good news is that if you try to choose your investments carefully — and subsequent chapters of this book give you the tools to do this — you should be able to minimize your losses. Ideally, your losses from any one investment may even be offset by the successes of your other investments.

Of course, if you're completely uncomfortable with the prospect of losing money, or if you need your money within five years, then investment vehicles such as stocks and corporate bonds aren't for you. You're better off putting your money into safer, more liquid places such as bank accounts and guaranteed investments, discussed in Chapter 2, or in a money market mutual fund, explained in Chapter 3.

Book IV

Investment Fundamentals

Realizing Gains through Compounding

Starting out as a first-time investor doesn't require a whole lot of money, which means that you don't need to wait until you've accumulated a large reserve of ready cash. You may ask: Why the big rush to start investing?

The answer is simple: You want to begin earning compound interest as soon as you can. Compound interest is actually the interest you earn on your interest. For example, if you invested $10,000 and earned 10 percent interest in the next year, your interest income would be $1,000. If you earned 10 percent again the following year, the $100 you would earn on the $1,000 (in interest you earned in the current year) would be considered compound interest.

Compounding is a compelling reason to start and keep investing for the long term because money left untouched reaps the greatest reward from compounding.

Table 1-1 shows you the power of compounding and how quickly even $100 saved or invested each month can grow under different interest rate scenarios.

Table 1-1	The Beauty of Compound Interest				
% Return	5 Years	10 Years	15 Years	20 Years	30 Years
0%	$6,000	$12,000	$18,000	$24,000	$36,000
5%	$6,829	$15,592	$26,840	$41,275	$83,573
8%	$7,397	$18,417	$34,835	$59,295	$150,030
10%	$7,808	$20,655	$41,792	$76,570	$227,933
12%	$8,247	$23,334	$50,458	$99,915	$352,992

To calculate how many years it will take to double your money as a result of compounding, use the *Rule of 72*. Just follow these steps:

1. **Determine what interest rate you think your money will earn.**

2. **Divide 72 by that interest rate.** The number you get is the number of years it will take to double your money.

For example, suppose that you believe you'll earn 8 percent annually in the coming years. If you divide 72 by 8, you can see that doubling your money will take nine years.

Focusing on a Goal

You can take the first step toward creating your investment plan by asking yourself a simple question: What do I want to accomplish? Actually, this step is your single most important move toward ensuring that your investment plan has a sound foundation. After all, these goals are the reason that you're launching a personal investment plan. So don't shirk this exercise. Dream away.

Perhaps you've always wanted to travel around the world or build a beach-front chalet. Or maybe you are interested in going back to school or starting your own business. Write down your goals. Your list of goals can serve as a constant reminder that you're on the course to success.

Don't forget the necessities, either. If you have kids who plan to go to college or university, you need to start preparing for that expenditure now. Your retirement plans fall into this category as well — now is the time to start planning for it.

Table 1-2 gives you a convenient format for writing down your goals. As you fill in Table 1-2, separate your goals into long-, mid-, and short-term time frames based on when you expect or need to achieve the goal. For example:

- Buying a vacation home or retiring ten or more years from now is a long-term goal.

- Sending your child to college or university in five to ten years is a mid-term goal.

- Buying a car in the next one to four years because you know your current model is likely to be on its last legs is a short-term goal.

As you jot down your goals, also write down their costs. Use your best "guesstimate"; or if you're not sure, search the newspaper for, say, the cost of a beachfront home that approximates the one you want to purchase. Leave the "Time and Monthly Investment" category alone for now — that column represents the next step, which you'll find more about shortly.

Table 1-2		My Goals
Time Frame	*Cost*	*Time and Monthly Investment*
Short-term:		
Mid-term:		
Long-term:		

Book IV

Investment Fundamentals

Okay, now for the tricky part. How much do you need to invest each month, and over what period of time, to achieve your goals?

Of course, you need to know an approximate rate of return before you can plan. Your rate of return will differ, depending on the sort of investment you choose. Research can help you accurately estimate your rate of return. (Chapters 2, 3, and 4 tell you how to go about getting this information for different types of investments.)

As an example, Table 1-3 shows you what you need to invest each month to earn $100,000 over different periods of time. Need $10,000 instead? Divide the monthly investment amount shown in Table 1-3 by 10. Want to save a million dollars instead? Simply multiply the amount by 10.

Table 1-3	Monthly Investments to Earn $100,000 at Varying Interest Rates		
Years	5%	8%	10%
5	$1,480	$1,350	$1,280
10	$640	$540	$480
15	$370	$290	$240
20	$240	$170	$130

If you're older, in retirement, or just plain more conservative (and like keeping a good bit of your money in accounts or investments that earn less interest), you may want to use a lower estimated interest rate in your calculations to reflect your situation.

If you're investing in another type of asset — real estate, for example — a real estate agent in your area can tell you the appreciation rate or the annual rate of return for properties in your area. You can use that rate as a gauge to estimate what you're likely to earn in future years.

For determining how much you need to sock away annually to meet your goals over a specific period of time, using a scientific calculator is easiest.

Starting Your Savings Now

Throughout the rest of this book, you'll find out about different types of investments that match your investment goals. To start out with any sort of investment, you need a cash reserve — and the amount varies, depending on your investment choice.

As you're doing your research and deciding which investments match your goals, start putting away $100 a month in an account earmarked for investment. By the time you determine the investing opportunities that best fit your needs, you should be well on your way to affording your investment.

Watching your dollars multiply can serve as motivation in itself: Your investment accounts may become as or more important to you than some of the other expenses that have eaten up your money in the past.

If you're the type who's been saving gobs of cash in a bureau drawer for a long time and now want to start earning real interest, you're one step ahead of the pack. You have the discipline. Now what you need is the knowledge and the tools.

The following chapters give you the tools you need to select investments and create an investment plan to meet all of your goals, including retirement. You also get the information you need to monitor your investments, so you can keep your plan on track.

Book IV

Investment Fundamentals

Chapter 2

Your Investment Choices: Savings Accounts, Tiered Accounts, and GICs

In This Chapter

▶ Sticking with the tried-and-true: savings accounts

▶ Tacking on more interest with tiered accounts

▶ Discovering GICs

*Y*ou can choose to be either a financial tortoise or a financial hare. As a financial hare, you can race ahead, spending everything you earn now, and have nothing later. Or, as a financial tortoise, you can pace yourself and spend responsibly, knowing that by spending a little less today, you can spend a lot more tomorrow. Assuming that you choose to be a financial tortoise, slowly and steadily socking away savings, where are you going to put those first dollars that you've set aside?

This chapter is about vehicles (investment options) that are appropriate for money that you don't want to put at great risk — for example, money that you have earmarked for emergency funds, or money that you're saving to buy a car, furniture, or a home within the next few years. By keeping your short-term money somewhere safe and convenient, you can feel comfortable putting your long-term money at somewhat greater risk. (Chapters 3 and 4 tell you about these kinds of riskier investments.)

Although they may not be the most exciting investments you'll ever make, savings accounts, tiered accounts, and GICs are worthwhile considerations for novice investors. Everyone should have some money in stable, safe investment vehicles. Savings accounts, tiered accounts, and GICs are basic savings tools and are the first step on your path to investing. These tools can help you build up the money that you need in order to start investing in other ways.

As you learn about investment vehicles through this book, you find out which ones are good for short-term investments and which are best for the long haul. How you invest your money depends largely on two factors: how long the money can remain out of your reach (time); and how much of it you can afford to lose (risk). Some investments are a lot riskier than others.

In this chapter, you find out about the safest investments for short-term money that you can't afford to lose, as well as what you need to know before you throw your hard-earned dollars into the pot.

Starting with Savings Accounts

Savings accounts are a form of investment — a very safe form. Although many banks don't pay interest on traditional chequing accounts, they almost always pay interest on traditional savings accounts. Most banks will offer a variety of accounts — some that combine an interest-bearing savings account with limited cheque-writing privileges.

For the most part, interest rates offered for traditional savings accounts differ only slightly from institution to institution. Don't expect too much, since the rates are at or near all-time lows. Today, the average savings account in Canada earns less than 1 percent daily interest. With this kind of return, it's no surprise more and more Canadians are choosing to sock money into slightly higher-yielding investments like money market mutual funds. (More on these in Chapter 3.)

When you further tack on inflation — even the very low rates seen in the past few years — that eats into your money over time, you might be asking yourself why you'd invest in a savings account at all.

There are several reasons to consider doing so. First, if you are a truly novice investor, a savings account can be the beginning of your learning process. You'll gain confidence when shopping around for the best possible interest rate, and again when you deal with the financial institution directly while opening the account.

Second, and more importantly, the money you invest in a savings account comes with an ironclad guarantee. Why? If the institution has Canadian Deposit Insurance Corporation (CDIC) insurance, your savings account is backed by the full strength and credit of the federal government. If the institution fails, the feds see that you automatically get your savings back — up to $60,000 per person, per institution, subject to some restrictions. As with any other insurance, you may sleep better knowing that it's there in the worst-case scenario.

Although putting your money in a savings account has serious limitations if it's your one and only investment strategy, having some of your money in a cash reserve makes sense. But as investments go, you wouldn't want to rely wholeheartedly on a savings account because the return on your investment is so low. Of course, factors such as fluctuating interest rates and the rate of inflation play a major role in how well your money does in this type of investment vehicle.

Web sites such as www.webfin.com publish lists of savings accounts interest rates at major Canadian financial institutions including banks, credit unions, and trusts.

Most banks charge a monthly or quarterly maintenance fee for a savings account. Some tack on an additional fee if your balance falls below a required minimum. In addition, you might be required to keep a savings account active for a specified time or face penalties.

Stacking Up Tiered Accounts

Some banks offer savings accounts with the added incentive of earning additional interest if your account balance remains consistently above a specified amount. This amount is usually at least $1,000, but it may be higher.

These types of accounts are often referred to as tiered, or as using deposit interest tiers. For example, with Scotiabank's "Scotia Gain Plan" interest rates are tiered and are up to 1 percent above the regular savings account rate. But daily balances below stated amounts (minimum $5,000) will be paid at the regular rate. At Royal Bank, the "Royal Money-Maker Plus" account pays about 1 percent interest on an account balance between $5,000 and $25,000. If you have between $25,000 and $60,000, that rate goes up to over 2 percent, and increases again to about 3.25 percent for accounts with anywhere from $60,000 to $100,000. The rates change weekly, so check for exact rates with your local Royal Bank branch.

Book IV

Investment
Fundamentals

Some tiered accounts pay no interest at all on balances below a certain threshold. Find out whether that's a realistic sum for you before opening this type of account. Also, be sure to find out if the higher rates of interest apply to your entire balance or just the portion above the minimum needed to receive that rate. Finally, keep in mind that transaction fees for tiered accounts tend to be considerably heftier than you would face with a traditional savings account.

Considering Guaranteed Investment Certificates

If your savings grow to the point where you have more money than you think you need anytime soon, congratulations! One of the places you can consider depositing some of the balance is a guaranteed investment certificate (GIC).

A GIC is a receipt for a deposit of funds in a financial institution. Like savings accounts and money market accounts, GICs are investments for security.

With a GIC, you agree to lend your money to the financial institution for a number of months or years. You can't touch that money for the specified period of time without being penalized.

Why would a financial institution need you to loan it money? Typically, institutions use the deposits they take in to fund loans or other investments. If an institution primarily issues car loans, for example, it's apt to pay attractive rates to lure money to four-year or five-year GICs, the typical car-loan term.

Generally, the longer you agree to lend your money, the higher the interest rate you receive. The most popular GICs are for six months, one year, two years, three years, four years, or five years. There is no fee for buying a GIC.

By depositing the money (a minimum of $500 at most Canadian institutions) for the specified amount of time, the financial institution pays you a higher rate of interest than if you put your money in a savings or chequing account that offers immediate access to your money. When your GIC matures (comes due), the institution returns your deposit to you, plus interest.

The institution notifies you of your GIC's maturation by mail or phone and usually offers the option to roll the GIC over into another GIC. When your GIC matures, you can call your institution to find out the current rates and roll the money into another GIC, or transfer your funds into another type of account.

Some institutions give you a grace period, ten days or so, to decide what to do with your money when the GIC matures. In most cases, though, you can specify in advance what should happen to the money by giving your bank instructions for maturation when you buy the GIC. At a CDIC-insured financial institution, your investment is guaranteed to be there when the GIC matures.

You may have heard about investment vehicles called term deposits. Depending on the financial institution, term deposits function in almost exactly the same way as GICs. In some cases, these names are used interchangeably.

Financial advisers say that GICs make the most sense when you know that you can invest your money for one year, after which you'll need the money for some purchase you expect to make. The main reward of investing in GICs is that you know for sure what your return will amount to and can plan around it. That's because GIC rates are usually set for the term of the certificate. Be sure to check on the interest rate terms though, because some institutions change their rate weekly.

Refer to Figure 2-1 to see how much money you can make by buying a guaranteed investment certificate versus investing in a savings account.

GICs are most useful as an investment when interest rates are high, as they were back in the 1980s. These days, consistently lower interest rates mean Canadians should at least consider other types of investments that are both safe and will probably earn more money over the same period of time.

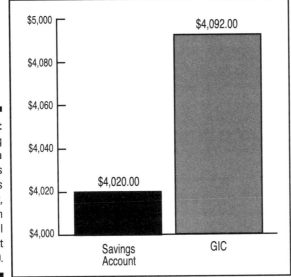

Figure 2-1: Comparing gains on a GIC versus a savings account, with an initial investment of $4,000.

Book IV

Investment
Fundamentals

The interest rates paid on GICs are contingent on many factors. While they do tend to reflect prevailing interest rates in the general market, GICs have administered rates, meaning financial institutions use discretion when setting them. For example, banks may increase rates during RRSP contribution season to attract investors. This also means rates are negotiable, depending on the size of the deposit and the relationship between the bank and the client.

Because of this flexibility, it pays to shop around for GIC specials to get the best interest rate. Remember to check out the rates at credit unions too.

If you want your money back before the end of the GIC's term, you will be heavily penalized, usually with the loss of several months' worth of interest. A second drawback is that GICs are taxable. The principal, or the amount you originally invested, is considered income. As well, whatever interest you earn on your principal (including earnings from the market-linked GICs discussed below) must be claimed as income, and is fully taxable on an annual basis. That means your financial institution will report the interest you earned during each tax year to the Canada Customs and Revenue Agency (CCRA). You will pay tax on that amount annually — despite the fact that you won't see the interest until the GIC matures.

If rates are low, you may want to purchase shorter-term GICs and wait for rates to rise. This way, you won't be tying up your funds for long periods of time while rates might be climbing. As another option, some banks might allow you to add money to a GIC account at the interest rate of that particular day. The advantage to this method is that if you open the account on a day when the rate is low, you can increase your earnings by adding money at a higher rate, later.

Before you buy a traditional GIC or term deposit, ask about the relatively new market-linked GICs being offered by many of Canada's big financial institutions. Market-linked GICs are tied to the performance of the stock market. Like GICs, your principal is guaranteed. You won't lose any of your original investment, no matter how much the stock market fluctuates. But with a market-linked GIC, instead of receiving a fixed rate of interest, your return depends on the value of the stock market during the term of your deposit. If the stock market performs well, this will probably give you a bigger return than you could get with a traditional GIC — although most financial institutions will impose a maximum cap. If the market plummets, however, you might end up with the same amount you invested in the first place.

See Table 2-1 for some suggested uses for entry-level investments.

Table 2-1	The Uses for Entry-Level Investments
Type of Investment	*Suggested Use*
Savings Account or Tiered Account (GIC) or Term Deposit	Tuck away some money in a traditional or tiered chequing or savings account to allow you to access it quickly for emergecies, such as car repairs or dentist bills.
Guaranteed Investment Certificate	GICs and term deposits are good investments if you are saving for larger-ticket items such as a down payment on a car or a major appliance items you don't intend to purchase for at least a year.

Chapter 3

RRSPs, Mutual Funds, and Your Investments

● ●

In This Chapter

▶ Finding out about RRSPs

▶ Having access to your RRSPs

▶ Realising your RRSP gains at retirement

▶ Mastering mutual funds

● ●

*T*he investment options discussed in this chapter are some of the most popular with Canadians — and the most useful. While in some cases your initial contribution isn't guaranteed the way it is in a savings account, the potential for growing your money is far superior. As well, mutual funds are managed by professionals, a fact that reduces the risk somewhat.

Parking Your Investments in Registered Retirement Savings Plans

Established in 1957, RRSPs, or Registered Retirement Savings Plans, were designed by the federal government to help Canadians invest for retirement. Anyone who earns income (as defined by the government) can place their investments into an RRSP plan, and you probably should too.

You set up your RRSP on your own, with a bank, mutual fund company or dealer, brokerage firm, credit union, trust company, insurance company or financial adviser. RRSPs can include almost anything you can think of, from aggressive growth stocks to conservative GICs. You can own as many RRSP plans as you want with a variety of institutions, but because you are often charged fees for each plan, it's wise to consolidate as much as possible.

Remember that long-term investments like those within an RRSP take advantage of long-term growth potential. That means, the earlier you start making contributions, the better. When you're in your 20s and 30s, retirement may seem impossibly far off — so far off, in fact, that it's hard to imagine planning for it now. However, if you want to retire in comfort, you have to think ahead.

Table 3-1 shows how financially beneficial it is to invest in an RRSP as early as possible. The first column shows the number of years before retirement the contributor started investing. The second column shows the accumulated balance at retirement, assuming annual contributions of $4,000 and an 8 percent annual return on investment.

Table 3-1	Investing Early for Retirement
Number of Years to Retirement	*Accumulated Savings at Retirement*
40 years	$1,123,124
30 years	$493,383
20 years	$201,691
10 years	$66,581
5 years	$29,343

Deciding not to contribute to an RRSP because you don't want to cut back on your take-home pay or telling yourself retirement is a long way off may prove to be a big mistake. Ultimately, you won't be paying yourself, and could risk ending up without enough money after you retire.

Discovering the key benefits of RRSPs

If you place your investments in an RRSP, your contributions offer two powerful, tangible benefits: First, an immediate tax deduction for the amount you've invested; and second, tax protection (a shelter) for the returns you will accrue on those investments within the RRSP until you withdraw the money at retirement.

Suppose that you earned $40,000 of taxable income this year, but made a $2,000 contribution to your RRSP. If your marginal tax rate (the highest rate of combined federal and provincial income tax you pay on the money you earn in a given year) is about 40 percent, you will achieve an immediate tax savings of $800 for this year, bringing your tax bill down from $16,000 to $15,200. That's money you will now be able to spend or, even better, invest.

Knowing how much you can contribute

Your RRSP contribution limit depends on your earned income. You are allowed to contribute a percentage of that income every year, up to a maximum dollar limit. Annual RRSP contributions cannot be greater than $13,500 in 2003. That limit rises to $14,500 in 2004 and $15,500 in 2005.

The limit can be greater if you have a carry-forward, meaning that you contributed less than your limit in previous years. The limit goes down if you are also contributing to a company pension plan or participating in a Deferred Profit Sharing Plan.

Your RRSP contribution limit is 18 percent of your prior year's *earned income*, less the prior year's pension adjustment reported on your annual T4. Earned income includes employment earnings; net income from self-employment; royalties; provincial disability pensions; alimony or separation allowances received; employee profit-sharing-plan allocations; and supplementary unemployment benefit plan payments (not Employment Insurance, or EI); *less* current year's loss from self-employment or an active partnership; deductible alimony and maintenance payments; and current-year rental losses.

Note: The government presented its 2003 budget on February 18, 2003. The proposed contribution limits are $14,500 for 2003, $15,500 for 2004, and $16,500 for 2005. In 2006 and thereafter, the limit will be capped at $18,000. In 2007, the $18,000 limit will be indexed for inflation. At tax time, check with your bank to confirm whether these proposed limits kicked in. In all likelihood, they will.

Deciding where to put your RRSP money

A very broad range of investment vehicles is eligible to go into your RRSP, including the following popular ones that are discussed in this book:

Book IV

Investment Fundamentals

- ✔ Deposits in savings or tiered savings accounts
- ✔ GICs and term deposits
- ✔ Stocks
- ✔ Bonds
- ✔ Mutual funds
- ✔ Mortgages

Depending on your risk tolerance, you can buy RRSPs that focus on different types of investments. Guaranteed plans invest in vehicles that guarantee you won't lose your principal, like GICs, and CDIC-insured savings accounts. With a guaranteed plan, you will know ahead of time exactly how much and how fast your money will grow. Variable-rate plans don't necessarily guarantee your initial investment, but can be very safe and offer far better returns. Those returns will fluctuate, however, since you can't predict the performance of the investment vehicles, like mutual funds or stocks. Keep in mind that with stocks and mutual funds, you have the added option of investing in a variety of fund types whose risk ranges from conservative to aggressive.

You don't have to choose just one kind of investment for your RRSP. In fact, unless your research tells you otherwise, you should invest only a certain percentage of your money in a high-risk investment, such as stocks. To determine what percentage of your money to invest in stocks, many financial advisers recommend that you subtract your age from 100. For example, if you're 25, you should invest 75 percent of your money in stocks.

When considering an overall investment portfolio, some financial planners advise using RRSPs for more conservative investments. The thinking here is that the tax-deferring power of your RRSP will compensate for lower returns. In other words, why jeopardize your retirement savings with high-risk investments when the real return on a more conservative RRSP investment may be only slightly lower?

Managing self-directed RRSPs

Most Canadians set up their RRSPs through a financial institution like a bank or mutual fund company. The institution puts your money into RRSP-eligible investment vehicles for you. Novice investors often choose this type of RRSP because they don't feel confident enough to do otherwise.

However, for those who want more control over their investment choices, you can set up what's called a self-directed RRSP, which allows you to pick and choose investment vehicles from wherever you want. Think of a self-directed RRSP as a shopping cart for the savvy investment consumer. Once you've chosen a particular investment, you place it in your cart to take advantage of the RRSP benefits discussed earlier.

You can register your self-directed RRSP with a financial institution or brokerage house, which becomes a trustee of the RRSP. In exchange, you may have to pay a yearly fee of about $100, although that fee is negotiable.

If you decide to set up a self-directed RRSP, you can transfer into it money you've already placed inside other RRSPs to create a single RRSP. To do so, you will have to fill out a special form provided by the federal government and pay a fee.

Even the savviest investment consumer needs advice. People with self-directed RRSPs should take advantage of the professional insights of a qualified financial planner to guide their strategy.

Contributing to spousal RRSPs

The government has made provisions within the RRSP system for spouses. The big advantage of a spousal RRSP is that it creates two separate sources of income, which generally results in tax savings when you retire. If one half of a couple earns a lot more money than the other, the spousal RRSP makes a lot of sense.

Let's say you are the higher earner. You set up a spousal RRSP in your spouse's name and contribute to it. In other words, you put in the money, but your spouse has legal control over it. Having done this, you reap two important benefits.

First, for every contribution, you will get a tax deduction (which will come in handy since you are being taxed at a higher rate on your higher income).

Second, and most importantly, when you have to withdraw money from the spousal RRSP at retirement, it will be taxed based on your spouse's lower income. Both of you benefit from a lower tax rate because the income has been split up, whereas all of the income would have been taxed at your higher rate if the money were coming solely out of your RRSP.

Contributing to a spousal RRSP does not preclude you from investing in your own RRSP, as long as the combined contribution does not exceed your allowable limit for that year. Spousal RRSPs can actually lengthen the number of years you will be able to contribute to an RRSP past age 69. How? People over 69 are still allowed to put money into their partner's spousal RRSP until the year that person turns 69.

Withdrawals from a spousal plan may be taxable in your hands if spousal contributions were made in either the year of the withdrawal or the two preceding years.

Establishing foreign content inside RRSPs

While the Canadian economy is among the most stable in the world, domestic investments may not grow as fast as those in bigger and more powerful markets like the U.S., or emerging markets like those in the developing world. This fact has not escaped either investors eager to increase their returns or our federal government, concerned with fostering the Canadian economy. The

Book IV

Investment Fundamentals

solution? The feds allow you to invest in foreign holdings inside your RRSP, but only up to a certain point. As of 2003, foreign investments can account for up to 30 percent of the book value of your RRSP. The *book value* is the exact dollar amount you've placed inside the plan — as opposed to the *market value,* which is the amount you could get if you cashed in the plan on any given day.

Borrowing from your RRSPs for a home or education

Most of the time, if you take money out of your RRSP before you retire, you pay income tax up front — what the government calls withholding tax. However, there are two instances in which the government lets you borrow from your RRSP tax-free and interest-free:

- **Home Buyer's Plan (HBP):** First-time home buyers (as defined by the federal government) can borrow up to $20,000 from their RRSP to finance their purchase through the HBP. This amount may double if you have a spouse with her or his own RRSP. However, the government has strict rules governing repayment, which must be completed within 15 years. Keep in mind, your HBP loan does affect the future gains you will miss out on for the period of time the money is outside your sheltered RRSP. For more on the HBP, see Book VI.

- **Lifelong Learning Plan (LLP):** Canadians wanting to go back to school to finish their education can withdraw up to $10,000 in a calendar year from an RRSP to finance full-time training or education for you or your spouse or common-law partner. You cannot use the LLP to finance your children's education. As long as you meet certain conditions each year, you can withdraw amounts from your RRSP until January of the fourth year after the year you make your first LLP withdrawal. You cannot take out more than $20,000 in total. You do not have to include the withdrawn amounts in your income, but you do have to repay these withdrawals to your RRSP over a period of no more than ten years. Any amount that you fail to repay when due will be considered taxable income for the year it was due. Like the HBP, your loan is interest-free and tax-free. But again, consider seriously the fact that the money you borrow will no longer be compounding inside your RRSP.

Borrowing for your RRSP

While conservative investors may feel nervous about borrowing to put away money for their retirement, borrowing to make an RRSP contribution can be a smart option. Many lending institutions eager to attract clients towards their investment products will offer loans for very low interest rates. Also, because your RRSP contribution is tax-deductible, you will probably be eligible for a tax refund that can then be used to pay off a portion of your loan.

The interest you pay on an RRSP loan is not, unfortunately, tax-deductible.

Cashing in your RRSP and the benefits of RRIFs

Unless they are locked into a fixed-term investment, you can withdraw funds from your RRSP anytime. The government imposes no penalty for withdrawal. However, if you withdraw funds before the RRSP matures during the year you turn 69, you will be fully taxed on the money you take out — unless you are participating in the government's Home Buyer's Plan or Lifelong Learning Plan.

The government extracts the income tax on withdrawals up front through a withholding tax (simply the government's means of collecting the income tax right away). For more on withholding taxes, see Chapter 6.

As mentioned above, all RRSPs mature the year you turn 69. You have three options when you convert, or dismantle, your RRSP. They are:

- ✔ **Converting your RRSP into a lump sum cash payout:** By the end of the calendar year following your 69th birthday, unless you've made other arrangements, your RRSP funds must all be withdrawn and face combined federal and provincial income tax. This tax will be levied up front through the withholding tax, and can be very steep since it varies upward depending on the size of the withdrawal.

- ✔ **Converting your RRSP into an annuity:** People who want the security of knowing they will have a stream of income for the rest of their lives can choose to use their RRSP funds to buy a life annuity. Sold by insurance companies, many annuities pay regular instalments of fixed income for life. Annuities are not like investments that can grow or shrink. The payments are fixed and can pose problems because they are inflexible to factors like inflation.

- ✔ **Converting your RRSP into a Registered Retirement Income Fund, or RRIF:** This allows you to bypass some of the problems faced when choosing either of the preceding options. First, an RRIF will extend the benefit of the tax shelter by allowing you to withdraw your funds over time rather than in a highly taxed lump sum. Second, an RRIF gives you flexibility, since you maintain your investments, which can continue to grow — possibly earning you more money for the times in your retirement when you might need more. With an RRIF, you are required to withdraw a minimum amount each year (the first year you buy the RRIF is exempt from this minimum).

Defining Mutual Funds

A mutual fund is managed by an investment company that invests (according to the fund's objectives) in stocks, bonds, government securities, short-term money market funds, and other instruments by pooling investors' money.

Mutual funds are sold in shares. Each share of a fund represents an ownership in the fund's underlying securities (the portfolio).

Investors can sell their shares at any time and receive the current share price, which may be more or less than the price they paid.

When a fund earns money from dividends on the securities it invests in or makes money by selling some of its investments at a profit, the fund distributes the earnings to shareholders. If you're an investor, you may decide to reinvest these distributions automatically in additional fund shares.

A mutual fund investor makes money from the distribution of dividends and capital gains on the fund's investments. A mutual fund shareholder also can potentially make money as the fund's share per share (called net asset value per share, or NAVPS) increases in value.

NAVPS of a mutual fund = Assets – Liabilities ÷ Number of shares in the fund

(Assets are the value of all securities in a fund's portfolio; liabilities are a fund's expenses.) The NAVPS of a mutual fund is affected by the share price changes of the securities in the fund's portfolio and any dividend or capital gains distributions to its shareholders.

Unless you're in immediate need of this income, which is taxable, reinvesting this money into additional shares is an excellent way to grow your investments, especially within your RRSP, where the gains you make will be sheltered from taxes.

Shareholders receive a portion of the distribution of dividends and capital gains, based on the number of shares they own. As a result, an investor who puts $1,000 in a mutual fund gets the same investment performance and return per dollar as someone who invests $100,000.

Mutual funds invest in many (sometimes hundreds of) securities at one time, so they are diversified investments. A diversified portfolio is one that balances risk by investing in a number of different areas of the stock and/or bond markets. This type of investing attempts to reduce per-share volatility and minimize losses over the long term as markets change. Diversification offsets the risk of putting your eggs in one basket, such as technology funds. (See Chapter 6 for a detailed discussion of diversification.)

A stock or bond of any one company represents just a small percentage of a fund's overall portfolio. So even if one of a fund's investments performs poorly, 20 to 150 more investments can shore up the fund's performance. As a result, the poor performance of any one investment isn't likely to have a devastating effect on an entire mutual fund portfolio. That balance doesn't mean, however, that funds don't have inherent risks: You need to carefully select mutual funds to meet your investment goals and risk tolerance.

The performance of certain classes of investments — such as large company growth stocks — can strengthen or weaken a fund's overall investment performance if the fund concentrates its investments within that class. If the overall economy declines, the stock market takes a dive, or a mutual fund manager picks investments with little potential to be profitable, a fund's performance can suffer.

Unfortunately, unless you have a crystal ball, you have no way to predict how a fund will perform, except to look at the security's underlying risk. If a fund has existed long enough to build a track record through ups and downs, you can review its performance during the last stressful market.

Fortunately for all investors, some companies use a statistical measure called standard deviation, which measures the volatility in the fund's performance. The larger the swings in a fund's returns, the more likely the fund will slip into negative numbers.

Periodicals that report on and rank mutual funds include All-Canadian Mutual Fund Guide and Canadian Mutual Fund Advisor, available on newsstands or at your library. Or check out www.morningstar.ca or www.globefund.com for similar information.

Considering different types of mutual funds

As you prepare to invest in mutual funds, you need to decide which type of funds best suit your goals and tastes. Basically, you have the following general types of mutual funds to consider:

- ✔ Equity funds, which invest in Canadian and foreign stocks

- ✔ Bond funds (also considered income funds), which invest in bonds

- ✔ Balanced funds, also called hybrid funds, which invest in both stocks and bonds

- ✔ Money market funds, which hold short-term investments

Book IV

Investment
Fundamentals

Table 3-2 gives you a sense of how many dollars investors allocated to different types of mutual funds in mid-2002 and the change in those numbers in just one year to mid-2003.

Table 3-2	Mutual Fund Assets in May 2002 and May 2003	
Fund Type	**Net Assets May 2002**	**Net Assets May 2003**
Canadian Equity funds	$102 billion	$84 billion
Bond and Income funds	$32 billion	$37 billion
Balanced funds	$68 billion	$65 billion
Foreign Equity funds	$104 billion	$75 billion
U.S. Equity funds	$31 billion	$28 billion
Canadian Money Market funds	$58 billion	$84 billion

*Source: The Investment Funds Institute of Canada (*www.ific.ca*)*

Each of these groups presents a wide variety of funds with different characteristics from which to choose. To help you further refine your search to match fund investments to your goals, the following lists offer a general look at some different types of funds available.

Equity funds also include:

✔ **Aggressive growth funds:** Managers of these funds are forever on the lookout for undiscovered, unheralded companies, including small and undervalued companies. The goal is to get in when the stock is cheap and realize substantial gains as it soars skyward. That dream doesn't always come true. But if you're willing to accept above-average risk, you may reap above-average gains.

✔ **Growth funds:** These funds are among the mainstays of long-term investing. They own stocks in mostly large- or medium-sized companies whose significant earnings are expected to increase at a faster rate than that of the rest of the market. These growth funds do not typically pay dividends. Several types are available, including large-, medium-, and small-company growth funds.

✔ **Value funds:** Managers of these funds seek out stocks that are under-priced — selling cheaply, relative to the stock's true value. The fund's manager believes that the market will recognize the stock's true price in the future. Stock price appreciation is long term. These funds don't typically turn in outstanding performance when the stock market is zooming along, but tend to hold their value a good deal more than growth funds when stock prices slide, so are generally believed to be good hedges to more growth-oriented mutual funds. These funds come in large-, medium-, and small-company versions.

✔ **Equity income funds:** These funds were developed to balance investors' desires for current income with some potential for capital appreciation. These fund managers invest mostly in stocks — often blue chip stocks — that pay dividends. They usually make some investments in utility companies, which are also likely to pay dividends.

✔ **Growth and income funds:** These funds seek both capital appreciation and current income. Growth and income are considered equal investment objectives.

✔ **International and global funds:** These two funds may sound like the same type of mutual fund, but they're not. International funds invest in a portfolio of stocks (international securities) outside of North America. Global funds, also called world funds, can invest anywhere in the world, including Canadian stock markets.

✔ **Sector funds:** The managers of these funds concentrate investments in one sector of the economy, such as financial services, real estate, technology, or precious metals. Although these types of funds may be a good choice after you've built a portfolio that matches your investment plan, they have greater risk than almost any other type of fund because these funds concentrate their investments in one sector or industry.

If you're uncomfortable with the potential for significant losses, make sure that a sector fund only accounts for a small percentage of your portfolio — say, less than 10 percent. Remember, however, that if you invest in a balanced portfolio, your other investments should hold their own if only one industry is impacted.

✔ **Emerging market funds:** The managers of these funds seek out the stocks of underdeveloped economies, such as Asia, eastern Europe, and Latin America. Finding undiscovered winners can prove advantageous, but an emerging market fund — also known as an emerging country fund — isn't a recommended mainstay for new investors because of the potential for loss. When these countries and economies suffer economic decline, they can create significant investor losses.

✔ **Region-specific or country-specific funds:** As their name implies, the managers of these funds look for the stock winners of one specific region or country of the world. Unless you have close relatives running a country somewhere and have firsthand knowledge about that land's economic prospects, you're wise to steer clear of these funds. The reason is simple: They have unmitigated risk from concentration in one area. For example, when Japan's economy declined in 1997, it sent mutual funds that invested exclusively in that country's companies tumbling by more than 40 percent.

Book IV

Investment Fundamentals

✔ **Index funds:** The managers of these funds invest in stocks that mirror the investments tracked by an index such as the TSX 300 Composite Index. Some of the advantages of investing in index funds include low operating expenses, diversification, and potential tax savings. Although they don't necessarily rely on the performance of any one company or industry to buoy their performance, they do invest in equities that represent a market — such as the Toronto Stock Exchange. If and when that market dips, as the S&P/TSX did between 2000 and 2003, it can dip significantly. The S&P/TSX went from a high of about 11,000 in mid-2000 to the 7,000 level in 2003, a staggering drop of over 35 percent in a relatively short period of time.

Bond funds are less risky than stock funds, but also potentially less rewarding. You can choose from the following types of bond funds:

✔ Government of Canada bonds

✔ Provincial bonds

✔ Corporate bonds

✔ Chartered Bank bonds

✔ International bond funds

Balanced funds are another investment option. These funds are a mix of stocks and bonds that are also called blended or hybrid funds. Generally, managers invest in about 60 percent stocks and 40 percent bonds. Balanced funds appeal to investors because even in bear markets, their bond holdings allow them to pay dividends. (A bear market is generally defined as a market in which stock prices drop 20 percent or more from their previous high.)

Money market funds are, arguably, the least volatile type of mutual fund. Fund managers invest in instruments such as short-term bank GICs, Government of Canada T-bills, and short-term corporate debt issued by established and stable companies. This type of mutual fund is ideal for people who may need to use the money to buy something in the short term like a down payment on a home. These funds are also a convenient place to pool money for future investment decisions.

Analyzing mutual funds

As you begin your search for mutual funds, make sure that your performance evaluation produces meaningful results. Performance is important because good, long-term earnings enable you to maximize your investments and ensure that your money is working for you. Gauging future performance is not an exact science.

When you evaluate funds, check out periodicals such as _Canadian Mutual Fund Advisor, All-Canadian Mutual Fund Guide,_ and _Investor's Digest of Canada,_ available by subscription, on newsstands, or at the library. A fund's prospectus, which you can request from a fund's toll-free phone number, also outlines the important features and objectives of the fund.

As an additional check, compare all your choice funds before making a final decision; avoid choosing one fund in isolation. A single fund can look spectacular until you discover it trails most of its peers by 10 percent.

Look for the following information when you select mutual funds:

- ✔ **One-, three-, and five-year returns:** These numbers offer information on the fund's past performance. A look at all three can give you a sense of how well a fund fared over time and in relation to similar funds.

- ✔ **Year-to-date total returns:** This is a fund's report card for the current year, minus operating and management expenses. The numbers can give you a sense of whether earnings are in line with competing funds, out in front, or trailing.

  Avoid the temptation to evaluate funds solely on returns to date. Past performance is no guarantee of future performance. Always look at the big picture, including the rest of the information on this list.

- ✔ **Maximum initial sales charges, commissions, or loads:** These are commissions you pay to a broker to buy a fund. A sales charge on a purchase, sometimes called a load, is a charge you pay when you buy shares. No-load funds don't charge sales loads. There are no-load funds in every major fund category. However, all mutual funds (whether load or no-load) have ongoing operating and management expenses.

  In Canada, front-end loads (sales charges you pay to your brokerage at the time you purchase your mutual fund shares) are negotiable up to about 5 percent, but you'll find a lot in the 2 percent range. Back-end loads (also called deferred sales charges or redemption fees, paid when you sell your shares) are higher, in the 6 to 7 percent range. Typically, the longer you keep your shares, the lower the back-end load, with the charge going down about 1 percent every year.

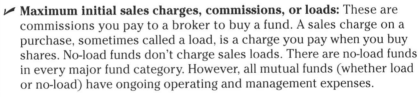
Book IV

Investment
Fundamentals

- ✔ **Annual expenses:** Also called management expense ratios (MERs), these include both the fees paid to a fund's portfolio managers and a fund's expenses. The MER is always calculated as a percentage of the fund's total assets and paid out of those assets. Before you settle on one fund, review the numbers on a few competitors. In general, the more aggressive a fund, the more expenses it incurs trading investments. Before you invest in a fund, be cautious if it has an extremely high MER compared to that of similar funds. You can find out how a fund's MER has fluctuated over the past five years by reading its annual report.

To develop a sense of how expenses can take a big bite out of earnings over the years, consider this example: A $10,000 investment earns 10 percent over 40 years with a 1 percent expense ratio, which yields a return of $302,771. The same investment with a 1.74 percent expense ratio returns $239,177, or $63,594 less.

✔ **Manager's tenure:** Consider how long the current fund manager (or managers) has been managing the fund. If it's only been a year or two, take that into consideration before you invest — the five-year record that caught your eye may have been created by someone who has already moved down the road. Fund managers move around often. In an ideal world, your funds are handled by managers with staying power.

✔ **Portfolio turnover:** This tells you how often a fund manager sells stocks in the course of a year. Selling stocks is expensive, so high turnover over the long run will probably hurt performance. If two funds appear equal in all other aspects, but one has high turnover and the other low turnover, by all means choose the fund with low turnover.

✔ **Underlying fund investments:** For your own sake, look at the top five or ten stocks or bonds that a fund is investing in. For example, a growth fund may be getting its rapid appreciation from a high concentration in fairly risky technology stocks, or a global fund may have many of its holdings here in the Canadian stock market. Neither of these strategies is a mortal sin if you know about and can live with it. If you can't, keep looking for a fund that matches your goals. Looking at underlying investments not only helps minimize your surprises as markets and economies shift, but also enables you to create a balanced portfolio.

Chapter 4

More Investment Choices: Stocks, Bonds, and Beyond

*T*he investments described in this chapter carry a great potential for return — but that possibility of return comes at a greater risk to your money. Stocks, bonds, and real estate are investment options whose value fluctuates with the market, meaning that the value of these investments can grow and shrink greatly. However, with the information in this chapter, you will be able to make good educated guesses about how to pursue these investments.

Sizing Up Stocks

A stock is a piece of paper that signifies that you own part of a company. The market price of a stock is directly related to the profits and the losses of the company. In other words, when the company profits, the worth of your stock increases. When the company falters and its profits decline, so does the worth of your stock.

Investors who buy stock own shares of the company. That's why they're called shareholders.

Understanding how stocks work

Companies issue stock to raise money to fund a variety of initiatives, including expansion, the development of new products, the acquisition of other companies, or the paying off of debt. In an action called an initial public offering (IPO), a company opens sale of its stock to investors.

An investment banker helps underwrite the public stock offering, that is, the investment banker helps the company determine when to go public and what price the stock should be at that time.

When the stock begins selling, the price can rise or fall from its set price depending on whether investors believe that the stock was fairly and accurately priced. Often, the price of an IPO soars during the first few days of trading, but then can later fall back to earth.

After the IPO, stock prices will continue to fluctuate based on what investors are willing to accept when they buy or sell the stock. In simple terms, stock prices are a matter of supply and demand. If everyone wants a stock, its price rises, sometimes sharply. If, on the other hand, investors are fearful that, for example, the company's management is faltering and has taken on too much debt to sustain strong growth, they may begin selling in noticeable volume. Mass sales can drive the price down. In addition to specific company issues, the price can drop for other reasons, including bad news for the entire industry or a general downturn in the overall economy.

Stocks are bought and sold on stock exchanges, such as the Toronto Stock Exchange (also known as the TSX) in Canada, as well as on exchanges around the world, like the New York Stock Exchange and the Tokyo Stock Exchange. Companies that don't have the cash reserves necessary to be listed on one of the exchanges are traded over-the-counter, which means that they receive less scrutiny from analysts and large investors such as mutual fund managers.

In addition, professional analysts who are paid to watch companies and their stocks can give a thumbs-up or a thumbs-down to a stock, which in turn can send stock prices soaring or plummeting. These stock analysts sit in brokerage firms on New York's fabled Wall Street and Toronto's Bay Street. The analyst's job is to watch closely the actions of public companies and their managers and the results those actions produce.

By carefully monitoring news about a company's earnings, corporate strategies, new products and services, and legal and regulatory problems and victories, analysts give stocks a buy, sell, or hold rating. Such opinions can have a wide-sweeping impact on the price of a stock, at least in the short term. Rumblings, real or imagined, can send the price of a stock, or the stock market overall, tumbling downward or soaring skyward.

The price of stock goes up and down — a phenomenon known as volatility — but if the news creating the stir is short-term, panic is an over-reaction. You don't want to sell a stock when its price is down, only to see it make a miraculous recovery a few days, weeks, or even months down the road.

Smart investors who have done their research and are invested for the longer term won't be impacted by short-term price dips or panics. Unless, of course, you use the opportunity to buy a stock you've already researched and were going to buy anyway. The old adage — buy low, sell high — holds as true today as it did 75 years ago.

How low can stock prices go? In October 1987, the much-watched Dow Jones Industrial Average (DJIA) tumbled by 22.6 percent in a matter of days. This rapid decline meant that the value of a $10,000 investment dropped to $7,740. Many stocks recovered, but some did not. On Bay Street, the S&P/TSX Index quickly lost 11.32 percent of its value. While the recent bear market was even more vicious, it took a period of years before it bottomed out.

You can lose all your money with a stock investment, and that risk is why you need to analyze your choices carefully. The three most basic types of risks associated with stock investments are:

✔ You may lose money.

✔ Your stocks may not perform as well as other, similar stocks.

✔ A loss may threaten your financial goals.

Stock investing carries certain risks, but they can be minimized by careful investment selection and by diversification, a technique for building a balanced portfolio, which you can investigate more thoroughly in Chapter 6.

Recognizing different types of stock

Companies issue two basic kinds of stock, common and preferred, and each provides shareholders with different opportunities and rights:

✔ **Common stock:** Represents ownership in a company. Companies can pay what are called dividends to their shareholders. Dividends are paid out from a company's earnings and can fluctuate with the company's performance. *Note:* Not all companies pay dividends.

Common stock offers no performance guarantees, and although this kind of stock has historically outperformed other types of investments, you can lose your entire investment if a company does poorly enough to wipe out its earnings and reputation into the foreseeable future. Common stock dividends are paid only after the preferred stock dividends are paid.

Book IV

Investment Fundamentals

✔ **Preferred stock:** Constitutes ownership in shares as well, but this stock differs from common stock in ways that reduce risk to investors, but also limit upside potential, or upward trends in stock pricing. Dividends on preferred stock are paid before common stock, so preferred stock may be a better bet for investors who rely on the income from these payments. But the dividend, which is set, is not increased when the company profits, and the price of preferred stock increases more slowly than that of common stock. Also, preferred stock investors stand a better chance of getting their money back if the company declares bankruptcy.

A company's stock is also categorized depending on its perceived expected performance. Basically, a company's stock falls into one of two categories: growth or value (see Table 4-1 for a summary of each). (A third category — income stocks — is not discussed here.)

Table 4-1 The Differences between Growth Stocks and Value Stocks

Investor Characteristic	Pros	Cons
Growth stocks	Investors anticipate higher profits in return for higher stock prices. The return on investment can be substantial and prove worth the risk	They are less likely to pay dividends; and if they do, they're typically lower than that of value stocks. Stock prices tend to be affected by negative company news and short-term market changes.
Value stocks	Investors anticipate that the company will experience a turnaround that will produce higher profits in the future. It costs fewer investment dollars to buy a dollar of their profits.	They may never realize the potential that investors project onto them.

Over time, you're likely to buy a mix of both types of stocks for your portfolio, so knowing the different characteristics of each is important. Understanding growth and value stocks can help you evaluate your options more carefully.

Growth companies are typically organizations with a positive outlook for expansion and, ultimately, stock prices that move upward. Investors looking for growth companies usually are willing to pay a higher price for stocks that have consistently produced higher profits because they're betting the companies will continue to perform well in the future.

Because they use their money to invest in future growth, growth companies are less likely to pay dividends than other, more conservative companies; when they do pay dividends, the amounts tend to be lower. An investor who buys a growth stock believes that, according to analysis of the company's history and statistics, the company is likely to continue to produce strong earnings and is therefore worth its higher price.

The stock of a growth company is, however, somewhat riskier because the price tends to react to negative company news and short-term changes in the market. Also, the company may not continue to produce earnings that are worth its higher price.

In contrast, value stocks are out of favour, left on the shelf by investors who are busy reaching for more expensive and trendier items. For that reason, you spend fewer dollars to buy a dollar of their profits than if you invest in a growth stock. When investors buy value stocks, they're betting that they're actually buying a turnaround story — with a happy ending down the road.

Value companies carry risk too, because they may never reach what investors believe is their true potential. Optimism doesn't always pay off in profits.

Identifying potential stock investments

What do you need to know to determine which stocks are potential investments? To get started, stick with stocks relating to your own interests or knowledge. If you frequent particular stores or restaurants and you use and like their products and services, find out if they are publicly held companies. Start identifying and watching these stocks. That advice doesn't mean that you should buy their stock right away. You still have some homework to do.

The following list tells you what to look for when investigating potential stock investments. Investment periodicals such as *The Investment Reporter, Investor's Digest of Canada,* and *Blue Book of Stock Reports,* along with the U.S. publication *ValueLine* (www.valueline.com) and any brokerage firm analyst report can provide you with much or all of the following pertinent facts and measures:

Book IV

Investment Fundamentals

✔ **Find out if the industry is growing.** Some industries aren't. News stories on the industry in question can tell you the state of the industry (also check out *The Globe and Mail Report on Business, National Post FP Investing,* or *Canadian Business* magazine). The company's annual report can also be a useful source for this kind of information.

Company shareholder departments can provide you with copies of annual reports and quarterly reports that companies must file. You can also find them at major public libraries, or on the Internet at www.sedar.com. Keep in mind that once you buy a stock, thereby becoming a shareholder, the company will be required by law to send you a copy of its annual reports.

✔ **Find primary competitors.** Don't look at a stock in isolation. A company that looks enticing by itself may look like a 100-pound weakling when you evaluate its strengths and weaknesses next to the leading competitors in the industry. Check out at least two competitors of any stock you're evaluating.

✔ **Check out annual earnings and sales.** This is key in deciphering how quickly a company is growing over one-year, three-year, and five-year time periods, and whether its earnings are keeping pace with sales. Look for growth rates of at least 10 percent.

✔ **Look at the stock's price-to-earnings (P/E) ratios.** This is the primary means of evaluating a stock. The P/E ratio is derived by dividing a stock's share price by its earnings-per-share. The result tells you how much investors are willing to pay for each $1 of earnings. Those stocks that have faster earnings growth rates also tend to carry higher P/Es, which means that investors are willing to pay through the nose to own shares. The value of a P/E ratio, however, can be subjective. One investor may think that a particular company's P/E ratio of 20 is high, while another may consider it low to moderate.

✔ **Find out the price-to-book value (P/B) ratio.** The P/B ratio is the stock's share price divided by book value, or a firm's assets minus its liabilities. This ratio is a good comparison tool and can tell you which companies are asset-rich and which are carrying more debt.

A low P/B ratio can be an indicator that a stock may be a good value investment.

✔ **Check out the stock's price-to-growth flow ratio.** This ratio is the share price divided by growth flow (annual earnings plus research and development costs) per share. This is a useful measure for assessing fast-moving companies, especially in the technology sector, where management often puts profits back into product development.

✔ **Look at the stock's PEG ratio.** The PEG ratio is a company's P/E ratio divided by its expected earnings' growth rate and is an indicator of well-priced stock.

✔ **Look ahead.** Projections of five-year annual growth rates and five-year P/E ratios can tell you whether analysts believe that the companies you're evaluating can continue to grow at their current rate, can beat it, or will start to fall behind.

Make a list of the stocks you are interested in and watch their performance over time. Doing so gives you a feel for how the stocks respond to different types of economic and market news. You can also see which stocks' prices move around and are more volatile.

So, does your own analysis indicate that you have a winner on your hands or a dog? If you're unsure, sit tight and watch what happens in the weeks and months ahead. Watching several stocks over a period of time not only tells you how well they're doing, or not doing, it can also show you how well you're honing your own stock analysis skills.

Bantering about Bonds

A bond is basically an IOU. When you purchase a bond, you are lending money to a government, municipality, corporation, federal agency, or other entity. In return for the loan, the entity promises to pay you a specified rate of interest during the life of the bond and to repay the face value (the principal) of the bond when it matures (or comes due).

When you buy a new bond from the original issuer (the entity to whom you're lending your money), you will purchase it at face value, also called par value, and you will be promised a specific rate of interest, called the coupon. If you buy a bond that's already been resold before maturity (from what's called the secondary market, where existing bonds are bought and sold), you may buy it at a discount (less than par) or at a premium (above par).

Bonds aren't like stocks. You are not buying part ownership in a company or government when you purchase a bond. Instead, what you're actually buying — or betting on — is the issuer's ability to pay you back with interest.

Understanding how bonds work

You have a number of important variables to consider when you invest in bonds, including the stability of the issuer, the bond's maturity or due date, interest rate, price, yield, tax status, and risk. As with any investment, ensuring that all these variables match up with your own investment goals is key to making the right choice for your money.

Be sure to buy a bond with a maturity date that tracks with your financial plans. For instance, if you have a child's post-secondary education to fund 15 years from now and you want to invest part of his or her education fund in bonds, you need to select vehicles that have maturities that match that need. If you have to sell a bond before its due date, you receive the prevailing market price, which may be more or less than the price you paid.

Book IV

Investment Fundamentals

In general, because they often specify the yield you'll be paid, bonds can't make you a millionaire overnight like a stock can. What can you expect to earn? That depends on a number of factors, including the type of bond you buy, and market conditions, like prevailing interest rates. What can you expect to lose? That depends on how safe the issuer is. The consensus, especially for beginning investors, is to steer clear of anything not rated A or above by the Dominion Bond Rating Service (DBRS) at www.dbrs.com.

Recognizing different types of bonds

Bonds come in all shapes and sizes, and they enable you to choose one that meets your needs in terms of your investment time horizon, risk profile, and income needs. First, here is a look at the different types of Government of Canada securities available:

- ✔ **Treasury bills:** T-bills are offered in 3-month, 6-month, and 12-month maturities. These short-term government securities do not pay current interest, but instead are always sold at a discount price, which is lower than par value. The difference between the discount price and the par value received is considered interest (and is taxed as income). For example, if you pay the discount price of $950 for a $1,000 T-bill, you pay 5 percent less than you actually get back when the bill matures. Par is considered to be $100 worth of a bond (which, although selling for a $1,000 minimum, is always expressed in a $100 measure for the purpose of valuation). The minimum investment for T-bills is $5,000, but you can subsequently purchase them in $1,000 increments.

- ✔ **Government of Canada bonds:** Unlike T-bills, Government of Canada bonds have fixed coupons that pay a specific interest at regular intervals (every six months). These bonds are longer-term offerings than T-bills, with maturities of between 1 and 30 years. Typically, the longer the term, the higher the interest paid. The minimum investment is lower than for T-bills, just $1,000. But they are also issued in larger denominations. The interest you earn on Government of Canada bonds is considered income and taxed as such. If the face value of your bond accrues, this is considered a capital gain.

- ✔ **Strip or zero-coupon bonds:** Strip bonds, so named because the coupon has been "stripped" from the bond's principal, work almost like T-bills. They are sold at a steep discount, and interest accrues (builds up) during the life of the bond. At maturity, the investor receives all the accrued interest plus the original investment. Strip bonds are guaranteed by the federal government, and can be sold anytime. As with T-bills, the difference between the discounted price you pay for a strip bond and the value at maturity is considered income, and is fully taxed.

- ✔ **Canada Savings Bonds (CSBs):** These have long been a fall investment ritual for Canadians. You purchase Canada Savings Bonds from your bank, trust, credit union, or investment dealer during the annual selling season, which runs from October 1 to April 1. The bond is registered to you and is non-transferable. The value of the bond itself never changes, so these bonds are not tradeable.

Quite simply, by buying a Canada Savings Bond, you are lending your money to the federal government in return for interest. With a regular-interest CSB, that gain is paid out once a year, on November 1, and is taxable as income. With compound-interest CSBs, your interest is reinvested until maturity, thereby compounding your gains, but, as of 1990, you still have to claim it as income each year. For more zest, the government also offers an indexed CSB, which takes into account rising interest rates. The bond's yield is based on the inflation rate plus a fixed rate of return. For more information on CSBs, visit the federal government's Canada Savings Bond Web site at `www.cis-pec.gc.ca`.

While Government of Canada bonds are some of the safest investment bets around — since they're guaranteed by the strength of the federal government — remember that risk and reward are tradeoffs that you need to look at in tandem. As with all investments, the safer the investment the less you're likely to earn or lose!

The following are other types of available bonds:

- **Provincial bonds:** Provincial governments issue both T-bills and bonds (short-, medium- and long-term), much like the federal government. While these are safe investments, bonds issued by provinces facing economic uncertainty, are considered slightly more risky by investors. In return for the added risk, they usually pay a higher yield.

- **Municipal bonds:** These are loans you make to a local government, whether it's in your city or town.

- **Commercial paper:** These are short-term debt instruments employed by both publicly owned Crown corporations (referred to as Government Guaranteed Commercial Paper) and private sector corporations. Like T-bills and strip bonds, they are sold at a discount, but yields tend to be higher.

- **Corporate bonds:** A growing area in Canada, these are issued by companies that need to raise money, including public utilities and transportation companies, industrial corporations and manufacturers, and financial service companies.

Corporate bonds can be riskier than either Canadian government bonds or provincial bonds because companies can go bankrupt. So a company's credit risk is an important tool for evaluating the safety of a corporate bond. Even if an organization doesn't throw in the towel, its risk factor can be enough to cause agency analysts to downgrade the company's overall rating. If that happens, you may find it more difficult to sell the bond early.

- **Junk bonds:** Junk bonds pay high yields because the issuer may be in financial trouble, have a poor credit rating, and are likely to have a difficult time finding buyers for their issues. Although you may decide that junk bonds or junk bond mutual funds have a place in your portfolio, make sure that spot is small because these bonds carry high risk.

Book IV

Investment Fundamentals

Although junk bonds may look particularly attractive at times, think twice before you buy. They don't call them junk for nothing. You could potentially suffer a total loss if the issuer declares bankruptcy. As one wag suggested, if you really believe in the company so much, invest in its stock, which has unlimited upside potential.

Identifying potential bond investments

Here's a look at some items you need to evaluate before investing in a fund:

- **Issuer stability:** This is also known as credit quality, which assesses an issuer's ability to pay back its debts, including the interest and principal it owes its bond holders, in full and on time. Although many corporations, the Canadian government and the provinces have never defaulted on a bond, you can expect that some issuers can and will be unable to repay.

- **Maturity:** A bond's maturity refers to the specific future date when you can expect your principal to be repaid. Bond maturities can range from as short as one day all the way up to 30 years. Make sure that the bond you select has a maturity date that works with your needs. T-bills and strip bonds pay interest at maturity. All other bonds pay interest twice yearly or quarterly. Most investors buy bonds in order to have a steady flow of income (from interest).

    The longer the maturity in a bond, the more risk associated with it — that is, the greater the fluctuation in bond value based upon changes in interest rates.

- **Interest rate:** Bonds pay interest that can be fixed-rate, floating, or payable at maturity. Most bond rates are fixed until maturity, and the amount is based on a percentage of the face or principal amount.

- **Face value:** This is the stated value of a bond. The bond is selling at a premium when the price is above its face value; pricing below its face value means that it's selling at a discount.

- **Price:** The price you pay for a bond is based on an array of different factors, including current interest rates, supply and demand, and maturity.

- **Current yield:** This is the annual percentage rate of return earned on a bond. You can find a bond's current yield by dividing the bond's interest payment by its purchase price. For example, if you bought a bond at $900 and its interest rate is 8 percent (0.08), the current yield is 8.89 percent — 8 percent or 0.08 ÷ $900 = 8.89.

- 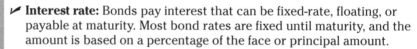 **Yield to maturity (YTM):** This tells you the total return you can expect to receive if you hold a bond until it matures. Its calculation takes into account the bond's face value, its current price, and the years left until the bond matures. The calculation is an elaborate one, but the broker you're buying a bond from should be able to give you its YTM. The YTM also enables you to compare bonds with different maturities and yields.

Don't buy a bond on current yield alone. Ask the bank or brokerage firm from whom you're buying the bond to provide a YTM figure so that you can have a clear idea about the bond's real value to your portfolio.

✔ **Tax status:** Outside your RRSP, the interest you earn on bonds is fully taxable as income. The difference between what you paid for a discounted bond and the value at maturity is also considered income. Gains you make on the value of a bond if you sell it before maturity are considered a capital gain. You will be taxed on 75 percent of your capital gains annually.

If you sell a Government of Canada, provincial, municipal, or corporate bond for more than you paid for it, you'll pay tax on the difference, which is considered a capital gain. The Canada Customs and Revenue Agency will tax you on 50 percent of that gain, for dispositions after October 17, 2000. This capital gains inclusion rate is likely to be in effect for the foreseeable future.

Investing in Real Estate

There are three ways that you can become a real estate investor: first, by buying your own home; second, by buying an investment property; and third, by investing in a real estate investment trust (REIT).

Although it's true that over time, real estate owners and investors have enjoyed rates of return comparable to the stock market, real estate is not a simple way to get wealthy. Nor is it for the faint of heart or the passive investor. Real estate goes through good and bad performance periods, and most people who make money in real estate do so because they invest over many years.

Buying your own home

Most people invest in real estate by becoming homeowners. Canadians have long been taught that the equity, which is the difference between the market value of your home and the loan owed on it, increases over time to produce a significant part of your net worth.

Unless you have the good fortune to live in a rent-controlled apartment, owning a home should be less expensive than renting a comparable home throughout your adult life. Why? As a renter, your housing costs will follow the level of inflation, while as a homeowner, the bulk of your housing costs are not exposed to inflation if you have a fixed-rate mortgage. And if you have a variable rate mortgage, you are enjoying rates that are near 30-year lows!

Book IV

Investment Fundamentals

Figure 4-1 illustrates the difference in expenditure when comparing owning and renting a home. This graph assumes that the homeowner has a 30-year, fixed-rate mortgage of 7.5 percent on $150,000, and the renter starts out with an $800 per month rent payment with annual increases of 4 percent.

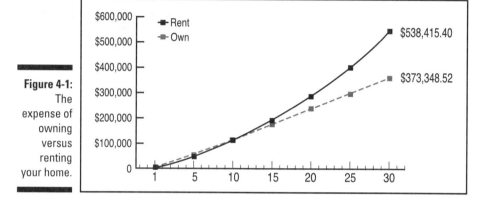

Figure 4-1:
The expense of owning versus renting your home.

Figure 4-1 shows that at the end of 30 years the renter has paid over $500,000, while the owner has paid less than $375,000. What's more, the owner has increased her equity, also called net worth. Owning your home can add to your sense of financial security as the economy fluctuates. In addition to the financial benefits, home ownership gives you more control over your own living space; for example, it allows you more freedom to decorate your home's exterior and interior according to your own tastes. And the federal government gives homeowners another major financial boost. How? Any profit made when you sell your primary residence is tax-free. This is called the principal residence exemption, and each Canadian family is entitled to one.

Buying an investment property

A second way to invest in real estate is to buy residential housing such as single-family homes or multi-unit buildings, and rent them. In many ways, buying real estate in this way isn't an investment; it's a business. Maintaining a property can easily turn into a part-time job. If you're a person who dreams of putting heart and soul into a property, however, it may be worth investigating. If you do decide to take this route, first, be sure that you have sufficient time to devote to the project. Second, be careful not to sacrifice contributions to your RRSP in order to own investment real estate.

Deciding to become a real estate investor depends mostly on you and your situation. Ask yourself the following questions: Is real estate something that you have an affinity for? Do you know a lot about houses, or have a knack for spotting up-and-coming areas? Are you cut out to handle the responsibilities that come with being a landlord? Do you have the time to manage your property?

Another drawback to real estate investment is that you earn no tax benefits while you're accumulating your down payment, whereas your RRSP gives you an immediate tax deduction as you contribute money to it. If you haven't exhausted your contributions to your RRSP, consider doing so before taking a look at investment real estate.

Investing in a real estate investment trust (REIT)

A *real estate investment trust (REIT)* is a "company." Although legally structured as a closed-end investment trust that owns, maintains, and manages real estate, most REITs boast an enterprising, internal management running a truly sophisticated organization. Most Canadian and U.S. REITs are publicly traded on major Canadian and U.S. stock exchanges. These public REITs have their own ticker symbols and trade the same way as common stocks do.

In North America, there are well over 200 publicly traded REITs to choose from, including over 20 from Canada. And in the same way that a mutual fund can provide you with a basket of publicly traded companies, a REIT lets you hold virtually any form of commercial real estate out there: office towers, malls, apartments, hotels, storage facilities, and even prisons! REITs buy real estate, manage it, develop it on their own (to a limited degree), or do a combination of these things.

During the recent bear market, investors flocked to REITs as a defensive haven of sorts. REITs also remain popular because they do the following:

✔ Provide generally positive returns over the long-term

✔ Expose investors to lower risk and provide higher stability relative to stocks

✔ Provide generous dividend yields when compared to like income-generating instruments

✔ Offer capital appreciation potential

✔ Possess distinct tax advantages (deferred tax payments and reduced tax rates)

✔ Trade quickly and easily on major exchanges

Book IV

Investment Fundamentals

✔ Represent a creative way to hold small chunks of real estate

✔ Benefit from good management in most cases

✔ Combine the best features of real estate, stocks, and mutual funds

✔ Are considered mainstream and proven by Canadian and U.S. investors

REITs have some very special and significant tax benefits to the unitholder. A portion of distributions from a REIT will not be immediately included in your current year's taxable income. However, in the current year, you are required to reduce your units' tax cost base by the amount paid or payable to you by a REIT. You will realize a higher capital gain (on a lower adjusted cost base) when the unit is sold at a future date. Depending on the REIT's structure and circumstances, you can receive up to 100 percent of the cash distribution in this tax-deferred manner. This deferral represents one of the key tax benefits associated with REITs. A second benefit is that when you do sell your REIT units, only 50 percent of the capital gain is included in your taxable income.

Of course, REITs have disadvantages, too, including the following:

✔ **Real estate risks:** Owning shares in a REIT carries the same investment risks as any real estate investment. If the property owned by the REIT is in trouble, so is the REIT.

✔ **Less profit than direct real estate investing:** That's the trade-off. Because REITs offer less risk than buying real estate on your own, they also offer a lower return on your investment.

When you're looking for a REIT to invest in, analyze it the way you would analyze a property. Look at the location and type of the property. If shopping malls are booming in Vancouver, and your REIT buys and sells shopping malls in Vancouver, then you'll do well. However, if your REIT invests in office buildings across the country and the Canadian office building market is overbuilt and having tough times, so will you.

Chapter 5

Monitoring Your Progress

●●

●●

*T*his chapter tells you how to assess the performance of your investments — or those you plan to buy — relative to their peers. It also provides you with tools to determine how the stock and bond markets, and the mutual funds that invest in them, are doing overall.

Checking Up on Savings Accounts and GICs

Chapter 2 suggests that these investments qualify as entry-level, or low-complexity, investments. The same holds true for monitoring their progress.

Traditional savings accounts and tiered accounts

Monitoring your savings account or tiered account is a lot like monitoring your chequing account. You receive statements from the institution (like your bank or credit union) that tell you your balance including accrued interest. Many institutions also have a telephone number — often toll-free — that allows you to access balance information by using your account number and your personal code number. In addition, more and more financial institutions have online banking that allows you to access your account information from your computer.

Guaranteed Investment Certificates

When you invest in a Guaranteed Investment Certificate (GIC), you receive an actual document that indicates the principal you invested, the interest rate, the length of time of the investment, and the final amount you will receive. Some institutions include your balance information on the statements you receive from other accounts you have with them, but not all do that.

The most important question with a GIC is what will happen to your money (both the principal and the interest you earn) when the GIC matures. This is your decision. Keep in mind, with GICs you've agreed to lock in your principal as well as the interest for a specified amount of time. What happens to that money after the term of the GIC is entirely up to you.

Banks and credit unions will generally ask for your instructions for maturity when you buy the GIC. You can instruct them to re-invest the money into another GIC, move it into a different investment, place it in a bank account, or have it returned to you. If the GIC is within your RRSP, you will be subject to a federal withholding tax (income tax you pay up front) if you decide to cash it in at maturity instead of reinvesting.

Most institutions send out a notice a few weeks before your GIC matures. If you want to change your instructions for maturity at that time (or anytime before the maturation date), call your financial institution and let them know.

Looking at Performance: The Indices

An index is a statistical yardstick used to gauge the performance of a particular market or group of investments. By tracking average prices or the movement of prices of a group of similar investments, such as small- or large-company stocks or bonds, an index produces a benchmark measure against which you can assess an individual investment's performance.

Think of using an index the same way that you may use a list of comparable home sales when you shop for a house in a neighbourhood. If the list of comparable homes shows you that the average three-bedroom house sells for $225,000, you can't expect to buy a similar house for too much less than that. At the same time, you don't want to pay too much more. In the same respect, the benchmarks produced by an index show you a reasonable performance target.

A return is an investment's performance over time. If you're looking at performance for a period of time, say five years, look for an average annual return. If the same mutual fund returned 10 percent over the course of those five years, its average annual return would be 10 percent. Its cumulative return, which simply totals an investment's performance year after year, would be 50 percent for those five years.

If an investment's performance over the course of a year is vastly superior or inferior to the appropriate index's return, you'll want to know why. Your investment may be outpacing its peers because it's a lot riskier. A mutual fund, for example, may invest in stocks or bonds that are far riskier than other funds it may resemble. On the other hand, an investment may be lagging its peers simply because it's a poor performer. Bear in mind, however, that you have to build a performance history over time to determine the character of a particular investment. Notice that in Figure 5-1, the mutual fund is performing below average, which may prompt you to sell that investment.

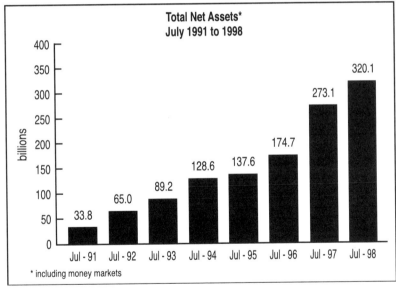

Figure 5-1:
A poor
performer.

The following sections offer a look at the indices that are likely to come in handiest as you try to determine expected performance from your investments.

Start by tracking an index that represents or follows your stock or mutual fund. After you become familiar with that index, pick up another index to follow. Be careful not to follow too many indices, though — it can become confusing and time-consuming.

Canadian indices

The number of Canadian stock, bond, and mutual fund indices continues to grow, with more specialized indices popping up over time. The ones described in this section are those you'll see on the daily business pages. Just about everyone in the investment world refers to them, and you will too.

The S&P/TSX Composite Index

The S&P/TSX Composite Index is the best recognized and most consulted Canadian index. It keeps track of the average performance of 300 Canadian large-company stocks trading on the Toronto Stock Exchange (or TSX), and is weighted according to market value. An index committee of the TSX reviews the companies periodically and may replace companies for several reasons, including, for example, bankruptcy.

The performance of member stocks is calculated daily, and acts as a daily measure of the market's rise or fall as well as an overall performance figure. These are the numbers you hear reported on the nightly news, see in newspapers, and can view on your computer screen if you log on to a personal finance Web site.

The S&P/TSX Composite Index tells you the average performance of the stocks in the index. This performance is reported as both numbers and percentages. If the TSX goes up, your newspaper might report that "the TSX went up 2 points or 6 percent today." When the stock market is doing well, the numbers and percentages go up. When it's doing poorly, they go down.

The index is divided into 14 industries and is further divided into sub-industries. Here is a list of the 14 main industries:

- Energy
- Financials
- Info technology
- Consumer discretion
- Consumer staples
- Healthcare
- Industrials
- Materials
- Telecommunications
- Utilities

✔ Gold

✔ Metals and mining

✔ Real estate

✔ Income trust

The S&P/TSX 60

Another heavily quoted Canadian stock index is the S&P/TSX 60 Index. This index follows 60 representative Canadian large-company stocks trading on the Toronto Stock Exchange. Some of the companies included in the S&P/TSX Composite Index, such as Alcan, TransCanada PipeLines Inc., and the Bank of Montreal, are also tracked by the S&P/TSX 60 Index. While both the Composite and the S&P/TSX 60 Indexes rise and fall daily, the S&P/TSX 60 Index tracks a much narrower range of companies, and is not as useful for investors who want a general benchmark against which to gauge their own stock's performance.

Scotia Capital Markets Universe Bond Index

If you're invested in the Canadian bond market, you won't be able to track the performance of your investments using a stock index like the S&P/TSX 60. You have to consult an index designed specifically to track bonds. In Canada, Scotia Capital Markets maintains the best-known bond index.

According to their own information sheets, Scotia Capital Markets would like its index to "reflect performance of the broad 'Canadian Bond Market' in a manner similar to the way the S&P/TSX Composite Index represents the Canadian equity market."

Begun in 1979, the universe bond index comprises almost 1,000 issues, including Government of Canada, provincial, municipal, and corporate bonds. You'll find the Scotia Capital Markets Universe Bond Index reported in daily newspapers alongside the major stock indices. The bond index is similarly calculated to reflect both number and percentage changes.

Book IV

Investment Fundamentals

The U.S. indices

While the Canadian indices will be most useful to you as an investor, it's also a fact that the American economy and its stock markets are considered the world leaders. Individual investors, business people, financial advisors and mutual fund managers all keep their eye on the performance of key U.S. indices when assessing their own progress in the market. You're sure to recognize at least one of the following key U.S. indices.

The Standard & Poor's 500

Also called the S&P 500, the Standard & Poor's index has become the dominant benchmark in U.S. investing in recent years. The S&P 500 tracks the performance of 500 stocks, comprising of 400 industrial companies, 40 utilities, 20 transportation companies, and 40 financial firms.

The S&P 500 is home to some of the best-known stocks in North America, including U.S.-based Microsoft and Dell. With so much fanfare, the S&P has become the index to beat for many mutual fund managers. Outperforming it is cause for celebration.

The Dow Jones Industrial Average

The Dow Jones Industrial Average (DJIA) tracks the performance of 30 companies that are among the largest companies and some of the most venerable stocks the U.S. stock market has to offer. If you own one of these stocks, such as Exxon or IBM, you'll want to know how your stock is faring compared to the average.

The results of the Dow are reported daily in newspapers across Canada, the U.S., and the world, as well as on news and financial Web sites. The results, which tell readers the average performance of the stocks in the index, are reported as both numbers and percentages. If the Dow goes up, your newspaper might report that "the Dow was up 4 points or 10 percent today." When the index goes up, investors are actively buying stocks and the stocks covered by the index are going up in value.

The Dow Jones is known all over the world, and serves as a daily report on how well the powerful U.S. economy is doing. After falling behind somewhat in the esteem of some critics for shying away from tracking high-tech stocks, the index has very recently been updated. While it still tracks the same number of companies — 30 to be exact — that number now includes computer giant Microsoft and retail giant Home Depot. It's important to look at the Dow relative to its index peers to get a sense about whether certain slices of the stock market are faring better or worse than others.

The Dow Jones Industrial Average is price-weighted — giving companies with a higher stock price more weight regardless of their size. Because of price-weighting, one company's stock can pull the index up or down significantly, even if that direction doesn't reflect the performance of the majority of the index's stocks. That price-weighting doesn't mean you can ignore the DJIA, which follows the performance of giants such as AT&T and General Electric, but you should understand how the average is determined.

The Nasdaq Composite Index

The Nasdaq is another widely quoted U.S. index. It is sometimes seen as a competitor to the S&P, but the Nasdaq Composite is actually very different. For starters, Nasdaq measures the stock performance of nearly 6,000 companies, over half of them in the high-tech and biotech arenas, and all of them found in the Nasdaq market. The index includes giant U.S. companies like Apple, Intel, MCI Communications, Cisco, Oracle, Sun Microsystems, and Netscape.

As a result, the Nasdaq index is a good deal more volatile than, for example, the Dow Jones Industrial Average and, perhaps, the stock market at large. It's also home to some of the bigger success stories of the 1990s, many of which are technology firms. The higher the potential for return an investment has, the more the risk it carries.

Just like the Dow Industrial Average and the S&P 500, the Nasdaq Composite gives the average performance of the stocks in the index both as numbers and percentages. If the Nasdaq goes up, your newspaper might report that "the Nasdaq was up 1 point or 3 percent today."

The Wilshire 5000

Want a good look at how the overall U.S. stock market is doing? The Wilshire 5000 tracks a huge universe of stocks — in fact, it lists almost every publicly listed stock, including those listed on the New York Stock Exchange, the American Stock Exchange, and the Nasdaq Composite. That's a pretty definitive look at the large-, medium-, and small-company stock markets.

This is not a must-read index, especially on a daily basis, but it is an index investors want to at least know about and have the option of viewing once in a while. It's the largest index going. It gives an investor a broad sense of how the U.S. stock market is faring overall and in which direction stocks are headed. More mutual funds have also started investing in stocks listed in the Wilshire 5000, which gives investors total U.S. stock exposure.

Remembering that Performance Is Relative

Everything is relative, regardless of which investment performances you're measuring. What may have been great performance a year ago may be considered good, bad, or indifferent today, depending on how the particular market you're invested in is doing.

Unless you have evidence of other negative indicators, don't knee-jerk into selling an investment just because its performance lags behind an index one year. You're investing for the long term. What's underperforming its index this year may well bounce back next year.

The trick to using indices is to be able to definitively tell how well the performance of your investments stacks up against that of their peers in the market you're in. With that know-how, you can answer questions like: Is this stock's performance average? Is this mutual fund's performance above average? Is this bond's performance poor?

Looking Rationally at Market Highs and Lows

You're investing hard-earned money, so you want to enjoy a sense of comfort and confidence in your investments' potential to perform as expected *over time*. The emphasis on the phrase over time is because chasing short-term performance can drive you crazy.

Investments can look mighty risky if you track their performance every day. In contrast, risk tends to flatten out a bit if you look at it year to year. In fact, since the late 1920s, few classes of investments have lost money over a ten-year period. Of course, some individual investments have lost money, but the general rule applies: Holding on to investments for a longer period of time will reduce your exposure to losses.

Do you want to avoid undue risk? Invest for the long term — or, at the very least, five years. If you need to tap your investments earlier than that, stick to shorter-term cash equivalents, such as money market mutual funds (which invest in high-grade bonds with shorter maturities) and guaranteed investment certificates.

Learning how to gauge the market is different from thinking you can predict the market. No one — not even the most savvy broker — knows with any real certainty how well or how poorly the market will fare in the future.

Reaching Your Goals

After you start investing, monitor your progress to ensure that you're on track. Make the anniversary of your first investment your day of financial reckoning (or at least that month).

When the day arrives, sit down and take an earnest look at what you're investing in, how much you're investing, whether or not your goals have shifted or changed completely, and whether or not you're saving enough (and earning enough on your investments) to reach your goals.

The ultimate measure of your portfolio isn't whether or not you're beating the benchmarks. It's whether or not you're reaching your goals. Are you? For example, if you determined at the outset that you needed to invest $500 a month and earn an average annual return of 9 percent, are you hitting your goal?

If you're meeting or beating your goals, you're in great shape. If you're not, identify what's wrong. Maybe you're not investing enough. You may have to pay off some bills so that you can find more money in your household budget to invest. Or you may find that your RRSP needs greater funding, so you have to increase the percentage of your pay you contribute each week or month.

To ensure that your investment plan is a workhorse that's pulling its weight, feed it. As you get raises at work, or come into "found" money — maybe a small inheritance, a bonus at work, or a tax refund — consider investing some or even all of these funds in your portfolio.

Knowing When to Sell

Of course, maybe one or more of your investments isn't performing up to your standards. This kind of letdown happens to the best of us, and you can count on a disappointment once or twice in your investment life. When underperformance hits home with one of your investments, take a deep breath and try to figure out what's happening.

Figuring out how long to hold on to an investment that isn't producing any growth is a challenge. You have to first determine what is keeping the investment on the rocks. The following sections offer a look at why an investment may be underperforming.

When you sell a stock, bond, or mutual fund, make sure that you find a suitable replacement and don't leave the cash lying in your chequing account, where it may be pilfered away by life's daily expenses.

Book IV

Investment Fundamentals

Is the economy the reason for your investment's slump?

Is the entire market taking its lumps? If so, your investment isn't immune. If one or more sectors of the stock market are taking a licking, consider the impact to your stock, bond, or mutual fund. A sluggish economy, or one that is in retreat, can play havoc with investments. Investments are long-term endeavours. Don't sell just because of an economic downturn. You'll take a loss.

An economic downturn can create a buying opportunity if it sends the price of stocks spiralling downward.

Is your stock falling behind?

If a stock is struggling, look at the company. Forget about what's happened to date for a moment. If you discovered the company again today, would you buy it? Do some future analysis on the company's prospects. Don't let your answer be clouded by negative feelings about the past few months or years. If you bought the stock because you believed that the company was well positioned for a turnaround due to new and competitive products or services, sales, profits, or other facets of its financial position, hang on a bit more. The last thing you want to do is take a loss on a stock that may turn around a few days or months after you give it the boot.

At the same time, if you decide you wouldn't buy the stock again today, or some of the economic reasons that attracted you to the stock in the first place haven't panned out, selling is okay.

Is your bond slipping behind?

If a bond is doing poorly, maybe because interest rates have risen (bond prices move in reverse of interest rates), ask yourself what cost you can expect from hanging on to the bond until maturity. Compare that expense with what it will cost you to sell the bond. If interest rates jump, say, to 9 percent, and you're hanging on to a bond paying 4 percent, you might well be better off selling the older issue and buying a new bond.

Is your mutual fund fumbling?

If your mutual fund isn't performing up to snuff, look at the fund manager's style. If the stock market is growth-oriented and your manager is a value manager who looks for bargains, you may be wise to hang on. Value-style investing comes in and out of favour, and you wouldn't want to miss the upside. Of course, if an inept mutual fund manager is the only reason you can find for the lagging performance, you can sell. Try to wait until a fund's performance has been impaired for at least two years in order to avoid unnecessary losses.

Chapter 6

Becoming an Effective Investor

*R*ight about now, you're probably feeling some sense of satisfaction. You've begun the enviable journey of building an investment plan and realizing your financial goals. Beyond the load of information you've absorbed already, some additional common-sense concepts can make your investing experience more productive and less mysterious. A few tricks of the trade also can help you become a more effective investor by guiding you around some of the pitfalls that trip up even the most earnest and dedicated investors.

Starting and Staying with a Diversified Investment Approach

The goal of diversification is to minimize risk. Instead of putting your eggs in one basket by investing every dime you have in one stock, one bond, or one mutual fund, you should diversify.

Diversification is a strategy for investing in a wide array of investments that ideally move slightly out of step with each other. For example, an investment in an international mutual fund might be doing poorly while an investment in a Canadian equity mutual fund is doing well. By investing in different sectors of the investment markets, you create a balanced portfolio. Parts of that portfolio should zig when other sections zag.

Table 6-1 shows the power of diversification by examining how three different diversified portfolios of money markets, bonds, and stocks can fare over time. The table also gives you a concrete idea of the investments that should go in a portfolio based on your own tolerance for risk. They're also a good way for you to measure whether your own portfolio is diverse enough for your own tolerance for risk or loss.

Table 6-1	Three Models of Diversification		
	Lower Risk/ Return Portfolio	*Moderate Risk/ Return Portfolio*	*Higher Risk/ Return Portfolio*
Makeup	20% money markets, 40% bonds, 40% stocks	20% money markets, 30% bonds, 50% stocks	20% money markets, 0% bonds, 80% stocks
Return for best year	22.8%	28.1%	35%
Return for worst year	–6.7%	–13.4%	–19.6%
Average annual return	9%	10.1%	10.9%

It's important to determine the percentage of stocks, bonds, and cash you want in your portfolio. In the stock and bond categories (or mutual funds that invest in these assets), it's also important not to load up on any one sector of the economy. So steer clear of the temptation to invest in three technology mutual funds, four Internet stocks, or six junk bonds — even if they're paying more than other investments.

The saying "no pain, no gain" also applies to the investment experience. You can avoid the prospect of experiencing any pain at all by investing only in Canada Savings Bonds and GICs that are federally insured. The price to be paid for that strategy: You may never lose money in the traditional sense, but you never gain much either, which means that you can still fall behind. You also run the risk of falling behind because of inflation, which eat ups about 1 to 3 percent of your purchasing power each year. If you only earn 4 or 5 percent a year on your savings or investments, you'll have a hard time preserving the capital you have, let alone growing it.

Developing a Dollar Cost Averaging Plan

No one can afford to have an investing plan forgotten or relegated to the back burner. You need to set up a plan for making set, regular investments. This way, you ensure that your money is working for you even if your best intentions are diverted.

Dollar cost averaging is a way to ensure that you make fixed investments every month or quarter, regardless of other distractions in your life. Dollar cost averaging is a simple concept: You invest a specified dollar amount each month without concern about the price per share or cost of the bond. The market is fluid — the price of your investment moves up and down — so you end up buying shares when they're inexpensive, some when they're expensive, and some when they're somewhere in between. Because of the commission cost to buy small amounts of stocks or bonds, dollar cost averaging is better suited for buying mutual funds.

In addition to helping you overcome procrastination about saving for investments, dollar cost averaging can help you sidestep some of the anxiety many first-time investors feel about starting to invest in a market that can seem too overheated or risky. With set purchases each month or quarter, you buy shares of your chosen investments regardless of how the market is doing.

Dollar cost averaging isn't statistically the most lucrative way to invest. Because markets rise more often than they decline, you're better off saving up your money and buying stocks, bonds, or mutual funds when they hit rock bottom. But dollar cost averaging is the most disciplined and reliable way to invest. Consider this: If you set up a dollar cost averaging plan now, then in 10, 20, or 30 years, you'll have invested every month in between and accumulated a pretty penny in the interim.

Most mutual funds let you start out on a dollar cost averaging plan (often called pre-authorized contribution or PAC plans for accounts inside your RRSP) for as little as $50 or $100 a month. The only catch is that you have to sign up to allow the fund to take the money from your chequing account each month. To find out if the funds you're interested in offer the service, look for the information in their prospectuses or call their toll-free shareholder services phone number.

Investing with Your Eye on Taxes

Unfortunately, with investing, as with just about any other activity that generates income, gains are taxable. The federal government collects all income tax for itself and on behalf of most provinces. As a rule, provincial income tax is calculated as a percentage of your federal income tax rate.

The fact that you will pay combined federal and provincial income tax on your investments should not deter you from trying to invest successfully. A good investor will come out ahead in the end. But you should realize now that you will pay taxes on investment gains. Consider the following tax implications for investments outside your RRSP.

Book IV

Investment Fundamentals

Savings accounts

Gains on simple savings accounts and tiered savings accounts are taxed as income. Banks and financial institutions report these gains to the Canada Customs and Revenue Agency (CCRA), just as all investment gains are reported.

GICs

The interest you earn on GICs must be declared as taxable income, and will be fully taxed on an annual basis. If, for example, your GIC is locked in for five years, that means you will pay tax each of those years — even if you haven't yet received any of the interest.

Mutual funds

With mutual funds, unfortunately, you have to pay tax each year on the interest and capital gains that the fund distributes to each of its shareholders. You also have to pay taxes on your own gains when you sell shares — another reason for a long-term buy-and-hold strategy.

Stocks

With stocks, you don't pay taxes on your gains until you sell your shares — a feature that fans of stock investing say is a clear advantage in the long run. The downside, however, is that when you do cash in shares down the road, your tax bracket or the tax rate may have increased.

Bonds

Price appreciation (if any) on a bond — whether it is a government or corporate bond — is taxable when the bond matures as a capital gain (you will pay tax on 50 percent of your capital gains annually). If your bond loses value, that loss is deemed a capital gains loss. You can apply that loss against other capital gains you report to CCRA.

The interest you earn on a bond is fully taxable annually. That rule applies even to compounded Canada Savings Bonds, where the interest is reinvested yearly, meaning you'll pay tax on interest you haven't yet received.

Tax-deferred investing with RRSPs

As Canadians, we have a very powerful tax-deferral tool in the form of RRSPs. Maxing out your contributions to your registered retirement savings plan really does boil down to a choice of paying yourself or paying CCRA.

As discussed in Chapter 3, the benefits of investing within an RRSP are twofold: First, all the contributions you make within your RRSP are tax-deductible — in other words, these contributions, up to the allowable limit, become an immediate deduction from your taxable income. Second, the government defers the tax bill for any gains you make on those investments, be they interest, capital gains, or dividends, until you cash in your RRSP.

Even after you turn 69, the tax-deferral power of your RRSP will keep working for you. How? You will have the opportunity to convert your RRSP into a registered retirement income fund (RRIF) and withdraw your funds over time rather than in a lump sum. You'll pay less this way, since the government charges less up-front income tax (called withholding tax) on smaller withdrawals. On top of that, the government gives you a pension income credit up to $1,000 annually, which reduces the amount of tax you owe for income you receive from qualifying pension income including RRSP funds.

Because interest-bearing investments are fully taxed at your marginal tax rate (the rate at which you are taxed on your last earned dollar of a given tax year), many investment advisers suggest these as your first choice to go inside an RRSP. Since capital gains are taxed at a lower rate (only 50 percent of the gain is added to your overall taxable income), these might be investments to keep outside your RRSP. Dividend-bearing investments from shares in Canadian equities are also taxed at a lower rate. That's because dividends represent a corporation's after-tax profits. To avoid double taxation, the federal government provides some tax relief in the form of a dividend tax credit, which reduces the rate at which your dividends from Canadian corporations will be taxed.

Calculating the dividend tax credit is a bit confusing (especially for residents of Quebec, who follow a different formula). For non-Quebec residents, you begin by grossing up (multiply upward) the amount of dividends you've received by 25 percent. Then you calculate federal income tax on that amount. Finally, you subtract the dividend tax credit (which is 13.33 percent of the grossed-up dividend) from the income tax you've calculated. In the end, you'll see that dividends are taxed at a lower rate than regular income. For those who can't stomach the calculations, keep in mind that dividend-paying Canadian corporations will send you a statement showing the grossed-up amount, as well as the dividend tax credit.

Book IV

Investment Fundamentals

The price you pay for tapping your retirement accounts early

Do not take money out of your RRSP on a whim, say, when you're changing jobs or feel the need for an extravagant vacation. If you make the withdrawal anyway and you're not age yet age 69, the money is considered income and is taxed as such by CCRA at your marginal tax rate. You'll also lose the tax-sheltered earning potential that the money bought you inside the plan.

Income tax on RRSP withdrawals is levied immediately when you take the money out. This way, the government gets its money up front, rather than waiting for you to file your tax return. This manner of extracting income tax is called a withholding tax, and is based on the amount you withdraw. As of the 2003 tax year, if you take $5,000 out of your RRSP, you'll be charged 10 percent withholding tax (unless you live in Quebec, where you'll have to pay more — 25 percent — since the province levies its own withholding tax). Between $5,001 and $15,000, that tax jumps to 20 percent (33 percent for residents of Quebec), and again to 30 percent for withdrawals over $15,000 (38 percent for residents of Quebec).

Since the withholding tax may not match the amount of tax you actually owe on the money you've withdrawn, you will still have to reckon with CCRA at tax time. Depending on your tax bracket, that will either mean paying more when you file your tax return, or, in some cases, getting a rebate for overpayment.

CCRA lets you borrow money from your RRSP for two specific purposes: a first-time home purchase (through what's called the Home Buyers' Plan or HBP); and post-secondary education (via the Lifelong Learning Plan or LLP). In both cases, the money coming out of your RRSP will not be subject to the withholding tax. However, there are specific rules governing when you must pay it back.

Before you borrow any money from your RRSP through the HBP or LLP, take into account the loss of tax-sheltered income growth you will suffer because of these withdrawals. In other words, even though you aren't paying any interest on the loan from your RRSP (as opposed to a traditional mortgage or student loan), you still pay indirectly. Depending on the amount and the length of time the money is out of your RRSP, this indirect loss of income growth could ultimately make a traditional bank loan the smarter choice.

Book V

Making Your Investments Work for You

The 5th Wave   By Rich Tennant

"I'm not sure — I like the mutual funds with rotating dollar signs although the dancing stocks and bonds look good too."

In this book . . .

Having decided what types of investments will work best for you (if you haven't decided, see Book IV), you're ready to start buying them and putting your money to work. Here you can find advice on selecting, buying, and monitoring your investments. This Book also helps you know where to look for the best mutual funds, stocks, and bonds, as well as how to keep track of their performance — online and off.

Here are the contents of Book V at a glance:

Chapter 1

Buying Mutual Funds

· ·

In This Chapter

▶ Growing to like discount brokers

▶ Picking a discount broker

▶ Discovering why banks are the simplest place to buy mutual funds

▶ Dealing with your bank

▶ Figuring out the different types of advisers

▶ Choosing the right adviser for you

▶ Checking out the advantages of dealing with an independent no-load company

▶ Counting the cost of going direct

· ·

*B*efore someone tries to sell you a mutual fund, or before you try to buy one on your own, you first have to decide whether you're a resolute do-it-yourself investor or a person who needs a person. Humanity can be divided into two groups: Those who want help with their investing and those who want to do it on their own. Funds are perfect for either approach. In this chapter, you'll find descriptions of the different companies and people you can go to for advice on selecting funds — or simply to have your purchase orders carried out. You can also read about a few of the advantages and drawbacks of each method of buying funds.

Checking Out Discount Brokers

Discount brokers are about the closest you can get, as yet, to investing heaven — they're cheap and simple. A discount brokerage account is a great place to build wealth for the long term because you can put almost any kind of investment into it — including mutual funds, shares, bonds, Canada Savings Bonds, or even your own mortgage. Next to the invention of the mutual fund itself, discount brokers have done more than any other financial innovation to open up the stock and bond markets to ordinary people. And best of all, discount brokers are great for keeping costs down, which is one of the most important determinants of investment success. Discounters are firms set up simply to carry out your buy-and-sell orders — charging low commission rates — and to provide an account in which you can hold your investments. They sometimes purport to offer lots of flashy services and information, some of which can actually be useful. But essentially, a discounter is just a bare-bones order-taking service.

In Canada, a minor price war broke out among discounters in the late 1990s as firms vied to come up with special offers, dancing dogs in neck ruffs, free trades, and extra services — which usually added up to a better deal for customers. Since then, though, the special promotions have died down — discounters have given up expensive gimmicks, sometimes even raised their rates, and concentrated their marketing more narrowly on getting the clients they really want, folks with plenty of cash. Picking a discount broker can be tricky, though. This chapter gives you the whole story — how discounters work, how they can save you more of your hard-won cash, how to pick the right one for you, and, finally, a few warnings about the horrible problems that some discount brokerage customers have run into.

Discovering what discount brokers are

A *discount broker* is a true broker in the sense that it's a firm set up simply to act as an agent. It collects a *commission* — that is, a transaction fee — when you buy or sell stocks, bonds, funds, and other investments. Yes, financial planners, insurance agents, and traditional stock brokers also take your orders in this way, but they also bill themselves as advisers and experts who get a fee for helping out. Nothing wrong with that as such — but their fees eat into your returns. A Canadian discount brokerage firm is nearly always an arm of a big bank, taking most orders over the phone or the Internet. In the United States, discounters execute your share-buying transactions for as little as US$8. In Canada, minimum charges for a single trade are generally C$25 and up. Discounters are perfect for mutual fund investors because they sell a huge range of funds with low sales commissions.

If you're absolutely certain that you're going to want personal advice from someone when you pick your funds, then skip this part of the chapter and jump ahead to the section, "Dealing With Your Friendly Neighbourhood Bank," for detail about banks and the services they provide. Discount brokers don't provide much advice, so if you feel you need help picking funds, you won't enjoy using one. In the same way, there's little or no "financial planning" on offer from a discount broker. Just a bare-bones account to hold your investments, and rock-bottom fees to buy and sell. The discounters may offer to sell you fancy packages of pre-selected funds, but there's not much personal advice about your situation.

Discounters, then, essentially offer a commodity. They employ a bunch of youngsters who are paid a wage for covering the phone and who don't traditionally get extra pay for persuading customers to buy things. In return for charging low commissions, discounters hope to attract enough business to turn a profit. That's why they're so keen to turn as much of their business as possible over to the Internet, where it can be automated.

In the not-too-distant past, discounters were subject to the provincial securities rule that obliges brokers to ensure that trades are suitable for the client. Like other people in the investment business who accept your money, they were supposed to follow the *Know Your Client* rule (the concept that people selling investments should recommend only securities that are suitable for the customer). However, securities regulators in Canada have since begun relaxing the requirement that trades through a discount broker must be vetted to find out whether they fit with the customer's risk tolerance and investment knowledge. That was after lobbying by the discounters, who claimed that having a human being check every trade slowed up the process too much. The message, for those who may have missed it, is this: When investing through a discounter, you're on your own, Dennis.

Getting set up with a discounter

Setting up an account with a discount broker is simplicity itself. You don't have to sit through a sales spiel or show that you have thousands to invest — just call them up, sign a few forms, open an account, and put some money in. Here are the basic steps:

- ✔ Call the discount broker you picked and ask for a new account application form or an RRSP application form. You can usually print it right off the firm's Web site.

- ✔ Sign and fill in the form, and send it back.

- ✔ Notice the dense pages of conditions that they make you sign. Guess what? They're not in your favour. But just about all discount brokers impose these convoluted terms — which essentially say that in the event of a disagreement the broker is always right — so you can't really escape.

- ✔ A discounter will pretty well accept your business no matter how poor you are. But you'll have to have the necessary cash in your account, Jack, before you make the first trade. For a fund, the minimum buy is nearly always $1,000.

- ✔ You never have to meet anyone face-to-face. The anonymity is relaxing, although you'll almost certainly get put on hold for a good stretch when problems occur in your account. And you'll get used to shouting at dazed teenage brokerage house slaves in a harsh barking tone.

Book V

Making Your Investments Work for You

✔ After that, just phone in your orders and check your account statement carefully. Always have them mail the trade-confirmation slip to you and check it against the order you placed.

Most discounters let you call up your account online, so just take a printout of the page and date it when you want a permanent record of your holdings and their value. They'll also mail you a monthly statement if you place orders or a quarterly one if you don't. Check these against your own records.

Using a discount broker is investing for grown-ups. There's no one around to hold your tiny hand or coo into your tight little rosebud of an ear that "the market always comes back." In return for the low commissions they charge, discounters are geared to provide little or no personal service.

Selecting a discounter

Don't get in a lather comparing the discounters' commissions and totting up their special offers. It's wonderful to see people in the investment business offering to cut their prices, but over the long term, saving $100 on a one-off basis doesn't amount to much. If you plan to simply buy and hold high-quality funds and stocks, it doesn't make a lot of difference if you've spent $100 or $200 in commissions building the portfolio. Yes, cheaper is always better, but fast and polite responses to your orders or questions, and investments that suit your needs, are all just as important as low rates.

At your service

The important thing is efficient, accurate, and prompt service — something that, sadly, discounters seem to have had a problem providing in the past. After a debacle in the hectic stock market of early 2000, when some clients said they were left on the phone for up to a week, the discount firms embarked on a hiring frenzy aimed at ensuring that they had enough staff to handle soaring demand.

If you've got the time and energy, you could pick a firm by opening two or even three separate accounts at different discounters at first — there are usually no fees for signing up as a client. After a year or so, you'll get a good feel for which discounter is most reliable and the easiest to use and you can transfer all of your assets there. Be sure to ask your family, friends, and work mates about their experience with discounters. If you keep coming across horror stories about a particular firm, then shop elsewhere.

Apart from commissions, the fee you're most likely to face at a discount broker is an annual administration fee of about $100 for an RRSP (often the fee is waived if your account is big enough).

Don't worry too much about picking the right discounter. If you make the wrong choice, you can switch later at the cost of a few weeks' wait and a fee of about $100. It's messy — and watch out for mistakes while they transfer your investments — but you have a right to move.

Book V

Making
Your
Investments
Work for
You

Finding the right discounter for you

A good source of information on discount brokers — and low-cost investing in general — is the Stingy Investor Web site (`www.ndir.com`). Run by avid number-cruncher Norman Rothery of Toronto, it offers a rundown of discounters' rates (although some of the information may be out of date from time to time).

Don't become obsessed with commission rates when choosing a discounter. Some have decided to market themselves as cut-price providers, offering minimum commissions for a stock trade that can run $25 or even less. That's a tremendous deal for investors; but remember that if you don't plan to trade stocks frequently, it's only of limited value. Look at the whole picture — including mutual fund commissions, service standards, and special options — before you make your choice.

Try calling the company a couple of times with questions. If you can't seem to get decent answers, then consider going somewhere else.

Some experts advise that you should use a discount broker not owned by your usual bank. That way, if there's ever a dispute over a trade, the broker can't just dip into your bank account and extract money.

How about a mutual fund discount broker?

Apart from the true discount brokers, which are licensed to deal in stocks and bonds as well as funds, investors also can choose from among dozens of "no-load" or "discount" mutual fund dealers that sell only mutual funds. These companies, which are often happy to buy and sell funds over the telephone, usually charge no commission on front-load funds, living off the rich trailer payment instead. Individual stockbrokers and financial planners also frequently offer to sell funds with no load.

Discount dealers will clearly save you money, and there's no reason not to go with one if you're happy with the level of service available and the selection of funds. But once again, don't let cost be the only deciding factor. There's no point saving yourself a one-off expense of 2 percent if the dealer subsequently doesn't give you enough advice and choice of products. Stick to a regular discount broker who's able to sell you shares and bonds as well as funds while also offering low commissions. And deal with a discounter that's a large multi-billion dollar organization so that you know the systems are in place to administer your account properly.

Dealing with Your Friendly Neighbourhood Bank

In the mid-1990s, if you asked an executive at a non-bank fund company why the banks didn't seem to be able to run a decent equity fund, he'd have curled his lip with scorn. "How," he would reply, "can the banks expect to get good stock picking out of their wretched nine-to-five wage slaves who ride the commuter cattle trains every morning from suburban wastes north of Toronto?" Well, those days are long gone. Banks have improved the returns from their stock funds and there are encouraging signs that they are finally reducing the costs charged to mutual fund investors. For one thing, banks have rolled out *index funds* — which simply track the entire market. And the Internet could turn out to be a marvellous device for further reducing costs, marking the dawn of a new age for the small investor.

Banks are a great place to buy mutual funds, especially if you just want a simple option that's also okay value. There are perks to keeping your investments where you keep your cash. If you use a bank to buy funds, your account statement is on the same recordkeeping system as your chequing account, which is very convenient, and no meddlesome prating salespeople are involved. This section shows why you can just go ahead and use your local bank branch for mutual funds if you want a quick solution. You won't get the best bargain going, but it'll do the job.

The good news about buying where you bank

Banks are the very simplest place to buy mutual funds: Just walk in and put your money into a selection of their house brands. But don't assume they're the best choice. A bank is a great place to start out buying funds, but you should certainly take a long hard look at what they can and can't offer.

Hey, you're busy, what with training your cat to play the xylophone ("No, the *left* paw!") and getting into the *Guinness Book of Records* for growing the longest nose hairs ever officially recorded (that old fool in Sinkiang-Uighur glued them in). So why not just make things easy on yourself and simply grab your mutual funds at the bank? Mutual fund buyers, especially rookies, can do well at the bank for a number of reasons.

One-stop shopping: Update your passbook and buy a fund

It's easy. Even if you don't have an account with a bank you can still walk into a branch, hand over a cheque, and sign up. Okay, it may take a couple of days to get an appointment with a *registered representative,* a bank employee who is licensed to sell funds, but after that the process should be painless. Once you've opened a fund account, most banks have telephone services for buying and selling funds, and nearly all offer telephone and Internet services that let you check your account balance and recent transactions.

Banks sell their own funds with no commissions or sales loads. That means all your money goes to work for you right away, and you can cash out at any time with no penalty (although some banks and other fund companies impose a short-term trading penalty, typically 2 percent, on those who sell a fund within 90 days).

You can set up a fairly decent mutual fund registered retirement savings plan — a tax-sheltered account of retirement money — at a bank in a half-hour flat by simply buying one of their pre-selected fund packages. Staff are trained to sell these mixtures, and questionnaires are designed to slot you into the right one, so you're likely to get a reasonable fit.

Keeping it together: All your eggs in one basket

Now that the banks have taken a healthy bite into the trust industry, you probably have your mortgage, line of credit, and chequing account at a bank. So buying mutual funds from the company that already holds the mortgage on your house means you get the luxury of dealing with the same bank employee for everything.

Offering to move your mutual fund business to a bank can radically improve your bargaining power when seeking a loan or mortgage. Bank employees get little chocolate soccer balls as rewards when their customers bring their investment portfolios to the branch. Use this to your advantage when looking to extend your credit, take a plunge into the real estate market, or buy a car. In today's competitive banking environment, an investor with a portfolio is a sought-after prize.

Not just a watering hole in the Namib Desert

The employees you deal with at a bank branch get wages, so they're not commission-driven jackals. But they usually sell only the house brand. And yes, they receive incentives to attract business, and yes, the banks tend to be vague on exactly what bonuses are paid.

For the most part, you'll find that banks are happy to sell you *index funds* — low-expense funds that simply track the stock- or bond-market index or benchmark. Index funds are such a good deal they should be part of every investor's arsenal, although you should also have between one-third and one-half of your stock market investments in traditional *actively managed* funds, featuring a person who buys and sells investments in search of trading profits.

Banks, unlike mutual fund companies that market their products through commission-paid salespeople, are able to make money from running index funds because they don't have to pay out those big commissions. Most offer index funds with expenses as low as 1 percent, compared with 2.6 percent on the average Canadian equity fund, for example. If you were to simply walk into a branch and open up a mutual fund account full of index funds like that, chances are that you'd do better than millions of mutual fund investors.

Banks fight for the right to serve you

The banks are hungry for your mutual fund business and they're willing to cut prices and improve service to get it. The fantastic growth of the Canadian mutual fund industry, with assets soaring to more than $385 billion in mid-2003 from less than $30 billion in 1990, has represented a migration of cash from bank savings accounts and guaranteed investment certificates into funds. The banks want to hold on to as much of that money as they can.

There's another reason why the banks are fund-mad: Remember that mutual funds are a wonderfully profitable and low-risk business. The management company just keeps raking off those 2-percent fees (plus expenses), no matter how well or badly the fund does. That must be a great comfort to unitholders of the average U.S. large-cap growth stock fund, for example, who lost an average of 19.1 percent of their money annually in the three years ending July 2003. Even large-cap value funds, the sort that Warren Buffett may hold, lost 1.98 percent annually during this dreadful three-year period. according to Morningstar.com.

Lending money, the banks' traditional way of making a profit, is more risky than selling mutual funds because borrowers can default and interest rates can jump, leaving the banks stuck with a pile of underpriced loans. So, more and more, banks are trying to become "wealth management" companies, and mutual funds are the name of that ball game.

Buyer beware: Banking cons

Nobody's perfect, and buying funds at a bank — either over the telephone or by going into a branch — has its drawbacks. Here, for your viewing pleasure, are the drawbacks of lining the pockets of nasal power-hungry guys from New Brunswick, the sort who become bank chairmen.

Few options

The big problem is lack of choice: The banks have dragged their feet on marketing other companies' funds because a banker likes sharing fees like a lobster enjoys taking a hot bath. That means customers are often stuck with the bank's line of products, which isn't always the strongest. More and more bank employees have personal finance training but most aren't specialists in the field. To get a full analysis of your situation, you may still have to go to a planner working for an independent firm.

The narrow selection of funds at many branches is the biggest problem with buying from a bank. All the big banks offer a full range of funds under their own brand name, but that doesn't necessarily mean that their Canadian equity or global equity funds will be any good. And even if you try to build a diversified fund portfolio by buying the bank's index funds and actively managed funds as well, there's always a risk that you're leaving too much money with just one investment team. Suppose that a particular coterie usually tends to get excited about flashy technology stocks — then you're likely to lose money when other investors get tired of such high-priced science fiction tales. You can get around this lack of *diversification* — the annoying word for spreading out your investments — by opening an account elsewhere as well, perhaps with another bank. Or you can at least increase your diversification by buying several of the bank's actively managed funds.

Overworked and underpaid: Not just you, some bankers too

Banks are busily blitzing their branch networks and cutting back on staff in search of higher profits, so it's getting harder and harder to talk to an actual human being unless you've got a whopping balance in your account. That's a drag and it's a disadvantage of going to a bank if you'd rather deal with a person than peck at the keyboard of a machine (what's wrong with you, anyway?).

Lack of pressure to perform

Customers who buy funds from a bank are isolated in the sense that the fund managers don't have brokers and other salespeople breathing in a damp, hot way down their necks, insisting on good returns. If a broker-sold fund's performance goes into the tank, salespeople get angry and embarrassed, because they have to face the clients they put into the loser. That's never a fun session. The sales force demands explanations from the manager. So the presence of salespeople probably serves to impose some discipline on fund companies. With bank funds where no brokers are involved, terrible performance used to drag on for years with little publicity or outcry.

Banks now take funds more seriously, meaning that problems get fixed fairly quickly, but bank fund unitholders arguably still don't have anyone looking out for their interests. Yes, nearly all mutual funds have "trustees" who theoretically are on the side of investors, but you won't find many fund trustees saying a single critical word about a fund's management or expenses. Most unitholders wouldn't know where to look for the trustees' names and no wonder: the fund companies hardly ever publicize their identities. You have to plow through the obscure "annual information form" for the fund, available on demand from your fund company, to identify the trustees. Securities cops are pushing to have the system fixed, but the fund companies are in no huge hurry to change the rules.

Another problem with buying funds from your bank is that, well, you're forced to deal with a bank. Phone calls get routed to voice-mail hell before they end up in the bottomless pit of general delivery, with Tats in shipping. Branches are being shuttered across the country, forcing customers to dial 1-800-PLS-HOLD or go to an Internet site (which saves the bank a packet). With all the branch cutbacks, employees are overworked. And they usually have to deal with all the other services and products that the bank delivers, and then face the whining, puking, and foot-stamping at home — not to mention the kids. So you won't get the sort of personal attention and time that a good financial planner or even stock broker delivers.

Stock Brokers, Financial Planners, and Advisers Aplenty

We may run out of water, out of brain surgeons, out of Vancouver Island marmots, and out of braying self-important financial journalists. But we'll never run out of mutual fund salespeople. At least 50,000 Canadians hold themselves out as financial advisers or planners in one way or another, and most of them are licensed to sell you mutual funds. They come in a bewildering range of guises, from DKNY-clad smoothies in the downtown core of big cities to hoser types in Molson sweatshirts wolfing down the free sandwiches at fund company lunches. And they give themselves a galaxy of names: financial consultant, investment counsellor, estate planner, financial adviser, investment executive, personal financial planner. Don't get worked up trying to figure out the differences among them. The fact is that the provinces' regulation of the financial planning game is still spotty, and hampered by power struggles among the competing groups, that outside Quebec just about anybody is free to call themselves anything.

This section describes the main types of fund salespeople and tells you about the advantages of using financial planners who charge only an upfront fee rather than collect commissions on the products they sell you, wrapping up with some basic tips on the right, and the wrong, way to pick an adviser.

Commissioned advisers

The vast majority of Canadians choose to go with a financial adviser who gets paid by a mutual fund company or insurance company for selling investment "products." In part, that seems to be a reflection of the nation's thrifty Scottish psyche: Unlike many Americans, Canadians would much rather have the expense of investing advice hidden from them, buried in the fee of a mutual fund or the cost of insurance. That way, it seems so much less painful than having to cut the adviser a cheque.

An obvious example of a commission-paid salesperson is the traditional *stock broker,* who makes money when you buy stocks, bonds, or funds. The broker gets a transaction fee or *commission* each time you put an order through.

- ✔ With stocks, the commission is added onto the cost when you buy or deducted from the proceeds when you sell — and your transaction confirmation should clearly show how much was charged. For example, when you buy or sell $10,000 worth of shares, you can expect to pay a sales commission of about $300.

- ✔ With bonds, the "commission" is normally a profit margin that's hidden in the price, just like buying a pair of jeans at the Gap. That's because brokers usually sell bonds to their clients that they already own themselves. No separate commission is charged or shown on your confirmation slip because the broker has already taken a markup.

- ✔ With funds, things get more complicated. But the essence of the system is that the broker (or financial planner or insurance salesperson) is paid by the fund company. The fund company, remember, charges an annual management fee — which is deducted from the assets of the fund — and pays roughly half of that out to the salesperson.

Commission-paid salespeople also include life insurance salespeople, whether independent or tied to a particular insurance company. In addition to life insurance, these agents are often licensed to sell mutual funds or the insurance industry's version of mutual funds, which are known as *segregated funds.* Segregated funds — so-called because their assets must be kept separate from those of the insurance company — carry guarantees to refund up to 100 percent of an investor's initial outlay.

Finally, there are Canada's thousands of financial *planners,* either in franchises, chains of stores, or small independent offices, whose bread and butter is the mutual fund.

Fee-charging advisers

The next group is far smaller but represents an excellent choice for those who don't mind signing a cheque to get advice. They're the *fee-charging* financial planners who aren't interested in selling products. In some cases, they'll help you to set up an account at a discount brokerage in which you can buy low-cost funds.

The drawback of going with a fee-charging planner is the pain of paying the freight, which can be substantial. It might be a percentage of your investments — typically 1 or 2 percent — or it can be an hourly charge that ranges from $50 an hour to a few hundred, depending on the complexity of your affairs.

With a fee-charging planner, you may have to make more choices about the investments you buy and the strategy you adopt. That's because the financial plan produced for each client is different, reflecting individual needs and wants, whereas commission-paid salespeople are often happiest suggesting a predesigned and relatively fixed package of funds that leaves you with few decisions to make.

Investors with substantial assets, in the hundreds of thousands of dollars, should strongly consider going with a fee-charging planner. Your accountant or lawyer may offer the service or may be willing to recommend someone. The fee will often run into several hundred dollars, but that's a bargain compared with the hidden cost of high mutual fund management fees levied by fund companies that sell through commissioned advisers.

A fee-based planner may produce a plan and then refer you to a commission-charging dealer — or even collect commissions on funds that you buy. That kind of double-charging adds another layer of complexity and fees, and it might not be the best deal for you. If the adviser is simply putting you into funds that pay commissions to salespeople, then what did you pay the advice fee for?

Salaried advisers

Thousands of financial advisers are being trained by the banks to take over the "wealth-management" needs of the aging baby boomers. They're generally on salary — plus bonuses if they can persuade you to put your savings into one of the bank's products, usually mutual funds or some other kind of managed-money program.

As explained earlier in this chapter, these bank employees are often limited in the products they can offer, and their training may not be as full as that of brokers or specialized financial planners. That means their advice should always be taken with a pinch of salt: they're employed to push the bank's products or sell funds that pay the bank a fat commission. Still, especially for investors with relatively simple needs and clear financial goals, the bank can be a great place to start off investing. Compared with the hard-driving world of brokers or financial planners, there's often little sales pressure. The product choices are simple, and having all of your money in one place makes for easy record-keeping.

But don't forget that you're doing the bank a favour by handing over your savings. That means you're entitled to a helpful and experienced bank employee, not some rookie or sleepyhead. And don't get railroaded into buying one of the fixed arrangements of funds that the banks love to pitch (it makes their administration much easier, for one thing). If you feel that none of the pre-selected packages meets your needs, then insist on a custom mixture of funds.

In general, the bank is the perfect first stop for starting-out investors with only a few thousand at their disposal. The banks are equipped to deal with small accounts and they have handy automated systems that allow you to check your account balance and transactions without waiting for someone to get back to you.

And the banks' employee training in investment advice is getting better all the time as the wealth-management business becomes vital to their future profit growth. Some banks even have qualified brokers available right in the branch who can sell you a range of stocks and bonds or funds from nearly every company.

 The blurred distinctions among all these types of commission-paid advisers make the whole business of looking for help confusing. But at least you have one thing going for you: Remember that if you buy mutual funds, your money is reasonably safe because it goes to the fund company instead of staying with the broker or dealer. So if you decide to dump your salesperson and his or her firm, you can simply shift the account elsewhere, after some whining and delays on the part of the old salesperson. Your money is doubly safe because even the fund company itself has to leave the fund's assets with a separate custodian for safekeeping.

 Make sure that you'll receive a statement at least twice a year from the fund company (ask to see a sample) so that you can be certain you're on the fund company's books. And make your cheque out to the fund company, not the salesperson. Finally, you should get transaction confirmations for your purchases from the company — alternatively, you can call the fund company itself to double-check that they have a record of your investment.

Finding the right professional

To fix yourself up with a well-trained and professional planner, make sure that he or she meets one or more of the following tests:

- ✔ **Membership in Advocis:** Advocis is Canada's largest association of financial advisors. It represents thousands of professional advisors and has members in 50 chapters across the country. Advocis members are to adhere to a strict Code of Professional Conduct, meet ongoing continuing education requirements, and are committed to putting the interests of their clients first. Making life simpler for investors, two former financial planning groups — The Canadian Association of Financial Planners and The Canadian Association of Insurance and Financial Advisors — merged in September 2002 to create Advocis, the brand name of The Financial Advisors Association of Canada (www.advocis.ca).

✔ **Completion of a recognized industry course:** These include courses that lead to the Certified Financial Planner (CFP) and Registered Financial Planner (RFP) designations. The CFP designation is administered and overseen by the Financial Planners Standards Council (FPSC). CFP licensees must meet the Council's standards in education, experience, examination, and ethics. Continuing education is required. The RFP designation used to be awarded by the Canadian Association of Financial Planners (CAFP), which merged into Advocis. The RFP program is now phased out.

✔ **Certified General Accountant (CGA):** An accounting designation granted to individuals who have fulfilled the educational and experience requirements of their provincial governing body. CGAs are trained in tax, accounting, and financial management. They are required to abide by a code of conduct and participate in a mandatory continuing education program.

✔ **Certified Management Accountant (CMA):** A person who passed the requirements of his or her provincial society of management accountants. CMAs are financial management professionals who combine accounting and strategic business management skills.

✔ **Chartered Accountant (CA):** Someone who has passed the national Uniform Final Exam. CAs have extensive training in tax and other areas of financial management and must adhere to a code of conduct.

✔ **Employment by a chartered bank or by a stock broker who is a member of the Investment Dealers Association of Canada:** If the person works for a bank, you can be sure of some supervision, although you should take nothing for granted. The banks have set up their own personal finance training system, but there's no guarantee that the person you get is particularly knowledgeable. If the broker works for an IDA brokerage firm, he or she could be incompetent or greedy, but at least you know that he or she has passed the Canadian Securities Course, the educational course given to all new stock brokers. Members of the public are also welcome to take this excellent course, virtually all of which may be useful to you. Call the Canadian Securities Institute, an IDA affiliate, at 416-364-9130 in Toronto or dial toll-free 1-866-866-2601 (English) or 1-866-866-2602 (French). The Web site is www.csi.ca. The IDA is a lobby group and disciplinary body for stockbrokers. If the person who wants to sell you mutual funds doesn't work for an IDA firm, then his or her employer should be in the new Mutual Fund Dealers Association of Canada — which was set up to catch mutual fund dealers who "fall through the cracks" with no industry-run body to keep an eye on them.

Unfortunately, you can easily come across bad planners, brokers, and advisers who have impressive qualifications or reputable employers. But at least you know that if they've gone to the trouble of getting trained, or they're under some kind of supervision from a large organization, then you're less likely to be stuck with a complete turkey.

The right way to pick an adviser

Finding an adviser is very much like picking a building contractor or nanny: word of mouth and your own gut instincts are among the best methods to use. So your first move should be to ask friends and relatives what they've done and whether they're happy with their advisers. And then go to see several candidates. Apart from qualifications and membership in a professional association, you should also check out a few more things.

Does the adviser seem curious about you and willing to answer questions frankly?

A good adviser will ask you questions about your income, life history, assets, financial goals, health, marital status, pension, and investment knowledge. If that doesn't happen, then you could be dealing with a sales-driven hotshot who's just looking to make commissions quickly. Shop elsewhere. And ask about sales commissions as well as the adviser's experience and training. Vague answers are a bad sign.

Does the adviser work for a firm with an adequate back office for client record-keeping and supervision?

Jargon alert — having an adequate "back office" is just a fancy way of saying that they are set up to administer clients' accounts and orders. Ask to see a typical client statement and ensure that the firm has a *compliance officer,* an employee who keeps an eye on the salespeople and the way they treat clients.

Does the adviser sell a broad range of products?

A planner who wants to talk about funds from just one or two companies is probably lazy. Nobody can be familiar with the products from every company, but you want someone with a good idea of what's out there. You also want an adviser who's knowledgeable about life insurance, or who can at least hook you up with an insurance expert.

Are the adviser's office, grooming, and general image professional?

Nobody's looking for Armani or marble halls, but sloppy-looking premises or a scruffy appearance are signs of someone who hasn't been able to attract many clients.

The wrong way to pick an adviser

Unfortunately, a lot of what passes for investor education is just a giant sales pitch. So-called "seminars" that purport to enlighten you on a particular topic such as preparing a will or taking early retirement are really just a way of getting lots of sales targets into a room. Wandering around a glitzy "exhibition" or "forum" for investors may be fun and even informative. But these events are also a lure for getting "prospects" — potential customers — into a nice concentrated bunch where they can be picked off easily. In fact, be careful about attending seminars if you're the excitable or gullible type. The colourful celebrity speakers who work the investment circuit are often masters of making their audience both greedy and afraid — and easy targets for the inevitable sales spiel from the salespeople who paid for the event.

If the phone rings with a broker, adviser, or planner offering to help, decline politely and hang up. Always. Such "cold calls" are a time-honoured method of drumming up business for brokers, and the salesperson calling may be perfectly legitimate. But responding to a random phone call out of the blue is an awful way of picking someone who's supposed to help you manage your money — such an important aspect of your life.

The telephone is still a favourite tool of those creatures that occasionally crawl out from under the rocks — the dishonest salespeople pushing "unlisted" and "over-the-counter" stocks or other "unregistered" investments that promise fantastic returns. Do yourself a favour and have some fun. Rent two wonderful movies about these crooked sales reptiles: *Glengarry Glen Ross,* based on David Mamet's play about sleazy real estate marketers, and *Boiler Room,* a movie released in 2000 that tells the tale of some Long Island junk-stock pushers. After watching those two great films, you'll be better equipped to deal with telephone sales pitches.

Buying Direct

Buying your funds directly from a fund company instead of from a bank or through an adviser is one of the more enjoyable and profitable ways of investing in funds. The company is directly answerable to you when you call or e-mail, and you can pull your money out with no strings attached if the managers don't make the fund go up. And best of all: You'll have no sales charges or *loads* to increase your expenses — companies that sell directly to the public without imposing sales commissions are called *no-load* fund marketers. This section examines buying direct, going through the pros and cons of this style of investing and taking you through a list of the top no-load players.

It's easy to get started — just call the companies or company you're interested in. They'll be pleased to send you the information about their funds. Table 1-1 lists the biggest no-load fund companies on the Canadian scene, their Web site addresses, and their assets. All are independent companies except for big Altamira Financial Services Inc., which was bought recently by National Bank of Canada. No-load fund managers treat you rather like discount brokers do. They have anything from one to dozens of telephone-answering staff who will handle your orders but don't know much about you. All you have to do to invest is call their number (often toll-free) and transfer some money or send a cheque. There's no wheedling, pawing salesperson in the shape of a broker, planner, or insurance agent, which means there are no fiddly and costly commissions to worry about. No-load companies are generally fairly big businesses and they can usually be relied on to send pretty reliable statements of your account. Sounds perfect, doesn't it? But first up, you have to make a choice between these two alternatives:

- ✔ The no-load direct sellers that offer truly low expenses but also come with a narrow selection and higher minimum investment.

- ✔ Altamira, with its wonderfully wide selection and low initial investment but higher expenses (which are in line with mutual fund industry averages).

Table 1-1	No-Load Direct Sellers in Canada	
Company	*Web Site*	*Assets (in $thousands, as of mid-2003)*
Phillips, Hager & North	www.phn.com	9,661,877
Altamira Financial Services	www.altamira.com	3,697,514
McLean Budden	www.mcleanbudden.com	657,973
Mawer Investment Management	www.mawer.com	610,113
Sceptre Investment Counsel	www.sceptre.ca	297,804
Saxon Group of Funds	www.saxonfunds.com	355,640

The advantages of buying direct

Using a no-load company that sells to the public is a halfway house between the lonely course of picking your own funds at a discount broker on the one hand and the comfy warm blanket of getting help from a bank employee or a salesperson who earns commissions on the other. When you go to such a salesperson (the option dealt with in "Stock Brokers, Financial Planners, and Advisers Aplenty," earlier in this chapter) or a bank (see "Dealing With

Your Friendly Neighbourhood Bank," earlier in this chapter), you get lots of assistance and help — but you usually pay for the advice in the form of higher annual costs imposed on your fund. And the selection that a bank or commission-paid salesperson carries is often limited to only a few dozen funds. At a no-load company, the people answering the phone will offer some advice and the expenses on their funds may be low. But the selection of funds on offer is once again limited to the company's own products, and that might be just a handful of funds. Discount brokers (see "Checking Out Discount Brokers," earlier in this chapter), whoopee, have lots of funds. They're the amusement park of funds. But you'll be riding that roller coaster alone, because you'll get hardly any help.

When you contact any fund company, no matter how it sells its products, ignore all of the marketing blather and ask for an application form and prospectus. Those two usually set out the stuff you need to know, such as minimum investment and annual costs. You can always slip 'em in the recycling bin later. Or toss them in that old rusty oil drum you use to burn garbage. (Don't the people next door complain about the choking greasy plume of smoke, by the way?)

There are important advantages to going with a no-load direct fund seller if you want a hassle-free solution. Here are the main ones.

More money in your pocket

The biggest plus of buying from a no-load company is the fact that you cut out the intermediary. No-load companies can charge you lower fees — although they don't always choose to do so. Because they don't have to pay an army of brokers — or cover the expense of running a sprawling network of bank branches — some direct sellers offer Canadian stock funds with annual expenses of 1.5 percent or less. That's much cheaper than most domestic equity mutual funds, which have total annual costs and fees closer to 2.5 percent. The more expensive fund is taking an extra 1 percent annually out of your mottled hide — over ten years, that difference adds up to 10 percent of your money.

Why one percentage point matters to you

If you were to invest $10,000 and earn a tax-free average annual return of 9 percent for a decade, you'd end up with $23,674. But the same $10,000 invested at a 10-percent rate of return, because the expenses were one percentage point lower, would grow to $25,937 — more than $2,200 more (see Table 1-2). That's why it's better to have a fund with a 1.5-percent annual expense ratio, rather than one with 2.5 percent in annual expenses. You can check a fund's expenses at the *Globe and Mail*'s mutual fund site, www.globefund.com, or look at your newspaper's monthly fund report.

Table 1-2	Think 1 Percent Doesn't Matter? That'll Be $2,263, Please	
Year	**Value at 9-Percent Return**	**Value at 10-Percent Return**
Initial investment	$10,000	$10,000
1st	$10,900	$11,000
2nd	$11,881	$12,100
3rd	$12,950	$13,310
4th	$14,116	$14,641
5th	$15,386	$16,105
6th	$16,771	$17,716
7th	$18,280	$19,487
8th	$19,926	$21,436
9th	$21,719	$23,579
10th	$23,674	$25,937

Advice for adults

Another advantage of going directly to a fund company is that you're treated like an adult rather than simply as a faceless consumer of the fund product. In other words, the company's Web site and mailings to investors often are more candid about performance. That's because many of the investors who use no-load companies tend to be independent souls who relish the low costs and are happy with the lower level of advice. They're the sort to demand complete reporting of performance.

If you're not satisfied with the performance of your no-load funds, or if you have queries, it's simple to just pick up the phone and call. You may not get the errant fund manager or a senior executive, but the representative who answers the phone will probably be able to give you some answers.

And best of all, buying no-load doesn't mean you have to give up getting advice altogether. Direct sellers often have staff who can advise you on choosing funds and even help you shape your overall investment strategy.

Make mine simple

Dealing with a fund company directly is simpler than buying a fund through a salesperson. You're not forced to relay your order or request via someone else, potentially causing confusion or delay. You can call up the company and buy and sell funds in your account right over the phone as well as asking for forms or other administrative help. Your relationship as a customer is clearly with the fund seller, not with an intermediary like a broker. That's great for you because:

- ✔ You have just one company to deal with and complain to if there's a mistake in your account. Or did you say you enjoyed muttering endlessly into voice mail, like a doomed character in an abandoned Samuel Beckett play?

- ✔ You get just one annual and quarterly statement of account.

- ✔ If you own several funds, it's handy to be able to check on their performance if they're all included in one company's mailings.

- ✔ You can switch money easily from fund to fund as your needs or assets change.

Allowing frequent trades

It's often tempting to move your money frequently from fund to fund in an attempt to catch rising stock markets and avoid falling ones. Just like it's hard to resist swerving really close to cops carrying out a roadside check to make 'em jump and scramble (they always see the funny side, bless them). Naturally, frequent traders love using no-load companies because there are no charges to switch their money in and out. That makes a no-load fund company the perfect choice if you fancy yourself someone with the ability to time movements in stock and bond prices — for example, every time the Canadian stock market goes up 20 percent in a year, you might decide to pull out of stocks. But no-load fund companies don't appreciate it when customers move their money around constantly, because it greatly increases the company's administration costs (all of those transfers must be accounted for). So they'll eventually crack down on you by limiting your trades. And you'll often get slapped with a charge of 2 percent of your money if you switch out of a fund within three months of buying it.

Still, if you want to try to outguess the markets and trade some money around every few months (even though it's often a bad idea), then direct and no-load may be the way to go. Here's why:

- ✔ The companies have people on staff to move your money from fund to fund quickly and easily.

- ✔ There are no sales charges to complicate the transfer of money or add to your costs.

Book V

Making
Your
Investments
Work for
You

✔ Buying the fund directly from the no-load fund company rather than through a discount broker or commission-paid adviser means your sale orders go directly into the fund company's system instead of through a discount brokerage employee. That speeds up the process and reduces the probability of mistakes in your order.

✔ You get an account statement and transaction confirmation slip in the mail directly from the no-load company and not through the discounter. That's simpler and more convenient for investors who are closely tracking their own performance.

Switching into and out of no-load funds through a discount broker can in fact cost you commissions, because discounters often impose small fees of around $35 each time you sell a no-load fund. A conventional broker won't welcome your business if you plan to chop and change your portfolio all the time, because of all the troublesome paperwork you create. Heavy and constant trading won't thrill even a no-load fund company. That's because trading raises administrative and mailing costs, which have to be paid by other investors. So with many companies, expect to pay a 2-percent penalty when you move money out of a fund within three months of buying it. And if you really go over the top, you may be banned from switching your money around or limited to a certain number of trades — say, one a month. How many trades are too many trades? There are no firm rules on what counts as heavy trading, but here are a few guidelines:

✔ An investor who moves some of his or her money from fund to fund twice a year or less would count as a light or infrequent trader.

✔ Someone who made between 2 and 12 trades a year would count as a medium trader.

✔ More than a dozen trades a year indicates that the investor is a heavy trader who thinks he or she can outguess the market.

A fund company is unlikely to cut off your buying and selling privileges unless you're trading very frequently — making changes to your portfolio every few days or every week. If you do get cut off and you can't resolve the situation, you may have to move your money to a discount broker that allows constant trading. But even if you buy through a discounter, the funds you're buying may well levy that 2-percent penalty if you sell a holding that was bought fewer than three months ago.

The penalty seems small but it reduces your return. Suppose that you decide that the Canadian stock market is set to boom because oil prices are rising (foreign investors see us as resource producers in toques, so they tend to buy into our market when prices for commodities, such as lumber, energy, and metals, are going up). You put $10,000 into a no-load company's Canadian equity fund, a fund that invests in stocks and shares (which in turn are a tiny slice of ownership of companies). The Canadian market goes up 10 percent in two weeks and my fund matches the rise in the broad market, boosting my investment to $11,000 — at which point you sell half of your holding in the fund, or $5,500. If the company slaps a 2-percent fee on investors who leave a fund after less than 90 days, then you'll receive a cheque for just $5,390, which is $5,500 minus 2 percent. Of course, your other $5,500 is still sitting in the fund.

How many trades are too many? Well, research seems to show that almost any level of chopping and changing reduces overall returns because most investors let emotion distort their judgment, leading them to do things at the wrong time. People sell when the market has slumped and is about to bounce back. And they buy after it has already shot up and is about to go on the slide.

Over time, share prices may tend to rise remorselessly as good companies thrive and the world economy grows, but the stock market also advances in sudden starts. If you happen to have sold your equity funds, following the dictates of your brilliant can't-lose trading strategy, just before one of those days, then you miss out on the profits. That said, there are a few times when it's a sensible idea to move money out of a fund, and holding the fund directly at a no-load company makes the process easier. Good times to move money include:

- ✔ When the fund has gone up so much that it now represents a huge portion of your portfolio. For example, if you've decided to keep just half of your money in shares, but one or more of your equity funds have produced a 100-percent return over the past year, then you probably have too much money riding on equities. Time to sell some of those stock funds.

- ✔ If you're foolhardy enough to bet on a *specialty* fund that invests in just one narrow section of the market, such as South Korea or financial-services shares, and you've been lucky enough to score a big profit. Such one-flavour funds tend to post huge crashes soon after their big wins — as investors go cool on the kind of stocks they hold. So think strongly about selling at least some of your units in a specialty fund as soon as it has a good year. No, don't just think about it: Pick up the phone and do it immediately.

- ✔ If your reason for holding the fund no longer applies. For example, a fund manager you like may have quit, or the fund may have changed its investment style.

Check your portfolio once or twice a year, and if it's out of line with your ideal mix of investments, then readjust it by moving money from one fund to another. For example, say you've decided that you want one-third of your $10,000 mutual fund collection in sure-and-steady government bonds — certificates issued by the government that pay interest and can be cashed in again at the issue price after a set number of years. The other two-thirds is in lucrative-but-dangerous stocks, those tiny pieces of ownership in companies. See Chapters 3 and 6 for more on stocks and bonds.

Book V

Making
Your
Investments
Work for
You

So your setup is:

$3,300 bond funds   33 percent of portfolio

$6,700 stock funds   67 percent of portfolio

$10,000 total portfolio 100 percent of portfolio

Say the bonds hold their value over the next year, remaining at $3,300, but the stocks rise 30 percent to $8,710, which gives you a mix of:

$3,300 bond funds   27 percent of portfolio

$8,710 stock funds   73 percent of portfolio

$12,010 total portfolio 100 percent of portfolio

This means you have too much riding on the stock market in relation to our original plan — almost three-quarters of the total pile. You can fix it easily by moving $663 out of your stock funds and into the bond funds, leaving you with a portfolio that looks like this:

$3,963 bond funds   33 percent of portfolio

$8,047 stock funds   67 percent of portfolio

$12,010 total portfolio 100 percent of portfolio

If you hold a super-volatile fund that invests in a narrow sector or region, such as a technology company or Latin America, it's a good strategy to move some money out of the fund if it shoots up in value. That way, you lock some profits before the inevitable crash. Holding such funds forever is of dubious benefit because they're at risk of losing money for long periods.

The drawbacks of buying direct

Most no-load mutual fund companies offer too few funds to really give you a diversified portfolio — that means an account with many different types of investment. Here are the main drawbacks to using a direct seller.

Significant levels of cash required

As mentioned at the start of this section, not everyone can go direct. As attractive as it seems to investors who are serious minimalists in terms of their need for guidance and their interest in paying fees to invest, you need a minimum amount of cash to play. This is obviously not the case with novice investors, or those in the process of building their portfolio. Although this type of investing may not be the right choice for you now, it is something to keep an eye on as your investing savvy, and your portfolio, grows.

Lack of choice

The main problem with direct purchase of funds is the narrow selection. Few direct sellers have more than one or two funds, so if you leave all of your money with the company you're at risk of seeing the market turn against that particular investment style.

A typical no-load fund company sells just a couple of funds of each type. Generally, there'll be:

- One or two stock funds
- One or two bond funds
- One or two global equity funds
- Perhaps a few specialty funds, such as one that buys only U.S. stocks

That's a small selection compared to buying from a broker, insurance salesperson, or financial planner, who can often sell you at least a dozen funds in each category. At a discount broker, you can buy hundreds of each.

You can avoid this lack-of-choice drawback by buying the direct seller's funds through a discount broker instead, if they're available. That lets you use the no-load seller's funds, with their nice low expenses, in combination with index funds or funds from other companies. However, your discount broker may not even carry a low-expense company's funds (because the discounter gets little or nothing in sales commissions).

Chapter 2

Types of Mutual Funds

*M*utual funds fall into four main categories, each of which is discussed in this chapter, but here is a quick breakdown:

✔ **Equity funds:** By far the most popular type of fund on the market, equity funds hold stocks and shares. Stocks are often called "equity" because every share is supposed to entitle its owner to an equal portion of the company. In May 2003, Canadians had $85 billion in Canadian equity funds, $75 billion in foreign equity funds, and another $28 billion in U.S. equity funds. These funds represent an investment in raw capitalism — ownership of businesses.

✔ **Balanced funds:** The next biggest category is balanced funds. They generally hold a mixture of just about everything — from Canadian and foreign stocks to bonds from all around the world, as well as very short-term bonds that are almost as safe as cash.

✔ **Bond funds:** These beauties essentially lend money to governments and big companies, collecting regular interest each year and (nearly always) getting the cash back in the end.

✔ **Money market funds:** They hold the least volatile and most stable of all investments — very short-term bonds that are issued by governments and large companies and usually provide the lowest returns. These funds are basically savings vehicles for money that you can't afford to take any risks with. They can also act as the safe little cushion of cash found in nearly all well-run portfolios.

Equity Funds: The Road to Riches

Equity mutual funds, which buy stocks and shares of companies, are perhaps the best route to riches that you'll ever find. Okay, marrying a 95-year-old hang-gliding suicidal millionaire in poor health may be quicker. But then there are all those whining rival heirs to fend off. Equity funds are a wonderful invention because they hold shares in a huge variety of (usually) great companies. So wide is the selection of holdings in most equity funds that if some of the businesses fail or stagnate, there are nearly always enough winners in the fund to pull you through.

Equity funds should be the core of just about anybody's investment portfolio, assuming he or she is investing for at least five years. Because the economy and well-run companies are almost certain to grow over time, stocks and shares can be the engine of growth for your money. If you want to earn decent returns on your cash over the long term, and you've decided to buy mutual funds, you're pretty well forced to buy equity funds. That's because they're the only type of fund that's likely to produce big returns, possibly 10 percent or more annually, in the long haul. And those are the types of returns that you need to defy inflation and build a substantial nest egg.

Yes, the stock market and the funds that invest in it can drop sharply, sometimes for years — you'll find some scary examples in this chapter. So make sure you've a good chunk of bond funds in your holdings as well. But there's strong evidence that equity markets pretty well always rise over periods of ten years or more, so equity funds are a relatively safe bet for buyers who are sure they can hold on for a long time without needing the money back at short notice.

Why investing in stocks is simple

Believe it or not, making money in the stock market is easy — in theory. You just buy *shares* — which are a tiny slice of ownership — in well-managed companies and then hold on to them for years. As the businesses you've invested in thrive, so do their owners, and that includes you as a *shareholder*. But when you actually try to select wonderful companies, things get complicated. For one thing, it's hard to tell which companies have genuinely bright prospects, because the managers of just about every corporation do a great job of blowing their little brass horns and making everything look wonderful in their garden. And like everything else, the stock market is subject to the whims of fashion. When investors decide that they love a particular company or industry, the shares usually go to fantastic heights. At that point, buying stocks turns into a risky game — because there's no point buying a great business if you pay four times what it's really worth.

Being fallible human beings, we constantly sabotage ourselves in the market. When everything is going well and shares are climbing to record highs, we feel all warm, fuzzy, and enthusiastic — and we stumble into the market just in time for the crash. And when the economy or the stock market is slumping, we get all depressed and sell our shares at bargain-basement prices — just when we should be grabbing more. But perhaps the biggest problem with investors is our innate belief that we're smarter than everybody else. Everybody else thinks the same thing, which means that lots of us are going to end up losers. You can try to make pots of money buying speculative technology companies or penny mining stocks or companies consolidating the pallet industry, but that's really gambling. True investing in stock markets is simply buying well-established, well-run businesses and holding the shares, ideally for years.

Mutual funds are one of the very best and easiest ways to make money from the stock market. That's because:

- They're run by professionals who are trained in the art of checking out businesses.

- They're set up to make it easy to put your money in and get it back.

- Best of all, funds hold a wide variety of companies, spreading your risk and giving you the chance to benefit from growth in a huge range of industries.

By handing your money over to a mutual fund company, you're saving yourself from yourself — if you aren't making the decisions, then you can't risk your savings on wild bets or crazy dreams.

The real kicker in stock market investing is figuring out whether a company is genuinely good — a quality outfit worth putting money into — and whether the price you're being asked to pay for shares is too high. Unfortunately, though, there may be no such thing as a true value for a company, because the numbers all vary so wildly according to the assumptions you make about the future. In that case, a stock is simply worth what people decide to pay for it on any given day. And that may not be very much: Stocks can dive for no apparent reason. It has happened to me, painfully, in my own personal investing. But there's one thing about the crazy volatile stock market that we should care about because it makes stocks and shares wonderful for ordinary people like us saving for the future. A gift, in fact, from the gods. Good companies thrive, their profits go up, and their stocks gain value over the long term.

Sometimes selecting a good company to invest in can be almost embarrassingly simple. If you shopped for a cordless phone in the early 1990s, you may have noticed that only two companies offered phones that could be described as beautifully designed, Canada's Nortel Networks Corp. and Japan's Sony Corp. High-quality design, like reliable service or clever marketing, is no accident — it requires talented people, and they don't stay long with badly run companies. Sure enough, an investor who bought either Nortel or Sony shares in early 1995 multiplied their money more than sixfold over the next five years.

Based on experience in the past century, you almost always win in the stock market over periods of at least ten years provided you stick to big, high-quality companies and you spread your risk by owning at least a dozen of them in different industries. Most equity mutual funds play it even safer by holding at least 50 different stocks (many hold 100 or more) so that they can be sure of buying and selling their holdings easily.

Remember, too: It's hard to lose money in the stock market as long as you buy well-run, large companies and hold them for long enough. Studies that looked at every ten-year period in the market during the 20th century found that stocks produced a profit in 99 percent of the periods, although that falls to 86 percent if you take inflation into account. Still, odds of six-to-one in your favour aren't bad.

Look at nearly any professionally run equity portfolio, such as a mutual fund, and you'll notice that it contains dozens and dozens of stocks. Why so many? Why doesn't the manager just buy his or her favourite half-dozen shares and run with that? One reason is that when the market turns sour on a company its stock tends to drop like a rock. So exposing a huge proportion of your fund to a single company is a bad idea. Getting stuck with a stock that nobody else wants is a fund manager's most ghastly nightmare. Whenever he or she offers the shares for sale, rival investment managers make sympathetic faces and gentle cooing noises — and then refuse to buy the garbage at anything but sub-bargain prices. Under provincial securities law, in order to protect investors, a mutual fund can have a maximum of one-tenth of its assets in a single stock. And most funds limit their exposure to single shares to 5 percent or less.

The ABCs of picking a fund

How do you pick those high-quality conventional funds, the ones that try to buy and sell stocks? Here are three basic rules, the ABCs of selecting a great equity fund:

- ✔ First, look for a fund that's full of companies from **A**ll industries — and, in the case of global funds, **A**ll major regions of the world.

- ✔ Second, insist that your fund holds lots of big, stable, and conservative companies — the type that investors call **B**lue-chip (because the blue chip is traditionally the most valuable in poker).

- ✔ Finally, look for a fund that has a habit of producing **C**onsistent returns over the years that aren't out of line with the market or with its rival funds.

The following sections take a closer look at these ABCs for picking core equity funds for your savings: Think **A**ll industries, **B**lue-chip holdings, **C**onsistent performance.

Select from all industries

A fund should hold companies from all, or nearly all, major industries, in order to spread risk — and to give unitholders a chance to profit if the stock market suddenly falls in love with a particular type of company. Here is one way to break down the industry groups:

Book V

Making
Your
Investments
Work for
You

- ✔ Banks and other financial companies, such as Citigroup, Royal Bank of Canada, or Deutsche Bank

- ✔ Natural resource processors, such as Imperial Oil Ltd., Alcan Inc., or Slocan Forest Products Ltd.

- ✔ Technology companies, such as Microsoft Corp., Intel Corp., or southern Ontario e-mail pager maker Research in Motion; cable-TV companies like Shaw Communications Inc. also fit in this group because they're battling the phone companies for control of the Internet access market

- ✔ Manufacturers of industrial and consumer products, such as drug maker Pfizer Inc. or General Electric Corp.

- ✔ Dull but steady utility and pipeline companies such as Alberta power generator TransAlta Corp. or pipeline system TransCanada PipeLines Ltd.; telephone companies such as AT&T and BCE Inc. also officially fit into this group, although in 1999 and 2000 they frantically tried to become Internet and entertainment companies, only to get caught in a financial vice as prices plunged for telephone calls.

- ✔ Retail and consumer service companies such as Canadian Tire Corp. and Wal-Mart Corp.

Not every group has to be represented in the top holdings of every fund, but a portfolio without at least one resource stock, financial services giant, or technology player among its biggest ten investments may represent a dangerous gamble. Why? Because of the ever-present chance that share prices in that missing sector will suddenly and unpredictably take off, leaving your fund in the dust. Avoid funds that make bets like that.

Hold blue-chip winners

Glossy mutual fund brochures often promise the sun, moon, and stars . . . but just look at the fund's top holdings. Whether the fund is Canadian, U.S., or international, at least two-thirds of its ten biggest investments should be big blue-chip companies that you or someone you trust has at least heard of. A list of the top stocks in any fund is readily available on the Internet. Look in the fund's marketing material or in the reports and documents given to unitholders. What you're looking for are big and stable firms, the type that offer the best prospect of increasing their shareholders' wealth over the years.

Talk is cheap and fund managers love to drone on about how conservative they are. But managers of supposedly careful funds can sometimes quietly take risks: They put big portions of the fund into weird stuff like resource stocks or Latin America to jazz up their returns and attract more investors. The list of top holdings is one of the most valuable pieces of information an investor has about a fund because it can't be faked or fudged (ruling out pure fraudulent reporting). If you don't see at least a few giant names — companies like BCE Inc., Coca-Cola Corp., Bank of Montreal, New York Times Co., General Motors Corp., GlaxoSmithKline PLC, or Toyota Motor Corp. in the fund's list of its biggest holdings — then the fund manager may be taking undue risks, fooling around with small or obscure companies.

Check out past performance, with caution

After you've satisfied the first two of these conditions, you should look at the fund's past performance. Begin by filtering out funds that have been around for fewer than five years, unless it's quite clear that someone with a record you can check has been running the money. Then look for consistent returns that aren't too much above or below the market. We all want to make lots of money, so leaving past returns until last may seem crazy, and exactly opposite to one's natural inclination. But it's the way sophisticated professionals do it. If the people in charge of a multi-billion-dollar pension fund are interviewing new money-management firms, for example, they'll ask first about the expenses and fees the money managers charge and also about the style and method the firms use to select stocks and bonds. Only then do the pros examine the past record of the managers — it's just assumed that they'll be near the average.

Measuring past performance is almost as impossible as determining the true value of a company's stock — it depends entirely on complex and varying assumptions and conditions. Here's an example: Legendary money manager Frank Mersch of Altamira Investment Services thrashed his competition for most of the early 1990s, playing resource stocks masterfully. He was a journalist's delight, always returning phone calls and providing pithy quotes. Everybody loved him, especially people with money in his fund. It soared more than 30 percent each year from 1990 through 1992, far ahead of the average Canadian stock fund. Who could blame you for deciding that Mersch was good — and for putting money into his fund? But then resource stocks slid when commodity prices fell, and Mersch missed out completely on the climb in financial stocks, which rose more than 50 percent in 1997 and again in 1998. The market and his once-beetle-like rivals left him behind, and by 1999 he had departed as manager of the fund. What happened? Did Mersch suddenly become dumb or did the market turn against him through no fault of his own — or was it simply that his luck changed? Such questions probably can't be answered accurately, so don't bother debating them. But again: Betting too heavily on yesterday's hot performers, hoping that they'll outrun the pack again tomorrow, is a good way to end up in a dud fund.

Don't get too hung up about hot results in the past. Mutual fund companies like to offer lots of funds so they can have a few big performers to bray about in the ads, but those returns are always partly a result of luck. And mutual funds, incidentally, are managed more recklessly than pension funds. There's always the temptation to jack up the risk and returns a little to get the money pouring in. With a pension fund, a manager is expected to stick to a certain set of goals and investing style, and the penalties are severe for taking unauthorized flyers. That's because you have a bunch of actuaries, pension experts with thin lips and no sense of humour, keeping a watery eye on a pension fund's portfolio. But retail investors usually don't have the knowledge or resources to check or worry whether a manager is sticking to the fund's prescribed style — say, lots of fast-growing companies with high-flying stocks.

You should find out what a fund's past performance has been and, above all, compare it with that of rival funds and the market as a whole. The simplest place to start is the *Globe*'s quarterly fund report (available monthly online at www.globefund.com). Remember to stick to funds that have been around for at least five years. You should also use the *Globe and Mail*'s fund Web site at www.globefund.com to check whether the fund has been near the top or bottom in each individual calendar year, to detect big swings in performance over time.

Newspaper reports supply the annual compound returns for every fund as well as for the average fund in its category and for the market as a whole. If you're interested in a fund, its compound returns should be above the average for its group, but if they're way above — for example, an annual return of 15 percent over five years while the average fund made less than 10 percent — then the manager is probably a risk-taker. Above all, though, be wary of funds whose returns over five and ten years are below those of the average fund: Such pooches have a dispiriting habit of continuing to bark and dig holes in the garden.

Balanced Funds

Ever have a really good roti — a West Indian treat packed with extra spices, tasty meat, and East Indian–style stuff like chickpeas? Remember the wonderful numb feeling of fullness afterward? Balanced funds are supposed to be a satisfying all-in-one meal like that. You hand your money over to the fund company or bank, and they make all of the decisions. A *balanced fund* is a nice broad mixture of many types of investment — the idea being that it'll never lose too much money. The manager usually invests the fund in a cautious blend of stocks, which are tiny pieces of ownership of companies, and long-term and short-term bonds, which are debts owed by governments and companies. Balanced funds are investment products you buy when you want nice steady returns of around 6 to 8 percent per year while avoiding losses as

Book V

Making Your Investments Work for You

much as possible. They're one of the mutual fund industry's most useful inventions and an excellent place for the nervous beginner to get going. This section introduces you to the main types of balanced funds, explains why they're a great way to start off in investing, and warns you about the problems you may run into.

Understanding balanced funds

Balanced funds are for busy people who want a one-decision product that they can buy and forget about. Imagine your family had a trusted lawyer or accountant who took care of all of your investing needs — the professional, if he or she was at all prudent, would end up putting the money into a judicious blend of bonds and stocks, with a healthy cushion of cash to further reduce risk. And that's the essence of a balanced fund — it includes a little bit of everything so that losses can be kept to a minimum if one type of investment falls in value. Balanced funds, which have been around since the dawn of the fund industry in the 1920s in one form or another, have attracted billions of dollars in recent years as confused investors decide to let someone else pick the right mix for their savings. As of May 2003, balanced funds had total assets of $66 billion, making them the fund industry's third-most popular product after Canadian equity and foreign equity funds.

Reviewing the asset mix of balanced funds

Want to have some fun? Call up a balanced fund manager and during the conversation suddenly shriek, "Watch out! The market's crashing." You're bound to get an entertaining reaction. That's because the people running balanced funds tend to be nervous types who loathe losing money. That's great for you if you're a worried investor who can't afford to take big hits. So put your money in a balanced fund if you want someone watching over it who also hates to see things drop in value. In mid-2003, most balanced funds in Canada had just over 50 percent of their assets in risky-but-lucrative stocks, but the majority had about 35 percent in dull-but-sure bonds. The rest was sitting on the sidelines in cash.

Remember the old rule that your portfolio's weighting in bonds plus cash should equal your age? If we assume that the average Canadian balanced fund has 55 percent in stocks and 45 percent in guaranteed investments like bonds and cash, then most balanced funds are suitable for investors aged about 45. So if you're younger, look for a slightly more aggressive mix, and if you're older, try to find something with more bonds.

A balanced fund should be a ready-made cautious investment portfolio. Yes, it may lose money — nothing is absolutely safe in investing — but it's unlikely to drop as much as 10 percent in a year. Just check the fund's mix of assets at the fund company's Web site or in its handouts. If there are plenty of bonds and cash, it's probably safe enough to buy.

Profitable plodders

The good news is that Canadian balanced funds have done a pretty good job of avoiding losses. The average fund in the group lost less than 2 percent annually in the grim three years ended May 2003, while the average Canadian stock fund fell about 4 percent per year. Over ten years, Canadian balanced funds produced a respectable annual average return of about 8 percent compared with about 9 percent for equity funds. Now, of course, a few weaklings got lost in that shuffle after they were merged into better funds, but that's not a bad showing. The fund industry, always remember, has a habit of quietly folding underperformers into its stars, cancelling the dogs' years of terrible returns. For example, Fidelity in the mid-1990s took a weak balanced fund and popped it inside its huge Fidelity Canadian Asset Allocation Fund. The old fund's poor returns vanished forever. It lives on for a while in the fading memory of strange people like me who love funds. But when we go to our cheap government-provided burial plots, the dud will be gone. It's always possible that you'll find yourself stuck in a similar underperformer. To minimize that risk, the best solution of all is to hold two balanced funds so that your entire portfolio doesn't suffer from weakness in one fund.

Don't worry: Balanced funds are all about simplicity. Until you make up your mind about your long-term investing plans, you'll almost certainly do fine over three to five years by simply buying a regular balanced fund, or two for more safety, and then forgetting about them.

Retiring with balanced funds

If you really want to adopt a simple approach, it's a great idea to use balanced funds in your *registered retirement savings plan (RRSP)* — a special account in which investment gains add up without being taxed until you take them out, usually at retirement. Balanced funds are a nice cautious mix, just the thing you want for your life savings. Younger investors can be more aggressive, putting nearly all of their money into stocks, but above the age of 35 it's a wise idea to own bonds as well. Nothing is forever. If you decide later that you want something else in your RRSP, maybe because the balanced fund you picked turned out to be a dog, then it should be a simple matter to shift the money to another fund or funds within the same RRSP or to another RRSP account without incurring taxes. (See Book VI for more about RRSPs.)

So if you just want a simple investment to buy and forget, go for one or two balanced funds. A balanced fund has a single unit value that's published daily in the newspapers and on the Internet, making the value of your holdings easy to check. Its return appears in the papers every month and on the Internet every day. And the performance is also published clearly by the fund company, or should be. As with any regular mutual fund, if you've bought a pooch the whole world can see, there'll be some pressure on the fund manager to improve it.

Book V

Making Your Investments Work for You

Steering clear of potholes: Consistently strong returns

Balanced fund managers' scaredy-cat caution has served investors well. As stocks slid in the first half of 2003 (until about May), the average balanced fund escaped with a modest loss of about 3 percent. The worst loss the group suffered in a recent full calendar year was back in 1994 when the average fund in the group slipped 2.4 percent. Even that loss wasn't really the fault of the managers. Interest rates jumped suddenly that year, slashing the value of the bonds they held. Otherwise, balanced funds have generated nice steady returns, just as they're supposed to. But remember that balanced funds and all other investors who own bonds have had a gale at their backs since the early 1990s, because the drop in inflation has made bonds steadily more valuable. (See Chapter 6 for more about bonds.) That's unlikely to happen again in coming years. With inflation low — at 4.3 percent in Canada in April 2003 — bonds will have a tougher time going up at the same pace. And that low inflation environment means that balanced funds could have difficulty keeping up with their flashier equity rivals.

If we move into an era of deflation (that is, falling prices), bonds will almost certainly become increasingly more valuable because the value of their steady payouts of cash rises consistently. In that case, which unfortunately could involve a very painful recession, balanced funds could easily outperform stock funds. But whatever happens, the point remains: A balanced fund is like "home safe" in a kids' game of tag in southern Ontario (the centre of the universe, as you know). It's a safe spot for your money, leaving you to get on with your life. (Okay, okay, what do you call it in Newfoundland? Squishy-jig or something, no doubt.)

Reviewing the problems with balanced funds

There are problems with balanced funds, both Canadian and global. Their fees and expenses are far too lavish, which scythes into investors' already modest returns. Fund companies have come up with their usual bewildering variety of products and combinations of products, waving magic wands and muttering incantations that evoke the gods of portfolio theory and the "efficient frontier." It may all be true, but one thing's for sure, Stuart: you're paying for it. All balanced products are basically porridge. Because returns from their different investments are mixed together in a gooey mess, it's hard to judge exactly how well the manager did on which asset.

High fees and expenses

The costs and fees charged to balanced fund unitholders are just too high. Fund companies already run big equity and bond funds, paying the salaries and expenses of the people who manage them, and they usually get those people to help select the stuff in their balanced funds. How much extra work is involved in that? The bond manager basically just does the same job again with his or her portion of the balanced fund, and the equity manager does the same. Some fat geezer in a huge black robe and cone-shaped hat decides what the asset mix will be and you're away to the races. But the average Canadian balanced fund vacuums up 2.5 percent of its investors' money each year, almost as bad as the 2.6 percent charged by the average Canadian equity fund.

Remember that the long-term annual return from balanced funds may be only about 6 percent, or even less. The long term, incidentally, means the rest of our lives, as economists like to say (it's the only joke they know). So, say inflation and taxes combined take 4 percent out of your annual 6 percent — then your real return is down to around 2 percent. So, for a tax-paying account, most of your real return from a balanced fund like Royal Bank's giant may go into fund expenses and fees.

Bewildering brews of assets

Fund companies know that many of their customers just want simple solutions they can buy and never look at again. So they've come up with a bewildering array of balanced combinations in which you can buy their wares. Many of these arrangements, such as Mackenzie Financial Corp.'s popular "Star" products, have their own unit values, making them look very much like mutual funds themselves. By mid-2003, there were more than 1,200 Canadian and global balanced products of all types, counting different "classes" of fund units as separate funds. In May 2003, Mackenzie had 24 Canadian and global balanced products in its Star lineup alone. It's enough to make you wonder how many Star investors, or even their brokers, would have had problems identifying exactly which one they owned.

Difficulty judging fund manager performance

A big difficulty with balanced funds, or any kind of casserole that you buy from a fund company, is that it's usually hard to know just what the manager did right or wrong. He or she may have blown it in bonds, or struck out in stocks, but it's impossible to work out from the comfortable-looking (you hope) overall return number that the company publishes. Some fund companies provide a commentary that at least gives you a clue as to what went right and what exploded in the manager's shiny little face. For many customers that's fine, because they couldn't care less what went on inside the fund as long as the return is reasonably good. And that's a perfectly sensible approach to take if you don't have the time or interest to look further into mutual funds. But balanced funds are opaque and mysterious, violating one of the huge virtues of mutual funds — the ability to check on performance easily.

Because it's difficult to check where balanced funds' profits came from, it's harder for you to pick the right fund. In other words, there's often no clear answer to the crucial question: How much risk did the manager take? Here's an extreme example of two imaginary funds to help illustrate the point.

Suppose that you're trying to choose between two balanced funds:

- First, the Tasmanian Devil Fund, which made an average 11 percent over the past ten years, enough to turn $10,000 into $28,394.
- And then, the Mellow Llama Fund, which made 9 percent a year. That turned $10,000 into $23,674, or almost $5,000 less.

What if the Devil Fund made its bigger profits by buying bonds and shares issued by risky little technology companies, whereas the Llama Fund owned shares and bonds from big and stable companies and governments? Most balanced fund investors would choose the second fund, because the danger of it crashing and losing, say, half of its value in a year — is so much less.

The Devil Fund, with its volatile but high-profit-potential stocks, may be suitable for an investor who doesn't need the money for years and can afford to take risks now. But it's not the right fund for an investor who may need the money at any time.

Bond Funds: Boring Can Be Sexy Too

Buying a *bond* means you're lending money to the government or company that issued the thing. The word "bond" means promise, indicating the borrowers have given their word that they'll be around to pay interest and refund the loan. All you're really entitled to get back are the periodic interest payments plus the return of all your money when the debt comes due. Dull, huh? Bond funds simply hold a bunch of these loans, collecting the interest cheques and cashing in the bonds when they mature. That means bond funds tend to plod along with modest returns, while stocks fly and crash from year to year. Equity (or stock market) funds, with their promise of apparently limitless growth, just seem so much more exciting. But remember that bonds along with stocks represent the two main financial assets you can invest in for the long term — while a little bit of cash on the side is an essential safety valve for nearly any portfolio. This section explains why you should own at least one bond fund and shows you how to pick a good one.

Discovering some great reasons to choose bonds

Here's why you must own some bonds or bond funds: Lending your money short-term, by popping it into a bank deposit or account, doesn't pay you enough. Okay, so you can invest most of your money in the stock market, but that's a recipe for losing most of your pile if the market goes into a huge dive. So we all should leave a portion on long-term loan to big, secure governments and companies. And the way to do that is to buy their bonds, which are essentially certificates representing interest-paying loans to the corporations or governments that issued the bonds.

Declining interest rates, a result of falling inflation, have put a tiger in the tank of bond funds for more than a decade. The average Canadian bond fund produced an annual compound return of 8.5 percent in the 1990s, not far short of the 9.6 percent return from Canadian equity funds. And stocks, remember, are supposed to perform much better than bonds to compensate for their extra risk. As of mid-2003, the ten-year average annual return from bond funds had slipped to about 7 percent — but that was mostly because the record no longer included 1991, when the average bond fund shot up almost 20 percent as inflation dropped sharply (bond buyers hate inflation because it erodes the value of the money they'll get back years hence when their bonds mature). That 7 percent didn't look too shabby when compared with the 9 percent average return from ever-risky Canadian equity funds. And in the scary three years ended June 2003, bonds came shining through: The average bond fund made 5.7 percent annually in the period, while the average Canadian stock fund lost about 5 percent per year.

But bonds will have trouble doing as well in coming years. Inflation was hovering at about 4 percent in mid-2003, meaning that it didn't have much more room to drop (unless we slide into scary deflation). That limited the scope for falling interest rates and higher bond prices. And if inflation and rates rise, then bond prices will drop, dragging down bond funds.

Get some sleep with bonds

Psychologically, having your entire savings in stocks is just too frightening for most normal people. The Standard & Poor's/Toronto Stock Exchange composite index dropped by one-fifth, or 20 percent, during one month (August 1998) as the economies of Russia and Asia threatened to go down the plughole. From August 2000 to August 2001, the index fell by more than 33 percent. Watching your life savings shrink at that speed would be no fun at all. Don't believe it? You will when you're sitting bolt upright at 4 a.m. reflecting on the minus signs next to those equity funds you thought couldn't miss "over the long term."

What goes up must come down, even the market

Sure, equities have always bounced back in the past. But stocks can go into a slump for years, just as they did in the inflation-and-recession-prone 1970s. From February 1966 to August 1982, a stretch of 16 long years, the Dow Jones Industrial Average of blue-chip U.S. stocks fell 22 percent in price.

Yes, America's blue-chip companies paid regular dividends during the period, reducing investors' losses. But it was still a horrible time to be in the market, a depressing and endless era of new lows.

Remember Japan and the way its market hit a euphoric peak in 1989 (just as technology and communication stocks all over the world did in 2000)? More than a decade later, the Japanese market was still down from its 1989 high.

Security if you hit a rough patch

You may lose your job, have legal troubles, or run into some disaster right in the middle of a periodic stock market slump. It would be ugly to be forced to tap into your serious money just after it's been carved up by a stock sell-off. So own some bonds. They serve as a giant, reassuring outrigger for your canoe, producing steady returns while holding their value.

Beware of falling prices

Finally, and perhaps most scary of all, companies and individuals all over the world are getting smarter and more efficient all the time. Why is that a problem? It means they're producing goods and services at ever-lower prices. Inflation in most wealthy countries has dropped to less than 3 percent from double figures in the 1980s, and it could keep right on falling until we're in an era of actual *falling prices*. If that happens, bonds and cash are likely to hold their value or even rise in price because the value of money will be rising (*inflation,* the opposite scenario, simply means that money is losing its purchasing power). In other words, deflation is a weird *Through the Looking Glass* world in which cash under the mattress becomes a solid investment that produces a real return.

Does a world of falling prices sound incredible? It's been happening all around us for years in computers, where prices drop and processing power increases every few months. Natural resource prices were in a slump for most of the 1990s as Russia and other poor countries flooded the market in a desperate bid to get U.S. dollars. Granted, there hasn't been an economy-wide slump in prices since the Depression of the 1930s, so nobody knows what it would be like — or what would happen to equity markets. But falling prices squeeze corporate profit margins like a vice, and declining profits are rat poison for stocks. From September 1929 to July 1932, as the Depression got going, the Dow fell by almost 90 percent. (That's not a typing error.) The Dow dropped to 41 from 381. So own some bonds.

Picking a good bond fund in thirty seconds

Selecting a superior bond fund boils down to two simple rules. It should hold plenty of high-quality long-term bonds, and it must have low expenses. You can find funds with low expenses, and check their holdings, at www.globefund.com — the *Globe and Mail*'s mutual fund Web site.

Here's more good news: You should own at least two Canadian and two global stock funds, because any equity manager can go into a slump for years. But you'll almost certainly do fine with just one bond fund, as long as it has low annual costs and is full of quality bonds. No big fund seller would allow its managers to make weird bets with a mainstream bond fund, such as buying 20-year paper issued by a bankrupt tin mine. The backlash from investors, the media, and possibly even regulators would be too great.

Book V

**Making
Your
Investments
Work for
You**

Insist on affordability

Demand modest annual expenses — less than 1 percent annually — with any bond fund. The returns from this asset class are relatively low, and likely to get lower in coming years because bonds are already trading at fat prices. So fund costs and fees must be kept down for the investor to be left with anything at all after taxes and inflation.

The average Canadian bond fund hits its unitholders for a criminal 1.8 percent annually, and there are plenty of funds in the group that grab 2 percent or more. That's ridiculous and here's why. In mid-2003, ten-year Canadian government bonds were offering a tiny annual yield of about 5 percent to investors who bought them and held them to maturity. Now, bond managers can sometimes increase returns by a few tenths of 1 percent by fancy trading, but unless interest rates drop rapidly over the next few years, it looks very much as though 5 percent or so is all that many bond portfolios are likely to make annually. Take a 2 percent expense ratio out of that, and you're left with only 3 percent. After inflation and taxes, in other words, bond fund unitholders could easily end up losing money in real terms.

So, in general, look only at bond funds with annual expenses of 1 percent or less. The funds with low expenses will almost all turn out to be no-load products that you buy directly from a bank or direct-selling fund company. That's because fund companies that sell through brokers, financial planners, and other advisers have to add on extra charges in order to have something left over to pay the salespeople; expect to pay an extra 0.75 percent annually on most broker-sold bond funds.

Look for quality in provincial and federal bonds

Buy a fund with plenty of high-quality long-term federal government and provincial bonds. A few super-blue-chip company bonds are okay, but remember that with business changing at the speed of Bill Gates's rubbery mind, today's corporate grande-dame could be tomorrow's bag lady. So go easy on the IBMs. If you're a bit nervous that inflation might come back, you want a middle-of-the road solution when it comes to bonds. So just get a bond fund that pretty well matches the SCM Universe Bond Total Return Index, an imaginary basket of typical high-quality bonds, calculated by huge stockbroker Scotia Capital Markets. The SCM Universe pretty well represents the entire Canadian bond market.

Why should you look for long-term bonds? If you have a home mortgage, you probably know that the best thing for you to do as a borrower in recent years has been to keep on renewing your mortgage for short terms at low rates instead of "locking in" for a longer term at a higher rate. But for lenders, such as buyers of a bond fund, the opposite strategy has been better. Lending long, by buying long-term bonds with ten or more years to run before they mature, has been the most lucrative approach because short-term interest rates kept dropping. Now the next ten years may be different, but you should still just buy a plain bond fund that's got plenty of long-term Canadian government bonds.

For the serious money portion of your portfolio, avoid risky "high-yield" bond funds or sleepwalking "short-term" bonds. The rule you apply should be this: Bet long-term as a lender because that's where the yield is. There's an old saying in the bond market: *Be long or be wrong.* If you want a compromise, buy a plain-vanilla bond fund whose average term to maturity is close to the SCM Universe Bond Total Return Index, which includes both short- and long-term bonds. Many fund companies and bond investors use the SCM Index as the benchmark with which they compare the performance and holdings of their funds.

Money Market Funds: Welcome to Sleepy Hollow

Money market funds are simply a safe parking spot for cash, designed to produce at least some sort of return. They generate a modest stream of income — annual returns from the group averaged just over 4 percent in the ten years ended June 2003. These funds invest in very short-term bonds and other fixed-income securities that usually have less than three months to go before they mature and the issuer pays the holders their money back. Money market funds are different in structure from normal mutual funds, and the way they calculate their returns can be confusing. But just use the same rules to pick one as you do with bond funds: Buy quality and, more than ever, insist on low expenses — 1 percent annually at the very most. As with all mutual fund investing programs, when buying a money market fund you should do more than just insist on low costs. Lean across the table — glaring at the hapless salesperson through bulging, insane eyes — part your spit-flecked, crusty lips, and scream for a reduction in expenses at the top of your voice. Otherwise, you won't make anything off a money market fund. This section shows you why money market funds are a great place to hold your cash while you wait to spend or invest it, as well as how to spot a good money market fund.

Book V

Making
Your
Investments
Work for
You

Understanding how money market funds work

Throughout this chapter and the preceding one, you've read a tonne of grim warnings about how you can easily lose money in mutual funds because of a drop in their unit price. Well, risking contradiction, that doesn't apply to the vast majority of money market funds because they are held steady at a fixed value, usually $10.

Some money market funds — especially the guaranteed type that promise to refund some or all of your money — have unit prices that do increase over time.

Keeping the unit price fixed isn't required by law, but it's the practice among fund companies. In theory, if short-term rates were to shoot up exponentially or the government's credit rating collapsed in some kind of unprecedented catastrophe, the fund company would let the value of your money market units drop. But by that time, you'll be too busy pitching bottles at the giant green spacecraft that just zapped your dog to worry much about it. In other words, woe betide the fund company that lets its money market fund units drop below their fixed value. Investors who buy this type of fund aren't known for their devil-may-care attitude to losses. It's more a kind of grim-glare-where's-my-money type of situation. So money market funds are rather like a guaranteed investment certificate: You're certain of getting your cash back, plus extra units that represent the interest you've earned along the way.

The interest is usually calculated daily but it's generally added to your account every month or when you sell your units. Money market funds, like nearly all mutual funds, however, beat the pants off GICs because they're "liquid." That's a bit of investment industry jargon that simply means you can "liquidate" or turn the investment into ready cash at a moment's notice. Unlike GICs, money market funds refund your money without penalty, usually at a day's notice.

As a guideline, the return from money market funds tends to be almost exactly the same as the return from one-year GICs. GICs earned an annual average of 4.1 percent in the ten years ended May 2003, essentially the same as the return from Canadian money market funds.

In other words, both fixed one-year deposits at the bank and money market funds gave you an annual yield of about 4 percent over a decade. That's only about half the 8 percent yearly return investors got from the average Canadian balanced fund, though — normally a pretty cautious mix of stuff from the stock market (which is always volatile) and bonds (which usually work in great slow cycles).

The *yield* is just the harvest you get on your money, expressed as a percentage of what you invested. So, a madcap biotech fund might go up 50 percent in a year — at huge risk — turning $1,000 into $1,500 (always assuming you were canny enough to sell out in time before it crashed). A money market fund in late 2000 offered an annual yield more like 4.5 percent, which would transform $1,000 into just $1,045 but at very little risk. But by mid-2003, as inflation stayed low, that yield had slumped below 2 percent, making money market funds much less attractive for investors. We're talking about a return of 20 bucks for tying up $1,000 for a year.

So remember that with a money market fund, you nearly always buy a set of units at a fixed price, usually $10 in Canada and $1 in the United States, and that unit price never changes. Your return comes in the form of extra units paid out to you along the way. You're not going to get wealthy soon with one of these funds. Just like bond funds, they're designed only to earn a steady and fairly predictable return. There's none of the flash, risk, and potential for big gains that you get with an equity fund. And fewer of those annoying broken-teeth incidents.

Selecting winning money market funds

Don't stay up all night picking a money market fund, because you've got a busy day ahead. A long day of sliding through sticky mud, trying to get a grip on infuriated ostriches. Money market funds tend to be pretty similar. In other words, there's no point chasing a big yield, because to get one the manager has to take more risk. If you're buying your other mutual funds at a bank or bank-owned discount broker, simply buy the bank's money market fund. There's enough competition in the industry to make it embarrassing for a bank to have its money market fund turn into a hound. If you're buying through a broker or other commissioned salesperson, his or her office is probably set up to put clients into a particular money market fund, probably from the fund company the salesperson's organization does the most business with. Since money market funds are just temporary holding spots for cash — or they constitute the low-risk, low-return "cash" portion of your portfolio — then one fund is pretty well as good as another.

Just make sure that you can find the money market fund listed in your daily newspaper, in a newspaper monthly report, or on the Internet. That way, you know you'll be able to track your holdings and check the accuracy of your account statement.

Choosing from a mix of money market funds

Some money markets are ultrasafe, sticking to government bonds. Others increase the risk level very slightly, and pick up about one-fifth of a percentage point in annual yield. Either choice is fine — it depends on your personality. Here's how to tell the two options apart:

✔ For their very nervous clients, the banks offer a superconservative "T-bill" fund that buys only short-term government bonds and government "treasury bills" (a type of bond with just a few months before it matures).

✔ For those willing to take a bit more risk, the banks offer slightly lower-quality funds — usually known simply as money market funds — that are allowed to increase their yield by buying things like corporate "commercial paper"; that is, short-term debt issued by big companies when they need a bit of cash to tide them over. These funds really aren't dangerous at all, because the companies that issue the paper they hold are nearly always blue-chip multinationals or their Canadian subsidiaries.

It would take a very nasty economic cataclysm indeed before any bank-run money market racked up losses big enough to force the bank to let the fund's unit price drop. So there's no significant difference between the two types of funds.

In the end, the extra bit of yield you get from a money market fund compared with a T-bill fund is very small. For example, the TD Canadian Money Market Fund, which is free to buy corporate securities, generated an annual return of 3.5 percent in the five years ended June 2003, only slightly higher than the 3.4 percent annual return from the TD Canadian T-Bill Fund, which must stick to government debt.

World travellers: U.S. money market funds

A handful of companies also offer foreign money market funds, either for investors who want to hold a lot of cash in U.S. dollars or for scaredy-cats who want a low-volatility investment that's safe from a drop in the Canadian dollar. Nearly all the funds in this group are bought and sold in U.S. dollars. The same rules apply to pick a fund. Look for low expenses if you want to end up with anything. Don't believe me? Look what happened to unfortunate investors in the AIM Short-term Income Fund. The fund's Canadian class B units came with annual expenses of 2.7 percent — which left investors with an average annual return of only 1.6 percent in the five years ended June 2003, compared with about 4 percent for the average U.S. money market fund. In other words, investors paid out more to the fund company than they got back in returns.

The average foreign money market fund has expenses of 1.2 percent, so refuse to pay anything more than that.

Is thin in? Watching those pesky expenses

Always remember that because the returns from money market funds are so thin, the slightest increase in expenses can leave you with nothing after taxes and inflation. So refuse to pay a sales commission when buying a money market fund. The broker or salesperson should be able to let you have it commission-free, especially if you're simply parking your money in the money market fund temporarily while you decide on a long-term home for it. Take five minutes to fire up www.globefund.com or check the listings in the monthly fund guide printed with your newspaper to check that the money market fund offered by your bank or salesperson has produced acceptable returns. It probably has. And remember that the average Canadian money market fund has expenses of 1.1 percent — you shouldn't be asked to pay more than that.

Examining Other Types of Funds

In mid-2003, more than 3,000 mutual funds totalling $387 billion in assets were held in over 50 million unitholder accounts in Canada. Each fund was different from the others, especially when it came to making money for investors in the fund. Don't let this bewilder you. All mutual funds can be grouped into one of a number of broad categories, starting with the categories of funds described earlier in this chapter (equity, balanced, bond, and money market). Here are some brief descriptions of other categories of funds, which will help you begin to eliminate the mystery from mutual funds:

- **Special equity or sector funds** limit themselves to investing in gold, real estate, science and technology, and almost any other industry according to the fund's guidelines. These funds tend to vary widely in value because they are not as diversified as other equity funds. In fact, some advisers consider them almost speculative in nature, and question their value inside an RRSP. Generally, these should make up no more than 5 or 10 percent of an RRSP's total value, and then only if you are a) young, b) ready to accept possible losses in your investment, or c) preferably both.

- **Dividend funds** invest in common and preferred shares of companies expected to pay high, long-term dividends. Some capital growth can be expected as well, but these funds primarily represent an opportunity to generate income.

- **Global or international funds** mirror other funds described previously in this list, except that they function almost exclusively outside of Canada. This makes them ideal for the foreign content of your RRSP, but beware: International funds may limit themselves to one country or region, such as India or Japan. They may also focus exclusively on developing or emerging markets, which includes Latin America and some Asian countries. Focusing on one region, or one type of country, defeats the prime purpose of investing beyond Canada, which is to build as much

Book V

Making
Your
Investments
Work for
You

diversification as possible into your RRSP. Better to choose funds that invest anywhere the fund manager finds the best prospects.

There are always exceptions, of course. Funds investing in the U.S. performed exceptionally well during most of the 1990s, reflecting that country's strong economic growth. But all well-managed global equity funds, such as AGF International Value, Spectrum Global Growth, CI Global, and others, had already invested heavily in the U.S. market. They profited from the U.S. market's growth. Unlike funds investing exclusively in the U.S., however, these global funds will be able to move elsewhere when the U.S. market is not performing as well as others.

✔ **Open** and **closed funds** describe the structure of the fund, not the investments they hold.

An *open fund* is the most common fund structure. It enables you or any investor to buy or sell shares in the fund at any time at the current unit price, which is based on the total net assets of the fund at the end of the day divided by the number of units in the fund. That's the price you'll receive per unit if you sell and the price you'll pay if you buy, and it's fixed by the market value of the fund's investments. Open funds have to keep a fair amount of cash or liquidable assets on hand in case more people want to sell their units than buy them. (There are other reasons as well, but this is a practical requirement.)

A *closed fund* is really like a separate company investing in other companies or securities on the market. Managers of closed funds invest money from shareholders just as they would in an open fund. But once the fund reaches its target investment limit, no further shares are issued. Instead, the fixed number of shares are bought and sold just like shares in IBM, Royal Bank, and Stelco. As a result, the price of the shares does not reflect the actual asset value so much as the *perceived* value of people who may want to own them. Units in closed funds are not as liquidable as open funds, so they're suitable for folks who limit their investments primarily to their RRSP. Until you build your investment knowledge, it's best to stay with open funds.

Other types of funds you may encounter include the following:

✔ **Pooled funds,** generally created for wealthy, sophisticated investors. If this includes you, why are you reading this book?

✔ **Segregated funds,** which are a combination of mutual fund and insurance policy, to prevent any loss of capital.

✔ **Labour venture funds** are designed for labour unions to use when investing in smaller companies just starting up. They offer attractive tax incentives and have finally begun producing reasonable results.

✔ **Royalty trusts** are a closed version of mutual funds that disperse income earned from their investments to the fund shareholders.

Chapter 3

The Essentials of Stock Investing

In This Chapter

▶ Understanding the difference between a stock and a company

▶ Discovering different kinds of stocks

▶ Navigating your way to successful stock investing

▶ Deciding whether long-term or short-term investments are right for you

▶ Looking at your objectives for investing

▶ Determining your investing style

Stock investing became all the rage during the late 1990s, when many Canadian investors watched their stock portfolios and mutual funds skyrocket in value as major North American markets experienced the fruits of an almost two-decades-long rising market (better known as a bull market).

Then came the dreaded bear market — complete with claws, sharp teeth, and three years of declining markets. Portfolios were mauled, chewed up, or worse. Investors with positive or even zero returns had downright bragging rights! Yet despite this recent roller coaster of a ride, over 40 percent of Canadians are still invested in stocks today. Some of these Canadians hold stocks directly; others hold them indirectly in their mutual and pension funds. Canadians are a resilient bunch: while many of us got scared, we did not jump ship en masse!

Investment activity in Canada and the United States is a great example of the popularity that stocks experienced during that time period. Yet people really didn't know exactly what they were investing in, or the risks. If they had had a clear understanding of what a stock really represents, perhaps they could have avoided some expensive mistakes.

The purpose of this chapter is not only to tell you about the basics of stock investing, but also to let you in on some sharp strategies and tactics that can help you profit from the stock market. Before you invest your first dollar, you need to understand the basics of stock investing.

It's Like Trading Cards!

The stock market is, well, a market of stocks. In essence, being in the market is like trading hockey cards. There is a buyer and a seller. The market is the schoolyard where buyers and sellers get together to trade cards. A sharp hockey-card trader (buyer) will try to guess which rookie player is the next Wayne Gretzky or Mario Lemieux. He or she will then try to obtain a future star player's rookie card and hope that that player scores a lot of goals, makes great saves, or is a solid defenceman. The card would almost certainly rise in value! The best price to pay is the lowest cash price, or the fewest cards traded away in return. The other trader and owner of the card (the seller) either will recognize greatness and ask a hefty price, or will fail to recognize talent and trade the card away for a song. In the hockey-card trading market (the schoolyard), you have kids who are buyers and kids who are sellers of cards. They may pay or get cash, and they may give up or get other cards.

The stock market is actually an established group of separate markets (many schoolyards in many countries) where Canadian investors can freely buy and sell millions of shares issued by thousands of Canadian and international companies. Like hockey cards, investors buy stocks because they seek gain in the form of appreciation (what happens when their stock, if held long enough, goes up in value — just like Wayne Gretzky's rookie card did), or income (some stocks pay income in the form of dividends), or both. (Sorry, no dividends are paid out by hockey players!) Those who already own stock may sell it to cash in and use the money for other purposes, like to trade coins. Either way, investors pay or get cash, or give up or get more stock with the proceeds. A market is made!

Why companies sell stock

Companies issue stock because they require money for a particular purpose. The first time a company sells stock to the public is known as an *initial public offering* (IPO), sometimes referred to as "going public." The most prominent new Canadian and U.S. stock IPOs are usually reported in the pages of financial publications, such as *The Globe and Mail*, the *National Post*, and *The Wall Street Journal*.

Generally, two types of companies go public by issuing stock:

- **An existing private company:** A company that is currently in operation as a private corporation but wants to expand.
- **A start-up company:** A company that is just starting up and decides to go public immediately to raise the capital necessary to establish itself.

Between the two, the safer situation for investors is the first type. That's because this kind of company has a proven track record — which hopefully includes growing sales, cash profits, and great ideas!

Why does a company go public? It goes public because it needs to raise the money necessary for its growth and financial success. More specifically, the money raised through a public offering of stock can be used for the following purposes:

- **To raise capital and finance expansion:** If ABC Corporation wants to increase its production capacity, it needs a new manufacturing facility. In order to raise the capital needed to build and operate the new facility, it may decide to sell stock to the public.

- **To invest in product (or service) research and development:** Many companies need money for research and development for a new invention or innovation.

- **To pay for the daily expenses of doing business:** Most companies have to pay for staff, benefits, utilities, and marketing efforts. Some companies may need additional operating capital until revenues from exciting new products and services catch up with and exceed expenses. (At least, that's the plan!)

- **To pay off debt:** The company may want to use the proceeds of a stock sale to pay off debt. Interest expense is the number-one financial anchor that causes companies to go bankrupt.

- **Miscellaneous reasons:** The company may need money for other reasons that are important for the health and growth of the enterprise, such as joint ventures and entry into brand-new lines of business.

Keep in mind that a stock offering doesn't always have to be in a first-time situation. Many companies issue stock in secondary offerings to gain the capital they need for expansion or other purposes.

Going public: It's no secret

When a private company wants to offer its stock to the general public, it usually asks a stock underwriter to help. An *underwriter* is a financial company that acts as an intermediary between stock investors and public companies. The underwriter is usually an investment-banking company or the investment-banking division of a major brokerage firm. The underwriter may put together a group of several investment-banking companies and brokers. This group is also referred to as a *syndicate.* Usually the main underwriter is called the *primary underwriter,* and others in the group are referred to as *subsidiary underwriters.*

Before a company can sell stock to the public, a couple of things have to happen:

✔ The underwriter or syndicate agrees to pay the company a predetermined price for a minimum number of shares and then must resell those shares to buyers such as their own clients (which could be you or me), mutual funds, and other commercial brokerages. Each member of the syndicate agrees to resell a portion of the issued stock. The underwriters earn a fee for their underwriting services. CIBC World Markets is one example of an underwriting company. Its investment-banking business works with companies to help them raise capital, grow, and invest.

✔ The underwriter sets a time frame to start selling the issued stock (this is the window of time that the primary market is taking place). The underwriter also helps the company prepare a preliminary prospectus that details the required financial and business information for investors, such as the amount of money being sought in the IPO, and who is seeking the money and why. (For details, see the section "Canadian regulators and toothless tigers" later in this chapter.)

The preliminary prospectus is referred to as the "red herring" because it usually comes stamped with a warning in red letters that identifies it as preliminary — a kind of disclaimer that the stock's price may or may not be changed as the final issue price.

The IPO stock usually isn't available directly to the public. Interested investors must purchase the initial shares through the underwriters authorized to sell the IPO shares during the primary market. After the primary market period — at the start of the secondary market — you can ask your own stockbroker to buy you shares of that stock. The *secondary market* is more familiar to the public and includes established, orderly public markets such as the Toronto Stock Exchange (TSX), the New York Stock Exchange, and the Nasdaq.

Canadian regulators and toothless tigers

The market for IPOs and all public stocks is regulated reasonably well in the United States by the Securities and Exchange Commission (SEC). The SEC sets the standard for disclosure and governs the creation of the prospectus. The prospectus must contain information such as the description of the issuer's business, names and addresses of the key company officers, key information relating to the company's financial condition, and an explanation of how the proceeds from the stock offering will be used.

In Canada, provincial and territorial securities administrators — also known as securities commissions — oversee and govern the securities industry. They possess broad powers under provincial statutes called *securities acts.* Securities commissions don't pass judgment on the worthiness of an investment. Rather, they try to provide assurance that companies offering securities furnish investors with good and complete disclosure of all key and relevant facts. Companies provide this disclosure through a prospectus, and subsequently through updates such as annual reports and other statutory declarations.

Regulators promote integrity in the stock market and help provide a more level playing field. While the Canadian stock market regulatory system is established and efficient, it is nowhere near as effective as its U.S. counterpart. That's because it's a lot easier to get away with corporate malfeasance in Canada than it is in the U.S. (names like Bre-X, Livent, and YBM come immediately to mind). Even after the Canadian system reveals illegal and questionable acts by public companies, the system is toothless — it has a bark, but no bite. For example, a judge recently meted out only light penalties on the former directors of YBM. Some observers felt that the punishment ought to have been greater, and several former directors were all smiles as they left the courtroom.

Relative to the U.S., very few corporate crooks in Canada wind up behind bars! Perhaps it's a lack of personnel, legislation, or political will that is at fault. At any rate, the road to full regulation in Canada remains long, and tougher measures are needed now.

Stock investors should know this so they can be proactive in identifying risks and in knowing their rights. It should also be noted that investment firms and their representatives must be registered with their respective provincial securities commission, either where they work or where they trade securities, and that they have to meet certain standards to become registered. Securities commissions can cancel the registrations of individuals or the firms they work for to protect your interests. They are also empowered to investigate matters, prosecute persons, freeze funds, hear facts, take evidence, impose penalties, and/or seize documents for examination. However, securities commissions can't compel a company or individual to repay investors. All they can do is halt trading in a security and deny the violator the right to trade securities in the province.

Although there is no federal regulatory body in Canada as there is in the U.S., each provincial securities commission is a member of the umbrella organization Canadian Securities Administrators. CSA members work to standardize securities law.

Book V

Making
Your
Investments
Work for
You

The securities industry self-regulates through bodies such as the Investment Dealers Association of Canada (IDA) and the Mutual Fund Dealers Association of Canada (MFDA). The Web sites of these Canadian organizations can be accessed at www.ida.ca and www.mfda.ca. Clearly, the Canadian stock investor is exposed to more investment risk than her U.S. counterparts. Self-regulation just doesn't fully meet the needs of the average investor!

Approval of the sale of stock by a provincial or territorial securities administrator doesn't mean that the administrator recommends the stock. Approval from an administrator means only that the sale of stock can go forward in accordance with provincial and federal laws. Approvals simply give some level of assurance that companies offering securities furnish investors with all the facts.

Defining a Stock

Stock represents ownership in a corporation (or company). Just like the owner of a car has a title that says he has ownership of a car, a stock certificate shows that you own a piece of a company. If a company issues stock of, say, 1 million shares and you own 100 shares, this means you have ownership equivalent to 1/10,000th of the company.

The physical evidence of ownership is a stock certificate, which shows what stock you own and how many shares. These days, investors rarely get the certificates in hand, direct from the company; instead, they simply trade through brokerage accounts (see Chapter 4 for lots of useful information on brokers) and shareholder service departments that hold the stock. Your brokerage statements tell you what you have — kind of like a bank statement. Such statements are sufficient today, when producing the actual stock certificate has become less necessary in our modern technological era than in the early days of stock investing.

There is a real distinction between the stock and the company. The company is what you invest in, and the stock is the means by which you invest. Some investors get confused and think that the company and its stock act as one entity.

Understanding your role as a shareholder

When you own stock, you become a *shareholder* (also known as a *stockholder*). The benefit of owning stock in a corporation is that whenever the corporation profits, you profit as well. For example, if you buy stock in ATI Technologies Inc. and ATI comes out with an exciting new computer graphics product that the public wants in massive quantities, not only does the company succeed but so do you, depending on how much stock you own.

Just because you own a piece of that company, don't expect to go to the company's headquarters and say, "Hi! I'm a part owner. I'd like to pick up some office supplies since I'm running low. Thank you and keep up the good work." No, it's not quite like that.

As a regular shareholder, you generally do not have the privilege of intervening in the company's day-to-day operations. Instead, you participate in the company's overall performance at a distance.

As an owner, you participate in the overall success (or failure) of a given company along with the thousands or millions of others who are *co-owners* (other investors who own stock in the company). The flip side is that if the company is sued or gets on the wrong side of the law you won't be in trouble — at least not directly. The company's stock value will be negatively affected and you'll most likely see a decline in the value of your stock, but you won't go to jail.

Knowing your rights as a shareholder

A stock also gives you the right to make decisions that may influence the company, such as determining the share price. Each stock you own has a little bit of voting power, so the more shares of stock you own the more decision-making power you have.

In order to vote you must attend an annual or special shareholders' meeting, or fill out a proxy ballot. The ballot contains a series of proposals that you may vote either for or against. Common questions concern who should be on the board of directors, whether to issue additional stock, and whether to acquire or be acquired by another company.

Cashing in on dividends

Dividends are a type of reward that companies pay to shareholders. When a company is a cash generator because of good sales and cost control, it builds its cash war chest. Some of this cash is kept to finance further growth or is utilized for other business purposes. But many companies will also distribute cash directly to shareholders in the form of a cash dividend.

Who makes this decision? The people who run a publicly traded company are the ones who may choose to "declare" a cash dividend. Specifically, a company's board of directors is responsible for declaring it. Once declared, a "date of record" or "record date" is set. The record date means that shareholders on record on or before that date are entitled to the dividend. Anyone buying the stock subsequent to that date must wait until the next dividend declaration to be entitled to receive a dividend (on the payment date). There are usually several weeks between the dividend declaration date and the date of record.

Stocks will trade "ex-dividend" (or no dividend) from the second trading day (a weekday) before the record date. This is important, because if you trade shares near the dividend date you should expect the share price to drop by roughly the amount of the dividend.

The board of directors can also declare a "stock dividend." Companies that don't regularly pay cash dividends often opt instead to pay dividends in the form of their own stock. A 5 percent stock dividend means that for every 20 shares of stock you own you obtain one new share as a dividend. You keep your same relative share of the book value of the company.

When a company declares a stock dividend, it keeps its accumulated cash. So, some companies prefer to issue a stock dividend to avoid paying out cash that they need to use elsewhere in their operations.

To recap, for typical Canadian dividends, the events in Table 3-1 happen four times per year.

Table 3-1		The Life of the Quarterly Dividend
Event	*Sample Date*	*Comments*
Date of declaration	January 15	The date that the quarterly dividend is declared by the company
Ex-dividend date	February 7	Starts the three-day period during which, if you buy the stock, you don't qualify for the dividend
Record date	February 10	The date by which you must be on the books of record to qualify for the dividend. All investors who are official shareholders on the record date will receive the dividend paid on the payment date regardless of whether they plan to sell the stock any time between the date of declaration and the date of record.
Payment date	February 27	The date that payment is made (a dividend cheque is issued and mailed to shareholders who were on the books of record as of February 10)

Chapter 4 shows you where to find dividend information.

Spotting stock value

Book V

Making
Your
Investments
Work for
You

Imagine that you like soup, and you're willing to buy it by the can at the grocery store. In this example, the brands of soup available on the shelves are like companies, and their prices represent the prices that you would pay for the companies' stock. The grocery store is the stock market. What if two brands of soup are very similar, but one costs 70 cents while the other costs 95 cents? Which would you choose? Odds are that you would look at both brands, judge their quality, and, if they were indeed similar, take the cheaper soup. The soup at 95 cents is overpriced. It's the same with stocks. What if you compare two companies that are similar in every respect but have different share prices? All things being equal, the cheaper price has greater value for the investor. But there is another side to the soup example.

What if the quality of the two brands of soup is significantly different but their prices are the same? If one brand of soup is flavourless and poor quality and priced at 70 cents and the other brand is tasty and superior quality and also priced at 70 cents, which would you get? I'd take the good brand because it's better soup. Perhaps the lesser soup might make an acceptable purchase at, say, 30 cents. However, the inferior soup is definitely overpriced at 70 cents. The same example works with stocks. A badly run company isn't a good choice if a better company in the marketplace can be bought at the same — or a better — price.

Comparing the value of soup may seem overly simplistic, but doing so does cut to the heart of stock investing. Soup and soup prices can be as varied as companies and stock prices. As an investor, you must make it your job to find the best value for your investment dollars.

Recognizing how market capitalization affects stock value

You can determine the value of a company (and thus the value of its stock) in many ways. The most basic way to measure this is to look at a company's market value, also known as market capitalization (or market cap). *Market capitalization* is simply the value you get when you multiply all the outstanding shares of a stock by the price of a single share.

Calculating the market cap is easy: it's the number of shares outstanding multiplied by the current share price. If the company has 1 million shares outstanding and its share price is $10, the market cap is $10 million.

Small-cap, mid-cap, and large-cap aren't references to headgear; they're references to how large the company is as measured by its market value. Here are the five basic stock categories of market capitalization:

- **Micro cap (under $250 million):** These are the smallest and hence the riskiest stocks available.

- **Small cap ($250 million to $1 billion):** These stocks fare better than the micro caps and still have plenty of growth potential. The key word here is "potential."

- **Mid cap ($1 billion to $5 billion):** For many investors, this category offers a good compromise between small caps and large caps. These stocks have some of the safety of large caps while retaining some of the growth potential of small caps.

- **Large cap ($5 billion to $25 billion):** This category is usually best reserved for conservative stock investors who want steady appreciation with greater safety. Stocks in this category are frequently referred to as "blue chips."

- **Ultra cap (more than $25 billion):** These stocks are also called "mega caps" and obviously refer to companies that are the biggest of the big. Royal Bank and Exxon Mobil are examples.

From the point of view of safety, the company's size and market value do matter. All things being equal, large-cap stocks are considered safer than small-cap stocks. However, small-cap stocks have greater potential for growth. Compare these stocks to trees — which tree is sturdier, a giant California redwood or a small maple tree that is just a year old? In a great storm, the redwood would hold up well, while the smaller maple tree would have a rough time. But you also have to ask yourself which tree has more opportunity for growth. The redwood may not have much growth left, but the small maple tree has plenty of growth to look forward to.

For beginning investors, comparing market cap to trees is not so far-fetched. You want your money to branch out without becoming deadwood.

Although market capitalization is important to consider, don't invest (or not invest) because of it. It is just one measure of value. As a serious investor, you need to look at numerous factors that can help you determine whether any given stock is a good investment. Keep reading — this book is full of information to help you decide.

Sharpening your investment skills

Investors who analyze the company can better judge the value of the stock and profit from buying and selling it. Your greatest asset in stock investing is knowledge (and a little common sense). To succeed in the world of stock investing, keep in mind these key success factors:

- ✔ **Analyze yourself.** What do you want to accomplish with your stock investing? What are your investment goals?

- ✔ **Know where to get information.** The decisions you make about your money and what stocks to invest in require quality information.

- ✔ **Understand why you want to invest in stocks.** Are you seeking appreciation (capital gains), or income (dividends)?

- ✔ **Do some research.** Look at the company whose stock you are considering to see whether it's a profitable company worthy of your investment dollars.

- ✔ **Understand how the world affects your stock.** Stocks succeed or fail in large part due to the environment in which they operate. Economics and politics make up that world, so you should know something about them.

- ✔ **Use investing strategies like the pros do.** In other words, how you go about investing can be just as important as what you invest in.

- ✔ **Keep more of the money you earn.** After all your great work in getting the right stocks and making the big bucks, you should know about keeping more of the fruits of your investing.

Common Approaches to Stock Investing

Before investing in stocks, ask yourself, "When do I want to reach my financial goals?" Stocks are a means to an end. Your job is to figure out what that end is — or, really, *when* it is. Are you seeking to retire in ten years, or next year? Are you paying for your kid's university education next year, or 18 years from now? The length of time you have before you need the money that you hope to earn from stock investing is one important factor that determines what stocks you should buy. Table 3-2 gives you some guidelines for choosing the kind of stock that's best suited for your goals.

Table 3-2	Matching Stock Types to Financial Goals and Investor Types	
Type of Investor	Time Frame for Your Financial Goal	Type of Stock Most Suitable
Conservative (worries about risk)	Long-term (more than five years)	Large-cap stocks and mid-cap stocks
Aggressive (high tolerance to risk)	Long-term (more than five years)	Small-cap stocks and mid-cap stocks
Conservative (worries about risk)	Intermediate-term (two to five years)	Large-cap stocks, preferably with dividends
Aggressive (high tolerance to risk)	Intermediate-term (two to five years)	Small-cap stocks and mid-cap stocks
Short-term	One to two years	Don't even think about stock investment!

Table 3-2 gives general guidelines, but keep in mind that not everyone can neatly fit into a particular profile. Every Canadian investor has a different personal situation, set of goals, and level of risk tolerance. Remember that *large-cap, mid-cap,* and *small-cap* just refer to the size (or market capitalization, also known as market cap) of the company. All things being equal, large companies are safer (less risky) than small companies. For more on market caps, see the section "Investing by Style" later in this chapter.

Investing by Time Frame

Are your goals long term or short term? Answering this question is important, because individual stocks can be either great or horrible choices depending on the term you're looking at. Generally, the term can be short, intermediate, or long. The following sections outline what kinds of stocks are most appropriate for each term length.

Investing in stocks becomes less risky as the necessary time frame lengthens. Stock prices tend to fluctuate on a daily basis, but they do have a tendency to trend up or down over an extended period. Even if you invest in a stock that goes down in the short term, you're likely to see it rise and even go above your investment if you have the discipline to wait it out and let the stock price appreciate.

Book V

Making
Your
Investments
Work for
You

Looking at the short term

Short term generally means one year or less, although some people say that short term means two years or less. You get the point.

All of us have short-term goals. Some are modest, such as setting aside money for a vacation next month or buying some furniture for the den. Other short-term goals are more ambitious, such as accruing funds for a down payment for a new home purchase within six months. Whatever the expense or purchase, you need a predictable accumulation of cash soon. If this sounds like your situation, stay away from the stock market!

Because stocks can be so unpredictable in the short term, they're a bad choice for short-term purposes. Be naturally sceptical whenever you hear market analysts saying things like "At $20 a share, XYZ is a solid investment, and we feel that its stock should hit our target price of $35 within six to nine months." You just know that someone will hear that and say, "Gee, why bother with 3 percent at the bank when this stock will rise by more than 50 percent? I better call my broker." The stock may indeed hit that target amount (and may even surpass that price), or it may not. Most of the time, however, the target price is not reached, and the investor is disappointed. The stock could even go down! But what if the money invested was meant to be used for an important short-term need? Remember, short-term stock investing is very unpredictable, and your short-term goals are better served with stable, interest-bearing investments (like GICs) instead.

During the raging bull market of the late 1990s, investors watched as some high-profile stocks went up 20 to 50 percent in a matter of months. Hey, who needs a savings account earning a measly 4 percent interest when stocks grow like that! Of course, when the bear market hit in 2000 and those same stocks fell 50 to 70 percent, suddenly a savings account earning a measly 4 percent interest rate didn't seem so bad after all.

Stocks, even the best ones, will fluctuate in the short term. No one can really predict the price movement accurately (unless they have some inside information), so stocks are definitely not appropriate for any financial goal that you need to reach within one year.

Considering intermediate-term goals

Intermediate-term refers to your financial goals that need to be reached within five years. If, for example, you need to accumulate funds to put money down for investment real estate property four years from now, some growth-oriented investments may be suitable.

Although *some* stocks *may* be appropriate for a two- or three-year period, not all stocks are good intermediate-term investments. There are different types and categories of stocks. Some stocks are fairly stable and hold their value well, such as the stock of much larger or established companies. Other stocks have prices that go all over the place, such as the stocks of untested companies that are just starting out and haven't been in existence long enough to develop a consistent track record.

If you plan to invest in the stock market to meet intermediate-term goals, large established companies or dividend-paying companies in much-needed industries (like food and beverage or electric utilities, for instance) are good choices for you. *Dividends* are payments made to an owner (unlike *interest,* which is payment to a creditor). Dividends are a great form of income, and companies that issue dividends tend to have more stable share prices as well.

Investing for the long term

Stock investing is best suited for making money over a long period. When you measure stocks against other investments in terms of five or (preferably) ten or more years, they excel. Even investors who bought stocks in the depths of the Great Depression saw profitable growth in their stock portfolios over a ten-year period.

In fact, if you take any 10-year period over the past 75 years, you'll see that stocks beat out other financial investments (such as bonds or bank investments) in every single 10-year period when measured by total return (taking into account reinvesting and compounding of capital gains and dividends)! As you can see, the long term is where stocks shine most. Of course, it doesn't stop there. You still have to do your homework and choose stocks wisely — because, even in good times, you can lose money if you invest in companies that go out of business.

Because there are many different types and categories of stocks, virtually any investor with a long-term perspective should add stocks to his investment portfolio. Whether you're saving for a young child's university fund or for your own retirement, carefully selected stocks have proven to be a superior long-term investment.

Investing by Style

When a lady was asked why she bungee-jumped off the bridge that spanned a massive ravine, she answered, "Because it's fun!" When someone asked the fellow why he went in a pool that was chock full of alligators and snakes, he responded, "Because someone pushed me." Your investment in stocks should not happen for any other reason except a purpose that you understand and buy into. That purpose should then translate into a corresponding investment style. If your purpose is to preserve your savings, then a conservative investment style is appropriate. Even if you invest because some adviser told you to, be sure that you get an explanation of how that stock choice fits your investment purpose and style.

Or consider the very nice, elderly lady who had a portfolio brimming with aggressive-growth stocks because she had an overbearing stockbroker. Her purpose, and style (which should be driven by her purpose), should have been conservative. She ought to have chosen investments to preserve her wealth rather than to grow it aggressively. Obviously, the broker's own purpose got in the way.

Stocks are just a means to an end. Determine your desired outcomes and then match your style to those outcomes. Following is a discussion of some classic and common investing styles.

Growth investing

When investors want their money to grow, they're looking for investments that appreciate in value. *Appreciate* is just another way of saying "grow." If you have a stock that you bought for $8 per share and now it's $30 per share, your investment has grown by $22 per share — that's appreciation.

Appreciation (also known as *growth* or *capital gain*) is probably the primary reason that people invest in stocks. Few investments have the potential to grow your wealth as conveniently as stocks. If you're looking to the stock market to make lots of money relatively quickly (and assuming you're not averse to assuming some risk), then growth investing is your ticket.

Stocks are a great way to grow your wealth, but they're not the only way. Many investors seek alternate ways to make money, but many of them are more aggressive and carry significantly more risk. You've probably heard about people who made a quick fortune in areas such as commodities (like wheat, pork bellies, or precious metals), options, and other more sophisticated investment vehicles. Keep in mind that you should limit risky investments to only a portion of your portfolio, such as 10 percent of your investable funds. Experienced investors, however, can go as high as 20 percent.

Income investing

Not all investors want to make a killing. Some people just want to invest in the stock market as a means of providing themselves with a steady income — they don't need stock values to go through the ceiling. Instead, they need stocks that perform well consistently. They want to preserve their existing level of wealth.

If your purpose for investing in stocks is to provide you with stable income, you need to choose stocks that pay dividends. Dividends are paid quarterly to shareholders on record.

Distinguishing between dividends and interest

A word of caution is called for here. Don't confuse dividends with interest. Most people are familiar with interest because that's how their money has grown for years in the bank. The important difference between the two is that *interest* is paid to creditors, while *dividends* are paid to owners. (Shareholders are owners — if you hold stock you're an owner, because stocks represent shares in a publicly traded company.)

When you buy stock, you're buying a piece of that company. When you put money in a bank (or when you buy bonds), you're really loaning your money. You become a creditor, and the bank or bond issuer is the debtor — as such, it must eventually pay your money back to you with interest.

Recognizing the importance of an income stock's yield

Investing for income means that you have to consider that investment's yield. If you're seeking income from a stock investment, you must compare the yield from that particular stock with alternatives. Looking at the yield is a way to compare the income you would receive from one investment with that from others. Table 3-3 shows some comparative yields.

Table 3-3	Comparing the Yields of Various Investments				
Investment	**Type**	**Amount**	**Pay Type**	**Payout**	**Yield**
Smith Co.	Stock	$50/share	Dividend	$2.50	5%
Jones Co.	Stock	$100/share	Dividend	$4	4%
Acme Bank	Bank GIC	$500	Interest	$25	5%
Acme Bank	Bank GIC	$2,500	Interest	$131.25	5.25%
Acme Bank	Bank GIC	$5,000	Interest	$287.50	5.75%
Brown Co.	Bond	$5,000	Interest	$300	6%

To understand how to calculate yield, you need the following formula:

Yield = Payout ÷ Investment amount

Book V

Making
Your
Investments
Work for
You

Yield enables you to compare how much income you would get for a prospective investment compared with the income you would get from other investments.

Jones Co. and Smith Co. are both typical dividend-paying stocks (in this example, presume that both companies are similar in most respects). But these two stocks have different dividends. How can you tell whether a $50 stock with a $2.50 annual dividend is better (or worse) than a $100 stock with a $4 dividend? The yield tells you.

Even though Jones Co. pays a higher dividend ($4), Smith Co. has a higher yield (5 percent). Therefore, if I had to choose between those two stocks as an income investor, I would choose Smith Co. Of course, if I truly wanted to maximize my income and didn't really need my investment to appreciate a lot, I would probably choose Brown Co.'s bond, because it offers a yield of 6 percent.

Dividend-paying stocks do have the ability to increase in value. They may not have the same growth potential as growth stocks, but at the very least they have a greater potential for capital gain than bank GICs or bonds.

Value investing

The great bear market of the first part of this decade appears to have played itself out. To say that it left a lasting impression on most Canadian investors would be an understatement. As a result of the bear market, observers noted a decided shift in what most investors seek. Momentum investing — where investors follow a herd of other investors after the next big thing — is passe. In fact, at the moment there really is no "next best thing," only a smattering of smaller "interesting" things!

Value investing is, on the other hand, a fundamental investing style that focuses on the strengths of an individual stock and the underlying company. Value investing is buying stocks as if you were buying the business itself. Value investors emphasize the intrinsic value of assets and current and future profits, and pay a price equal to or less than that value.

The ultimate question about value investing is this: "What am I buying — and what am I paying for it?" Canadians who recognize the importance of that fundamental investing question typically adopt, or are amenable to, a value-investing style. It's different from growth investing, and different from income investing, yet value investing has elements of both. Tremendous value may be found in an income stock at its current price. Value can also be indicated in a growth stock, as long as the price is right relative to its higher risk. Value can be measured in at least three basic ways.

Book value per share

The first way to determine value is to measure a stock's book value per share. Book value is the amount that one share of a company's common stock would be worth if the powers-that-be were to liquidate the company, pay the amounts owed, and divide the remaining cash among the shareholders. (This assumes that the book value determined by accountants is roughly the same as the street value of assets held, and the real current value of liabilities owed.)

Over the past few years, it has been typical to see Canadian stocks average about 5:1. This means that shares of Canadian companies are currently priced at an average of about five times a company's worth. This is a high level in our opinion, so you want to look for stocks that are reasonably priced relative to this benchmark.

Price ÷ earnings ratio

The second way to measure a stock's value is by using the price ÷ earnings ratio. This is the multiple a stock trades at as compared to its annual earnings. If a company earned $1 per share last year and its stock is currently selling for $10, its price ÷ earnings P/E ratio is 10:1, or 10.

In the S&P 500 index, the average P/E ratio over the past few years has been about 23, based on the most recent actual earnings of companies that make up that index. While this is not its highest level in history, it's still pretty close!

Keep in mind that you should consider the P/E ratio in the context of the growth prospects of the company you're considering for investment. A company that sells at a P/E of 10 — below market averages — may not be desirable if it has exhibited annual growth in earnings of only 3 percent. Yet, a stock boasting a higher current P/E multiple of 20 might be still be considered desirable if it's demonstrating a great trend of annual earnings growth of 35 percent per year or more! Also consider a stock's P/E ratio in the context of the stock's industry group. A stock selling at a P/E of 12 will be attractive if the average P/E among other stocks in its industry is hovering at 19.

Dividend value

A third way to measure a stock's value is the stock's dividend. You may do well if you can find stocks that meet the prior two criteria and also pay dividends. That would be the icing on the cake! Consider past or expected future increases in the stock's dividend payout.

You don't have to use the value-investing approach for *all* of your investments. Depending on your goals, it's okay to mix investing styles.

Take this advice from Warren Buffett: "For some reason, people take their cues from price action rather than from values. What doesn't work is when you start doing things that you don't understand or because they worked last week for somebody else. The dumbest reason in the world to buy a stock is because it is going up."

Oh, and one other thing. How can you spot the value investor at a cocktail party? Easy. He's the only one talking about an actual company while all the other guests stand around discussing the stock market.

Chapter 4

Before You Get Started with Stocks

. . . .

In This Chapter

▶ Exploring financial issues you need to know about to be a well-informed investor

▶ Interpreting stock tables

▶ Revisiting dividend news

▶ Finding out what brokers do

▶ Telling the difference between full-service and discount brokers

▶ Selecting a broker

▶ Learning about online brokers

▶ Exploring the types of brokerage services and accounts

. . . .

K nowledge and information are two critical success factors in stock investing. (Isn't that true about most things in life?) People who plunge headlong into stock investing without sufficient knowledge of the market, types of risks, and current information in particular quickly learn the lesson of the speeding skier who didn't find out ahead of time that the ski run he was on was actually closed due to rock hazards (ouch!). In their haste to avoid missing so-called golden investment opportunities, investors too often end up losing money.

There's no such thing as a single (and fleeting) magical moment, so don't feel that if you let an opportunity pass you by you'll always regret that you missed your one big chance. The stock market is an entity that opens and closes every day. Tomorrow's opportunities may not even be imaginable today. Resist the urge to jump at what seem to be golden investment opportunities unless you really know what you're doing. Don't chase stocks that are having an upward price run but lack solid fundamentals. A better approach is to first build your knowledge by finding quality information. Then buy stocks and make your fortunes more assuredly. Where do you start and what kind of information should you acquire? Keep reading.

Reading (and Understanding) Stock Tables

The stock tables in major business publications, such as the *National Post* and *The Globe and Mail,* are loaded with information that can help you become a savvy investor — *if* you know how to interpret them. You need the information in the stock tables for more than selecting promising investment opportunities. You also need to consult the tables after you invest to monitor how your stocks are doing. If you bought HokySmoky common stock last year at $12 per share and you want to know what it's worth today, check out the stock tables.

If you look at the stock tables without knowing what or why you're looking, it's the equivalent of reading *War and Peace* backward through a kaleidoscope. Nothing makes sense. But to help you make sense of it all (well, at least the stock tables), Table 4-1 shows a sample stock table for you to refer to as you read the sections that follow.

Table 4-1			Deciphering Stock Tables					
52-Wk High	52-Wk Low	Name (Symbol)	Div	Vol	Yld	P/E	Day Last	Net Chg
21.50	8.00	SkyHighCorp (SHC)		3143		76	21.25	+.25
47.00	31.75	LowDownInc (LDI)	2.35	2735	5.7	18	41.00	-0.50
25.00	21.00	ValueNowInc (VNI)	1.00	1894	4.5	12	22.00	+.10
83.00	33.00	DoinBadlyCorp (DBC)		7601			33.50	-.75

Every newspaper's financial tables are a little different, but they give you basically the same information. However, even though it is updated daily, this section is not the place to start your search for a good stock; actually, it should be where it ends. The stock tables are the place to look when you know what you want to buy — or you already own a particular stock — and you're just checking to see the most recent price.

Each item gives you some clues about the current state of affairs for that particular company. The sections that follow describe each column to help you understand what you're looking at.

52-week high

Book V

Making
Your
Investments
Work for
You

The column labelled "52-Wk High" (refer to Table 4-1) gives you the highest price that a particular stock has reached in the most recent 52-week period. The value in knowing this is so that you can gauge where the stock is now versus where it has been recently. SkyHighCorp's (SHC) stock has been as high as $21.50, while its last (most recent) price was $21.25, the number listed in the "Day Last" column. (Flip to the "Day last" section for more on understanding this information.) SkyHighCorp's stock is trading very high right now, because it's hovering right near its overall 52-week-high figure.

Now, take a look at the DoinBadlyCorp's (DBC) stock price. It seems to have tumbled big time. Its stock price has had a high in the past 52 weeks of $83, but it's currently trading at $33.50. Something just doesn't seem right here. During the past 52 weeks, DBC's stock price fell dramatically. If you're thinking about investing in DBC, find out why the price fell. If the company is a strong one, it may be a good opportunity to buy it at a lower stock price. If the company is having tough times, avoid it. In any case, research the company and find out why its stock has declined.

52-week low

The column labelled "52-Wk Low" gives you the lowest price that particular stock has reached in the most recent 52-week period. Again, this information is crucial to your ability to analyze a stock over a period of time. Looking at DBC in Table 4-1, you can see that its current trading price of $33.50 is right about where its 52-week low is. So far, DBC doesn't look like a real catch.

Keep in mind that the high and the low prices just give you a range for how far that particular stock's price has moved within the past 52 weeks. They could alert you that a stock has problems, or they could tell you that a stock's price has fallen enough to make it a bargain. Simply reading the 52-week high and 52-week low columns isn't enough to determine which of those two things is happening. They basically tell you to get more information before you commit your money.

Name and symbol

This is the simplest column. It tells you the company name (usually abbreviated) and the stock symbol assigned to the company. Once you have your eye on a stock for potential purchase, get familiar with its symbol.

Knowing the symbol makes it easier to find it in the financial tables, which list stocks in alphabetical order by symbol. Stock symbols are the language of stock investing, and you need to use them in all stock communications, from getting a quote at your broker's office (even by touch-tone, using only your phone's buttons and no voice) to buying stock over the Internet.

Dividend

Dividends are essentially payments to owners (shareholders). On a more nitty-gritty level, here's how dividend information appears in stock tables (shown under the "Div" column in Table 4-1), and what you should look for.

If — and this can be a big if — a company pays a dividend, it's shown in the dividend column. The amount you see is the annual dividend quoted as though you owned one share of that stock. If you look at LowDownInc (LDI) in Table 4-1, you can see that you would get $2.35 as an annual dividend for each share of stock that you own. The dividend is usually paid quarterly. If you own 100 shares of LDI, the company would pay you a dividend of $58.75 each quarter ($235 total per year).

A healthy company strives to maintain or upgrade the dividend for shareholders from year to year. In any case, the dividend distribution is very important if you're a stock investor who also seeks income. For more about investing for income, see Chapter 3. Companies that don't pay dividends are bought by investors primarily for growth. For more information on growth stocks, see Chapter 3.

Volume

Normally, when you hear the word *volume* on the news, it refers to how much stock is bought and sold for the entire market. ("Well, stocks were very active today. Trading volume at the TSX was 270 million shares, and the NYSE hit 2 billion shares.") Volume is certainly important to watch, because the stocks that you're investing in are somewhere in that activity. For your purposes here, though, the volume (the "Vol" column in Table 4-1) refers to the individual stock.

Volume tells you how many shares of that particular stock were traded that day. If only 100 shares are traded in a day, then the trading volume is 100. SHC had 3,143 shares change hands on the trading day represented in Table 4-1. Is that good or bad? Neither, really. Usually volume for a particular stock is mentioned in the business news media when it is unusually large. If a stock normally has volume in the 5,000 to 10,000 range and all of a sudden has a trading volume of 87,000, then it's time to sit up and take notice.

Keep in mind that a low trading volume for one stock may be a high trading volume for another stock. You can't necessarily compare one stock's volume against that of any other company. The large-cap stocks like Nortel or Home Depot typically have trading volumes in the millions of shares almost every day, while less active, smaller stocks may have average trading volumes in far, far smaller numbers.

The main point to remember is that trading volume that is far in excess of that stock's normal range is a sign that something is going on with that stock. It may be negative or positive, but something newsworthy is happening with that company. If the news is positive, the increased volume is a result of more people buying the stock. If the news is negative, the increased volume is probably a result of more people selling the stock. What are typical events that cause increased trading volume? Some positive reasons include the following:

- **Good earnings reports:** A company announces good (or better than expected) earnings.

- **A new business deal:** A company announces a significant and favourable business deal, such as a joint venture, or lands a big client.

- **A new product or service:** A company's research and development department creates a potentially profitable new product.

- **Indirect benefits:** A company may benefit from a new development in the economy or from a new law passed by Parliament.

Some negative reasons for an unusually large fluctuation in trading volume for a particular stock may include the following:

- **Bad earnings reports:** Profit is the lifeblood of a company. If a company's profits fall or disappear, you'll see more volume.

- **Governmental problems:** The stock is being targeted by government action (such as a lawsuit or Ontario Securities Commission probe).

- **Liability issues:** The media report that a company has issued a recall notice concerning a defective product, or has a similar problem.

- **Financial problems:** Independent analysts report that a company's financial health is deteriorating.

The bottom line is to check out what's happening when you hear about heavier than usual volume (especially if you already own the stock).

Yield

In general, yield is a return on the money you invest. However, in the stock tables, *yield* ("Yld" in Table 4-1) is a reference to what percentage that particular dividend is to the stock price. Yield is most important to income investors. It is calculated by dividing the annual dividend by the current stock price. In Table 4-1, you can see that the yield du jour of ValueNowInc (VNI) is 4.5 percent (a dividend of $1 divided by the company's stock price of $22). Notice that many companies have no yield reported; because they have no dividends, yield cannot be calculated.

Keep in mind that the yield reported in the financial pages changes daily as the stock price changes. Yield is always reported as if you're buying the stock that day. If you bought VNI on the day represented in Table 4-1, your yield would be 4.5 percent. But what if VNI's stock price rose to $30 the following day? Investors who bought stock at $30 per share would obtain a yield of just 3.3 percent. (The dividend of $1 would then be divided by the new stock price, $30.) Of course, because you bought the stock at $22, you essentially locked in the prior yield of 4.5 percent. Lucky you. Pat yourself on the back.

P/E

The P/E ratio indicates the ratio between the price of the stock and the company's earnings. P/E ratios are widely followed and important barometers of value in the world of stock investing. The P/E ratio (also called the "earnings multiple," or just "multiple") is frequently used to determine whether a stock is expensive (a good value). Value investors find P/E ratios to be essential to analyzing a stock as a potential investment. As a general rule, the P/E should preferably be 10 to 20 for large-cap or income stocks. For growth stocks, a P/E no greater than 30 to 40 is preferable.

In the P/E ratios reported in stock tables, *price* refers to the cost of a single share of stock. *Earnings* refers to the company's reported earnings per share as of the most recent four quarters. The P/E ratio is the price divided by the earnings. In Table 4-1, VNI has a reported P/E of 12, which is considered a low P/E. Notice how SHC has a relatively high P/E (76). This stock is considered too pricey, as you're paying a price equivalent to 76 times earnings. Also notice that the stock DBC has no available P/E ratio. Usually this lack of a P/E ratio indicates that the company reported a loss in the most recent four quarters.

Book V

**Making
Your
Investments
Work for
You**

Day last

The "day last" (or "close") column tells you how trading ended for a particular stock on the day represented by the table. In the stock table in Table 4-1 earlier in this chapter, the stock LDC ended the most recent day of trading at 41. Some newspapers report the high and low for that day in addition to the stock's ending or closing price for the day.

Net change

The information in the net-change column ("Net Chg" back in Table 4-1) answers the question "How did the stock price end today compared with its trading price at the end of the prior trading day?" Table 4-1 shows that SHC stock ended the trading day up 25 cents (at $21.25). This tells you that SHC ended the prior day at $21. On a day when VNI ends the day at $22 (up 10 cents), you can tell that the prior day it ended the trading day at $21.90. You get the idea.

Discovering Why Closing and Dividend Dates Matter

Reading and understanding the news about dividends is essential if you're an *income investor* (someone who invests in stocks as a means of generating regular income). Paying particular attention to important dividend dates helps you benefit as an investor.

To begin, you should be aware of the fact that there are three business days between the date of execution of a trade and the "closing" or "settlement" date. The closing or settlement date is the date on which the trade is finalized, usually three business days after execution. Similar in concept to a real estate closing, it's the official date on which you are the proud new owner (or happy seller) of the stock.

There are also three business days between the ex-dividend date and the date of record. This information is important to know if you want to qualify to receive an upcoming dividend. Timing is important, and the following example is the best way to explain it.

Say that you want to buy ValueNowInc. (VNI) in time to qualify for the quarterly dividend of 25 cents per share. Assume that the date of record (the date by which you have to be an official owner of the stock) is February 10. You have to execute the trade (buy the stock) no later than February 7 to be assured of the dividend. If you execute the trade right on February 7, the closing date would occur three days later, on February 10 — just in time for the date of record.

But what if you execute the trade on February 8, a day later? Well, the trade's closing date would be February 11, which would occur *after* the date of record. Because you wouldn't be on the books as an official shareholder on the date of record, you wouldn't get that quarterly dividend. In this example, the February 7 ÷ 10 period is called the *ex-dividend period.*

Going for Brokers

When you're ready to dive in and start investing in stocks, you first have to choose a broker. It's kind of like buying a car: You can do all the research in the world and know exactly what kind of car you want to buy; still, you have to buy it through a car dealer. Similarly, when you want to buy stock, your task is to do all the research you can to select the company you want to invest in. Still, you need a broker to actually buy the stock, whether you buy in person or online.

The broker is the intermediary between you and the world of stock investing. The broker's primary role is to serve as the vehicle through which you either buy or sell stock. The brokers referred to in the following sections are organizations such as TD Waterhouse, E*Trade Canada, Merrill Lynch HSBC Canada, and many others that can buy stock on your behalf. Brokers can also be individuals who work for such firms. Although you can buy some stocks directly from the company that issues them, to purchase most stocks you still need a broker.

The primary task of brokers is the buying and selling of stocks, but they can perform other tasks for you, including the following:

- ✔ **Providing advisory services:** Investors pay brokers a fee for investment advice.
- ✔ **Offering limited banking services:** Brokers can offer features such as interest-bearing accounts and cheque writing.
- ✔ **Brokering other securities:** Brokers can also buy bonds, mutual funds, and other investments on your behalf. Keep in mind that the word *securities* refers to the world of financial (or paper) investments and that stocks are only a small part of that world.

Personal stock brokers make their money from individual investors like you and me through various fees, including the following:

- ✔ **Brokerage commissions:** This is a fee for buying and/or selling stocks and other securities.

- ✔ **Margin interest charges:** This is interest charged to investors for borrowing against their brokerage account for investment purposes.

- ✔ **Service charges:** These are charges for performing administrative tasks and other functions. Brokers charge fees to investors for RRSPs, for mailing stocks in certificate form, and other special services.

There is a distinction between personal stock brokers and institutional stock brokers. Institutional brokers make money from institutions and companies through investment banking and securities placement fees (such as initial public offerings and secondary offerings), advisory services, and other broker services. Personal stock brokers generally offer the same services to individuals and small businesses.

Distinguishing between Full-Service and Discount Brokers

There are two basic categories of stock brokers: full-service and discount. The type you choose really depends on what type of investor you are. In a nutshell, full-service brokers are suitable for investors who need some guidance, while discount brokers are better for those who are sufficiently confident and knowledgeable about stock investing to manage with minimal help.

Full-service brokers

Full-service brokers are just what the name indicates. They try to provide as many services as possible for investors who open accounts with them. When you open an account at a brokerage firm, a representative is assigned to your account. This representative is usually called an *account executive,* a *registered rep,* or a *financial consultant* by the brokerage firm. This person usually has a Canadian securities licence and is knowledgeable about stocks in particular and investing in general.

What they can do for you

Your account executive is responsible for assisting you, answering questions about your account and the securities in your portfolio, and transacting your buy and sell orders. Here are some things that full-service brokers can do for you:

✔ **Offer guidance and advice.** The greatest distinction between full-service brokers and discount brokers is the personal attention you receive from your account rep. You operate on a first-name basis, and you disclose much information about your finances and financial goals. The rep is there to make recommendations about stocks and funds that are hopefully suitable for you.

✔ **Provide access to research.** Full-service brokers can give you access to their investment research department, where you can get in-depth information and analysis on a particular company. This information can be very valuable, but be aware of the pitfalls.

✔ **Help you achieve your investment objectives.** Beyond advice on specific investments, a good rep gets to know you and your investment goals and *then* offers advice and answers your questions about how specific investments and strategies can help you accomplish your wealth-building goals.

✔ **Make investment decisions on your behalf.** Many investors don't want to be bothered when it comes to investment decisions. Full-service brokers can actually make decisions for your account with your authorization. This service is fine, but be sure to require them to explain their choices to you.

What to watch out for

Although the full-service brokers, with their seemingly limitless assistance, can make life easy for an investor, you need to remember some important points to avoid problems:

✔ Brokers and account reps are still salespeople. Most are honest; some are complete shills. No matter how well they treat you, they're still compensated based on their ability to produce revenue for the brokerage firm. They generate commissions and fees from you on behalf of the company. (In other words, they're paid to sell you things.)

✔ Whenever your rep makes a suggestion or recommendation, be sure to ask why and request a complete answer that includes the reasoning behind the recommendation. A good adviser should be able to clearly explain the reasoning behind every suggestion. If you don't fully understand and agree with the advice, don't take it.

✔ Know that working with a full-service broker costs a bit more than a discount broker. Discount brokers are paid simply for performing the act of buying or selling stocks for you. Full-service brokers do that and more. Additionally, they provide advice and guidance. Because of that, full-service brokers are more expensive (through higher brokerage commissions and advisory fees). Also, most full-service brokers expect you to invest at least $5,000 to $10,000 just to open an account. Grrrr.

✔ Handing over decision-making authority to your rep can be a possible negative because letting others make financial decisions for you is always dicey — especially when they're using *your* money. If they make poor investment choices that lose you money you may not have any recourse, because you authorized them to act on your behalf.

✔ Some brokers engage in an activity called churning. *Churning* is basically buying and selling stocks for the sole purpose of generating commissions. Churning is great for brokers but bad for customers. Sometimes a broker may do a lot of trading in the account. The account may show little in terms of investment success but cost you dearly in commissions. Churning generates a lot of activity for the primary purpose of making more money for the broker (not for you!).

Some of Canada's full-service brokers include Merrill Lynch HSBC Canada, RBC Dominion Securities, and TD Waterhouse Investment Advice. Of course, all brokers now have full-featured Web sites to give you further information about their services. Get as informed as possible before you open your full-service account. A full-service broker should be there to help you build wealth, not make you . . . uh . . . broker.

Discount brokers

Perhaps you don't need any hand-holding from a broker. You know what you want, and you can make your own investment decisions. All you want is someone to transact your buy/sell orders. In that case, go with a discount broker. Discount brokers, as the name implies, are cheaper to engage than full-service brokers. They don't offer advice or premium services, though — just the basics required to perform your stock transactions.

If you choose to work with a discount broker, you must know as much as possible about your personal goals and needs. You have a greater responsibility for conducting adequate research to make good stock selections, and you must be prepared to accept the outcome, whatever that may be. Because you're advising yourself, you can save on costs that you would have incurred had you paid for a full-service broker.

You should also note that most Canadian discount (and full-service) brokers are also online (Internet) brokers (discussed in the section, "Researching Online Brokerage Services," later in this chapter.) Conventional discount brokers (such as TD Waterhouse and Scotia McLeod Direct Investing) have offices throughout Canada that you can walk into and speak to customer service staff face-to-face. You can transact in person, over the phone, or through the Internet. That's the sort of thing that makes them conventional. Pure online discount brokerage firms (like E*Trade Canada) have essentially the same services, but without the walk-in offices and automated telephone trading. They're a little unconventional, and that's just the way they like it!

What they can do for you

Conventional discount brokers share many of the same primary advantages over full-service brokers, including the following:

- **Lower cost:** This lower cost is usually the result of lower commissions.

- **Unbiased service:** Because discount brokers offer you the ability to transact your buys and sells only without advice, they have no vested interest in trying to sell you any particular stock.

- **Access to information:** Established discount brokers offer extensive educational and research resources at their offices or on their Web sites.

What to watch out for

Of course, doing business with discount brokers also has its downside:

- **No guidance:** Because you've chosen a discount broker, you *know* not to expect guidance, but the broker should make this clear to you anyway. If you're a knowledgeable investor, the lack of advice is considered a positive thing — no interference.

- **Hidden fees:** Discount brokers may shout about their lower commissions, but commissions aren't their only way of making money. Many discount brokers charge extra for services that you may think are included, such as issuing a stock certificate or mailing a statement. Ask whether they assess fees for maintaining RRSPs or fees for transferring stocks and other securities (such as bonds) in or out of your account, and find out what interest rates they charge for borrowing through brokerage accounts.

- **Minimal customer service:** If you deal with an Internet brokerage firm, find out about its customer service capability. If you can't transact business at its Web site, find out where you can call for assistance with your order.

Choosing a Broker

There are a few other issues to resolve before choosing a broker. Once you have decided whether to go the full-service or discount broker route, you have to make sure that you select a brokerage firm that's a member in good standing of one of Canada's self-regulatory organizations, or SROs. With big-name brokerages that you recognize, this is no big problem — all are probably in good standing. But with smaller brokerages you need to check this out. Another thing to do before choosing a broker is to assess and revisit your personal investing style (see Chapter 3). Both issues are discussed next.

Examining self-regulatory organizations (SROs) in Canada

Canadian stock exchanges and the Investment Dealers Association of Canada (IDA) represent Canada's SROs. An SRO has been provided with legislated authority and the responsibility to regulate its member firms. They ensure that SRO members meet standards governing stocks and other securities. SROs regulate markets and trading, as well as firms that are members, their employees, and their business practices. They do this by establishing rules regulating how stock markets must operate. They monitor and visit brokers and other investment dealers on a periodic basis to ensure that mandated rules of operation (such as those concerning solvency) are followed. SROs investigate suspected infractions by sending out investigators and compliance officers to review things a bit further when necessary.

The provincial securities commissions have a national group that works toward making securities regulations consistent and standardized across Canada. This group is called the Canadian Securities Administrators (CSA). It's a good function to have, but offers nowhere near the power wielded by the more independent regulators of U.S. stock markets. As a result, options and remedies to the Canadian individual stock investor are limited. You should note that although the IDA is an SRO, it regulates member firms operating mostly in the bond and money markets, not the equity markets that stocks are part of.

 To find out if a firm is a member of an SRO, check out the Web sites (under Member Firms) of the Investment Dealers Association (www.ida.ca), or TSX (www.tsx.ca). You can also contact these organizations the good old-fashioned way — by phone!

Revisiting your personal investing style

Before you choose a broker, you need to analyze and re-assess your personal investing style. Once you know yourself and the way you invest, then you can proceed to finding the kind of broker that fits your needs. It's almost like choosing shoes; if you don't know your size, you can't get a proper fit. (And if you get it wrong you can be in for a really uncomfortable future.)

Consider Bob and Ed. Both men are knowledgeable, confident, and competent investors, so they each choose a discount broker — makes sense. Bob likes to trade stocks very frequently. Ed is a buy-and-hold type, but he likes to use margin. *Trading on margin* means using the stocks and other securities in your brokerage account as collateral to purchase more shares. Which discount broker is suitable for which investor?

Say that there are two discount brokers, JumpCo and StayCo. JumpCo charges $9 per trade, while StayCo charges $25. However, when it comes to margin trading, JumpCo charges 10 percent, while StayCo usually charges a full percentage point lower.

In this example, JumpCo is better suited to Bob's style of investing, while StayCo is better for Ed. Because Bob likes to trade frequently, the commission charge makes it more economical. Ed will pay a higher commission, but he'll eventually make his money back through lower margin-interest costs.

This example clearly illustrates how different investors can benefit by analyzing themselves and then choosing an appropriate broker.

Making the decision

When it's time to choose a broker, keep the following points in mind:

- ✔ Match your investment style with an SRO-member brokerage firm that charges the least amount of money for the services you're likely to use most frequently.

- ✔ Compare all the costs of buying, selling, and holding stocks and other securities through a broker. Don't look only at commissions; compare other costs, too, such as margin interest and other service charges.

- ✔ Contact a few firms before making your selection. Ask them if they are currently seeking accounts like yours. Ask for and call a few references to find out about the broker's strengths and weaknesses.

- ✔ If you selected the full-service-firm route, ask for a recommendation of one or more brokers at the brokerage who would be appropriate to handle your account, and interview them.

- ✔ Read articles that compare brokers in publications and newspapers such as *Canadian Business* and the *National Post.*

Your broker will influence your finances in a big way, so take the time to get to know her and decide whether this is the person for you.

Finding brokers is easy. They're listed in the Yellow Pages as well as in many investment publications and on financial Web sites.

The Canadian Investor Protection Fund (CIPF) is overseen by the Canadian investment industry and provides coverage for Canadians making investments through its members. It insures brokerage accounts similar to the way the Canada Deposit Insurance Corporation (CDIC) insures bank accounts. CIPF limits coverage provided for a customer's general accounts equal to $1,000,000 to losses related to securities and cash balances. However, the amount of cash losses that you can claim as part of this limit is restricted, and other important coverage restrictions exist. Check out the CIPF Web site (www.cipf.ca) for full and detailed information. By the way — you aren't covered if the market corrects!

Book V

**Making
Your
Investments
Work for
You**

Investing is no more than the allocation of capital for use by an enterprise with the idea of achieving a suitable return. He or she who allocates capital best wins!

Researching Online Brokerage Services

Investing online through the Internet has flourished for several reasons. Online investing, via an online brokerage service, lets you buy and sell stocks and other financial instruments using your personal computer and an Internet connection. As mentioned before, most online broker services are provided by traditional full-service and discount brokers. Several factors contribute to the rapid growth of online investing.

Understanding why online investing is popular

First, the Internet provides quick and easy access to raw investment information (such as a stock quote) as well as refined information (such as a broker's analysis of a company, or other information services previously available only to investment professionals). Second, by eliminating the need for actual brokers or advisers online brokers can offer commission rates that are lower than offline brokers charge. For example, buying 500 shares of Bombardier through a traditional full-service broker could cost you about $100 in commissions. Online, the cost is about $35. Easy account access is another reason for the popularity of online investing. Online brokers conveniently provide you with access to your account and the ability to place orders anytime and anywhere in Canada (or abroad) as long as you have an Internet connection. Finally, control of the investment process appeals to many investors. You can research a company, buy shares in it, monitor its progress, and chat with other shareholders in that company to hear their opinions.

Getting online trading services for less

As you may have guessed, no two online brokerage services are alike. Furthermore, individual brokerages may change their services and fees to keep pace with their competitors. To find the online broker that best meets your needs, you must investigate the prices, services, and features that various brokers offer.

Make certain that your brokerage doesn't charge you for services that are free elsewhere, or are hidden. Some hidden fees may include:

- ✔ Higher fees for accepting odd-lot orders (orders that include increments of less than 100 shares)
- ✔ Fees for sending out certificates (some firms charge $50 per certificate)
- ✔ Fees to close your account
- ✔ Fees to withdraw funds from your trading account.

Trading online at a discount

You can't measure broker service with a formula. You have to look at both financial and non-financial criteria.

Cost is one factor. Definitely look at how much each broker charges in commission at different volumes of trades. Also assess the quality of online trade execution by talking to others who use a service you are considering. Are real-time quotes available? Is research material available? What is the overall ease of use of the service? Does the broker provide online screening tools?

Product selection is another important factor. You want to be able to trade things like guaranteed investment certificates, gold and silver certificates, municipal bonds, futures, Canadian and foreign equities, and so on. A list of investment products to consider is provided later in this chapter.

Response time should be quick. Some online brokers boast trade execution times of less than nine seconds! Phone each firm to see how long it takes for the broker to respond. E-mail each broker under consideration with a few questions; ask for an application to be sent by mail. Again, evaluate the response time.

Table 4-2 lists several discount brokerage services in Canada.

Book V

Making
Your
Investments
Work for
You

Table 4-2   You Can Trade at a Discount

	Minimum Online Trade Fee	Minimum Automated Telephone Trade Fee	Minimum Broker Assisted Trade Fee
BMO InvestorLine 1-800-387-7800 www.bmoinvestorline.com	$25 for up to 1,000 shares	$25 for up to 1,000 shares	$40 minimum price per trade
CIBC Investor's Edge 1-800-567-3343 www.investorsedge.cibc.com	$25 for up to 1,000 shares	$25 for up to 1,000 shares	$43 minimum price per trade
Disnat 1-800-268-8471 www.disnat.com	$29 for up to 1,000 shares	Not available	$42 on orders of up to $2,000
E*Trade Canada 1-888-872-3388 www.canada.etrade.com	$26.99 minimum	Not available	Online trade fee plus $35
Merrill Lynch HSBC Canada 1-866-865-4722 www.mlhsbc.ca	$29 for up to 1,000 shares	Not available	$40 minimum per trade
National Bank Discount Brokerage 1-800-363-3511 www.nbc.com	$24.95 for up to 1,000 shares	$24.95 for up to 1,000 shares	$40.95 minimum per trade
Royal Bank Action Direct Brokerage 1-800-769-2560 www.actiondirect.com	$29.95 for up to 1,000 shares	$35 for up to 1,000 shares	$43 minimum per trade
Scotia McLeod Direct Investing 1-800-263-3430 www.scotiabank.com	$25.95 for up to 1,000 shares	$25.95 for up to 1,000 shares	$34.95 minimum per trade
Sun Life Securities 1-800-835-0812 www.sunsecurities.com	$29 for up to 1,000 shares	Not available	$43 minimum per trade
TD Waterhouse 1-800-465-5463 www.tdwaterhouse.ca	$29 (TalkBroker) or $29 for up to 1,000 shares	(Web Broker or Wireless) to 1,000 shares	$35 (Telemax) for up $43 minimum per trade

Understanding Brokerage Accounts

Once you start investing in the stock market, you have to somehow actually *pay* for the stocks you buy. Most brokerage firms offer investors several different types of accounts, each serving a different purpose. The following sections present three of the most common types. The basic difference boils down to how particular brokers view your creditworthiness when it comes to buying and selling securities. If your credit isn't great, your only choice is a cash account. If your credit is good, you can open either a cash account or a margin account.

To open an account, you'll have to fill out an application and submit a cheque or money order for the minimum amount required.

Cash accounts

A *cash account* is just what you think it means. To begin trading, you must deposit a sum of money along with the new account application. The amount of your initial deposit varies from broker to broker. Some brokers have a $10,000 minimum, while others will let you open an account for as little as $75.

With a cash account, your money has to be deposited in the account before the closing (or "settlement") date for any trade you make. The closing occurs three business days after the date you make the trade (date of execution).

In other words, if you call your broker on Monday, October 10 and order 50 shares of CashLess Corp. at $20 per share, then on Thursday, October 13 you'd better have $1,000 in cash sitting in your account (plus commission). Otherwise, you'll be charged interest at rates as high as 19 percent, and your next trade will be blocked by the credit department!

If you have cash in a brokerage account (remember, all accounts are brokerage accounts, and "cash" and "margin" are simply types of brokerage accounts), see whether the broker will pay you interest on it and how much. Some offer a service in which uninvested money earns money market rates.

Margin accounts

A *margin account* gives you the ability to borrow money against the securities in the account to buy more stock. Once you're approved, your brokerage firm gives you credit. A margin account has all the benefits of a cash account plus this ability of buying on margin.

For stock trading, the margin limit is 50 percent. In other words, if you plan to buy $10,000 worth of stock on margin, you need at least $5,000 in cash (or securities owned) sitting in your account. The interest rate that you pay varies depending on the broker, but most brokers generally charge a rate that is several points higher than their own borrowing rate.

Why use margin? Margin is to stocks what mortgage is to buying real estate. You can buy real estate with all cash, but many times using borrowed funds makes sense.

Option accounts

An *option account* gives you all the capabilities of a margin account (which in turn also gives you the capabilities of a cash account) plus the ability to trade stock and index options. When you open an options account, the broker usually asks you to sign a statement that you are knowledgeable about options and are familiar with the risks associated with them.

Chapter 5

Buying and Selling Stocks

. . . .

In This Chapter

▶ Basing your strategy on your needs

▶ Deciding where to allocate your assets

▶ Recognizing when to unload your stocks

▶ Looking at different types of brokerage orders

▶ Using trailing stops to protect your profits

▶ Trading on margin to maximize profits

▶ Making sense of going short

. . . .

Stocks are a means to an end. What end are you seeking? You should look at stocks as tools for wealth building. Sometimes they're great tools, and sometimes they're awful. It depends on your approach. Some stocks are appropriate for a conservative approach, while others are more suitable for an aggressive approach. Sometimes stocks aren't necessary at all. Golly! A stock investing book that suggests that stocks aren't always the answer! That's like a teenager saying, "Dad, I respectfully decline your generous offer of money for my weekend trip."

Placing an Order to Buy or Sell Stocks

Investment success isn't just about picking rising stocks; it's also about how you go about doing it. Frequently, investors think that good stock picking means doing your homework and then executing that purchase or sale. However, you can take it a step further, to maximize profits (or minimize losses). As a stock investor, you can do so by taking advantage of techniques and services available through your garden-variety brokerage account. (See Chapter 4 for more on brokerage accounts, and a bit about fruits and vegetables, too.) This chapter presents some of the best ways you can use these powerful techniques — useful whether you're buying or selling stock. In fact, if you retain nothing more from this chapter than the concept of *trailing stops* (see the section "Trailing stops"), you'll have gotten your money's worth.

Orders you place with your stock broker neatly fit into two categories:

- ✔ **Time-related orders:** Time-related orders mean just that; the order has a time limit. Typically, these are used in conjunction with conditional orders. (For an example, see the "Keeping a Line on Limit Orders" section later in this chapter.) The two most common time-related orders are day orders and good-till-cancelled (or GTC) orders, which are explained in their own sections later in this chapter.

- ✔ **Condition-related orders:** A condition-related order means that the order should be executed only when a certain condition is met. Conditional orders enhance your ability to buy stocks at a lower price, to sell at a better price, or to minimize potential losses. When stock markets become bearish or uncertain, conditional orders are highly recommended. A good example of a conditional order is a *limit order.* A limit order may say, "Buy SlapShot Company at $45." But if SlapShot Company is not available at $45 (this is the condition), then the order isn't executed.

Get familiar with both kinds of orders, because they're easy to work with and invaluable tools for wealth building and (more importantly) wealth saving!

Using a combination of orders helps you fine-tune your strategy so that you can maintain greater control over your investments. Speak with your broker about the different types of orders you can use to maximize the gains (or minimize the losses) from your stock-investing activities. You also can read the broker's policies on stock orders at the brokerage Web site.

Calling It a Day Order

A *day order* (a time-related order) is an order to buy a stock that expires at the end of that particular trading day. If you tell your broker, "Buy BYOB Inc. at $37.50 and make it a day order," you mean that you want to purchase the stock at $37.50. But if the stock doesn't hit that price, your order expires at the end of the trading day unfilled. Why would you place such an order? Maybe BYOB is trading at $39, but you don't want to buy it at that price because you don't believe the stock is worth it. Consequently, you have no problem not getting the stock that day.

When would you use day orders? It depends on your preferences and personal circumstances. There are few events that cause us to say, "Gee, I'll just try to buy or sell between now and the end of today's trading action." However, you may feel that you don't want a specified order to linger beyond today's market action. Perhaps you want to test a price. ("I would like to get rid of stock A at $39 to make a quick profit, but it's currently trading at $37.50. However, I may change my mind tomorrow.") A day order is the perfect strategy to use in this case.

By the way, if you make any trade and don't specify time with the order, most (if not all) brokers automatically treat it as a day order.

Understanding Good-till-Cancelled (GTC)

A *good-till-cancelled (GTC)* order is the most commonly requested order by investors. Although GTC orders are time-related, they are always tied to a condition, such as when the stock achieves a certain price. The GTC order means just what it says: The order stays in effect until it is transacted or until the investor cancels it. Although the order implies that it could run indefinitely, most brokers do have a time limit to it. The time limit could be 30 days, 60 days, 90 days, or longer. Ask your broker about his particular policy on GTC orders.

A GTC order is usually coupled with conditional or condition-related orders. For example, say that you want to buy ASAP Corp. stock but you don't want to buy it at the current price of $48 per share. You've done your homework on the stock, including looking at the stock's price-earnings ratio, price to book ratio, and so on, and you say, "Hey, this stock isn't worth $48 a share. I would only buy it at $36 per share." You think the stock would make a good addition to your portfolio, but not at the current market price — it's overpriced or overvalued according to your analysis. How should you proceed?

Well, you wouldn't put in a day order to get the stock at $36. To go from $48 to $36 in a day means that the stock would need to fall by 25 percent. The odds are against that happening (unless you know something that we don't). However, the odds that such a decline could happen over a period of a few weeks or a few months are much better. If you want that stock at your price and you are patient, ask your broker to do a "GTC order at $36." This means that your broker will buy the shares if and when they hit the $36 mark (or until you cancel the order). Just make sure that your account has the funds available to complete the transaction.

The bottom line is that GTC orders are very useful, so you should become familiar with your broker's policy on them. While you're at it, ask whether any fees apply. Many brokers don't charge for GTC orders because, if they happen to result in a buy (or sell) order, they generate a normal commission just as any stock transaction would. Other brokers may charge a small fee. In many cases, if a fee is charged it's credited against the commission should the transaction occur. Fee or no fee, the GTC order is meant to protect you from further losses or to help you lock in a profit.

When you want to buy

In recent years, people have had a tendency to rush into buying a stock without giving some thought to what they could do to get more for their money. It doesn't occur to some investors that the stock market can be a place for bargain-hunting consumers. If you're ready to buy a quality pair of socks for $16 in a department store but the sales clerk says that those same socks are going on sale tomorrow for only $8, what would you do — assuming that you're a cost-conscious consumer? Unless you're barefoot, you're probably better off waiting. The same point holds true with stocks.

Say that you want to buy SOX Inc. at $26 but it's currently trading at $30. You think that $30 is too expensive, but you're happy to buy the stock at $26 or lower. However, you have no idea whether the stock will move to your desired price today, tomorrow, next week, or even next month. In this case, a GTC order is appropriate.

When you want to sell

Remember the socks you bought? Well, what if you have a hole in your sock (darn it!)? Wouldn't you want to get rid of it? Of course you would. If a stock's price starts to unravel, you want to be able to get rid of it as well.

Perhaps you already own SOX (at $25, for instance) but are concerned that market conditions may drive the price lower. You're not certain which way the stock will move in the coming days and weeks. In this case, a GTC order to sell the stock at a specified price is a suitable strategy. Because the stock price is $25, you may want to place a GTC order to sell it if it falls to $22.50, to prevent further losses. Again, in this example GTC is the time frame, and it accompanies a condition (sell when the stock hits $22.50).

Placing Market Orders

When you buy stock, the simplest type of order is a *market order* — an order to buy or sell a stock at the market's current best available price. It doesn't get any more basic than that.

Here's an example: Beliveau Inc., is available at the market price of $10. When you call up your broker and instruct him to buy 100 shares "at the market," the broker will implement the order for your account, and you pay $1,000 plus commission.

Book V

Making
Your
Investments
Work for
You

Current best available price" is the phrase used because the stock's price is constantly moving, and catching the best price can be a function of the broker's ability to effectively process the stock purchase. For very active stocks, the price change can happen within seconds. It's not unheard of to have three brokers simultaneously place orders for the same stocks and get three different prices because of differences in the broker's capability. (Some computers are faster than others.) The price difference within these seconds usually isn't worth getting concerned about because the difference amounts to pennies. It would matter to day traders and those who buy huge amounts of stock, but it's not a consequential difference to the everyday stock investor.

The advantage of a market order is that the transaction is processed immediately, and you get your stock without worrying about whether it hits a particular price. For example, if you buy Beliveau, Inc. with a market order, you know that by the end of that phone call (or Web site visit), you're assured of getting the stock. The disadvantage of a market order is that you can't control the price that you pay for the stock. Suppose that you learn that Beliveau, Inc. is currently trading at $10 per share. You call your broker to place an order. If the stock jumps to $11 per share before you finish ordering, you end up buying it for $1 more than you figured. Then again, you could get it for $9 if the price moves downward. With a fast-moving stock, you may get it at a significantly higher price than you planned. Conversely, if you're selling a particularly volatile stock, you might lock in a sale price lower (or higher) than you expected if the price changes before you finish your sale.

Market orders get finalized in the chronological order in which they're placed. Your price may change because the orders ahead of you in line caused the stock price to rise or fall based on the latest news.

Stop! I Order You!

A *stop order* (or *stop-loss order,* if you own the stock) is a condition-related order that instructs the broker to sell a particular stock only when the stock reaches a particular price. It acts like a trigger, and the stop order converts to a market order to sell the stock immediately.

The stop-loss order isn't designed to take advantage of small, short-term moves in the stock's price. It's meant to help you protect the bulk of your money when the market turns against your stock investment in a sudden manner.

Say that your Beliveau, Inc. stock rises to $20 per share and you seek to protect your investment against a possible future market decline. A stop-loss order at $18 will trigger your broker to sell the stock immediately if it falls to the $18 mark. In this example, if the stock suddenly drops to $17 it will still trigger the stop-loss order, but the finalized sale price will be $17. In a volatile market, you may not be able to sell at your precise stop-loss price.

However, because the order automatically gets converted into a market order, the sale will be done, and you avoid the impact of any further declines in price of the stock.

The main benefit of a stop-loss order is that it prevents a major decline in a stock that you own. It's a form of discipline that is important in investing in order to minimize potential losses. Investors can find it agonizing to sell a stock that has fallen. If they don't sell, however, the stock often continues to plummet as investors continue to hold on while hoping for a rebound in the price.

A stop-loss amount is usually set at about 10 percent below the market value of a stock. This percentage gives the stock some room to fluctuate, which most stocks tend to do on a day-to-day basis.

Trailing stops

Trailing stops are an important technique in wealth preservation for seasoned stock investors and can be one of your key strategies in using stop-loss orders. A *trailing stop* is a stop-loss order that the investor actively manages by moving it up along with the stock's market price. The stop-loss order "trails" the stock price upward. As the stop-loss goes upward, it protects more and more of the stock's value from declining.

To illustrate trailing stops with a real-life example, say that in 1999 you bought ATI Technologies (ATY) at $25 per share. As soon as you finished buying it, you immediately told your broker to put a stop-loss order at $22 and make it a good-till-cancelled (GTC) order. Think of what you did. In effect, you placed an ongoing (GTC) safety net under your stock. The stock can go as high as the sky, but if it should fall the stock's price will trigger a sell order at $22, at which point your stock will automatically be sold, minimizing your loss.

If ATI goes to $50 per share in a few months, you can call your broker and cancel the former stop-loss order at $22 and replace it with a new (higher) stop-loss order. You simply say, "Please put a new stop-loss order at $45 and make it a GTC order." This higher stop-loss price protects not only your original investment of $20, but also a big chunk of your profit. As time goes by and the stock price climbs, you can continue to raise the stop-loss price and add a GTC provision. Now you know why it is called a trailing stop: It trails the stock price upward like a giant tail. All along the way, it protects more and more of your growing investment without limiting its upward movement.

Some investment experts advocate setting a trailing stop of 10 percent below your purchase price. Many investors who invest in very volatile stocks may put in trailing stops of 20 or 25 percent. Is a stop-loss order desirable or advisable in every situation? No. It depends on your level of experience, your investment goals, and the market environment. Still, stop-loss orders are appropriate in most cases, especially if the market seems uncertain (or you do!).

A trailing stop is a stop-loss order that you actively manage. The stop-loss order is good-till-cancelled, and it constantly trails the stock's price as it moves up. To successfully implement trailing stops, keep the following points in mind:

✔ **Brokers usually don't place trailing stops for you automatically.** In fact, they won't (or shouldn't) place any type of order without your consent. Deciding on the type of order to place is your responsibility. You can raise, lower, or cancel a trailing stop order at will, but you need to monitor your investment when substantial moves do occur, and to respond to the movement appropriately.

✔ **Change the stop-loss order when the stock price moves significantly.** Hopefully, you won't call your broker every time the stock moves 50 cents. Change the stop-loss order when the stock price moves around 10 percent. When you initially purchase the stock (say, at $90 per share), request the broker to place the stop-loss order at $81. When the stock moves to $100, cancel the $81 stop-loss order and replace it at $90. When the stock's price moves to $110, change the stop-loss order to $100, and so on.

✔ **Understand your broker's policy on GTC orders.** If your broker usually has a GTC order expire after 30 or 60 days, you should be aware of it. You don't want to risk a sudden drop in your stock's price with the stoploss order protection. If your broker's time limit is 60 days, note it so that you can renew the order for additional time.

✔ **Monitor your stock.** Trailing stops is not a "set it and forget it" technique. Monitoring your investment is critical. Of course, if it falls, the stop-loss order you have will prevent further loss. Should the stock price rise substantially, remember to adjust your trailing stop accordingly. Keep raising the safety net as the stock continues to rise. Part of monitoring the stock is knowing the *beta,* which you can read more about in the next section.

I beta you didn't know this

To be a successful investor, you need to understand the volatility of the particular stock you invest in. In stock-market parlance, this is also called the beta of a stock. *Beta* is a quantitative measure of the volatility of a given stock (mutual funds and portfolios, too) relative to the overall market, usually the S&P 500 index. Beta specifically measures the performance movement of the stock as the S&P moves 1 percent up or down. A beta measurement above 1 is more volatile than the overall market, while a beta below 1 is less volatile. Some stocks are relatively stable in their price movements; others jump around.

Because beta measures how volatile or unstable the stock's price is, it tends to be uttered in the same breath as "risk" — more volatility indicates more risk. Similarly, less volatility tends to mean less risk.

Table 5-1 shows some sample betas of well-known companies (as of March 2002):

Table 5-1		Looking at Well-Known Betas
Company	*Beta*	*Comments*
Petro Canada	.55	Is less volatile than the market. If the S&P moves $10, Petro-Canada would move only $5.50.
Yahoo!	2.63	Is almost three times more volatile than the market.
Public Service Enterprise Group	.07	Statistically considered much less volatile than the market.

You can find a company's beta at Web sites that usually provide a lot of financial information about the company, such as Yahoo!Finance (finance.yahoo.com). Once there, type in your stock ticker symbol, and click the Profile icon. That's where you'll find the beta.

The beta is useful to know because it gives you a general idea of the stock's trading range. If a stock is currently priced at $50 and it typically trades in the $48–$52 range, then a trailing stop at $49 doesn't make sense. Your stock would probably be sold the same day you initiated the stop-loss order. If your stock is a volatile growth stock that could swing up and down by 10 percent, you should more logically set your stop-loss at 15 percent below that day's price.

The stock of a large-cap stock in a mature industry tends to have a low beta — one close to the overall market. Small- and mid-cap stocks in new or emerging industries tend to have greater volatility in their day-to-day price fluctuations; hence, they tend to have a high beta. (You can find an explanation of capitalization in Chapter 3.)

Keeping a Line on Limit Orders

A *limit order* is a very precise condition-related order, implying that there is a limit either on the buy or the sell side of the transaction. You want to buy (or sell) only at a specified price. Period. Limit orders work better for you if you're buying the stock, and they may not be good for you if you're selling the stock.

Usually there are no special fees for limit orders. Brokers make their money when the order is triggered. At that point, the transaction (buy or sell) would generate a regular commission. However, policies and fees can vary depending on the brokerage. Some Internet brokerages actually charge a small fee for limit orders because they charge low commissions. They may credit the fee against the sell or buy commission if the order is triggered. (This is also true of stop orders, which are discussed earlier in this chapter.)

Book V

**Making
Your
Investments
Work for
You**

When you're buying

Just because you like a particular company and you want its stock doesn't mean that you're willing to pay the current market price. Maybe you want to buy Beliveau, Inc., but the current market price of $20 per share isn't acceptable to you. You prefer to buy it at $16 because you think that price reflects its true market value. What do you do? You tell your broker, "Buy Beliveau with a limit order at $16."

Of course, you don't know exactly when the stock will hit your price of choice. In this example, stock in Beliveau, Inc. may hit $16 by the end of the day or sometime next month or possibly never. A limit order must have a specified time period in which it can transact. You have to specify whether it is a day order (good for the day) or a GTC order, which is discussed in its own section earlier in this chapter. Unless you know some bad news about the company that the rest of the market doesn't (in which case a day order is advisable), the better option is to make it a GTC limit order. If and when the stock goes to $16 during the time your GTC order is in effect, the order to buy will automatically be performed, and you receive a trade confirmation notice.

What happens if the stock experiences great volatility? What if it drops to $16.01 and then suddenly drops to $15.95 on the next move? Actually, nothing, you may be dismayed to hear. Because your order was limited to $16, it can be transacted only at $16, no more or less. The only way for this particular trade to occur is if the stock rises back to $16. However, if the price keeps dropping, then your limit order won't be transacted and may expire or be cancelled.

When you're buying a stock, many brokers interpret the limit order as "buy at this specific price or better." Presumably, if your limit order is to buy the stock at $10, you'll be just as happy if your broker buys that stock for you at $9.95. This way, if you don't get exactly $10, because the stock's price was volatile, you'll still get the stock at a lower price. Speak to your particular broker to be clear on the meaning of the limit order.

When you're selling

Limit orders are activated only when a stock hits a specific price. If you buy Beliveau, Inc. at $20 and you worry about a decline in the share price, you may decide to put in a limit order at $18. If you watch the news and hear that Beliveau's price is dropping, you may sigh and say, "I sure am glad that I put in that limit order at $18!" However, in a volatile market, the share price may leapfrog over your specified price. It could go from $18.01 to $17.99 and then continue its descent. Because the stock price never hit $18 on the mark, it isn't sold. You may be sitting at home satisfied (mistakenly) that you played it smart, while your stock plummets to $15 or $10 or worse! It's best to have a stop-loss order in place.

Pass the Margin, Please

Margin means buying securities, such as stocks, by using funds you borrow from your broker. Buying stock on margin is similar to buying a house with a mortgage. If you buy a house at the purchase price of $100,000 and put 10 percent down, your equity (the part you own) is $10,000, and you borrow the remaining $90,000 with a mortgage. If the value of the house rises to $120,000 and you sell (for the sake of simplicity, closing costs aren't included in this example), you will make a profit of 100 percent. How is that? The $20,000 gain on the property represents a gain of 20 percent on the purchase price of $100,000, but because your real investment is $10,000 (the down payment), your gain works out to 200 percent (a gain of $20,000 on your initial investment of $10,000).

Buying on margin is an example of using leverage to maximize your gain when prices rise. *Leverage* is simply using borrowed money to increase your profit. This type of leverage is great in a favourable (bull) market, but it works against you in an unfavourable (bear) market. Say that a $100,000 house you purchase with a $90,000 mortgage falls in value to $80,000 (and property values can decrease during economic hard times). Your outstanding debt of $90,000 exceeds the value of the property. Because you owe more than you own, it is negative net worth. Leverage is a double-edged sword.

Marginal outcomes

Suppose that you think that the stock for the company Mergatroid, Inc., currently at $40 per share, will go up in value. You want to buy 100 shares, but you have only $2,000. What can you do? If you're intent on buying 100 shares (versus simply buying the 50 shares that you have cash for), you can borrow the additional $2,000 from your broker on margin. If you do that, what are the potential outcomes?

If the stock price goes up

This is the best outcome for you. If Mergatroid goes to $50 per share, your investment will be worth $5,000, and your outstanding margin loan will be $2,000. If you sell, the total proceeds will pay off the loan and leave you with $3,000. Because your initial investment was $2,000, your profit is a solid 50 percent, because ultimately your $2,000 principal amount generated a $1,000 profit. (This example leaves out charges such as commissions and interest paid on the margin loan, which can be as high as 10 percent.) However, if you pay the entire $4,000 up front — without the margin loan — your $4,000 investment will generate a profit of $1,000, or 25 percent. Using margin, you will double the return on your money.

Leverage, when used properly, is very profitable. However, it is still debt, so understand that you must pay it off eventually.

If the stock price fails to rise

If the stock goes nowhere, you still have to pay interest on that margin loan. If the stock pays dividends, this money can defray some of the cost of the margin loan. In other words, dividends can help you pay off what you borrow from the broker.

Having the stock neither rise nor fall may seem like a neutral situation, but you pay interest on your margin loan with each passing day. For this reason, margin trading can be a good consideration for conservative investors if the stock pays a high dividend. Many times, a high dividend from $5,000 worth of stock can exceed the margin interest you have to pay from the $2,500 (50 percent) you borrow from the broker to buy that stock.

If the stock price goes down, buying on margin can work against you. What if Mergatroid goes to $38 per share? The market value of 100 shares will be $3,800, but your equity will shrink to only $1,800 because you have to pay your $2,000 margin loan. You're not exactly looking at a disaster at this point, but you'd better be careful, because the margin loan exceeds 50 percent of your stock investment. If it goes any lower, you may get the notorious *margin call,* when the broker actually contacts you to ask you to restore the ratio between the margin loan and the value of the securities. See the following section for information about appropriate debt to equity ratios.

Maintaining your balance

When you purchase stock on margin, you must maintain a balanced ratio of margin debt to equity of at least 50 percent. If the debt portion exceeds this limit, then you'll be required to restore that ratio by depositing either more stock or more cash into your brokerage account. The additional stock you deposit can be stock that's transferred from another account.

If, for example, Mergatroid goes to $28 per share, the margin loan portion exceeds 50 percent of the equity value in that stock — in this case, because the market value of your stock is $2,800 but the margin loan is still at $2,000. The margin loan is a worrisome 71 percent of the market value ($2,000 divided by $2,800 = 71 percent). Expect to get a call from your broker to put more securities or cash into the account to restore the 50 percent balance.

Book V

Making Your Investments Work for You

If you can't come up with more stock, other securities, or cash, then the next step is to sell stock from the account and use the proceeds to pay off the margin loan. For you, it means realizing a capital loss — you lost money on your investment.

Margin, as you can see, can escalate your profits (on the up side), but magnify your losses (on the down side). If your stock plummets drastically, you can end up with a margin loan that exceeds the market value of the stock you used the loan to purchase. In the emerging bear market of 2000, many people were hurt by stock losses, and a large number of these losses were made worse because people didn't manage the responsibilities involved with margin trading.

If you buy stock on margin, use a disciplined approach. Be extra careful when using leverage, such as a margin loan, because it can backfire. Keep the following points in mind:

- ✔ **Have ample reserves of cash or marginable securities in your account.** Try to keep the margin ratio at 40 percent or less to minimize the chance of a margin call.

- ✔ **If you're a beginner, consider using margin to buy stock in large companies that have a relatively stable price and pay a good dividend.** Some people buy income stocks that have dividend yields that exceed the margin interest rate, meaning that the stock ends up paying for its own margin loan. Just remember those stop orders.

- ✔ **Constantly monitor your stocks.** If the market turns against you, the result will be especially painful if you use margin.

- ✔ **Have a payback plan for your margin debt.** Margin loans against your investments mean that you're paying interest. Your ultimate goal is to make money, and paying interest eats into your profits.

Going Short and Coming Out Ahead

The vast majority of stock investors are familiar with buying stock, holding on to it for a while, and hoping its value goes up. This kind of thinking is called *going long,* and investors who go long are considered to be *long on stocks.* Going long essentially means that you're bullish and seeking your profits from rising prices. However, astute investors also profit in the market when stock prices fall. *Going short* (also called *shorting a stock, selling short,* or *doing a short sale*) on a stock is a common technique for profiting from a stock price decline. Investors have made big profits during bear markets by going short. A short sale is a bet that a particular stock is going down.

To go short, you have to be deemed (by your broker) creditworthy — your account needs to be approved for short selling. When you're approved for margin trading, you're probably set to sell short, too. Speak to your broker (or check for this information on the broker's Web site) about limitations in your account regarding going short.

Because going short on stocks has greater risks than going long, beginning investors should avoid shorting stocks until they become more seasoned.

Most people easily understand making money by going long. It boils down to "buy low and sell high." Piece of cake. Going short means making money by selling high and then buying low. Huh? Thinking in reverse is not a piece of cake. Although thinking of this stock adage in reverse may be challenging, the mechanics of going short are really simple. Consider an example that uses a fictitious company called DOA, Inc. As a stock, DOA ($50 per share) is looking pretty sickly. It has lots of debt and plummeting sales and earnings, and the news is out that DOA's industry will face hard times for the foreseeable future. This situation describes a stock that is an ideal candidate for shorting. The future may be bleak for DOA, but promising for savvy investors.

You must understand brokerage rules before you conduct short selling. The broker must approve you for it, and you must meet the minimum collateral requirement, which is typically 50 percent of the shorted stock's market value. If the stock generates dividends, those are paid to the owner of the stock, not to the person who is borrowing it to go short. (See the next section, "Setting up a short sale," to see how this technique works.) Check with your broker for complete details.

Setting up a short sale

This section explains how to go short. Say that you believe that DOA is the right stock to short — you're pretty sure its price is going to fall. With DOA at $50, you instruct your broker to "go short 100 shares on DOA." (It doesn't have to be 100 shares; that's just an example.) Now, here's what happens next:

1. **Your broker borrows 100 shares of DOA stock, either from his own inventory or from another client or broker.**

   That's right. The stock can be borrowed from a client, no permission necessary. The broker guarantees the transaction, and the client/owner of the stock never has to be informed about it, because he never loses legal and beneficial right to the stock. You borrow 100 shares, and you'll return 100 shares when it's time to complete the transaction.

2. **Your broker then sells the stock and gives you the money.**

   Your account is credited with $5,000 (100 shares × $50) in cash — the money gained from selling the borrowed stock. This cash acts like a loan on which you're going to have to pay interest.

3. **You use the $5,000 for a little while.**

   Your broker has deposited the $5,000 in your account. You can use this money to buy other investments.

4. **You buy the stock back and return it to its rightful owner.**

   When it's time to close or "cover" the transaction (either you want to close it, or the owner of the shares wants to sell them, so you have to give them back), you must return the number of shares you borrowed (in this case, it was 100 shares). If you buy back the 100 shares at $40 per share (remember that you shorted this particular stock because you were sure its price was going to fall) and these 100 shares are returned to their owner, you make a $1,000 profit. (To keep the example tidy, brokerage commissions aren't included.) By selling short, you made money when the stock price fell!

Oops! Going short when prices grow taller

You may have guessed that there was a flip side to the wonderful profitability of selling short. Presume that you were wrong about DOA and that the stock price rises from the ashes as it goes from $50 to $87. Now what? You still have to return the 100 shares you borrowed. With the stock's price at $87, that means that you have to buy the stock for $8,700 (100 shares at the new, higher price of $87). Ouch! How do you pay for it? Well, you have that original $5,000 in your account from when you initially went short on the stock. But where do you get the other $3,700 ($8,700 less the original $5,000)? You guessed it — your pocket! You have to cough up the difference. If the stock continues to rise, that's a lot of coughing.

How much money do you lose if the stock goes to $100 or more? A heck of a lot. As a matter of fact, there's no limit to how much you can lose. That's why going short can be riskier than going long. With going long, the most you can lose is 100 percent of your money. However, with going short, you can lose more than 100 percent of the money you invest. Yikes!

Because the potential for loss is unlimited when you short a stock, you should use a stop order (also called a *buy-stop order*) to minimize the damage. Better yet, make it a good-till-cancelled order, discussed earlier in this chapter. You can set the stop order at a given price, and if the stock hits that price you buy the stock back so that you can return it to its owner before the price rises even higher. You still lose money, but you limit your losses.

Watching out for ticks

Short sellers should be aware of the *uptick rule,* which states that you can enter into a short sale only when the stock has just completed an uptick. "Tick" in this case means the actual incremental price movement of the stock you're shorting. For a $10 stock that was just $9.95 a moment ago, the 5-cent difference represents an uptick. If the $10 stock was just $10.10 a moment before, the 10-cent difference is a downtick. The amount of the tick doesn't matter. So, if you short a stock at the price of $40, the immediate prior price must have been $39.99 or lower. The reason for this rule (a Canadian and U.S. securities regulation) is that short selling can aggravate declining stock prices in a rapidly falling market. In practice, going short on a stock whose price is already declining can make the stock price fall even more so. Excessive short selling can make the stock more volatile than it would be otherwise.

Chapter 6

Investing in Bonds

*N*ext to mutual funds, bonds are the most confusing investment option for the majority of Canadians. That's because bonds have a mystique about them — with the exception of Canada Savings Bonds (CSBs), which many people use as a means of forced savings.

Bonds are not as complex as you may think, and by the time you reach your mid-30s, they deserve a place in your investment portfolio, in one form or another.

What Is a Bond?

Bonds are a simple idea made complicated by time. Essentially, a bond is an IOU issued by a corporation or a government in exchange for cold, hard cash. Here's an easy way to understand bonds.

If a friend asks to borrow a hundred dollars from you until the end of the month, she may offer an IOU promising to pay you back on that particular day. Bonds aren't much different, especially if your friend agrees to pay you interest on the loan.

But suppose your friend wants to borrow the money for a little longer than a month — say, 30 years? That changes things quite a bit.

First, you would hope she'll still be your friend in 30 years, and that she'll be around to pay back the loan. Also, instead of waiting 30 years for the entire amount to be repaid plus interest — which would be a pile of interest — you would probably appreciate receiving a series of interest payments from time to time. That's when the one big IOU becomes a series of little IOUs, promising to pay interest on the loan once or twice a year. Each small IOU would have a date on it, indicating when the payment was due. You would agree to give each small IOU back to your friend on its date in exchange for cash payment, representing interest earned on the loan.

If you needed cash before the term of the loan was up, you could obtain it by selling the IOU to someone else. If this third person knows nothing about your friend, and has doubts about her ability to repay the loan, it will influence the price they are willing to pay for the IOU. Familiarity and trust reduces the risk and raises the price; unfamiliarity and distrust increases the risk and lowers the price. All bonds work essentially the same way.

The date on which a bond/IOU must be paid is called its *maturity date,* and the difference between the price paid for the bond and its value at maturity, divided by the number of years between then and now, equals the annual interest (see Table 6-1).

Table 6-1	Interest Calculation on Bond's Issue Date
Price you pay for the bond:	$1,000
Value of the bond at maturity:	$2,000
Difference in value:	$1,000
Number of years to maturity:	10
Annual interest earned ($1,000 divided by 10):	10%

These days, with interest rates hovering near 30-year lows, 10 percent guaranteed interest is very appealing for a high-quality bond. In fact, if the *issuer* of the bond — whoever borrowed the money in the first place — is well known, with a good credit rating, people would pay more for this bond if you were selling it, lowering the actual annual interest rate. If you offered this bond, you may be paid $1,400 for it, earning you an immediate $400 profit (see Table 6-2).

Book V

Making
Your
Investments
Work for
You

Table 6-2	Interest Calculation If Rates Drop	
Price you received for the bond:		$1,400
Value of the bond at maturity:		$2,000
Difference in value:		$600
Number of years to maturity:		10
Annual interest earned ($600 divided by 10):		6%

But if interest rates suddenly skyrocket, as they did in the 1980s when you could earn 14 percent a year from money in your savings account, your 10 percent annual interest will be almost an insult. So you'll receive *less* for the bond than you paid in order to earn *more* in annual interest (see Table 6-3).

Table 6-3	Interest Calculation If Rates Rise	
Price you received for the bond:		$500
Value of the bond at maturity:		$2,000
Difference in value:		$1,500
Number of years to maturity:		10
Annual interest earned ($1,500 divided by 10):		15%

Notice three things here:

✔ Nothing about the bond has changed except its selling price. The company or government issuing the bond is the same; the maturity date is the same; the face value of the bond is the same. The only difference is the current interest rate available from other sources.

✔ You can make money from bonds in two ways. First, from the interest they earn for you, and second, from buying and selling bonds just as you would buy and sell any other item.

✔ Bond prices and interest rates are opposite riders on the same teeter-totter — when one goes up, the other drops. So the bond you buy today for $1,000 may be worth substantially less next month if the interest rate climbs higher. If the interest rate on bonds you hold is high enough, and the life of the bond is long enough, this shouldn't be a major concern to you. But it illustrates that a risk exists even with so-called "guaranteed" bonds.

Understanding what a bond represents

When a government or corporation issues bonds — basically a batch of IOUs borrowing money to expand the business, pay debts, improve facilities, and for other practical reasons — it is faced with a number of decisions:

- ✔ How much money do we need to raise? (Always a prime concern)
- ✔ How long can we take to pay it back? (Usually from 5 to 30 years)
- ✔ How much annual interest will we have to pay? (Determined by current interest rates and the level of risk involved)

Government-guaranteed bonds are not always issued by governments. Back in the early 1980s, when interest rates soared through the stratosphere, you could purchase Ontario Hydro bonds, guaranteed by the Government of Ontario, that paid *14 percent annual interest for 25 years!* Since mortgages were earning close to 20 percent in annual interest, this wasn't quite as dramatic as it sounds. But interest rates go up and down over time, and clever (or well-advised) investors stocked up on Hydro bonds. When interest rates dropped, the other end of the teeter-totter took off. Investors sold the bonds at a fat profit and moved the money into equity-based mutual funds. None of this is rocket science among sophisticated investors, of course. But you don't have to be sophisticated to take advantage of these opportunities. You just have to read books like this one to understand the basic principles. So keep reading!

After bonds are issued by a company through an investment dealer, they are traded the same as any other commodity, from pork bellies to uncut diamonds. The price people will pay to obtain the bonds is based, as with commodities, on how much profit the buyer believes he can make and how much risk is involved.

For example, bonds issued or guaranteed by a government are low risk because most governments can always find a way to pay their debts — they simply raise taxes. But since government-guaranteed bonds carry minimum risk, they don't have to pay high interest to attract your money.

Bonds issued by a corporation whose reputation is less than perfect, or whose coffers are not filled with gold bars, must pay higher interest to match the risk involved.

Looking at gilt-edged, blue-chip, and junk bonds

Book V

Making Your Investments Work for You

Bond rating services, such as Dominion Bond Rating Service (www.dbrs.com) are companies that employ experts who spend their career evaluating bonds and the firms or governments issuing them, assigning each a rating based on the risk involved. A bond whose likelihood of being paid at maturity is about as certain as the sun rising tomorrow morning is rated AAA. A niggling doubt may reduce it to A+ or A. Serious concerns will topple a bond down to a C or D rating.

✔ **AAA- and AA-rated bonds** are considered high-grade, with little risk of default. They include bonds guaranteed by federal and provincial governments as well as the bluest of blue-chip companies.

✔ **A- and BBB-rated bonds** represent moderate risk, and are usually issued by large corporations.

✔ **BB- and lower-rated bonds** carry a more serious risk of default, meaning you could lose your entire investment in them. Bonds in this category are marketed as high-yield bonds, more familiarly called *junk bonds.*

A bond's rating has a direct impact on the price the market will pay for the bond, and the amount of interest the bond must earn to attract investors. In that sense, bond rating services are like handicappers at a horse race, telling you which nag is likely to finish in the money. If you go along with their views, your odds of winning may be better, but the amount of money the cashier pays for your ticket will be lower.

Gilt-edged bonds are rated AAA or AA. These are issued by federal or provincial governments and large, well-managed companies with excellent reputations, usually referred to as *blue-chip* firms. In Canada, this includes corporations such as Bell Canada, IBM Canada, Loblaw Companies Limited, and chartered banks. It can also include corporations whose reputations may have been tarnished in recent years, such as the former Ontario Hydro, but whose payment of their bonds is guaranteed by the government.

The bonds that most Canadians are familiar with are Canada Savings Bonds (CSBs), which may seem like a wise addition to your RRSP. Except that they weren't eligible for an RRSP unless they were called *Canada RRSP Bonds.* Then their name was changed to *Canada Premium Bonds.* Isn't government wonderful?

Whatever their current name, CSBs for RRSPs pay compound interest (the interest you earn this year earns its own interest next year), are 100 percent guaranteed by the Government of Canada, and can be purchased by anyone who has had a permanent residence in Canada for at least six months. The minimum purchase for RRSP-eligible bonds is $500, and they are available in denominations of $500, $1,000, $5,000, and $10,000.

Junk bonds — or *high-yield* bonds, as they are known in more polite circles — are at the other end of the risk scale from CSBs. These IOUs, which tend to have short maturity dates and pay very high interest rates, may be issued by companies as a means of financing the takeover of another firm. The odds of the company covering these bonds may still be in your favour, but the risk of losing your entire investment remains.

Between these two extremes are bonds issued by lesser corporations that may or may not be around with the money they owe you when the bonds reach maturity. These include smaller but solid companies such as Domtar and Interprovincial Pipeline, and it's worth obtaining professional advice before deciding to risk your funds in them.

The lower a bond's alphabetical rating, the higher the interest it pays. In mid-2003, bonds rated BB, which is edging into junk-bond territory, averaged 7.75 percent, or about 3 percent more than top-rated bonds. Bonds three notches lower, at the CC level, were averaging 17.34 percent interest. Pretty tempting? Yes, but if the company issuing the bond defaults, you are left holding a very pretty piece of paper — and nothing more.

Junk bonds can pay *very* impressive interest rates. It may be appealing, when everyone else is promising a paltry 5 percent annual interest for their bonds, to invest a few bucks in a junk bond promising annual interest of 12 to 16 percent. If faced with this opportunity — probably not by a qualified professional financial adviser, by the way — take a long walk around the block before reaching your decision. If you still want to throw your money at some junk bonds, take another walk . . . and another. In the end, the decision is yours. But don't make it without a lot of thinking and a lot of walking.

Knowing why strip bonds are a good choice

A bond's small IOUs, which pay interest once or twice a year, are called *coupons* and come attached to the bond itself. The world is filled, or so we are told, with cackling millionaires whose days consist of removing bonds from their vaults and clipping off the coupons, which they can spend like cash. Try not to think about them right now. . . .

Bonds consist of coupons, which represent the scheduled interest to be paid over the life of the bond, and the *residual,* which is the original (or *par*) value of the bond. If you own a $100 (par value) Government of Canada bond paying 8 percent annual interest and maturing on January 1, 2020, it includes coupons dated December 1 and June 1 for each year between the date it was issued and its maturity date. Each coupon is worth $4.00, representing 4 percent of the par value; two coupons each year produce 8 percent annual interest.

But nobody says you must have all the coupons and the residual in one piece on the bond. Each can be removed and traded at whatever value buyers and sellers agree upon for them.

When coupons and the residual have been removed from a bond, the bond is undressed. It's actually called *stripped* — but bonds can be dull stuff for some people, so think of them as naked if it makes them more interesting. (Even *strip* sounds a bit risqué in some tonier circles, where you may hear them referred to as *zero-coupon bonds.*)

Actually, coupons are no longer physically stripped from a bond. Instead, they are *book-based,* which means they exist only as an entry in a centralized financial registry system called the Central Depository System (CDS).

Both the coupons and the residual have a fixed value on their maturity date. Will you pay that price to purchase them before that date? Of course not. How can you make money by paying $100 today for something that will be worth $100 in 5, 10, or 20 years? You will pay *less* than the amount shown on the coupon or residual. The difference between the price you pay today and the price it will be worth on its maturity date, divided by the number of years between now and then, equals the annual interest earned. In other words, it works precisely like a regular bond, but without regular interest payments.

Strip bonds are popular choices investments for a bunch of reasons, and they belong in the RRSP of anybody over age 35. Here's why:

- Strip bonds pay higher interest than guaranteed investment certificates.

- You know exactly how much interest you will earn between now and the bond's maturity date.

- Strip bonds are more liquid (you can sell them when necessary) than GICs, which lock you in for periods from six months to five years. Try cashing in your GIC before it comes due and you'll pay a fat penalty.

- Government-guaranteed strip bonds are even more secure than a GIC. GICs are guaranteed by the Canada Deposit Insurance Corporation to a maximum of $60,000 per account. But federal and provincial governments guarantee their bonds for the full amount.

- Strip bonds represent extra value for RRSP holders, since they hold no appeal for investors who buy bonds as a source of regular income. Hold a strip bond outside your RRSP and you are required to declare the increase in value each year on your income-tax return. This means you'll pay tax on the profit, even though you are years away from actually pocketing it! In a tax-deferred RRSP, this doesn't apply. The result: Strip bonds appeal to a smaller segment of the market, which lowers their price and raises the interest they pay.

✔ When you purchase strip bonds, you'll receive a disclosure document indicating limits on their liquidity, marketability, tax implications, custodial arrangements, and safekeeping issues. None of these is critical to RRSP owners who plan on keeping the bonds within their RRSP until maturity.

Deciding between short-term or long-term

Short-term bonds, maturing in two years or less, provide you with flexibility. The interest they produce will be relatively low, but they'll be converted into cash fairly soon, opening up new opportunities.

Long bonds, shorthand for "long-term," are the same size as short models — "long" indicates a maturity date far into the future. They pay higher interest rates than short-term bonds, because long-bond buyers want protection against the danger of inflation between the day they buy the bond and the day it matures. The longer the term, the higher the risk of inflation.

Long bonds are almost as flexible as short-term bonds, since there will always be a market for quality bonds. The question is, at what price? A rise in interest rates will reduce the price you can get for your bonds if you decide to sell them.

How to Buy Bonds

Bonds are available from banks, trust companies, credit unions, caisses populaires, full-service brokerage houses, and licensed financial advisers. Most of the discount brokerages listed in Chapter 4 (see Table 4-2) also allow you to buy and sell certain types of bonds. Strip bonds are a little more difficult to obtain, although your self-directed RRSP administrator can purchase them for you. TD Canada Trust sells strip bonds. So do independent and bank-owned investment brokers such as BMO Nesbitt Burns and Merrill Lynch, and full-service financial planners including The Financial Planning Group, Money Concepts, and others.

Although it's wise to hold good bonds to maturity within your RRSP, there may come a time when you want their cash value before that date. This means you will be selling your bond on the secondary market, which is like a used car lot for bonds. The price you receive for your bond will depend on a number of factors, all as variable as the wind. These include the following:

Book V

Making
Your
Investments
Work for
You

✔ **Current interest rates:** If they have risen since you purchased the bond, you will receive less than you might expect. If they have dropped, you'll make extra profit.

✔ **The bond's maturity date:** Short-term bonds tend to earn lower interest.

✔ **Bond features:** Some bonds come with extra features (or, as they may say in a used-car lot, "optional extras"). These include callable bonds — the lender reserves the right to pay you back before the maturity date — and extendable bonds, which means you could wait a little longer than you thought.

✔ **The creditworthiness of the lender:** If a company's fortunes have fallen since the bond was issued, the bond's price will drop to reflect this.

Remember the "No Free Lunch" Rule

No matter who sells you a bond — stripped, well-dressed, or junk — they are not doing it because they like your curly hair and sweet smile. They're doing it to make a profit. This probably does not qualify as headline news, but it should concern you because the profit margin charged by the bank, trust company, or broker selling you the bond is both hidden and negotiable.

Most brokers, if you ask about commissions on bonds, will claim they don't charge any. They may say something like "We agreed on a ten-year stripped bond at 4.87 percent and that's what you received, with no commissions charged." Trouble is, when the brokerage firm purchased it on your behalf, the bond didn't pay 4.87 percent; it paid perhaps 5.25 percent. The difference? The broker paid *less* to buy the bond so the lower purchase price would have produced *more* interest earned between now and the bond's maturity date. How much more? That depends. But pay attention: If you sell the bond before its maturity date, your broker will pay you less than full market price, producing a lower earned annual interest than you might expect. So you pay a commission buying the bond and a commission selling it. Or, to put it succinctly: You lose coming and going.

All in all, you could wind up losing 2 full percentage points from the interest earned on your bond, without even knowing about it. Instead of earning you 7 percent annually, the bond earns you little more than 5 percent annually.

Does this make your broker, financial adviser, or self-directed RRSP administrator crooked? No, it's just the way things are done in the bond market. Bonds for small investors are bought and sold according to the interest they earn, not according to the actual purchase price.

But losing as much as 2 percent in annual interest should concern you — especially since you can do something about it. Here's what to do:

- ✔ Get details on the recommended bond from your adviser or investment counsellor. Write down the name of the company or government that issued the bond, the date of issue, its value, the maturity date, and, if possible, the series number.

- ✔ Ask your financial adviser or the counsellor who purchases the bonds for you to provide information on her firm's bond-commission policy. Refuse to believe that a policy does not exist. Every major investment dealer has guidelines on bond commissions. If your adviser stonewalls you, inform her that you're prepared to ask other firms the same question, looking for the best deal. Make it a threat and follow through. (It's always a buyer's market for RRSP owners.) Hey, it's your money, not theirs.

- ✔ Contact a discount brokerage such as TD Waterhouse. Ask for the price and point spread of the bond recommended by your adviser, providing all the data you have. The difference will be your adviser's commission rate.

- ✔ Demand that your broker or adviser confirm the commissions being earned on the bond she wants you to purchase, and the amount by which it reduces your earned interest. A difference of 0.50 percent between the two yields is acceptable. You owe your adviser something for her service, after all. Just don't overpay. Example: The bond price paid by your adviser's firm yields 5.75 percent annual interest; at the price you pay for it, the bond earns 5.25 percent. That's reasonable. Anything greater than 0.50 percent is like having your pocket picked.

All these demands and action by you will not generate unbridled delight from your financial adviser. Tough. It's your money, your future, and you have every right to know what something is really costing you. Simply remind your adviser that she is supposed to be working for and with you — not against you.

Chapter 7

Screening Mutual Funds Online

● ●

In This Chapter

▶ Using online screening tools to find mutual fund values

▶ Investigating top screen sites

▶ Using an online broker

▶ Knowing when to sell

● ●

*T*his chapter gives you all the basic online tools for identifying mutual fund candidates, describing five types of online screening tools that can help you choose the mutual fund that best meets your needs. These mutual fund screens vary from simple to more advanced; you should find that the best online mutual fund screen is the one that includes the criteria that are most important to you.

What Am I Screening?

Before you can screen mutual funds, you have to know where to find the large online mutual fund databases:

✔ **GLOBEfund** (www.globefund.com), shown in Figure 7-1, has a large database of mutual fund profiles, which are essentially fact sheets. GLOBEfund also has an online portfolio tracking tool to help you place a current value on your mutual fund holdings. With this feature, you don't have to wait until the end of the month to find out what your holdings are worth. An available filtering tool lets you specify what type of fund you wish to find, how large the fund is, what the fees are, and other selection criteria. (More on the actual screening process is discussed later in this chapter.)

✔ **The Fund Library** (www.fundlibrary.com) lets you access detailed profiles on a wide array of Canadian mutual funds. At this site, you can also set up a portfolio or watch list of mutual funds you wish to track, and personalize the way you want to view this information. The Fund Library also has discussion forums to let you chat online with other mutual fund investors, and lets you access vast educational resources in their online learning centre. Its fund rating tool will help you make the right mutual fund choices.

✔ **Morningstar Canada (**www.morningstar.ca**)** has a comprehensive listing of just about any Canadian mutual fund available. The information is free, but you are asked to register by providing a bit of general information about yourself. Once you have access, you can track your holdings with Morningstar's portfolio manager tool to help you analyze the mix and value of your holdings. The sister Web site at www.morningstar.com lets you do the same type of analyses as the Canadian site, but also gives you information on about 13,000 U.S.-based mutual funds. You can also learn about investing in mutual funds sold outside North America.

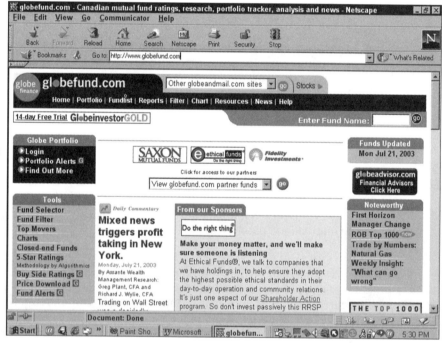

Figure 7-1: GLOBEfund has comprehensive information about mutual funds that are offered in Canada.

How to Screen Mutual Funds Online

The Internet provides a variety of mutual fund screening tools that sort thousands of U.S. and Canadian mutual funds by criteria that you select. For example, you may want one type of fund for your children's education — something long-term because you don't need the money for 10 to 20 years — and a different fund for your retirement to help you get a steady stream of income and to reduce your current tax liabilities. With online screening tools, you can evaluate several funds that meet your financial needs.

Most investment screening Web sites are free. But there's always an exception. Morningstar Canada's (www.morningstar.ca) BellCharts feature is just about the most powerful mutual fund screening tool available for Canadian funds. But it will cost you a fee. Subscription rates are accessible on the Morningstar Canada Web site.

Screening a list of mutual funds residing in a database is an inexpensive way to isolate mutual funds that meet your special criteria. Be wary that some databases list funds incorrectly or have outdated information; however, they are useful for pruning a long list of candidates to a manageable short list.

Some mutual fund screening programs — for example, Quicken's Mutual Fund Finder (www.quicken.com/investments/mutualfunds/finder/) and MSN Investor (moneycentral.msn.com/investor) — are for beginners. Others, such as BellCharts (offered through Morningstar Canada), require a bit of practice. Some mutual fund screens, such as at BellCharts, allow you to download the data to your spreadsheet so that you can do additional analysis.

Each screening site uses different criteria to sort mutual funds. You have to decide which criteria you care about and then use the site that offers the criteria you want. Any way you look at it, the selection of the right mutual fund is still up to you.

Here's an overview of the features of a few mutual fund screens that are best for beginning online investors:

✔ **Morningstar Canada (**www.morningstar.ca**)** has a screening tool called Fund Selector (see Figure 7-2), which lets you screen and create a short list of Canadian mutual funds by fund sponsor, fund category, load type, RRSP eligibility, fund assets, management expense ratio, Morningstar rating, and rate of return. At Morningstar Canada's home page, click the Fund Selector icon.

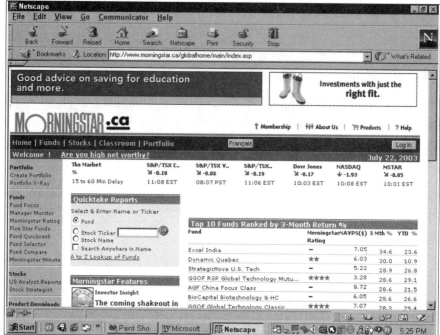

Figure 7-2:
Morningstar
Canada has
a Canadian
mutual fund
performance
screen
called Fund
Selector.

- ✔ **Morningstar U.S.** (www.morningstar.com) offers a free, independent service that evaluates mostly U.S. mutual funds. Its screening tools are even more selective than those found at Morningstar Canada.

- ✔ **Webfin** (www.webfin.com) has a basic screener of Canadian mutual funds. You can select criteria around the type of fund, fund company, RRSP status, management fees, and yield.

- ✔ **Microsoft MoneyCentral Investor** (moneycentral.msn.com/investor) is free and has lots of features. You can select from a predefined fund search or perform a custom search using criteria that you define. The MoneyCentral Fund Finder lets you search a database of over 8,000 funds. The custom search criteria include the fund family name, investment focus, the fund's historical performance, overall rating, the minimum initial investment, risk ranking, and load status.

The following mutual funds screens are great for more experienced investors:

- ✔ **SmartMoney** (www.smartmoney.com) lets you reveal desirable investment opportunities by helping you research over 12,000 U.S. mutual funds and screen from over 60 criteria. You can view your results in different ways, save your favourite screens for repeated use, and further analyze funds using SmartMoney's fund snapshots and advanced charting and technical analysis tools. You can also use one of its pre-defined SmartMoney Fund Screens, and create a spreadsheet and download an extensive report on all your funds. The site charges a fee for this extensive service.

✔ **Thomson Investors Network** (www.thomsoninvest.net), shown in Figure 7-3, has free mutual fund (and stock) screens. On the home page, click Funds. Next, click Fund Screening and select the characteristics of the mutual fund you are seeking. Click Show Results to enter your choices and see your results. This site lets you screen both Canadian and U.S. funds. One drawback is that you can't copy search results to a spreadsheet program.

Book V

Making Your Investments Work for You

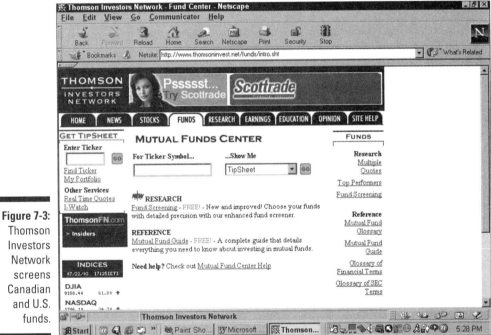

Figure 7-3: Thomson Investors Network screens Canadian and U.S. funds.

Buying Mutual Funds Online: No Broker Needed

When you have decided which mutual fund best suits your portfolio, you can purchase it without a broker. All you have to do is contact the company directly. Table 7-1 lists a few online mutual fund companies. The table shows the name of the mutual fund company and its Internet address.

Table 7-1	Examples of Online Mutual Fund Sources
Company	*Web Site Address*
AGF	www.agf.com
AIC Funds	www.aicfunds.com
Altamira	www.altamira.com
Fidelity Funds	www.fidelity.com
Greenline Mutual Funds	www.tdcanadatrust.com
Mackenzie Funds	www.mackenziefinancial.com
Talvest	www.talvest.com

Buying Mutual Funds Online: Using an Online Broker

You can purchase mutual funds through registered representatives of banks, trust companies, stock brokers, discount brokers, and financial planners. To purchase mutual funds via the Internet, go to a broker's Web site.

Register by completing the online application form. You have to provide information about your income, net worth, Social Insurance Number, and the type of account you desire. Sometimes you can open an account based on the quality (creditworthiness) of your information. However, to have a fully functioning account, brokerages are required to have your signature on file. After they have your signature on file, you can buy or sell as much as you want.

After you open your account, you can log on to the Internet, go to your brokerage Web site, and enter orders by completing the online form. You can access your account at any time, check all your investments, and monitor your investments by using online news or quote services.

You have the following options for selecting a broker, virtually all having an online array of services:

✓ **A deep-discount broker:** The least-expensive type of broker ($7 to $15 per trade); no recommendations; contacting a human if an error occurs is often difficult.

✔ **A discount broker:** Less expensive than full-service brokerages; no recommendations; minimal human contact.

✔ **A full-service broker:** Full commissions, recommendations, advice, and personal service.

Here are a few examples of online brokers:

✔ **E*Trade Canada** (`www.etrade.ca`) charges no fee as long as funds are held for at least 90 days (otherwise, a 1 percent or $39 minimum fee applies). However, the fund companies may charge fees themselves. This broker lets you trade over 3,200 mutual funds.

✔ **Merrill Lynch HSBC Canada** (`www.mlhsbc.ca`) offers no fee (over 1,200 funds) and for-fee trades for thousands of mutual funds. The company also trades stocks, bonds, and options.

Selling Mutual Funds Online

If your fund becomes one of the worst performers, consider selling. You need to look at more than just the fund's rating, though. Here are a few guidelines for determining when to sell a fund:

✔ Look at the performance of comparable mutual funds. If a similar fund's overall performance is down 10 percent but your fund is down 16 percent and its performance consistently trails its peers, it may be a loser.

✔ If your fund has drifted from its original investment objectives, then it's not meeting your asset allocation goals. You'll lose all the benefits of diversification if you have two mutual funds investing in the same asset class.

✔ Keep track of changes in your fund's management. If the fund hires a new money manager, that person may have a different investment strategy.

✔ You may want to sell if your mutual fund's management expense ratio (MER) has crept up, or if you inherited the fund. High MERs reduce your returns and make the fund less profitable than similar funds with lower expenses.

✔ In a volatile market, you may discover that you are a more conservative investor than you imagined. If you can't sleep at night, sell your fund.

✔ You are going to pay taxes on your capital gains. If one of your mutual funds is posting negative returns, you may want to consider selling it to offset your tax liabilities.

- ✔ If the fund increases by three or four times its original size in a short time period and its performance starts to decline, you may want to sell. As the fund keeps growing and growing, the professional money manager can't invest in the securities he or she knows and loves best, so the fund may start to acquire poor- or average-performing assets.

- ✔ Consider your needs. If you purchased the fund for a specific purpose and your life circumstances change, you should sell the fund and purchase one that meets your needs — even if the fund is doing well.

Funds that underperform in the short term can still be sound investments. For example, some Canadian funds did not outperform the TSX in the past three years, but their average total returns over the past three years exceeded 20 percent.

Chapter 8

Internet Stock Screening

● ●

In This Chapter

▶ Becoming familiar with online stock screens

▶ Building your first stock screen

▶ Locating online and PC-based stock screens

▶ Using prebuilt stock screens

▶ Getting online stock recommendations from the experts

● ●

*S*tock screening boils down to finding the answer to one fundamental question: "Which stock (of all stocks) should I buy right now?" Of course, finding the answer to this question requires asking many more specific questions about stocks — questions that are difficult to answer without the help of computerized databases.

This chapter shows how you can use the Internet and PC-based stock screening tools to whittle down the universe of stocks to a manageable few candidates. You can then analyze your short list of stocks for a few gems that may bring you above-average returns. This chapter also tells you where to find daily or weekly results of prebuilt stock screens.

Finding the Best Stock Electronically

Screening is a process that permits investors to locate and distill information within a larger set of information. The Internet provides many screening tools to help you prospect stock issues. The goal of stock screens is to point out which stocks are worth your research and analysis time.

Some people believe that using a stock screen is like panning for gold. You use your computer to screen ("pan") for investment "nuggets" from a long list of possibilities. The individual investor sets the objectives of any single screen. Different people get different results because no two people have exactly the same selection criteria or investment philosophy.

Overall, the benefit of stock screens is that they let you generate your own ideas — ideas that generate profits based on your investor savvy. Stock screening programs allow you to go beyond finding good stock investments and assist you in finding the very best stocks.

To identify investment candidates, the stock screen uses your preset criteria, such as *growth* (stocks that are expanding faster than the market or their peers); *value* (stocks that have strong financial statements but are selling at prices below their peers); or *income* (stocks that provide higher than average dividends).

Depending on the criteria you select, you may have to run several iterations of the stock screen. For example, your first screen may result in several hundred possibilities. Because you can't investigate and analyze so many candidates, you have to run a second screen of these results. This fine-tuning should lead to a manageable list of investment candidates that you can research and analyze — perhaps between 10 and 20. It is likely that you can quickly pare this number down by using common sense and your investment experience.

Choosing the criteria for your first stock screen

Typically, you build a stock screen by accessing an online stock screening tool and filling out an online form. You can find examples of the variables used in these forms later in this chapter, in the section "Important ratios for screening stocks." The first stock screen that you develop may include quantifiable variables that you believe are the most important — for example:

- ✔ **Earnings growth:** The percentage of change between current earnings and earnings for the last quarter or last year.

- ✔ **Recent earnings surprises:** The difference between predicted and actual earnings.

- ✔ **Price–earnings (P/E) ratio:** The current price of the stock divided by the earnings per share — that is, net income divided by the total number of common shares outstanding. Value stocks have P/E ratios below 10 or 12, and growth stocks have P/Es above 20. Technology stocks can have P/E ratios above 30 and still be considered good value if their current and expected growth rates are high.

- ✔ **Dividends:** The annual cash dividend paid by the company.

- ✔ **Market capitalization:** The number of outstanding shares multiplied by the current stock price of those shares. Market capitalization is sometimes abbreviated to cap. This value is a measurement of the company's size. Firms with high market capitalization are called "large-cap" and companies with low market capitalization are called "small-cap."

Fine-tuning your stock screen

Book V

Making
Your
Investments
Work for
You

After you select your initial screening criteria, you click Submit, Sort, or a similar command. A list of stock candidates appears. Often this list includes several hundred stocks. This number is still too large to research, so you should narrow this list by selecting more variables.

You may have some special knowledge about the industry you work in. You may have used certain products over the years and can use your knowledge to your advantage. However, keep in mind that a good product doesn't necessarily mean a good company. You may want to filter out companies that you just don't understand. You may also want to filter out companies about which you lack information. Without at least some basic information, you can't perform a complete analysis.

Using your stock screen results

After you complete your second stock screen and sort the data, you should have a list of about 10 to 20 companies. Start a file for each firm and begin to gather data for your analysis. At this point, you may discover through company-related news or press releases that some companies aren't worth additional research — a finding that further reduces your short list. For example, the company may have filed for bankruptcy, or it may be targeted for federal investigation. Maybe the company recently paid a large fine for shady dealings, or the executive management was recently indicted for fraud, misconduct, or some other crime.

Important ratios for screening stocks

Every industry has its own language, and the financial industry is no exception. The following sections offer definitions of the key terms that the finance industry uses for stock screening variables. They are worth knowing as you build and fine-tune your own stock screens.

Beta

Beta is the measurement of market risk. The beta is the relationship between investment returns and market returns. For example, risk-free Canada Savings Bonds have a beta of 0. If the beta is negative, the company is inversely correlated to the market — that is, if the market goes up, the company's stock tends to go down. If a stock's volatility is equal to the market, the beta is 1. In this case, if the stock market increases 10 percent, the stock price increases 10 percent. Betas greater than 1.0 indicate that the company is more volatile than the market. For example, if the stock is 50 percent more volatile than the market, the beta is 1.5.

Book value

Book value is the original cost, less depreciation of the company's assets, less the outstanding liabilities. (*Depreciation* or *amortization* is the means by which an asset's value is expensed — or spread — over its useful life for accounting and tax purposes.)

Cash flow to share price

The ratio of *cash flow to share price* is the company's net income plus depreciation or amortization (expenses not paid in cash) divided by the number of shares outstanding. For companies that are building their infrastructure (such as cable companies or new cellular companies) and, therefore, don't yet have earnings, this ratio may be a better measure of their value than earnings per share (EPS).

Current ratio

Current ratio is current assets divided by current liabilities. A current ratio of 1.00 or greater means that the company can pay all current obligations without using future earnings. The *quick ratio* is current assets minus inventory, divided by current liabilities. It measures the readiness of a company to meet its current obligations in a matter of days.

Debt-to-equity ratio

To determine the *debt-to-equity ratio,* divide the company's total amount of long-term debt by the total amount of equity. (*Equity* is defined as the residual claim by shareholders of company assets after creditors and preferred shareholders have been paid.) This ratio measures the percentage of debt the company is carrying. Many firms average a debt level of 50 percent. Debt-to-equity ratios greater than 50 percent may indicate trouble. That is, if sales decline, the firm may not be able to pay the interest payments due on its debt.

Dividends

Dividends are paid quarterly out of retained earnings. However, some high-growth companies reinvest earnings and don't pay dividends.

Dividend yield

Dividend yield is the amount of the dividend divided by the most current stock price. You can use dividends as a valuation indicator by comparing them to the company's own historical dividend yield. If a stock is selling at a historically low yield, it may be overvalued. Companies that don't pay a dividend — many Canadian technology stocks don't declare dividends — have a dividend yield of zero.

Earnings per share (EPS)

Earnings is one of the stock's most important features. After all, the price you pay for a stock is based on the future earnings of the company. The consistency and growth of a company's past earnings indicate the likelihood of stock price appreciation and future dividends. *Earnings per share* is often referred to as EPS.

Market capitalization

Market capitalization is calculated by multiplying the number of outstanding shares times the current stock price of those shares. Market capitalization is sometimes called *market value.*

P/E ratio

You calculate the *price–earnings ratio* by dividing the price of the stock by the current earnings per share. A low P/E ratio indicates that the company may be undervalued. A high P/E ratio indicates that the company may be overvalued.

Price-to-book value

Price-to-book value is the current price of the stock divided by the book value. If the current stock price is below the price-to-book value, the stock may be a real bargain. On the other hand, impending unprofitability or unjustified levels of intangible assets (such as goodwill) may be the reason.

Return on equity (ROE)

Return on equity (ROE) is usually equity earnings as a proportion of net worth. You divide the most recent year's net income by shareholders' equity (*shareholders' equity* is assets minus liabilities) to calculate the ROE.

Shares outstanding

The term *shares outstanding* refers to the total number of shares for a company's stock. To determine the firm's outstanding shares, you need the most recent data. The shares outstanding can be calculated by taking issued shares on the balance sheet and subtracting treasury stock. *Treasury stock* is stock issued but not outstanding by virtue of being held (after it is repurchased) by the firm.

Using Online Stock Screens

Web-based stock screens can require between 2 and 30 variables. Their computerized stock databases can include anywhere from 1,100 stocks to more than 9,000 stocks. As well, some computerized stock databases are updated daily, weekly, or monthly. The best stock screen is the one that includes your personal investment criteria. A few examples follow:

✔ **Yahoo! Finance** (`finance.yahoo.com`) has one of the most comprehensive stock screens available on the Internet. After you click on the Screener feature, you can choose from an array of criteria to help you find an appropriate stock. Examples of criteria include share price, industry sector, multi-year performance, beta, sales, and several key ratios. This Web site feature can screen both Canadian and U.S. stocks, and is free.

✔ **Adviceforinvestors.com** (`www.adviceforinvestors.com`) has stock screens geared to Canadian companies. A monthly subscription fee of about $10 applies to the basic subscription option. You have up to 20 screening criteria to select from including share price, exchange, industry, revenue, assets, price-earnings, and performance. This site also lets you access technical indicators to see where the stock price may be headed in the future. Click Stock Screening from the home page to access this tool.

✔ **GLOBEinvestor.com** (`www.globeinvestor.com`) has Canadian and U.S. stock screens (see Figure 8-1). Criteria include North American stock exchange, industry sector, share price, and performance. The service is free, and lets you view current and most recent quarter information about companies that met your criteria and were listed for you. From the list, you can click on handy icons to access a given company's financial statements, profile, and more.

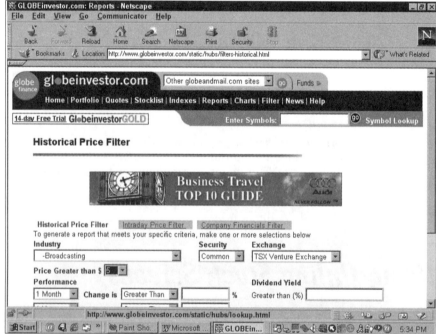

Figure 8-1:
GLOBEin-
vestor.com
lets you
screen
information
about
Canadian
companies.

Book V

Making
Your
Investments
Work for
You

✔ **Multex Investor's NetScreen** (`www.multexinvestor.com`) allows you to screen for stocks by using any of over 20 variables. To access the stock screen, go to the home page and click Screening Center. This stock screen features comparisons of variables, user-defined variables, comparison of variables to a constant, use of a variable more than once, and use of operators (greater than, less than, equals, and so on). The database is updated weekly. Your screening results are limited to no more than 200 companies at a time. Some of the larger inter-listed Canadian companies (such as Nortel, JDS Uniphase, and ATI Technologies) are covered. You can also use their prebuilt screens available within their Power Screener feature.

✔ **Microsoft MoneyCentral Investor** (`moneycentral.msn.com/investor`) is free and has lots of features. You can select from more than 500 criteria to quickly create a list of companies that meet your standards, or, if you'd rather, you can use a pre-existing search and modify it to suit your needs. If you find a company in the results list that looks interesting, it's easy to export the symbol to your portfolio so you can keep an eye on it. Once you have crafted just the right search, you can save it and run it again later. You can vary the number of matches you'll see in the results list from 1 to 100, or change the sort order by just clicking a column heading. You can also use Investment Matcher, a way to find companies with a similar market cap, average daily volume, price-to-sales ratio, and other specific criteria.

✔ **Nasdaq** (`www.nasdaq.com`) has its own stock screening tool, but it's limited to companies listed on Nasdaq-AMEX and the NYSE. It uses most of the variables mentioned in this chapter, and the database is updated daily. The screening tool is free.

Using Stock Screening Software

PC-based stock screens use their own stock screening software and databases. The advantage of these programs over Web-based stock screens is that they use hundreds of variables to screen stocks. PC-based screens are also a lot faster!

Equis International — MetaStock (`www.metastock.com`) is an example of a technical analysis software product that includes a stock search engine, real-time charting, and an analysis tool. The program is compatible with Microsoft Office, which means that you can download data to an Excel spreadsheet or embed charts in Word. You set the rules to identify trends and highlight important ratios. Click on a Canadian or U.S. stock price, and the program links your Internet browser to a free Web site that provides the current stock prices. When you purchase the software, you receive a CD-ROM with a historical database of more than 2,200 different U.S. securities, Canadian stocks, mutual funds, futures, and indexes. The price of MetaStock 8.0 is US$449, and can also be purchased under monthly or annual subscription rates.

Figure 8-2 shows the home page of MetaStock software. The makers of MetaStock use their software program to make stock recommendations. For example, they show the top five stocks that had the biggest gains over the past week, measured on a percentage basis. For example, a $20 stock that increases in price to $25 has a 25-percent gain.

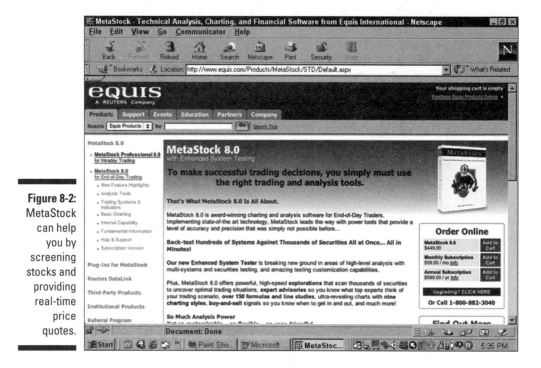

Figure 8-2: MetaStock can help you by screening stocks and providing real-time price quotes.

Using those Terrific Prebuilt Stock Screens

The Internet provides many prebuilt stock screens that use preselected criteria. Some of these screens may make your work easier because they already include the investment criteria that you feel are most important.

✔ **The Motley Fool** (www.fool.com) offers a weekly discussion of its stock screens of U.S. companies. Stocks are listed alphabetically as well as by descending percentages.

✔ **Quicken.com — Popular Stock Searches** (www.quicken.com/investments) uses a large database of stocks to help power its 41 variable screening tool. Figure 8-3 shows the Quicken.com prebuilt stock screen for Popular Searches (at the Search entry page, just click Popular Searches).

Book V

Making Your Investments Work for You

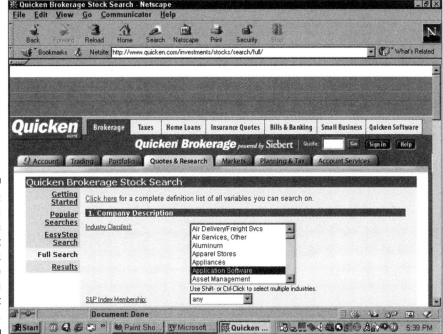

Figure 8-3:
Quicken provides prebuilt stock screens to help you select stocks.

Quicken's Stock Evaluator compares your search results and explains the benefits and limitations of using each variable as a stock-selection criterion. The prebuilt stock screens are divided into three categories:

- **Popular Search:** Uses preset criteria that match the most popular investing strategies.

- **EasyStep Search:** Walks you through six steps that use important variables one step at a time. Each step provides definitions about the variable and shows why the variable is important in your stock search.

- **Full Search:** Uses 33 variables on one page and many advanced search options.

✔ **Zacks** (www.zacks.com) is one of the very few Web sites on the Internet that has a screening tool for Canadian stocks. It allows you to screen stocks on the Toronto Stock Exchange, where most Canadian public companies are listed. Their top-rated stocks have almost always outperformed the S&P 500 Index over the last ten years.

Chapter 9

Valuing Bonds Online

- -

In This Chapter

▶ Making sense of why bond values change

▶ Determining the value of any type of bond

▶ Discovering the easiest way to determine your bond returns

▶ Buying and selling bonds

▶ Using a hot strategy for reducing bond risk

- -

*T*his chapter shows you how to analyze a variety of fixed-income investments, exploring the benefits of savings bonds, explaining new regulations, and discussing the limitations of this type of investment. For online investors who wish to know how to pay the right price for a bond, or when to bail out of one, this chapter shows how to value all types of bonds and determine bond yields (returns). Doing so may sound complicated, but with a little practice you'll be calculating your returns in no time. This chapter also provides a hot strategy that can protect you from interest-rate risk.

Treasury Securities and You

The federal government sells Canadian treasury securities to the public in order to pay off maturing debt and raise the cash needed to operate the Canadian government. The Bank of Canada auctions them every other week. There are three general types of treasury securities, in both Canada and the United States. A U.S. treasury bill, which is a popular form of treasury security, has a minimum purchase requirement of US $10,000. Canadian treasury bills require minimums from $5,000 (for terms of 6 to 12 months) up to $25,000 (for 30- to 60-day terms). A U.S.-denominated Canadian treasury bill (guaranteed by the Canadian government) has a minimum requirement of US $100,000. The chief difference between the U.S. and Canadian treasury securities, as seen in the following list, is the life of the obligation.

✔ **Treasury bills (T-bills)** mature in three months, six months, or one year. Treasury bills are purchased at a discount, so interest is actually paid. For example, you'll write a cheque for $10,000 and the government refunds the discount (which equals the interest rate determined at). In other words, your return is the difference between the purchase price and the maturity value.

✔ **Treasury notes (Canada notes)** are considered intermediate-term securities and mature in 2 to 10 years. Canada notes are denominated in U.S. dollars and provide interest payments to note holders.

✔ **Treasury bonds (Canada bonds)** are long-term securities that have maturities ranging from 10 years to 30 years. They are sold by auction to securities dealers and banks.

Government information is often written in a way that makes purchasing treasuries seem more difficult and complex than it really is. But don't get discouraged. For more information about understanding and purchasing Canadian and U.S. treasury securities, refer to the following online resources:

✔ **Bank of Canada** (www.bankofcanada.ca)**:** This comprehensive site provides auction dates and news about Canadian treasury securities. It also has information about bonds, currency, inflation, financial markets, rates, and statistics. The Bank of Canada publishes rationale behind interest rate and monetary policy, which is critical information that investors can react to and capitalize on.

✔ **BondCan** (www.bondcan.com)**:** This site provides detailed overviews about the bond market from a Canadian perspective. You can access a glossary of bond jargon, as well as a Bonds 101 feature that will help you better understand fixed income securities and markets. In addition to its periodic commentary and outlook features, it provides links to other Web resources dealing with Canadian and foreign bonds.

✔ **CIBC Economics Online** (http://research.cibcwm.com/res)**:** CIBC's online economics site, shown in Figure 9-1 (click on Economics and Strategy), lets you access research and overviews about Canadian government bonds, interest rates, and the provincial, national, and global economies. It publishes key economic indicators, forecasts, and statistics. You can access free and valuable industry analyses and economic commentary from the experts. The Week Ahead feature is especially valuable since it tells you what important economic news to expect in the coming month, and this information can help you better hone your investing strategy.

Book V

Making
Your
Investments
Work for
You

Figure 9-1:
CIBC's
market
overviews
help you
determine
where the
Canadian
and global
economies
are likely to
go.

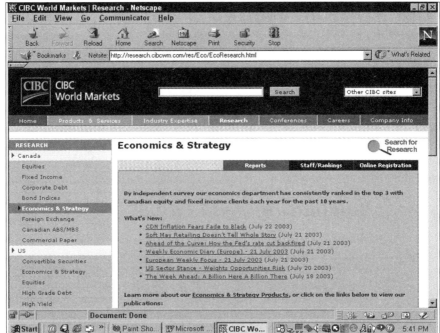

🖙 **GovPX** (www.govpx.com)**:** This site provides 24-hour real-time quotations
of U.S. government securities. The leading site also provides active lists
of treasury bonds, notes, and bills with each financial instrument's
coupon rate and maturity date. Lists include buyers' bid prices, sellers'
asking prices, changes from the prior trading day, and yields. It also has
useful links to related sites.

🖙 **Quote.com Street Pricing** (finance.lycos.com)**:** This site provides free
quotes for U.S. and Canadian treasury securities (treasury notes, bonds,
and bills) and government agency securities. Specific information
includes maturity dates, interest rates and spreads, yield, and price
changes. To get there, click on the Funds folder, and then again on the
Bonds feature.

🖙 **Zero coupon bonds and strips**
(www.ny.frb.org/pihome/fedpoint/fed41.html)**:** Here you can get
an explanation of these more sophisticated treasury securities from the
Federal Reserve Bank of New York. Once there, check out how the Fed
works, scan the statistics, and access some important economic
research and data. It's all free!

The Math of Bonds

The bond market is dominated by institutional investors (insurance companies, pension funds, mutual funds, and so on) that account for 80 to 85 percent of all trading. However, the impact of individual investors can also be felt through the purchases of mutual funds that specialize in bonds.

The following section shows the valuation process of bonds and the relationship of interest-rate changes to the value of bonds, providing several easy-to-use approaches that take the mystery out of determining your bond yield.

Calculating bond values

One such approach is calculating the value of a bond.

A bond issued by a corporation is called a *debt instrument.* The bond states how the debtholder (investor) is repaid. Generally, these terms are normal debt arrangements. The borrower makes interest payments and then pays the principal at a predetermined date. Several things make bonds complicated, such as provisions to convert the bonds to common stocks at a predetermined stock value or terms that allow the bond issuer to retire the bond before maturity.

The value of a bond is based on the investor's overall assessment of the bond's worth at a given point in time. The receipt of future interest payments, the repayment of principal, and the credit rating or riskiness of the bond usually drive these assessments. You aren't obligated to hold a bond until maturity, and bonds are traded freely in the marketplace.

Calculating the value of a bond involves determining the present value of the interest payments and the eventual recovery of the principal. *Present value* means discounting the future cash flow to calculate how much you're willing to pay today for those future receipts.

At times, calculating the yield on bonds can seem more complicated than it really is. For example, if you purchase a one-year treasury bill for $9,500 and redeem it in 12 months at full face value ($10,000), your gain is $500 (subject to Canadian income tax). To determine your yield, use the following formula (assuming your holding period is one year):

Face value – Price / Price = Annual return

$10,000 – $9,500 / $9,500 = 0.526 or 5.26%

See the section "The easy way to value your bond returns" later in this chapter, where you can calculate the yield for a bond that has a maturity term greater than one year. Yield is a key performance indicator for bonds.

Creating yield curves

Book V

**Making
Your
Investments
Work for
You**

A *yield curve* is a diagram that illustrates the relationship of bond yields to maturities on a specific day. Yield curves can be used to decide which type of bond is best for your financial objectives. Bond yields and maturities are posted daily at the *Globe and Mail*'s Web site (www.globeandmail.com) and at the *Wall Street Journal* Interactive Web site (www.wsj.com). Go to their respective business sections to find the link.

On a piece of graph paper on the horizontal axis, plot the maturities oftreasury securities from left to right starting with the shortest maturity of 30 days to the longest maturity of 30 years. Then on the vertical axis, plot the yield of each treasury security. Next, connect the dots to make a yield curve. See the curve descriptions in the following list to find out what your results indicate:

- ✔ If the short-term rates are higher than the long-term rates, then the yield curve becomes *inverted,* or has a downward swing to it, which tells you that this situation tends to be *bearish* for the market. In times like these, monetary policy is likely to be tight; the Bank of Canada or Federal Reserve will push up short-term rates.

- ✔ If the short-term rates are lower than the long-term rates, then the yield curve is *positive,* or has an upward swing to it, which usually indicates that investors are willing to tie up their money in long-term commitments to reap higher rewards.

- ✔ If the short-term rates and the long-term rates are the same (or nearly the same), then the yield curve appears to be flat.

The yield curve approach also works for other types of bonds, such as government agency, municipal, or corporate bonds. Remember that you need to include in the curve only bonds with the same level of risk, such as all AA-rated corporate bonds.

The easy way to value your bond returns

Bonds are often quoted at prices that differ from their stated (or *par*) values, a situation that can be troublesome for investors who want to determine the yield of the bond. Still, many ways exist to calculate the yield value of a bond. The *approximate yield to maturity (YTM)* method provides the easiest way to determine a bond's current yield.

To calculate the approximate yield to maturity, you need the following information:

- ✔ Annual interest payment (I)
- ✔ Principal payment (P)

✔ Price of the bond (B)

✔ Number of years to maturity (M)

Using these values, you calculate the approximate yield to maturity (YTM) by using the following formula:

$$YTM = \{I + [(P - B) \div M]\} \div [(0.6 \times B) + (0.4 \times P)]$$

For example, what is the yield to maturity on a 12-year, 7-percent annual coupon, $1,000 par value bond that sells at a discount for $942.21? Here are the calculations:

$$YTM = \{70 + [(\$1,000 - \$942.21) \div 12]\} \div [(0.6 \times \$942.21) + (0.4 \times \$1,000)]$$

$$YTM = [70 + (57.79 \div 12)] \div (565.33 + 400)$$

$$YTM = (70 + 4.82) \div 965.33$$

$$YTM = 74.82 \div 965.33$$

$$YTM = 0.0775$$

$$YTM = 7.75\%$$

If your required rate of return is 8 percent, you should *not* purchase the bond because the approximate yield to maturity (7.75 percent) doesn't meet your financial requirements. Conversely, if the bond has a return that is equal to or greater than 8 percent, the bond meets your objectives and is a "buy" candidate.

Note: If the value of the bond is discounted (that is, sells below its par value — in this case, below $1,000), the yield to maturity (YTM) is greater than the 7-percent coupon rate.

More Online Bond News, Rates of Return, and Advice

For more information about bond markets, commentary, rates, and news, see the following online resources:

✔ **E*Trade Canada** (www.etrade.ca) provides a daily and weekly Bond Market Commentary that includes financial data about bonds, and discusses political, economic, and other events that can affect the price of bonds. Check out a new feature called Bond Marketplace where you can search out and buy from an inventory of bonds and other fixed income securities. It's a great source for information about bonds.

Book V

Making
Your
Investments
Work for
You

✔ **SmartMoney.com** (www.smartmoney.com), shown in Figure 9-2, provides key interest rates, bond market updates, a bond calculator, and a glossary. Educational articles include bond strategies, short-term bond investing, bond allocation, and a bond primer. Yup, this site is the "James Bond" of bondsites.

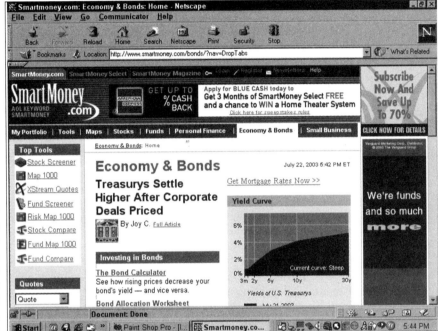

Figure 9-2:
SmartMoney
.com is a
good place
to learn
more about
bonds.

Where to Buy Bonds

Tens of thousands of Canadians own bonds of various stripes. In fact, about $1 billion of Canada Savings Bonds are sold each year. Three sources exist for purchasing CSBs and other bonds:

✔ **Banks, credit unions, and other financial institutions:** Many Canadian financial institutions are qualified as savings-bond agents. These agents accept the payments and the purchase orders for Canada Savings and other bonds, and forward the orders to the Bank of Canada (or, in the case of U.S. savings bonds, to a Federal Reserve bank).

✔ **Employer-sponsored payroll savings plans:** More than 5,000 Canadian employers participate in employer-sponsored payroll savings plans, and some chartered banks offer Canada Savings Bonds through installment plans.

- ✔ **Federal Reserve banks:** If you want to buy U.S. savings bonds, you can write to a regional Federal Reserve bank and ask for an application. The "Fed" allows you (even though you are a Canadian) to purchase savings bonds by mail. A U.S. Savings Bond page can be found at the Web site for the Federal Reserve Bank of New York (www.ny.frb.org/pihome). This site provides the addresses of the 12 regional Federal Reserve banks. (Of course, you can also buy U.S. savings bonds through most Canadian financial institutions.) You can also purchase treasury securities through the Fed's Internet purchase program, *Buy Direct!,* or by calling 1-800-943-6864. Tender forms and payments may also be submitted electronically through your financial institution or government securities broker or dealer.

How to buy 'em

You can get more information about buying and selling Canadian treasury bills and Canada Savings Bonds by going to the Bank of Canada's Web site (www.bankofcanada.ca). You can even see if there is an unclaimed bank account or unredeemed bond in your name!

Canadians who invest in U.S. treasuries and savings bonds can obtain all the order forms, instructions, auction dates, auction results, and other related information at the Bureau of the Public Debt Web site (www.publicdebt.treas.gov). You can download and print forms, send e-mail requests for forms, or ask that forms be mailed to you. The ability to purchase U.S. treasury securities without a broker is a great money-saving feature for investors. Check out the special rules for Canadians who wish to buy U.S. securities.

Rolling over, cashing in, or selling your treasury securities

Canadian and U.S. treasury bills mature at various intervals of time. When your treasury bill matures, you have two choices. First, you can roll over your investment and reinvest in the face value of another T-bill (with the same or a different maturity). Second, you can cash in and have the proceeds deposited to your holding account. For example, say that your $15,000 T-bill with a maturity term of 13 weeks matures. You can elect to reinvest in another $15,000 T-bill for 13, 26, or 52 weeks. If you choose not to reinvest your $15,000 at maturity, your holding account is credited with $15,000, or a cheque for $15,000 is sent to your home.

Book V

Making
Your
Investments
Work for
You

A third T-bill disposition option exists. You can sell your treasury securities before they mature, through a broker. But this will cost you extra money in commissions.

If you need to sell your U.S. treasury security, the U.S. federal government will help you. You can sell directly through Treasury Direct — without a broker. The government gets quotes from different dealers and offers you the best price. The fee starts at US$25 for each security sold, but many securities are also offered for free. You can even have the proceeds from the sale of the treasury security deposited directly into your chequing account, less the transaction fee. While you're at their Web site (www.publicdebt.treas.gov/sec/secbsr.htm), also check out their bond calculator, commentary, and primers on treasury securities.

Book VI
Somewhere over the Rainbow: Retirement Planning

The 5th Wave   By Rich Tennant

"That reminds me – I have to figure out how to save for retirement *and* send these two to college."

In this book . . .

You can never be sure of anything — which makes planning for your retirement even more vital than ever. Exerting as much control as possible over your financial future and being prepared, both financially and emotionally, to deal with the unforeseen, are two ways to deal with inevitable change. For the vast majority of Canadians — those of us who are neither permanently nor outrageously wealthy — an RRSP is perhaps the best way of preparing financially for the future.

This Book is for people who want down-to-earth guidance on accumulating enough money via an RRSP to live reasonably well through their retirement years. It's about building your RRSP, the largest, most liquidable asset you and most other Canadians will ever own. And it's about helping you avoid mistakes by alerting you to their presence before you encounter them.

Here are the contents of Book VI at a glance:

Chapter 1

Getting Started with Your RRSP

. . . .

In This Chapter

▶ Understanding the basic principles and benefits of RRSPs

▶ Countering RRSP procrastination

▶ Calculating your maximum contribution

▶ Maximizing foreign content

▶ Making contributions regularly

▶ Borrowing to save

▶ Claiming your tax benefit

. . . .

Canadians may grumble about many government decisions, but Ottawa deserves a round of applause for creating the *Registered Retirement Savings Plan (RRSP)* way back in 1957.

By the way, an RRSP is not an insurance plan. It is not a savings bond. It is not a pension plan. And it is not a ticket that you buy today and present to the government when you are 65 years old, in return for a cheque and a pat on the head for being a good citizen.

An RRSP is an *investment*. Like all investments, it demands your attention from time to time. Also, an RRSP is not guaranteed to deliver X amount of money if you contribute Y dollars to it every year for Z years. Its growth will vary over the years, and the amount you have when you retire will be based on the amount of money you put into it, the number of years you keep adding to it, the attention you pay to managing it, the quality of advice you receive in caring for it, and, like it or not, a smattering of good luck.

Basic Principles of RRSP Investing

One of the joys of managing your RRSP is the satisfaction you gain from taking control of your financial future. This needn't be as complicated as you may expect.

It begins with three basic principles of investing. You can apply variations to these according to your own interest and comfort level, but understanding and applying these three concepts is the secret of investing success:

- **Diversification:** This is just another way of saying "Don't put all your eggs in one basket." If you invest all of your RRSP contributions, for example, in five-year GICs paying 6 percent annually, you might feel pretty smug . . . until you discover at the end of the five years that the stock market rose an average 12 percent annually over the same period. And if you sank every RRSP penny into shares of a South Korean manufacturing company, the Asian financial crisis of 1998–99 would have had you lying awake at night in a cold sweat, watching your hard-earned dollars sink in value.

  The solution is to *diversify* your RRSP among various investment alternatives including GICs, bonds, equity-based investments (meaning you own shares in companies traded on the stock market), and other alternatives. Diversification adds security to your RRSP and lets you sleep better at night. You need a minimum amount in your RRSP to take advantage of diversification — $10,000 say — and a formula based on your own comfort level. Here's the guideline to help you craft your own diversification formula: The percentage of "guaranteed" investments — GICs, T-bills, bonds, and so on — held in your RRSP should not exceed your age until you are within sight of retirement. It's just a guide, of course, but a good one to remember.

- **Liquidity:** Having a $1,000 diamond ring on your finger is not the same as having a certified cheque for $1,000 in your pocket. While their value may be identical, the cheque is much more *liquid* than the diamond ring, which means it can be converted into cash more easily. Keeping a portion of your RRSP in liquid investments makes it easy to withdraw money from your RRSP to meet an emergency or for certain qualified reasons. Liquidity grows more important as you near retirement, but it also enables you to change the recipe of your RRSP investment, which means you can diversify your investments more easily.

  Savings accounts, short-term GICs, and certain kinds of mutual funds provide high liquidity. You pay for this convenience with generally low returns from your investment.

- **Growth versus income:** Think of two kinds of trees — an oak tree and an apple tree. If you plant the oak tree and your sister plants the apple tree, you'll each benefit in different ways over the years. You can watch the oak tree grow steadily taller until it becomes a strong, sturdy source of shade and, eventually, wood that you can use to heat your home or build furniture. Meanwhile, your sister will be harvesting apples each year.

  Some investments are like that — one provides long-term growth, and the other rewards you on a regular basis over the years. Generally, the younger you are, the more focused you can be on growth. Combining both, by the way, is one more kind of diversification.

Excuses, Excuses

In spite of the benefits of an RRSP, many people choose to ignore them. It's always easy to find reasons for justifying this attitude. How many of the following excuses have you heard . . . or used?

✔ I'm too young.

✔ I just got married.

✔ I just got a mortgage.

✔ My house is my retirement plan.

✔ My spouse/partner has an RRSP.

✔ We're starting a family.

✔ I can't afford it.

✔ RRSPs are too confusing.

Here are some powerful counterarguments to these excuses:

"I'm too young." No, you're not. If you're old enough to read this book and have any source of income, you're old enough to make an RRSP contribution. Sure, retirement is many years away. But look at your RRSP contributions as a form of savings. Over the years, you'll receive great satisfaction in having those funds tucked away where the Canada Customs and Revenue Agency (CCRA) can't get at them, and where they'll eventually grow by leaps and bounds.

"I just got married." Now that the honeymoon is over, it's time for you to face reality. The CCRA, you may have noticed, didn't send you a wedding gift and doesn't offer special breaks to married couples. For example, unlike U.S. citizens, Canadians cannot file a joint tax return, dividing their income and lowering their marginal tax rate. But you can both benefit from an RRSP, beginning right now. If one of you is earning substantially more than the other, consider a spousal RRSP. (See Chapter 2 for details.)

"I just got a mortgage." That's a long-term financial commitment. Over the years, your mortgage will slowly decrease with each payment. If you are able to set aside even a small amount — as little as $50 each month — you can begin building an RRSP, which will move in the opposite direction as your mortgage, growing in value as the mortgage shrinks. Imagine the day when your mortgage is finally paid off and your RRSP is in the six-figure range, ready to provide you with a comfortable income. Imagine the good feeling you'll have. (And don't forget those tax advantages.)

Book VI

Somewhere over the Rainbow: Retirement Planning

"My house is my retirement plan." A house isn't a retirement plan — it's shelter and warmth, with a little pride thrown in. Real estate booms of the past (along with a few aggressive real estate agents) convinced many Canadians that their home wasn't just their castle but the foundation of their investment portfolio. This is nonsense, as anyone who got caught in a bursting local real estate bubble can attest to. If you suddenly need the cash that's locked into your house, being caught in a downward real estate cycle can cost you a lot of money and heartache. This is by no means a warning against owning your own home. In fact, owning good properties is a good thing. But as a source of retirement income, it doesn't compare with a liquid and flexible RRSP. You buy your home with after-tax dollars (what's left of a loonie when federal and provincial income tax has been deducted); you invest in an RRSP with before-tax dollars (the money you've earned and expect to keep).

"My spouse/partner has an RRSP." All right, let's get brutal about this. First, it's lovely to assume that you and your partner will spend the rest of your lives together, but that's still just an assumption. Canadian family law provides for an even distribution of assets, including an RRSP. This means that, in the event of a separation, each of you owns half the RRSP benefit you need. Next, if both of you have earned income, you are jointly enjoying only half the tax benefit available to you. Everyone with earned income should have an RRSP. There's plenty of upside and virtually no downside.

"We're starting a family." Somewhere amid expenses for diapers, toys, clothing, day care and other associated costs, try to find a few dollars for an RRSP. Parents do themselves and their children a favour by acquiring a savings habit and sharing it with their kids. When your offspring are old enough, you can explain how the money is contributed and invested, and together you can watch how it grows over the years. This will make it easier for your children to pick up the habit for themselves, including opening their own RRSP. Besides, think how much peace of mind they'll enjoy knowing Mom and Dad will face retirement with adequate assets . . . meaning you won't be a burden to them in the future.

"I can't afford it." This is one we can all relate to. Each of us has limits on the amount of money left over after taxes, rent or mortgage payments, food, transportation, and so on. Here are three ways to deal with this particular excuse:

- It doesn't take much to get started — as little as $50 each month, for example, will enable you to invest in mutual funds. That's equivalent to the cost of a coffee and doughnut each working day. Invest the same amount in a mutual fund, and you'll improve your financial outlook and (probably) reduce your waistline.

- Arrange an automatic RRSP contribution through your employer (called a *source deduction*), bank, trust company, or credit union and reduce the impact on your budget. If you prefer to have your employer handle the paperwork, call your local CCRA office and ask for a source-deduction form. You and your employer complete the form and your employer forwards it to the CCRA.

- ✔ If taxes are the biggest single bite out of your income each month, isn't that the best place to begin saving money? An RRSP enables you to reduce your taxes while saving money. What's more, if you qualify for a tax refund, you can use it for part of next year's contribution.

"RRSPs are too confusing." Not anymore. That's why you're reading this book, remember?

Determine Your Maximum Contribution

Book VI

Somewhere over the Rainbow: Retirement Planning

The federal government places no limits on the amount of money you can accumulate tax-free inside your RRSP, but it limits the amount you can contribute into it each year. This amount is based on your earned income for the year in which the RRSP contribution is credited. Because many people don't know how much income they have earned until the year is over, RRSP rules permit contributions made up to the end of February to be claimed against the previous year's income. This fits neatly between the end of the calendar year and April 30, the deadline for filing your income tax return. Most Canadians don't get around to making their RRSP contributions until around Groundhog Day, which is why everyone living between Newfoundland and Nanaimo cannot escape being bombarded with RRSP information from banks, trust companies, mutual funds, and probably Cousin Fred between Christmas and March 1.

Of course, you needn't wait until the end of February to make your RRSP contribution. You can actually put money in your RRSP as early as January 1 of the year in which you claim an RRSP deduction from your income. That gives you 14 months to act — from January 1 of one year all the way to February 28 the following year. By acting sooner than the deadline, you avoid the traditional rush and panic. And by investing the funds 14 months earlier, you get an extra year's growth. Over 25 years or so, the benefits of this extra year can mean literally tens of thousands of dollars more in your RRSP.

The current calculation for maximum RRSP contributions is 18 percent of earned income to a maximum of $13,500. This is expected to remain in effect through the 2003 taxation year. Then it is scheduled to climb to $14,500 for 2004 and $15,500 for 2005. After the 2005 tax year, the maximum contribution will be indexed to inflation.

If you are a member of a company pension plan or deferred profit-sharing plan (DPSP), your maximum RRSP contribution is reduced, because it would represent a major unfair advantage to you over those Canadians who are unable to participate in such plans. This includes people such as wretched ink-stained freelance writers, for example, which means this is one Canada Customs and Revenue Agency ruling with which those of us who took part in the creation of this book have absolutely no problem. . . .

Canada Customs and Revenue Agency limits

Each spring and summer, Canada Customs and Revenue Agency sends all taxpayers a *Notice of Assessment,* which establishes the maximum contribution you are allowed for the current year. So, an assessment you received in June 2003 would show the maximum you are able to contribute and deduct from your 2003 income for tax purposes. Remember, you will have until the end of February 2004 to make the contribution and until the end of April 2004 to file your tax return.

The CCRA's Notice of Assessment includes their evaluation of any retirement benefits you earned from being a member of a company pension plan or DPSP. This evaluation, and its impact on your RRSP contribution limit, is called your *pension adjustment,* or *PA factor.* Subtracting the PA factor from 18 percent of your taxable income produces the maximum RRSP contribution permitted to you.

The PA factor changes according to the type of pension plan or DPSP your employer provides:

- A *defined benefit plan* pays you a retirement income based on your years of service with the company and your income level. Your PA factor with a defined benefit plan is calculated according to the future value of the plan, using your previous year of employment.

- A *defined contribution* or *money purchase plan* has no fixed benefit when you retire. You and your employer both contribute to the plan each year, and the amount of income paid to you by the plan when you retire is dependent on the total value of the plan at that time. If you belong to this type of plan, your maximum RRSP contribution will be 18 percent of your earned income less the amount contributed to the plan by both you and your employer.

- A *deferred profit-sharing plan* is built up from money placed in the plan by your employer, based on the company's profits for that year. Your PA factor under this plan will equal the total DPSP contribution (up to a maximum limit) made on your behalf. This will be subtracted from 18 percent of your earned income for that year.

Table 1-1 illustrates examples of income levels and contribution limits for four individuals with varying incomes.

Andy had $30,000 earned income in 2003 and belongs to no pension plan.

Allison had $40,000 earned income in 2003 and belongs to a money purchase pension plan. Between them, she and her employer contributed $2,500 to her plan in the same year.

Arthur had $75,000 earned income in 2003 and belongs to a DPSP. His company contributed $5,000 to his DPSP in 2001.

Amanda had $90,000 earned income in 2003 and belongs to no pension plan.

Table 1-1	Maximum RRSP Contributions, 2003		
Name	*Income*	*PA Factor*	*Maximum*
Andy	$30,000	N/A	$5,400
Allison	$40,000	$2,500	$4,700
Arthur	$75,000	$5,000	$8,500
Amanda	$90,000	N/A	$13,500

Calculating Andy's maximum RRSP contribution is easy — 18 percent of $30,000.

Allison's maximum contribution was reached by taking 18 percent of her earned income — $7,200 — and subtracting the total contributions to her money purchase pension plan from that amount, leaving $4,700.

Arthur's RRSP contribution was reached by subtracting the $5,000 earned by his DPSP from 18 percent of his earned income (18 percent of $75,000 = $13,500), for an $8,500 maximum.

Amanda did very well — but 18 percent of her $90,000 earned income exceeds the $13,500 maximum that applies to everyone. Even if Amanda made a million dollars last year, she would be restricted to $13,500.

Since the maximum RRSP contribution is scheduled to climb to $14,500 for 2004 and $15,500 for 2005, and assuming the same income and PA factor figures apply, Amanda will be able to contribute up to the higher maximums in those respective years. For Andy, Allison, and Arthur, there will be no change, again assuming the same figures apply.

A little room for going over the limit

Believe it or not, the folks at Canada Customs and Revenue Agency agree that we live in an imperfect world. Mistakes can be made. Rules can be changed. Murphy's Law can still apply. And any one of us, or even the CCRA itself, can miscalculate now and then and — horrors! — contribute more money to an RRSP than is allowed under the rules.

That's why Canadians are permitted to contribute up to $2,000 more than allowed in any taxation year. If this occurs, you simply deduct the over-contribution from the amount permitted in the following taxation year.

For example: If your RRSP contribution limit for one year, based on 18 percent of your earned income less any PA factor, is $5,000, you are allowed to contribute up to $7,000 without penalty. If you do so, and your RRSP limit remains at $5,000 for the following year, the $2,000 over-contribution is subtracted from that year's $5,000 contribution limit, reducing it to $3,000. If you think you can deduct the entire $7,000 from your earned income, generating a fatter tax refund, forget it. You cannot deduct more than your limit — in this case, $5,000. (However, if the extra $2,000 that you overcontributed is invested early and wisely within your RRSP, you enjoy the benefit of positive tax-free returns.) You can apply the over-contribution to the following year, however. So, for tax purposes, your $3,000 allowable contribution in 2002 becomes a $5,000 deduction from earned income in that year, because you have carried the over-contribution forward.

What happens if you over-contribute more than the $2,000 limit? Ottawa gets nasty, that's what. You must withdraw the excess funds from your RRSP before you can claim any further contributions to it. And to make its point, the CCRA slaps a penalty of 1 percent per month on over-contributions made beyond the $2,000, until you get it out of your plan.

By the way: No one under 19 years of age is permitted to over-contribute to their RRSP. One more source of adolescent angst. . . .

If you are currently employed and plan to retire in the next few years, you may be eligible to place a *retiring allowance* in your RRSP. A retiring allowance is any money awarded to you by your employer when you leave work permanently for any reason. It includes payments made to you in recognition of your years of service, as well as any unused sick-leave pay; it does not include unused vacation benefits. The formula is a little complex because Ottawa has tinkered with the rules over the years. It works like this:

For each year of service between 1989 and 1995, you are allowed to contribute up to $2,000 to your RRSP beyond your normal contribution limits within 60 days of the end of the year in which you received the retiring allowance (basically, the same time frame used for standard RRSP contributions).

For each year of employment prior to 1989 in which your employer did not make contributions to a pension plan on your behalf, or did not make deposits in a deferred profit-sharing plan, you are permitted an additional $1,500 contribution.

Here is why it will pay to see your accountant before transferring a substantial amount of money from a retiring allowance to your RRSP: The amount of the retiring allowance transferred to your RRSP does not affect the calculation of your RRSP contributions for that year. But any portion of the allowance transferred to an RRSP and claimed as a deduction must be added back to your taxable income for the purpose of calculating the *alternative minimum tax (AMT)*, which has a basic deduction of $40,000. If AMT is payable, it can be recovered up to seven years in the future to the extent, in any year, that your income tax liability is greater than the AMT liability. So you could face some unexpected taxes unless you obtain qualified advice. Accountants know all about this stuff. Thank goodness.

Years of employment after 1995 do not qualify you for any retirement allowance contributions, and any part of a calendar year is counted as a full year. An example: Sam began working for a small-town daily newspaper in October 1963 and retired in March 1991. The newspaper maintained no formal pension plan but awarded lump-sum payments and credited sick leave not taken during employment. Sam's 28 years of employment thus qualified him to contribute 28 (total years of employment) × $2,000 + 26 (years of employment without a pension plan prior to 1989) × $1,500 = $95,000. This amount, shown on Sam's last T4 slip, will be offset by a standard RRSP contribution receipt.

Book VI

Somewhere over the Rainbow: Retirement Planning

A second chance to contribute

The most common problem people encounter, especially in the early years of their career, is not contributing too much to their RRSP but rather contributing too little. Fortunately, the Canada Customs and Revenue Agency provides a break by permitting you to catch up with bigger contributions later. If your contribution limit for this year is $7,500 and you can only afford to contribute $5,000, the $2,500 difference isn't lost; it's *carried forward* indefinitely in something called *unused deduction room.* Next year, or at any year in the future, you can add the amount in your unused deduction room — sounds like a storage area in a mathematics warehouse, doesn't it? — to your deduction limit and increase your contribution. So if next year's contribution limit remains at $5,000, you are eligible to carry forward the $2,500 from the previous year, contribute $7,500, and deduct the full amount from your taxable income.

Wherever possible, however, it's best to maximize and start enjoying the benefits of tax-free compound interest growth from the earliest possible date.

Is it possible to justify contributing less than the maximum RRSP contribution, even when you can afford it? Perhaps. For example, you could use part of the money set aside for your RRSP to pay down a high-interest credit card balance instead. Some credit cards carry an 18 percent interest rate, and it's difficult to obtain that kind of growth from investments these days. You can always catch up in the future, using your unused deduction room.

But if you do, you are losing both the tax-deduction benefits of an RRSP and delaying the tax-free compound-interest growth. Here's an even bigger concern: Governments, you may have noticed, have a habit of changing rules that benefit taxpayers. Nowhere is it written that the carry-forward option for RRSPs will remain part of the RRSP program forever. If the federal government chooses to eliminate this rule sometime in the future, those delayed contributions will be gone and you will have no chance to catch up. Ever.

So, as Janis Joplin used to advise (in a slightly different context): Get it while you can!

The Foreign-Content Factor

In the past, one of the most vexing RRSP rules was the one that restricted the portion of your RRSP that you are permitted to invest outside Canada, in foreign bonds or in shares of foreign companies. Until 2000, the limit of foreign content in an RRSP was 20 percent, ridiculously low. This has now been raised to a more realistic 30 percent of the *book value* — the original cost of your investment — in foreign stocks, bonds, and mutual funds.

Some people believe this is still too low, and they have a point. After all, the best way to maximize long-term growth — consider "long-term" to mean five years or more — is through investments in equities or shares in companies. History has proven that equity investments, over the long haul, provide the biggest returns. True, the stock market has its ups and downs, as you no doubt are aware. But the general trend is always up, and the longer you hold quality investments in equities, the higher their value can be expected to rise.

The problem faced by RRSP owners is that Canada represents barely 3 percent of the world's total value of traded stocks. What's more, stock markets in many countries have risen faster and higher than our own in the past decade. So every dollar invested outside Canada has a better chance of being worth much more, and much sooner, than a dollar invested in Canadian stock markets.

Another problem for RRSP investors is the nature of the Canadian economy. While Canada is an industrialized nation, a good deal of our industry is linked directly to resources — mining, lumber, petroleum, and similar activities. Resources are the raw material of other industries. When the economy begins to move, resources are in demand and their prices rise. As the economy flattens out, the demand for resources drops along with prices (and profits for the resource-based companies). All of this puts resource investments on a perpetual roller-coaster ride, making investment a more risky and stomach-churning exercise in Canada than elsewhere.

Some Canadians believe Ottawa should remove all limits from foreign investment in RRSPs. This may be good in theory, but not necessarily good in practice, especially as you approach retirement age. Here's why:

Foreign investment exposes you to both more opportunities and additional risk. The additional risk, in this case, is foreign exchange rates. Any change in the value of the Canadian dollar affects the value of your foreign investment, which rides the opposite end of an unpredictable teeter-totter. When the value of the loonie drops against the currency of another country, all your investments in that country are suddenly worth more in Canadian dollars. If the loonie rises, as it did sharply in mid-2003, the value of your investment drops in proportion.

Book VI

Somewhere over the Rainbow: Retirement Planning

Currency changes are neither good nor bad news. They're simply unpredictable. If you invested every penny of your RRSP in U.S. assets, for example, and the loonie rises 5 percent against the Yankee greenback, your original investment drops by an equal amount.

Monthly Contributions versus Lump-Sum Payments

The first wise decision you can make in providing yourself with future financial security is to open an RRSP, if you haven't already. The second wise decision you can make is to arrange regular contributions each month throughout the year instead of waiting to make a lump-sum contribution at the last minute — like, ten minutes to midnight on February 28.

What makes this such a wise decision?

First, monthly contributions become almost painless. It's much easier to adjust your budget to 12 relatively small amounts over a full year than absorb a major *whack!* each February.

Next, regular contributions give you an opportunity to ponder where and how to invest your RRSP contributions. Last-minute decisions tend to be second-rate decisions, and if you don't make up your mind where to invest your money until the late-February last-minute rush each year, the growth of your RRSP is sure to suffer.

Finally, monthly contributions enable you to benefit from *dollar-cost averaging*, a neat trick where you make your investment over a series of year-round equal payments. Because no one is wise enough to recognize the bottom price of any mutual fund or common share (that is, the best time to leap into a growing market), nor are they wise enough to know when the top price has been reached (that is, the best time to get out while the gettin' is good), dollar-cost averaging is the next best thing. When unit prices are lower you purchase more shares, and when the prices are higher you acquire fewer shares. And you are able to accomplish this trick because you're investing a regular series of equal payments that purchases shares when the market is high or low.

If you must make a last-minute lump-sum contribution, by all means do so. But try to adapt to regular monthly contributions if possible.

Will two people, contributing exactly the same amount of money to their RRSP and investing it exactly the same way, have identical RRSP values? Not necessarily.

If you make a lump-sum payment at the end of the year in December, and your twin sister contributes the same amount 12 months earlier in January, you both qualify for the deduction in the same year. But your sister's 12-month head start means her RRSP will grow faster as time goes by. How much faster?

Assuming that you each contribute $1,000 annually and earn interest at 10 percent, at the end of five years your RRSP is worth $6,105 and your sister's will have a balance of $6,715. After ten years, your sister has $17,531 in her RRSP while you have just $15,937. And if you both maintain the same contribution level and earn the same annual interest, after 30 years your sister's RRSP will have a value of $180,943 compared with your $164,494. The difference? The 12-month head start she took each year. And that $15,000 advantage could generate enough retirement income for your sister to enjoy a few weeks in Florida each winter, leaving you back in Canada to shovel snow and read her gloating postcards.

Deductions at source

If your employer automatically deducts income tax from each paycheque, your deductions are made *at source*. This is also an easy and more convenient way to make regular contributions to your RRSP throughout the year. While you won't enjoy the delicious thrill of receiving a fat tax refund each spring, unless you make a lump-sum supplementary contribution (assuming you have room in your RRSP limits) your net pay will be increased. That's because your employer will be authorized to lower your income tax deductions to reflect your RRSP contributions.

It is up to you, not your employer or Canada Customs and Revenue Agency, to take the initiative to have your employer reduce your income tax with each paycheque, reflecting your monthly RRSP contributions. Write to the source deductions division of your district taxation office (your employer can provide the address) and ask the CCRA to authorize the lower tax level. Include details such as the full address of your employer and a copy of a receipt confirming your RRSP contributions issued by the bank, trust company, credit union, mutual fund, or other holder of your RRSP assets. Be sure to mention other sources of earned income if you have any.

When the CCRA is satisfied that your request qualifies, they will authorize your employer to reduce the income tax withheld from your paycheque each month, boosting your take-home pay.

If you belong to a group RRSP administered by your employer, the income tax payments withdrawn from your salary already reflect your RRSP contributions, so there is no need to alert the CCRA.

Book VI

Somewhere over the Rainbow: Retirement Planning

Borrowing to save

The idea of borrowing money in order to save it doesn't make sense unless you save it in an RRSP. If borrowing is the only way to max out your RRSP contribution for the year, it becomes a very attractive move, *provided you pay back the loan in a year's time.* You are no longer allowed to deduct the interest on money you borrow to make an RRSP contribution. (Until 1981, you were. See what is meant about the Feds changing the rules now and then?) But borrowing the money to make your RRSP contribution is a much wiser move than making no RRSP contribution at all. And if you have put off making a contribution until the RRSP deadline, it makes even more sense.

Suppose it's mid-February and you want to contribute $5,000 to your RRSP before the February 28 deadline arrives. If you are in a 40 percent marginal tax bracket, the $5,000 deduction will earn you a $2,000 tax refund when you file your return in April. Hey, don't pass it up! So what do you do? You visit a local bank, trust company, or credit union, and tell them you want to borrow $5,000, which you will invest in an RRSP with their organization. You want to spread payments over 12 months, you expect to receive a favourable interest rate, and you would be especially pleased if they would delay the due date of the first payment by three months. If you are a local resident, steadily employed, and have a credit rating at least as good as your dog's, the financial institution will agree to these terms. If they don't, walk out the door and visit another bank/trust company/credit union where you ask for the same terms. You'll get them.

When the paperwork for the $5,000 is finished, assign it to an RRSP with the same people who loaned you the money. They will issue a receipt entitling you to deduct the entire $5,000 from your tax return. (You may have to wait two weeks or more for the receipt to arrive.) Based on your 40 percent marginal tax rate, this will generate a $2,000 refund from Canada Customs and Revenue Agency — which, if your timing is good, arrives in the mail around the same time your first loan payment is due. Apply the entire amount to the loan balance, and you now have $5,000 in your RRSP and owe just $3,000 to the bank.

There's more. You'll be paying interest on the balance, and the annual interest percentage will likely be more than your RRSP earns over the year. But *you are paying interest on a declining balance for your loan;* each monthly payment reduces both the amount you owe and the interest you pay. Meanwhile, *the $5,000 in your RRSP is earning interest on a rising value.* After six months, for example, the balance of your loan could be just $1,500 (assuming that you applied your tax refund to the original amount) and the value of your RRSP could be $5,125. In another six months your loan will have vanished. But the $5,125 in your RRSP is like that pink bunny with the drum. It keeps growing and growing and growing. . . .

RESPs

A recent Canada Customs and Revenue Agency wrinkle provides another source of RRSP contributions to some people under certain circumstances. It concerns *Registered Education Savings Plans (RESPs),* created to help parents and grandparents save for a child's education. RESPs have been around for a few years, but a change in the rules now benefits RRSP holders.

Previously, if funds in an RESP were not used by the designated child for post-secondary educational purposes, the contributor to the plan could recover only the money invested in it; all other funds went to the government. As of 1999, if the RESP beneficiary chooses not to obtain a post-secondary education, contributors can roll the entire value of the plan, up to a maximum of $50,000, into their RRSP or a spouse's RRSP, provided the plan is at least ten years old and sufficient contribution room exists in the designated RRSP.

Catching up big-time

Some banks offer RRSP loans that enable you to catch up on the unused contribution room you may have created over the years. You can actually get your hands on as much as $50,000 for this purpose, although $15,000 to $20,000 is more realistic. What's more, you can take up to 15 years to repay the loan. Is this a good idea?

It depends. If you are in a 40 percent tax bracket, a $15,000 catch-up contribution — making up for several years when you failed to make the maximum contribution permitted each year — will produce a $6,000 tax refund. If you apply this to the loan and reduce the balance to $9,000, if the bank or trust company agrees to charge interest at *prime rate* (say around 7 percent), and if you stretch the payments over 15 years, your monthly payments are a tolerable $173. Meanwhile, your RRSP balance is immediately $15,000 fatter and grows free of tax.

Sounds good. But remember that you'll be paying back $1,876 in loan interest over the years, which is $1,876 unavailable for future RRSP contributions. Remember too that a bank's prime rate can fluctuate. Any significant rise in interest rates will boot your monthly payments higher, which could put a strain on your cash flow.

The bottom line? Weigh your options, measure your confidence level about future earnings, and be sure to shop around. RRSP loans to people with good credit ratings are considered very low risk, so you have a right to demand the lowest available interest rate.

Book VI

Somewhere over the Rainbow: Retirement Planning

Claiming Your Deduction

Making an RRSP deduction makes you feel good twice. First you feel good soon, when you receive your tax refund cheque from Canada Customs and Revenue Agency. Then you feel good later, when your RRSP contributions have grown over the years into a healthy nest egg.

But believe it or not, there is a way to feel even better about your refund. Here's how it works:

The CCRA does not insist that you submit your RRSP contribution receipt, qualifying you for lower taxes, in the same tax year in which you made it. You can, if you wish, tuck the receipt into your sock drawer and leave it there for a few years. Why in the name of the Minister of Finance would you want to do this? Because it could earn you a bigger deduction later.

Suppose your earned income was $30,000 this year, and you made a $2,000 contribution to your RRSP. That income level puts you in the 28-percent tax bracket, so the $2,000 contribution produces a $520 tax refund ($2,000 × 28 percent). But you're confident that your income will rise to $40,000 over the next year or two, placing you in the 40 percent tax bracket. Now the $2,000 contribution produces an $800 tax refund ($2,000 × 40 percent), or $280 more. That's not a bad deal.

People who take time from work to enjoy a sabbatical or to have children can also benefit from delaying their deduction. While taking time off and earning little if any income, there is limited benefit in filing a deduction. But back at work again, when the income level jumps, the RRSP receipt pays off with a bigger deduction.

Both of these situations — a potentially much larger annual income in a year or two, and a return to full employment — can justify a delay in claiming your RRSP deduction.

Is there a downside? There is always a downside in life. Instead of waiting, you could claim your deduction now and use an immediate tax refund to pay down high-interest credit card balances — always a smart move — or invest the money outside your RRSP. There is also the danger of falling prey to the dreaded "Close the loophole!" cry from Ottawa, which means they yank back something they awarded you in the past before you have had a chance to enjoy it — in this case, the opportunity to claim delayed deductions.

Chapter 2

What to Expect from Your RRSP

. . . .

In This Chapter

▶ Calculating growth over the years

▶ Dealing with inflation

▶ Determining how much you should accumulate

▶ Finding out what's attractive about spousal RRSPs

▶ Using your RRSP as collateral

▶ Knowing what happens to your RRSP if you leave the country

. . . .

Contributing as much as you can afford to your RRSP year after year is one heck of a good idea, as you have probably figured out if you have read this far. But growing your RRSP isn't like raising mushrooms in your basement; you can't just toss a shovel or two of goodies at it from time to time and assume it'll take care of itself.

Making regular contributions is only the first part of your plan. The second part is finding ways to maximize the growth of your investment, year after year. This is the part that makes many Canadians nervous or confused, and perhaps a bit of both. A successful RRSP strategy requires work, and that turns off a lot of people. Unless you already have some investment experience, the very mention of terms such as *diversification, debt instruments, asset allocation,* and *equities* can make your eyes glaze over.

The responsibility of making decisions about their RRSP frightens some people. Mention mutual funds or stock markets to many Canadians, and they picture a giant neon sign flashing "Risk! Risk! Risk!" in red letters. Too bad they can't see the other side of that sign. It glows in a rich, gold colour and spells out "Reward! Reward! Reward!"

Don't be intimidated by the fear of risk. You can't avoid it entirely. But you can manage it to your benefit. How?

- ✔ **By learning some basic rules:** The investment options you face are not all that complex, and the principles are easy to grasp by anyone who can read a bank statement.

- ✔ **By understanding the principles of basic investing:** Using this knowledge to make wise decisions can make an astonishing difference to the value of your RRSP.

- ✔ **By realizing that taking charge of your investments can be both satisfying and fun:** You can take comfort in the rewards of making good decisions, and gain experience when your decisions don't pay off quite as well as you hoped.

Actively managing your RRSP by applying basic investment principles, supported by qualified professional assistance, will produce results far richer in the long term than an RRSP that consists entirely of cash savings, guaranteed investment certificates (GICs), and guaranteed bonds. Count on it.

Growth Expectations

When RRSP owners realize the impact of long-term growth, they become enthusiastic about taking charge of their investments, seeking an extra 2 or 3 percent advantage each year. Perhaps a 2 percent improvement doesn't sound all that impressive to a baseball player's batting average. But over the long term, an RRSP that earns 12 percent annually instead of 10 percent can make the difference between a "getting by" retirement and a near-luxurious lifestyle.

How much difference can your RRSP decisions make to the amount of money you have when you retire? Check out Table 2-1.

Table 2-1	Impact of RRSP Investment Decisions Original Investment: $5,000		
Investment	*Percentage Growth*	*10 Years*	*30 Years*
Canada Savings Bonds (CSBs)	6.5%	$9,385.69	$33,071.83
Canadian mutual funds	8.8%	$11,621.41	$62,782.25
International mutual funds	11.0%	$14,197.10	$114,461.48

If you had invested your RRSP in eligible Canada Savings Bonds ten years ago, your RRSP would have produced growth of 6.5 percent each year since you bought the bonds. Not bad? Consider this: Money invested in a typical Canadian equity-based mutual fund would have returned an average growth of 8.8 percent each year, a 2.3 percent annual improvement over the bonds. And the same amount of money invested in a typical international equity-based mutual fund would have awarded you a whopping 11.0 percent average annual return over that same ten-year period.

A $5,000 investment growing at 6.5 percent annual compound interest would grow to $9,385.69 over this ten-year period. The same amount of money growing at 8.8 percent annually over the same ten-year period would be worth $11,621.41.

And if you could earn 11 percent from your $5,000, you would have $14,197.10. The difference over 30 years is even more impressive.

So don't consider a 2 or 3 percent improvement in your RRSP growth insignificant. Over the long term, that kind of advantage can be a gold mine.

Book VI

Somewhere over the Rainbow: Retirement Planning

The Spectre of Inflation

Back in the days of the voyageur fur traders, North American native tribes believed an evil spirit prowled the northern woods. On the coldest, darkest nights of the year, the spirit would emerge from the forest and devour all the food gathered by the tribe to sustain them through the winter. If it were famished enough, the spirit would begin consuming the people themselves. Only when the beast was satisfied did it return to its hiding place. The tribes would take a long time to recover, and they would never forget the evil spirit, lurking somewhere in the darkness, ready to creep back into the village at any time.

Economists and investors fear a similar legendary beast, called inflation. From time to time the inflation beast arrives, and the devastation is massive. Its last appearancc was in the early 1980s, when interest rates shot beyond the 20 percent level, leading to business failures, mortgage foreclosures, and financial disaster for anyone living on a fixed income, other than those who lived on interest income that was fixed at high rates! Inflation leads to higher prices for goods and services, which triggers demands for higher wages and salaries, which produces higher prices . . . and the merry-go-round keeps spinning.

Large-scale inflation is created by a number of factors that are fascinating to economists and as interesting as a pile of bricks to the rest of us. Fortunately, the last decade has seen relatively low rates of inflation, averaging about 2 percent per year. The world economy may be able to sustain these low rates indefinitely, or so we hope — other than those who rely on income generated by high interest rates!

But inflation is always around in small amounts, and even low levels can affect your long-term RRSP goals. Just as the 2 percent difference is a long-term shot in the arm to the growth of your RRSP, a steady 2 percent rate of inflation means you'll need substantially more money in the future to enjoy the same degree of comfort you experience today.

Suppose that you plan to stop working in 20 years, and you estimate that a retirement income of $40,000 a year should do just fine. Sounds good. But you're measuring that income with *today's* dollar value. Over time, inflation lowers the value of every dollar you earn or accumulate each year. If inflation averages 3 percent annually over the next 20 years, the lifestyle you can enjoy today with a $40,000 annual income will cost you $72,244 a year when you retire. If inflation jumps to an average of 5 percent annually between now and then, you'll need $106,132 to enjoy a life that costs $40,000 today (see Table 2-2). By the way, historically, our economy has endured an average 5 percent annual inflation rate.

Table 2-2	Income Growth to Match Inflation			
	Amount Needed to Match $40,000 Income Today			
Inflation Rate	*5 Years*	*10 Years*	*15 Years*	*20 Years*
3%	$46,371	$53,757	$62,319	$72,244
4%	$48,666	$59,210	$72,038	$87,645
5%	$51,051	$65,156	$83,157	$106,132

Don't fret — inflation also brings a few investment opportunities with it. But the long-term impact of even relatively low levels of inflation should alert you to two rules of life, retirement, and the whole darn thing:

- Maximize the contribution level and growth of your RRSP.
- Actively manage your RRSP so that you can respond to unforeseen events and opportunities.

How Much Will You Need?

Of all the questions asked by RRSP investors, this is perhaps the most difficult to answer. Why? Because it involves so many variables, including the following:

- **Your lifespan:** How long do you expect to live after retirement? (*Note:* "As long as possible" doesn't count.)
- **Your age when you retire:** Will you be 55? 60? 65? Older?

> ✔ **Your retirement lifestyle:** Will you read and garden? Travel often as
> globetrotters? Remain in your own home, or sell it and move to smaller,
> less expensive quarters? Do you plan to work part-time?
>
> ✔ **Your financial situation:** Will your home be mortgage-free, or will you
> still be making those pesky payments? Will you be facing substantial
> balances on high-interest credit cards?

The answers to these questions are yours to determine. There is no "one size
fits all" secret to estimating the retirement income you'll need. All you can do
is accept some basic assumptions and proceed from there, making adjustments
as you go along. Here are a few guidelines that most economists and financial
advisers agree upon:

Book VI

**Somewhere
over the
Rainbow:
Retirement
Planning**

> ✔ **Expect that you will need only 70 percent of your current income to
> sustain the lifestyle you enjoy today.** Some advisers say 80 percent, and
> others suggest as low as 40 percent, depending on the lifestyle you
> choose. Remember, you'll be spending less on job-related expenses such
> as clothing, commuting, and lunches. A paid-up mortgage and grown
> children will cut your living costs even further. So 70 percent of what you
> currently earn makes a reasonable figure for a comfortable retirement.
>
> ✔ **Assume at least some income from government sources.** Current
> maximum C/QPP benefits for those retiring at 65 are about $10,000
> annually. Start drawing benefits at age 60 and it drops to around $7,000 a
> year; delay retirement to age 70 and it rises to the $13,000 level.
>
> ✔ **Plan on living to the ripe old age of 90.** A few generations ago, this was
> a rare life expectancy for average Canadians. But given better medical
> care and the awareness of maintaining a healthier lifestyle — no smoking,
> regular exercise, annual check-ups, and improved diet — it's not such an
> outrageous goal. If you retire at age 55, this means 35 years of retirement
> ahead of you, which may be longer than your entire working career.
>
> ✔ **Assume a conservative return on your RRSP balance after retirement
> of 8 percent annually and an average annual inflation rate of 5 percent.**
> This will generate an average 3 percent in annual growth after inflation.
> Now estimate the retirement income you'll need — say, $40,000 per year,
> plus any government benefits listed above — and multiply by 25.

Hang on, because the answer is $1 million. But depending on your age and
your determination, this is not quite as unreachable as you may think. If your
current age is 25 and you are able to generate a conservative 8 percent growth
from your RRSP, it takes an annual contribution of $3,860 to reach that magic
million at age 65. Earn 12 percent each year from your RRSP — not an
unreasonable level over the very long term — and you need only $1,300 each
year in your plan.

If you're currently 35 years old, you'll need to sock away $8,830 each year earning 8 percent annual growth, or $4,140 each year if you can obtain 12 percent annual growth, to reach a million dollars at age 65. If you hold off until age 45 to launch your RRSP program, it will take $21,850 (at 8 percent) or $13,380 each year (at 12 percent) to accumulate a million.

- ✔ If the prospect of generating a million bucks in today's dollars sounds too daunting, make some adjustments. Do you really want to live in a large urban house when you retire? If your home is mortgage-free, you'll manage to keep virtually every penny of its value when you sell it, which helps to make up any shortfall between your RRSP value and that magic million. Your annual income needs will drop even lower by eliminating all the maintenance costs associated with your house.

- ✔ If you're married, and either you or your spouse earns substantially more income than the other, you can reduce the retirement income you'll need by cutting your income-tax level through a spousal RRSP, described in the upcoming section, "Spousal RRSPs and Income Splitting."

To calculate the amount you need to sock away to reach a million dollars, see this book's Appendix.

Paying Attention

If the biggest RRSP mistake made by most Canadians is failing to maximize their contribution each year, the second biggest mistake is not actively paying attention to the health of their investment. Like any growing thing, from carrots to kids, RRSPs thrive with attention, guidance, and general TLC. And who benefits? You do, with a larger nest egg to generate more retirement income.

Don't make the mistake of assuming your RRSP task ends with your annual contribution, or that your tax refund cheque is the biggest benefit you enjoy. Paying attention to the growth of your RRSP, with a review every six months, can make an immense difference over the years. And you don't need a financial guru standing at your elbow, either. All it takes is a basic understanding of a few rules, a strategy you can follow, and a little advice now and then from a qualified adviser.

Spousal RRSPs and Income Splitting

If you are married or in a common-law relationship, it pays to understand spousal RRSPs and their benefits. Canada Customs and Revenue Agency provides few breaks for married couples, but one pops up in the RRSP rules. It provides the option of contributing to a *spousal RRSP,* which doesn't generate benefits today but delivers major reductions in income tax down the road.

A spousal RRSP permits you to place your RRSP contribution into a plan belonging to your partner. This cannot be used to increase your qualifying RRSP contribution limit; if your limit is $5,000 and you place it all in an RRSP belonging to your spouse, there is none left over for your own plan in that year. So why bother? Because a spousal RRSP favours couples in which one spouse earns significantly more income than the other. If the high-income spouse contributes only to his or her RRSP, it will produce substantially more income when retirement day arrives *and* attract substantially more tax to be paid. Here's an example:

Jeff and Jean are the same age and have been married for 12 years. Jeff is a sales executive, and Jean is an artist. Each year, Jeff makes his maximum contribution to his RRSP — about $15,000 on average. Jeff and Jean feel this substantial investment is all they will need to build a hefty RRSP balance when they retire at age 55, and they are correct. If the plan is wisely invested and grows at a reasonable 10 percent annually, Jeff's RRSP will sport a healthy $900,000 balance by the time he is 55 years of age. They expect the $900,000 to produce 5 percent of its total value annually as retirement income, which means they will be earning — and paying tax on — $45,000 each year. But this entire amount will be earned in Jeff's name, and will be taxed accordingly. Using current income-tax rates, this will mean returning $14,465 to Ottawa every year as income tax, leaving them $30,535 as net income.

Book VI

Somewhere over the Rainbow: Retirement Planning

But if Jeff divides his annual $15,000 contribution into equal amounts, putting $7,500 in his RRSP and $7,500 into Jean's, they would still have the $900,000 nest egg, divided equally between the two plans, with each plan valued at $450,000 (assuming the same 10 percent average annual return for both plans). Instead of one income, the two plans generate separate incomes for each spouse, producing a different tax picture. The two separate incomes still total $45,000, but the total family income is taxed at $22,500 for Jeff and $22,500 for Jean. The lower figure triggers a lower tax rate; each spouse now pays about $6,000 in income tax each year, leaving them with a $33,000 net income — which will be like getting a $2,500 annual gift from the CCRA. Over 20 years, that's $50,000 in income-tax payments Jeff and Jean will avoid.

There's more. Every Canadian with pension income can claim an annual $1,000 pension income tax credit. If both spouses earn income from their own RRSP, the couple can claim $2,000 total instead of $1,000 if only one partner has RRSP income.

Having a spousal RRSP may also help you avoid the Old Age Security (OAS) clawback, a voracious beast that starts consuming 15 cents out of every dollar earned above an annual retirement income level — currently $55,309 — reducing your OAS payment to nil when your retirement income reaches the magic amount of $89,948. If your spouse is younger than you, and you expect to have earned income beyond age 69 — the age limit for making RRSP contributions — you can contribute to your spouse's plan and still claim the tax benefit because your individual incomes will be sufficiently low.

The CCRA's definition of a spouse is "a person of the opposite sex to whom the individual is married or with whom the individual has cohabited in a conjugal relationship for a period of at least one year, or less than one year if the two individuals are the natural or adoptive parents of a child." This, however, is currently under review and may change. Check with the CCRA to confirm the definition if you are unsure of your situation.

Here are some things you should know about a spousal RRSP:

✔ One more time: Having a spousal RRSP does not increase the total amount of the contribution you are allowed to make. If your limit is $5,000 and you place $4,000 in a spousal plan, this leaves only $1,000 for your plan.

✔ The money you contribute to your spouse's RRSP belongs to your spouse. But if he or she withdraws the funds from the spousal plan within three years, it is taxed as your income. For this reason alone, it is wise to keep your spouse's RRSP separate from his or her own plan, if one exists.

✔ If you and your spouse separate, the existence of a spousal plan will have no bearing on the division of assets if you reside in a province with family law provisions. Under these provisions, all shared assets accumulated during the relationship are divided equally — including both personal and spousal RRSPs.

✔ Income splitting to reduce taxes on your retirement income is a key benefit of a spousal RRSP. How big is the benefit? It depends on these factors:

 • What will be the taxable income and income-tax rate of the contributing spouse after retirement? (If it is less than that of the owner of the spousal plan, there is no benefit to be gained; you are simply dancing in circles, which may seem like fun but doesn't get you anywhere.)

 • What will be the annual income generated from the spousal RRSP?

 • How stable is the marriage?

Pledging Your RRSP as Collateral

The value of your RRSP represents an important asset to you, one that you can expect to grow substantially with time. Banks, trust companies, credit unions, caisses populaires, and other organizations love folks with assets. In fact, people with money to lend favour people with assets so much that they charge them a lower interest rate on borrowed money, as long as the loan is backed with *pledged assets,* or *collateral.*

So, can you pledge some or all of your RRSP as collateral for a loan and qualify for lower interest rates? And if you can — should you?

Canada Customs and Revenue Agency says you can pledge some or all of your RRSP as collateral for a loan, but they do not encourage you to do it. If you pledge any or all of your RRSP assets as collateral, the fair market value of those assets held in your RRSP will be added to your taxable income for the year. If you assign $10,000 of your RRSP's value to a bank as collateral for a loan, the CCRA acts as though you had withdrawn the same amount (or fair market value) in cash, and taxes you accordingly. When the loan is paid off and you no longer need the assets as collateral, you can deduct the amount previously included in your income minus any losses suffered over the term of the loan.

It's all very complex and fraught with danger — too much, in fact, to justify unless the reduced interest rate earned by using your RRSP is substantial. Besides, most financial institutions will not accept RRSP assets as collateral. They do, however, consider anyone with a good-sized RRSP balance to be a better-than-average credit risk, and adjust the interest rate charged on the loan downward to reflect this.

Here's one situation where it makes sense to use your RRSP assets as collateral, if you can find a financial institution to go along with it:

Suppose that you find yourself suddenly unemployed for a short time. You may be tempted to withdraw money from your RRSP to cover essentials such as mortgage or rent, food, utilities, and so on. Unfortunately, once the funds are out of your RRSP, they cannot be put back in again when you find a new job. But if you borrow enough money to carry you over and pledge a portion of your RRSP as collateral, you can begin paying the loan back when you are employed again. When the loan is repaid, the pledge of your RRSP as collateral is lifted, you claim the deduction and any losses, and you haven't lost a thing.

This is probably the only time when using your RRSP this way makes sense. And only for a very short time.

Leaving the Country

What happens to your RRSP and all those tasty tax benefits if you leave Canada for employment in another country, such as the United States? It depends on where you go, and whether the move is considered temporary or permanent.

Book VI

Somewhere over the Rainbow: Retirement Planning

If you leave the country to accept temporary employment in the U.S., you can continue to make RRSP contributions as long as you are still considered a Canadian resident under the Canada/U.S.A. tax treaty. Your employer or a tax accountant can provide the necessary documentation. If you commit to full residency and employment in the U.S., and you pay income tax there, you can no longer make contributions to your plan. Nor, by the way, can you transfer its assets to an Individual Retirement Account (IRA), roughly the U.S. equivalent to an RRSP. You can, however, continue to maintain your RRSP in your absence, and its value will continue to grow free of Canadian tax. To escape U.S. tax on the growth of your RRSP assets, you need a special tax form obtainable from a qualified tax accountant.

What about cashing in your RRSP while living in the U.S.? Only if you're a glutton for tax punishment. First, Canada Customs and Revenue Agency will slap a 25 percent withholding tax on the proceeds. Then Uncle Sam will tax you on the entire value your RRSP earned between the day you left Canada and the day you closed your RRSP. You may even be subject to U.S. income tax as well.

Chapter 3

Your RRSP Strategy

· ·

· ·

A self-directed RRSP will provide you with either a small sense of exhilaration — hey, you're in charge of your own future! — or a substantial dose of anxiety ("Hey, I'm in charge of my own future!").

The best way to make the most of it is by setting a strategy to maximize your RRSP growth over the years. Relax, you're not planning the D-Day invasion of Europe. You're just evaluating some basic facts, such as your age, the number of years remaining before you retire, the amount of annual contributions you'll be able to make, and the *risk threshold* that makes you comfortable while building the value of your RRSP.

Planning for your retirement income is like plotting a long journey. You start by deciding where you want to go and when you want to arrive there. Then you determine any stops you may need to make along the way, including a few to ensure you're still on the right course. That's really what an RRSP strategy is all about. Start with a goal (the total value of your RRSP when you retire); choose your route (the contributions and investments you'll make over the years); decide on some overnight stops (short-term goals); and schedule a pause now and then to confirm your progress (periodic investment reviews).

Of course, the RRSP journey for some people is a 30-year-plus excursion, which is not exactly a weekend trip to the cottage.

Investments Suitable for Your RRSP

Remember the three groups of investment types: liquidable (cash and its equivalent), income (bonds, GICs, and mortgages), and growth (stocks and mutual funds). Almost any investment based on these characteristics is accepted by the Canada Customs and Revenue Agency for use in your RRSP.

Things you *cannot* hold in your RRSP (the CCRA prevents it):

- ✔ Foreign cash
- ✔ Collectible items such as coins, artwork, stamps, and antiques
- ✔ Mutual funds not registered with the Canada Customs and Revenue Agency
- ✔ Commodities, futures, and complex options
- ✔ Real estate
- ✔ Investments in small, privately held companies

Things you *shouldn't* hold in your RRSP (common sense prevents it):

- ✔ **Annuities:** Annuities produce a steady income over a fixed period of time, purchased with a single large payment. They're a possible alternative to other options when you eventually retire, but they have no place inside an RRSP. Their tax-free growth status carries no benefit because everything in your RRSP grows free of immediate taxation anyway. What's more, annuities pay hefty commissions to the people who sell them, and they carry large administration fees. Avoid them. (For more on annuities, see Chapter 5.)

- ✔ **Limited partnerships:** Some investment salespeople may propose a limited partnership (LP) as a suitable RRSP investment. Some people may suggest removing your own appendix too. For the record, an LP enables managing partners of a company or real estate development to use Other People's Money (in this case, yours) as capital. Later, when the term of the agreement is up, the investors and partners share in the profits.

    Sound like a good idea? It's not. LPs are sold through brokers and financial consultants who earn commissions as high as 10 percent, skimmed off the top of your initial investment. Management fees and other expenses are deducted from the operation each year, and the LP managers — who are paid by these fees and expenses — decide the amount to pay themselves. Sound bad? It gets worse. Unlike mutual funds, you can't vote with your dollars, because LPs are not liquid. Their term is usually from seven to ten years, and you cannot take your money out — whatever may be left of it — before the term is up. LPs have had a notoriously checkered history over the last two decades. If an adviser seriously proposes an LP for your RRSP investments, do two things: Say no . . . and look for a new financial adviser.

Matching Your Investment Mix to Your Goals

The ideal RRSP does not match the opinions or reflect the preferences of anyone. Instead, it meets the unique needs of its owner — that's you.

Your RRSP should change with time, just as you will. As you age, your priorities shift, you grow wiser in the ways of the world, and you tend to conserve your energy a little more. That's a good way to describe the changes you'll want to make to your RRSP over time. All of these changes, of course, will be influenced by your personal comfort level, your investment sophistication, and your risk threshold. That's what makes the ideal mix of liquidable, income, and growth investments unique to you.

This section tackles your concerns, and the changes to your RRSP basic recipe you may want to make, decade by decade.

Book VI

Somewhere over the Rainbow: Retirement Planning

- ✔ **Up to age 25, you're fancy-free.** Retirement is an eon or two away, your income is limited, and your attentions are elsewhere. Still, this is the time when you can earn maximum rewards from every RRSP dollar you invest. This is the time to go for growth. You don't need income from your RRSP, and you don't need much liquidity. The vast majority of your investments should be growth-oriented, even if they are subject to wide fluctuations in value. For example, you may want to choose *sector funds,* which are mutual funds investing in specific industries, such as entertainment, communications, and health care. These funds are subject to wild swings in value, but if the underlying quality is good, they are a route to maximum RRSP growth.

- ✔ **From age 25 to 35, you acquire commitments.** You may be married with children and a mortgage, and deeply involved in your career. You have more income, but more expenses as well. The needs of your RRSP reflect your new commitments, now geared for steady growth to maturity. Some of the riskier growth investments that appealed to you ten years ago aren't as attractive, and a little liquidity in your plan, enabling you to obtain cash if needed, wouldn't hurt at all.

- ✔ **From age 35 to 45, the word is reality.** You are approaching your maximum income level, and your RRSP contribution limits have risen accordingly. Most of all, your RRSP is now worth a fair amount of money — and that's good, because all those people who appear in advertisements promoting retirement benefits start looking like you and your friends. Your major concern is holding on to all the money your RRSP has earned over the years, and that means more income and security. You still need growth, but now you prefer sure and steady improvements rather than fast-paced, jerky motions — kind of like your changed taste in music.

- ✔ **From age 45 to 55, the horizon draws closer.** Perhaps you're an empty nester by now. In any case, you relish each increase in your RRSP's value and look for all the guarantees you can get. It's a time of consolidation and preparation. Income investments are especially attractive, and GICs you once sneered at for their low earnings now find a place in your plan. After all, they are guaranteed and predictable, which, you've come to learn, is something that life is not.

- ✔ **From age 55 to 65, it's harvest time.** You focus on both "topping up" your RRSP before converting its assets to retirement income and locking in as much as possible with reduced-risk investments. Growth and liquidity are still factors, but you are more conscious about holding on to what you have.

Keeping the three basic investment groups in mind — liquidable, income, and growth — the following sections examine the various options that deliver these qualities in various proportions. These are the raw ingredients of your recipe. Later, you can add a little spice if you like.

Savings accounts

You may have had one of these since you were a child. Besides being safe, they are also highly liquidable, as you know if you ever took a hammer to your piggy bank. But money in your piggy bank tended to grow mouldy, and not much else. Savings accounts provide not much more than that these days, yet too many Canadians open an RRSP savings account, plunk their loonies into it, and call the whole process "retirement planning." It's not. Savings accounts pay little more than the rate of inflation, which means no growth and no income. A little liquidity in your RRSP goes a long way, but you can enjoy its advantages in better places than a savings account.

GICs

Along with savings accounts, *guaranteed investment certificates (GICs)* are one way for a bank, trust company, or credit union to borrow money from you. In return, they generate interest payable either when the GIC term — from six months to ten years — is up, or on a regular basis — monthly, semi-annually, or annually. These are known as *fixed-income* investments.

Some RRSP owners believe in GICs the way people believe in heaven: they're convinced that nothing better exists. Sorry. Until you build substantial funds in your RRSP or approach retirement, many investment options are better for your RRSP than large quantities of GICs.

Bonds

A bond is basically a GIC with more class. Bonds pay higher interest, can be sold with relative ease (for high liquidity), and some even come with a guarantee. They are admittedly more complicated than GICs. Essentially, a bond is an IOU issued by a corporation or a government in exchange for cold, hard cash that they can use to expand business, pay debts, improve facilities, and for other practical reasons. It's worth learning about them in detail. To do so, check out Chapter 6 in Book V.

T-bills

The *T* stands for treasury, which means your government needs a short-term loan to get it through the weekend. T-bills, bought and sold by brokerage houses, pay rates comparable to guaranteed bonds. They are not intended for long-term investments, which makes them both highly secure and very liquid. You can obtain longer-term benefits from T-bills by investing in money market mutual funds trading in T-bills and selected high-quality bonds issued by large corporations.

Book VI

Somewhere over the Rainbow: Retirement Planning

Stocks

Here's where we enter sweaty-palm territory for investment novices. Too many Canadians associate the words *stock market* with the word *Crash!* That's because a slow and steady rise in the Toronto Stock Exchange (TSX) and other stock markets never makes the front page of most newspapers, but a major drop in stock prices suddenly becomes big news.

The facts: Nothing provides better long-term growth prospects for your RRSP than a mix of shares in quality companies, in Canada and around the world. Choosing the companies in which to invest, however, demands knowledge, experience, patience, and a little luck now and then. The best advice when you're just starting your RRSP is, don't try this at home. That's what mutual funds are for (discussed in the next section.)

When you purchase a *common stock,* you own a piece of that company and are investing in its future prosperity. The price of the stock will fluctuate with the financial successes or setbacks of the company, influenced by the economy and the sentiments of the market. Some companies, like some people, are more popular than others, even though they share similar characteristics with the less popular companies. Popular companies see their stock value rise and remain more immune to world events and the state of the economy.

Many companies issue two kinds of stock: *common shares* and *preferred shares.* They're a little like flying economy or first-class. Owners of preferred shares are first in line when the dividends are handed out. Owners of common shares have to wait until after the preferred shareholders have been paid their dividends.

Mutual funds

Suppose that you had $25,000 in your RRSP, and you liked the idea of having someone manage it for you on a continuous basis. Every day, this manager would review your account before deciding which stocks, bonds, or other investments to buy and sell, based on the manager's knowledge, experience, and access to huge volumes of research information. In return, you would pay the manager about 2 percent of the value of your RRSP each year.

It's a nice idea, except that 2 percent of $25,000 won't get the job done. But if a thousand people like you pooled their RRSPs, the total would amount to $25 million, and 2 percent of that is $500,000 annually. Now you have a manager's attention — and, with a little tweaking here and there, you also have a *mutual fund.*

In reality, $25 million is a tiny mutual fund these days. Many Canadian mutual funds reach several billion dollars in *managed assets,* the money entrusted to them by investors. The skills of the fund manager should produce a substantially higher annual return for investors than they could earn on their own, more than making up for the annual fee paid to the manager. This is why the amount of money invested by Canadians in mutual funds exploded from a few hundred million dollars in 1980 to more than $475 billion in mid-2003.

Mutual funds provide the best opportunity for inexperienced investors to build their RRSP value over time. They also provide an excellent way to diversify your investments in several different ways. But they are not foolproof, and choosing the best fund for your needs takes some investigation by you, as well as some consultation with your financial adviser. (For more about mutual funds, see Chapters 1 and 2 of Book V.)

Mortgages — yours and others

A mortgage is a legitimate investment for an RRSP, as long as it is secured by real estate within Canada — such as your own home, for example. Does this mean you can use cash from your RRSP to finance the mortgage on your home and actually pay yourself with monthly mortgage payments? As a matter of fact, it does. Hey, why doesn't everybody do that? Here's why:

- ✔ It's a complex operation involving a mortgage trustee, real estate appraiser, legal counsel, and mortgage insurance.

✔ It involves several high-priced people, all of whom expect to be paid, to set up the mortgage inside your RRSP. It also involves a separate self-directed RRSP fee each year.

✔ You need at least $50,000 in cash or liquidable assets (plus that much room in your mortgage) to make it worthwhile, and at least $75,000 to make it attractive.

✔ You cannot charge an excessive interest rate on the mortgage to build your RRSP. Canada Customs and Revenue Agency says the interest rate must be "comparable" to current rates in the marketplace. If your bank offers you a 10-year mortgage at 7.5 percent interest, that's the amount you should set for your RRSP mortgage.

Book VI

Somewhere over the Rainbow: Retirement Planning

Yet there are some advantages. Mortgage rates are always a few percentage points above GICs, with similar security. And you can also use RRSP cash to fund a mortgage for someone else, including a son or daughter. But do you want to?

If your RRSP plans are just getting rolling, the mortgage option is not for you — at least, not for a few years. When the value of your RRSP hits six figures, you may want to review it, however.

Contributions in kind

Until now, the focus has been on making contributions in cash to your RRSP. But there is another alternative, called *contributions in kind*. A contribution in kind simply means transferring any eligible investment held outside your RRSP into your plan, where any earnings it produces are subject to deferred taxation, just like other RRSP investments. If you own, inherit, or otherwise acquire some Canadian bonds (including Canada Savings Bonds, or CSBs), mutual funds, eligible mortgages, or shares in Canadian companies (or in foreign companies, up to 30 percent of your total RRSP value), you can move them into your RRSP and claim a deduction.

This is even better than it sounds. Suppose you've been purchasing Canada Savings Bonds over the years instead of contributing to your RRSP, and you have accumulated $5,000 worth of CSBs. Now you want to begin your RRSP, but don't have cash on hand to make a contribution. No problem. Launch your RRSP with the CSBs as your opening contribution, and claim a $5,000 deduction from your income for the year (assuming you have that much contribution room, of course). If you're in the 40 percent tax bracket, this produces a $2,000 tax refund, and you have another $2,000 to add to your plan.

You can enjoy the same benefits if Uncle Herbie decides to give you a gift of his shares in Gold Brick Mining, Inc. Assuming that they qualify as an RRSP investment, you can roll them into your plan and earn a tax refund. The amount you can claim is equal to the value of the shares, or any qualifying investment, on the day you transferred them into your RRSP.

Here's where things can get tricky. If Uncle Herbie paid ten dollars per share for the gold mine stock, and each share was selling for 20 dollars on the day you transfer them into your RRSP, a light goes on at the Canada Customs and Revenue Agency. After all, the value of the shares has doubled since Herbie purchased them. That's a capital gain, and capital gains are taxable even though you have not sold the shares for a profit. Thus, you'll be assessed tax on the increase in the share value as soon as the shares are transferred to your name. The CCRA calls this *deemed disposition*. If the shares also increase in value between the day they are transferred and the day you put them in your RRSP, this will be taxed as well. It's probably still wise to make the contribution this way; just be prepared for the tax it triggers.

You can even use your RRSP as a form of pawnbroker, in times of need. No, it won't loan you 20 bucks against your watch or wedding ring. But if you own eligible securities such as stocks, bonds, or mutual fund shares outside your RRSP, and you're strapped for cash on a fairly short-term basis, you can transfer the securities into your RRSP and withdraw an equal amount in cash. Your securities continue to grow in value, but now the growth is tax-deferred. You have the cash you need to tide you over and, when the cash crisis is past, you can buy the securities back again. This gets a bit tricky, so you'll want a little professional assistance. But it can be done.

Over-Contributing and Under-Contributing

Some RRSP rules are set in concrete. Others kind of float on foam rubber. If you have the cash available, and if you enjoy shaking things up a little, this is one area where you can bend the rules to your benefit.

Putting too many eggs in your basket (or, you can never have too many eggs)

If you believe in taking every advantage offered you, consider again the benefit of contributing more to your RRSP than the Canada Customs and Revenue Agency officially allows.

As mentioned in Chapter 1, tax regulations allow you to exceed your contribution by up to $2,000 at any time up to retirement. This is cumulative, by the way, not an annual limit. When you retire, you adjust the balance of your RRSP by claiming the excess as part of your final RRSP contribution. If in your final year of making RRSP contributions your limit is $8,000, you must subtract any over-contribution from that amount to arrive at your actual maximum contribution limit.

The idea was to provide RRSP owners with a margin of error, so they could avoid the severe penalty of 1 percent per month on excessive RRSP contributions, which doesn't kick in until the $2,000 limit is exceeded.

Over-contributing to your RRSP has benefits. You'll have an extra $2,000 growing tax-sheltered within your plan for several years. If it grows at an average 10 percent annually, after 20 years your $2,000 will be worth about $15,000, which is $15,000 more than if you had strictly abided by the rules.

Drawbacks? There are always drawbacks.

First, this assumes that you are young enough to wait 20 years before collecting this particular bonus. Trouble is, people in their mid-30s are often too strapped for cash to even meet their maximum permitted annual contribution, so going $2,000 over it, even once, could be a stretch.

Next, use the $2,000 up and you have no margin for error. Every loonie you happen to contribute over your limit in the future brings with it a penalty of 1 percent per month.

Should you over-contribute? Sure, if the extra dollars are available and you are careful to monitor your contributions in the future, avoiding that nasty penalty.

Book VI

Somewhere over the Rainbow: Retirement Planning

Putting too few eggs in your basket

In contrast with excess contributions, most Canadians find they don't have enough funds on hand to reach their RRSP limit. This creates carry-forward amounts, which appear on the CCRA's Notice of Assessment sent to you after you file your income tax return.

Making up some of this unused contribution room is a good idea — but where can you find the money? Here are four possible sources:

- ✔ **Year-end bonuses:** If you receive year-end bonuses from your employer, as much as $10,000 can be contributed directly to your RRSP tax-free, providing you have contribution room.

- ✔ **Contributions in kind:** You can use RRSP-eligible investments held outside your plan, such as stocks, bonds, and mutual funds, to make up unused contribution room.

- ✔ **Your tax refund:** Roll it into your RRSP immediately to absorb at least some carry-over and start building your plan balance.

- ✔ **Borrow the money:** Take out a loan as long as you can pay off the balance within 12 months (see Chapter 1).

Review Your Progress

The administrator of your self-directed RRSP will issue statements either each month or each quarter. This is not junk mail — take a few moments to review each statement and file it away with others for reference. Here's what your statement will include, and what you should take the time to review:

✔ **A summary of your account:** Look for any change in asset value (the total value of everything in your RRSP). Is your RRSP worth more or less than on your previous statement? If more, how much (if any) was generated by new contributions? If less, did you expect a drop due (almost exclusively) to fluctuations in the value of your mutual funds?

✔ **A summary of your contributions:** The statement will include contribution activity both since your last statement and during the year to date. Look for confirmation that your contributions are being registered.

✔ **Plan growth:** Look for the increase in the value of your self-directed RRSP since placing it with the bank, trust company, investment firm, or other administrator.

✔ **Foreign content:** Look for maximum (30 percent) foreign investment through bonds and mutual funds.

✔ **Transactions:** Look for a record of all transactions in your RRSP since you received your last statement. This includes new contributions, any buying or selling of investments (bonds, mutual funds, and so on) held in your RRSP, and any rollover of GICs or T-bills that have matured since your last statement. Did you authorize these trades or renewals? Do you understand why they were made?

✔ **Account valuation:** Look for both the *book value* (what you paid for them originally) and *current value* (what you would get for them if you sold them on the date of your statement) of all the individual assets held in your RRSP, including GICs, T-bills, bonds, mutual funds, and other investments. Which ones have risen since the last statement? Which ones have fallen in value? How comfortable are you with this?

✔ **Cash balance:** Look for excessive amounts of cash. A few hundred dollars is probably not worth being concerned about. If it approaches $1,000 or more, find better ways of earning money from it through the purchase of T-bills or money market funds, which are almost as good as cash but earn more interest. (Cash can build up in your account from various sources, including dividends from stocks you own in your RRSP, unallocated contributions, or other reasons.)

How to Read Your RRSP Statement

Each RRSP administrator has a slightly different statement format, but they all include certain key areas of information. Please remember that *your RRSP statement is not junk mail.* It is in your selfish interest to review it briefly as soon as you receive it, and scan it in detail on a regular basis. You should also file copies in a safe place. Figure 3-1 shows the first page of an actual RRSP statement from a bank-owned brokerage to one of its RRSP customers (we've changed the brokerage and customer's name, but not the figures).

Here are some points to note about the first page of the RRSP statement shown in Figure 3-1:

Book VI

Somewhere over the Rainbow: Retirement Planning

ANYBANK CANADA, INC.
2001 Walla Walla Blvd, Toronto, ON M5R 3K5

Registered Retirement Savings Plan
Statement of Account

March 2001

Currency: **CANADIAN DOLLARS**

ANY BANK SELF–DIRECTED RRSP
TRUST COMPANY ACTING AS TRUSTEE

Account number

This statement is for
March 1 to
March 30, 2001

Your last statement was for
February 1 to
February 28, 2001

SUMMARY OF YOUR INVESTMENTS

in Canadian dollars

	Value on Feb 28, 2001 ($)	Value on Mar 30, 2001 ($)	% of total value on Mar 30, 2001
Cash and cash equivalents	542.03	543.11	1.3
Fixed income	37,228.66	37,311.71	87.5
Equities	—	—	—
Mutual funds	5,062.00	4,766.85	11.2
Other	—	—	—
Total investments	**42,832.69**	**42,621.67**	**100.0**

SUMMARY OF YOUR RRSP CONTRIBUTIONS

	First 60 days of the year ($)	Balance of the year ($)	Total year to date ($)
Contributions made by you	0.00	0.00	0.00

SUMMARY OF YOUR FOREIGN CONTENT

Revenue Canada allows you to hold up to 30% of the total book value of your account in foreign investments, with no tax penalty.

	Book value ($)	% of total book value on Mar 30, 2001
Canadian investments	25,656.65	83.6
Foreign investments	5,047.13	16.4
Total book value	**30,703.78**	**100.0**

page 1 of 2

Figure 3-1:
The opening page of an RRSP statement includes account summary information.

✔ It was not an especially good month for this RRSP investor, or for the market generally. The total value of her plan dropped by over $200. But she has a long way to go before retiring, and building her RRSP is not an unbroken straight line.

✔ Almost 90 percent of her RRSP is invested in fixed-income investments — in this case, government strip bonds. They're safe and secure, which helped avoid larger losses during this down-market period for equities. But at 42 years of age, she is much too young to have such a large portion in low-earning investments like these.

✔ No contributions were made to her RRSP during the first two months of 2001. She makes a lump-sum contribution near the end of each year. A series of 12 monthly contributions would be better, providing her with the advantages of dollar-cost averaging.

✔ The plan has just $5,047.13 in foreign content, representing 16.4 percent of the plan's total book value. With her next contribution, the RRSP owner should either sell some of her strip bonds or begin expanding her foreign portion closer to the 30 percent foreign-content limit, perhaps with a conservative, but often well-performing global equity fund.

Figure 3-2 breaks down the plan contents in detail. A few things to note:

✔ The government strip bonds are laddered, maturing in 2006, 2008, and 2009, respectively.

✔ The bonds do not indicate their annual percentage yield. You have to figure that one out for yourself. The 2006 Government of Canada bond, for example, was purchased for $7,747.50 (book value); was worth $11,080.50 on March 30, 2001; and can be cashed for $15,000 on December 1, 2006 (face value). In the 5$\frac{1}{2}$ years until its maturity date, the bond will earn just under $4,000 — or about 6.4 percent annually, based on its current value.

✔ The Fidelity Focus Health Care Fund slipped almost $300 in value since it was purchased. It's a good long-term sector fund, not a core equity fund.

Remember, this is only a one-month snapshot of constantly changing asset values. By March 2003, Canadian equities were, as a whole, still losing money, interest rates and inflation remained low, and the market was still reeling from a very nasty and sharp-toothed bear market that lasted over three years. Assuming this RRSP owner was 15 to 20 years from retirement, what would you advise her to do?

✔ Sell the strip bonds and buy a broadly based Canadian equity mutual fund while stock prices are depressed?

✔ Sell the mutual fund at a loss and buy safer, more secure strip bonds?

 ✔ Sell some bonds and the mutual fund, and hold cash or T-bills until things settle down?

 ✔ Just grin and bear it?

Notice how it is always easier to make decisions about other people's money?

ANYBANK CANADA, INC.
2001 Walla Walla Blvd, Toronto, ON M5R 3K5

Registered Retirement Savings Plan
Statement of Account

March 2001

Currency: CANADIAN DOLLARS

Book VI

Somewhere over the Rainbow: Retirement Planning

▮ DETAILS OF YOUR INVESTMENTS — CANADIAN DOLLARS

We have identified foreign investments with the letter F.

Cash and cash equivalents	Book value ($)	Value on Mar 30, 2001 ($)
CASH	543.11	543.11

Fixed income	Face value segregated s custody c ($)	Book value ($)	Price per $100 on Mar 30, 2001 ($)	Value on Mar 30, 2001 ($)
CPN GOVERNMENT OF CANADA DUE DEC 01 2006	15,000 s	7,747.50	73.870	11,080.50
CPN NEWFOUNDLAND & LABRADOR HYDRO DUE DEC 15 2008	11,860 s	4,981.20	63.356	7,514.02
CPN NFLD LAB HYDRO DUE JAN 14 2009	29,707 s	12,384.84	63.006	18,717.19
Total fixed income		25,113.54		37,311.71

Mutual funds	Number of shares or units segregated s custody c	Book value ($)	Price per share or unit on Mar 30, 2001 ($)	Value on Mar 30, 2001 ($)
FFIDELITY FOCUS HEALTH CARE FUND DSC	261.197 s	5,047.13	18.250	4,766.85
Total Canadian dollar investments		30,703.78		42,621.67

▮ DETAILS OF YOUR ACCOUNT ACTIVITY — CANADIAN DOLLARS

Date	Activity	Description	Number of shares or units	Price per share or unit ($)	Added to (deducted from) your account ($)	Cash Balance ($)
Mar 1		Cash balance				542.03
Mar 16	Interest	INTEREST ON CREDIT BALANCE AT 2 3/4% 02/16 THRU 03/06				0.78
Mar 16	Interest	INTEREST ON CREDIT BALANCE AT 2 1/4% 03/07 THRU 03/15				0.30
Mar 30		Cash balance				543.11

page 1 of 2

Figure 3-2: More specific account activity appears on page two of this RRSP statement.

When It Makes Sense to Invest in Your Employer

Should you hold shares of the company you work for inside your RRSP? Some employers encourage this idea, but beware the possible consequences of investing too much in one place. Spending a large portion of your RRSP on shares in your employer's firm means you are relying on the company for income, benefits, and retirement funds. If the company has bad times, you could lose all three.

It makes sense to spend your RRSP contributions on shares of your employer's company under these conditions:

✔ You are totally confident that the company is well-managed and maintains a strong market position. In other words, your company is a market leader and is virtually debt-free.

✔ The company offers you shares at a discounted price. (It should be at least 10 percent to make it worthwhile.)

✔ The company offers you a *share purchase plan,* where it matches your contribution — usually on a 50 percent basis. So, for every dollar you spend to buy shares for your RRSP, the company adds 50 cents.

✔ You limit the value of its shares to no more than 20 percent of the total value of your RRSP.

Chapter 4

Withdrawing Money from Your RRSP

*I*t may burrow its way into your mind gradually, or it may spring full-blown when you open your RRSP statement someday and realize that you have more assets in your plan than you expected. The temptation may be to withdraw some funds now instead of waiting for retirement, or to borrow a few dollars — it's your money, after all — and arrange to pay it back later. You may even like the idea of using your RRSP assets as a mortgage on your home.

All of these options, and a few others as well, may present themselves. What do you do? The general answer is the same one you were told as a child: Resist temptation. If you've managed to do this without fail, you may not need this chapter. But if your hand slipped into the cookie jar from time to time, you should absorb the advice and guidelines carefully.

Why Your RRSP Is Not for a Rainy Day

The biggest risk as your RRSP builds is to think of it as an emergency stash, a lump of money you can use when there's not enough cash in the bank or room on your credit card. It's your money, after all, and no one will scold you for getting your hands on it years ahead of time. But if you do, you'll lose three ways.

Sharing your withdrawal with CCRA

Your first loss will be in withholding tax deducted even before you get your hands on the cash. This is just the beginning of Canada Customs and Revenue Agency's penalty for being impatient. The entire amount you withdraw will be added to your taxable income for the year, and while the withholding tax will be credited, you will almost certainly pay even more at tax time according to your tax bracket (see Table 4-1).

Table 4-1	Withholding Tax Rates on RRSP Withdrawals	
	Canada (Excluding Quebec)	*Quebec*
Up to $5,000	10%	21%
$5,001 to $15,000	20%	30%
$15,001 and up	30%	35%

If you withdraw $10,000 from your RRSP, you'll actually receive only $8,000, because 20 percent, or $2,000, is sent to the CCRA to be credited on your income-tax return for the year. In Quebec, you'll pocket just $7,000, even though your RRSP is now $10,000 poorer.

If you must withdraw funds (and only in dire circumstances, remember) make it in amounts of $5,000 or less, on consecutive days, to reduce the immediate tax impact. If you withdraw $5,000 today and $5,000 tomorrow, you'll receive a net amount of $9,000; withdraw the $10,000 all at once and you'll receive a net of $8,000.

Stunting your RRSP's growth

Your second loss is the potential tax-sheltered growth you would have enjoyed inside your RRSP. This can be enormous and, in time, will dwarf the immediate funds you obtain (see Table 4-2).

Table 4-2	Future Cost of Early RRSP Withdrawals (Assuming Annual Compound Returns of 10 Percent)		
Amount	*In 10 Years*	*In 20 Years*	*In 30 Years*
$1,000	$2,600	$6,730	$17,450
$5,000	$12,970	$33,640	$87,250
$10,000	$25,940	$67,280	$174,550

If you're currently 30 years from retirement, the $5,000 you withdraw for today's needs will reduce your RRSP's value by almost $90,000 when you're ready to use it. That's a hefty price to pay on top of the income tax assessed.

Book VI

Somewhere over the Rainbow: Retirement Planning

Squandering contribution room: No double dipping

Finally, the third loss is contribution room in your RRSP. The $5,000 you withdraw today cannot be made up later. It was based on previous income levels, and no amount of future income or pleading to the CCRA will return it.

Financial emergencies arise, of course. But unless and until every other alternative has been explored, it simply does not make sense to take funds out of your RRSP to meet them.

The added risk of spousal RRSP withdrawals

Withdrawing funds from a spousal RRSP is fraught with even more risk. Only the planholder is permitted to take money from a spousal RRSP, and if no contributions have been made to the spousal plan within three years of the last contribution, the withdrawn funds will be taxed as the contributor's income, not the planholder's. Thus, if you contribute to your spouse's RRSP this year and he or she withdraws money from it any time during the next two years, the Canada Customs and Revenue Agency taxes the money as though it went directly into your pocket. Exceptions to this rule are the following:

✔ The parties are living apart due to a breakdown in the relationship.

✔ The contributing spouse has died.

✔ Either spouse is a non-resident.

✔ The planholder transfers the money to purchase an annuity, which cannot be accessed for three years.

✔ The money is transferred to an RRIF.

✔ The money is transferred to a Registered Pension Plan and not withdrawn for three years.

Combining RRSPs and RESPs

RRSPs have siblings, including *RRIFs,* or *Registered Retirement Income Funds* — more about them in Chapter 5 — and *RESPs,* or *Registered Education Savings Plans.* The objective of RESPs is to provide parents and grandparents with the opportunity to accumulate funds to cover the cost of higher education for their children and grandchildren. While RESP contributions cannot be deducted from taxable income the way RRSP contributions can, the money remains tax sheltered. As though to make up for the lack of tax benefits, the federal government adds an extra 20 percent of annual RESP contributions, to a maximum of $400 annually.

Here's where your RRSP comes in: If you open an RESP for your child and he or she decides not to pursue a higher education, you can transfer up to $40,000 from the RESP into your RRSP or a spousal RRSP. This can be done if

✔ The RESP has been in place for at least ten years.

✔ The child has reached age 21 and will not be attending an institution of higher learning.

✔ Contribution room exists in the RRSP or spousal RRSP (if no contribution room exists, the RESP funds are returned to the contributor, subject to income tax plus a 20 percent penalty).

This makes an RESP a very attractive prospect. Your contributions build tax-free, helped along by government assistance, and if your pride and joy decides to become a street vendor instead of a doctor or lawyer, you can soothe your disappointment by bumping up the value of your RRSP.

RESP rules

Keep these guidelines in mind as you merrily sock away dollars for your little one(s).

The maximum annual RESP contribution you can make is $4,000 per child. Twenty percent of however much you contribute over a one-year period is matched by the federal government — to a maximum of $400. (This may not sound like much, but over time, it can really build up.)

A few more points to remember:

✔ There is a lifetime cap on the RESP's value, at $42,000 per child. And because the maximum life of the plan is 25 years, your pride and joy had better head off to school by then, or better yet, be back and graduated so they can start paying you back.

✔ Any missed required payments will be included in income for that year, and subject to tax.

✔ Just as with RRSP contributions, you have the first 60 days of a year — that is, until the end of February — to make a repayment and have it credited to the previous year.

✔ You can withdraw principal at any time without taxation. However, you may have to pay back a portion of the government grants that you received.

✔ Interest paid on cash borrowed to contribute to an RESP is not tax deductible.

If your child doesn't go to Ivory Tower College, aside from transferring the funds to an RRSP, you can get your original capital contributions back, tax-free. And you can get the plan earnings back if the plan has been in place for at least ten years, with returned earnings taxable to you, the contributor.

The Lifelong Learning Plan and Your RRSP

If your kids decide not to pursue their education past high school, this does not mean that you can't. In fact, the government's Lifelong Learning Plan enables you to finance an education for either you or your spouse with money from your RRSP without subjecting it to income tax or penalty. The maximum withdrawal permitted from each plan is $20,000 over a four-year period. Other rules include the following:

✔ You must be enrolled, on a full-time basis, in a qualifying educational program before March of the year following the withdrawal.

✔ A *qualifying educational program* is one at a university or college, or certain training programs of at least three months' duration and including at least ten hours of instruction or course work per week.

✔ The amounts withdrawn for this program are repayable to the RRSP in equal installments over a ten-year period.

✔ The first payment is due either during the last year you were enrolled in the program or during the sixth year after you made your first withdrawal under this program, whichever is earliest.

The Home Buyers' Plan and Your RRSP

If you have built up funds in your RRSP and have yet to purchase your first home, here's another way to put the money to use before your retirement years. The *Home Buyers' Plan (HBP)* is a loan from your RRSP to you, free of tax and interest payments. To qualify, you or your spouse must not have owned a home and lived in it as your principal residence for five years prior to making the application.

The Canada Customs and Revenue Agency counts "five years" this way, when it comes to the HBP: Take the four years preceding the year you withdraw the money, plus the period of the year you make your withdrawal, ending 31 days prior to the date you take the money out of your RRSP. Clear? Good.

The exception to the five-year rule applies where disabled family members are concerned. If you already own your own home, you can use the HBP to purchase a home that provides better accessibility for a disabled and dependent relative if he or she qualifies for the Disability Tax Credit.

You normally get one opportunity to use this plan. Here's how it works:

✔ The property you are purchasing must be in Canada and must not have been owned previously by you or your spouse.

✔ It must be occupied as your principal residence within one year of buying it.

✔ The home can be existing or brand-new.

✔ The home can be detached, semi-detached, a townhouse or condominium, a mobile home, an apartment, or a share in a co-op housing corporation where ownership is transferable.

✔ Both you and your spouse may borrow up to $20,000 each from your individual RRSPs.

✔ Funds contributed to your RRSP within 90 days of the loan cannot be withdrawn for this program. Thus, make a contribution to your RRSP on February 28 and it cannot be applied to the Home Buyers' Plan until June 1.

✔ Annual repayments to your RRSP must be made on or before December 31 of each year (but, as with RRSPs, any payment made within the first 60 days of the year can be credited to the previous year).

✔ Repayments begin in the second calendar year following the calendar year in which the withdrawal is made. (Repayments on loans made in the year 2003 must begin in 2005.)

✔ Annual repayments will be determined by dividing the amount borrowed by 15. Thus, a deduction of $20,000 from your RRSP under this plan will require annual repayments of $1,333.33.

✔ Repayments are kept separate from contributions and are not tax-deductible.

✔ Repayments are made to the financial institution administering your RRSP and must be accompanied by a special RRSP Repayment Form available from your bank, trust company, or whoever is holding your RRSP for you. This is to prevent the money from being credited as a regular, tax-deductible RRSP contribution.

✔ Repayments larger than the scheduled amount will reduce subsequent payments by a proportional amount.

✔ Miss an annual repayment and you're in deep doo-doo with the CCRA. The missed repayment will be declared as taxable income for that year. And, as a second slap on the wrist, the money will be deemed a permanent withdrawal, which means you can never put it back in your RRSP. Yikes!

Does this make the HBP worthwhile? It will for many people. From its inception in 1992 to the end of 2003, about 600,000 Canadians had taken advantage of it. Should you?

Buying your first home is as much an emotional decision as an economic one, and no one can put a price on another person's emotional satisfaction. Unless you can sweet-talk a relative or friend into providing an interest-free loan to help acquire your dream home, the Home Buyers' Plan is your only alternative. Just keep these serious drawbacks in mind before taking this step:

✔ Once the money is out of your RRSP, it is not building through compound interest. This inevitably reduces the value of your plan over time . . . by a significant amount.

✔ What happens if you find yourself unable to manage the repayments? You'll suffer that two-pronged penalty of both paying income tax on the missed repayment and not being allowed to return it to your RRSP. It probably means you won't be making any RRSP contributions either. Consider this: If you had difficulty raising money to purchase your home by other means, how will you be able to handle mortgage payments, maintenance, RRSP repayments, *and* RRSP contributions unless your income takes a major leap?

✔ Do not count on the value of your home increasing over time, making up for lost growth in your RRSP as a result of taking out this loan. Given the constant fluctuations in property values, you shouldn't count on it happening.

All in all, the program has more drawbacks than benefits. But if you still feel the way to your dream home is through your RRSP, applications for the Home Buyers' Plan can be obtained from a Canada Customs and Revenue Agency office.

Book VI

Somewhere over the Rainbow: Retirement Planning

Bowing Out Early

It may hit you while reviewing an especially rewarding RRSP statement or while sitting in traffic on your way to work, breathing the fumes of the car ahead of you. You may get the idea while on vacation, or upon hearing of the early demise of an old friend or school chum.

Wherever and whenever it occurs, at some point around 50 or beyond, you'll ask yourself: "Why am I still working? Why don't I turn my RRSP assets into something that will produce an income, and leave the rat race?"

It's a question only you can answer, along with assistance from your spouse, family, and financial adviser or investment counsellor. But before you go that far, here are some items to review:

- ✔ Take stock of your entire financial situation. Review your debts (including mortgage) as well as your RRSP assets.

- ✔ Do you have any other retirement income from private pensions? Will it enable you to retire early? Will there be a penalty (in reduced benefits) if you do?

- ✔ Will you be totally retired or do you plan to work part time? If so, how much will you earn? Is this realistic?

- ✔ Review the estimated percentage of current income you'll require (see Chapter 2).

- ✔ Consider carefully the benefits of holding off retirement for a year or more. At middle age, about half your RRSP assets should be in equities. If the stock market is currently at a low ebb, this could reduce your expected retirement income. It may turn around and boost your nest egg substantially by this time next year. If the markets are galloping along, the reward for delaying retirement could be substantial. For example, if your equities total $300,000 and the market returns 20 percent over the next year, that's a growth of $60,000 in this sector alone.

- ✔ Some investment counsellors suggest a fake "retirement trial" for a few weeks. You'll still be working, but try to live on only the amount of income you expect to have during retirement. (You can do this on paper, if you like.)

Retirement is no longer a 65-and-out proposition for most people. Careful long-term management of your RRSP provides you with options, and options create freedom.

Chapter 5

The Time Has Come to Cash In!

· ·

In This Chapter

▶ Facing the end of your employment career

▶ Winding down your RRSP

▶ Deciding whether to continue working

▶ Evaluating your options: Lump sum, annuity, or RRIF

▶ Understanding RRIFs

▶ Withdrawing money from your RRIF

▶ Dealing with LIFs and L-RIFs

▶ Maintaining growth in your RRIF

▶ Choosing strategies for growth *and* income

▶ Measuring other income sources

▶ Ensuring you make objective decisions about your retirement and your RRIF

· ·

*A*fter years of paying into your RRSP, you'll make a decision somewhere, sometime, to turn the tables on your plan so that it will begin paying you. These payments will form part of your retirement income.

Your decision to begin drawing benefits from your hard work and diligence will be based on economics and emotions. In all likelihood, the larger your RRSP balance, the smaller the emotional impact. Leaving your work career, after all, is a little like taking your first parachute jump: No matter how carefully you have planned, there is always the risk that something can go wrong.

The End of Your RRSP as You Know It

You can begin drawing income from your RRSP assets at any stage of your life. Some people choose to do this in their 50s, expecting CPP (Canada Pension Plan) benefits to (they hope) kick in as early as age 60, supplemented (they hope again) with OAS (Old Age Security) benefits at age 65. Others enjoy the luxury — or bear the necessity — of continuing to contribute to their RRSP well beyond traditional retirement age.

The life of your RRSP winds up at the end of the calendar year in which you turn 69. This, by the way, is a brick-wall deadline. If you do not make some arrangement to convert your RRSP into an income-producing investment by that date, Canada Customs and Revenue Agency assumes you have deducted the entire amount as one lump sum and taxes you accordingly. If you think the income tax you pay on your annual salary is substantial, wait until you see the size of your tax bill on a lump-sum income that could total several hundred thousand dollars in one year. So ignore this date at your peril.

Until age 69, you can manage to be semi-retired, draw income from previous RRSP assets, and contribute to an RRSP — all at the same time. Income from a part-time job qualifies for RRSP contributions, which is one way to counter the risk of inflation.

Consider the following situation: You decide to retire at age 60, with RRSP assets that are able to generate about $20,000 income annually. Added to the pension you're entitled to, and taking early CPP benefits, you have about $44,000 in annual income. However, because you still have a few years to go before the age 69 cut-off, you may decide to continue working in a part-time capacity, start contributing to a new RRSP, and reap the benefits of your hard-earned $20,000 RRSP income.

Suppose you accept a part-time opportunity that pays $1,250 per month, or $15,000 annually. The work not only provides extra income (up to $59,000 annually — see Table 5-1) but also enables you to open a new RRSP, contributing almost $3,000 annually to it and taking a tax benefit as a result. You will be able to do this, if you choose, until you turn 69, potentially providing you with an extra $40,000 or so in new RRSP assets.

By accepting the job after the end of the calendar year in which you first begin drawing CPP benefits, you won't affect your government pension income. If you do both in the same calendar year, Ottawa taxes back the CPP payments; Ottawa permits you to both earn an income and keep all your CPP benefits beginning the calendar year *after* your first CPP benefit.

Table 5-1	Earning and Saving Your RRSP Assets
Source	*Amount*
Old RRSP income	$20,000
CPP	$6,000
Private pension	$18,000
Part-time work	$15,000
Total	$59,000

Moving from RRSP to RRIF

Whenever you choose to begin cashing in on your RRSP assets, you must convert them to one or a combination of three alternatives: a lump-sum payment, an annuity, or a Registered Retirement Income Fund (RRIF).

For almost everyone, the choice will be either an annuity or an RRIF. Withdrawing your RRSP assets in a lump sum triggers income tax on the entire amount. There may be times when this makes sense to some people, but I can't think of any.

If you've been successful at managing your assets through a self-directed RRSP and still feel comfortable doing so, your best choice to produce retirement income will likely be a *Registered Retirement Income Fund,* or *RRIF.* A RRIF is similar in operation to an annuity and provides a better opportunity to generate more income. For example, you can build inflation protection into your RRIF through diversification and laddered GICs (guaranteed investment certificates).

Do you have private pension benefits or deferred profit-sharing plan assets from your working career? If they're not locked in, you can roll them into your RRSP assets when converting them to an RRIF, which gives you more investment clout with fewer administrative fees and headaches.

Two more pluses for RRIFs: They provide almost total flexibility, which will enable you to take advantage of certain economic conditions; and with careful management they can provide a lump-sum estate for your beneficiaries.

How an RRIF Works

The easiest way to grasp the concept of an RRIF is to consider it an RRSP in reverse. Over many years, you paid the RRSP. Now the RRSP pays you. You manage these two investment vehicles differently, but perhaps not as much so as you may expect. The biggest change is a shift in emphasis from growth to income, although you still need to pay attention to your plan's growth to counter the risk of inflation and avoid outliving your money.

Rules for RRIF withdrawals

In case you may want to leave all your RRIF assets inside the plan, building to Everest heights of value . . . well, you can't. You must withdraw a minimum amount (sometimes called a *minimum annual payout,* or *MAP*) from your RRIF each year, measured as a percentage of the assets in your plan at the end of the previous year. The amount varies with your age, as shown in Table 5-2.

Table 5-2	Minimum Withdrawals from RRIF by Age (Percentage of Assets)				
Age	*Minimum*	*Age*	*Minimum*	*Age*	*Minimum*
69	4.76%	78	8.33%	87	11.33%
70	5.00%	79	8.53%	88	11.96%
71	7.38%	80	8.75%	89	12.71%
72	7.48%	81	8.99%	90	13.62%
73	7.59%	82	9.27%	91	14.73%
74	7.71%	83	9.58%	92	16.12%
75	7.85%	84	9.93%	93	17.92%
76	7.99%	85	10.33%	94	20.00%
77	8.15%	86	10.79%	95+	20.00%

Example: If your RRIF value is $400,000 at the end of the year in which you turn 69, you have to withdraw at least 5 percent of that amount, or $20,000, the following year, when you are 70. The financial institution managing your RRIF can arrange to make payments to you during the year according to your direction. (You can always take out more than the minimum amount, of course.) At the end of each year, if you have not withdrawn the minimum amount, a cheque will be issued to you making up the difference.

If your spouse is younger than you, you can base the minimum withdrawal amount on your spouse's age, leaving more of your RRIF assets tax-sheltered to continue building in value.

No income tax is withheld when withdrawing the annual minimum from your RRIF. Taxes are withheld, however, on amounts exceeding the minimum. Using the example above, if you withdrew $25,000 instead of the minimum $20,000, income tax would be applied to the $5,000 above your minimum at source (that is, withdrawn by the financial institution managing your RRIF and paid to the Canada Customs and Revenue Agency on your behalf). All RRIF income, of course, is subject to income tax, and a return must be filed.

Look for income, but keep your eye on growth

While you were building your RRSP assets, you could see the difference a few percentage points of annual returns made over time. When managing your RRIF, the impact can be just as dramatic and, best of all, more immediate. If you can manage to boost the average annual returns from your RRIF from 4½ percent to 8 percent, as shown in Table 5-3, both your retirement and your estate will be substantially wealthier. The withdrawal levels are the minimum annual amounts set by Canada Customs and Revenue Agency.

Table 5-3		RRIF Returns by Age and Percentage Return			
		4½ Percent Return		*8 Percent Return*	
Age	*Percentage*	*Fund*	*Withdrawal*	*Fund*	*Withdrawal*
65	4.00%	$300,000	$12,000	$300,000	$12,000
66	4.17%	$301,209	$12,550	$311,486	$12,979
67	4.35%	$301,909	$13,126	$322,870	$14,038
68	4.55%	$302,051	$13,730	$334,061	$15,185
69	4.76%	$301,581	$14,361	$344,951	$16,426
70	5.00%	$300,443	$15,022	$355,417	$17,771
71	7.38%	$298,577	$22,035	$365,318	$26,960
72	7.48%	$289,444	$21,650	$366,429	$27,409
73	7.59%	$289,294	$21,274	$367,160	$27,867
74	7.71%	$271,117	$20,903	$367,472	$28,332
75	7.85%	$261,908	$20,560	$367,324	$28,835

Launch your RRIF with $300,000, accept 4½ percent returns, make minimum annual withdrawals, and at age 70 you'll be required to take just over $15,000 from a balance of $300,000. Get an 8 percent annual return — from income plus growth — and at age 70 your minimum withdrawal will be almost $3,000 higher, *plus your RRIF will have increased in value by over $55,000.* If you can achieve this level of growth with a reasonable degree of risk, why not?

During your working years, you probably looked for ways to raise your salary level from time to time. Improving your education, adding new work skills, and changing employers are the most common techniques used in search of a bigger paycheque. Why not maintain the same approach with your RRIF? The tactics are different, of course, and since your basic expenses are likely fixed, you don't need a constantly growing amount of money each year. But some careful planning and periodic reviews can put several thousand dollars in your pocket each year from the same nest egg.

These current economic times present a challenge to RRIF owners looking for more income. Inflation remains low, which is a good sign. But low inflation also means low interest rates, which makes it difficult to obtain high returns from some RRIF assets. In mid-2003, five-year interest rates from GIC-based RRIF investments fluttered around the 4 percent mark, while one-year GIC rates hovered a full percentage lower. If you've managed to accumulate $200,000 in your RRIF, these interest-rate levels would produce an annual income of just $7,000 before eating into your principal. At that level, annuities begin to look pretty good, even with all their disadvantages.

Remember our old friends Risk and Reward? If you want to increase your earnings from the RRIF above a paltry 3 to 4 percent annually, you'll have to accept some risk. But this is not an easy time in your life to accept risk. You need both solid financial advice and an awareness of your own risk-tolerance level. Fortunately, by now you've spent many years getting to know both, so some of these decisions may be a little easier to make than you think.

Looking at Other Options, Part 1: Annuities

A generation or so ago, back when many Canadians considered life insurance almost a basic requirement, annuities were very popular. Promoted and managed by insurance companies, annuities could be purchased with the funds built up inside *whole-life insurance plans.* Whole-life insurance, thanks to higher premiums, provided both immediate life insurance coverage and a cash-value pot of gold on your 65th birthday. (The alternative to whole-life insurance, known as *term insurance,* provides only a lump-sum payment to your beneficiary and no cash value when you reach 65.)

Millions of Canadians chose whole-life insurance as a means of saving for the future, and in the process made the insurance companies very wealthy indeed. Part of the sales pitch used by insurance salespeople was that the money claimed by the policyholder at age 65 could be used to purchase an annuity from the same insurance company. An annuity is a contract that guarantees a series of payments in exchange for a lump-sum investment. The size of the payments depends on a number of factors, including the following:

- The amount of money used to purchase the investment

- The age of the person purchasing the annuity (the annuitant)

- The annuitant's gender

- The length of time the payments are guaranteed (anywhere from five years to the lifespan of the annuitant)

- Whether or not the annuitant chooses to continue the payments to his or her surviving spouse

Book VI

Somewhere over the Rainbow: Retirement Planning

In other words, you paid the insurance company while you worked, and the insurance company paid you after age 65. Or, to put it cynically: When you are paying insurance premiums, the insurance company is betting you will live; when you are collecting an annuity, the insurance company is betting you will die. Either way, money flows through the hands of the insurance company, providing it with many opportunities to make a profit.

Annuities began to fall out of favour around the same time that Canadians realized they could buy term insurance at a much lower premium price than whole-life insurance. They could invest the difference themselves and beat the insurance companies at their own game. Annuities continue to be popular with folks who prefer not to get their hands dirty and have their minds cluttered with investment decisions. They prefer to choose among various annuity options and settle down to a fixed income for the rest of their life. Market turbulence? Risk versus reward? Income versus growth? To an annuitant, those are all someone else's concern.

With an annuity, all your decisions are made up front; the most critical is choosing whom to purchase the annuity from. Annuity payments fluctuate not only according to the firm providing the annuity, but also according to the date you purchase the annuity. The $100,000 you invest in an annuity this month could purchase more or less of an income for you next month. Whether you choose to wait, hoping the rates will rise, or buy now, fearing the rates will fall, *you are locked in for life*. That's the minus side of annuities.

Annuities are calculated on the basis of the monthly income paid per $50,000 or $100,000 originally invested, and are influenced by various factors and options (see Table 5-4).

Table 5-4	Factors Influencing Annuity Payment Rates	
Factor	*Payments Increased*	*Payments Reduced*
Age	Older	Younger
Gender	Male	Female
Guaranteed term	5 years	10 years (or longer)
Surviving spouse	Excluded	Included

Table 5-5 provides some idea of the range of annuity payments provided by major Canadian insurance companies for a male in good health as of mid-2003. These rates change day to day, so don't expect them to be exactly on the mark when you read this. But if no major economic event has occurred between now and then, these rates may still be in the ballpark.

Table 5-5	Ten-Year Guaranteed Monthly Annuity Payments per $100,000 Invested, by Age of Annuitant (as of May 2003)			
Male	*Age 55*	*Age 60*	*Age 65*	*Age 70*
Canada Life	$579.10	$624.17	$682.76	$753.95
Empire Life	$573.94	$627.57	$696.68	$767.99
Equitable Life	$584.70	$630.78	$690.94	$765.33
Great-West Life	$537.17	$579.33	$634.84	$703.28
Imperial Life	$569.71	$613.35	$671.28	$743.43
Manulife Investments	$564.93	$612.00	$675.50	$749.45
Maritime Life	$573.26	$622.26	$685.15	$760.25
Standard Life	$554.61	$601.33	$661.63	$735.62
Sun Life Assurance	$568.93	$610.85	$666.85	$735.85
Transamerica Life Cda	$587.54	$633.88	$695.33	$770.87

Source: Cannex, May 12, 2003

Using this payment schedule, a man aged 60 with RRSP assets of $400,000 could guarantee at least ten years of monthly income, before taxes, as low as $2,317.32 (if he chose Great-West Life) or as high as $2,535.52 (if he chose Transamerica Life Canada). Should he die before the guaranteed period expired, the payments would continue to his beneficiary to the end of the guaranteed period.

Based on the $400,000 original investment used to purchase the annuity, the Transamerica Life Canada annuity would generate an annual income of $30,426.24, which equals an annual return of 7.6 percent. Five-year GIC rates at the time were hovering around 4 percent annually, so this sounds very attractive . . . until you remember that this form of annuity contains no protection against inflation, which could quickly erode the spending power. Annuities indexed to inflation are available, but they would generate substantially less income than the example shown here.

Book VI

Somewhere over the Rainbow: Retirement Planning

A couple of other points worth considering:

- ✔ That $30,426.24 annual income, guaranteed for ten years, means the insurance company is on the hook for only $304,262.40 if you croak before the ten-year guarantee is up. Even if the insurance company generates the current GIC rates of 4.5 percent annual return from your $400,000, it will earn $180,000 over the same ten years, for a total of $580,000. Is this a good deal for you? Perhaps, if peace of mind is your sole concern.

- ✔ Annuity payments aren't quite as volatile as the stock market, but they vary a surprising amount over relatively short periods of time. Transamerica Life, for example, paid 60-year-old males looking for a ten-year guarantee $607.32 per $100,000 per month in mid-1999. Less than four years later, 60-year-old males were collecting almost $30 per month more for the same amount under the same conditions from the same company.

- ✔ Waive the ten-year guarantee, which means payments cease when you die, and you don't increase your income all that much. Canada Life, for example, will pay you only another $15 per month per $100,000. Should you die after receiving just one payment, the insurance company cleans up and probably throws a party in your honour. Big deal. Take the guarantee.

For comparison's sake, Table 5-6 presents annuity rates for females from the same companies and for the same guaranteed term, posted on the same day. Notice that the rates are slightly lower, reflecting the longer life expectancy of females.

Table 5-6	Ten-Year Guaranteed Monthly Annuity Payments per $100,000 Invested, by Age of Annuitant (as of May 2003)			
Female	*Age 55*	*Age 60*	*Age 65*	*Age 70*
Canada Life	$538.57	$573.84	$621.40	$684.58
Empire Life	$540.46	$583.18	$641.13	$707.91
Equitable Life	$551.27	$588.95	$639.27	$705.72
Great-West Life	$506.16	$540.23	$586.21	$647.24
Imperial Life	$536.42	$571.72	$620.00	$684.94
Manulife Investments	$527.06	$565.34	$615.92	$684.89
Maritime Life	$533.69	$574.18	$627.83	$697.69
Standard Life	$525.30	$564.51	$617.43	$688.03
Sun Life Assurance	$534.75	$570.23	$613.39	$676.49
Transamerica Life Cda	$551.25	$588.06	$638.45	$705.99

Source: Cannex, May 12, 2003

Why such a wide range in annuity payments?

Approach two different insurance companies for their annuity rates, and you'll discover different levels of payments — sometimes a substantial difference (see Tables 5-5 and 5-6). What accounts for such a wide range? Three things:

- ✓ **Tables of mortality:** Insurance companies employ actuaries who spend their entire careers estimating how long people will live. Each company's actuaries can arrive at different estimates, and the company who decides you will live longest will offer you the smallest annuity.

- ✓ **Interest rates:** The money you use to purchase your annuity is invested by the insurance company. Wise investments generate bigger returns, which enable the insurance company to pay you a bigger annuity.

- ✓ **Guarantees:** The cost of annuity options you choose, including guaranteed terms and surviving-spouse payments, are priced differently by each insurance company according to the expected risk.

As you can see, to earn the most income from an annuity it helps to be older (you won't be expected to live as long) and male (ditto), with a shorter guaranteed term and payments that cease upon your death. Payments due to you during the guaranteed term can be left to a beneficiary in the event of your death.

Should you choose an annuity for your retirement income?

Perhaps, if the following applies to you:

- ✔ You have relatively small retirement savings that must generate an income for a very long time because you are relatively young, your family has a history of living to a ripe old age, or both of these factors.

- ✔ You want the peace of mind that comes from knowing you will have a fixed amount of income.

- ✔ You prefer to avoid making any decisions when it comes to investing your money.

But be aware of these drawbacks:

- ✔ You lose control of your savings and the returns they can generate for you.

- ✔ Lump-sum withdrawals — to deal with a financial emergency, for example — are not permitted.

- ✔ The rate of return will be lower than the rates available from quality mutual funds. If the stock market begins generating high annual returns, in the vicinity of 20 percent, and your annuity is returning only 6 or 7 percent, you'll just have to stand on the sidelines and watch.

- ✔ Unless you choose an indexed annuity, inflation could seriously erode your income over the years (but remember that indexed annuities also pay substantially less money to you each month).

- ✔ If you don't choose a guaranteed term or a surviving spouse option and you die shortly after the annuity begins (it happens more often than you may think), neither your beneficiaries nor your estate receive a penny.

- ✔ Choosing various options, such as guaranteed terms, payment to a surviving spouse, and so on, reduces your annuity income.

- ✔ Your annuity decision is locked in — literally for the rest of your life. So don't make it in haste, and be sure to discuss your decision with your spouse, your family, and your financial adviser before signing on the dotted line.

Looking at Other Options, Part II: LIFs and L-RIFs

If you're entitled to private pension benefits that are *locked in* (often referred to as a *locked-in retirement account,* or *LIRA*), you're faced with another decision. At one time, locked-in pensions accrued during your working years provided no withdrawals; the total amount of your pension was used to purchase an annuity, with all the drawbacks reviewed earlier in this chapter.

Various provinces, beginning with Quebec, saw the unfairness of this restriction years ago and introduced legislation permitting locked-in pension benefits to be converted into a *life income fund,* or *LIF.* Think of a LIF as a locked-in RRIF. You determine how to invest and manage your LIF in the same way you handle your RRIF, and you must be 55 years of age before you can make any withdrawals. The same minimum payouts apply for LIFs and RRIFs, but a LIF adds a restriction to the maximum amount you can withdraw. This is to ensure that assets remain in the LIF when you turn 80 and you are required to use money left in your LIF to purchase a life annuity.

This is where things get complicated.

Unlike the fairly simplified formula for determining minimum withdrawals from an RRIF, the calculations for maximum withdrawals from a LIF in most provinces may remind you of high-school algebra:

Maximum LIF withdrawal = B $\times$ M $\times$ F

B is the *balance* in your LIF account on January 1 of the year you withdraw the money.

M is the number of *months* remaining until you turn 90.

F stands for *factor,* based on a combination of current long-term Canadian bond rates and 6 percent annual returns.

Alberta, Saskatchewan, Manitoba, and Ontario tweak the LIF idea with a *locked-in retirement income fund,* or *L-RIF,* which does not require you to purchase a life annuity at age 80. Each province sets its own withdrawal formula for L-RIFs. In Ontario, for example, L-RIF owners can simply withdraw the previous year's investment return from their L-RIF. This ensures that some assets from their L-RIF will remain in their estate when they die.

If you have a LIRA, consult with your financial adviser, investment counsellor, or the pension fund administrator for maximum withdrawal guidelines in your province.

Benefiting from Other Income Sources

Even after converting your RRSP assets into an income-producing plan, a number of other sources of money remain available to you. How you choose them and use them is up to you.

Your C/QPP benefits

When you turn 60, you are eligible for early C/QPP (Canada/Quebec Pension Plan) benefits. The formula sets full benefits at age 65, reducing them by one-half percent for each month under the threshold age. Thus, at age 60, you are entitled to 70 percent of full C/QPP benefits (5 years = 60 months $\times$ $\frac{1}{2}$% = 30% subtracted from 100). Similarly, if you delay applying for C/QPP benefits past your 65th birthday, the benefits rise by one-half percent monthly.

Book VI

Somewhere over the Rainbow: Retirement Planning

Should you apply early? The consensus is a resounding "Yes!" for two reasons. First, if you wait until 65 to receive benefits, it takes a long time for the increased C/QPP payments to catch up with those lost five years. At current benefit rates, for example, you'll receive about $126,000 in total payments over the 20 years between age 60 and age 80. Wait until you're 65 to receive them and you'll be paid $134,000 over the 15 years between age 65 and age 80. Few people believe it's worth waiting five years to obtain a paltry $8,000 more in total benefits.

The second reason for applying early is the usual uncertainty about any government benefit. It may be withdrawn or seriously modified at any time. If you have been paying into it through all your working years, you are entitled to its benefits. Go get 'em. Just remember that your benefits won't begin appearing in your mailbox automatically when you turn 60 years of age. You must apply for them, preferably about six months in advance of your 60th birthday. Applications are available from your local office of Human Resources Development Canada (HRDC), or call 1-800-277-9914. Information is also available on HRDC's Web site at www.hrdc-drhc.gc.ca.

Your home

Along with the money built up in your RRSP/RRIF, your house represents a substantial asset. For many people, its value is at least as high emotionally as it is economically. If you have raised your family, with all the attendant pain and pleasures, under the same roof for a few decades, selling your home can be a wrenching decision to make. Yet from a financial standpoint alone, your house, especially if it is mortgage-free, is both an underused asset and an ongoing expense. The equity in your home could be producing at least $5,000 annual income for each $100,000 of value, without depleting the principal by a penny.

Whether you choose to remain in the family home or another alternative is not a decision to be taken lightly, and it probably needn't be made right away either. So review all the following options, choose the one that you're most comfortable with at the moment, discuss it at length with your partner and family, and give it a good deal of thought.

✔ **Stay where you are.**

Pros: Comfort, security, no emotional stress, old friends and neighbours nearby.

Cons: Maintenance costs, physical labour needed for upkeep, no active use of equity.

✔ **Stay where you are and generate income from a reverse mortgage.**

Pros: Same as the preceding, plus active use of equity in home.

Cons: Maintenance costs and upkeep continue, possibility of little or no estate value remaining. (Check out Chapter 4 in Book III for more information about reverse mortgages.)

✔ **Sell current home, purchase smaller home or condominium, perhaps in less expensive neighbourhood or community.**

Pros: Reduce or eliminate maintenance and upkeep, opportunity for new friends and activities, some assets available for investment or income generation.

Cons: Moving expenses, perhaps some emotional stress, distance from friends and family, possible loss of rewarding activities such as a garden and workshop.

✔ **Sell current home and rent.**

Pros: Eliminate maintenance and upkeep, all home equity is available for investment or income generation.

Cons: Rental expense/drain on income.

✔ **Rent current home, move to apartment or other facility.**

Pros: Equity in home generates new source of income while maintaining asset value.

Cons: Maintenance, upkeep, tenant relationships, distance from family and friends.

A Step-by-Step Approach to Making Decisions

Retirement is an emotional time, a mix of contrasting feelings that range from anticipation and achievement to uncertainty and regret. The feelings you experience, and the way you deal with them, are yours alone. You may want, however, to impose some sort of structure on the decision making to assist your objectivity. Here are several things you should do:

- ✔ **Take your time.** Unless it's the end of the year in which you turn 69, you don't need to rush into converting your RRSP into an RRIF or annuity. So give yourself some time to think things over. What are the priorities of your retirement? Will you travel a lot? Buy toys such as a new car, a boat, or a home workshop? Spend more time in your garden or performing volunteer work? Are you concerned about leaving a fat inheritance to your children or grandchildren, or to charity? You had goals during your employment years, and you should set goals in retirement. It helps when making decisions about your RRSP assets.

- ✔ **If you don't need an RRIF income right away, don't use it.** You may take a part-time job or have some private pension income or assets outside your RRSP to live on for a while. If that's the case, and you are still under 69 years of age, don't be in a rush to convert your RRSP to an RRIF. If you can leave it alone for a year or two, it will continue to build value sheltered from tax.

- ✔ **Consider splitting your C/QPP benefits.** This is an option available to couples where one spouse has a substantially larger income than the other. The spouse with the higher income can have up to 50 percent of his or her income transferred to the other spouse, reducing income-tax levels.

- ✔ **Set up a total review of your RRSP portfolio.** Do it sooner, rather than later. Call your financial adviser or investment counsellor and ask for a complete review of all your assets — RRSP, home equity, life insurance, private pension income, non-registered investments, the works. Give yourself at least an hour to discuss and evaluate them all. Include your spouse in the session. Then consider how each fits into your strategy.

- ✔ **Don't limit your investment horizon.** In your 60s and 70s, you could need a retirement income for another 20 years or more. That qualifies as a long-term investment horizon, which deserves the same kind of investment tactics you used when building your RRSP. So don't overlook equity investments, especially quality growth-oriented mutual funds, as a means of building your RRIF assets and a hedge against inflation.

- ✔ **You can still make investments — and should.** Past age 69, you can't enjoy the tax-sheltered advantages of an RRSP, but that's no reason to avoid investing with available income if you have it. With two incomes, these investments should be made by the spouse with the lower income, to reduce income-tax levels.

Book VI

Somewhere over the Rainbow: Retirement Planning

Things to ask yourself before finalizing your RRIF investment mix

Are you planning any major changes to your lifestyle? Perhaps you're shopping for a vacation condominium, or you've come into a major inheritance. Or the change has been for the worse: You've lost your spouse, or your health has deteriorated substantially. How will any of these events affect your economic needs?

Have economic conditions changed? If inflation leaps out of the bushes and begins chewing up savings, or the stock market is riding either a severe bearish or wild bullish trend, this will influence your economic decisions.

Has your income tax status changed significantly? This is likely to be the result of assets held outside your RRIF. For example, if you sell your home and invest the proceeds, these earnings will be added to your RRIF income and could bump your marginal income tax to a higher bracket.

Are you worrying more about your investments? During your working years, it was easier to accept volatility and paper losses in your RRSP than it will be after you retire. When those same dollars are put to work earning you a living, their ups and downs are a little harder to deal with. If that's the case, perhaps you should exchange some growth and income in your RRIF for a little more security.

Have you maintained a balance in your RRIF investments? Paying attention to the relative size of equities and bonds in your RRSP has probably maintained the balance that feels best for you. RRIF owners can become a little neglectful of this aspect, so check once a year to ensure the balance between secure investments — GICs, bonds, T-bills — and equity investments matches your strategy and comfort level.

Do you still need the same rate of return? You may be delighted when you discover a portion of your RRIF is churning out 15 or 20 percent in average annual returns, but remember that this kind of growth usually involves risk and volatility. Are the returns worth it? Should you shift more emphasis to security?

Have your goals changed? Sitting on your back porch each day may have been fun for the first several months, but if you have an urge to see more of the world or satisfy a craving for a sailboat, this puts new pressure on the performance of your RRIF investments. How badly do you want that new toy? How much pressure can you accept?

Appendix

Your Personal RRSP Planner

In This Chapter

▶ Determining how much you need to retire comfortably

▶ Enjoying the relief when you realize the amount is reachable

*T*he chartered banks are pleased to help you plan for your retirement in various ways, such as providing methods of calculating the assets needed to meet your anticipated income. This generic version of a widely used formula assumes a 3 percent annual inflation rate and an 8 percent annual return on your investments over a 20-year retirement period. Those are fairly conservative measurements, but hey, we Canadians have always been a little cautious when it comes to planning for the future.

Step 1:   How much annual income will you need? (Assume 70 percent of your current income): $_____

Step 2:   From Column A in Table A-1, find the number of years until you plan to retire, choose the corresponding **Growth Factor for Income** from Column B, and write it here: _____

Step 3:   Multiply Step 1 by Step 2:_____

Step 4:   What is the current value of your RRSP? _____

Step 5:   From Column C in Table A-1, choose the **Growth Factor for Investments** that matches the number of years until you retire and write it here: _____

Step 6:   Multiply Step 4 by Step 5 and write it here: _____

Step 7:   Subtract Step 6 from Step 3 and write it here: _____

The last figure you calculate is the amount you'll need to contribute each year until you retire.

Table A-1	Growth Factors	
A	B	C
Years to Retirement	Growth Factor for Income	Growth Factor for Investments
35	0.1440	0.0572
30	0.1947	0.0610
25	0.2697	0.0667
20	0.3875	0.0756
15	1.5912	0.0910
10	1.0100	0.1226
5	2.2901	0.2194

Once you're done, you'll likely realize that putting away the amount in Step 7 on a yearly basis isn't going to be the monolithic task you at first thought. When you follow the process back to the somewhat intimidating amount in Step 1, you can nevertheless breathe a little easier, as you realize, "Yes, I can do this."

Book VII
Estate Planning

"I know I should tidy up, but I'm convinced that as long as I'm this disorganized I can't die yet."

In this book . . .

We usually can't tell very far ahead what day our world will end. But we can plan ahead against that day — and there are good reasons for doing so. Planning ahead involves creating an estate plan and making a will, power of attorney, and living will. An estate plan is a strategy for increasing the amount of cash and property you own in your lifetime, and for giving it to others after your death (sometimes even before your death). A will is a legal document that comes into effect when you die and sets out the plan you've made to give your property to others. A power of attorney is another legal document. It gives a person you choose the ability to handle your financial affairs when you're still alive but you can't handle them yourself. A living will, also a legal document, gives a person you choose the ability to make decisions about your personal care when you're still alive but you can't make them yourself.

Estate planning and wills were not invented for controlling people who want to keep their hands on their property after they're dead. (Well, they weren't invented just for never-say-die controllers. . . .) They were invented for people who want to make sure that, after their death, life goes on fairly smoothly — financially if not emotionally — for their family and friends.

Here are the contents of Book VII at a glance:

Chapter 1

Estate Planning Basics

· ·

· ·

*H*ere's the good news about estate planning, right up front: You have an estate! You don't have to be a sports star or to have inherited old family money to have an estate or to need to do estate planning.

Now for the bad news about estate planning: It forces you to think about death — and not just in an abstract philosophical kind of way. It forces you to think about your own death. It also forces you to think about leaving family and friends behind, when they still need you to be there.

You're probably not going to enjoy the estate planning process very much, but this chapter explains why you should do it even though it's not a lot of fun. And after you've done it, you'll feel a kind of virtuous glow because you've taken important steps to make things easier for the people you care about when you die.

What Exactly Is Your Estate?

Before you start wondering why the butler and chauffeur didn't show up for work this morning, here's a little more detail about what your estate is.

Your estate is made up of everything you own. That makes sense so far, right? But in legal terms, your debts — everything you *owe* — are also part of your estate, since what you own must be used to pay off your debts when you die. (For a quick start at taking stock of your estate, see Chapter 1 in Book I.)

Everything you own (referred to in law and accounting as your *assets*) includes the following:

- A home, cottage, or other real estate
- A boat, a car, or other motor vehicles
- Any money you have in cash, bank accounts, or certificates of deposit
- Any investments you hold, such as shares, bonds, or mutual funds
- Your valuable personal belongings, such as computers, stereo systems, TV and VCR or DVD player, jewellery, artwork, antiques, silver and fine china, or collectibles such as a complete set of Elvis Plays Las Vegas memorial plates
- Your other belongings that may have value only as part of your household, such as furniture, kitchen utensils, linens, and clothing
- Any business you run as a sole proprietor or partner

Everything you owe includes the following:

- A mortgage on your home or other real estate
- Personal loans that have not been paid off
- Business loans made to you personally (if you're a sole proprietor or partner, you and your business are one and the same)
- Unpaid credit card balances
- Other unpaid bills
- Unpaid income taxes

Also, some other things, while not technically part of your estate, need to be taken into account when you think about who has to be looked after by you and how much they'll need to keep going:

- **Life insurance:** If you have a life insurance policy, when you die either your estate or an individual (or individuals) you name as beneficiary, whichever option you have chosen, will receive the insurance proceeds.
- **Pension plans:** If you are a member of an employee pension plan, your spouse or a person you name as beneficiary may be entitled to receive after your death a pension or a one-time payment.
- **Government benefits:** Your spouse and/or children may be entitled to receive either a pension or a one-time payment from the Canada Pension Plan, Old Age Security, Veterans' Affairs, or Workers' Compensation after your death.

Besides being what you own and owe, your estate is also a legal being that comes into existence on your death — sort of like a ghostly lingering reminder of you. It has some of the same legal rights that you had when you were alive, such as the right to enter into contracts and to sue and be sued. It also has some of the duties you had, the principal one being the duty to pay income tax. Various places in this book may discuss your estate's activities, so don't let it throw you for a loop.

Why Do You Need to Do Estate Planning?

Notice that this section is not titled, "Do You Need to Do Estate Planning or Not?" You do need to do it, so don't argue. And here are the main reasons why you need to plan your estate. You want to make sure that when you die:

✔ You have done everything in your power to see that your family has enough money to manage without you — it takes planning to set aside and invest money for your family (see Books IV and V) and to make sure that you have enough insurance.

✔ Your property goes to the people *you* want to have it — if you die without a valid will, the provincial government decides who gets your property based on rules set by provincial law, and it may well not go to the people you have in mind (see Chapter 3 for a discussion about beneficiaries).

✔ A person *you* choose will look after your estate — without a valid will, there will be no executor named by you who will have the automatic right to look after your estate; instead, someone (usually a family member) will have to apply to the court to be appointed to look after it (see Chapter 3 for more about choosing an executor).

✔ You have a say in who will look after your children — if both you and the children's other parent die, a will is the best way to let your surviving family and the courts know whom you would like to care for the children (see Chapter 3 for more about taking care of your children).

✔ Your debts can be paid with the least damage to your estate — if you make no plan for payment of your debts, there may not be enough cash available to pay them. If you leave no will, the person appointed to look after your estate will have to sell some of your property to get the necessary cash, without any guidance from you about what to sell and what to keep in order to give to a particular family member or friend.

✔ The capital gains taxes your estate has to pay will be as low as possible — when you die your estate is taxed as if you had sold everything you owned just before you died, and without proper tax planning the bill can be high (see Chapter 2).

Book VII

Estate Planning

✔ The probate fees your estate has to pay will be as low as possible — in almost all provinces, probate fees are calculated according to how much your estate is worth; with advance planning, you can reduce the value of your estate for probate purposes, and so reduce these fees.

✔ The future of any business you own has been looked after — you need to plan ahead, whether you want your business to carry on and who should look after it, or you want it to be sold and how much you want to for it (see Chapter 3).

Here's a final, even more morbid, reason to plan your estate. As part of the process, you can let your family know what you'd like done with your body. (Oddly enough, your body is not part of your estate, unlike the other things that belonged to you when you were alive; it belongs to your executor or, if you have no executor, your closest relative.) You can make your wishes known about organ donation (yes or no) and funeral arrangements (plain oak casket or the King Tut special, burial or cremation, flowers or donations to a favourite charity), so your family members don't have to go through the stress of making choices they think you'd approve of. You may end up saving your family members from fighting.

What Tools Are Used in Estate Planning?

Uh oh, things are starting to sound technical here. So we're going to need "tools" to do this estate planning business, are we? Like what? A level to make sure that all family members are treated equally? A shovel to beat off Canada Customs and Revenue Agency?

Actually, the tools here are a little less physical . . . although it's probably not a bad idea to keep that shovel handy. Once you know what your estate consists of and what you want to give to whom, you can choose some estate planning tools to help you do what you want.

The most commonly used estate planning tools are the following:

✔ **A will:** A will is a written, signed, and witnessed document that states how you want your property to be given away after you die, and appoints an *executor* to look after your property and debts after your death. You can find out more about wills, including how important it is to have a lawyer prepare yours, in Chapter 4.

✔ **Gifts given during your lifetime:** A gift is a transfer of all of your rights over a piece of property. Once you make a gift, you no longer have the right to hold on to the thing given or to sell it or to take it back from the person you gave it to or to leave it to another person in your will. Giving a valuable gift usually has tax consequences for the giver. "Tax consequences" is a fancy way of saying "tax payments."

✔ **Trusts:** A trust is another way to give property away during your lifetime. But instead of giving the property directly to the person you want to have the use of it (the *beneficiary*), you give the property to another person you choose (a *trustee*) to hold and look after it for the use of the beneficiary. Why, you may be asking, would anyone want to do a weird thing like this? The main reason is to prevent the beneficiary from having total control of the property (for example, if the beneficiary is a child, or mentally disabled, or hopeless about business matters; or if you want one person to have use of the property in the short term but want a different person to become the owner of the property at a later date). There can be income tax benefits to setting up a trust. If you decide to set a trust up, you'll need a professional — an estates and trusts lawyer or a tax lawyer, to advise you and to do the paperwork.

✔ **Joint ownership of property during your lifetime:** Joint ownership while you're alive allows you to control who gets the jointly owned property when you die. You can own property jointly with another person (or with other people) in all provinces except Quebec. All sorts of property (real estate, bank accounts, mutual funds, or other investments) can be owned in this way. When you die, your share in the property will automatically pass to the surviving owner. It's not necessary to mention the property in your will in order to pass it on to the surviving joint owner. In fact, you can't deal with joint property by will even if you want to.

✔ **Life insurance:** Life insurance is a kind of bet that you make with an insurance company. You're betting that you'll die, and the life insurance company is betting that you won't. If the life insurance company loses, it has to pay up on the bet — that is, the proceeds of the policy. A life insurance policy helps you ensure that your family has enough money after you die to replace the income you'll no longer be around to earn, or to help them pay off taxes or other debts without using up your estate. The downside (apart from the fact that in order to win the bet you have to die)? Many insurance policies end when the insured reaches retirement age — in other words, just when your chance of winning starts to improve.

Book VII

Estate Planning

When Should You Make an Estate Plan?

Most people put off estate planning because they don't want to face the certainty of dying. Some people are even afraid that doing some estate planning makes them more likely to die. As a public service, here are some scientific facts about estate planning and death. Statistics do indeed show that 100 percent of people who have planned their estate die. However, statistics also show that 100 percent of people who *haven't* planned their estate die. You can now rest assured that there is no cause-and-effect relationship between estate planning and death. There is however a cause-and-effect relationship between a lack of estate planning and wasted time, trouble, and aggravation for the people you care about.

Since estate planning isn't going to kill you, when's the best time to do it? You should make an estate plan as soon as you have any significant property (and you care who's going to get it) or as soon as there is anyone who is financially dependent on you, whichever happens sooner. You are legally able to make a will when you're quite young — as soon as the age of 18 (even younger in some limited circumstances). Don't assume that estate planning is something to do when you're "old," because you don't have to be old to die; you just have to be alive. Anyway, if we waited until we were "old," none of us would ever do any estate planning: No matter how old we get, we don't think of ourselves as old. Old is what other people get.

Going through the estate planning process once is not the end of the matter. Estate planning is a continuing process because you have to change your estate plan as changes occur in the following areas:

- ✔ **In your personal life:** You should review your estate plan if you marry. Have a look again when you have children, and as they grow up, leave home, and start to earn their own living. Think about changing your will if your spouse or partner dies, if you divorce, or even if you separate and meet someone new.

- ✔ **In your business life:** If you start a business, alone or with others, you should review your estate plan to make sure it deals with your business's debts, as well as with the decision of whether your business will fold or carry on under new management when you die.

- ✔ **In your executor's life:** You may need to change your will if the person you have named as your executor is no longer willing or able to take on those duties, or if you decide that you need someone with more sophisticated business or investment skills. (Not to knock Cousin Joe — he's a good guy — but does he know a stock option from a distributor cap?)

- ✔ **In the value of your property:** If the value of the property you own goes way up or down in value, you may want to make changes to your estate plan to deal with the change in the taxes your estate will have to pay and with the debts your estate may have. You may also want to re-think how you've divided up your property in your will if you're trying to treat everyone equally.

- ✔ **In the law:** Between the time you plan your estate and the date you die, there will almost certainly be changes to tax law, family law, and estate law that may require changes to your estate plan. It's hard to keep tabs on the law — unless you're an eagle-eyed lawyer — so it's a good idea to have a lawyer review your estate plan every now and then.

Should You Get Professional Help?

In a word, yes! Estate planning, including cookie-cutter will-preparation kits, is dangerous territory for the do-it-yourselfer. The law in these areas is very complicated. Mistakes are all too easy to make.

If you make a mistake in preparing or signing your own will and power of attorney, they may not do what you want them to do, or, even worse, they may be totally invalid. And don't even think about what will happen if you make a mistake in planning to reduce the taxes on your estate.

But naturally you're worried about the cost of professional help. Will you have anything left in your estate after you pay for it? Obviously, cost will be related to the amount of work you want done. If you have a large estate and need to make complex arrangements to reduce taxes, sure, it will be expensive. On the other hand, a will is a real bargain as far as legal services go. Most lawyers look on wills as "loss leaders." They hope the executor will ask them to do the legal work for the estate after you die, so they don't charge very much to do the will. And the very best lawyers even avoid wishing for your demise!

Lawyers are not the only professionals who can help you in planning your estate. Although a lawyer (or, in Quebec and British Columbia, a notary) with experience in will preparation should always be used to draft the actual legal documents and can usually give you much of the estate planning advice that you need, other professionals can also help in the financial, investment, and tax-saving part of the planning process. They include

- Professional accountants
- Accredited financial planners

You may also be able to get advice from people or institutions you may deal with while building or planning your estate, such as

- Insurance agents or brokers
- Trust companies or banks
- Stockbrokers and mutual fund agents or brokers

Even with professional help, the more you know the better. That's where this book comes in handy, taking you through the process of estate planning and preparing a will and other documents so that you can get the most out of your professional advisers.

Book VII

Estate Planning

Chapter 2

The Taxman Cometh:
Taxes and Your Estate

. . . .

In This Chapter

▶ Discovering how your estate will be taxed

▶ Discovering the tax strategies for estate planning

▶ Knowing what tax-avoidance strategies are available only after your death

▶ Pre-planning to pay your estate's tax bill

. . . .

There are no "death taxes" or "inheritance taxes" in Canada (Yay!), but that doesn't mean that no taxes are payable following a death (Boo!). Taxes at death can be quite substantial, but with proper estate planning you can keep them to the minimum possible. Alas, before you can do any planning, you need to understand basic tax. That's what this chapter is about.

Taxes on an Estate

When you die, you may be gone, but you're not forgotten by the tax authorities. Under income tax law, your estate is born as a brand-new taxpayer that comes into existence on the date of your death.

Your estate (via your executor) has to file estate tax returns annually, starting from the year in which death occurred until the year in which the last property of the estate is given out to the beneficiaries. Filing has two purposes:

✔ To report income of the estate so that it can be taxed in the estate

✔ To give the Canada Customs and Revenue Agency (CCRA) information about distributions of income from the estate to beneficiaries, so the income can be taxed in the hands of the beneficiaries

Estates are taxed in much the same ways as individuals. So you have to know something about how individuals are taxed before you can know how estates are taxed.

In Canada, individuals pay federal and provincial income tax on their *income* and on their *capital gains.* Examples of income are the following:

- Salary or wages
- Commissions
- Tips
- Rental payments received
- Interest payments received
- Dividends on shares
- Profits from an unincorporated business

Capital gains are profits from the disposition (such as a sale or a gift) of *capital property,* which is property with a long-term value, such as the following:

- Shares in a corporation
- Real estate (but not your *principal residence,* which is what your home usually is — see "Should You Put Your Money into Your Principal Residence?" later in this chapter)
- Valuable art, jewellery, collectibles, or antiques

Income and capital gains are taxed differently. Income tax is calculated on the full amount of an individual's income. Capital gains tax is currently calculated on one-half of a capital gain.

Understanding capital gains

Tax on capital gains, rather than tax on income, is usually the big thing people have to worry about when they're doing estate planning. A taxpayer can make a capital gain by disposing of capital property for more than it cost, or have a capital loss by disposing of capital property for less than it cost. (See the section, "Capitalizing on capital losses," later in this chapter to find out what you do with a capital loss.)

Calculating taxable capital gains

It's easiest to explain how to calculate a capital gain by starting with a sale of capital property. And in everyday life, most capital gains arise from a sale. The amount of a capital gain on a sale is calculated by looking at two things:

✔ The cost of the capital property, which is the purchase price plus other costs of acquiring the property (such as legal fees, commissions, licensing fees, the cost of borrowing money to buy the property, and the cost of improving the property). The cost of capital property, once all of these things are taken into account, is called the *adjusted cost base.*

✔ The amount received on the sale of the capital property, which is the selling price minus the cost of selling the property. The cost of selling includes such things as repairs, advertising, legal fees, and commissions. This sale amount, once everything is taken into account, is called the *adjusted sale price.*

A capital gain (or capital loss) is the difference between the adjusted sale price and the adjusted cost base. If the adjusted sale price is higher than the adjusted cost base, you have a capital gain. If it's lower, you have a capital loss.

Only a portion of any capital gain is taxable. That portion is added to your income and is taxed as part of your income at standard income tax rates. The portion has changed from time to time. Before 1972, capital gains weren't taxable at all. Then for many years, one-half of a capital gain was taxable. Recently, three-quarters of a capital gain has been taxable. But in the year 2000, the portion has fallen twice — first to two-thirds and then again to one-half. (And don't even try to guess what may happen by the time you're reading this book!) For capital gains made on or after October 18, 2000, one-half of any capital gain is your *taxable capital gain,* and is added to your income. If you made a capital gain before October 18, 2000, you should check with CCRA to find out what portion of the gain is taxable.

(The calculation of the capital gain or loss is a bit more complicated if you used the property for business purposes and claimed *capital cost allowance* — that's depreciation, or a gradual loss in value — against the property. In that case, you'll need to talk to CCRA or get advice from an accountant.)

If it walks like a capital gain and it quacks like a capital gain . . .

Don't assume that you have a capital gain only by selling something you have bought. You can also end up with a capital gain on capital property

✔ That you didn't buy — that is, it was given to you as a gift, or you inherited it, or you received it as part of an employment package (such as shares or stock options).

✔ That you didn't sell — that is, you gave it away to someone as a gift, or you moved it from an investment account into your RRSP.

✔ That you own at the time you die — Canadian tax law makes the peculiar assumption that immediately before you die you dispose of all of your capital property (this is called a *deemed disposition*).

Book VII

Estate Planning

When you become the owner of property in a way other than buying it, tax law says that you acquired the property for its *fair market value* (the going price in the open market) on the day the property came into your possession.

When you give away capital property, tax law says that you are disposing of the property at fair market value. Even though you're not actually getting a cent for your property, you're triggering a capital gain (or loss) that has to be reported in your income tax return for the year. And when that happens, you — or your estate, if you're dead — have to come up with cash to pay the tax on the capital gain.

If you trigger a capital gain on property that you didn't buy in the first place or sell in the second place, how the heck are you supposed to figure out what the capital gain is? Well, you have to find out what the fair market value of the property was when you got it and when you disposed of it. This is easy with publicly traded stocks, for example, because a broker can tell you what a stock was worth on any given day. But suppose that you inherited a cottage from your parents and then gave it to one of your children. With property such as real estate, art, or jewellery, you'd have to get an expert's appraisal of the value at the time of acquisition and/or disposal.

And now for a strange tax fact: If you've owned property for many years (a family cottage or shares in a corporation, for example), for capital gains purposes you're responsible for the increase in value of the property only since December 31, 1971, referred to by CCRA as "V-Day." (V is for valuation, *not* victory over CCRA.) That's because capital gains were not taxable in Canada before that date. As a result of this change, owners of capital property don't have to go back any further than that when they're figuring out the adjusted cost base of their property.

Capital gains tax and spouses

A taxpayer ordinarily has to pay capital gains tax whether the property is sold or given away, or "deemed" (by CCRA) to have been disposed of, if the capital property has gone up in value. However, there is an exception when a taxpayer transfers property to his or her spouse. No capital gain is triggered.

Spouses, for tax purposes, are deemed by CCRA to be two people who live together in a *conjugal* (marriage-like) relationship and have done so continuously for at least 12 months. They don't have to be married to each other. The two people can be of the same sex.

When a taxpayer transfers property to a spouse, the spouse automatically steps into the shoes of the taxpayer and gets the original adjusted cost base of the capital property along with the property. It is as if the spouse acquired the property at the same time and for the same price as the taxpayer did. This is called a *spousal rollover.* (Isn't this a great name? Unfortunately, that's as far as the income tax people went, and there is no spousal heel or spousal stay or spousal sit-up-and-beg in tax law.)

There is an automatic rollover — of the property, you understand, not of the spouse — any time a taxpayer transfers property to a spouse during the marriage (or marriage-like relationship). When the spouse ultimately sells the property, he or she includes one-half of any capital gain, calculated using the *original* adjusted cost base, in his or her income. (CCRA can *attribute* the capital gain back to the spouse who originally owned the property; in other words, make that spouse pay the capital gains tax.) A taxpayer who doesn't think this whole idea of rollovers sounds like a heck of a lot of fun can choose not to have one.

Capitalizing on capital losses

Are you thinking how much fun it would be to take out the garbage just about now or clean the cabinet under the bathroom sink? You can't leave yet. Your torment is only beginning. This section tells you about capital losses. To remind you, a taxpayer has a capital loss by disposing of capital property for less than it cost.

Question: You have to pay tax on one-half of a capital gain — but what do you do with a capital loss?

Answer: If you have a capital loss in the same year that you have a capital gain, you can deduct the capital loss from the capital gain before calculating your taxable capital gain. If your capital loss is more than your capital gain, you have taxable capital gains of zero in that year. However, you can use a capital loss to reduce only *a capital gain* in that year; you can't use a capital loss to reduce *income* in that year. What you can do is carry any extra capital loss back to any of the preceding three years to reduce taxable capital gains you had earlier. You have to file a new return to get back tax you paid in the preceding year or years. If you still have any unused capital losses, you can carry them forward indefinitely.

Now here's an amazing thing. Canadian tax law actually gives you a reason to die (other than the ordinary ones of sheer annoyance or apoplexy) if you have capital losses larger than your capital gains. In your very last income tax return, which is filed after you're dead, capital losses can be used to reduce income!

Special rules apply to capital losses in your last or *terminal* return. That's the return filed by your executor for the tax year in which you die. In the terminal return, capital losses must first be used to reduce capital gains, but if any losses are left over, they can be used

- ✔ First, to reduce your other income in the taxation year in which you die, and

- ✔ Then to reduce your other income in the taxation year before the year you die.

This gives you a whole new perspective on your inexorably approaching death, doesn't it?

Taking in taxable income

This tax primer has concentrated on calculation of capital gains so far because it's the most important stuff to know about if you're estate planning. However, the rules about calculation of taxable income have a bearing on RRSPs (Registered Retirement Savings Plans) and RRIFs (Registered Retirement Investment Funds) if they're a part of your estate, so this section discusses a bit about income now.

Calculating taxable income

In the annual tax return, a taxpayer is required to list his or her income from all sources, including employment income or income from an unincorporated business, pension income, amounts withdrawn from an RRSP or RRIF, benefits from various sources, investment income, and rental income. These different types of income are added together to arrive at the taxpayer's *total income.*

Taxpayers are allowed certain *deductions* from their total income to arrive at their *taxable income,* the income on which federal and provincial income tax is calculated. Allowable deductions include the following:

- ✔ RRSP contributions

- ✔ Annual union or professional dues

- ✔ Attendant care expenses that allowed the taxpayer to earn income

- ✔ Certain child care expenses

Understanding tax brackets

Individual taxpayers don't pay tax on their taxable income at one single rate. Instead, they can pay tax at up to four different rates. As income increases, the percentage rate at which it is taxed also increases in steps, or by brackets. It's hard to generalize about the combined rate of federal and provincial tax, because provincial tax rates vary from province to province, and both federal and provincial rates change from time to time. In fact, federal tax rates were last reduced for the 2001 taxation year, and the February 2003 federal budget contained no tax rate increases. At the same time, some provincial tax rates are changing too (and not always down). Roughly speaking, as of 2003, the tax brackets are as follows:

- ✔ If your taxable income is up to approximately $30,000, you'll pay tax at a combined rate of about 24 percent. However, the basic personal exemption tax credit reduces the tax payable on approximately $8,000 of this amount to $0.

- ✔ If your taxable income is between approximately $30,000 and approximately $60,000, you'll pay tax at a rate of about 24 percent on taxable income up to $30,000 and at a rate of about 34 percent on taxable income between $30,000 and $60,000.

- ✔ If your taxable income is between approximately $60,000 and $100,000, you'll pay tax at a rate of about 24 percent on taxable income up to $30,000, at a rate of about 34 percent on taxable income between $30,000 and $60,000 and at a rate of about 39 percent on taxable income between $60,000 and $100,000.

- ✔ If your taxable income is over approximately $100,000, you'll pay tax at a rate of about 24 percent on taxable income up to $30,000, at a rate of about 34 percent on taxable income between $30,000 and $60,000, at a rate of about 39 percent on taxable income between $60,000 and $100,000 and at a rate of about 47 percent on taxable income over $100,000.

Book VII

Estate Planning

Keep in mind that these are very rough estimates. So don't trust us, check the combined federal/provincial rate in your province. Also keep in mind that the February 2003 federal budget proposes to raise the 2004 income tax thresholds to $35,000 in the lowest bracket, $70,000 in the middle bracket, and $113,804 in the highest tax bracket.

Should You Leave Everything to Your Spouse?

In order to make use of this strategy, you first have to have a spouse. (See "Capital gains tax and spouses," earlier in this chapter for how CCRA defines "spouse.") But don't put tax avoidance above your own personal happiness — don't acquire a spouse just so that you can minimize estate taxes. If you do, you may be found floating face-down in the bathtub some day, while your spouse is seen elsewhere drinking champagne and waving around your life insurance policy.

If you already have a spouse, you may want to leave everything to him or her anyway, no matter what the tax consequences are. On the other hand, you may be thinking about leaving some or all of your estate to your children, grandchildren, or others. So this section looks into the pros and cons of leaving property to your spouse.

Dealing with capital property

Your capital property is subject to capital gains tax. Capital property, as explained earlier in this chapter, is property with long-term value, and you are deemed by CCRA to have sold all of your capital property for its fair market value just before you die (a *deemed disposition*). If what you owned went up in value after you got it, your estate will have a capital gain, one-half of which is taxable.

This rule about your capital property does not apply to any property that you leave to your spouse in your will. The gift of the property in your will is not treated as a disposition of the property at its current value. Instead, there is an automatic spousal rollover, and the gift is treated as a disposition of the property at its original cost to you. (If you've already forgotten what spousal rollovers are, you can refresh your memory back in the "Capital gains tax and spouses" section earlier in this chapter.) When you dispose of your property for the same price at which you bought it, there is no capital gain. So because of the spousal rollover, your estate will not have to pay any capital gains tax on the transfer.

But when your spouse decides to sell the property, or when your spouse dies, he or she is taxed on the increase in the value of the property from the time you got the property, not from the time *he or she* got the property.

It's clear that if you leave all of your property to your spouse, your estate will not have to pay any capital gains tax at all. But what if you don't want to leave everything to your spouse? What if you want to leave something to your children? Is there any way that the spousal rollover can help you? In fact, there is. You can still take advantage of the spousal rollover by leaving property that is subject to capital gains tax to your spouse while leaving property that is not subject to capital gains tax to your children or others.

The spousal rollover applies when you leave your property directly to your spouse. It will also apply if you leave your property in trust for your spouse in your will if the will is drafted so that

- Your spouse has the right to receive all of the income earned by the trust for the rest of his or her life, and

- No one but your spouse has the right to receive any of the income or the property of the trust as long as your spouse is alive.

Distributing RRSPs and RRIFs

A Registered Retirement Savings Plan (RRSP) contribution is fully deductible from the taxpayer's income. You don't pay any income tax on money that you earn that you put into an RRSP. So if you have income in a particular year of $40,000, and you make an RRSP contribution of $3,000 in that year, your income is reduced like magic to $37,000 for that year. Whenever you withdraw money from your RRSP, it's taxed as income in the year of withdrawal.

So if you have income in a particular year of $40,000 and you withdraw $3,000 from your RRSP that year, your income is increased to $43,000 for that year. When you reach age 69 (actually, you get to the end of the year), you have to withdraw everything from your RRSP, but you can roll it over into a Registered Retirement Investment Fund (RRIF) so that you don't have to pay tax on the income that has accumulated in the RRSP over the years. You then have to make annual withdrawals from your RRIF and pay tax on those withdrawals as income.

Death of a taxpayer

A taxpayer who dies is deemed by CCRA to have cashed in all RRSPs (and also RRIFs) before dying, and the full amount of the RRSPs or RRIFs must be added to income in the terminal return.

Now here's the first twist. For estate planning purposes, an RRSP or RRIF is not treated simply as cash in the estate if it's given as a gift in your will or it's directed to someone you've named as beneficiary of your RRSP or RRIF. When tax has to be paid on the RRSP or RRIF amounts that are added to income, the tax doesn't come straight out of the RRSP or RRIF. The tax comes first out of ordinary cash in your estate. So what can happen when you give someone your RRSP or RRIF is that the person gets the full amount of money in the RRSP or RRIF, but anyone who was supposed to get cash from your estate gets less because it's being used to pay the tax on the RRSP or RRIF.

Now for the second twist. If you make your spouse the beneficiary of your RRSP or RRIF and the proceeds are paid into your spouse's RRSP or RRIF, the money in the RRSP or RRIF is not added to your estate's income and no tax will be payable by your estate or by your spouse. (And your spouse will still have the right to make his or her usual RRSP or RRIF contribution.) If you name your estate as beneficiary of your RRSP or RRIF and your spouse is the beneficiary of your estate, the money in your RRSP or RRIF will be taxed in the hands of your spouse and no tax will be payable by your estate, as long as your spouse and your executor file a *refund of premium* form with CCRA. Your spouse will have the right to avoid paying tax on the proceeds by depositing the RRSP or RRIF proceeds into his or her RRSP or RRIF. (Again, your spouse will still have the right to make his or her usual RRSP or RRIF contribution.)

Likewise, if you name a child or grandchild who is financially dependent on you as a beneficiary of your RRSP or RRIF, or you leave the RRSP or RRIF to him or her in your will, your estate will not have to pay any tax as long as the beneficiary and your executor file a refund of premiums form. The full amount of the RRSP or RRIF will be taxed as income in the hands of your child or grandchild. (The way in which the amount will be taxed depends on whether your child or grandchild is under the age of 18 and/or suffers a physical or mental disability.)

As you keep seeing, life — or death — is simple if you want to leave everything to your spouse. Your estate will not have to pay any tax. But supposing you don't want to leave everything to your spouse? You may have good and valid reasons; it's no one's business but yours. Anyway, supposing you'd like to leave something to your children or even a friend? You can use your knowledge about how RRSPs and RRIFs are taxed to make sure that both your spouse and someone else of your choice will get the most out of your estate while CCRA gets the least.

What's the best way to pass on your RRSP or RRIF?

If you want your spouse to get the money from your RRSP or RRIF, it is usually better to make him or her the beneficiary of the plan rather than having the plan go through your will because

- Your spouse will be able to get the money more quickly if he or she is named as the beneficiary.
- Your estate's probate fees will be lower (we discuss probate fees later in this chapter).
- The money will not be used to pay the debts of your estate.

If you want someone other than your spouse to get the money from your RRSP or RRIF, it's usually not a good idea to name that person as beneficiary of the plan. It's usually not even a good idea to leave the RRSP or RRIF directly to that person in your will. It's probably better to name your estate as beneficiary of your RRSP or RRIF and simply divide your estate among the people you choose.

Should You Put Your Money into Your Principal Residence?

Just to recap, so that this concept is etched permanently into your brain no matter how much you'd like to forget it, when you dispose of capital property at a profit you trigger a capital gain, and capital gains tax becomes payable. A home, cottage, or vacation property is a form of capital property. As with all other kinds of capital property, when you die you will be deemed to have sold the property the day before you die. If the property went up in value after you got it, there will be a capital gain.

Now with most capital property, one-half of that capital gain would be taxable. But if this home or cottage or vacation property is your *principal residence,* your estate won't have to pay any capital gains tax.

Book VII

Estate Planning

What is a principal residence?

Here again is yet another incredibly boring definition that will lead you to a tax secret. A principal residence can be any residential property that you inhabit or your spouse or your child ordinarily inhabits during the year. It does not have to be your main residence. Your cottage or vacation home can qualify as a principal residence as long as you occupy or your spouse or at least one of your children occupies the property for some time during the year.

There is a catch here. The catch is that, since 1982, a family is allowed only one principal residence each year. If you own only a house or only a cottage, the one property you own will be your principal residence. But what if you own both a house and a cottage? In that case, when you sell or give away the property — or die, more to the point — you (or your executor) must choose one of them to be your principal residence and to qualify for the capital gains exemption.

But can you make use of the principal residence exemption?

Because of the principal residence exemption, you can leave your principal residence to anyone you choose without worrying about your estate (or anyone else) having to pay capital gains tax on it. Whoopee!

If your only objective in planning your estate is to keep your taxes to a minimum, and if you've carefully followed and understood everything you've read in this chapter about taxes and your estate, you're thinking right now that you'll leave your principal residence to your children and leave your spouse some other property that's subject to capital gains tax. Great plan — start the engines and see if it will fly.

If you have only one residence

If you have only one property that qualifies for the principal residence exemption, and that property is your family home, you probably want to leave the property to your spouse, not to your kids. If you do that, there's already an automatic spousal rollover that keeps your estate from having to pay capital gains tax, so the principal residence exemption doesn't add anything extra here.

And if you and your spouse own your family home as joint tenants (as most couples do), you can't leave your home to your kids even if you want to. That's because when you die, your share of the home will automatically pass to your spouse, no matter what your will says. Your share of the home will not become part of your estate.

All in all, you won't be able to make much use of the principal residence exemption if you own only one residential property.

If you have two residences

The principal residence exemption can be very useful, however, if you own more than one residential property. If you own a home and a cottage, for example, you can take advantage of the principal residence exemption to leave your home to your spouse and your cottage to your children. Your estate will not have to pay any capital gains tax on your home because of the spousal rollover. Your estate will not have to pay any capital gains tax on the cottage if your executor names your cottage as your principal residence.

Simplicity is a relative concept as far as taxes are concerned, but things are fairly simple if you never use your principal residence exemption from capital gains tax until you die. However, things will work out very differently if you have used your principal residence exemption in the past. That's because you can only have one principal residence in any given year.

Should You Give Things Away Now?

There are many reasons why you may want to give things away to others before you die:

- ✔ You may take pleasure in watching them enjoy your gifts while you're still alive. Conversely, you may take sadistic pleasure in watching some of your friends and relations seethe because you gave gifts to others and nothing to them.

- ✔ You may own property that is too expensive or too much trouble for you to keep up any more.

- ✔ You may hope to keep your family from fighting over how to divide your estate after you die.

- ✔ You may hope to save taxes either for yourself now or your estate later.

If you're dead set on giving your property away while you're still alive, there are a couple of ways to do it. You can make an absolute gift of the property by giving away full or part ownership of it, or you can create a trust and transfer the property to the trust.

At the moment, however, this section looks at the tax reasons for giving your things away while you're still alive. The two major possible tax advantages to giving things away are

- ✔ To reduce the capital gains tax your estate will have to pay when you die. Your estate pays capital gains tax as if you sold everything you owned on the day before you die. So, the less you own at the time you die, the less tax your estate will have to pay.

- ✔ To reduce your income tax now. If you give away property that is earning income, the income earned by the property in the future will be paid to the new owner and should be taxed in the hands of the new owner.

Notice that these things are *possible* advantages. The balance of this section takes a look at each of them a little more closely, because neither of them is a sure thing.

Book VII

Estate Planning

Will you actually reduce capital gains tax for your estate?

There is a capital gains tax advantage for the estate only if you give away capital property that has increased in value. There is no capital gains tax advantage to giving away cash or cash-like investments such as GICs or treasury bills, because they do not go up in value, and so your estate will not have to pay any capital gains tax on the deemed disposition of these items when you die.

While it's true that if you give away capital property that has increased in value, your estate will not have to pay any capital gains tax later; however, you may have to pay capital gains tax now! (And if the gift is to your spouse, and your spouse sells the property at a profit before you die, CCRA has the power to attribute the capital gain back to you; in other words, tax you as if the capital gain is yours.)

It doesn't usually make sense to pay taxes now if you can put them off until later. However, you may be willing to pay some capital gains tax now if you believe that the property will increase in value a lot more before you die. It may also make sense to give away property now if you have a capital loss that you can use to offset the gain, so that no tax will be payable.

Will you actually reduce your income taxes now?

Even though the new owner of the property will receive the income from the property, *you* may still have to pay the tax on it. Depending on whom you give the property to, CCRA may attribute the income back to you and tax you as if the income continues to be yours. (CCRA will tax the income in the hands of the person who will pay tax at the higher rate.) Here's what CCRA can do:

- ✔ If you give income-producing property to your spouse or to a trust for your spouse, CCRA has the power to tax you on any interest or dividend income or any capital gains from that property in the future.

- ✔ If you give income-producing property to a child or grandchild under the age of 18, CCRA has the power to tax you on any interest or dividend income from the property in the future (but your child or grandchild will be responsible for any future capital gains). You cannot be taxed on the income earned by property that you transfer to your adult child or grandchild.

Are you quite sure you want to give away your property? If the tax consequences of giving away your property don't put you off generosity, there's still a little more to think about. Whatever your reasons for considering giving your money or property away while you're still alive, you should ponder the matter before you give up control over property that's important to you. And you must also keep enough money and property for yourself that you don't go from being financially independent to being dependent on others.

Should You Freeze Your Estate?

You may have heard people use the term *estate freeze* and wondered what they were talking about. Estate freeze can be used to describe any of several estate planning techniques that are used to reduce the capital gains tax that you would otherwise have to pay when you leave capital property to your children or grandchildren when you die. They are used for capital property that is expected to increase a lot in value in the future.

Estate freezes are all designed to transfer your property out of your hands so that you cap the amount of capital gains tax you'll ever pay. (You may have to pay capital gains tax on the current value of the property.) If the property goes up in value in the future, whoever gets the property from you — usually someone in the next generation or even the one after that — will have to pay capital gains tax on that future increase.

There are really complicated estate freezes and less complicated estate freezes. There are no simple estate freezes. Following are just a few types of estate freezes.

A gift as estate freeze

A gift of your property to a child or grandchild is a relatively simple form of estate freeze. When you give your property to your child or grandchild, you pay capital gains tax exactly as if you sold the property at its current fair market value. Your child or grandchild has to pay the tax on any capital gains that accumulate in the future.

Don't forget that you may get stuck paying annual taxes on income from the property as long as your child or grandchild is under 18!

A sale as estate freeze

Another way of creating an estate freeze is to sell your property to your child or grandchild at its current fair market value. You pay the capital gain based on the sale price of the property, and your child or grandchild will have to pay any future capital gains when the property is sold or otherwise disposed of. You can set up the transaction so that your child does not pay you right away but instead gives you a *promissory note,* which is a document in which your child promises to pay the sale price when you demand it. The advantage of using a promissory note is that that you don't have to pay tax on the entire sale price at once; CCRA lets you spread out the capital gain over up to five years.

If you don't, in fact, want any money from your child or grandchild, you don't ever have to demand payment during your lifetime. (You'll still have to pay the capital gains tax either in a lump or spread out over five years.) Your child or grandchild will have to pay your estate the amount of the promissory note when you die (and can buy life insurance on your life to get the money to do so) unless you forgive the promissory note in your will.

A trust as estate freeze

In another form of estate freeze, you can set up a trust that you manage for your children or grandchildren and give property to the trust. This will allow you to keep some control over the property. You have to pay capital gains tax as if you sold the property at its fair market value when you handed it over to the trust. You won't have to pay the tax on future capital gains; it will have to be paid by either the trust or the beneficiaries of the trust, depending on the circumstances:

- ✔ If the trust sells the property and continues to hold the proceeds of sale in trust, the trust will pay the tax.
- ✔ If the trust sells the property and pays the proceeds of sale to the beneficiary, the trustee decides whether the trust or the beneficiary will pay the tax.
- ✔ No tax is payable when the trust ends and the trustee transfers the property to the beneficiary, but the beneficiary takes over the property at the trust's adjusted cost base. (You can find more about what an adjusted cost base is in the section "Understanding capital gains," earlier in this chapter.) When the beneficiary disposes of the property, he or she is taxed on the capital gain from the time the property was transferred by you to the trust.

A corporation as estate freeze

In all three of the preceding types of estate freeze, you have to pay tax now as the cost of handing over responsibility for future capital gains tax to your children or grandchildren. There is one type of estate freeze in which you don't have to pay any capital gains tax until you die — an estate freeze involving a corporation. This kind of estate freeze is very complicated and is usually used to pass on a business or real estate investments.

You create a corporation and transfer ownership of property to the corporation in return for shares in the corporation. You give your children shares in the corporation as well. The corporation is organized using different classes of shares; you take shares that give you voting rights and control over the corporation, and you give your children shares that go up in value as the property goes up in value. If the estate freeze is set up properly, there is a rollover (similar to a spousal rollover) when you transfer your property to the corporation, and the transfer doesn't trigger any capital gains tax at the time.

When you die, your estate pays capital gains tax on the value of your shares in the corporation — which will be the same as the value of the property when you transferred it to the corporation. If your children ever sell their shares, they will pay capital gains tax based on the increase in the value of the property from the time it was transferred into the corporation. (If the corporation, which is separate from the humans who control it, sells the property, it will pay capital gains tax based on the increase in value of the property from the time it was transferred to the corporation. The proceeds from the sale, less the cost of paying the tax, could then be paid out to the shareholder children in the form of dividends.)

Estate freezes involving trusts or corporations are not do-it-yourself projects. If you are thinking about an estate freeze, you need professional tax and legal advice. And if you have to stop to think about whether you can afford to pay for fancy advice, trust us, you don't need to think about an estate freeze — you don't have enough money to make an estate freeze worthwhile!

Should You Donate Something to Charity?

If you leave money or property to a registered charity, your estate will be able to claim a tax credit in your terminal tax return against the income tax it would otherwise have to pay. Your estate will be allowed to claim a tax credit of 17 percent of the first $200 in donations and 29 percent of donations from $200 up to the full amount of your taxable income reported in your final tax return. The amount of tax that your estate would otherwise pay is reduced by the amount of this tax credit.

If the charitable donations in your will are more than your net income in your final tax return, your executor has the right to refile your tax return for the year before you died and use the remainder of the donation to get a tax credit to reduce that year's taxes after the fact. (Your estate will get a refund.)

It is important to know how to make charitable donations in the right way in order to get the maximum tax benefits possible. The ways of donating include:

- **Gifts of cash made by will:** You can make a gift of a specified amount of money to the charity, or you can give the charity a share or percentage of the value of the residue of your estate — the *residue* is what's left in your estate after your executor pays your debts and taxes and hands out the gifts of cash and property that you made to named individuals.

- **Gifts of specific property made by will:** Instead of leaving cash to a charity, you can leave specific property to the charity (a gift in kind) — for example, stocks or other securities, real estate, artwork, or a motor vehicle.

- **Gifts of life insurance:** If you think that there won't be enough money in your estate to fund the charitable donation you'd like to make, you can donate the proceeds of a life insurance policy on your own life to the charity you've chosen. There are two different ways to do this:

  - You can donate the insurance policy to the charity while you are still alive.

  - You can hold on to your insurance policy and either name the charity as the beneficiary of the policy, or name your estate as the beneficiary and leave the charity an amount of money equal to the life insurance proceeds in your will.

- **Gifts of RRSP or RRIF proceeds:** You can donate the proceeds of your Registered Retirement Savings Plan or Registered Retirement Investment Fund to charity. If you do, you can either name the charity as the beneficiary of the RRSP or RRIF or you can name your estate as the beneficiary and leave the charity an amount of money equal to the proceeds of the plan or fund in your will.

- **Charitable gift annuities:** You can make a donation to a charity while you're still alive in return for an annuity. An *annuity* is an investment bought from a financial institution, usually an insurance company. You pay the financial institution a lump sum in return for its promise to pay you a fixed amount of money every year for either a set number of years (a *fixed term annuity*), until you die (a *life annuity*), or until both you and your spouse die (a *joint life annuity*).

- **Charitable remainder trusts:** In a charitable remainder trust, you put income-producing property into a trust and get the income from the property for as long as you (or you and your spouse) are alive. The charity gets the trust property when you (or the second of you and your spouse) die.

- **Memorial donations:** If you want to donate to charity after your death, asking for memorial donations is a way of getting others to make the donation. It's not exactly cheating; you could think of it as "leveraging" your death. Or you could think of it as exercising power from beyond the grave (or urn) to encourage others to be charitable.

When the Taxman Finally Arriveth . . . With the Bill

In this chapter, you've discovered a number of ways that you may be able to reduce the tax that your estate will have to pay on the property you own when you die. But unless you leave everything to your spouse, your estate will have to pay something. To be prepared for that unhappy time, you should:

✔ Estimate how much tax your estate will have to pay in your terminal return.

✔ Decide where the money will come from to pay it.

✔ Plan so that the wrong person doesn't get stuck with the bill.

Estimating the tax

You can't know what property you will own when you die or what it will be worth. All you can do is estimate your taxes (over and above your usual tax bill) based on your present situation. To keep your estate plan current, you'll need to do this from time to time. Start by going to the "Your Net Worth" table (Table 1-1) in Chapter 1 of Book I and making a list of everything you own.

Make a list of everything that you are *not* leaving to your spouse. Don't worry about property that will not be subject to capital gains, such as cash, GICs, treasury bills, or your principal residence. Estimate your capital gain for each remaining piece of property by doing the calculation shown in Table 2-1.

Table 2-1	Estimate Your Capital Gains	
	Current fair market value of property	$_____
−	Estimated costs to sell, if any	$_____
=	Adjusted sale price	$_____ (A)
	Purchase price of property (or fair market value of property when you acquired it, if you didn't buy it)	$_____
+	Costs of buying (if any)	$_____
=	Adjusted cost base	$_____ (B)
	A − B = Capital gain	$_____
x	50% (or x 0.50) = Taxable capital gain	$_____ (C)

When you have done this calculation for everything you own, add the taxable capital gains figures together for your total taxable capital gains and call it amount (D).

Now you know how much your taxable capital gains will be, but you're not finished yet. You haven't taken into account the tax you will have to pay on any RRSPs or RRIFs that you do not leave to your spouse. Remember that the full value of your RRSPs and RRIFs will be taxed as income received by your estate. So add together the balances in all of your RRSPs and RRIFs and add that total to your taxable capital gains total. That combined total is the amount on which your estate will be taxed as a result of the gifts you are making in your will.

Use Table 2-2 to do the rest of the calculation.

Table 2-2   Add Deemed Income from Gifts of RRSPs and RRIFs

Total taxable capital gains	$_____	(D)
+ RRSPs and RRIFs not left to spouse	$_____	
= Amount in your estate that is subject to tax	$_____	(E)

Finally, estimate the tax rate that will be applied to the capital gains and RRSPs and RRIFs. (For estimating purposes, you can do this here the lazy way.) After you dispose of all your capital property the day before you die, and after all of your RRSPs or RRIFs are rolled in, there's a very good chance you'll have made it into the top tax bracket. So assume a tax of 50 percent — if that's not true in your case, you'll be too embarrassed to tell anyone anyway. Use Table 2-3 to calculate your taxes.

Table 2-3   Calculate the Actual Amount of Tax Payable in Your Terminal Return

Amount in your estate (over and above your final year's income) that is subject to tax	$_____	(E)
x 50% = Tax payable	$_____	

Where will the money come from?

Once you have an idea of how much tax your estate will have to pay, think about where the money will come from to pay it. CCRA doesn't like to wait to be paid — although your executor may be able to work out a deal with them if there is difficulty in paying the tax owing right away. Here are some options for paying the tax bill:

- ✔ Your estate may be rolling in cash and there will be enough of it to pay the tax.

- ✔ If your estate does not have enough cash to pay the tax, it may have valuable property that can be sold and turned into cash. If you would like your executor to sell (or not to sell) specific property, you should leave instructions in your will to that effect.

- ✔ If there is not enough cash in the estate or you don't want non-cash property in your estate sold, you'll have to buy enough (additional) life insurance to cover the expected tax bill.

- ✔ If your estate owes tax money and simply does not have enough cash or property to cover the bill, CCRA can go after the executor personally if he or she transferred cash or property out of the estate to the beneficiaries before the taxes were paid. But if the executor didn't do that and there still isn't enough money to pay the taxes due in the terminal return, the tax authorities have to go whistle. They can't get it out of your executor or surviving family or friends.

Book VII

Estate Planning

Make sure the wrong person doesn't get stuck with the bill

You may have heard of situations in which one beneficiary receives a piece of property while another beneficiary gets stuck paying the taxes. That's because of a rule of estates law that the taxes and other debts of your estate are to be paid using the residue of your estate (anything you have not left as a specific gift to a specific individual) first, then out of cash gifts to specific individuals, then out of non-cash gifts (they'd have to be sold for cash, of course). Keep that in mind when you plan your gifts under your will. You can plan around this in several ways:

✔ Make sure that you have enough cash, through insurance or otherwise, to pay all of your taxes so that gifts of cash to named individuals are not affected.

✔ Divide your estate among your beneficiaries in shares instead of leaving them specific property. That way they'll share equally in losses to tax or debt payments.

✔ State clearly in your will that the person who gets a particular piece of property is responsible for any taxes on that property. Then you won't run into the problem of one person getting the property and another person footing the tax bill.

Chapter 3

Creating an Estate Plan

· ·

In This Chapter

▶ Deciding whom you want to provide for after you're gone

▶ Deciding whom you are required to provide for after you're gone

▶ Understanding what an executor does

▶ Choosing your executor

▶ Knowing what will happen to your children after your death if you make no plans

▶ Choosing someone to look after your children if you die

▶ Finding out about the duties of a testamentary guardian

▶ Deciding whether to sell your business or keep it in the family

▶ Considering when to sell or turn over control of your business

· ·

*C*aptain on the bridge! That's you, the captain of your ship of estate. In the preceding chapters, you can find out about the reasons for estate planning, income tax concerns, and the main estate planning tools. If you've read them, your response was probably a hearty yo ho ho, and a bottle of rum. Now it's time to start using what you've learned — perhaps learned painfully (rum will do that to you) — and begin to create an estate plan.

The first step will be to assemble a crew for your estate — your beneficiaries (the people you will provide for in your estate plan) and your executor (the person who will manage your estate after you've sailed into the sunset).

Accounting for Your Beneficiaries

When you die, you have to give away everything you own. That means figuring out whom to give it to. This is the tricky part of estate planning — you can reward those who've been good to you and punish those who haven't by giving a gift here, withholding a gift there. Some people make a sordid hobby out of picking their beneficiaries, and then they proceed to revise their choices on an almost daily basis, according to who has pleased them or ticked them off most recently. Perhaps it's their twisted way of wielding power.

Not everyone can afford the fantasy of planning their estate just to get even with their family, friends, and acquaintances. Most people have better things to do with their time. They have obligations, and those obligations may extend past the end of life. Sometimes, feelings and obligations match exactly, and you can choose a beneficiary without any trouble at all. But in other cases, the feelings and obligations are completely at odds (feelings: good, obligation: none; or feelings: bad, obligation: heavy), and it becomes more difficult to make choices. In this section, you find what you need to help you think about how to choose your beneficiaries, possibly including some people you wish were at the bottom of the sea.

In choosing your beneficiaries — and in deciding what to give them — you have to consider

✔ Whom you really *want* to provide for and whom you merely *have* to provide for

✔ Your reason for providing for them

✔ The best way to do the providing

The people you want to provide for

Unless you have the misfortune of coming from a totally dysfunctional family, it won't be difficult to settle on the people you actually *want* to give your money and belongings to. (And if you do hate everyone you know and would be keelhauled before you gave any of them a nickel, with luck you'll be able to leave everything to charity — preferably one that will really get up their noses.)

Rounding up the usual suspects

Take a look around you to see the beneficiaries whom you'll want to provide for. They're the people you live with or spend your time with. As noted in Chapter 1, who these people are may vary with your stage of life:

✔ When you're young and single, they're parents, brothers and sisters, friends, a charity, or a combination of these.

✔ When you marry or settle into a serious relationship, it will probably be your spouse or partner whom you want to get all or most of what you own.

✔ When you have young children, they'll likely be first on your mind.

✔ If you divorce, your children or other relatives will be at the top of the list, and your former spouse may or may not be right off it.

✔ Once your children are grown up and self-sufficient, grandchildren or a favourite charity may attract your attention.

What's your reason for giving?

There are many different reasons to include certain family members or friends in your estate plan. The particular reason you have in each case will affect what you decide to give and how you go about giving it.

You may want to include someone in your estate plan in order to

- ✔ **Provide ongoing support.** Your spouse or children, or some other relative or friend, may need your financial assistance. It may take the bulk of your estate to do it.

- ✔ **Help meet a particular goal.** Finishing a university degree, starting a business, or buying a house requires cash. A gift of a specific amount of money will do the trick.

- ✔ **Say thank you.** An employee may have been very loyal, or a friend may have been especially kind when you were sick or in some kind of trouble. A gift of money or one of your personal possessions may be the answer.

- ✔ **Pass on a family heirloom.** You may have received furniture, photographs, or papers from your parents or grandparents that have been in the family for generations or that have special significance for your family. You'd like the heirloom to go to a relative who will value it and pass it on in turn.

- ✔ **Leave a memento.** A family member may have admired a piece of your jewellery or a friend may have shared your passion for collecting belly dancer figurines. A gift of a particular item would be appropriate.

- ✔ **Show that he or she was in your thoughts.** A gift of one of your personal possessions or a small sum of money will be appreciated.

Book VII

Estate Planning

What's the right tool for making the gift?

The most obvious way to give to your survivors is to leave money or property in your will. But, as discussed in Chapter 1, there are other ways of providing for your beneficiaries:

- ✔ **Life insurance:** You can name someone as beneficiary of a life insurance policy, and your beneficiary will receive the insurance proceeds directly.

- ✔ **RRSPs and RRIFs:** You can name someone as beneficiary of your RRSP or RRIF, and your beneficiary will receive the RRSP/RRIF proceeds directly.

- ✔ **Pension plans:** If you are a member of an employee pension plan, you may be able to name a beneficiary to receive a pension after your death or a one-time payment.

- ✔ **Joint ownership of property:** If you own property jointly with another person, when you die your share in the property will automatically pass to the surviving owner, without your having to mention the property in your will.

That's the how. Now what about the when? When do you want the person to get the money or property? Timing will also affect your choice of estate planning tool. You may want to provide for someone

- ✔ **While you're alive:** That means a gift or a living trust.

- ✔ **Immediately after your death:** That means making a gift in your will or naming the person as a beneficiary of your life insurance policy or your RRSP or RRIF.

- ✔ **After you die but not until someone else also dies:** You may want your children to inherit your property, for example, but not until after the death of your spouse. That means setting up a trust in your will to give your spouse the use of the property during his or her lifetime, and to hand the property over to your children when your spouse dies.

- ✔ **After you die but not until the person reaches a certain age:** You may not want your children to have total control over the inherited property until they are 25 years old, for example. That means setting up a trust in your will to keep your money invested for your children until they turn 25, and then to give them the property outright.

Should you give to children directly or indirectly?

If you have children under the age of majority to deal with, you have some special concerns. You must decide whether to provide for them by making a gift to the children themselves or by making a gift to their parents (and benefiting the children by a trickle-down effect).

If you are married with young children, you certainly want to make sure that your children are supported after you die, but that doesn't necessarily mean that you have to give money to them directly by naming them as beneficiaries of your will and/or insurance policies. You can achieve your purpose by leaving your estate to your spouse, who will use it to support your children.

If you're dubious about what your spouse will do with the money, then you must name your children as beneficiaries to make sure that they are provided for. But if you want to leave money for your children, you must set up a trust in your will that will invest the money for the children, pay out income and capital as necessary, and turn the entire fund over to the children when they grow up.

If you give a large sum of money directly to a minor child (under age 18 or 19, depending on the province), the provincial government will step in and put the money into a trust. The trust will be managed by a government official (called the *public trustee* in most provinces) and turned over to the child when he or she comes of age. Many people aren't all that keen on the way the provincial government manages their tax dollars and would be less than thrilled to have the government managing their personal money.

If you have grandchildren, nephews and nieces, or other children whose lot in life you'd like to improve, the question still arises — do you want them to benefit directly or indirectly? If you want the child to have a direct benefit, you can make a gift to be held in trust until the child comes of age.

If you have education in mind, you can even set up a Registered Education Savings Plan to help out the child with university or college expenses. If you think it would be better to benefit the child indirectly, you can give a gift to the child's parents and make the entire family's finances healthier.

The people you have to provide for

There are some people in your life whom you see more as ballast than crew. They're the people you have to provide for even though you may not want to — they have to be in your estate plan too.

You may think that you can do what you like with your property when you make your will, but you're wrong. For centuries, people making wills could do pretty much what they wanted — they had the *right of testamentary freedom*. However, since the early years of the 20th century, certain limits have been placed on that freedom. Nowadays when you're making plans, you have to take into account the possibility that, once you've passed on, claims will be made against your estate by

- People who are dependent on you for support
- Your spouse
- People you've promised to provide for

People who are dependent on you for support

Have you been giving money to certain family members or old pals for years and think it's high time they stood on their own two feet? So far, you've never been able to work up the nerve to tell them you're turning off the tap, but you're looking forward to doing just that in your will. Well, there's some bad news for you — death is no certain escape from those relatives and friends who have attached themselves to you like barnacles.

Whatever province you live in, there is a law to make sure that your *dependants* — certain people you are required by law to support — will be looked after out of your estate.

The definition of a dependant varies from province to province. In some provinces, only children or legally married spouses can be considered dependants. In other provinces, unmarried spouses, parents, grandparents, or siblings can also qualify as dependants.

A person won't necessarily be considered a dependant just because he or she is related to you. The person must also be someone whom you were supporting (or under a legal obligation to support) at the time of your death. Likewise, a person won't be considered a dependant just because you were supporting him or her before you died. There must also be a recognized relationship between the two of you.

For example, your deadbeat friend who has been sleeping on your basement sofa and whose car loan you have been paying for the last six months would not qualify as a dependant. But your own child under the age of majority would qualify as a dependant whether or not you are providing support for him or her.

Provincial law allows a dependant to make a claim for support from your estate if you do not leave him or her enough money in your will. A judge would decide whether to provide for a dependant out of your estate by looking at things such as that person's other sources of income and ability to earn a living.

Dependants are given a fixed period of time, usually six months, in which to make a claim by starting a court action. Your executor cannot legally start giving your estate away to your chosen beneficiaries until the time limit for these claims has passed and no claim has been made.

Once someone has made a claim, your executor will not be allowed to give anything to your beneficiaries without first getting a court order, or else getting the consent in writing of everyone who has the right to make a claim against your estate as a dependant. If your executor does give any of your estate to your beneficiaries without consent or a court order, the executor could really land in the drink. He or she may personally have to pay the dependant if there's not enough money left in the estate.

If you have been supporting someone, or know or think that you have a legal obligation to support someone, tell your lawyer when you're making your will. Your lawyer can determine whether or not that person has the right to make a claim against your estate as a dependant. If the person does have a right, you should probably leave enough money in your will to support him or her. (Your lawyer will be able to help you figure out how much that is.)

There's not much to be gained by trying to leave a dependant out of your will. A dependant with any gumption will get the money out of your estate anyway — and your other beneficiaries won't get anything until the claim has been dealt with.

Your spouse

In addition to being able to make a claim against you as a dependant, in some provinces, your spouse may have rights to claim a minimum share of your estate. Some provinces have passed family law legislation that is designed to give a surviving spouse the same rights to a division of property that a spouse would have on a marriage breakdown. So if you're thinking that death would be a cheaper escape from your marriage than divorce, think again.

Like dependants, your spouse has a fixed period of time, usually six months, in which to make a claim by starting a court action. Your executor can't legally give any of your estate to your chosen beneficiaries until the time limit has passed without a claim, unless your spouse consents. If your spouse does make a claim, your executor will not be allowed to give anything to your beneficiaries until his or her claim is settled, unless your spouse consents. If your executor does give any of your estate to your beneficiaries without consent, the executor may personally have to pay some or all of any amount that a court later awards to your spouse.

It looks like "'til death do us part" is a bit off the mark, doesn't it? Even if you're looking forward to death as a way of fleeing the clutches and financial demands of your spouse, if you live in a province that gives spouses a right to a share of an estate, you have to leave your spouse the required amount.

When you talk to your lawyer about making your will, your lawyer will ask if you are married or separated. He or she will tell you whether or not your spouse has the right to make a claim for a share in your estate. If your spouse does have a right, you'll probably have to leave him or her enough money to satisfy it. (Again, your lawyer will be able to help you figure out how much that is.) As with your dependent relatives, there's little to be gained by trying to leave your spouse out of your will.

Book VII

Estate Planning

People you've promised to provide for

Generally speaking, if you promise a person that you'll make a provision in your estate, he or she can't force your estate to carry through on your promise. That only goes for ordinary, run-of-the-mill promises, though. If your promise is contained in a contract, the person to whom you made the promise may be able to make a claim against your estate.

This kind of promise is most commonly found in separation agreements. A separation agreement may contain a promise by one of the spouses that

> ✔ His or her estate will continue to make support payments to a spouse and/or children. If you have made this kind of promise, you should make sure that you earmarked enough money in your estate for support payments. (Your lawyer will probably suggest that in your will you give your executor the right to try to negotiate a one-time payment to replace ongoing payments.)

✔ He or she will maintain a life insurance policy in a specific amount naming the spouse and/or children as beneficiaries, failing which the estate will be required to pay a fixed amount of money to the spouse and/or children. If you have made this kind of promise, you should make sure that you've got that life insurance in place!

If you have signed a separation agreement, show it to your lawyer when you go to talk about preparing your will.

The people you decide not to provide for

Finally, there are people in your life who've walked the plank — these are the people you don't want to give anything to, don't legally have to give anything to, and don't intend to give anything to. In your estate plan, you should pay attention to them as well.

What if you don't want to leave anything to someone who is a close relative? You've got your reasons. Perhaps you've already given a gift of money or property, or you believe that he or she doesn't need your money and property but other relatives do. Maybe you once made a substantial loan that was never repaid. Or maybe you just can't stand this person, and the two of you have been quarrelling for years.

A close relative who feels entitled to be included in your will may be tempted to go to court to try to have your will set aside after your death. If your will does get set aside, then you have no valid will — and provincial rules about who shares in your estate if you die without a valid will (that is, if you die *intestate*) take effect. Depending on how close this relative is and what other relatives survive you, he or she may manage to get a chunk of your property.

It may be a wise idea to offer an explanation in your will if you are leaving a close relative little or nothing. If you don't say anything at all about this person, the troublemaker could argue to the court that failing to remember him or her at all was evidence that your mind was in tatters when you made your will. If you mention the person and give a reason for cutting him or her out, it will make an attack from that quarter more difficult.

Understanding Your Executor

You get to be captain on your ship of estate, but you need someone to carry out your orders when you're down in Davy Jones's locker. That's what your executor is for.

It will give you a jaunty, nautical air if you refer to your executor as your "XO" (no, it doesn't mean love and kisses; it stands for *Executive Officer*). Or possibly, it may send your family looking for your power of attorney and living will, convinced that you are no longer mentally capable of managing your own affairs.

What does an executor do?

Before you can decide whom to name as your executor, you should know what it is your executor will have to do. Not everyone is cut out to be an executor, so you'll want to choose yours carefully.

Your executor (called a *liquidator* in Quebec and an *estate trustee with a will* in Ontario) must do the following:

- **Make your funeral arrangements.** An executor usually checks to find out whether you left any instructions, and consults with the family about what you might have liked, but the executor has the legal responsibility to make your funeral arrangements and has the final say about them.

- **Collect information about your estate.** Your executor has to get a reasonable amount of information about the property you own and your debts (including the approximate value of both) in order to apply for letters probate, and locate and gather in your property.

- **Protect the property of your estate.** Your executor has to make sure that valuables (house, car, jewellery, artwork, and so on) are kept safe, and that the property of the estate is properly insured. If you leave behind a business or investments that need active attention, your executor has to look after them personally or else hire a skilful person to manage them.

- **Apply, if necessary, for *letters probate*** (known in Ontario as a *certificate of appointment of estate trustee with a will*). In order to administer your estate, your executor must be able to prove to the world that he or she has the legal authority to do so. The best proof is letters probate, a document from the provincial surrogate or probate court certifying that your will is valid. (Your executor may or may not have to apply for letters probate depending on the size and complexity of your estate.) In order to get letters probate, your executor will have to estimate the value of your estate and have the estate pay probate fees (in almost all provinces, probate fees are based on the total value of your estate).

- **Gather in the property belonging to your estate.** Your executor will have to track down everything that you owned and that now belongs to the estate, and, if necessary, transfer the registration of things that were in your name into the estate's name (real estate, vehicles, bank accounts, investments). Property that your executor must track down includes insurance proceeds, pension benefits, and survivors' benefits that are owed to your family.

Book VII

Estate Planning

✔ **Make an inventory of the property in your estate and value the property.** Your executor has to have a reasonably good idea of the value of your estate in order to get letters probate. But in order to complete your terminal tax return, your executor will have to know your exact income in the year you died, as well as the exact present value of your capital property *and* its value when you got it (for capital gains tax calculations). See Chapter 2 for more on capital gains taxes.

✔ **Keep the money and investments in your estate properly invested.** Your executor has to stash your cash in a safe place until he or she pays the estate's debts and taxes and distributes the remainder of the estate to the beneficiaries. An executor has to choose conservative, low-risk investments, unless you give special instructions in your will (for example, that playing the futures market is okay). Your beneficiaries can sue your executor for making bad investments and reducing the value of the estate before it's given to them.

✔ **Pay debts and taxes.** Your executor must find out whom you owed money to (your creditors) and then pay them, and must also file your terminal income tax return and any outstanding past returns (and, as time passes, estate tax returns) and pay income taxes due. All payments come out of the estate, not the executor's pocket.

✔ **Distribute your estate to the beneficiaries.** Your executor has to hand over the property in your estate to your beneficiaries, following the instructions in your will. If your will creates a trust naming your executor the trustee, he or she will continue to hold onto the trust property and manage it on behalf of the beneficiaries of the trust, in accordance with the instructions in the will.

✔ **Account to the beneficiaries.** Your executor will have to give a statement to the beneficiaries that sets out what money and property were received and paid out on behalf of your estate.

What are the legal responsibilities of an executor?

Your executor is a kind of trustee who must do the following:

✔ Follow the instructions set out in your will.

✔ Obey provincial laws about trusts.

✔ Act with the greatest trust, loyalty, and honesty.

✔ Deal with the property of the estate the same way a reasonably prudent businessperson would handle his or her own property.

- ✔ Act in the best interests of the beneficiaries and not favour some beneficiaries over others.

- ✔ Carry out duties personally and not pass them off to someone else (although it's okay for the executor to have professionals working for him or her, such as having a lawyer get letters probate or an accountant prepare tax returns or a broker give investment advice).

- ✔ Not try to make a personal profit from the estate or get a good deal for himself or herself on property from the estate.

Choosing your executor

So far, what you know about an executor is this: An executor has to perform fairly complex tasks, such as arranging your funeral and looking after and valuing real estate, investments, and personal possessions; has to manage the finances of your estate; has to deal with a lawyer or a court office to get letters probate; has to keep track of everything that comes into and goes out of your estate; and has to make sure your beneficiaries get what you want them to get. And an executor has to do all these things with honesty and loyalty, and do them as well as a reasonably careful businessperson would do them when dealing with his or her own property. (Read the upcoming section, "What can happen if you choose the wrong executor?" to find out what can go wrong if you make the wrong choice.)

Clearly, acting as an executor is not going to be as easy as falling out of a crow's nest. That means you don't want to choose someone who's going to have trouble fulfilling the role because his or her business or management skills are too limited to deal with the kind of property you're leaving. You also don't want to choose someone who won't want the job (a person named as executor doesn't have to accept) or who doesn't have time to do it. Likewise, you'd prefer to avoid someone who's not likely to last as long as your estate — if you set up a trust for young children, for example, you don't want to name an executor who has one foot in the grave. Last but not least, you don't want an executor who's going to have trouble getting along with one or more of the beneficiaries, or who may find it hard to treat certain beneficiaries fairly.

Have a look at your potential crew members. Does anyone there fill the bill? There's no need to panic just because your family and friends are normal human beings instead of lawyers, accountants, bankers, or entrepreneurs. Most executors do not administer the estate all on their own. They hire a lawyer and perhaps an accountant to carry out many of these tasks. So if your estate is relatively simple, anyone who is honest and has good common sense and at least enough sophistication to work with a lawyer and/or accountant can be your executor.

Book VII

Estate Planning

If you think it will take more than one person to handle the challenge, you can name two or more individuals as co-executors. If your estate is complex, you can name a trust company such as Royal Trust or Canada Trust (their services may be expensive) as your executor, or as a co-executor with an individual. If you decide to go for co-executors, though, keep in mind that they have to act unanimously unless you say in your will that they don't. Then think about which would be worse — requiring your executors to agree about everything, or letting each one act alone?

Oh, and by the way, you should think about naming an alternate executor, especially if you've chosen to go with a single executor. If you don't name an alternate executor and the executor who's your only choice dies before you or refuses to act, someone will have to come forward and apply to the court to be made the administrator of your estate. If your executor dies after you and you haven't named an alternate executor, your executor's executor will become your executor.

When your executor's not quite up to the job

Suppose you feel that you have to name some particular person as your executor in order to avoid hurting his or her feelings deeply, even though he or she isn't quite up to the job. Your spouse, for example, may be very offended at being rejected for the post.

You can take steps while you're alive or in your will to help the landlubber executor — throw a lifeline, as it were. For example, you can pair this executor with a more skilled and experienced executor by naming a more business-savvy friend or relative as co-executor. If your estate is complicated and has enough money to pay the extra fees involved, you can name a trust company, or a professional, such as your lawyer or accountant, as co-executor. Or you could start introducing your executor to your affairs gradually while you're alive and well (and hope you don't kick off before the executor gets the hang of them). You could also put together a team of professional advisers (lawyer, financial consultant, accountant, and broker) and let your executor know they'll be available to help when the time comes.

What can happen if you choose the wrong executor?

Your executor is the linchpin of your estate plan. If you choose the wrong one, your plans can be seriously messed up. For example, an executor who is unwell or old and feeble when you die may drop out or die before his or her duties are completed. But that's not really such a big problem. One way or another, you'll still end up with an executor (your alternate executor, for example). But executors can do worse than get sick or bite the dust. An executor who performs the job incompetently or dishonestly can be bad news, big time.

An incompetent executor may:

- Fail to file appropriate tax returns, leading to extra tax payments in the form of interest and penalties, and extra attention from CCRA.

- Fail to take advantage of various tax-saving strategies such as making an RRSP donation or tax-free rollover of certain qualified assets to your spouse, or taking advantage of unused capital losses, with the result that your estate loses money to the tax authorities unnecessarily.

- Pay debts that should be challenged (so your estate loses money) or fail to pay all of your legitimate debts (so your estate is sued).

- Make poor investment decisions, so your estate doesn't increase in value as it could or even loses money.

- Distribute your estate before your debts and taxes are paid (with the result that the executor may have to pay some of them personally — ha ha, serves the twit right).

- Distribute your estate to the wrong beneficiaries or in incorrect shares or amounts.

A dishonest executor may:

- Steal money from your estate, either by pocketing estate money outright or by overpaying himself or herself for services as the executor.

- Put his or her interests ahead of those of your estate, for example by buying property from the estate for a low price, or by directing paid estate-related work to himself or herself, friends, or family.

- Deliberately favour one beneficiary over another.

Your solution: Make sure you've got an alternate executor — and, if necessary, a trust company as an objective and impartial executor of last resort.

Looking Out for Your Children

Fairy tales were scary when you were a kid, even when they had a happy ending. Now that you have kids yourself, some of the fairy tales are even scarier because you find it harder to believe in the happy ending. And the scariest of all fairy tales are the ones about orphaned children.

Book VII

Estate Planning

It won't help to hide under the covers or to ask for a night light to be left on. You may as well know what will happen to your children under the age of majority if you die before them — and what you can do to try to make sure they'll be safe and well cared for even though you're not there.

Before getting into what will happen to the kids if you die, here's what the law says about who cares for the kids when their parents are still alive. This will delay the stuff about orphans, which you really don't want to hear about, and make it easier to understand when you get there.

In every province, both living parents are the guardians of their children. That means that they are both responsible for caring for the children and they both have the right to make decisions about how the children are raised — where they should live, what faith they should be raised in, where they should go to school, and what medical treatment they should have.

This two-parent, two-guardian arrangement is hunky-dory if both parents live together. Things get a little less hunky-dory and a little more complicated if the parents are separated or divorced. Then they will have to agree who will have custody of the children.

Custody and guardianship mean pretty much the same thing. The person who has custody of the children is the person with whom the children live and who cares for the children and makes the decisions that affect their lives. (This can be viewed as a responsibility or a privilege, depending on how your day has gone so far. By the way, what was that crashing noise coming from the kitchen?) The parents may agree that they will continue to share custody in some way — such as joint custody, which allows both parents to have a say in how the children are raised — or they may agree that only one of them will have custody.

If separated parents can't come to an agreement about custody, the courts will decide for them. Judges often prefer joint custody arrangements. If that's impossible because the parents won't cooperate, judges make their decisions by assuming that both parents have an equal right to care for their children but that custody should go to the one who can care for them best.

You can't put the scary part off any longer because this is a book about wills and estate planning, not about baby and child care. The balance of this section tells you what will happen to your kids following your death if you make no plans for their care, starting with the least upsetting scenario; but matters will rapidly go downhill after that.

If one parent dies but the other is still alive and has custody

What happens to the children on the death of the first parent depends on the custody arrangements that existed beforehand.

If the parents were sharing custody — either because they were living together as a family, or because, although separated or divorced, they had agreed to a joint custody arrangement, or because a court had ordered a joint custody arrangement — the surviving parent simply carries on as sole guardian of the children.

If one parent dies and that parent had sole custody

If the parent who died had sole custody of the children, there are a number of things that could happen:

- Someone, perhaps the surviving parent, the new spouse of the parent who died, or a grandparent will come forward and offer to look after the children.

- More than one person — surviving parent, new spouse, grandparents, and maybe other relatives — will put in dibs on the kids and there will be a long, drawn-out, expensive fight over who gets to care for them. If the kids are this lovable, they may have a future in the entertainment business.

- No one will offer to take the children. The surviving parent may not want them and there may be no other close relatives or friends who feel a moral obligation towards them — or else everyone who *may* feel a moral obligation is already acquainted with the children. Having enjoyed the spectacle of them tearing around like banshees when they were not murdering each other over the TV, the toys, or the right to monopolize the bathroom, all potential caregivers run screaming in the opposite direction. Sadly, this may also be the case if a child has a disability and needs extra care.

If only one person wants custody

There may be only one person interested in caring for the children. Or the entire family may have discussed the situation and agreed that a particular family member should care for the children.

The person who wants custody or guardianship of the children will have to apply to the court for a formal custody order. In a few provinces, a surviving parent who was not a guardian (because of an agreement or court order giving custody to the other parent alone) automatically becomes the guardian and does not legally need a court order. But even when there is no legal requirement to get a court order, a formal order may be necessary to allow the guardian to

- ✔ Receive any money for the children's care and upbringing that was left by the parent who died.
- ✔ Register the children in school.
- ✔ Consent to medical treatment on behalf of the children.

When an application for custody is made, the court has a duty to make sure that the person applying is capable of looking after the children and has a reasonable plan for their upbringing. This is true even if no one comes forward to oppose the application.

If there's a custody battle

If the kids are popular and a fight erupts over who gets them, it will be up to the court to decide who gets custody. The judge hearing the application will base his or her decision on the best interests of the child. This means that the judge will want to hear about such things as:

- ✔ The family relationship between the children and each person claiming custody.
- ✔ The emotional ties between the children and each person claiming custody.
- ✔ The existing living arrangements between the children and any person claiming custody.
- ✔ The ability of each person claiming custody to look after the children.
- ✔ The plans of each person claiming custody for the care and upbringing of the children.
- ✔ The stability of the family life of each person claiming custody of the children.
- ✔ The children's point of view — in some provinces, they are even entitled to a lawyer to put their interests forward.

How these factors would play out in an actual custody battle would depend on the particular circumstances of the case. A biological parent has a real advantage, even if he or she was not the greatest parent before the other parent's death. Unless the surviving biological parent is seriously unfit to look after a child, the courts will likely grant him or her custody. The only competition to watch out for is a relative or friend with whom the children lived before the death of the first parent. And the preferences of an older child are very important.

If no one wants the kids

If there are no family members or friends who are willing and able to look after the children, the children will be considered *children in need of protection* under the province's child welfare legislation.

We don't operate orphanages in Canada anymore, so put out of your mind the sad picture of your children trudging up the steps of some grey and soulless institution. But don't worry: plenty of other sad pictures can replace it. The children will be placed in the care of a child and family services agency, which will try to find them a foster home. (They make an effort to keep families together in one foster home, but it's not always possible.) The children may be adopted, especially if they're quite young, perhaps by the foster parents or perhaps by someone else.

Child and family services agencies are fairly careful about picking foster parents, and they keep an eye on the children in foster care. The adoption process is quite lengthy and is geared toward investigating the adoptive parents to make sure they're fit. But there's no doubt about it, even a kind foster family or adoptive family isn't the same thing as *your* family.

Children who are not adopted are on their own as soon as they come of age (18 or 19 depending on the province). If they inherited property from the parent who died and that parent made no special trust provisions, the children will also receive the property as soon as they come of age. So your teenagers could be running around with no one to supervise them and their pockets full of cash — or with nothing in their pockets at all.

Book VII

Estate Planning

If both parents are dead

Now for the orphans. If the children have only one surviving parent who then dies, or if both parents die at the same time, the result will be the same. There is no person who has an automatic right to take over custody of the children.

The options are the same as in the circumstance of the death of a parent who has sole custody of the children. If both of the children's parents are dead:

✔ One person may offer to look after the children. It will be up to the courts to decide whether that person is suitable — and if he or she is not, then the children will be turned over to the child and family services agency as a child in need of protection.

✔ Several people may offer to look after the children and then there will be a custody battle over them — but in this case no one has the advantage of being the children's parent, so the outcome of the fight may be harder to predict. With luck, at least one of the people who want custody will be someone the courts think is fit to have custody.

✔ No one may offer to look after the children. Then, once again, the children will be handed over to the child and family services agency.

Appointing and safeguarding a testamentary guardian

A *testamentary guardian* is a person appointed in a parent's will to look after the children. In almost every province, a parent can appoint a testamentary guardian — but making the appointment won't necessarily dissolve all parental worries. The effect of appointing a guardian depends on the province the family lives in and whether or not there is a surviving parent.

If the other parent survives the testator

If the parents shared custody of the children and only one parent dies, the surviving parent will continue to be the guardian of the children. It doesn't matter that the parent who died named a different guardian-by-will — the deceased parent can't terminate the surviving parent's right to be guardian of the children. In some provinces, the appointment of the guardian has no effect at all in these circumstances, and in most other provinces, the surviving parent can go to court to remove the guardian named by will. In a couple of provinces, the guardian-by-will can act as guardian, but has to act jointly with the surviving parent.

If the parent who died had sole custody of the children and the other parent survives, the surviving parent does not automatically become the guardian. But neither does the guardian appointed by will. Anyone who wants custody of the children will have to go to court to get it, and if there's more than one person asking for custody, they'll have to duke it out in front of a judge.

The surviving parent has the better chance of getting custody unless he or she is really an unfit parent. If the parent is unfit, then the guardian appointed by will may get the nod, so too if the children have been living safely and happily with the guardian. But because the judge has to decide what to do based on the best interests of the children (see the section called "If there's a custody battle" earlier in this chapter), not on the wishes of the people asking for custody, it's possible that the judge won't give custody to either the surviving parent or the guardian appointed by will.

If one parent is already dead and then the second parent dies

If the second parent to die appointed a guardian-by-will, in almost all provinces, the guardian will get custody of the children if the guardian agrees to the appointment — unless someone else applies to be guardian (and/or asks the court to remove the testamentary guardian). Then it's up to the courts to choose the guardian.

In some provinces, it's up to the courts even if no one else wants custody or objects to the guardian: the appointment under the will lasts for only 90 days. During that time the guardian-by-will must apply to the court for a formal custody order. In the other provinces, there is no legal requirement for the guardian under the will to get a court order granting custody. However, such an order may be necessary or at least desirable if the guardian wants to receive money left for the children's care, to register the children in school, or to consent to medical treatment for them. Financial institutions, schools, and doctors are apt to want proof of guardianship, and it's more reassuring to them to see a court order than a will.

If a guardian is appointed by will but other relatives and friends want custody in spite of the testator's choice, then everyone goes roaring off to court. In choosing among the various applicants, a judge doesn't have to decide that the guardian under the will is unfit before picking someone else to have custody. The judge will take the testator's wishes into account, but will make a choice based on the best interests of the children. (This takes you back to the section on custody battles again.)

Sounds like the guardian-by-will may spend more time in court than with the kids. A testator who doesn't want the chosen guardian to feel oppressed (or bankrupt) from the very beginning should include a provision in the will that the estate will pay the guardian's legal costs.

What you can do to safeguard your choice of guardian

You looked your family and friends over and chose as testamentary guardian the person you thought would best care for your children. But when you're gone, your choice won't necessarily be respected. People you rejected out of hand may show up yelling "Me, me!" and the judge (who's never met you, your kids, or any of the would-be guardians) may second-guess you and make his or her own choice. Is there any way you can get a little more control over the situation?

You may have noticed that "the best interests of the children" is a recurring theme when it comes to awarding custody of children. In order to make your choice of guardian stick, you can try to arrange things so that the court will be convinced that going with your choice will also be acting in the children's best interests.

Book VII

Estate Planning

How do you perform this trick? (No, flying monkeys are not the answer.) You have to start while you're still alive. When you choose someone to be guardian, if possible choose a person whose relationship with your children satisfies a good number of the "best interests of the children" factors. Look for a potential guardian who

- Is a relative (by blood or marriage).
- Has strong emotional ties with the children.
- Is living with the children (if not, then a person with whom the children would like to live — of course, your children may be at a stage when they'd like to live with anyone except you).
- Is able to look after the children.
- Can come up with good plans for the care and upbringing of the children.
- Lives in a stable family relationship.

And don't forget that the potential guardian should be someone who'll agree to be guardian. Make sure you ask before sticking a name in your will. "Sneak-up" or surprise guardianship doesn't work too well.

What if you don't know anyone who has a close relationship with your children — the kind of relationship the court will be looking for when deciding whether your choice of guardian is okay? Then it's time to get to work and create such a relationship. Keep in touch with whichever members of your family you consider fit to look after your kids, and encourage some bonding between them and the children. If your family looks hopeless, see whether any of your friends are suitable. And don't pin your hopes on just one individual — you may want to name an alternate guardian in your will in case your first choice gets cold feet. Faraway children look greener.

The duties of a guardian

In fairy tales, the duties of a fairy godparent are pretty much restricted to showing up in the nick of time to rescue the child hero/heroine just when all seems lost. A guardian works harder and gets less time off. And doesn't get a magic wand that actually turns mice into pumpkins.

Guardian of the person and guardian of the property

If a person is appointed the guardian of a child and nothing is said to limit the guardian's appointment, that person has the right and the responsibility to

- Care for the child and make decisions about how the child is raised (have custody of the child), and
- Look after the child's property.

It is possible, however, to appoint one person to care for the child (to be the child's *guardian of the person*) and another person to look after the child's property (to be the child's *guardian of the estate* or *guardian of the property*). In a will, it is usual to name a guardian of the person, and to make the executor the guardian of the property. The two guardians may be the same person or they can be different people.

Instructions for the guardian (s)

Instructions to the guardian of the property are usually left in the will. It's best to set up a testamentary trust for minor children, and then the person looking after the property will be your trustee.

Instructions to the guardian of the person should be discussed face to face with the guardian. The better your chosen guardian knows you and your children, the more likely it is that he or she will know your values and have a sense of the way you would like your children to be raised. You may also want to leave a detailed letter for the guardian with your will, in which you set out your wishes about your children's general upbringing, their religious training and education, and the values you would like them have (fiscal conservative with a strong social conscience or bleeding heart liberal? Pepsi or Coke? Barney or Thomas the Tank Engine?). These instructions are not legally binding, but they will give the guardian some guidance and perhaps comfort. The letter will also be a useful tool in the guardian's hands when your children claim that if their parents were still alive they would have let them ____ (fill in the blank).

Book VII

Estate Planning

Protecting Your Business

Nearly two million Canadians own their business or professional practice, either alone or with others. Are you one of them? And have you ever dreamed of your business being handed down from generation to generation . . . your portrait hanging on the boardroom wall . . . maybe even a bronze statue of you outside the head office . . . your descendants and their employees speaking of you in reverential tones as "our founder"?

Maybe that's not your fantasy at all. Maybe you'd just as soon your kids didn't follow you into the business you're in. But even so, you'd probably like to pass its value on to your family by selling the business and leaving them the money.

This much is sure: If you own your own business, deciding what to do with it is an important part of your estate planning. And deciding what to do isn't the end of it — you've got to take action, too. Whatever your decision about your business, it's much more likely to work out if you make plans than if you leave everything to chance.

Your main choice lies between keeping your business in the family and selling it to someone outside your family. However, it's not necessarily up to you to decide what to do with your business.

If you're a sole proprietor or the sole or majority owner of the shares of a corporation, the decision is pretty much yours. You own the business and you can do what you like with it. You'll have the power to hand it over to your family if that's what you want to do, or to sell it if you prefer.

If you are a partner in a business or a minority shareholder in a corporation, your choices are more limited. Your business associates very probably have a big say in what's going to happen.

You may already be sold short

If you have partners or if you have fellow shareholders who together hold more shares in the corporation than you do, you don't have total control over your business. Whether you want to sell or you want to bring your family in, your partners or the other shareholders will want to stick their oar in. They may be able to prevent you from sharing ownership of the business with family members or passing ownership on to them. And they may be able to prevent you from selling your ownership interest to an outsider.

If your business is a partnership

To be frank, it's rather unlikely that you will be able to transfer your interest in a partnership to a family member either during your lifetime or on your death.

You can transfer your partnership interest in an ongoing business to someone else (including a family member) only if your partners consent to the transfer. And they won't consent unless they think exchanging you for your family member is good for the business and for them as well. If there's a partnership agreement, it may require you to transfer your interest directly to your partners if you want out. And you can't add a new partner or partners without the consent of your existing partners.

If you die while still a partner in a business, you can't just leave your partnership interest to a family member and assume that he or she will take your place. If you have a partnership agreement, it probably only requires your partners to pay your estate for your interest. It almost certainly doesn't say that the partnership has to take on someone you choose to replace you. If you don't have a partnership agreement, the partnership dissolves on your death. Then your family members simply inherit your share of any property belonging to the partnership. It would be up to your former partners and your family to decide whether they wanted to re-form the partnership together.

If your business is a corporation

If your business is a corporation, you have to bring in new owners by transferring shares in the corporation to them. Anyone can buy shares in a public corporation on the stock market (although usually only the very rich can buy enough shares to get any kind of control over the business). But in a private corporation — which is the only kind of corporation you would be turning over to your family or selling to an outsider — the shareholders and/or the directors of the corporation have to give their consent before shares can be transferred. If you're not the only shareholder or not the majority shareholder of your corporation, it may be difficult or impossible to persuade all the necessary people to allow you to transfer your shares to a family member, or to anyone else for that matter. Just like partners, shareholders and directors don't want new owners wandering in off the street. (You'd also need consent to get the corporation itself to give or sell new shares to your family member.)

In addition, if you're thinking of selling, it's highly unlikely that an outsider would want to buy a minority share in a private corporation, even if the other shareholders agreed to the purchase. Actually, your family member might not thank you for a minority interest either. The only real market for minority shares in a private corporation is the other shareholders of the corporation.

Book VII

Estate Planning

You may have options

If you're a sole proprietor or majority shareholder in a corporation, you're going to be able to decide for yourself whether to bring family members into the business — or whether to sell the business and pass its value on that way.

If you're bullish on keeping your business in the family, you may be interested to know that you're in the minority of Canadian business owners. Experts who surveyed a sample of family-owned Canadian businesses with annual revenues of at least $1 million revealed that only one-third of owners thought it was important to keep the business in the family.

But if you're not afraid to buck a trend and you'd still like to hand down your business to your family, brace yourself for a bear market. Another survey, this one by the Family Firm Institute, an international organization that assists family businesses, showed that only about 30 percent of family-owned businesses survive into the second generation, 12 percent into the third generation, and 3 percent into the fourth generation and beyond. Of all family businesses in Canada, only 2 percent have passed through four generations or more. So even if nothing's stopping you from passing your business on to your children, your chances of creating a commercial dynasty are small.

So what's the plan here? You've got a choice. Should you try to keep the business in the family, or should you sell? In order to make your decision, you'll have to start thinking about the nature of your business, the abilities and interests of your children, and your own temperament.

Look at your business

The characteristics of your business itself may determine whether or not it can be passed successfully on to the next generation. If it can't, the recommendation is: Sell. If you could use a little help pondering this matter, here are some points to consider:

- ✔ Must your business be operated by someone with special training or expertise? If you are a licensed professional or a skilled tradesperson, your business probably can't be carried on by a family member who isn't qualified in that trade or profession.

- ✔ Can your business get along without you or are *you* the business? Is your business based solely on your particular skills, talents and/or personality? If that's the case, it may be that *no one,* inside or outside your family, can take it over successfully. It only has value — income value — as long as you're running it, and there may be no value to pass on.

- ✔ How much is your business worth as a going concern? Is it worth enough to pass it on to all of your children who are interested in sharing in it? In other words, will they all be able to earn a decent living from it, either right away or after they've used their skills to expand it? Or will they starve? If the business won't support them, you would be doing them a favour to sell it and pass on the proceeds instead.

- ✔ How much has your business gone up in value since you started it? Selling your interest in your business or transferring it to a family member other than your spouse could trigger a capital gain or loss. (See Chapter 2.) If your business is a corporation, up to $500,000 of any capital gain may be tax free because of the capital gains deduction permitted under the *Income Tax Act* for qualifying small business corporations. If your business is a sole proprietorship or partnership, there's no deduction available. Will you have enough other money and property (or life insurance) to pay the tax on any capital gain that pops up when you give your business to your children? If you don't, selling your business may be the only way you'll get the money needed to pay the tax due.

Look at your family (1): The advancers

Assume that your business meets the requirements to be handed on to your children. Every family has its advancing and declining issues, and the character and talents of your family members will determine whether it's wise or even possible to pass your business on to the next generation.

First of all, is there anyone in your family who is interested in taking over your business *and* who has the talent and ability to be successful? If your only child or all of your several children have the desire and the talent to carry on, you could be all set to start dynasty building.

Do none of your children have the talent to carry on (whether interested in doing so or not)? Again, you're all set — to sell to an outsider. There's no point in letting your children take over just to run the business into the ground. It will be best for them if you sell the business and give them the money to finance other enterprises they're better suited for.

But those two scenarios aren't the end of the possibilities. What if . . .

- You have several children, and they're all interested but only some are talented. Do you cause family strife by taking on some and rejecting the others? If you believe that taking on only some of your children will cause a lot of harm to your family, and you care more about your family than about your business, then you should consider a sale.

- You have several children with the interest and talent (whether they represent all of your children or only some of them). Do they get along well enough with each other that it's safe to bring them all in? Have their dispute resolution skills improved since they fought as children over the TV remote and whose turn it was to walk the dog? If they can't get along well as people, they'll have trouble getting along as partners, and an enforced partnership is almost certainly doomed.

- You have talented, interested children who get along well with each other. But are they capable of working with and learning from you? Will they be willing to wait until you are ready to hand control over to them, or will they try to force you out of the business before you are ready?

One last (somewhat gloomy) thought here: If it's a commercial empire you have in mind, even if your children get along well enough to cooperate as partners themselves, they may have trouble cooperating when it comes time to choose among their own children as their successors. That's the stage at which the McCain family business came unglued. There's a reason for that old expression, "Shirtsleeves to shirtsleeves in three generations"!

Look at your family (2): The decliners

If you have more than one child and you decide (for various reasons, not restricted to those discussed above) to turn your business over to one or some of them rather than to all of them — what are you going to do about the children who've been left out of the business?

Your business has value. It may even be the most valuable thing you own. You may not care that you're not treating all your children equally in your estate plan by cutting some of them out of the business. But it's bound to cause trouble, and you may not want to increase your family's volatility (or turn your family into a hornet's nest). But then again, you may care very much about acting fairly towards everyone.

There are solutions to the problem of an unequal distribution of your estate, short of selling the business to an outsider, to save yourself a lot of grief. Here are some of them:

- ✔ You may have enough other money and property or enough life insurance that you'll be able to divide your estate equally among your children anyway.

- ✔ You may decide to make a gift of only part of the value of the business, and require your chosen successor to buy the rest of the business's value from you or your estate — so that you have enough money to leave equal shares to your other children. (Before you go for this solution, consider whether the business generates enough income for your child to be able to afford the purchase price you're asking. You don't want to sink your successor into debt.)

- ✔ You may decide to give ownership of the business to all of your children on the understanding that only one of your children will operate the business. In this case you have to consider whether the business is profitable enough to support several owners, and whether the silent partners are capable of actual silence.

Look at yourself

Now, what about you? Can you do whatever is necessary to ensure a smooth transfer of control of your company to your children? Are you a floor trader at heart, working for yourself alone? Or are you the kind of person who can give up control of your business before you die, if that's what it will take to make the transition successful? Ask yourself:

- ✔ Can you bring yourself to choose a successor at all?

- ✔ Are you truly willing to involve your children in the ownership and/or control of your business before you retire?

- ✔ Are you capable of working *with* and perhaps *for* your children, rather than always being the boss?

If you answered "no" to any of these questions, you're probably not a good candidate for founder of a dynasty. Neither was a "very foolish fond old man."

Timing is everything: When should you hand things over to your family?

If you're going to hand over ownership of your business to your family, when should you do it? There are a number of things to take into account:

- When can you afford to retire from the business? If you don't have other income and investments to live on, and if your successors won't make enough from the business to pay you for it while they run it, you may have no choice but to hang on to the business yourself until you die.

- When can you afford the tax on the capital gain? If your business has gone up in value, you may have to pay capital gains tax when you transfer ownership of the business. If you don't have sufficient other money and property to be able to pay the tax without having to liquidate the business, you may have to hold on to the business until you die. At that point, life insurance you've bought for the purpose will help your estate cover the tax on the capital gain.

- Do you expect your business to continue to go up in value? If so, you may want to consider some form of estate freeze fairly soon that involves transfer of ownership (although not necessarily control) away from you. (See Chapter 2 for more on estate freezes.) If you do an estate freeze on your business, you may or may not have to pay capital gains tax on the current value of the business. But either way, future increases in value will belong to your children and will not be taxable in your hands. Your children will not have to pay any tax on increases in value until they dispose of the business.

Even if you decide that you can't afford to hand over ownership before you die, you should consider handing over control of your business — or at least partial control — while you're still alive. Bringing your family into the business while you're still around will increase their chances of successfully carrying on the business because

- They will have the opportunity to learn about the business from an expert — you.

- Your clients or customers will have an opportunity to get to know your children and transfer their trust and loyalty (now yours alone) to them.

Book VII

Estate Planning

Timing is everything: When should you sell?

If you are planning to sell your business, you want to sell it for the highest possible amount. So you want to sell it when it's most valuable. Is that when it's a going concern? Or when you're finished with business life — well, with life in general — and your executor may be selling off just the business's property?

Most businesses are worth more as a going concern than as a collection of assets. And usually your business will be worth even more as a going concern if you're still around. A business that's in business has *goodwill,* which can be loosely defined as the intangible value of the high likelihood that customers will keep coming back. If you stick around for a while after a new owner takes over, the customers are more likely to do that. For another thing, you can offer a buyer your expertise by agreeing to stay on while the buyer learns the ropes and gets to know your customers.

And there's yet another reason to sell while you're alive. You can arrange to have the sale price paid to you in instalments spread out over several taxation years, and so reduce the tax payable on any capital gain. If you cling to your business until you die, you are deemed to have disposed of it at your death. Then your estate has to receive the full proceeds all at once and pay any taxes due in that same taxation year. This will come at a really bad time because you're deemed to have disposed of your non-business assets as well, and your estate will have to pay tax on any resulting capital gains. Just for fun, don't forget that everything in your RRSPs not left to your spouse will be considered income and be taxed as well.

Transferring or selling a sole proprietorship

A sole proprietorship is fairly easy (from a legal point of view) either to transfer or sell. The business is essentially the assets (property) that the proprietor owns personally and uses to carry on the business. Once the sole proprietor has decided what to do, then he or she can act right away.

Keeping it in the family

If you want to hand over your business to a family member during your lifetime, you'll have to legally transfer ownership of all of the assets of the business. (You'll trigger a capital gain for yourself if your assets have gone up in value.)

If you want to hand over your business on your death, you will need a properly drafted will leaving the assets of the business to your chosen successor(s). (See Chapter 4 for more on wills.)

If you've decided on an estate freeze, you'll need to make extra plans. An estate freeze is a lot more complicated than simply handing over your assets during your lifetime or leaving them in your will. (See Chapter 2 for more on estate freezes.)

You'll probably want your successor to get not only the assets of the business but also all of the debts of the business. If you're giving your business away during your lifetime, you'll have to make some arrangements with your successor and your creditors for the payment of your business debts. If you're giving your business away in your will, your estate will be responsible for paying its debts. That could have the effect of reducing other family members' share of your estate — so take this into account when you're making your estate plan.

Selling outside the family

Selling to an outsider is much the same as transferring to a family member — you transfer ownership of the assets used in your business to the purchaser and make arrangements for the payment of your business debts.

At the time of the sale, you'll want some tax advice about reducing the taxes payable on any capital gain you've triggered by the sale. For example, you may be able to arrange for the price to be paid to you in instalments spread out over several taxation years.

Selling a partnership

If you're a partner in a business, your best plan probably is to have your partners buy your interest when you retire or die. That means you need a *partnership agreement* that deals specifically with retirement and death.

If you have no partnership agreement or you have one but it doesn't deal with retirement and death issues, your partnership will simply dissolve when you leave or die (the exception is a *declared partnership* in Quebec). If you have a two-person partnership, it will dissolve when you leave or die whether or not you have a partnership agreement. Once you reach the point of retirement or death, you (or your estate) will be at a disadvantage when it comes to negotiating a price for your interest in the partnership or your share of the partnership assets. That's because your partners aren't required to buy you out, and they may not have the money to buy you out anyway. And they have to agree before you can sell to an outsider — assuming you can find one who wants to join this partnership.

To prevent this financially unpleasant situation from coming to pass, you need a partnership agreement that deals with what happens when a partner wants to leave or retire or die. And you need it now, before you're actually ready to leave or retire or die.

You'll need to speak to a business lawyer about this, but your agreement should have:

- ✔ A buy-out clause *or* a buy-sell clause. If one partner wants out, either the rest of the partners buy that partner out or (usually only in small firms) that partner buys out all the other partners. (If no one is willing to buy, then the partnership is dissolved.)

- ✔ A retirement clause. The other partners buy out a partner who wants to retire. The clause will say how the price of the buy-out is to be calculated (the buy-out money will probably have to be borrowed).

- ✔ A clause that requires the other partners to buy the interest of a partner who has died from the dead partner's estate.

- ✔ A clause that requires the partners to have life and disability insurance on each other. The insurance proceeds can help fund a buy-out triggered by the death or disability of a partner.

It's possible, but uncommon, to have a partnership agreement that allows partners to sell their partnership interest to an outsider if the other partners approve of the new partner.

Transferring or selling a corporation

To transfer or sell your ownership interest in a corporation, you have to transfer or sell shares in the corporation. That sounds easy enough, but it isn't always that easy in practice.

Keeping it in the family

If you are the only or the majority shareholder in your business corporation, you're free to transfer your shares to whomever you like. You don't need anyone's consent if you're the sole shareholder or the majority shareholder. So you'll simply sign the shares over to your family member while you're alive, or leave the shares in your will.

If you're just one of the shareholders and are not the majority shareholder, you'll need the consent of at least some of the other shareholders and/or the directors of the corporation to hand over your shares to anyone. If you want to be able to give or leave your shares to a family member, it is critical that you have a *shareholders' agreement* that says you can do that. You'll need to negotiate the agreement with your fellow shareholders before the time comes for you to make your dynasty-building move. The other shareholders may want their children to come into the business as well, so there could be interesting times ahead for the corporation.

Selling to an outsider

If you are the only shareholder or the majority shareholder, again you can do whatever you like with the corporation. You're free to sell it to the buyer of your choice. (Unhappy minority shareholders might have a right to complain to the court about what you're doing, however.) You can sell a business corporation either by selling all of the corporation's assets or by selling its shares.

Whether you choose an asset sale or a share sale will depend largely on the tax consequences for you — consult your lawyer and accountant before you start negotiating a deal with a buyer.

If you are not the only shareholder or the majority shareholder, for all practical purposes your market is limited to your fellow shareholders or the corporation. But if you want to sell to either, you'll need to do some advance planning because without a shareholders' agreement in place,

✔ Neither the shareholders nor the corporation are automatically required to buy your shares.

✔ Neither the shareholders nor the corporation are required to offer a fair price for your shares.

✔ Even if the corporation and/or the shareholders want to buy your shares, they may not have enough money.

The upshot is, you want a shareholders' agreement that requires the other shareholders or the corporation to buy your shares from you or your estate and that says how the price is to be calculated. The agreement should also require the shareholders to be insured (life and disability insurance) so that there will be money to fund a share purchase on the death or disability of a shareholder. (If you just leave and don't die, the shareholders or corporation will probably have to borrow money to pay for your shares.) You may also want the agreement to give you or your estate the right to terminate the corporation's existence, so you can get your share of the corporation's property if the other shareholders or the corporation can't buy your shares.

Book VII

Estate Planning

Chapter 4

Reading and Understanding a Will

. . . .

In This Chapter

▶ Discovering that formal wills are not written in English

▶ Learning what a will says, in translation

▶ Learning the rules about how a will is signed and witnessed

▶ Finding out about do-it-yourself wills

. . . .

*I*f you don't have a will, there's no way you can put your estate plan into action. In fact, if you don't have a will, your estate could be in a real mess. A person who dies without a will is said to have died intestate. You can die intestate by never making a will at all, or by making a will that turns out to be invalid (because you are not legally capable of making a will or because your will is not properly signed and witnessed). If you die intestate, here are some of the consequences:

✔ Your property will be given away according to rules set by provincial law.

✔ There won't be an executor, carefully chosen by you, who will have the automatic right to look after your estate.

✔ Your estate may lose money while it is being administered.

✔ The property of your estate may not be given away in the form you'd like (even if it were going to the people you'd like).

✔ Your estate will probably end up paying more in taxes.

✔ If any of your beneficiaries are under the age of majority, any property that goes to them has to be managed by the provincial government.

✔ Your wishes about who will look after your children when you're gone may not be made known.

So that you don't end up in a state of intestate (so to speak), this chapter moves estate planning from theory to practice. You find out why you need a will, examine a sample will, and discover what the heck each section of it means.

Get Ready, Get Set, Get Lost

Reading a standard will prepared by a lawyer is like turning on the hyperdrive and blasting out of the familiar solar system. It's very easy to get lost! But with a little training (from this chapter), you won't find yourself drifting helplessly and searching for a familiar landmark when you look for the first time (or the tenth time) at your own will.

A standard will can be very short or can go on for pages and pages. It is usually at least several pages long and contains a series of numbered paragraphs. Although every will is tailored to the needs of the individual, wills often follow a standard pattern. You can expect to find clauses that:

- Identify the testator, the person making the will (you).

- Revoke (cancel) all previous wills, to make it clear that this will replaces any earlier will you made.

- Name the executor, the person who will administer your estate.

- Leave all of your property to your executor in trust. (Please remain calm and do not unbuckle the restraints of your zero-gravity chair, as ignition is imminent. This isn't a scam dreamed up between your lawyer and your executor to grab your estate. The executor, as the trustee of your estate, is given a kind of ownership of the property in the estate after you die but has to hand the property out according to the instructions in your will.)

- Tell the executor to pay all valid debts, claims, and taxes of the estate.

- Tell the executor to give your beneficiaries (people and/or charities you've chosen to receive gifts) whatever is left in the estate after the debts, claims, and taxes have been paid.

- Give the executor certain legal and financial powers to manage your estate — power to keep or sell property in the estate, to invest cash, and to borrow money.

- Name someone to have custody of minor children, if you have any.

Taking a Close Look at a Will

In the rest of this chapter, you'll work through what a complete standard will may look like. The first thing you'll notice is that it is not written in English. It's mostly written in Englatin, with some medieval French thrown in. You'll also notice that it follows the simple rule, "Why use one word when three will do?" As well, when it comes to sentence length, enough is never enough, and punctuation is almost totally banned (especially if it may put a sentence out of its misery). After you review the will in all its glory, you can go through it paragraph by paragraph, translated into English, and figure out what's going on.

There is no one-size-fits-all will. Each person's will has to meet the needs and objectives of that particular person. So first, here are the details you need to know about this will's testator, John Robinson, and about his wishes.

John Robinson is married to Maureen Robinson. They have a grown-up daughter, Judy, and two younger children, Penny and Will. And who knows, they may have more children, depending on plot requirements and available alien technology.

John wants to leave his state-of-the-art atomic force microscope to his colleague, Dr. Zachary Smith; $10,000 to his daughter Judy; and $2,500 to the Alpha Prime Foundation to Save All Humanity Resident in Canada (a CCRA–registered charity). He wants to leave everything else to his wife, if she is still alive when he dies. If his wife dies before he does, he wants to divide his estate among his children and wants each minor child's share of the estate to be held in trust until the child is 21 years old.

Book VII

Estate
Planning

He wants his wife to be his executor if she is still alive when he dies. If his wife dies before he does, he wants his daughter Judy to be his executor. He wants his executor to have broad powers to deal with his estate and to be able to use her own judgment about what to do — because you never know when an intergalactic financial opportunity or disaster may occur.

Now that you've met John Robinson, have a look at Figure 4-1 to see what a sample will for him might look like. If you try reading it at all, your eyes will probably cross around Paragraph III(a), and the rest of the will will go by in the kind of blur you normally associate with space travel at warp speed. Then you'll slowly move in for a closer look at the sample will, hopefully making it comprehensible in a language spoken by humans.

THIS IS THE LAST WILL AND TESTAMENT of me, JOHN ROBINSON, of the City of Jupiter 2, in the Province of an Unknown Part of the Galaxy.

I.   I REVOKE all former wills and other testamentary dispositions made by me.

II. I NOMINATE, CONSTITUTE, AND APPOINT my wife, MAUREEN ROBINSON, to be the executor and trustee of this my will, provided that if my said wife shall have predeceased me or shall survive me but die before the trusts hereof shall have terminated or shall refuse or be unable to act or to continue to act as such executor and trustee, then I nominate, constitute, and appoint my daughter, JUDY ROBINSON, to be the executor and trustee of this my will in the place and stead of my said wife. I hereinafter refer to my executor and trustee for the time being as my "trustee."

III. I GIVE, DEVISE, AND BEQUEATH all of my property of every nature and kind and wheresoever situate, including property over which I may have a general power of appointment, to my trustee upon the following trusts, namely:

(a) To pay out of the capital of my general estate my just debts, funeral and testamentary expenses, and all estate, inheritance, succession duties, or taxes whether imposed by or pursuant to the law of this or any other jurisdiction whatsoever that may be payable in connection with any property passing (or deemed to pass by any governing law) on my death or in connection with any insurance on my life, or in connection with any gift or benefit given or provided by me either in my lifetime or by survivorship or by this my will or any codicil hereto, and whether such taxes and duties be payable in respect of estates or interests which fall into possession at my death or at any subsequent time; and I authorize my trustee to commute or prepay any such taxes or duties.

(b) To deliver to ZACHARY SMITH, if he survives me, my Atomic Force Microscope.

(c) To pay to my daughter, JUDY ROBINSON, if she survives me, the sum of TEN THOUSAND DOLLARS ($10,000).

(d) To give to the Alpha Prime Foundation to Save All Humanity Resident in Canada, located in Ottawa, Ontario, Canada, the sum of TWO THOUSAND FIVE HUNDRED DOLLARS ($2,500) for its general purposes. I declare that the receipt of the person who professes to be a treasurer or other proper officer for the time being of this charitable organization shall be a sufficient discharge to my trustee therefor.

(e) To pay, transfer, and assign the residue of my estate to my wife, MAUREEN ROBINSON, if she survives me for a period of thirty days, for her own use absolutely.

(f) If my said wife predeceases me or survives me but dies within a period of thirty days of the date of my death, to divide the residue of my estate into as many equal shares as there shall be children of mine then alive, and I declare that if any child of mine should then be dead and if any issue of such deceased child should then be living, such deceased child of mine shall be considered as alive for the purpose of such division.

My trustee shall set aside one of such equal shares as a separate trust for each child of mine who shall be living at the division date and shall keep such share invested and the income and capital or so much thereof as my trustee in her uncontrolled discretion considers advisable shall be paid to or applied to the benefit of such child until he or she attains the age of twenty-one years when the capital of such share or the amount thereof remaining shall be paid or transferred to him or her, any income not so paid or applied in any year to be added to the capital and dealt with as part thereof. If such child should die before attaining the age of twenty-one years, such share, or the amount thereof remaining, shall be held by my trustee in trust for the issue of such child who survive him or her in equal shares per stirpes. If such child should leave no issue him or her surviving, such share or the amount thereof remaining shall be held by my trustee in trust for my issue alive at the death of such child in equal shares per stirpes.

IV. I AUTHORIZE my trustee to use her discretion in the realization of my estate, with power to sell, call in, and convert into money any part of my estate not consisting of money at such time or times, in such

Figure 4-1: A sample will for John Robinson.

such manner and upon such terms, and either for credit or for part cash and part credit as she may in her absolute discretion decide upon, or to postpone such conversion of my estate or any part or parts thereof for such length of time as she may think best. My trustee shall have a separate and substantive power to retain any of my investments or assets in the form existing at the date of my death at her absolute discretion without responsibility for loss to the intent that investments or assets so retained shall be deemed to be authorized investments for all purposes of this my will.

V.   I DECLARE that my trustee when making investments for my estate shall not be limited to investments authorized by law for trustees but may make any investments which in her absolute discretion she considers advisable, and my trustee shall not be liable for any loss that may happen to my estate in connection with any such investment made by her in good faith.

VI.   MY TRUSTEE may make any division of my estate or set aside or pay any share or interest therein, either wholly or in part, in the assets forming my estate at the time of my death or at the time of such division, setting aside or payment, and I expressly declare that my trustee shall in her absolute discretion fix the value of my estate or any part thereof for the purpose of making any such division, setting aside or payment, and her decision shall be final and binding upon all persons concerned.

VII.   SUBJECT AS herein specifically provided, if any person other than a child of mine should become entitled to any share in my estate before attaining the age of majority, the share of such person shall be held and kept invested by my trustee and the income and capital, or so much thereof as my trustee in her absolute discretion considers advisable, shall be used for the benefit of such person until he or she attains the age of majority.

VIII.   I AUTHORIZE my trustee to make any payments for any person under the age of majority to a parent or guardian of such person or to anyone to whom she in her discretion deems it advisable to make such payments, whose receipt shall be a sufficient discharge to my trustee.

IN WITNESS WHEREOF I have to this my last will and testament, written upon this and 1 preceding page, subscribed my name this 11th day of June, 20__.

SIGNED by the testator, JOHN ROBINSON,)
as his last will, in the presence of us,   )
both present at the same time, who at   )
his request, in his presence and in the   )   _____
presence of each other have hereunto   )   John Robinson
subscribed our names as witnesses.   )

WITNESS:

Signature: _____

Name: _____

Address: _____

Occupation: _____

Signature: _____

Name: _____

Address: _____

Occupation: _____

Book VII

Estate Planning

Identification

> THIS IS THE LAST WILL AND TESTAMENT of me, JOHN ROBINSON, of the City of Jupiter 2, in the Province of an Unknown Part of the Galaxy.

This part is easy. It identifies the document as a will and the testator as John Robinson. It also identifies his city and province of residence. Pat yourself on the back for understanding everything perfectly so far.

Revocation of other wills

> I.   I REVOKE all former wills and other testamentary dispositions made by me.

The making of a will generally cancels any previous wills. Clause I makes it clear that the testator does intend to cancel them. "Other testamentary dispositions" would include a *codicil,* an addition to an existing will that revises some part of the will. (**Note:** In the farthest western reaches of our galaxy, a codicil is a hallucinogenic fungus. It would be wise not to confuse the two.)

Naming the executor

> II. I NOMINATE, CONSTITUTE, AND APPOINT my wife, MAUREEN ROBINSON, to be the executor and trustee of this my will, provided that if my said wife shall have predeceased me or shall survive me but die before the trusts hereof shall have terminated or shall refuse or be unable to act or to continue to act as such executor and trustee, then I nominate, constitute, and appoint my daughter, JUDY ROBINSON, to be the executor and trustee of this my will in the place and stead of my said wife. I hereinafter refer to my executor and trustee for the time being as my "trustee."

Clause II appoints John's wife, Maureen, to be his executor. If Maureen dies or is unwilling or unable to act as John's executor or to complete the executor's work, John appoints his daughter Judy to be executor. (For more information about choosing an executor and what an executor does, see Chapter 3.)

John named an alternate executor for Maureen (Judy), but has not named an alternate executor for Judy. (He was probably running out of trustworthy adults, and trust companies have not caught on much beyond the orbit of Pluto.) If Maureen dies and then Judy dies, Judy's executor will become John's executor.

After this clause, you may lose track of the executor and wonder if she has fallen into a black hole. She hasn't, she's just changed her name. This clause names the executor as both executor and trustee, and the executor is referred to as "the trustee" for the rest of the will. That's because the next clause sets up a trust for all of the property in John's estate and the executor is the trustee who deals with the property.

Leaving property to the executor in trust

> III.   I GIVE, DEVISE, AND BEQUEATH all of my property of every nature and kind and wheresoever situate, including property over which I may have a general power of appointment, to my trustee upon the following trusts, namely:

Clause III gives all of John Robinson's property to his executor, not for her own benefit but for the benefit of the people who will eventually receive the property under the will. These are the people to whom John's estate owes money, and the beneficiaries.

A "general power of appointment," in case you were wondering, is a very old-fashioned right over property that you rarely find in Canada anymore.

John's instructions to his trustee about what to do with the property in trust are set out in the lettered sub-paragraphs that follow this clause.

Book VII

Estate Planning

Payment of debts

> (a)   To pay out of the capital of my general estate my just debts, funeral and testamentary expenses, and all estate, inheritance, succession duties, or taxes whether imposed by or pursuant to the law of this or any other jurisdiction whatsoever that may be payable in connection with any property passing (or deemed to pass by any governing law) on my death or in connection with any insurance on my life, or in connection with any gift or benefit given or provided by me either in my lifetime or by survivorship or by this my will or any codicil hereto, and whether such taxes and duties be payable in respect of estates or interests which fall into possession at my death or at any subsequent time; and I authorize my trustee to commute or prepay any such taxes or duties.

Paragraph (a) directs the executor (now of course known as the trustee) to pay all legitimate (valid) debts, claims, and taxes of John Robinson's estate, including the cost of his funeral. Most of the paragraph deals with the different ways that taxes might become payable. The executor is given the right (by John, not by Canada Customs and Revenue Agency) to use her judgment about the timing of tax payments — she can put off paying (*commute*) or pay in advance (*prepay*).

Payment of debts and taxes is the executor's first responsibility. Nothing can be given to the beneficiaries until it is clear that there is enough money in the estate to pay the debts and taxes. If there is not enough money to cover them *and* the full amount of the gifts to the beneficiaries, the gifts to the beneficiaries will be reduced.

Distributing the remaining property to the beneficiaries

After the executor pays the debts and taxes of John's estate, she must give the remaining property to the beneficiaries according to John's instructions. First, she must give the specific gifts John made in his will. After the specific gifts are made, she must distribute the *residue*. The residue is what is left after debts, claims, taxes, and estate administration expenses have been paid and the specific gifts have been given out.

Specific gifts

John's will contains three specific gifts, one of personal property and two of cash.

> (b)   To deliver to ZACHARY SMITH, if he survives me, my
>   Atomic Force Microscope.

This gift of property is worded in a typical way. There will be a gift only if Zachary Smith is alive when John dies. If Dr. Smith dies before John, Smith's heirs are not entitled to the gift. The microscope will become part of the residue of John's estate and go to other beneficiaries of John's.

Even though paragraph (b) doesn't say so, there will also be a gift only if John owns the microscope when he dies. If he doesn't own it at the time of his death, Dr. Smith will get nothing since the will does not provide for an alternate gift to him.

> (c)   To pay to my daughter, JUDY ROBINSON, if she survives me, the
>   sum of TEN THOUSAND DOLLARS ($10,000).

This is a typical gift of cash to an individual. There will be a gift only if Judy is alive when John dies. If Judy dies before John, her heirs will not be entitled to take the gift. The cash will become part of the residue of John's estate.

And there will be a gift only if there is $10,000 left in John's estate after his executor pays the estate's debts and gives Dr. Smith the microscope.

> (d)   To give to the Alpha Prime Foundation to Save All Humanity Resident in Canada, located in Ottawa, Ontario, Canada, the sum of TWO THOUSAND FIVE HUNDRED DOLLARS ($2,500) for its general purposes. I declare that the receipt of the person who professes to be a treasurer or other proper officer for the time being of this charitable organization shall be a sufficient discharge to my trustee therefor.

This is a typical gift of cash to a charity. Chapter 2 has a bit more on gifting to charities.

In the second sentence of paragraph (d), John is saying that the executor has done all that is expected of her if she gives the money to the charity and gets a receipt for it from someone who appears to be an officer of the charity. This paragraph is designed to protect the executor from liability if the person she pays the money to turns out to be the wrong person.

Gift of the residue

> (e)   To pay, transfer, and assign the residue of my estate to my wife, MAUREEN ROBINSON, if she survives me for a period of thirty days, for her own use absolutely.

Book VII

Estate Planning

John is leaving the residue of his estate (what's left after payment of his debts and taxes and the gifts to Dr. Smith, Judy, and the Alpha Prime Foundation) to his wife Maureen. "For her own use absolutely" means there are no strings attached — she can do whatever she likes with the property she receives. (An alternative would be to give her the use of the property for her lifetime and then give it to the children.) But she only gets the residue if she lives for at least 30 days after his death. If she dies before John dies or less than 30 days after John dies, she will not inherit. Now what's that all about?

Suppose John and Maureen were in a cosmic radiation accident together. Without paragraph (e), Maureen would inherit from John even if she outlived him by only 15 minutes. The residue of John's estate would go to Maureen, and then would immediately become part of Maureen's estate and would be disposed of according to the provisions in *her* will. So John's property would be given to the people named by Maureen, not by John! Even if John and Maureen both name the same beneficiaries (as husbands and wives very often do), the property would have to pass through first John's estate and then Maureen's estate. That would result in extra work and expense.

Thirty days is the standard time period used in wills. There's no magic to the number 30 nowadays, but it was probably once considered a reasonable length of time to wait to see whether the second of two people who were injured or who sickened at the same time was going to live or die.

Alternative gift of the residue

> (f)   If my said wife predeceases me or survives me but dies within a period of thirty days of the date of my death, to divide the residue of my estate into as many equal shares as there shall be children of mine then alive, and I declare that if any child of mine should then be dead and if any issue of such deceased child should then be living, such deceased child of mine shall be considered as alive for the purpose of such division.

What happens if Maureen Robinson dies before John does? Who gets the residue of the estate then? Paragraph (f) gives the answer, and it's an eyeful.

If Maureen dies before or within 30 days after John dies, John's estate is to be divided equally among his children. If John's children all survive him, and John has no other children by that point, then each of the three children will get one-third of the residue.

Then the next question is: What happens if a child also dies before John does? After all, some days there's an evil plasma creature lurking behind every rock.

When John was considering how to pass his estate on to his family, he had to think about whether the share of a child who died before him would simply go to his surviving children or whether it would go to any children that his deceased child had. This paragraph shows that John ended up deciding to divide a deceased child's share among that child's own children.

Here's an example of how this paragraph might work itself out, given the following situation:

> John dies, as the result of an unfortunate misunderstanding with a native of the planet Zifpox. At the time of his death, Maureen is already dead (unexpected meteorite shower, no shower cap) as is Judy (the espresso on the planet Tryffl is unbelievably strong). Penny and Will, John's two other children, are both in their 20s. Will has a son, Robby. Judy is survived by her two daughters, Blawp and Spingo.

The residue of John's estate would be distributed like this:

- ✔ Penny will receive one-third of the residue.

- ✔ Will will receive one-third of the residue (and his son will receive nothing).

- ✔ Blawp and Spingo will receive Judy's one-third share and it will be split equally between them, so each of John's granddaughters will receive one-sixth of the residue.

Trust for children under the age of 21

> (f)   *continued*   My trustee shall set aside one of such equal shares as a separate trust for each child of mine who shall be living at the division date and shall keep such share invested and the income and capital or so much thereof as my trustee in her uncontrolled discretion considers advisable shall be paid to or applied to the benefit of such child until he or she attains the age of twenty-one years when the capital of such share or the amount thereof remaining shall be paid or transferred to him or her, any income not so paid or applied in any year to be added to the capital and dealt with as part thereof. If such child should die before attaining the age of twenty-one years, such share, or the amount thereof remaining, shall be held by my trustee in trust for the issue of such child who survive him or her in equal shares per stirpes. If such child should leave no issue him or her surviving, such share or the amount thereof remaining shall be held by my trustee in trust for my issue alive at the death of such child in equal shares per stirpes.

Book VII

Estate Planning

The paragraphs are getting worse. It may be time to turn on the neutron shields for protection.

The rest of paragraph (f), which should not be approached without full anti-particle gear, tells John's executor what to do if any of John's children or grandchildren are under the age of majority (18 or 19, depending on the province or solar system) when John dies. Remember that a minor child cannot receive property directly. In Canada, if no trustee is named, then the provincial public trustee is supposed to look after a minor child's inheritance.

John instructs that the share of any minor child (or grandchild), including any interest earned on the share, is to be held in a trust set up specifically for the child, with John's executor as trustee. The share, plus interest, is to be turned over to the child when he or she turns 21. John could have instructed his executor to turn over the child's share as soon as the child reached the age of majority. However, he thought that any child would be better able to handle the inheritance at a slightly older age. And when you factor in light-speed travel, it could take John's executor the additional two or three years just to figure out how old everyone is anyway.

Until the child turns 21, John instructs his executor to use her own judgment about how much of the money to give to or spend on the child.

Finally, if a child dies before reaching the age of 21, that child's share will be divided among his or her children, if any. If the child has no children, then his or her share will be divided among John's other surviving children. If one of John's children has died (under 21) but has produced children, then the share that would have gone to John's child will be divided among those children. If you're wondering where all of this comes from . . . because frankly you don't see it there . . . part of what is said is an expansion of the two little words "per stirpes." This Latin phrase, meaning "through the descendants," says that if one of your children dies before you, your deceased child's children will get their parent's share, divided up among them.

Executor's powers

From this point on, the will mainly natters about giving the executor powers to deal with the estate. These include such things as the power to keep property of the estate in its current form instead of turning it into cash, the power to invest the estate's cash as the executor thinks best, the power to borrow money on behalf of the estate, and the power to buy property from the estate.

Turning the estate's property into cash

IV.	I AUTHORIZE my trustee to use her discretion in the realization of my estate, with power to sell, call in, and convert into money any part of my estate not consisting of money at such time or times, in such manner and upon such terms, and either for credit or for part cash and part credit as she may in her absolute discretion decide upon, or to postpone such conversion of my estate or any part or parts thereof for such length of time as she may think best. My trustee shall have a separate and substantive power to retain any of my investments or assets in the form existing at the date of my death at her absolute discretion without responsibility for loss to the intent that investments or assets so retained shall be deemed to be authorized investments for all purposes of this my will.

In clause IV, John gives his executor the power to keep any of the property of the estate in the form it's in when John dies, instead of selling it for cash. He also gives the power to delay turning property of the estate into cash. Under provincial law, an executor must turn all of the property of the estate into cash as quickly as possible — unless the will contains the powers given here.

Investments

> V.   I DECLARE that my trustee when making investments for my estate shall not be limited to investments authorized by law for trustees but may make any investments which in her absolute discretion she considers advisable, and my trustee shall not be liable for any loss that may happen to my estate in connection with any such investment made by her in good faith.

In clause V, John has given his executor very broad powers to decide how to invest any cash in the estate. Instead of restricting her to the very safe investments permitted under provincial trust legislation, John is allowing his executor to invest in any type of investment she thinks will be good. (This is wise, because provincial legislation has never seen the Intergalactic Stock Exchange during a trading session. It's true that you can easily lose your shirt and three of your five eyes, but, on the other hand, investors have been known to triple their pseudopod holdings in a single 20-second "trade blast.") John has also given his executor absolution: As long as she makes her investment decisions honestly, she will not be financially responsible to the beneficiaries if any of the investments lose money.

Distribution in kind

> VI.   MY TRUSTEE may make any division of my estate or set aside or pay any share or interest therein, either wholly or in part, in the assets forming my estate at the time of my death or at the time of such division, setting aside or payment, and I expressly declare that my trustee shall in her absolute discretion fix the value of my estate or any part thereof for the purpose of making any such division, setting aside or payment, and her decision shall be final and binding upon all persons concerned.

Book VII

Estate Planning

If it turns out that more than one beneficiary will share in the residue of the estate (which will happen if Maureen dies before or within 30 days of John's death), John's executor will have to divide the residue of the estate into the correct number of shares. Under this will, the shares have to be of equal value (from paragraph III(f)).

John's estate may include some cash (in various currencies), some stocks, some rocks (picked up en route), his residence/vehicle, furniture, extraterrestrial art objects, and household goods. The only totally fair way to distribute the estate in equal shares would be to sell everything and split the cash. But, as with most estates, there are items that the beneficiaries would like to keep in the family. John, in clause VI, says that the executor can use her own judgment to decide to distribute some or all of the residue in its existing form. She'll be able to give each beneficiary a combination of cash and other property as long as the value of each beneficiary's share amounts to the correct percentage of the total value of the residue. If the beneficiaries can't agree on the value of individual pieces of property, the executor may have to get a professional valuation.

Dealing with minors

John's will contains two more clauses to help his executor deal with beneficiaries who are minors.

> VII. SUBJECT AS herein specifically provided, if any person other than a child of mine should become entitled to any share in my estate before attaining the age of majority, the share of such person shall be held and kept invested by my trustee and the income and capital, or so much thereof as my trustee in her absolute discretion considers advisable, shall be used for the benefit of such person until he or she attains the age of majority.
>
> VIII. I AUTHORIZE my trustee to make any payments for any person under the age of majority to a parent or guardian of such person or to anyone to whom she in her discretion deems it advisable to make such payments, whose receipt shall be a sufficient discharge to my trustee.

Clause VII sets up a trust for anyone who may end up inheriting property under John's will while still a minor, but who is not already covered by the trust that looks after John's children and grandchildren. This is the ultimate "what-if?" clause because it addresses the possibility that when John dies his wife is dead and all of his children are dead without having left any grandchildren. John has not said where he wants his estate to go if that happens. As a result, his estate would be divided under provincial intestacy laws and might eventually reach a distant relative under the age of majority. If he has no relative, his estate will *escheat to the Crown* (become the property of the provincial government). If the estate escheats, this trust clause will be totally unnecessary — except on a small planet circling the star Tau Ceti, where the government is formed by citizens in the larval phase of development.

Clause VIII talks about the mechanics of making payments on behalf of beneficiaries who are minors. Since payments cannot be made directly to a minor, this clause gives the executor authority to make the payment to the minor's parent or guardian or to anyone else whom the executor considers suitable (for example, a school requiring payment of tuition fees, or Rigellian space pirates holding the minor hostage).

Signing provisions

IN WITNESS WHEREOF I have to this my last will and testament, written upon this and 1 preceding page, subscribed my name this 11th day of June, 20__.

SIGNED by the testator, JOHN ROBINSON,)
as his last will, in the presence of us,   )
both present at the same time, who at   )
his request, in his presence and in the   )   John Robinson
presence of each other have hereunto   )   _____
subscribed our names as witnesses.   )

WITNESS:

Signature: _____

Name: _____

Address: _____

Occupation: _____

Signature: _____

Name: _____

Address: _____

Occupation: _____

Book VII

Estate Planning

This final clause says how many pages long the will is. That's so nobody will be able to slip an extra page in after John has signed (yes, there are people and life forms in this universe who would tamper with a will).

The clause also says the date on which John signed the will. It is important to include the date, since a new will revokes all wills that John made earlier. Without dates, it will be impossible to know which will came first if John has more than one signed will.

There's a strange blather beside the place for John's signature about how the will was signed with everyone in everyone else's presence. It almost sounds like the testator and witnesses are a troupe of contortionists. It's actually a description of the proper signing procedure for a will.

Chapter 5

Power of Attorney and Your Living Will

*Y*ou've got an estate (or else you're in the process of creating one), and that means you have all kinds of affairs to transact. You work to produce income, you make investments, you buy and sell property, you take out insurance, and you make a will. What would happen to you (and your estate) if you were no longer able to rush around attending to your affairs because you were physically or mentally disabled?

It's not uncommon for people to be disabled for a period of time — in some cases for years — before they die. It's not a scenario any of us likes to confront. For some people, disability is worse to face than dying. While you're in the process of planning how to care for your family and friends after you die, you should also make plans to care for yourself and them if you become disabled.

This chapter tells you why you need documents (a *power of attorney* and a *living will*) that allow someone of your choice to manage your finances and make decisions about your medical care if you become disabled before you die.

Power of Attorney: The Solution to Your Management Problems

A person is considered to be mentally incapable of making legal and financial decisions when he or she is not able to understand information that is relevant to making a decision, or is not able to appreciate what is likely to happen as a result of making the decision.

If you become mentally incapable of looking after your own affairs, there are a surprising number of things you won't be legally able to do. You won't be able to enter into contracts — and that will cut off your personal ability, for example, to

- Buy or sell investments.
- Buy insurance.
- Buy or sell real estate.
- Buy or sell big-ticket items like a car.
- Open a bank account or rent a safety deposit box.
- Take out a mortgage.
- Rent an apartment or make arrangements to go into a seniors' residence or a nursing home.

They'll probably still take your cash down at the grocery store or pharmacy, and your bank may let you withdraw small amounts of money at reasonable intervals. But many merchants and almost all banks will get very nervous if you don't appear to be mentally coherent and you want to do something involving even a moderately large sum of money.

Other people you want to deal with may well go along with you too, if you don't look too glassy-eyed or talk too strangely (this is especially true if you transact business by mail or e-mail). However, there are two problems with this:

- You may, in your vacantness, want to enter into a contract that is harmful to you, or the other party to the contract may want to take advantage of your state of mind to defraud you.
- Even if the contract is perfectly fair, it can be challenged and set aside if someone realizes that you were not mentally competent when you entered into it.

If you are mentally incapable, you will need someone else to conduct your legal and financial affairs for you all the time. If you are physically disabled, you may need someone else to conduct your legal and financial affairs for you only some of the time. In order to give someone else the ability to look after your affairs, you need to prepare a *power of attorney.* A power of attorney is a document that gives another person authority to handle legal and/or financial affairs of the person who signs the document.

Before going any further, here is an important vocabulary section. A power of attorney isn't known as a power of attorney in every province. This chapter uses the term power of attorney throughout, but, depending on the province, it may be known as a *power of attorney for personal property,* a *power of attorney for financial decisions,* a *mandate,* or a *representation agreement.* Similarly, this chapter refers to the person who makes and signs the power of attorney as the *principal,* although, depending on the province, this person might also be known as the *donor* or the *grantor.* Finally, this chapter refers to the person chosen by the principal to handle affairs as the *attorney,* although, again depending on the province, this person might be known as the *attorney in fact,* the *agent,* the *donee,* the *mandatary,* or the *representative.*

Got it together now? The principal wants another person to look after the principal's legal and/or financial affairs, so the principal signs a power of attorney document appointing the person of his or her choice to be the attorney.

A power of attorney must be created when you are mentally capable. To be considered mentally capable of creating the power of attorney, you must be capable of knowing the value and kind of property you own and of understanding the powers that you are giving to another person.

Book VII

Estate Planning

Powers of Attorney Come in Different Models

A power of attorney is quite flexible in its use. You don't have to be mentally or physically incapable to want one, you just have to want someone else to look after a legal or financial matter for you.

Examples, anyone? You can create a power of attorney that gives your accountant the power to handle all of your affairs for a short period while you're out of the country and out of reach, or one that gives your daughter the authority to sell your cottage, or one that gives your son the authority to instruct your lawyer what to do in a lawsuit you've started, or one that gives your nephew the authority to make deposits and withdrawals in your bank account. You can also create a power of attorney that gives a relative, friend, or professional adviser the power to look after all of your affairs for the rest of your life.

A power of attorney has no flexibility in one respect, though: It ends as soon as the principal dies. It cannot take the place of a will, and it cannot override the provisions of a will. And an attorney cannot make a will on behalf of the principal.

Enduring or continuing power of attorney

An ordinary power of attorney is valid only as long as the principal is mentally competent. It automatically ends when the principal becomes mentally incompetent. For many people, of course, this is exactly the point at which they want the power of attorney to come into play.

This would be a much shorter chapter if there were no answer to this problem. Luckily, there is an answer, and unluckily, this chapter is quite long. The answer is the *enduring* or *continuing* power of attorney. It is intended to continue in effect even after the principal becomes mentally incompetent. What's needed to turn an ordinary power of attorney into an enduring power of attorney is a specific statement in the power of attorney document that the power of attorney is intended to continue after the principal becomes mentally incompetent.

General or specific power of attorney

A power of attorney can be *general* or *specific*.

A general power of attorney gives the attorney power to make many or all financial and legal decisions on the principal's behalf. In most provinces, a general power of attorney gives the attorney authority to make any financial or legal decision that the principal could make, and to do any financial or legal act that the principal could do — except prepare or change the principal's will. The principal can impose limitations on the attorney's power when the document is prepared. But if the principal does not do so, the attorney has complete power to manage the principal's affairs. That includes, for example, receiving money and paying bills; opening and closing bank accounts; making bank deposits and withdrawals; making and cashing in investments; buying, mortgaging, and selling property; and hiring and firing workers (such as caregivers) for the principal.

A specific power of attorney gives the attorney power to carry out the transactions mentioned in the document. For example, it could allow the attorney to do personal banking, or to deal with stated sources of income such as investment income and dividends, or to carry out a particular activity such as selling a vacation property.

In Quebec, the situation is somewhat different. A power of attorney (called a *mandate*) only automatically gives the attorney (called the *mandatary*) the authority to make decisions and take actions that are necessary to preserve the principal's property, and it strictly limits the way in which the attorney can invest the principal's money. In addition, the attorney must get a court order to sell any of the principal's property. A Quebec power of attorney document must give the attorney "full administrative powers" in order to create a general power of attorney like that discussed above.

Banking power of attorney

Banks have specific power of attorney documents for banking matters. You can usually get a form at your local branch, and, if you only want to make a specific power of attorney for banking, you don't need to go anywhere else to get a power of attorney. In fact, even if you have a general power of attorney prepared by your lawyer, your bank may insist that it needs a power of attorney for banking in its own form. You (or your attorney armed with a general power of attorney) may have an uphill climb to convince the bank employees that a general power of attorney includes a banking power of attorney.

If your bank refuses to accept the general power of attorney and insists on its own banking power of attorney, the bank's form should be checked over by a lawyer before you sign it, to make sure that it doesn't cancel the general power of attorney.

 Since it may be too late for you to sign a banking power of attorney by the time your general power of attorney is needed, you should have a discussion with the manager of your bank branch at the time you're having a general power of attorney prepared. Ask whether the general power of attorney will be acceptable. If it looks like the bank is going to be stubborn, take the bank's form for the banking power of attorney to your lawyer for review.

Book VII

Estate Planning

What's in a Power of Attorney?

The power of attorney document differs from province to province. In most provinces, though, a power of attorney document usually

- ✔ **Names the attorney(s).** If more than one attorney is being appointed, the document should say whether the attorneys may make decisions alone or whether they must agree on all decisions. Sometimes, a power of attorney also names a substitute attorney who takes over if the original attorney is unable or unwilling to carry out the required duties.

- ✔ **Cancels previously made powers of attorney.** If there is an earlier power of attorney in effect and the principal wants it to continue in effect, the later document must make that clear. (It's this cancelling clause in the banking power of attorney that can lead to trouble if you've already got a general power of attorney.)

✔ **Sets out the powers the attorney is to have.** The attorney can be given all powers the principal has, or any part of the principal's powers — such as the power to carry out certain types of transactions (for example, banking) or the power to deal with certain types of property (for example, investments or real estate).

✔ **Indicates whether or not the power of attorney remains in effect after the principal becomes mentally incompetent.** If the document says nothing about this, then it ends when the principal becomes mentally incompetent. If it is meant to continue in effect, the document must say so in the words required by the law of the province in which the power of attorney is to be used.

✔ **States when the power of attorney comes into effect.** A power of attorney can come into effect immediately or at some time in the future. In some provinces it comes into effect as soon as it has been signed and witnessed. (To prevent the attorney from acting before the principal is ready to hand over the reins, the principal can have a third person — say the principal's lawyer — hold onto the document until the principal becomes mentally incapable.) In other provinces, the principal can decide when it will come into effect — on a specified date or on the happening of a specified event (usually the mental incapacity of the principal).

If the power of attorney is to come into effect when the principal becomes mentally incapable, in some provinces the power of attorney document can say how it's to be decided that the principal has become incapable (for example, by the opinion of the principal's doctor or lawyer). If the document doesn't say anything about how to decide, then the provincial statute governing powers of attorney applies. In some provinces, the statute says that two doctors must agree that the principal is incapable. In other provinces, the statute says that a court must decide.

✔ **Says whether the attorney is to be paid.** In most provinces, the attorney is not entitled to be paid unless the power of attorney says so. If the attorney is to be paid, the document may set out the amount or the provincial government may set the rate.

✔ **Makes conditions about how the attorney is to exercise his or her powers.** The document can say that the attorney has to invest in certain types of investments, or consult with or report to the principal's family members or financial advisers, or keep financial records in a certain form.

What's Involved in Preparing a Power of Attorney?

The main thing that's involved in preparing a power of attorney is a visit to your lawyer (or, in Quebec, a notary).

There's no legal requirement that a lawyer has to prepare the power of attorney document, however. It's perfectly legal for a person to write out his or her own version, or fill out a pre-printed form.

However, the strongest recommendation is that you *not* go the do-it-yourself route, though. A power of attorney is much like a will — there are special rules about who can be an attorney and who can be a witness, and it also takes some legal knowledge to know what to put in the document and what to leave out. The following sections include some of the things that can go wrong for do-it-yourselfers.

The attorney

For the most part, choosing an attorney is not difficult. The attorney can be anyone who has reached the age of majority (18 or 19, depending on the province) and is mentally competent. Alternatively, the attorney can be a financial institution (usually a trust company).

Book VII

Estate Planning

Choose an attorney whom you trust and who you think would make the same kinds of decisions about your financial matters that you would make.

However, there can be some traps waiting for the principal who doesn't get legal advice and assistance:

- ✔ In some provinces, an attorney who is the spouse of the principal may run into trouble if he or she later tries to mortgage, sell, or otherwise transfer the family residence. Under the family law statutes in some provinces, *both* spouses must consent to such a transaction. One spouse won't be able to use a power of attorney to give the other spouse's consent to such a transaction. (That's to make sure that, for example, a devoted wife is not using the power of attorney to transfer or mortgage the family residence out from under her adored husband.) So it may turn out, in your province, that your spouse is not the best person to be your attorney if your family home may have to be sold or mortgaged.

✔ If the principal wants to name more than one attorney, the principal has to state in the document whether each attorney can act alone or whether the attorneys must act together. If you don't say anything, they must act together.

✔ The principal may forget to name a substitute attorney in case the first choice is unwilling or unable to take on or continue the job.

The powers

A principal may well find it useful to have the help of a lawyer to give the attorney the proper powers. A do-it-yourself principal may make mistakes because:

✔ For the power of attorney to remain valid after the principal becomes mentally incompetent, there has to be specific wording in the document. If the required wording isn't used, the power of attorney may end just when it will be needed.

✔ If there is an earlier power of attorney that the principal wants to remain in effect (for example, a general power of attorney), a later power of attorney (for example, a banking power of attorney) must not contain a *revocation* clause that cancels the earlier one.

✔ If the principal wants to limit the attorney's powers in some way, or have the attorney show financial records to someone for review, that has to be dealt with specifically in the document.

✔ If the power of attorney is going to be used in connection with real estate, special wording may be required, as well as special signing procedures. In some provinces, the people witnessing the signing of the power of attorney may then have to swear an oath before a commissioner or notary public that they are the witnesses.

✔ If the principal has property in another province, one power of attorney may not be enough — a second power of attorney, valid in the other province, may have to be prepared.

The process

It's just as important to get the details of creation of the power of attorney right as it is to get the right words in the document. A lawyer will make sure that all the legal requirements for properly giving a power of attorney are met.

The principal must be in the right state

A lawyer will make sure that the principal has reached the age of majority (easy) and is mentally competent to give a power of attorney (harder). Your lawyer won't let you sign a power of attorney document if you're mentally incompetent — there wouldn't be much point, because it wouldn't be valid if you sign it while incompetent. If your lawyer has doubts about you, he or she may even refer you to a doctor for an examination before agreeing to assist you in creating a power of attorney. This is a safeguard to make sure that you know what you're doing when you give another person power over your financial affairs.

If someone later questions whether you were mentally competent when you signed the document, your lawyer will be able to give evidence that you were. Why would someone challenge your mental competence at the time you signed? Because that person doesn't like the attorney you chose or the decisions the attorney is making. If that person could prove to a court that you were not mentally competent when you made the power of attorney, the power of attorney would be declared invalid from the beginning. There is much less likely to be a challenge if you had a lawyer help you prepare and sign the document because a lawyer wouldn't ordinarily let you sign if you weren't right in the head.

The document must be signed and witnessed

A power of attorney has to be properly signed and witnessed, just as a will does. In most provinces, two witnesses must be present when the principal signs the document and then the witnesses must also sign the document. The principal and the witnesses must all be present together to watch each other sign. (In some provinces, only one witness is required.) In some provinces, the witnesses may have to swear before a commissioner or a notary public that they are the witnesses.

The purpose of these rules is to make sure that no one is forging the principal's name on the power of attorney, or sneakily getting the principal to give a power of attorney without knowing it, or forcing the principal to give the power of attorney against his or her will.

The witnesses must be eligible

Anyone who witnesses the signing of a power of attorney has to be eligible to be a witness. In almost all provinces, the witnesses must not be the attorney, the attorney's spouse, the principal's spouse, or the principal's child. Further, in some provinces only specified people such as judges, justices of the peace, lawyers, and doctors can act as witnesses.

The purpose of this rule is to make sure that the witnesses don't have their own stake in creating the power of attorney. Independent witnesses presumably won't help anyone to forge a power of attorney or force the principal to sign a document against his or her will.

The attorney needs to know when it's time to take over

Finally, the attorney may need a lawyer's help to decide when the power of attorney can be used.

In provinces where the power of attorney comes into effect as soon as it is signed, the principal may want to instruct his or her lawyer to hold the power of attorney document and not give it to the attorney until the principal is mentally incapable. Then the attorney needs to know when to call up the lawyer and ask for the document. This is a matter you and your attorney should discuss with your lawyer.

In provinces where the power of attorney can come into effect when a particular event happens, the principal may state that the event is mental incapacity. Again, the attorney may need to talk to a lawyer to decide whether the event has happened. The principal may even have stipulated that his or her lawyer should decide when it has happened (the usual alternative is to have the principal's doctor decide).

If the power of attorney is intended to come into effect when the principal becomes mentally incompetent and the document says nothing about how it's to be determined that the principal is incompetent, the attorney may need a lawyer's assistance to find out what the provincial law says about determining incompetence. In some provinces two doctors are needed to give evidence, in others a court has to review the evidence and make a decision.

Making Your Wishes Known through a Living Will

The preceding section told you what to do so that your legal and financial affairs will be properly managed if you become unable to look after them yourself. However, if you can't look after your affairs, you probably can't look after yourself either. So who's going to look after you?

Although there's no such thing as universal legal and financial care in Canada, there is such a thing as universal health care. If you need to be looked after physically, you will be. If you need to be treated in a hospital, you'll be admitted to a hospital and treated — if there's a bed for you. If you need to live in a nursing home, a space will be found for you, once you get to the top of the waiting list. If you need home care, health care workers will come (although perhaps only eventually and occasionally).

So you don't really have to worry about making plans to get access to health care. (Or at any rate there's no point in worrying.) The thing you have to worry about is telling health care workers what you want. If you're sick or injured or dying, you may not be physically or mentally capable of telling anyone your wishes. When that time comes it may turn out that you don't care what happens to you. But you probably care now — so this is when you should make your arrangements for a second-in-command who'll speak for you and tell everyone what you would say if you could.

If you're conscious and mentally capable, you make your wishes about medical treatment known by telling your doctor and/or family what you want. If you can't speak, you may have to write your wishes. If you can't speak or write, you may have to talk with your eyes.

If you're not fully conscious or not mentally capable, the way to make your wishes known is by having prepared a *living will* while you were conscious and capable. A living will lets an earlier, mentally capable, version of yourself speak through another person when the later version of you can't.

A living will can do two things:

- ✔ It can appoint someone to make health care decisions for you.
- ✔ It can tell the appointed decision maker what decisions you would like made.

In some provinces, a living will is intended to deal with medical treatment only. In others, it can also deal with personal care decisions about things such as housing, food, hygiene, clothing, or safety. You can find out more about living wills in your province from your lawyer, your provincial law society, or provincial government.

A living will comes into effect only when you're not mentally capable of giving consent to or refusing medical treatment. In most provinces, living wills are legally recognized and the instructions in a living will must be followed. They override the wishes of a patient's family, in the same way that the wishes of a mentally competent patient override the wishes of the patient's family. Even in provinces that haven't yet legally recognized living wills, the instructions will quite probably be followed too.

It would be too much to ask all the provinces to get together and use the same vocabulary about living wills. So there's a different name for a living will in almost every province. Depending on the province, the living will may be called a *personal directive*, a *representation agreement*, a *health care directive*, a *power of attorney for personal care*, a *mandate*, a *directive*, or an *authorization*. Also depending on the province the appointed decision maker may be called an *attorney for personal care*, a *proxy*, an *agent*, a *representative*, a *substitute decision maker*, or a *mandatary*. This chapter refers to a living will and a substitute decision maker.

Book VII

Estate Planning

What does a living will say?

The living will form is different in different provinces, but generally you'll find that the form covers several standard points.

It names the person who will speak for you

Some people appoint just one substitute decision maker to make decisions on their behalf. Others appoint two or more decision makers, usually to make sure that someone will be available when needed rather than to create a safeguard against one person making the wrong decision. If you appoint more than one substitute decision maker but want one person to be able to act alone if a decision has to be made quickly, your living will should say that any substitute decision maker can make a decision individually. But if you want group decisions in case they're safer, the living will should say that the substitute decision makers must agree on all decisions.

Some people appoint a back-up substitute decision maker in case the original substitute decision maker can't or won't act. This is probably wise, because you can't know what the future holds for your substitute decision maker any more than you can know what it holds for you.

See the section, "Not everyone is eligible to be a substitute decision maker," later in the chapter to find out who is eligible to act as your substitute decision maker.

It may cancel a previous living will

When you make a living will and name a substitute decision maker and give instructions about your health care, you normally want to revoke or cancel any previous living will you made. After all, you're making a new one because you've changed your mind about what you want done or whom you want to decide on your behalf.

It may list what health care decisions can be made

If provincial law allows a variety of decisions to be made by a substitute decision maker, a living will could give power to make all health care decisions, or (for example) power only to make decisions about medical treatment or power only to make decisions about food, safety, and hygiene.

It gives instructions about health care treatment

If you live in a province that allows you to give a substitute decision maker the power to make decisions about different aspects of your health care, you could give a variety of instructions. You could say, for example, that if possible you would prefer to be cared for at home instead of in a hospital or nursing home. You could say that you'd like to be cared for in your daughter's home rather than your son's. You could say that you want to be bathed daily, and that you want to be dressed instead of being left in pyjamas. You could say that if you develop a tendency to wander and get lost you would prefer to have a caregiver with you at all times rather than being restrained in a locked area or a chair or bed with straps. You can give instructions about anything that concerns you or occurs to you. Whether it will be possible to carry out your instructions when the time comes is a question for another day.

The instructions you give about medical treatment are a different matter. They tend to be geared less towards everyday life and more towards the question of how long you want to live and in what state. Your substitute decision maker is not going to have a lot of trouble deciding to consent to routine maintenance for you. You don't need to sweat over giving instructions to have your blood pressure taken by the nurse in a nursing home.

Your instructions to the substitute decision maker about medical treatment could be very general — for example, you could instruct that you don't want any treatment that

✔ Will not cure you, and

✔ Will not improve your quality of life if it prolongs your life.

Book VII

Estate Planning

Or your instructions could be more specific — for example, that you do not want to be put on a ventilator or given CPR if you are in a permanent coma or vegetative state and suffer respiratory failure or heart failure. In fact, your instructions can be even more specific than that. You could run down a list of injuries and diseases and state in each case what treatment you would or would not consent to. That might be kind of a fun thing to do on a rainy afternoon.

TIP

If you're specific in your instructions, you'd better say how much discretion your substitute decision maker has to make a different decision. You might not want to miss out on a new medical treatment that could have you back on your feet in no time flat, or you might prefer not to be given experimental treatment that would be unpleasant but would provide little permanent benefit.

If you actually have a particular disease or condition when you make your living will, make sure that you and your substitute decision maker understand how the disease or condition is likely to progress, what the available treatment options are, what they involve, and whether they're likely to be successful. Talk to your doctor, or do research in a library or on the Internet.

It may give instructions about organ and tissue donation

Your instructions to your substitute decision maker can also include your wishes for organ and tissue donation. You should know, however, that if you give advance consent to organ or tissue donation and members of your family are opposed when the time comes, the hospital will probably not accept your donation.

How do you make a living will?

You can fill out a do-it-yourself form to make a living will. You don't have to have a lawyer (or, in Quebec, a notary). However, it's better to have a living will prepared by a lawyer. A lawyer will act as an objective person who can help you decide what instructions you want to leave and who can help you choose the best person to be the substitute decision maker. In addition, a lawyer won't forget to use any special language that the province wants in a living will.

A lawyer will also make sure that you are legally capable of making a living will, that your substitute decision maker is legally eligible to act, and that any special formalities in the making or signing of the document are observed.

You have to be legally capable of making a living will

In some provinces you can make a living will if you are as young as 16, while in others you must have reached the age of majority (18 or 19, depending on the province).

To make a valid living will you must also be mentally capable. In some provinces this means that you must be able to "understand the nature and effect of the living will," and in others that you must be able to "make health care decisions by being able to understand and appreciate the consequences of treatment choices." That's the law . . . but if you're nutty as a fruitcake or comatose, a lawyer won't make a big inquiry into your understanding and appreciation.

Not everyone is eligible to be a substitute decision maker

There are not a lot of qualifications required for a substitute decision maker. In some provinces a person as young as 16 can be named a substitute decision maker, while in others the person must have reached the age of majority (18 or 19, depending on the province).

The substitute decision maker, just like a patient who gives consent, must be mentally capable of understanding and appreciating the consequences of medical treatment choices and decisions. The substitute decision maker has to be mentally capable when called upon to act. That's one reason why it may be a good idea to name more than one substitute decision maker, or to name an alternate.

In Ontario, a person who is being paid to provide health care or residential, social, training, or support services for a person cannot be appointed as that person's substitute decision maker.

Whom should you choose as your substitute decision maker? First, go for someone you feel confident will carry out your wishes. Second, choose someone who isn't going to feel devastated and guilty if he or she has to make a non-life-affirming decision about you. Discuss your wishes in advance not only with your chosen substitute decision maker but also with your whole family so that your decision maker will be supported rather than attacked by your (other) relatives.

Formalities involved in making a living will

You have to sign and date your living will. (If you're physically unable to sign, someone else may sign on your behalf.) Some provinces don't require that a living will be witnessed unless it was signed by someone on your behalf, while others require one witness or even two witnesses (depending on the province) to your signature. Again, ask your lawyer or check with your provincial law society or provincial government for more information.

In cases when a witness is (or witnesses are) required, the substitute decision maker cannot be a witness. Neither can the spouse of the person making the living will or the spouse of the substitute decision maker. The purpose of these rules is to prevent a person from being forced to make a living will or being forced to choose a particular substitute decision maker. The theory is that this sort of thing is less likely to happen if the living will is witnessed by people who have a little distance from the person making the living will and from the proposed substitute decision maker.

Book VII

Estate Planning

After you've made a living will

There's no use making a living will if nobody knows what it says or can find it when it's needed. Your substitute decision maker could have a lot of trouble persuading your doctor or the hospital that he or she has the right to make decisions without the living will to show. Once you've made a living will, give the original to the substitute decision maker — or at the very least tell the substitute decision maker where to find the original.

Put the original of your living will in a safe place, but do not put it in your safety deposit box! Chances are that your substitute decision maker wouldn't be able to get into your box after you became either physically or mentally incapable.

Give a copy of your living will to your doctor(s) for the record. You may also want to give copies to other family members and/or your lawyer.

If you're suffering from a particular disease or condition, keep up to date on what medical treatment is available. You may want to revise your living will to give different instructions if there are significant advances in treatment. And don't forget to revise your living will if something happens to your substitute decision maker.

Appendix A

Prepare to Meet Your Lawyer

● ●

*T*o plan your estate properly and carry out the plan, you need a lawyer. While you're in the planning stages, your lawyer will be able to help you prepare a complete estate plan that answers all your needs by taking you through the foreseeable possibilities about your future and your family's future. When you're ready to put your plan into action, your lawyer can draft your will and other legal documents, such as a power of attorney and a living will, that reflect your wishes.

Use the form in this appendix to make sure your lawyer has all the information necessary to do the best job possible for you.

INFORMATION ABOUT YOU

Have you ever made a

- ☐ Will?
- ☐ Power of attorney?
- ☐ Living will?

If so, you should bring the documents to your meeting with your lawyer.

INFORMATION ABOUT YOUR FAMILY

Marital Status

Are you currently

- ☐ Single? If you are living with someone, bring any cohabitation agreement you have signed.
- ☐ Planning to marry? If so, bring any marriage contract you have signed or are thinking of signing.
- ☐ Married? If so, bring any marriage contract you have signed.
- ☐ Separated? If so, bring any separation agreement you have signed or are thinking of signing, and any court orders that have been made.
- ☐ Divorced? If so, bring your divorce decree and any separation agreement and court orders.
- ☐ Widowed? If so, bring a copy of your spouse's will.

Your Children

	Child #1	Child #2	Child #3	Child #4
Name				
Date of birth				
In your custody or another's				
Disabilities or special needs				

Bring any documents, such as a separation agreement or court order, that affect your relationship with your children.

Who would you like to look after your underage children if both parents are dead?

_____

Your Grandchildren

	Grandchild #1	Grandchild #2	Grandchild #3	Grandchild #4
Name				
Date of birth				
Disabilities or special needs				

Other Family Members or Friends (whom you have a moral obligation to support financially)

	Person #1	Person #2	Person #3
Name			
Date of birth			
Disabilities or special needs			

Pets to Be Cared For

	Pet #1	Pet #2	Pet #3	Pet #4
Name				
Date of birth				
Special needs				

INFORMATION ABOUT YOUR PROPERTY

Real Estate

	Property #1	Property #2	Property #3
Address			
How is it owned (by you alone, by you and another)?			
Approximate value			

Vehicles

	Vehicle #1	Vehicle #2	Vehicle #3
Description			
How is it owned (by you alone, by you and another)?			
Approximate value			

Bank accounts

	Account #1	Account #2	Account #3
Location			

How is it owned
  (by you alone, by
  you and another)? _____   _____   _____

Approximate balance _____   _____   _____

RRSPs and RRIFs

	Plan/Fund #1	Plan/Fund #2	Plan/Fund #3
Location	_____	_____	_____
Beneficiary named	_____	_____	_____
Approximate value	_____	_____	_____

Pension Plans

	Plan #1	Plan #2	Plan #3
Employer	_____	_____	_____
Beneficiary named	_____	_____	_____
Approximate value	_____	_____	_____

Investments (bonds, GICs, shares, mutual funds, etc.)

	Investment #1	Investment #2	Investment #3

Description
How is it owned
  (by you alone, by
  you and another)?
	_____	_____	_____

Approximate value	_____	_____	_____

Life Insurance

	Policy #1	Policy #2	Policy #3
Insurance company	_____	_____	_____
Beneficiary named	_____	_____	_____
Face amount of policy	_____	_____	_____

Valuable Personal Possessions (electronic equipment, art, antiques and heirlooms, jewellery, silverware, furs)

	Possession #1	Possession #2	Possession #3	Possession #4
Description	_____	_____	_____	_____
How is it owned (by you alone, by you and another)?	_____	_____	_____	_____
Approximate value	_____	_____	_____	_____

Furniture and Household Contents

How are they owned (by you alone, by you and another)? _____

Approximate value _____

Money Owed to You

	Amount #1	Amount #2	Amount #3
Owed by	_____	_____	_____
Owed because of	_____	_____	_____
Due on	_____	_____	_____
Approximate amount	_____	_____	_____
Supporting documents (mortgage, contract, court order, etc.)	_____	_____	_____

Your Business

Description _____

Address(es)_____

_____

_____

How is it owned (sole proprietorship, partnership, corporation) and what is your share?

_____

Book VII

Estate Planning

Approximate value (of assets less liabilities if sole proprietorship or partnership, of shares if corporation)

_____

INFORMATION ABOUT YOUR DEBTS

Mortgages

	Mortgage #1	Mortgage #2	Mortgage #3
Address of property	_____	_____	_____
Name and address of mortgagee	_____	_____	_____
Approximate outstanding balance	_____	_____	_____

Loans

	Loan #1	Loan #2	Loan #3
Description (car, line of credit, etc.)	_____	_____	_____
Name and address of lender	_____	_____	_____
Approximate outstanding balance	_____	_____	_____

Outstanding Taxes and Penalties

CCRA	_____
Property taxes	_____
Other	_____

Family Law Support Orders

	Family member #1	Family member #2	Family member #3
Amount of payment	_____	_____	_____
Frequency of payment	_____	_____	_____
Probable end date	_____	_____	_____

Court Judgments against You

Amount of judgment _____

Date of judgment _____

Have you ever declared bankruptcy? _____
If so, bring those documents to your lawyer.

OTHER ADVISERS

Lawyer

Name _____ Address _____

Kind of work done for you _____

Accountant

Name _____ Address _____

Kind of work done for you _____

Bank Manager

Name _____ Address of bank branch _____

Kind of work done for you _____

Broker

Name _____ Brokerage _____

Address _____

Kind of work done for you _____

Financial Adviser

Name _____ Address _____

Kind of work done for you _____

Book VII

Estate Planning

Other

Name _____   Address _____

Kind of work done _____

LIFE INSURANCE AND PENSIONS

Life Insurance

	Policy #1	Policy #2	Policy #3
Description	_____	_____	_____
Beneficiary	_____	_____	_____

Pension Plans

	Plan #1	Plan #2	Plan #3
Description	_____	_____	_____
Beneficiary	_____	_____	_____

YOUR WISHES FOR YOUR WILL

Your first choice(s) for executor(s) _____

Alternate choice(s) for executor(s) _____

Specific Gifts

Personal Effects

	Item #1	Item #2	Item #3	Item #4
Description	_____	_____	_____	_____
Beneficiary	_____	_____	_____	_____

Real Estate

	Property #1	Property #2	Property #3	Property #4
Description	_____	_____	_____	_____
Beneficiary	_____	_____	_____	_____

Vehicles

	Vehicle #1	Vehicle #2	Vehicle #3
Description	_____	_____	_____
Beneficiary	_____	_____	_____

RRSPs and RRIFs

	Plan/Fund #1	Plan/Fund #2	Plan/Fund #3	Plan/Fund #4
Description	_____	_____	_____	_____
Beneficiary	_____	_____	_____	_____

Investments

	Investment #1	Investment #2	Investment #3	Investment #4
Description	_____	_____	_____	_____
Beneficiary	_____	_____	_____	_____

Cash

	Amount #1	Amount #2	Amount #3	Amount #4
Amount	_____	_____	_____	_____
Beneficiary	_____	_____	_____	_____

Pets

	Pet #1	Pet #2	Pet #3	Pet #4
Name of pet	_____	_____	_____	_____
Beneficiary	_____	_____	_____	_____

Family Business

Description _____

Beneficiary _____

Other

Description _____

Beneficiary _____

Book VII

Estate Planning

Residue

(What's left over after you have made all your specific gifts)

If you have a spouse: Would you like all the residue to go to your spouse, would you like none of the residue to go to your spouse, or would you like some of the residue to go to your spouse and some to others? _____

_____

If you have children:

How would you like to divide your estate among them? _____

_____

What should happen to one child's share if that child dies before you? _____

_____

If your children are young, until what age should their shares be held in trust? _____

How should a child's trust fund be used? (For example, not used until child comes of age, used for child's education, paid out to child as a regular allowance, etc.)

_____

If you have grandchildren:

How do you want them to share in your estate? _____

What should happen to one child's share if that child dies before you? _____

_____

If your grandchildren are young, until what age should their shares be held in trust? _____

How should the grandchildren's trust fund be used? (Not used until child comes of age, used for child's education, paid out to child as a regular allowance, etc.)

_____

If you have no immediate family:

Would you like to give friends or other relatives a share of your estate? _____

Names of friends or relatives _____

_____

What should happen to someone's share if he or she dies before you? _____

_____

Would you like to give something to charity? _____

Name of charity or charities _____

Approximate amount you would like to give _____

Is there anyone you wish to exclude from your will who might expect to be mentioned in your will?

_____

YOUR WISHES FOR YOUR POWER OF ATTORNEY

Your first choice(s) for your attorney(s)_____

Your alternate choice(s) for your attorney(s) _____

When would you like the power of attorney to come into effect — immediately, when you become physically disabled, suffer from minor mental disability, or suffer from major mental disability?

_____

Do you want the power of attorney to give your attorney(s) all the powers that you have to deal with your affairs, or would you like to limit the attorney(s)' powers?

_____

YOUR WISHES FOR YOUR LIVING WILL

Your first choice(s) for your substitute decision maker(s): _____

Your alternate choice(s) for your substitute decision maker(s): _____

What are your wishes about prolonging your life or hastening your death?_____

_____

_____

Book VII

Estate Planning

Appendix B

Instructions for Your Executor

· ·

*Y*our executor has a lot to do when you kick the bucket, including collecting your important documents, making your funeral arrangements, and generally making sure your wishes for your estate are followed in letter and in spirit. You can find more about the duties of an executor at great length in Chapter 3.

Use the form in this appendix to make sure your executor can get a running start on the job.

INSTRUCTIONS TO MY EXECUTOR

My will:

You will find the original of my will in the following place: _____

_____

The following are my wishes for organ and tissue donation:

☐ I wish to donate the following: _____

_____

☐ My consent to donation documents can be found in: _____

☐ I have notified the following registry that I would like to donate:_____

☐ I wish to donate my body:

☐ I have contacted the following institution to pre-arrange body donation:

_____

☐ I have not contacted any institution but would like to donate my body to:

_____

☐ I do not wish to any of my organs or tissues to be donated.

☐ I do not wish to donate my body.

The following are my wishes for my funeral:

If pre-arrangements have been made:

I have pre-arranged my funeral at the following funeral home: _____

☐ I have prepaid my funeral.

☐ I have not prepaid my funeral.

My funeral has been pre-arranged but not pre-paid and I would like it to be paid out of the following bank account(s) or insurance policy or benefit plan:

_____

_____

My documents relating to pre-arrangement or pre-payment can be found in:

_____

_____

I own a plot at the following cemetery: _____

☐ I own the plot alone.

☐ I own the plot with the following person:

My documents relating to the plot can be found in: _____

If no pre-arrangements have been made:

☐ I would like to use the following funeral home: _____

☐ I leave it to you to choose a funeral home.

I would like my body to be treated in the following way:

☐ Embalmed   ☐ Not embalmed

☐ Made up   ☐ Not made up

I would like to be buried in the following clothes: _____

_____

If possible, I would like to have the following item(s) buried with me: _____

_____

I would like my obituary to appear in the following papers: _____

_____

☐ _____ I have written my obituary. You will find it in:

_____

☐ I would like the following person or people to write my obituary: _____

_____

☐ I do not want a visitation.

☐ I would like a visitation.

☐ For the visitation, I would like my coffin to be open.

☐ I do not want an open coffin.

☐ I would like a funeral service.   OR   ☐ I would like a memorial service.

If necessary, I would like my funeral service delayed a reasonable length of time to permit the following people to attend:

_____

_____

I would like the following person to officiate at my service: _____

If he or she is not available, then my second choice is: _____

I would like the funeral service to be held at: _____

_____

I would like the following kind of service: _____

Book VII

Estate Planning

I would like the following passage(s) to be read at the service:_____

_____

_____

_____

I would like the following music played at the service: _____

_____

I would like the following person or group to play the music at the service: _____

_____

I would like the following hymns sung at the service: _____

_____

_____

I would like the following prayer(s) to be said at the service: _____

_____

_____

_____

☐ I don't want anyone to deliver a eulogy.

☐ I would like the following person or people to deliver a eulogy: _____

_____

I would like the following people to be pallbearers at a funeral service: _____

_____

_____

I would like the following people to be ushers at a funeral or memorial service:_____

_____

_____

I would like a reception following the funeral, to be held at: _____

_____

☐ I would like memorial donations instead of flowers.

☐ I would like mourners to be given the choice between memorial donations and flowers.

Disposal arrangements, if no pre-arrangements have been made:

☐ I would like to be buried.

☐ I would like to be buried in the following cemetery: _____

_____

☐ I leave it to you to choose a cemetery.

☐ I would like a monument:

☐ An upright stone

☐ A marker

Description of the stone or marker I would like: _____
_____

I would like the following engraved on my monument: _____
_____
_____

☐ I would like to be cremated:

☐ I would like my ashes to be scattered at: _____
_____

☐ I would like my ashes to be buried at: _____
_____

☐ I would like my ashes to be put in a columbarium at: _____
_____

If my ashes are buried or put in a columbarium, I would like the following engraved on my
monument:
_____
_____

☐ I realize it is difficult to do, but I would like to be buried at sea if possible:

My preferred location is: _____
_____

☐ Other instructions for disposal of my remains: _____
_____
_____

☐ I would like a memorial tree planted for me at: _____
_____

☐ If possible, I would like a memorial plaque put up for me at: _____
_____

I would like the following engraved on the memorial plaque:_____
_____

Book VII

**Estate
Planning**

Other instructions for a memorial: _____
_____
_____

Payment

I would like the cost of my funeral and disposal to be paid out of the following bank account(s), insurance policy, or benefit plan:

Appendix C

Inventory for Your Executor

* *

*W*hen you die, your executor will arrive on the scene and immediately need lots and lots of pieces of paper. Not making sure that your executor will have what she needs will really make her regret your death.

Use the form in this appendix to prepare an inventory of your important documents and where your executor can find them.

INVENTORY FOR MY EXECUTOR

Inventory made as of: _____ / _____ / _____
DATE/MONTH/YEAR

The original of my will is located in: _____

_____

The name and address of my lawyer: _____

_____

The name and address of my financial adviser or accountant: _____

_____

The name and address of my insurance agent: _____

_____

I have a safety deposit box at the following bank or trust company:

Name and address of bank	Location of key

My important documents (e.g., investment certificates, bonds, share certificates, ownership documents, loan documents, valuations of property, etc.) include the following:

Document	Location

I have money in the following bank accounts:

Address of bank	Account number	If joint account, joint owner is

I own the following RRSPs or RRIFs:

Name of institution	Description

I am a member of an employee pension plan at the following institutions:

Institution name and address	Plan name or number

I own the following life insurance policies:

Name of insurance company	Face amount of policy	Named beneficiary

I have a stock portfolio with the following broker: _____

For stocks owned jointly, the joint owner is: _____

I own or rent the following real estate:

Address	If jointly owned, joint owner is	If mortgaged, mortgagee is

Book VII

Estate Planning

I own or lease the following vehicles:

Description of vehicle	Location	If jointly owned, joint owner is

I own personal property that is kept outside my residence(s):

Description	Location

The following property is being held by me but belongs to someone else:

Description of property	Name and address of owner

I am owed money by the following people or organizations:

Name of debtor	Description of debt	Amount owed

I owe money to the following:

Name of creditor	Description of debt	Amount owed

WARNING! I have concealed valuable property in the following places (so be careful about throwing anything out!):

Book VIII

Taking Care of Business

The 5th Wave   By Rich Tennant

In this book . . .

Starting a business: The final frontier.

Your entrepreneurial mission: To explore new products and services. To seek out new markets, new customers, and new suppliers. To boldly go into business for yourself.

And as you boldly go, who knows where you might end up? To keep from ending up lost in space, you need help setting up your business — choosing the right vehicle, charting the right course, and taking off with the right payload. This Book gives you a head start on your voyage, and helps with the speed bumps along the way.

Here are the contents of Book VIII at a glance:

Chapter 1

Show Me the Money: Sourcing Financing for Your Business

- -

In This Chapter

▶ Calculating how much money you need to set up your business

▶ Estimating how much first-year cash you need

▶ Forecasting your cash flow

▶ Sourcing financing for your business

▶ Looking at the risks of financing

- -

*I*f you're starting a business, you need money. Maybe just a little bit, and maybe you already have it; maybe a lot and you're going to have to scout around for it. In any case, you need to know exactly how much money to hunt for, where to hunt for it, what you're going to have to do to bag it, and what it will cost you.

Your Business Needs Capital

You'll have to spend money to get your business to the point where it can begin operating. These are *start-up expenses* or *capital expenses,* things you need to do or buy to get your business rolling — and very few of them are free. You'll need money for the following:

✔ To acquire or protect the right to use an idea in your business

✔ To identify the nature of your business — researching and developing your product, doing market research, and organizing initial promotional activities

✔ To set up your business as a legal entity:

  • And while you're hanging out at the lawyer's, you'll need money for any additional work your lawyer does for you, such as preparing standard documents for your business to use.

- Not to favour lawyers over accountants, you'll also need money for initial advice and assistance from an accountant about the form of your business and how best to structure it to keep accounting difficulties and taxes to a minimum (see Chapters 3 and 4 for more about taxes and accounting).

✔ To buy equipment and other capital assets (items that last over one year) for your business — use Table 1-1 to calculate your start-up capital asset costs

✔ To locate your business in its own premises

✔ To buy an existing business

Table 1-1	Start-Up Plan — Expenses for Capital Assets and Other Items
Furniture and furnishings	Total Cost $
List individual items such as:	Cost of individual items:
Desk	$
Chairs	$
Light fixtures, etc.	$
Computer hardware and software	Total Cost $
List individual items:	Cost of individual items:
	$
	$
Web site design	$
Business stationery (graphic design, materials, and printing)	$
Special equipment for your business	Total Cost $
List individual items, such as	Cost of individual items:
Vehicles	$
Machinery	$
Cost of initial inventory (for a retail business)	$

Table 1-2 helps you add up the cost of everything related to start-up.

Table 1-2	Start-Up Expenses for a Custom-Built Business
Your initial capital (the money you've already got in your pocket that is required for your business enterprise)	$
Licensing a product to manufacture or use or sell, or patenting your own invention	$
Researching and developing your product or service	$
Initial promotional activities	$
Legal and accounting fees for business setup	$
Purchase of equipment (from Table 1-1)	$
Purchase price and legal fees if you buy property for your business premises	$
Leasehold improvements and legal fees to review the lease, if you rent business premises; or renovation costs if you set up a home office	$
Total new capital (add up initial capital plus the costs you've listed)	$
Total capital required (subtract initial capital from total new capital). This is how much you need but don't have at the moment.	$

If you're buying a business instead of building your own, your table of start-up expenses will look like Table 1-3.

Table 1-3	Start-Up Expenses If You Buy an Existing Business
Your initial capital (the money you've already got in your pocket to buy a business)	$
Purchase price of business	$
Professional fees (lawyer, accountant, broker, valuator, and so on) associated with the purchase	$
Total new capital (add up initial capital plus the price of the business plus professional fees)	$
Total capital required (subtract initial capital from total new capital). This is how much you need but don't have at the moment.	$

Book VIII

Taking Care of Business

Your Business Needs Operating Funds

Once you've figured out the capital requirements of your business, you're still not ready to carry on business . . . at least not for very long. You also have to work out how much money you'll need to run the business on a basis (actually a month-to-month basis). These are called *operating expenses*. After your business is generating a steady income, your revenues will cover all or most of your operating expenses. But until then, you'll need to borrow money to pay for things such as:

✔ Salaries

✔ Lease or mortgage payments

✔ Utilities such as telephone, hydro, and water

✔ Insurance premiums

✔ Property taxes, if you own your business premises rather than rent them

✔ Ongoing professional fees (legal, accounting, advertising, publicity)

✔ Cost of running any vehicles

Projecting your expenses and revenues

For some of your operating expenses you'll be able to write down a fairly accurate estimate from a supplier (such as a landlord, accountant, or insurance agent). For others (such as utilities and maybe salaries), you'll just have to guess.

After estimating your expenses, you have to estimate how much revenue you'll bring in to cover your expenses. This step will give you a better grasp of how much money you really need to borrow for monthly operations.

It's a lot easier to project your expenses than your revenues. But you can make a guess at your revenues by making some assumptions. The usual assumptions are

✔ The number of customers or clients you'll get, and

✔ The average amount of each sale or transaction.

Multiply these two figures together to estimate sales. (Make a note to yourself about how you chose the figures you're using. You'll need to add that information as a footnote to your *forecast of income and expenses*.)

Preparing a forecast of income and expenses

The figures discussed in the previous section get plugged into a forecast or projection of income and expenses. Take a look at Table 1-4.

Table 1-4	Forecast of Income and Expenses (for the first year of operation)
Income	
Sales or revenues	$
Other	$
Total Income	$
Expenses	
Salaries and benefits	$
Owner	$
Employee(s) (if any)	$
Lease payments	$
Advertising	$
Market research	$
Insurance	$
Utilities (electricity, heat)	$
Telephone, fax, and Internet	$
Professional services	$
Legal	$
Accounting	$
Vehicle operation and maintenance	$
Other	$
Total Expenses	$
Net Profit or **Loss** (deduct total expenses from total income)	$

Book VIII

Taking Care of Business

After filling out this table you should have a reasonable idea of what your operating expenses will be for your first year of business, and whether you can expect that, by the end of the year, your revenues will cover your expenses or that you'll be in the hole (and how deep the hole will be).

Projected cash flow

It's not enough to know how much you need to operate your business, you also have to know *when* you need the money. The timing of income and expenses rarely match each other exactly, so you can't necessarily expect to be able to pay your expenses out of the income you're making. Your income may come in a lump once a year or a few times a year, whereas your expenses are likely to be fairly steady on a month-by-month basis. By preparing a *cash flow statement,* you'll know when you may need bridge financing to keep the business afloat. This is especially true during the first year or so of your business's existence, before income is steady or before you've been able to put aside some profits to operate the business between infusions of income.

Many of your expenses won't change from month to month (lease or mortgage payments, for example), and others may be predictable even though they change during the course of the year (a snow removal contract during the winter months, or salaries for extra staff during a busy season). But if you had trouble estimating your total annual income, you'll have even more trouble estimating how it will come in month by month. Give it a shot, though, taking into consideration that your monthly income will probably increase over the course of the first year as your business gets established. Your business may have seasonal highs and lows too. An accountant, for example, can probably expect a seasonal high just after she files client income tax returns and the bills go out for tax preparation services rendered; a business that sells cards and gifts can probably expect highs just before Christmas, Valentine's Day, and Mother's Day.

You'll find an example of a projected cash flow statement to use as a guide in the sample business plan in the appendix. Table 1-5 doesn't have room for all 12 months plus an annual total, so it shows only some representative months. (When you prepare your cash flow statement, however, you should fill in all 12 months.)

Table 1-5	Projected Cash Flow Statement					
	Jan	Feb	March...	Nov	Dec	Year
Income:						
Cash sales						
Receivables						
Total income						
Expenses:						
Salaries						
Lease						
Advertising						
Market research						
Insurance						
Utilities						
Telephone						
Professional						
Other						
Total expenses						
Cash flow						
[Subtract monthly expenses from monthly income. If it comes out a negative number, put brackets around the number.]						
Cumulative cash flow						
[Move from left to right adding the previous month's cash flow to the following month. For January, you will have the same number as for the January cash flow, but for February, you will add the cash flow numbers for January and February together; for March, you will add January, February, and March together, and so on. Again, put brackets around negative numbers.]						

Book VIII

Taking Care of Business

After filling out Table 1-5, you'll have some idea of how many months of the first year you'll need a loan to pay your operating expenses (from the cash flow line), and at what point your revenues will start reducing your need for a loan (from the cumulative cash flow line).

Sources of Financing for a Start-Up Operation

Now you know, more or less, how much money you need to start up and run your business for the first year. You just don't know where you're going to find that money. Generations of businesspeople have wondered the same thing, so by now there's a standard list of sources of money. The sources include:

- Personal assets
- Money from friends and family
- Borrowed money:
    - Credit card
    - Mortgage on home or vacation property
    - Commercial loans (capital and operating)
    - Micro-credit loans
- Credit:
    - Suppliers
    - Customers
- Sale of accounts receivable
- Grants and loans from government
- Investment from external sources
    - Angel investor (some are sinister!)
    - Venture capital company

That's a respectable-looking list — somewhere among all these possibilities you should be able to find a buck or two.

Mix-and-match financing

Most businesses need a combination of financing. For example, besides using personal assets and money from friends and family to get started,

- To get equipment, a business may need
    - A capital loan, and/or
    - A conditional sales agreement, and/or
    - A lease

> ✔ To get operating funds, a business may need
>
>   • A line of credit and/or
>
>   • Payment in advance from customers and clients, and/or
>
>   • Credit from suppliers
>
> ✔ To make leasehold improvements, a business may need a capital loan

So you'll likely be dealing with several sources of financing. That means you should read *the balance of this chapter carefully.*

Personal assets

Most entrepreneurs start off using at least some of their own money. Look around and see what money you have handy — or what property you could turn into cash — to finance your business start-up. Keep in mind that you still need money to live on while you're getting your business off the ground. You're not going to be a very effective CEO if you're starving or sleeping on the street.

Look for the following resources that you may already have available:

> ✔ Money in bank accounts
>
> ✔ Bonds
>
> ✔ Stocks — but if they've increased in value since you acquired them, you'll have to declare a *capital gain* on your next income tax return and could end up taking a tax hit
>
> ✔ RRSPs — but remember that you'll have to add any amount you withdraw to your income for the year, and you could end up paying tax on it if you earn other income
>
> ✔ Personal property or real property you can sell, such as vehicles, jewellery, collectibles, art, a vacation home, or even your real home. If property other than your real home (your *principal residence*) has increased in value since you acquired it, you'll have to declare a capital gain on your income tax return and may have to pay tax

Money from friends and family

Friends and family may be willing to lend money to you, or they may be willing to give it to you flat out. Think very carefully, however, before asking relatives and friends for money. If your business tanks and you can't repay them, they'll probably stop speaking to you. Then you'll have not only no business, but also no one to give you any sympathy either.

If you do go ahead, make a formal arrangement with the lenders, for two reasons — first, so that they can get something back if you're successful or if you go bust (a document will provide the evidence they need to make a claim against your business as a creditor); and second, so that they can't demand their money back just when you desperately need it. If the money or property is a gift, the giver should sign a document stating that the money or property is a gift and is yours absolutely to do with what you like. If the money is a loan, you should have a contract (a *promissory note*) with the lender setting out

- The amount of the loan
- Whether interest is payable on the loan and, if so, at what rate
- How and when the loan is to be repaid (for example, a schedule of payments)
- Whether the lender wants *security* for the loan (something the lender can take in exchange if the loan isn't repaid), and what the nature of that security is. Security could include a mortgage against your home, or the taking of shares in your corporation, or a promise from someone else associated with you or the business that he or she will repay the loan if you don't (this is a *guarantee*).

Money borrowed from commercial lenders

Commercial lenders are banks, trust companies, credit unions, caisses populaires, finance companies, and insurance companies. They've got lots of money . . . if you can just get your hands on it.

Many commercial lenders can also help you get access to funds from the *Business Development Bank of Canada* (visit their Web site at www.bdc.ca for more information about their lending activities) and from the federal government's *Canada Small Business Financing (CSBF)* program. Most small businesses starting up or operating in Canada are eligible for CSBF loans, as long as their estimated annual gross revenues do not exceed $5 million during the fiscal year in which they apply for a loan. For more information about CSBF loans, go to the Strategis Web site (strategis.ic.gc.ca).

Credit cards

If you need to borrow from a bank, your first thought may be to use your credit cards. It's easy — no application forms to fill out, no waiting, no business plan to prepare, no intimidating interview with a bank manager. You may even have a high enough limit on your card(s) to get as much money as you need.

Don't do it! The interest rate on credit cards is astronomical compared to the interest rate you'll pay if you borrow in a more business-like fashion — probably at least double and maybe triple. You have better options.

Mortgage on your home or vacation property

If you own real property and it isn't already mortgaged to the hilt, you can borrow against that property by taking out an additional *mortgage*. If you're thinking of mortgaging property, consider these factors:

- **What's the property worth?** Will mortgaging it get you as much money as you need? You probably won't be able to borrow its full unmortgaged value.

- **Is the property already mortgaged?** If it is, there may not be enough *equity* (unmortgaged value) in the property for you to get as big a loan as you need.

- **Do you need someone else's legal consent to mortgage the property?** You do if you have a co-owner. Even if you're the only owner, if you're married, in most provinces your spouse will have to give consent to the transaction before you'll get any money (sometimes even if it's not your family home that you're borrowing against).

- **Can you afford to lose the property if your business fails?** If you *default* on your loan (don't pay it back on time), the lender has the right to take the property — and either keep it or sell it to cover your unpaid loan. (If it's sold, you'll get the excess over the outstanding amount of the loan plus legal fees.)

Business loans

If you're borrowing because you need money to purchase capital assets for your business, you'll apply for a *capital loan*. If you're borrowing because you need money to cover the ongoing costs of running your business, you'll apply for an *operating loan*. You can go looking for either kind of loan from a commercial lender. But choose a branch that regularly handles small business clients, if you can find one — if the branch staff are only used to making deposits and withdrawals, they won't know what to do with you . . . and the easiest thing will be to show you the door.

Banks, most credit unions, and many trust, loan, and insurance companies can make a loan under the Canada Small Business Financing (CSBF) program for capital expenses including the purchase or improvement of real property, leasehold improvements, and the purchase or improvement of equipment. The federal government partially guarantees CSBF loans, so lenders are more willing to lend, and owners don't have to provide personal assets as security.

The chances are good that at some point you'll want a business loan, so the following sections tell you about loans in detail.

Book VIII

Taking Care of Business

Principal and interest

The amount of money the lender gives is called the *principal* or *principal amount* of the loan. The amount the borrower pays for the use of the money is called *interest.* (You're not going to find an interest-free loan if you deal with anyone other than your mother.) Interest is calculated as a percentage of the principal. If you are charged *simple interest* on the loan, you pay interest only on the principal you've borrowed. So if you borrowed $100,000 at 10 percent, you'd owe $10,000 in interest per year.

But commercial lenders charge *compound interest* on a loan if the terms of repayment stretch past the time the interest is actually due. Compound interest is interest on the principal *and* on the interest owing. When you're charged compound interest, you end up with a higher interest rate (the *effective interest rate*) than the rate you're quoted (the *nominal interest rate*). And the more often the interest is *compounded* or *calculated,* the higher the real interest rate.

Interest can be compounded on any basis the lender chooses — daily, weekly, monthly, semi-annually, annually. If you borrowed $100,000 at 10 percent compounded monthly, your real interest rate would actually be 10.47 percent. And in commercial loans, unlike consumer loans, the lender doesn't have to tell the borrower the total amount of interest payable over the life of the loan (the *cost of borrowing*).

Repayment of the loan

It's likely that you'll take out either a *term loan* or a *line of credit.* Capital loans are usually term loans. Operating loans usually come in the form of a line of credit. If you have a term loan, the lender sets a schedule for regular repayment of principal and interest.

If you have a line of credit, also known as *overdraft protection,* the lender (which is normally your bank) tops up your business account if there's not enough in the account to cover a cheque. Then when you make a deposit to your business account, the money is automatically applied to pay down the loan. You may also be required to make regular payments or make a deposit to the account within a fixed period of time to cover the overdraft.

A line of credit is usually a *demand loan,* which means that the lender can demand payment in full at any time, not just after you've missed a payment. However, if you make your payments on time, demand will not be made — unless you do something to lead the lender to believe that your business is in trouble. The lender also usually requires you to sign blank promissory notes, which it fills in as the line of credit goes up. The promissory note provides evidence of what you owe, and the lender can also sue you on the note if you don't pay the loan.

Non-repayment of the loan

Lenders don't take it for granted that borrowers will pay up on schedule — or ever. They know they could sue the borrower for failing to pay, but they also know that suing someone is expensive and time-consuming, and even if they win the lawsuit it's often difficult to collect the money. So to make life easier for themselves, lenders usually require borrowers to give *security* or *collateral*. When a borrower gives security, he legally gives the lender the right to take specified property from the borrower if the borrower doesn't make his payments. The lender usually sells the property to pay off the loan. Typically, lenders take security on such property as

- Real estate — security will take the form of a *collateral mortgage* or *charge* or, in Quebec, a *hypothec*

- Equipment and other non-land assets — security may take the form of a *chattel mortgage,* known in some provinces as a *specific security agreement*

- Accounts receivable, also known as *book debts,* which is money that customers or clients owe the borrower — security can take the form of *an assignment of accounts receivable,* which gives the lender the right to collect debts owing to you if you default on your loan

- Inventory — the lender may be able to take security under *s. 427 of the Federal Bank Act* if you are borrowing from a chartered bank

If you have a capital loan, the lender will probably want security over the capital property (real estate or equipment) you're buying. If you have a line of credit or overdraft protection, the lender may want security over your business's accounts receivable and inventory.

Other forms of security that a lender may ask for include

- **A general security agreement:** This gives a lender security over almost all of the borrower's existing and future assets (usually excluding real property, but including equipment, vehicles, machinery, inventory, accounts receivable).

- **A debenture:** This is much like a general security agreement, except that only a corporation can give a debenture as security for a loan, and a debenture usually includes real property as well as other assets.

- **A pledge of shares** (or of bonds or debentures) which are the personal property of the borrower or a guarantor: For example, if the borrower is a corporation, the lender may want a pledge of shares of the corporation from the shareholders who have guaranteed the loan. Then, if the borrower does not repay the loan, the lender can take control of the corporation.

And lenders don't always stop at taking security. Sometimes they want (instead of or in addition to security) a *guarantee*. A guarantee is a promise by someone other than the borrower that if the borrower doesn't pay up, the *guarantor* (the person or business giving the guarantee) will repay the loan. For example, if the borrower is a corporation — especially a corporation that doesn't have much in the way of assets — the lender may ask for a guarantee from the individuals associated with the corporation, such as the shareholders or the directors. A bank can also ask for security from the guarantor, such as a *collateral mortgage* on the guarantor's home.

If the borrower does not meet the lender's criteria to receive a loan, the lender may be willing to go ahead with the loan if someone who *does* meet the criteria agrees to *co-sign* the loan. Unlike a guarantor, a *co-signor* can be required to repay the loan even if the borrower is capable of repaying the loan himself.

Micro-credit funds

Micro-credit is a small loan (under $25,000, often only a few thousand dollars), available to individuals with a low income, to help them start up a very small business. (They're often targeted toward young people, or women, or new immigrants, or the disabled; and/or they may be targeted toward a restricted geographical area.) They can be used for capital investment or operating funds. They often offer, besides money, business courses and networking opportunities.

For more information about micro-credit and especially where to find some, go to the excellent federal government site, Strategis (strategis.ic.gc.ca).

Credit from suppliers and clients

Maybe you didn't realize you could put your customers and suppliers to work for you as lenders.

Suppliers

If you are buying equipment or machinery, you may be able to finance the purchase through a loan from the vendor, a *conditional sales agreement,* or a *lease.* The vendor will probably want a down payment and security (for example, a chattel mortgage if the vendor is loaning you the money), and will want to be repaid on a regular schedule, as would a commercial lender.

If you're buying inventory or supplies, you may be able to get financing through a credit arrangement. Suppliers may offer 30, 60, or 90 days to pay, with a discount if payment is made within a shorter time. (Two problems here: first, because you're a start-up without a credit history, suppliers may not want to extend credit and may instead want cash on delivery from you; and second, the effective interest rate you pay on the money you're "borrowing" by not taking the discount is high — in the range of 20 to 30 percent or more.) Suppliers may also sometimes offer a loan, or else a sale on *consignment* (you don't pay the supplier until a customer purchases a consigned item). If you buy inventory on credit, the supplier may want to take security in the form of a *purchase money security interest.*

Customers

You may well be able to get your clients or customers to finance the work you do for them by getting them to pay a deposit or *retainer* (that's what professionals call a deposit) and/or instalment payments as you do the work (instead of waiting to be paid when everything's finished).

Sale of accounts receivable

You can sell your recent accounts receivable at a discount for instant cash. This is called *factoring* and it's more expensive than borrowing — it can be a lot more expensive — but you don't have to show that your business has revenue and you don't have to put up security. The factor pays you a percentage of the value of your receivables immediately, collects the receivables, deducts fees, and sends you the balance. (Depending on your arrangement with the factor, your customers needn't know they're dealing with a factor instead of with your business.)

The initial percentage you get from the factor will depend on things like the value of the receivables, number of customers, and credit-worthiness of the customers — it can run anywhere from about 90 percent down to 30 percent. In "recourse" factoring, the factor can look to you to cover any bad debts, while in "non-recourse" factoring (which is, naturally, more expensive) bad debts are the factor's problem. Factoring is available from factoring companies, finance companies, and some banks. It's traditionally used in the apparel, textiles, carpets, and furniture industries, but it's not restricted to those industries.

Government loans and grants

You too may be able to snarf up some money from the public trough to start and run your business! There are lots of government assistance programs — to browse, go to the Canada Business Service Centre site at www.cbsc.org/english/finance where you can search for federal or provincial programs. For example, you may be able to get some repayable or even non-repayable money from:

- ✔ Human Resources Development Canada, if you need to hire or train an employee

- ✔ The Industrial Research Assistance Program (IRAP) of the National Research Council (http://irap-pari.nrc-cnrc.gc.ca/english/), if you need to research and develop a new technological product or service

- ✔ Canada Council for the Arts, if your business involves artistic creation (like writing, painting, music, performance)

- ✔ Industry Canada, for various initiatives

Arm's-length investment

For some businesses, a start-up loan isn't much use. If you take out a loan, you have to pay it back — usually beginning right away — and your business, even though it has fantastic prospects over the next few years, won't be able to generate cash revenues for some time *and* it needs a cash infusion (perhaps a big one) to get started at all.

So maybe what you need is *seed financing* or *seed capital* from an investor such as an *angel* or a *venture capital firm,* rather than a loan from a lender.

Seed capital provides money for such things as

- ✔ Proving that an idea or invention actually works in practice as well as it does in theory (*proof of concept*)

- ✔ Protecting intellectual property (usually through a patent)

- ✔ Completing a *prototype* (working model) of a product or invention

- ✔ Doing market research

- ✔ Creating strategic partnerships with other businesses or with potential customers

- ✔ Hiring experienced managers for the business

- ✔ Creating a business plan

- ✔ Hunting down even more capital that's required to start the business operating

The great majority of start-up businesses don't need seed capital for these kinds of things. And even start-ups that do aren't that likely to get outside investment in the business. Most requests for investment get rejected either because there are limited financial prospects for the business or because the managers of the business don't have the necessary skills to run the business successfully. But this section tells you about outside investors anyway.

Angel investors

If you go around talking about angel investors, chances are most people will think you've been out in the sun too long. You'll get the same kind of reaction as if you mentioned that aliens are broadcasting messages to you through the fillings in your teeth.

Angel investors actually do exist, however. They are individuals, often successful businesspeople, who want to invest their own money in promising new businesses, usually in the same field the angel comes from (many or most come from a high-technology or biotechnology background), and usually in businesses in their own geographic area.

What angels offer

Angels usually invest an amount in the range of $10,000 to $150,000, although some may go as high as $500,000 or more if they've got the money and they like the business's prospects. Besides providing money, angel investors also take an interest in the running of the business. Because they're experienced, they may be able to help you find customers and sell your product, put you in touch with suppliers and professional advisors, and prepare you and your business to hunt for the next round of financing.

What angels are looking for

Angels are looking for a good return on their investment in your business — typically 30 percent compound annual returns. Not many business owners even plan for their business to grow that aggressively, much less are capable of making it happen. Angels are also looking for *equity in* (a share in the value of) your business and the right to be involved in major decisions and to get frequent status reports.

Where to find an angel

Heaven? Sure, but maybe closer than that. Network in your own business community and ask around about angel investors. Finding one at all is a matter of luck, and if you do find an angel, he or she won't necessarily be interested in investing in your kind of business. Learn as much as you can about an angel before approaching him or her, and customize your pitch to match the angel's interests.

Book VIII

Taking Care of Business

Venture capital

Venture capital is money that's available for risky investments if there's a good chance of getting a high return on the investment. There's about $6 billion in venture capital floating around in the Canadian economy at the moment, and in the past few years, venture capitalists (VCs) have poured about $1 billion per year into businesses. However, that doesn't mean that you'll be able to get any of it. Venture capitalists are ridiculously fussy about whom they give their money to.

What kind of business opportunities is a VC looking for?

Venture capitalists are typically looking for three things:

- ✔ **A large market opportunity** — one that will provide very high returns within a fairly short time, about five to seven years (the majority of investments are made in technology)

- ✔ **Good managers** — or at least one good and committed manager who will be able to recruit a strong management team

- ✔ **A strategic plan about building the business** — one that includes a lucrative *exit strategy* (see "What a VC wants in return," later in this chapter) for the venture capitalists

What a VC can offer

Like angel investors, venture capitalists offer money, management expertise, and connections — to other money, to professional advisors such as lawyers and accountants, and to suppliers and potential customers.

What a VC wants in return

To put this section in perspective, venture capitalists are also known, affectionately of course, as *vulture capitalists*. What they usually want is

- ✔ At least a 25 percent return on investment; and they're really thrilled at the prospect of getting a 300 to 500 percent return (a *home run*)

- ✔ Significant ownership of the business — usually 20 percent or more of the business's equity, plus their own pet director(s) on the board of directors

- ✔ A lucrative exit strategy within five to seven years. Exit strategies include the following:

  - An *initial public offering* (IPO)

  - Sale of the business to another corporation

  - A company *buy-back* (the business or business owners buy back the VC's share of the corporation)

  - A *write-off* of the investment (as lost money) — although clearly this is not "lucrative"

Where to find a VC

Venture capital firms, unlike angels, are very easy to find. You can get a list of them by going to the Canadian Venture Capital Association Web site (www.cvca.ca), and from there you can link to the home Web site of each association member. You'll be able to get contact information, as well as some information about the interests and expectations of each member, from their Web site. Finding them, of course, does not necessarily mean getting money from them.

Chapter 2

So Long and Thanks for All the Cash

In This Chapter

▶ Getting money from a commercial lender

▶ Finding out what's required — an application or a full business plan

▶ Getting help to write a business plan

▶ Learning (at tedious length) what goes into a business plan

Sometimes preparing an application to get money involves filling out a form created by the lender, and sometimes it involves preparing a business plan — a much trickier hoop to jump through. Most of this chapter focuses on a formal business plan because it's a lot more difficult to prepare a business plan than to fill out an application form.

Preparing a business plan is usually looked upon as a thoroughly intimidating activity, so this chapter has a comforting title, instead of a title ("DON'T PANIC!") that may have tipped you off, but you would have bypassed the chapter completely.

Don't Panic!

All business books contain a chapter on writing a business plan. It's required writing. You can't get a licence to publish a business book unless you include a chapter on business plans.

However, to get you off on the right foot, this chapter starts by telling you why you should not panic at the thought of having to read the chapter — or of having to prepare a business plan.

First reason not to panic

You don't always have to prepare a formal business plan to get money. When you're looking for money, the first thing you should do (after identifying a source of money) is contact the source and find out what documentation they want in order to consider your request. Especially for smaller amounts of money (say, under $35,000 to $50,000), the source may want only a limited amount of information about your business. (See "Tackling an Application Form," later in this chapter.) Or the source may not need a full-strength business plan and instead be willing to settle for a mini business plan (see "A mini business plan," later in this chapter).

Second reason not to panic

Most business books put the business plan chapter almost at the very beginning, where it's especially unnerving. Who knows how many people have decided not to go into business because they couldn't face writing a business plan as the first step in starting a business? And nobody's able to put together a description of their business and an analysis of the marketplace, and financial statements, before they've even thought about their product or service, their business organization, what equipment they'll need and where they'll be located, and what sources of funding are available to them.

By the time you get to this business plan section, you've done a lot of the work needed to create a business plan — and you didn't even know you were doing it. Besides that, after going through Chapter 1, you're much more motivated to work to get some money.

Third reason not to panic

Here's yet another reason not to panic: Even if you have to prepare a business plan, you don't have to prepare the business plan on your own. If you don't feel like doing this all by yourself, you can visit your trusty bow-tied accountant. Your accountant should be able to put together at least the financials for your business plan after talking to you for a couple of hours about your business and what you're planning to do with it.

There are also consultants who can write a business plan for you. (You can expect to drop several thousand dollars on a consultant.) It would probably be best to use a consultant who has lots of experience in the field of your business, rather than one who simply specializes in writing business plans in any industry.

You can find consultants (you can find consultants galore, most likely) by asking around among your business acquaintances, or approaching your provincial Canada Business Service Centre (CBSC) or a municipal or regional economic development office for their help or their suggestions about whom to contact. You can also get in touch with a university business school — MBA students run assistance programs and for a modest fee will work with you on a business plan.

Taking Your First Step

Before you write down a word or add up two numbers, contact the source of financing you're interested in. Tell them how much you want to borrow and in what form, and then ask about the application process. If they say you just have to fill out a form, get the form. If they say you have to prepare a business plan, ask if they have any guidelines or forms to show what they want to see in the business plan. If they don't, you have to do it yourself — but this chapter offers a lot of help about the form and content of a business plan.

Tackling an Application Form

You may only need to fill out quite a short, simple application form to apply for the money you need. Typically, an application form will ask you to give information about how much money you want and what you're planning to use it for, and also about:

- The business's primary financial institution (it may or may not be the institution you're requesting the loan from)
- The name, trade name, and address of your business
- The form of your business (sole proprietorship, partnership, or corporation)
- The nature of your business
- How long the business has been established, and how many employees it has
- Financial problems and setbacks your business has experienced, such as claims from creditors and lawsuits, and whether the business has ever been in receivership or declared bankruptcy.

Book VIII

Taking Care of Business

The application form will also ask for a summary of financial information about your business, including:

✔ Total gross annual sales or revenues for the preceding fiscal year (if you've been in business for more than a year) or as projected for the year ahead (if you're a start-up)

✔ Net after-tax profit or loss (for the preceding fiscal year if you've been in business for more than a year, or as projected for the year ahead if you're a start-up)

Be prepared to provide the financial statements themselves. For information about preparing financial statements, see Chapter 4.

Finally, the application form will ask for information about the owner(s) of the business, including:

✔ Names and addresses

✔ Income in the preceding year (as reported on the owner's tax return)

✔ A list of each owner's assets and debts. (In the "Sharing Financial Information" section later in this chapter, you'll find a personal balance sheet that will show you the kind of information the lender has in mind.)

For a start-up business, the decision whether to lend will be based as much on the owner's personal financial status as on the business's, because start-up businesses normally don't have much in the way of assets.

If the owner has no assets, the lender will be very reluctant to lend the business any money. Probably the best indicator of whether you'll get the loan is whether you own a home (one that's not 100 percent mortgaged already). The lender will feel much more comfortable giving you money if it can take back a mortgage as security. (See Chapter 1 for more about security for a loan.)

Introducing: The Business Plan

Sometimes there's no other way — if you want money, you'll have to prepare a business plan to submit to the lender.

A business plan sets out how much money you want and what you're going to do with it, describes your business, places it within the context of the industry it belongs to, examines the marketplace and competition and sets out a strategy for competing in the marketplace, and provides detailed financial information about your business.

A lender or investor looks at a business plan to see whether it's safe to put money into your business. If your business is well thought-out, it's more likely to be successful, generate a profit, and be able to repay the lender or investor.

When you show someone a business plan, you're revealing a lot of important information (important to you, at least) about your business. If you want to impress on the potential lender or investor that this information shouldn't be broadcasted around the solar system, you may want to ask the lender or investor to sign a confidential disclosure agreement before looking at the business plan. You don't want to see Trudy, the banker's friend, starting up her own new business that's based on *your* rejected business plan!

What Goes into a Business Plan?

Books and even chapters about business plans are often incredibly detailed and seem to be written for businesses that are looking for huge amounts of money to expand businesses already in operation. They're intimidating, and by the time you get to the end of the book or chapter you feel like there's no point in writing a business plan because you don't have an MBA and you don't understand the marketing and accounting jargon.

Don't twist yourself into knots about writing a business plan. Although almost every book or article you read about creating a business plan will tell you a somewhat different way to set the plan up, all business plans contain, in the long run, the same quite understandable information.

A full-scale business plan

If a lender is looking for the whole shebang, business-plan-wise, here's the information required:

Book VIII

Taking Care of Business

- ✔ How much you want from the person who's reading the business plan and what you're going to do with it

- ✔ A description of what your business does, and a description of the industry your business is part of

- ✔ An explanation why your business can compete successfully, and your strategy for competing (that is, for marketing your product or service)

- ✔ A description of how your business runs or will run on a day-to-day basis, including information about the business's managers

✔ Financial information about your business, including projections about income and expenses (as a start-up, you won't have much in the way of a financial history), and also about your personal financial status — so the lender or investor can decide whether it's safe to invest. A lender or investor will expect to be paid back out of profits of the business or (if the business doesn't generate enough profits) out of the sale of what the business owns — and/or what *you* own.

A mini business plan

If the lender doesn't want to know every last detail about your business (and who can say whether the lenders who *do* want to know every detail actually read the business plan from cover to cover?), you need to prepare only a short version of a business plan. A mini business plan would cover any given topic more briefly, and it may include only:

✔ How much you want from the lender and what you'll do with it

✔ Name and address of the business, form of business, and how long it's been established

✔ The nature of your business, and what its goals are

✔ A basic analysis of your market and competition, including disclosure of information sources

✔ Pro forma financial statements (prepared using various assumptions about sales and costs)

How Much You Want (Your Objective)

You should say right up front how much money you want and what you're going to do with it. You should also say right up front how this money will increase the profits or value of the business so that the loan can be repaid or the investment can provide a return.

No, it's not rude or pushy to start by saying what you want. You'll save your potential lender or investor time and annoyance. No one with money wants to plod through pages of information without knowing beforehand why they're plodding. They'll want to assess what you want against what you have — and against what they have to offer — from the very beginning of your plan.

Describing Your Business

Next, the plan describes your business, and how your business fits into the larger industry that it's part of.

Your product or service

Start with what your business does — what product it manufactures or sells or what service it provides.

For example, if you're firing up a bakery operation, you'll describe the baked goods you're going to produce and your potential customers. If you're setting up a bookkeeping practice, you'll describe the services you plan to offer and to whom.

If your business has an intellectual property component — for example, if you're

- manufacturing a product that's patented or whose design is registered as an industrial design, or
- distributing or selling a product under a licence agreement or marketing a product under a trademark

then your plan should describe the status of protection of the product or service. For instance, if your product or method is patented, say so and mention its patent number, or if a patent has been applied for, say that a patent application is pending; if you're distributing a patented product, talk briefly about the licence agreement you have.

For a business that needs money to start manufacturing a product, you should be prepared to show a potential lender or investor working drawings and designs of the product.

The goals of your business

While your immediate goal is to get your business set up, you presumably also have other goals on the way to success. An investor would like to know where you're headed. So your plan should outline your short-term goals and your long-term plans.

Book VIII

Taking Care of Business

In the case of the bakery, for example, your short-term goal may be to produce ten dozen loaves of bread per day within a month of starting the operation and distribute them through five local independent food stores. A longer-term goal may be to produce 100 dozen loaves per day and distribute them through a grocery chain with stores around your city. Your ultimate goal (for the moment) may be to expand your baking operation to the point that it supplies bread for the grocery chain throughout the province; or it may be to franchise your bakery and sell franchises across the country.

If you think your business may attract a lot of interest from the world at large (and not just from your doting family and satisfied customers) and will need a large amount of invested money to expand and function properly, your long-term goal may be to become a publicly traded company. Publicly traded companies are able to raise money by offering their shares to the public through a stock exchange.

If you think your business is likely to be of great interest to one or more large corporations in the industry, and that a large corporation would show its interest via a nice fat offer to buy you out, your long-term goal may be to sell your business to a larger business.

Your business within the industry

Your business won't be operating in isolation. Even if you haven't thought about it that way, it's part of some fairly large-scale industry. Your bakery is part of the baked goods industry; your bookkeeping practice is in a small corner of the accounting industry; your computer program for hunting down certain kinds of information on the Internet is part of the computer software industry. The lender or investor you approach may not know much about the industry at all and will need background information to make a decision.

So you need to write a short profile of the industry. To do this you'll have to conduct some research by contacting industry associations, or reading industry publications, or searching for newspaper and magazine articles, or going through Statistics Canada data.

Here are some of the things you should think about including in your profile:

- **The size of businesses in the industry:** Some businesses are mainly made up of large multinational corporations, like the pharmaceutical industry; some are mainly made up of national corporations, like the Canadian banking industry — although you're probably not thinking of starting up a bank; others may have a mix of large and small businesses, like the legal and accounting industries; and some mostly consist of small businesses, like the personal services industry.

- **The total volume of sales in the industry and the total value of sales:** You're just going to have a small piece of the pie to start with, but it's good to show that the pie is nice and big.

- **Any legislation, regulations, and standards that apply to the industry's products or services:** For example, the manufacture of food and drugs is heavily regulated by the federal government; travel agencies are regulated by provincial governments; cafes are regulated and inspected by municipal governments.

- **Trends in the industry:** It may be growing, or shrinking, or shifting its focus from certain products or services to others; or it may be facing stricter government regulation, or it may be about to be deregulated.

- **The main challenges and problems the industry faces:** Is it being forced to compete globally instead of nationally? Is it losing customers because it isn't meeting changing customer needs? Has it priced its goods or services out of the larger marketplace? Is it sluggish because it hasn't upgraded old infrastructure?

- **The future of the industry:** Will it stay much as it is but expand — or contract? Will it change significantly in response to consumer demand or new legislation?

By the way, don't make this stuff up. It's easier and more fun to make it up, true, but it's a bad move. It will make you look light-minded and untrustworthy if anyone finds out. And since you're not making it up, you should footnote facts and opinions that you state to show their source. If a lender or investor wants more information about the industry, he, she, or it should be able to locate your references.

Once you've finished your industry profile, you have to discuss how your business fits into the industry. Are you going to create a product that will revolutionize the industry, or even make it obsolete? Are you going to take advantage of a gap and expand your business to become a major player? Are you going to quietly but competently fill a little niche? How will industry trends affect your business's chance of success? How will your business meet the industry's challenges? How will your business fit into the industry's future that you've projected? This section is going to give you quite a mental workout! But preparing it will make you reflect on a lot of points that are important to your business success.

Book VIII

Taking Care of Business

Why your business can compete successfully

After you've described your business world, you have to show that you can survive in it by competing successfully. In trying to figure out how well you'll be able to compete, you have to consider both the market for your product or your service, and your competition in the marketplace.

Your market

You need to know a reasonable amount about the market for your product or service so that you'll be able to

- ✔ Identify your target market for the product or service
- ✔ Identify your portion of the total target market (it's probably not going to be the total market, at least not to begin with)
- ✔ Identify marketing strategies (covering things such as prices, distribution, and business promotion)

Your target market

There are different ways of determining your target market. One is geography. Your target market may be the people (or businesses) within a geographic area. For example, if you run a retail business, you may see your target market as the people who live within walking distance or a short driving distance of your store. If you're distributing a product, you may have a distribution agreement with the manufacturer that allows you to distribute the product within your province or within a region (for example, the Atlantic provinces, or the Vancouver area, or specified towns in northern Ontario). If you're the sole manufacturer of a product that's in demand (say, a hula-hoop during a hula-hoop craze), your geographic market may be the entire country or the entire continent.

Another way of determining your target market is by the characteristics of your customers or clients — for example, sex, age, interests or needs, and/or income level if your customers or clients are individuals; kind of business and/or annual sales if your customers are other businesses.

Your share of the target market

Besides figuring out who or what your target market is, you have to try to estimate what share of the target market your competitors hold and what share you can capture. This is guesswork unless there are very few competitors on the scene. As an example, if you open a convenience store in a residential area where there are no other stores, you've got a good chance of getting a very big share of the target market (the inhabitants of the residential area). But — to take an example from the opposite end of the spectrum — if you're planning to sell T-shirts over the Internet (a huge total market), you may never be able to estimate your market share or a competitor's with anything approaching accuracy because many businesses are competing in a fickle market.

If you're looking for a large sum of money, it would be worth your while to have a professional marketing study done to examine in detail the size of the market, the existing competitors in the market, and the market share your business may expect to capture.

Marketing strategy

When it comes to identifying a marketing strategy, there are lots of details to take into account. They include

- **Your planned method(s) of selling and/or distributing your product or service:** Are you going to sell direct to the end user, or are you going to go through a third party (such as a manufacturer's agent or a distributor or a retailer, if you're a manufacturer)? If you already have contracts or partnerships with individuals or businesses or governments who are going to buy or distribute your product or service, mention them here.

- **Your location (if it has an impact on marketing):** Your location is important if, for example, you're a retail store or service relying on walk-in customers, or if you provide a product that can be shipped only short distances to customers, or if you need to project an image to customers that can be achieved in only a certain area. It's not particularly important if you provide a service or product without needing face-to-face contact with your customers or clients — for example, if you run a call-centre operation. Then it's fine to be in an industrial plaza in the middle of nowhere, as long as you can get workers to agree to walk through dark alleys.

- **Your strategy for promoting the product:** This covers things like

  - **Your business image:** How are you going to present your business? Are you going to package it around a logo or trademark? Are you going to build it around a concept (such as one-stop errand running if you're starting up a rent-a-spouse business) or a special product? Are you going to promote it as an essential for your target market (such as a business-district spa for businesswomen)?

  - **Your advertising message:** What's your message, and your method and budget for getting the message out? Methods may include TV and radio spots, newspaper ads, billboard and signs, flyers distributed around neighbourhoods or to local businesses — or even just word of mouth. The method should be appropriate to the target market and to the image you want your business to project.

Book VIII

Taking Care of Business

- **Your public relations plan, if any:** Do you have a plan for approaching the media (in the hope that they'll write about you or interview you on TV news or a business program or a lifestyle show) and organizing events to attract media and/or customer attention? Media approaches may include press releases, contacts with acquaintances or friends-of-friends, or cold calls.

- **Your sales strategy:** How are you going to set your basic price? (Generally speaking, it should be high enough to cover your costs of providing the product or service and earn you a profit, and low enough that your competitors are not underpricing you.) What other pricing procedures are you going to use to attract customers and clients? (Possibilities include gifts, coupons or two-for-one offers, special sales to groups, or special rates for large purchases of your product or time.)

- **Finding and keeping customers:** What's your plan for coming up with leads to find new customers and clients? (Tried and true methods include advertisements, arranging for other individuals and businesses to refer clients to you, and buying customer lists.) Are you going to make presentations to prospective clients or customers? (What will the content of the presentation be, and how will you jazz it up to give it impact?) How are you going to satisfy the customers you do get? (Think about a returns policy, guarantees, or product service provided on the premises.)

Your competitors

You need to know your market, but you also need to know your competitors. If you can't beat them at their own game, that will be the end of you.

In this part of your business plan, you'll:

- ✔ **Fearlessly name your competitors:** Remember, though, you're talking about your competitors in your target market and not all the competitors in the total market. If you're starting a dog-walking business, your competitors aren't every personal-service provider in the province, or even every dog-walker in the city, just the dog-walkers in the neighbourhood you plan to service. For now.

- ✔ **Describe the similar products or services available from the competitors:** What are the strong points about the competing products or services, and what are the weak points? What problems exist with the competition's product or services?

- ✔ **Explain why customers will buy the product or service from you instead of something similar from the competition:** Describe the strengths of *your* product or service.

Strong points of either the competitors' businesses or your business may include:

- ✔ Higher quality of services or product
- ✔ Innovative nature of the product or service (being the first to provide a product or service can give the provider a competitive edge — but keep in mind that the first provider isn't necessarily the best provider)
- ✔ Lower cost of services or product
- ✔ Better distribution system
- ✔ Better management
- ✔ Better customer service — efficient, fast, friendly
- ✔ Better service guarantees that accompany the product or service
- ✔ Location that's more convenient for customers or clients
- ✔ Loyalty of an established base of customers or clients
- ✔ Loyalty of customers or clients to a particular brand
- ✔ Access to a client/customer base that hasn't been tapped yet

Weaknesses are the flip side of these matters — such as higher cost of the product, poorer quality of the service, less convenient location, and so on.

Don't overdo describing your competitors' strengths or your own weaknesses. You don't want to deep-six your business proposal by presenting the competition as unbeatable or you as a lost sheep among the coyotes. But you do want your potential investor to know that you've taken an objective look at the market and your chances of turning a good profit.

How Your Business Runs (Management and Operations)

Book VIII

Taking
Care of
Business

Investors are amazingly curious about how you will run your business. Some even go so far as to say that they care less about the product or service the business provides than they do about who's in charge. Poor management can destroy even a great idea, while good management can nurture a less-than-fantastic idea along the path to success.

Business info and history

You're allowed to start with the easy stuff about your business:

- ✔ Address, telephone and fax numbers for the business, and e-mail address
- ✔ A statement about the form of your business (sole proprietorship, partnership, or corporation)
- ✔ A description or picture of any business logo, design, trademark, or trade name you're using
- ✔ A brief history of the business, including the date of business start-up

Business managers

Then you get down to the nitty-gritty: Who's running this show? Here the key people are listed (it may be a short list) and their titles, if any:

- ✔ **The owner(s) of the business:** The sole proprietor of a sole proprietorship, the shareholders of a corporation, the partners in a partnership
- ✔ **The manager(s) of the business:** For example, the managing partner of a partnership, or the CEO (chief executive officer) of a corporation — and the compensation the manager is to receive. Each manager's *CV (curriculum vitae, or resume)* should accompany the business plan. And it should show that the manager has relevant business experience. If you're a novice at running a business, your CV should at least show that you've got related work experience and/or that you've attended some courses or workshops on setting up and managing a business. If you're starting a complex business or one that requires a lot of money (hundreds of thousands or millions of dollars) at the outset, don't fool around playing CEO if you're not a seasoned professional. Investors won't look at your business unless you've got a professional with a track record in place.
- ✔ **Key employees of the business:** For example, the person responsible for sales and marketing or the person in charge of research and development
- ✔ **If the business is based on an idea, the inventor(s) or creator(s) of the idea:** For example, the inventor of a drug or medical device, or the designer of a product that the business is going to manufacture. If at all possible, you want the creative brain behind the business to come along with the business. Have an inventor or creator provide a CV to attach to the business plan.

- **Professional advisors of the business:** The lawyer, accountant, publicist, advertising firm

- **Investors already on board:** These could be you (via your bank account, investments, sale of property, and so on) and your family and friends who loaned you cash or contributed equipment; or your bank that gave you a start-up loan, or some other arm's-length investor

Business operations

If it's relevant to your business — for example, if you're a manufacturer or if you service products — you should also provide information about

- Your facilities or physical plant or infrastructure

- Your equipment and methods of operation (including any intention to be ISO-9000 certified)

- Your materials and supplies, and their sources

Sharing Financial Information

In the finance section of your business plan you're going to crunch the numbers to show that you've got a good chance of making a profit, or at least of paying back the loan or generating a return on the investment. This is a spot where lenders or investors will become extremely eagle-eyed because they want to be pretty sure that they'll get their money back someday, one way or another.

You do this part of the business plan through *spreadsheets* (financial tables created by software packages such as Excel or Lotus 1-2-3) rather than written text.

Specifically, investors will want to know:

- How much money the business needs to get up and running (or to expand, if this isn't a start-up operation) — in other words, what the present *capital requirements* of the business are.

- How many assets the business already has (how much property it owns, such as money, real estate, equipment, and valuable contracts such as licence agreements and leases) and how many liabilities it has (how much it owes, such as mortgages, loans, and accounts payable) — this is the *balance sheet.*

✔ What the projected profit of the business is — how much the business will earn and how much it will cost the business to earn that amount. Or to put it another way, what the income and operating expenses will be (this is a *statement of income and expenses*). You may also have to show when the income comes in and when payment of expenses goes out, with a *cash flow statement*.

✔ What assets the principals of the business have and what liabilities — this means preparing a *personal balance sheet* for each owner of the business. A loan for your business will actually be a personal loan if your business is a sole proprietorship or a partnership. And even if your business is a corporation, there's a good chance you'll be asked to guarantee a business loan personally if your business doesn't generate enough profit and doesn't have enough assets to sell to repay the loan. If you're not a good loan risk personally, the whole deal may fall through.

If your business has been in operation for two or three years and isn't a start-up, you'll also be expected to provide *balance sheets* for the preceding years and *income* (or *profit and loss*) *statements*. See Chapter 4 for more about these statements.

Capital requirements of your business

Chapter 1 has details about calculating the capital requirements of your business. You'll find a table there that will help you to prepare a statement of your start-up capital needs.

Assets and liabilities of your business

The assets and liabilities of your business are set out in a balance sheet. Chapter 4 explains balance sheets and how to prepare them.

Projected income and expenses of your business

You can find information about preparing a forecast of income and expenses in Chapter 1, including a table to help you work out your forecast of income and expenses for the first year of business.

Your personal capital

The lender or investor may well be looking to you to pay up if your business can't. If so, you'll be asked to provide a *personal balance sheet*, often called a *statement of net worth*, listing your own assets and liabilities. This provides a snapshot of the financial you. Table 2-1 shows an example of a personal balance sheet.

Table 2-1	Personal Balance Sheet
Assets:	
Cash	$
Investments	$
Cash-value life insurance	$
Real estate (home, cottage)	$
Vehicles	$
Personal property	$
Personal loans	$
Other	$
Total assets	$
Liabilities:	
Mortgages	$
Personal loans	$
Credit card balances	$
Other personal debts (e.g. unpaid property taxes, unpaid income taxes, outstanding bills, child support)	$
Monthly bills	$
Total liabilities	$
Net worth (total assets minus total liabilities)	$

Book VIII

Taking Care of Business

Offering References

You're exhausted now but you're not finished. As a final touch, a lender or investor may like to know more about your business reputation (or if you don't have a business reputation yet, your personal reputation) — but not from you. So be prepared to provide, if asked, the names of two or three people the lender or investor could speak to — for example, your bank branch manager if you've dealt with him or her for some time, or other business people you've dealt with over the years (probably best not to name your competitors here — or your mother). If you've never been in business for yourself before, you could name an employer or a customer or client you worked with. Ask your references for permission before you give their names. At the very least, you don't want them to be taken by surprise when a lender calls up for a chat about you.

If your business venture revolves around marketing a new technology (say, new computer software or hardware), a lender or investor would probably like to have the names of a couple of people who know the field and who can give an opinion about the commercial potential of your technology. Again, avoid giving the name of a competitor.

The Final Product

After you've put together a first draft of your business plan, you should ask someone with business experience whose judgement you trust to read the plan and comment on it. Then you revise the plan and polish up the prose. You can see how an entire business plan is supposed to look by going to the sample business plan in this Book's appendix. Your final version of the plan will include the following:

- ✔ Cover
- ✔ Title page
- ✔ Table of contents
- ✔ Executive summary
- ✔ The plan itself
- ✔ Financial statements

Cover

Don't get carried away with something expensive, or covered with decorations. Just buy a plain paper cover — preferably in a conservative colour.

Executive summary

If your plan is more than three or four pages long (excluding financial charts), you need to provide a summary at the beginning of the plan so that the reader can decide even more quickly whether to talk to you or simply toss your plan in the circular file. The summary should

- ✔ State the amount of money required and what you will do with it
- ✔ Briefly describe the business
- ✔ Describe the business's product or service
- ✔ Summarize income projections

Book VIII

Taking
Care of
Business

Chapter 3

Paying Your Dues: All about Taxes

. . . .

In This Chapter

▶ Learning about income tax

▶ Finding out about sales taxes

▶ Revisiting payroll taxes

▶ Looking at other business taxes

. . . .

*O*ne of the unpleasant realities of being in business is that you are expected to pay taxes. Every level of government — federal, provincial, and municipal — wants something. You will have to pay:

- ✔ **Income taxes** — to the federal and provincial governments
- ✔ **Sales taxes** — to the federal and provincial governments
- ✔ **Payroll taxes** — to the federal and provincial governments
- ✔ **Business taxes** — possibly to the federal and provincial governments, and more likely to your municipal government

Taxes are not only hard to dodge, they are also complicated and difficult to understand. It's impossible to explain taxes fully in just one chapter. In fact, you can still be pretty muddled (not to mention shell-shocked and bored within an inch of death) after reading whole books about taxes. So in this chapter, you get just enough information to let you know the kinds of taxes you have to pay and when you have to pay them, and with a bit of advice thrown in about keeping your income tax to a minimum.

Income Taxes

Individuals and corporations must pay taxes on income to both the federal and provincial governments. The Canada Customs and Revenue Agency (CCRA) collects both federal and provincial income tax from individuals (human beings, that is) in every province except Quebec, and from corporations in all provinces except Alberta, Ontario, and Quebec, where the provincial governments collect their own corporate income taxes.

A business can also be taxed on its *capital gains.* A capital gain is the profit made on the sale or other disposition of *capital property.* Capital property is property acquired to be held onto rather than resold right away. Examples of capital property could include commercial real estate bought for use in a business, or shares in a corporation. A start-up business isn't likely to have capital gains while it's a going concern, so you won't find any discussion of capital gains in this chapter. But a business may have capital gains or capital losses when the business is sold or is wound up.

What income is a business taxed on?

You will be pleased to know that you're not taxed on every cent your business earns. Your income taxes are calculated only on the *profit* your business makes. Your business's profit is its *gross income* (or *revenue* — the money the business takes in) minus its legitimate *expenses* (the money spent or expenses incurred in order to earn the income).

The lower your business's profit, the less tax you will have to pay. So the question is how *legally* to keep your profits as low as possible for tax purposes. There are only two ways to have low profits (and therefore low taxes). One is to keep your business revenues as low as possible and the other is to make your legitimate business expenses as high as possible.

Unfortunately, you can't minimize your business revenue without cheating because you are required by law to report everything your business earns. So the only way legally to reduce your profits and your tax payable is to maximize your legitimate business expenses. It is therefore critical to know what deductions you are entitled to. Over the next few pages, you'll find out what is considered to be business income and what is considered to be a legitimate business expense.

Everyone wants to pay as little tax as possible. Tax *avoidance* is paying as little tax as is legally possible. Tax *evasion,* on the other hand, is failing to pay taxes that are legally owing — and it's a crime. Income tax laws are complicated and change constantly, so you need expert tax advice from an accountant and/or tax lawyer to make sure that you avoid as much tax as you can without evading any tax. You also need advice to make sure that any tax-avoidance scheme you come up with will actually work.

What is business income?

According to the CCRA, business income includes money earned or valuable property received from any activity you engage in as part of your business. Business income includes

- Fees charged to your clients for services you provide, excluding any sales tax you charged

- The purchase price charged to your customers for goods you sell, excluding any sales tax you charged

You are required to report to the CCRA all income earned by your business during the taxation year.

What are legitimate business expenses?

The CCRA allows you to deduct from business income most reasonable expenses you pay in order to earn that income. Since the only legal way to reduce your profits — and therefore your taxes — is to maximize your legitimate business expenses, it's very important to know what your legitimate business expenses are. They include:

- Mortgage interest and property taxes on real property you own and use for your business (see below, under the heading "Home office expenses," if you run your business out of a home you own)

- Rent if you lease your business premises (see "Home office expenses," if you run your business out of your rented home)

- The cost of labour and materials for any minor repairs or maintenance done to property you use to earn income

- The cost of leasing equipment used in your business

- The cost of buying or manufacturing the goods you sold during the year

- Delivery, freight, and transportation expenses

- Insurance premiums you pay to insure any buildings, machinery, and equipment you use in your business

- Utilities such as telephone, electricity, heat, and water

- The cost of office expenses and supplies — small items such as printer ink cartridges, stationery, pens, pencils, paper clips, and stamps

- Some of the expenses of running a motor vehicle that you use to earn business income (for more information, see below under the heading "Car expenses")

Book VIII

Taking Care of Business

- Interest you pay on money that you borrow to run your business

- Annual licence fees and levies (such as municipal business taxes) to run your business

- Annual dues or fees for membership in a trade or commercial association (but not if the main purpose of the club is dining, recreation, or sporting activities)

- Legal, accounting, and other professional fees

- Management and administration fees to operate your business, including bank charges

- Expenses for advertising your product or service

- Travel expenses to earn business income

- Fifty percent of business meals, beverages, and entertainment

- Salaries and benefits you pay to employees, as well as your portion of Canada Pension Plan and Employment Insurance premiums (see the heading "Employee salaries," below, for more information)

You may have noticed that this list includes only leased equipment, and purchased office supplies of a minor kind such as pens and paper. More important items that you purchase (rather than lease) such as a computer, phone system, fax machine or other office equipment, furniture, and larger items such as buildings or vehicles can't be fully claimed in the year of *purchase* as business expense. That's because these items, which are *capital property,* will continue to be useful to your business for more than one taxation year. However, since these items *depreciate* (wear out or lose their usefulness over time), you can claim a percentage of the cost as a business expense each year over a period of several years until the entire cost has been claimed. The amount you are allowed to claim on *depreciable capital property* each year as an expense is called *capital cost allowance,* and there's a special place on the income tax form for calculating the exact amount of capital cost allowance you can claim in a given year.

Many of your business expenses are clearly only for your business, such as the cost of an ad in the newspaper or lease payments on machinery used to create the product you sell. But there are other items that you may use both for your business and personally — for example, a cellphone, a computer, or your car. When you calculate your business expenses, you are not allowed to claim any part of the expense that relates to your personal use of the item. You can deduct only the portion of the expense that relates to your business use. For example, if you use half of your monthly airtime on your cellphone for business calls and half for personal calls, you can claim as a business expense only the amount paid for the business calls.

Home office expenses

If you operate your business from your home, you are allowed to deduct expenses for the business use of your home. This allows you to get a tax deduction for a portion of your home expenses (which you would have to pay anyway).

For the costs to be deductible, your home office must either

- Be your main place of business, or,
- If it's not your main place of business, be used *exclusively* for business purposes and be used on a regular basis for meeting clients or customers in connection with the business

If your home office meets one of these two tests, you can deduct a percentage of the following costs:

- Mortgage interest and property taxes (if you own) or rental payments (if you rent)
- Utilities such as heat, electricity, and water
- Maintenance costs or condo fees
- Home insurance

To figure out the percentage you're allowed to deduct, calculate what percentage of your home you use for your business. Divide the area of your office by the total area of your home. So, for example, if your home is 1,500 square feet in area, and the room you use exclusively for business is 300 square feet in area, then you can deduct 20 percent of your home costs. Or you may divide the number of rooms occupied by your business by the total number of rooms in your home. For example, if you have four rooms in your apartment and you use one of those rooms exclusively for business, then you can deduct 25 percent of your home costs.

You can use the home office deduction to bring your business income down to zero, but not to put your business into a loss position, or to increase a loss that already exists. Once you reach zero, any home office expenses that are left over can be applied against business income in future years.

Car expenses

You are allowed to deduct the expenses of running a motor vehicle that you use to earn business income. These expenses include:

- Fuel and oil
- Maintenance and repairs
- Insurance

Book VIII

Taking Care of Business

✔ Licence and registration fees

✔ Leasing costs or interest paid on money borrowed to buy the vehicle (but note that if your vehicle is a passenger car, there is a limit to the amount you are allowed to claim)

✔ Capital cost allowance, if you own the motor vehicle (again, if your vehicle is a passenger car, there is a limit to the amount you are allowed to claim)

If you use your car for both business and personal purposes, only the portion of your car expenses that relate to your business activities is a legitimate business expense. Use the following formula:

$$\frac{(\text{Total car expenses} \times \text{kilometres driven for business purposes})}{\text{Total kilometres driven}} = \begin{array}{l}\text{Allowable} \\ \text{business} \\ \text{expense}\end{array}$$

Employee salaries

You can deduct the salaries you pay to your employees, as well as the portion that you pay of their Canada Pension Plan and Employment Insurance contributions. You can also deduct the cost of any benefits you provide to your employees, such as health insurance and life insurance.

Hiring a family member may be a good way to reduce your business income taxes. By paying your spouse or child or parent a salary, you reduce profits and therefore taxes payable. Your family member will have to pay tax on the salary, but will pay less tax than you or your business would, as long as his or her tax rate is lower. By shifting some of the profit to your family, you increase your family's after-tax income even though total income remains the same.

You can employ family members in your business and deduct the salary as a legitimate business expense if:

✔ You actually pay the salary, and

✔ The family member actually does work that is necessary for the business, and

✔ The salary you pay is reasonable in comparison to what you would pay someone else

If you are a sole proprietor or a partner, you or your partners are not employees of the business, so you cannot deduct any salary or draw taken. In order to be employees and run the business, you have to incorporate. However, there are other tax advantages to being a sole proprietor or partner, so don't go rushing off to incorporate.

How much tax will you pay?

The amount of tax you will pay depends on the form of your business. That's because sole proprietorships and partnerships are taxed differently from corporations.

If your business is a sole proprietorship or partnership

If you carry on business as a sole proprietor, from the tax point of view the business's income is considered to be your personal income. If you carry on business in a partnership, your share of the business's income is also considered to be your personal income.

You report your (or your share of the) business's profits or loss in your personal income tax return. (See below under the heading "When and how do you have to pay?" for more about how this is done.) Your business does not file a separate tax return.

If your business has made a profit, the profit (or your share of the profit) is included in your personal income and is taxed as personal income. If your business has suffered a loss, the loss (or your share of the loss) is subtracted from your personal income from other sources for the year. That means that a business loss reduces your total income.

If you have a business loss but you have no other income for the year, or if the loss from your business is greater than your income from other sources, you can carry the loss back and apply it against income you earned in the past three years, or you can carry it forward and apply it against income you earn in the next seven years.

Your federal and provincial income tax is calculated as a percentage of your total personal income, including your business profits or loss. Your tax rate depends on your total income — as your income goes up, so does the percentage at which it is taxed.

Federal tax rates are the same across the country, but provincial tax rates vary from province to province. As a result, the *combined rates* of federal and provincial tax vary across the country. You can find exact information about the combined federal and provincial tax for your province at PricewaterhouseCoopers Tax News Network Canada at www.ca.taxnews.com, but in the meantime, here's a rough idea of what you'll have to pay. In the 2003 taxation year, depending on the province,

✔ If your taxable income is up to about $30,000, you'll pay tax at a combined rate of about 20 percent, including the favourable impact of a basic personal exemption of approximately $8,000.

✔ If your taxable income is between $30,000 and $60,000, you'll pay tax at a rate of around 20 percent on taxable income up to $30,000 and at a rate of 34 percent on taxable income between $30,000 and $60,000.

✔ If your taxable income is in the range of $60,000 and $100,000, you'll pay tax at a rate of about 20 percent on taxable income up to $30,000, at a rate of about 34 percent on taxable income between $30,000 and $60,000 and at a rate of about 39 percent on taxable income between $60,000 and $100,000.

✔ If your taxable income is about $100,000, you'll pay tax at a rate of around 20 percent on taxable income up to $30,000, at a rate of about 34 percent on taxable income between $30,000 and $60,000, at a rate of about 39 percent on taxable income between $60,000 and $100,000 and at a rate of about 47 percent on taxable income over $100,000.

These are very rough estimates, so check the combined federal/provincial rate in your province to get a more accurate picture.

If your business is a corporation

If your business is incorporated, the corporation is a taxpayer that has to file its own income tax return (see below under the heading "When and how do you have to pay?" for more about how this is done) and pay tax on its profits.

Unlike individuals, whose tax rate increases in steps or brackets with the amount of income earned, corporations are taxed at a *flat rate*. Depending on the province, the combined federal and provincial tax rate ranges from about 36 to 44 percent. However, the federal *small business deduction* reduces the tax rate to between 15 and 21 percent on the first $200,000 of business income earned by a *Canadian-controlled private corporation*. (A Canadian-controlled private corporation is exactly what it sounds like — a private corporation controlled by Canadian shareholders.) The tax rate on a Canadian-controlled private corporation's business income between $200,000 and $300,000 ranges between 25 and 39 percent, and on income over $300,000 the tax rate goes back up to between 36 and 44 percent (again depending on the province).

The small business deduction generally does not apply to a corporation's income from interest, dividends, rents, or royalties.

If your corporation suffers a loss, the loss can be carried back and applied against profits made in the past three years, or carried forward and applied against profits made in the next seven years. (The corporation's loss cannot be applied to reduce your personal income for tax purposes.)

The tax authorities aren't finished with you after they tax your corporation. If you receive any money from the corporation in the form of salary, benefits, a bonus, or dividends, you have to report that money as income on your personal income tax return and pay tax on what you receive. (See the heading above, "If your business is a sole proprietorship or partnership," for tax rates.) Salary, bonus, or benefits are taxed at your personal tax rate. Dividends are also taxed at your personal tax rate, but come with a *dividend tax credit* that limits the tax to a maximum of about 33 percent (the figure varies by province). The tax credit recognizes the fact that dividends are a distribution of corporate profits on which the corporation has already paid taxes.

When and how do you have to pay?

Every Canadian taxpayer is required to file an income tax return each year and pay whatever taxes are owing. The type of return you file, your deadline for filing it, and the deadline for paying your taxes depend on your form of business organization.

If your business is a sole proprietorship or partnership

If you carry on business as a sole proprietor or in a partnership, your profit from the business is considered to be your personal income and is reported in your personal tax return — the standard T1-General Form. Your business does not file a separate tax return. Instead you complete a Form T2124, Statement of Business Activities (or T2032, Statement of Professional Activities, which looks much the same), and include it as part of your personal tax return. The form gives details of your business's income and expenses. You include the business's profit (or loss) as part of your income.

Individual taxpayers must file their personal income tax returns and pay any taxes owing by April 30 of the year following the taxation year. (That means, for example, filing your income tax return for 2003 by April 30, 2004.) If you are self-employed and are a sole proprietor or a partner, your tax return is not due until June 15 following the end of your business's *fiscal period* or taxation year (which for most partnerships and sole proprietorships must be the same as the calendar year). However, your taxes must still be paid by April 30. So even if you're not ready to prepare your income tax return, you have to estimate how much tax is owing and send that amount in by April 30 with a letter setting out your Social Insurance Number and what the payment is for. (If you estimate wrong, you'll have to pay interest from April 30 on the amount you didn't pay but should have.)

Don't for a minute think that just because you are self-employed and not receiving a paycheque, the CCRA will sit back and wait to be paid all of the taxes you owe on April 30. Self-employed taxpayers are required to pay their tax by quarterly instalments. After your first year of making a profit on which you have to pay at least $2,000 in tax, the CCRA will send you an instalment notice telling you that you have to start paying taxes on a quarterly basis, and thereafter it will send you quarterly reminders to pay up. The CCRA calculates your instalment payments, but you don't have to pay those amounts. You can estimate your income for the year and pay one-fourth each quarter. But if you underestimate the amount of tax you owe, you will have to pay interest on the amount by which your instalments fall short.

If you have to make quarterly instalment payments, salt away in a special bank account the amount you'll owe at the end of each quarter, so that you don't accidentally spend it.

In the first year that your sole proprietorship or partnership makes a profit, don't forget that you're a taxpayer even though you don't have to pay taxes until April 30 of the following year! Estimate (generously) how much money you'll owe in taxes on each month's income, and put that amount into an interest-earning bank account or into treasury bills or GICs so that you'll have it ready to pay on April 30 *and* you'll have earned some interest income on it.

If your business is a partnership with six or more partners, the partnership must also file a partnership information return — Form T5013. (An information return is not a tax return. It is not used to calculate how much tax is payable, but to give the CCRA information to ensure that tax information for the partnership is being properly calculated and reported by each of the partners.) The partnership information form must be filed by March 31.

If your business is a corporation

If your business is incorporated, the corporation is a taxpayer and has to file its own income tax return — Form T2, Corporation Income Tax Return — together with information from the corporation's financial statements. (See Chapter 4 for more about financial statements.) Form T2 serves as both a federal and provincial income tax return — except in Alberta, Ontario, and Quebec, where a separate provincial corporate tax return must also be filed.

The corporation will have to file a corporate income tax return within six months after the end of the corporation's fiscal period or taxation year. Unlike a sole proprietorship or partnership, a corporation can choose any date for its year-end.

You will also have to file your personal income tax return. Your return must be filed by April 30, because you are not considered to be self-employed when you're running your business through a corporation.

A corporation must pay income tax in monthly instalments unless the tax payable for the year or the previous taxation year is $1,000 or less. (During the corporation's first taxation year, no instalment payments have to be made.) The CCRA does not calculate the amount of the instalments — you must do that yourself, basing your payment on one of the following:

- ✔ An estimate of the tax payable in the current year, or

- ✔ The tax paid in the previous year, or

- ✔ A combination of the tax paid in the previous year and the year before that

If the corporation owes more income tax than it paid in its monthly instalments, it must pay the balance within two months after the end of the corporation's fiscal year (three months if the corporation is a Canadian-controlled private corporation, eligible for the small business deduction, and with an income of less than $200,000). Notice that the due date to pay the balance of the tax is earlier than the deadline for filing the corporation's income tax return.

If you've engaged in conduct unbecoming

Whether your business is a sole proprietorship, partnership, or corporation, if

- ✔ You don't make your instalment payments on time

- ✔ You don't pay enough in instalment payments, or

- ✔ You don't pay any balance of tax owing by the due date — April 30 for individuals, and two (or three) months after the fiscal year end for a corporation

then you will have to pay interest at about 10 percent on taxes that are overdue.

You may have to pay a *penalty* if

- ✔ Your accumulated interest charges for any year are more than $1,000

- ✔ You file your income tax return late

- ✔ You fail to report income, or

- ✔ You knowingly or carelessly make false statements or omissions on your tax return

Penalties start at 5 percent of unpaid taxes — but they don't stop there.

Book VIII

Taking Care of Business

What records must you keep?

Any corporation or individual who carries on a business, or is required to pay or collect income taxes, must keep books and records that allow the amount of taxes payable to be calculated and checked. You must hold onto these books and records for at least six years after the taxation year they relate to.

To make it easier to prepare your tax returns when they are due, you should keep organized books and records throughout the year as well as hanging on to your invoices and receipts. You can keep actual account books, or you can use small-business bookkeeping and accounting software. Chapter 4 has more about accounting for your business.

What if you're audited?

When you file your or your corporation's income tax return, it is reviewed by the CCRA. When the CCRA completes the review it issues a *notice of assessment,* which sets out the amount of tax payable for the year. The CCRA has the right to *reassess* your return later, and can go back and reassess your returns for the past three years (or longer, if they suspect fraud) and ask you for more money. If you disagree with the CCRA about the amount it says you have to pay, you (personally or through your accountant) can object to the assessment or reassessment, and try to persuade the CCRA that you don't owe as much as they say by showing them documents that support your objection and even by visiting the local Tax Services Office in person to argue your case. This can go on for some time, because the CCRA usually takes a while to digest any communication from a taxpayer.

A tax audit is different from (and worse than) an assessment or reassessment. In an audit, the CCRA goes over all your records, including records you weren't required to send in with your tax return, to see whether you've declared all of your income and deducted only legitimate expenses.

Tax returns of corporations and self-employed taxpayers are more likely to be audited than those of taxpayers who are employees, because businesses have more opportunities to evade taxes by hiding income or inflating (or even making up) expenses.

On an audit, you will have to prove all of your income and expenses by presenting receipts. So just in case you're audited, you should keep receipts that are dated and show what business activity they relate to.

If you are audited, the CCRA will notify you by letter that your tax return for a stated year, or years, has been selected for review. The letter will ask you to provide specified information within 30 days (although you can ask for an extension if you need more time).

If you get an audit letter, speak to your accountant immediately. If you don't already have an accountant, this would be a good time to get one! You can respond to the request on your own, or you can (and probably should) hire an accountant or tax lawyer.

The auditor will then arrange a face-to-face meeting (your accountant or even your lawyer can be present), during which you may be asked to justify some of your expense claims. You'll respond by showing the auditor your supporting records and receipts. You should have your records organized so that you are able to answer the auditor's questions. Be cooperative and polite, even if you're feeling cranky and angry. (There's no point in irritating a person who has the power to assess additional taxes, not to mention interest and penalties, against you.)

When the auditor is finished, he or she will send you a letter setting out proposed changes to your income tax return, and giving you time either to accept the changes or dispute them. (To dispute the proposed changes, you will have to provide new information that you didn't have for the auditor.) Then the CCRA will send you a notice of reassessment setting out what you owe and when it's due.

If you accept the reassessment, you have to pay the balance by the due date. If you can't pay by the due date, you can contact the collections department of the CCRA to make other arrangements for payment. You can apply to the Fairness Committee at the CCRA to have any penalties or interest set aside. If you disagree with the reassessment, you can file a notice of objection with your local Tax Services Office within 90 days after the date of the reassessment.

Collecting Sales Taxes

The federal government and every province except Alberta require sales tax to be charged when goods are sold or services are provided. The federal sales tax is the Goods and Services Tax (GST). GST and provincial sales tax (PST) are charged separately in all provinces except Nova Scotia, New Brunswick and Newfoundland, which have combined their provincial sales taxes with the GST into a Harmonized Sales Tax (HST). Provincial sales taxes range from 7 to 10 percent, GST is 7 percent, and HST is 15 percent.

Provincial sales tax

Businesses that sell goods or provide services on which PST has to be charged are responsible for collecting the tax from the buyer of the goods or services. Businesses are required to *remit* (send) the collected taxes to the provincial government on a regular basis. In every province except Quebec (where sales tax works more like GST, see below), the tax is payable by the final consumer only, so businesses do not have to pay PST on goods that will be resold (although they must pay PST on goods bought for their own use).

If your business will be selling goods or providing services on which PST must be charged, you must register with your provincial government's department or ministry of finance. You will be given a registration certificate and provincial tax number. You will have to file periodic (usually monthly) returns with the ministry of finance, in which you report the amount of tax collected and remit the tax. For more information about PST in your province, check the Web site for your provincial Canada Business Service Centre or for your provincial government.

Your business must keep proper books and records to document the amount of tax collected, and you are subject to audits by the provincial government.

If you fail to file returns, collect taxes as required, or remit the taxes collected, you may be charged an interest penalty. You may even be charged with an offence and hauled into court.

Goods and Services Tax

GST applies to almost all goods sold and services supplied anywhere in Canada. Unlike PST, which is paid only by the ultimate consumer, GST is charged to everyone along the production and sale chain — from the supplier of the raw materials, through the manufacturer, wholesaler, and retailer, down to the consumer. While everyone is charged the tax, the government keeps only the tax paid by the ultimate consumer. Everyone else in the chain is allowed to claim a refund on the GST they paid (called an *input tax credit*).

You'll find plenty of information about the GST on the CCRA Web site at www.ccra-adrc.gc.ca.

GST categories

GST must be charged when goods and services are "supplied" — whether by sale, rental, barter, or gift. There are three categories of "supplies":

1. Supplies that are taxable at 7 percent, which include all supplies that don't fall into the second and third categories — so there's a good chance that whatever goods or services you're providing are in the first category.

2. Supplies that are taxable at 0 percent, which include prescription drugs and medical devices, basic groceries, international travel and transportation, precious metals, and farm and fishing products and equipment.

3. Supplies that are *tax-exempt,* which include health care, personal care, child care or educational services, and financial services.

Are there crazy people running the Goods and Services Tax department of the federal government? Why would you tax supplies at 0 percent . . . and what on earth is the difference between supplies that are taxed at 0 percent and supplies that are tax-exempt? Well, the GST people may indeed be crazy, but there's a certain method to their madness. The supplier doesn't collect GST from customers if supplies are taxed at 0 percent or if supplies are tax-exempt. But if a business provides zero-rated supplies, it can still claim a refund on the GST it paid to get goods and services, whereas if a business provides tax-exempt supplies, it can't.

Registering for the GST

If your business provides GST-taxable goods and services *and* has annual revenues of more than $30,000, you *must* register for the GST. Otherwise you *may* register. Once you register for the GST you must charge GST to your customers and remit it to the CCRA, and you can claim a refund on the GST you pay to get goods and services. If you don't register for the GST, you don't have to charge GST, but you can't claim a refund, either.

Register for the GST even if your revenues are less than $30,000. You'll be able to get back the GST paid on the goods and services your business buys. Besides, you don't really want your customers to know that your business's annual revenues are less than $30,000.

You register for the GST by applying to the CCRA for a *business number.*

Collecting and remitting GST

When you invoice a customer or client for goods or services you provide, you have to invoice for GST, as well. You calculate GST on the full price your customer pays, including any customs or excise duties and transportation taxes — but excluding any provincial sales tax, and not taking into account any discounts for early payment of your invoice or interest charged for late payment.

Book VIII

Taking Care of Business

You must report the amount of GST collected and remit it to the CCRA on a regular basis. How often you remit depends on your business's annual sales, as follows:

- ✔ If your annual sales are less than $500,000, you must remit GST quarterly, and you must report annually although you can choose to report quarterly; you can also choose to report and remit monthly.

- ✔ If your annual sales are between $500,000 and $6,000,000, you must report and remit GST quarterly, although you can choose to report and remit monthly.

- ✔ If your annual sales are more than $6,000,000 (here's hoping!), you must report and remit GST monthly.

On the GST form, you show the GST your business charged on the goods and services it provided, as well as the GST your business paid on the goods and services it bought. The difference between what you charged and what you paid is the amount you must remit to the government. If you paid more than you charged, you are entitled to a GST refund.

You must keep books and records, including invoices, to document the GST collected and any refunds claimed, for six years.

If you fail to report or remit GST as required, you will be charged interest and penalties. If you willfully fail to pay, collect or remit GST, you can be charged with an offence, and if you're convicted you can be fined or imprisoned.

Harmonized Sales Tax

Hey, what's that sound? Could it be "The Ride of the Valkyries"? Actually, it's the humming of the Harmonized Sales Tax (HST), the name given to the combined GST and provincial sales tax charged in Nova Scotia, New Brunswick, and Newfoundland.

If your business supplies goods or services in these provinces, no matter where in the country your business is actually located, you are required to collect and remit 15 percent HST to the CCRA. When you register for GST, you're also registered for HST, which works the same way as GST.

Payroll Taxes

Payroll taxes are taxes levied by the federal government and some provincial governments on businesses with employees. The federal payroll taxes are Employment Insurance (EI) and Canada Pension Plan (CPP). Employers must make contributions to EI and CPP on behalf of their employees, as well as withholding and remitting the employees' contributions. Provincial payroll taxes include health insurance and workers' compensation premiums.

Business Taxes

In addition to income taxes, sales taxes, and payroll taxes, federal, provincial, and municipal governments levy other business taxes:

- ✔ The federal government levies a *large corporation tax* on corporations with over $10 million of taxable capital in Canada

- ✔ Some provincial governments levy a tax on the *paid-up capital* of corporations. Paid-up capital is the total amount paid to the corporation for all the shares that have been issued to shareholders.

- ✔ Municipalities levy taxes on businesses. Businesses that own real estate in the municipality have to pay property taxes, but in some municipalities even businesses that rent rather than own are required to pay taxes. These taxes may be based, for example, on the annual rental value of the property or the square footage of the premises or the value of the business's stock-in-trade.

Your accountant can tell you more about these matters, or you can contact your federal, provincial, and municipal governments or visit their Web sites.

Chapter 4

Close Encounters with Accounting

In This Chapter

▶ Learning why accounting is important for your business

▶ Finding out what records to keep and how to keep them

▶ Learning the basics of bookkeeping

▶ Being introduced to financial statements

*T*o be successful, a small business owner has to keep track of what the business earns and what it spends, and what it owns and what it owes. That means that every small business owner has to know something about accounting. But you don't need to go through an entire accounting course here — just the absolute basics. If you find yourself yearning for more information than provided here, you can turn to *Accounting For Dummies*.

What's Accounting and Why Is It Important?

Accounting is the main language of business and its essence is to keep track of, and report on, financial transactions. Specifically, it's a process that begins with the collecting and recording of information about transactions and continues with sorting of the transactions by category and ends in the preparation of financial statements and income tax returns. Accountants call this process the *accounting cycle*. Some of the steps in the accounting cycle will be carried out by you, others will be carried out by your bookkeeper and/or your computerized accounting system, and still others will be carried out by your accountant.

Accounting is important in the day-to-day operation of your business because it helps you:

- Collect your accounts
- Pay your bills
- Pay your taxes
- Keep track of your inventory
- Prevent theft and fraud by your associates, employees, and customers

It is also important in the long term because it helps you:

- Assess how your business is doing
- Collect the information you need to plan and make decisions
- Give lenders the information they want before they will lend you money
- Give investors the information they want before they will invest in your business
- Give a buyer the information he or she wants to see before buying your business.

Starting with Bookkeeping

Bookkeeping is the information-gathering and record-keeping aspect of accounting. No matter how much professional or computer help you intend to have with your bookkeeping, it is up to you to keep track of all the financial transactions of your business — such as making sales, buying inventory, paying salaries, and borrowing money.

Your first chore as a bookkeeper is to keep all the pieces of paper, such as invoices, sales slips, and credit card slips, that document business transactions (and the more organized you are about it, the better). You should also keep a record of these transactions. Your second chore is to buy a green cap, so you can look like a bookkeeper, too!

Saving pieces of paper

Every financial transaction of your business should be documented by a piece of paper.

- ✔ **Whenever your business provides a service or sells a product:** You should generate an invoice. (You may have the kind of business where you prepare invoices only on a weekly or monthly basis.) Most off-the-shelf accounting software is able to generate invoices. If you're in a retail business, your cash register may generate a sales slip or invoice when you ring up the sale, or you may have to write up an invoice by hand. Send or give the invoice to the customer or client, and keep a copy for your records.

- ✔ **Whenever your business incurs an expense or makes a payment:** No matter how small the payment, you should get a bill, invoice, or receipt. If it's not clear what the receipt relates to, or the date the payment was made, it is important for tax and accounting purposes to make a note on the receipt identifying the business purpose of the transaction more clearly.

For income tax purposes, you have to keep a copy of both the bill and a copy of your cheque as proof of payment.

You must save every last one of these pieces of paper, which accountants and bookkeepers refer to as *source documents*. You can just throw all of them into a file, and let your bookkeeper and/or accountant sort them out later (and charge you for the extra work), but it makes more sense for you to set up some sort of system for filing them by category. For example, you may want to set up separate files for:

- ✔ Invoices you give to your customers when you provide a service or product
- ✔ Inventory purchases
- ✔ Office supply expenses
- ✔ Car expenses
- ✔ Entertainment expenses
- ✔ Accounting expenses

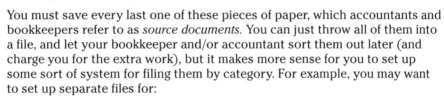

Recording your transactions

The next step in the bookkeeping process is to make a written record of the financial transactions, taking the information from your source documents.

Open a business bank account

If you want to keep track of and have a record of your business transactions, you should open a bank account that is just for your business. Open a separate account even if your business is a sole proprietorship or partnership. (If you're a sole proprietor or partner, your business is not legally separate from you as an individual.) You may think that it doesn't matter if your business and personal accounts get mixed up — but once you're finished with this chapter, you'll come around to the point of view that it's best to keep your business affairs to themselves.

The bank account should be a chequing account that gives you a monthly statement and that automatically returns your cancelled cheques. Unless you will be using a computerized accounting program that will prepare and keep track of your cheques (see following section), order cheques for your new account, and get a *cheque register.* (This little booklet for recording transactions in your account usually comes with your new cheques or can be wheedled out of a teller at your bank or trust company.)

Pay into and out of your business account

Whenever you receive a payment for goods or services provided by your business, deposit the entire amount immediately in your business account. Enter the payment received in your cheque register.

As much as you possibly can, make any payments for your business by cheque. If you like to make payments by credit card, consider getting one card that you use for nothing but business purposes. Always pay your monthly bill for that card out of your business account.

If you have just one credit card for both personal and business purposes, you can pay the monthly bill out of your personal account and then write a cheque to yourself on your business account for the business portion of the bill. On the cheque stub for the total repayment, make a note of the individual amounts and the supplier's name — that way your accountant (or your auditor — see Chapter 3) won't have to go through your personal records to verify your expenses. Similarly, if you happen to make a cash payment out of your personal pocket for a business expense, write yourself a cheque on your business account to repay yourself.

Whenever you make a payment, enter it in your cheque register.

If you operate this way, you automatically create a record of all your business's income and expenses. In accounting language, you are *recording entries* into a *cash receipts and cash payments journal.*

Cash accounting or accrual accounting?

When you record a business transaction in your cheque register, you are not recording the transaction until you actually make or receive a payment. This is called *cash accounting* — you record income when you actually receive it and expenses when you actually pay them.

Cash accounting is an *accounting method.* An accounting method is supposed to match up your income and expenses in a consistent way. *Cash accounting* is based on the receipt and disbursement of cash, and is used mostly by very small businesses. *Accrual accounting* is another, more common accounting method used by most medium- and large-sized businesses. In *accrual accounting,* you record income when you earn it (for example, when you send out an invoice for the service performed or product supplied), and you record expenses when you incur them (for example, when you receive the benefit of a service or product). You may actually receive the cash income or pay the expenses at some later time. The accrual method of accounting seeks to *match* (another accounting principle) the period the expense is incurred to the period benefiting from that expense.

Once you choose an accounting method, you're not supposed to change back and forth.

Speak to your accountant about whether to use cash accounting or accrual accounting in your business. Service providers usually use the cash method, while retailers usually use the accrual method. You will have to report your business income on an accrual basis for income tax purposes.

If you use accrual accounting in your business, you will have to keep another set of records to record sales when you make them (called a *sales journal*) and purchases when you make them (called a *purchases journal*).

Sorting your income and expenses by category

The next step in the accounting cycle is to sort your business's financial transactions into categories. You need to know what categories your income and expenses fall into in order to prepare your income tax returns and financial statements, and in order to keep track of how your business is doing and to make decisions and plans.

Sorting your income

All money your business receives is not identical. For example, when you receive a payment from a customer or client, most of it will be payment for your product or service, but some of it will be payment of GST/HST and/or provincial sales tax.

Your business may receive other kinds of money, as well, such as

✔ Advances from the bank under a loan to your business

✔ Refunds for goods your business has purchased and returned

✔ Payment from an insurance policy for losses your business has suffered

✔ Refund of a security deposit given when you entered into a lease

✔ Money you or your family invest in the business

You need to sort income by category, because different kinds of income are treated differently in preparing financial statements and for tax purposes.

Sorting your expenses and other payments

You also need to sort your expenses and other payments by category, because different kinds of expenses are treated differently in preparing financial statements and for income tax purposes. (See Chapter 3 for more about expenses and taxes.)

Here are some of the categories of expenses you will want to keep track of:

✔ **General expenses to run your business:** This would include things such as

- Rent

- Interest on borrowed money

- Legal and accounting fees

- Office supplies

- Professional or trade association fees

- Wages paid to employees (including deductions)

These *operating expenses* are fully deductible from income in the year the expense occurred. They are sometimes called *overhead*.

✔ **Costs incurred to produce a product you manufacture:** These costs are fully deductible from income in the year the cost occurred too, but they show up in a different place on financial statements, so you may as well stick them in a different category from the beginning.

✔ **Inventory:** The cost of buying inventory is also fully deductible from income, but it too has a special place on a financial statement.

✔ **Auto expenses:** If you use a vehicle partly for business purposes and partly for personal purposes, only the business portion is deductible. So you'll want to keep auto expenses separate from other expenses so that you can calculate the deductible portion at the end of the year.

✔ **Home office expenses:** You can deduct only a portion of your home rent or mortgage and utilities if you're running your business out of your home. So keep these expenses separate from other business operating expenses.

✔ **Business entertainment:** Only 50 percent of a business entertainment expense is deductible from income, so don't just toss it into the general expense pile.

✔ **Capital purchases:** These are purchases of capital property, which is property with a long-term (over one year) value, such as equipment, vehicles and furniture. You can deduct only a specified percentage as _capital cost allowance_ for tax purposes (also known as _depreciation_ for accounting purposes). So definitely don't let your capital purchases get mixed up with your operating expenses. (See Chapter 3 for more about capital cost allowance.)

✔ **GST/HST payments:** You'll want to keep track of the amount you pay for GST/HST separately, so that you can incorporate input credits into your calculation of how much you owe at the end of each quarter.

In accounting language, these categories are called _accounts_.

Record-keeping

In order to sort your income and expenses by category, you need to keep separate records for the different types of income received by your business and the different types of expenses incurred by your business. (This is in addition to keeping a cheque register.) Ask your accountant about the categories your business needs to keep track of.

At a minimum, you'll need different file folders to hold the source documents for each category. But you should also keep a written record of income and expenses. At the most basic level, you could keep these records on sheets of lined paper. At a slightly more sophisticated level, you could keep the records in account books purchased from a business supply store such as Grand and Toy or Staples/Business Depot or Office Depot. (Account books are specially lined.) These days, however, most businesspeople use accounting software, which creates the records automatically from the entries that you make. Whichever way you do it, the same purpose is served and the same record is created.

Handling the bookkeeping burden

As you can imagine, proper bookkeeping involves a great deal of detailed work. How are you going to get it done? You have three options.

Keep your own books manually

This tried-and-true method is cheap and easy to set up (you can buy manual bookkeeping ledger and journal systems, with directions, from any office supply store), but difficult and time-consuming to maintain.

You have to make all of the journal entries by hand, and then *post* the changes to the proper *accounts.* If you need to generate a summary or financial statement, you have to work it out yourself.

If you decide to go this route, you should ask your accountant to help get you started.

Keep your own books using accounting software

You can use accounting software designed primarily for personal and business use, such as Quicken or Microsoft Money, or a more sophisticated system designed with small businesses in mind, such as MYOB (Mind Your Own Business), QuickBooks, or Simply Accounting.

The personal-use systems are basically electronic cheque registers, with the added ability to sort expenses into categories and to generate income statements and balance sheets. When you enter your business's financial transaction into the computer, the program will post the changes to the appropriate accounts automatically.

A good business system will also generate sales invoices, track and report GST/HST/PST, track and age your accounts receivable, help keep track of your inventory, and compute employee payroll.

Ask your accountant (the guy with the brown bowtie) for advice on the accounting software that's best for your business. You should also consider speaking to a computer geek to make sure that you have the computer required to support the software you need to buy, and to ensure that the software is installed properly. Try to get the accountant to meet the computer consultant to get them to properly match your computer system to your accounting needs. Besides, geeks and nerds like each other's company!

Use a freelance bookkeeper

If you can't or don't want to do your bookkeeping yourself, get someone to do it for you. When you first start your business, you probably won't need — or be able to afford — to hire a full-time bookkeeper. It makes more sense to contract with a freelance bookkeeper who will work only the number of hours that your business actually needs.

Your accountant is your best source for finding a bookkeeper. In fact, your accountant probably has a bookkeeper with whom he or she works on a regular basis and who is familiar with the accountant's requirements.

Your bookkeeper and accountant can decide whether to work with a manual or a computerized bookkeeping system.

Practising Inventory Accounting

If you're not in a pure service business, one of the things you want your accounting system to do is to keep track of your inventory so that you know when to buy replacement inventory, and also what kind and how much. You need to know what sells and what doesn't in order to know what to buy in the future.

The best way to get this information is by using inventory-tracking software. If you have a retail business, you want a point-of-sale system that makes adjustments to your inventory records when sales are entered at the cash register. As noted in the section, "Handling the bookkeeping burden," earlier in this chapter, some computerized bookkeeping packages include inventory-tracking features. If you prefer a low-tech approach, ask your accountant to help you develop a manual inventory-tracking system.

Whatever system of inventory tracking you use, be sure to do physical counts of your inventory two to four times a year. Compare the results of your physical count with what is shown in your financial records. Any gaps may indicate theft, damage, or other forms of loss.

Valuing your inventory

In addition to knowing what you have in your inventory, you need to know how much it's worth. This isn't easy to figure out if you bought identical inventory items at different times and prices throughout the year. (You can't just shrug this question off because it affects the cost of goods figure in your income statement and the inventory figure in your balance sheet.)

Since it is generally impossible to identify your inventory really specifically, you address this question by using one of two accounting methods. The *First In, First Out (or FIFO)* method assumes that the inventory you bought earliest is sold first. Under this method, you value your inventory at the most recent price you paid for it. The *Last In, First Out (or LIFO)* method assumes that the inventory you bought last is sold first. Under this method, the value of your inventory is based on the oldest item in it. Your accountant will advise you which method you should use. For income tax purposes, you have to use the FIFO method.

Monitoring with Internal Controls

Think no one associated with or working for your business will ever stick his or her hand in the till? Think again. Although shoplifting gets more attention, internal theft and fraud cost businesses far more each year. In consultation with your accountant, establish and enforce *internal controls,* a system of checks and balances, to discourage and detect both honest mistakes and dishonesty. Here are some examples of internal controls:

- ✔ Inspecting and counting shipments from suppliers before paying for them
- ✔ If you have associates or employees, requiring two signatures on cheques over a certain amount
- ✔ If you have associates or employees, having outsiders or employees who aren't normally involved do surprise inventories and compare them with inventory records
- ✔ Having one person record sales and collections while another person records and takes the deposits to the bank
- ✔ Requiring every associate or employee to take a vacation, during which time someone else does that person's job.

Historical Financial Statements

There are historical financial statements and forward-looking financial statements. Historical statements report actual results of the operation of the business after they've taken place. The income statement and balance sheet are the main types of historical financial statements. Forward-looking statements (sometimes known as *pro forma* financial statements) are used to plan for the future, and they include forecasts of income and expenses and cash flow projections.

The income statement and the balance sheet are the main types of historical statements. You use these statements to track the progress of your business and help you plan for the future.

Creating financial statements

If you have accounting software that prepares financial statements and you've faithfully recorded all your transactions, you'll be able to generate accurate financial statements by clicking a button.

It's also perfectly possible to create financial statements by hand. (In the bad old days, this was the only way to create them.) The following sections about income statements and balance sheets explain the process to you in case you want to try it yourself — but mainly so you'll have an idea of what's going on inside your computer — or your accountant's head.

The income statement

The *income statement,* also called a *profit and loss statement,* sets out the business's revenues (or income or sales) and expenses over a stated period of time (a specific month, quarter or year). The business's *revenues* are the money that its customers or clients pay for its products or services. Its *expenses* are the costs incurred in doing business. The business's profits equal its revenues minus its expenses.

How do you prepare it?

In Table 4-1, you'll find instructions for preparing an income statement. If you are in a retail or manufacturing business, start with Gross Sales (which is all the money you took in minus GST/HST charged) and then deduct the Cost of Goods Sold, which is what you paid directly for your inventory, either to buy it or manufacture it — Gross Sales minus Cost of Goods Sold equals Gross Profit. (If you are a service business, you will not have a cost-of-goods-sold expense.) Then set out and add up all of your expenses of operating the business other than those directly related to creating or acquiring the product you sell (that's your overhead), and subtract the total from Gross Profit to find your Net Income or (Net) Profit before taxes are taken into account.

What can it tell you?

By comparing the current year's (month's or quarter's) Gross Sales figures to the previous year's (month's or quarter's), you can tell whether your sales are going up or down. By comparing current Expenses to previous Expenses, you can tell which of your expenses have gone up or down.

By looking at your Gross Profit and Expenses together, you'll see whether you're generating enough through sales to cover your operating costs.

By dividing your Net Income or Profit by your Gross Sales, you'll find out what your *return on sales* is. That gives you an idea about how efficiently your business turns a dollar's worth of sale into a profit.

Book VIII

Taking Care of Business

Table 4-1	Statement of Income and Expenses		
	Prior Year (or month or quarter)	**Budget (for current year or month or quarter)**	**Current Year (or month or quarter)**
Gross Sales MINUS **Cost of Goods Sold** EQUALS **Gross Profit**	As a start-up, you won't have a prior year, month, or quarter until you've been in business for a while.	Your budget is the projected statement of income and expenses that you prepared before the start of this year. See below for forecasting income and expenses.	These are the actual figures from the records you've kept for the period.
Expenses (such as) Accounting/legal, Bank charges, Depreciation, Insurance, Marketing, Rent, Telephone, Wages **Total Expenses**			
Net Income or **Profit** (before income tax) (Subtract Total Expenses from Gross Profit)			

You prepare a budget for an upcoming period by preparing a forecast of income and expenses. It is meant to be a realistic prediction of the revenue you will earn and the expenses you will incur over that period. Before you start your business, your income and expense forecasts are based on a combination of research and hope. (It's a lot easier to project your expenses than your revenues before your business is actually up and running. Chapter 1 has some advice about forecasting income and expenses.) After your business has been in operation for a year, you'll be able to make your forecasts based on past performance and your knowledge of trends in your field.

By dividing your Gross Profit by total sales made to find your *gross profit margin*, you can see how much profit you earned on sales before taking into account your costs of selling the products and administering your business. The higher the gross profit margin, the more breathing room your business has to cover the residual costs required to get your product or service out the door.

By dividing your Net Income or Profit by your total sales, you can find your *net profit margin* or *profit margin*. A low net profit margin may indicate that the business isn't being efficiently or economically run.

The acceptable profit margin varies with the type of business, and you should be able to find out through your professional or trade association what a decent profit margin is for your type of business.

The balance sheet

The balance sheet lists a value for everything a business owns (its *assets*) and everything it owes (its *liabilities*) as of a specified date, usually the last date of the company's *fiscal* (financial) year, referred to as its *year-end*. It's called a balance sheet because the total assets have to equal the total liabilities (including the owner's equity). (If you come up with a balance sheet where assets don't equal liabilities, you haven't created an *imbalance sheet,* you've just done it wrong.)

How do you prepare it?

You create a balance sheet by setting down the value of the business's assets and liabilities in a recognized order.

Start with assets, which are categorized as *current assets* or *fixed assets.* Current assets are cash or assets that are intended to be and can be converted into cash easily. Fixed assets are assets the business intends to hold onto for a long period of time.

Then list liabilities, categorizing them as *current liabilities* or *long-term liabilities.* Current liabilities are debts that are expected be paid within a year, such as accounts payable, current wages, current taxes, and the current portion of long-term debt. Long-term liabilities are debts that will not be paid off within a year. *Owner's equity* — what a business is worth after its debts are deducted from its assets — is also considered a liability. (It's that double-entry accounting thing again.) Take a look at Table 4-2.

Book VIII

Taking Care of Business

Table 4-2	Balance Sheet		
	Prior Year (month, quarter)	*Budget*	*Current Year (month, quarter)*
Assets			
Current Assets			
Cash Accounts receivable Inventory			
Total Current Assets			
Fixed Assets			
Furniture and fixtures Equipment			
Total Fixed Assets			
Total Assets			
Liabilities			
Current Liabilities			
Accounts payable Short-term debt payable			
Total Current Liabilities			
Long-term Liabilities			
Long-term debt payable			
Total long-term liabilities			
Total Liabilities			
Owner's Equity or **Net Worth** (Subtract Total Liabilities from Total Assets)			
Total Liabilities and **Net Worth** (add Total Liabilities and Net Worth together)			

What can it tell you?

By dividing the Total Liabilities (the total debts of your business) by the Owner's Equity or Net Worth, you'll get the *debt-to-equity ratio* of your business. This ratio will tell you what percentage of the business you own and what percentage your lenders own. Generally speaking, you don't want the ratio to go above 1:1 (that is, you own as much of your business as your lenders do). If it goes above 2:1 (your lenders own twice as much as you do), you may find it difficult to borrow money because even the most optimistic lender can't be sure of getting the money back out of the business. Keep in mind, though, that if you have too little debt, you may not be realizing the full potential of your business — because you can use borrowed money to expand and improve your business and make it more profitable.

By dividing Current Assets by Current Liabilities, you'll find your *current ratio*. It tells you how *liquid* your business is — how quickly you can come up with cash if you need to. A 1:1 ratio means that your business has a dollar in current assets to cover every dollar of current liabilities. You don't want to fall below 1:1, and you'd like to stay at 2:1 or higher. By dividing the Current Assets minus Inventory (that is, only Cash and Accounts Receivable) by the Current Liabilities, you'll come up with the *quick ratio*. The quick ratio will give you an idea how quickly you can come up with cash without selling off your inventory. You want your quick ratio to be at least 1:1.

By dividing the Net Income or Profit (from the income statement) by the Net Worth of the business (from the balance sheet), you can find out what your *return on equity* or return on investment is. You'd like a return at least equal to what you'd get if you just sold the business, invested the cash and collected interest or dividends. (But if you look at your return on equity and panic because it's low, remember to take into account any money you are getting from the business as salary.)

Cash Flow Projections

Income and expenses rarely match each other exactly. Your income may come in a few times a year, whereas your expenses are likely to be fairly steady on a month-by-month basis.

As a result, it's not enough to know how much money your business is going to earn. You must also know when you are actually going to receive it. Likewise, it's not enough to know how much money you'll need to operate your business. You also have to know when you'll need it. A cash flow projection charts not only how much money you can expect to receive and pay, but when.

You use a cash flow projection when you first start your business to help you calculate how large an operating loan you need until you can establish an income flow that more closely matches the amount and timing of your expenses.

Cash flow projections remain useful, if not essential, even after your business is established. While some of your expenses are fixed and occur on a regular basis, you have some control over the timing of other expenses. Cash flow projections help you plan, both to put off expenses you have control over until you expect to have the income to cover them, and to borrow money to cover expenses you can't put off. You should make cash flow projections for at least six months into the future, updating them every month.

If you borrow money, the lender will want to see your cash flow projections to help decide whether and when you'll be able to repay the loan.

Chapter 1 has more about cash flow, including an explanation of how to build a cash flow table. For an example of a cash flow table, see the Sample Business Plan in this Book's appendix.

Hiring an Accountant

So, does your business need an accountant? If you've paid the slightest attention to anything in this chapter, you'll be screaming "Yes!" Although you don't have to have an accountant as a permanent member of your staff, you need to consult an accountant on an ongoing basis:

- ✔ **To help you set up your bookkeeping system** — either a manual or computerized one, and to build in internal controls to help reduce errors and to prevent and detect theft and fraud

- ✔ **To prepare various financial statements** — such as budgets, cash flow statements, income statements, and balance sheets, based on a review and analysis of financial data

- ✔ **To prepare your income tax returns** — based on a review and analysis of financial data in the context of income tax law

- ✔ **To deal with the CCRA from time to time** — if you experience difficulties arising out of your income tax returns or with respect to your GST or employer remittances

Anyone can call himself or herself an accountant. What you absolutely want is a professional accountant. In Canada, there are only three types of recognized professional accountants — *chartered accountants, certified general accountants,* and *certified management accountants.* These accountants have a professional designation and belong to government-recognized and self-regulating bodies, just as lawyers (the guys with yellow suspenders) do.

✔ **Chartered accountants (CAs)** are regulated by provincial institutes of chartered accountants. They must have a Bachelor of Commerce or equivalent university degree, complete 30 months of supervised employment, take a series of professional courses, and pass a number of examinations, including a nationally administered Uniform Final Exam.

✔ **Certified general accountants (CGAs)** are regulated by provincial associations of general accountants. They must have a university degree, take a series of distance learning courses through the Certified General Accountants Association, complete between two and three years of supervised employment, and pass a series of examinations.

✔ **Certified management accountants (CMAs)** are regulated by provincial societies of management accountants. They must have a university degree, pass a CMA entrance examination, and complete a two-year program while gaining practical experience by working in a management accounting environment. Most CMAs are managers who are employed by businesses, but there are also consulting CMAs who offer strategic and financial management accounting services to the public on a fee-for-service basis.

Book VIII

Taking Care of Business

Chapter 5

Mayday, Mayday: When Your Business Springs a Leak

In This Chapter

▶ Making a plan when you can't repay a debt

▶ Dealing with lack of funds to pay your rent or mortgage

▶ Coming up with a strategy when you can't pay your taxes

▶ Deciding when to declare bankruptcy

*W*hen you can't avoid trouble, you have to deal with it. So this chapter is meant to help you face your problems head-on, make an objective assessment of the situation, and try to come up with a plan of action.

But remember that there are ways you can avoid some of the trouble discussed in this chapter in the first place:

✔ Don't borrow more money than you can realistically expect to repay on schedule

✔ Do a credit check on customers before you do the work

✔ Follow up on collections after you send a bill

✔ Take care not to do shoddy work or provide defective products

✔ Always have contracts in writing that you understand

✔ Perform your contracts properly

Your Business Can't Make a Payment that's Due

If you borrow money, you're expected to repay it. If you don't repay, the lender is liable to get a little exercised. But what the lender can do depends on the nature of the lender and the loan, as discussed in the following sections.

A payment on a loan from a non-commercial source

You got extra money from a family member or friend to set up your business (see Chapter 1) but the lender doesn't feel so charitable now — maybe he needs the cash desperately, or maybe you've ticked her off by not taking her canny business advice.

Besides giving you the cold shoulder or not inviting you over for dinner anymore, the lender can sue for return of the money. This is true whether or not there's a written contract. An *oral contract* (a contract made through conversation) is as valid as a contract in writing. It's just harder to prove the terms of an oral contract because no one wrote them down. Your lender is legally able to tell the court about the conversations you had when the loan was made (the terms of the loan agreement will be the lender's word against yours), can require other people who have heard you talk about the loan to repeat in court what they heard, and can show to the court documents such as a note or letter you wrote to the lender acknowledging the loan or saying that you would pay the money back.

So don't ignore the lender or tell him to buzz off. If you have no money to pay now, try to reach some kind of agreement:

- See if the lender will agree to wait a few weeks or months until you do have the money, or

- See if the lender will agree to accept smaller payments over a longer term, or smaller payments now and "balloon" payments later to make up for the smaller payments now, or

- Offer something other than money in full or part payment of the loan — something you own or the business owns, or your services for free, or

- Offer security for the loan, such as a mortgage on property you own; or offer a share in your business (although doing these things could create more problems for you in the long run)

Then put into writing the agreement you've reached, and sign it and have the lender sign it. Each of you should get an original of the signed agreement.

A payment on a loan from a commercial source

If you have a commercial loan, you probably agreed to pay it off in instalments, so you may think that not being able to pay one instalment is not such a big deal. You're wrong. Most commercial *term loans* (see Chapter 1) have an *acceleration clause*. That means that the lender can demand that you repay the entire loan as soon as you miss one payment by more than a few days. And if you have a *line of credit* (see Chapter 1), it's probably repayable *on demand* — so you don't even have to miss one payment before the lender has the right to tell you to repay the full amount.

If a lender makes a demand for repayment and you can't repay, the lender has the right to sue you for the outstanding amount of the loan, plus interest owing, plus the lender's costs of collecting the debt from you. If you've given *security* for the loan (a right against property — again, see Chapter 1), your agreement with the lender probably allows the lender to *realize on the security* after you miss a payment. That means that the lender, after demanding repayment of the loan and waiting a few days for payment,

- ✔ Can take property you offered as security and either keep it or sell it (or start a lawsuit for possession of the secured property if you won't let the lender have it)

- ✔ Can demand that a person who *guaranteed* the loan pay back the loan (plus interest)

- ✔ Depending on the terms of the loan agreement, may be able to *appoint a receiver/manager* to take possession of the secured property and sell it

If a lender seizes secured property, you may have the right for a short period (a couple of weeks) to get the property back by paying what you owe plus interest and costs. If the lender sells the property, it has to make sure that it gets a fair price, and afterward has to account to you for the property. It's not allowed to keep more than it's owed (don't forget that this includes interest and the costs of taking and selling the property), and it has to pay you any surplus from a sale.

If you know that you don't have the money to make a payment, but you think that you'll have money soon to get back on track, try the following:

✔ First, try to see if you can find the money for the payment from another source. Unless you're on really good terms with your commercial lender and have the lender's trust and adoration, it's probably best not to let the lender know that you're in a bit of trouble. The lender may panic and pull the plug on your loan, and on any other dealings you have with that lender.

✔ If you can't get money from another source, talk to your lender before the due date of the payment that you're going to miss. The lender may agree to overlook your default for a short time, especially if you offer some additional security (if you've got anything left that's not already being used for security, that is — if you don't, the lender may accept security from someone else, such as a personal guarantee from a relative or associate).

Be careful about borrowing more money and offering more security for a loan that you're already having trouble repaying! You may just be digging yourself deeper into a hole, and in the long run you may lose more.

If you're in a really bad financial position and you don't think that a little extra money or a little extra time is going to do anything but delay bigger trouble, you should think about making a proposal to all of your creditors or even going bankrupt (see the section, "Your Business Is Insolvent," later in this chapter).

A payment for an asset bought on credit

If you've bought assets (such as equipment or vehicles or furniture) for your business and are paying for them over time, you've almost certainly entered into a financing agreement such as a *chattel mortgage, conditional sales agreement, purchase money security interest,* or a *lease with an option to purchase.* If you stop making your payments, the other party to the financing agreement can

✔ Sue you for the full amount still left to pay (plus interest)

✔ Seize the asset and sell it (and account to you after the sale)

Find out whether the financer is willing to give you more time to pay (and then try to find some money) — that's about all you can do.

A payment under an equipment lease

If your business leased assets instead of buying them outright or on time, you're not in any better position if you stop making your regular payments. The terms of a commercial asset lease normally don't allow you to stop making your lease payments for any reason — and that includes the fact that the asset is broken or defective and the fact that you have no money. You have to make all the payments for the full term of the lease. If you miss a payment, the *lessor* can

- ✔ Sue you for the full amount owed under the lease
- ✔ Seize the asset (and, if you have an option to purchase, sell it and account for the proceeds to your benefit)

Once again, about the only thing you can do is try to negotiate more time to pay, and look for some money to pay with.

You've Personally Guaranteed a Debt for Your Business and Your Business Can't Pay

If you've given a personal guarantee for a business loan and your business can't make a payment, the lender can demand payment from you. If you don't pay, the lender can sue you for the full outstanding amount of the loan, plus interest. If you gave security (such as a mortgage on your home) as well as guaranteeing the debt, the lender can realize on the security.

If you've co-signed a loan with your business, the lender doesn't even have to wait for your business to miss a payment — it can demand that you make the payment instead, because you're equally responsible for the loan from the get-go.

Note that if you're a member of a partnership, in most provinces the partners are individually responsible for paying debts of the partnership if the partnership itself can't pay. This is commonly referred to as "joint and several" partner liability.

Your Business Can't Pay Its Rent

If you can't pay the rent owing under your commercial lease, your landlord has a variety of nasty things it can do to you including

- ✔ Sue you for *arrears of rent* (rent owing) or for *damages* (money compensation) for breach of the lease, while letting you stay on under the lease
- ✔ Retake possession of the premises and terminate the lease (in which case, although the landlord can sue for arrears of rent before termination, it can't sue for any rent due after the date of termination)

- Retake possession of the premises and terminate the lease with notice for future loss of rent (then the landlord can sue for arrears of rent before termination and also for damages for future loss of rent after the date of termination. If the landlord makes a reasonable effort but can't find another tenant, or another tenant who's willing to pay as much as you agreed to pay, the landlord can sue you for the entire shortfall over the rest of the term of your lease)

- Retake possession of the premises without terminating the lease, and re-letting the premises acting as your agent (you remain responsible for the rent, minus whatever the landlord collects from the new tenant)

- *Distrain* (seize and sell your property on the premises) to satisfy arrears of rent. In most provinces, if you remove your property from the premises to keep your landlord from getting its hands on it, the landlord can seize the property wherever it is (if the landlord can find it) within the next 30 days and can have you pay a significant penalty for being such a sneak.

If your landlord terminates your lease, retakes possession of your premises or distrains, you may want to see a lawyer to find out whether the landlord is within its rights. Landlords sometimes ignore the fine print of the law, and you may have some rights of your own. For example,

- In most provinces, a landlord cannot terminate a lease for non-payment until the rent has been unpaid for 15 days or more (and it can't terminate for other reasons without giving you proper notice and a chance to fix whatever the landlord is complaining about).

- If the landlord terminates, you can go to court to get the termination set aside — if you can pay the arrears of rent.

- A landlord can't distrain until the day after the rent was due, and has to carry out the *distraint* (also known as a *distress*) during daylight hours.

- In most provinces, when the landlord distrains it can't seize fixtures, cash, property that belongs to others (such as inventory on consignment), or perishable goods, and it has to leave tools you use in the business up to a value of $2,000.

- The landlord has no right to distrain if it has already got a judgment for arrears of rent, or has terminated the lease or locked you out, or if you and the landlord have agreed that the lease is at an end.

Your Business Can't Pay a Mortgage on Real Property

If you took out a mortgage to buy real property for your business and you can't make your payments, the *mortgagee* (the lender) has the right in many provinces to *foreclose* on the mortgage (become the legal owner of the property), or to sell the property — under court supervision in a *judicial sale,* or privately under a *power of sale.*

If the mortgagee starts a legal action for foreclosure or judicial sale, you can stop it by paying off the entire mortgage, or in some cases by paying the payment(s) you missed plus a penalty. If you can't pay the entire mortgage immediately, you can ask the court for a delay (from about two to six months) in order to come up with the money. You can also stop foreclosure by asking for judicial sale. If the foreclosure goes through, in most provinces your mortgage debt is cancelled and you don't owe the mortgagee anything, even if the property is worth less than the debt you owe (but on the other hand the mortgagee doesn't owe you anything if the property is worth *more* than the debt you owe). If the property is sold in a judicial sale, any money left over after payment of the mortgage debt plus interest plus legal costs is yours; but if there's a shortfall, the lender can require you to make it up.

Most mortgagees prefer to act under a power of sale, if they can, because they don't have to go to court to sell the property. The lender has to notify you that it's going to exercise its power of sale, and you'll be given a short time (about a month) to stop the sale by paying off the mortgage or in some cases by making up the payment(s) you missed. As with a judicial sale, the proceeds from the sale will be used to pay the outstanding amount of the mortgage, as well as interest and costs; if there's a shortfall, the mortgagee can sue you for it, but if there's money left over, the mortgagee has to return it to you.

If the mortgagee wants to sell the property, find out whether it will let you try to sell the property yourself first. Buyers may think they can get a good deal and may offer a lower price when they see it's a judicial sale or sale under a power of sale. The more money the property sells for, the less you'll owe the mortgagee or the more you'll get to keep.

Book VIII

Taking Care of Business

Your Business Can't Pay Its Taxes

The Canada Customs and Revenue Agency (CCRA) has a *statutory lien* against the personal property (as opposed to real property, or real estate) of a taxpayer who does not pay taxes or remittances that are due. This lien lets the government seize your business's personal property — which is your personal property, if you're a sole proprietor or partner — after giving 30 days' notice (during the notice period you can pay up and avoid the seizure).

If you own real property in a municipality and you don't pay your property taxes, the municipality will add interest charges and penalties to your property tax bill. If you *still* don't pay your taxes, the municipality has the right to sell your real property after a period of time has first elapsed, the length of the period depending on the municipality. (The municipality doesn't get to keep all the money from the sale, only the amount that you owe in taxes.)

Your Business Is Insolvent

Your business is *insolvent* if it owes at least $1,000 and cannot pay its debts as they become due. There's nothing wrong with being insolvent in itself (apart from the fact that you have no money), but if you're insolvent, you're in danger of being forced into *bankruptcy*. A creditor to whom you owe more than $1,000 and who has no security from you for the debt can *petition* your business into bankruptcy if your business commits an *act of bankruptcy* — such as not paying a debt when it's due or not complying with a court order to pay a creditor who's won a lawsuit against the business, or telling a creditor that you're not going to pay your debts, or hiding or disposing of property to avoid paying a creditor.

If you're dealing with unsecured creditors

If you're insolvent, what can you do before someone petitions you into bankruptcy? You can try to reach some kind of agreement with your creditors — for example, that they'll give you more time to pay, or accept part payment of your debt. Put any agreement into writing. By the way, your creditors won't likely be interested in cutting you some slack unless your business has decent prospects.

 If your business does have prospects, it may be wise to get some advice from a lawyer who specializes in insolvency, or from a *trustee in bankruptcy* who deals with businesses (rather than with consumers). Your advisor may recommend making an informal offer to your creditors, or a formal *proposal* under the *Bankruptcy and Insolvency Act* (see the next section).

If you're dealing with secured creditors

If you're insolvent and a secured creditor notifies you that it's going to realize on its security, you should consider making a formal proposal under the *Bankruptcy and Insolvency Act.* If you do nothing at this point, your secured creditors are going to make off with the secured property, and you probably need it to keep your business running. You should get a trustee in bankruptcy to advise you and to file in bankruptcy court a *notice of intention to make a proposal.* Once the notice is filed, your business has some protection from secured and unsecured creditors for at least a month:

- ✔ Creditors can't seize any property.

- ✔ Companies that supply things such as electricity, heat, water, and telephone can't cut off service.

- ✔ Parties to contracts with your business can't terminate the contracts or invoke acceleration clauses (an acceleration clause makes a debt you're paying off in instalments come due all at once).

On the downside, you have to pay cash up front for any supplies you buy.

After you file your notice of intention, you have to file the actual proposal, and then your creditors meet within about three weeks to vote on it. Here's another downside to the proposal process: if your secured creditors reject the proposal (even if your unsecured creditors don't), they can immediately realize on their security. In addition (as if you needed an addition at this point), your business is deemed to have made an *assignment in bankruptcy* (a transfer of its property to the trustee in bankruptcy) and will be officially declared bankrupt.

You can choose to go bankrupt

You can be forced into bankruptcy, but you can also choose to go into bankruptcy by making an assignment in bankruptcy. Why would you actually want to go bankrupt? Well, once you're declared bankrupt by a court, your trustee in bankruptcy deals with your creditors. You don't have to look at their intimidating faces anymore. Your trustee will make arrangements to sell the business's property to pay the debts. And you'll be able to start over again.

If you're carrying on business as a sole proprietorship or a partnership, you'll go bankrupt as an individual. If you're carrying on business as a corporation, the corporation will go bankrupt. As an individual you'll probably be discharged from bankruptcy after nine months, and if you receive an *absolute discharge*

Book VIII

Taking Care of Business

almost all of your debts are cancelled. (If you receive a *conditional discharge* you'll still be responsible for repaying certain debts — income taxes for example.) A corporation can't be discharged until it has paid all its debts, but you can always start up a new corporation (however, you may find that the creditors you stiffed won't be very anxious to deal with your new corporation).

See the next section for more (yum!) about bankruptcy.

Bankruptcy

Once the bankruptcy court has made an order that your business is bankrupt, it appoints a trustee in bankruptcy. The trustee becomes the legal owner of all the unsecured property that formerly belonged to your business (and to you if your business is a sole proprietorship or a partnership) and it uses the property to pay off debts. Your secured creditors keep their rights over secured property. It doesn't go to the trustee.

If you're a sole proprietor or partner and you go bankrupt, you'll be allowed to keep some personal property — about $5,000 worth (more in some provinces) of clothing, furniture and "tools of your trade."

If your business is a corporation and you're a director, you may not escape having to make some payments personally if your business goes bankrupt. You'll be held responsible for up to six months' worth of unpaid wages for employees, for unpaid amounts owed to the CCRA for income tax and GST/HST, Canada Pension Plan and Employment Insurance, and for unpaid provincial sales tax owed to your provincial department or ministry of finance. And that's on top of paying any business loans for which you gave a personal guarantee.

If your business disposed of any property to save it from creditors, you can be personally charged with a criminal offence. And your trustee in bankruptcy can sue to get his hands on property that was improperly transferred away from the business, so that it can be distributed among the creditors.

If a person or business is an undischarged bankrupt, he, she or it can't borrow more than $500 without telling the lender about the state of bankruptcy (and not telling is an offence punishable by a fine or imprisonment). If a person is an undischarged bankrupt, he or she cannot be the director of a corporation.

Appendix

Sample Business Plan

● ●

*H*ere is a sample business plan for your review. The elements of this plan will help you understand how important this document is for every small business. They may seem like a lot of work to create — but business plans are an essential blueprint for where you want your business to go!

Sample business plan reprinted courtesy of Palo Alto Software, www.paloalto.com, 1-800-229-7526.

January 2001

This sample business plan has been made available to users of *Business Plan Pro*™, business planning software published by Palo Alto Software. Names, locations and numbers may have been changed, and substantial portions of text may have been omitted from the original plan to preserve confidentiality and proprietary information.

You are welcome to use this plan as a starting point to create your own, but you do not have permission to reproduce, publish, distribute or even copy this plan as it exists here.

Requests for reprints, academic use, and other dissemination of this sample plan should be emailed to the marketing department of Palo Alto Software at marketing@paloalto.com. For product information visit our Website: www.paloalto.com or call: 1-800-229-7526.

Copyright Palo Alto Software, Inc., 1995-2002

Confidentiality Agreement

The undersigned reader acknowledges that the information provided by
_____ in this business plan is confidential; therefore, reader agrees
not to disclose it without the express written permission of _____.

It is acknowledged by reader that information to be furnished in this business plan is in all
respects confidential in nature, other than information which is in the public domain through
other means and that any disclosure or use of same by reader, may cause serious harm or
damage to _____.

Upon request, this document is to be immediately returned to _____.

_____Signature

_____Name (typed or printed)

_____Date

This is a business plan. It does not imply an offering of securities.

Table of Contents

Business Solutions Consulting

1.0 Executive Summary

Business Solutions Consulting (BSC) is a start-up consulting firm focused on serving the comprehensive needs of businesses in the full range of the business cycle.With a core staff of experienced professionals and a team approach to most consulting projects, BSC will be able to offer a more balanced quality service than many of its competitors.

BSC offers a list of services for business owners to choose from, depending on their particular business needs. This includes; business and marketing plan preparation, financial search and procurement, IT consulting services, management development, human resources advising, and etc.

BSC will have a focus on start-up businesses, preferably in the earlier stages of operation. Small and mid-sized businesses make up a sizable majority of U.S. and international markets. BSC prefers to establish a relationship with a younger operation and continue to nurture that relationship over the long term.

Competitors in the forefront of the marketplace typically offer many of the same services as BCS. These services include information-based consulting, integration and management services. Services are designed to increase clients' operations effectiveness through reduced cost, improved customer service, enhanced quality of current product lines and services, and a more rapid introduction of new products and services. Competitors also offer industry-specific expertise to objectively evaluate, select, develop, implement, and manage information systems, networks, and applications.

BSC's co-owners, Andrew B. Christiansen and David E. Fields, will each provide $50,000 that will cover the bulk of the start-up expenses. The rest of the required financing will come from the Small Business Administration (SBA) 10-year loan in the amount of $100,000. Combined, these funds will be sufficient to cover the company's expenses throughout the first year of operations, which is the most critical from the cash flow standpoint.

BSC's Break-even Analysis is based on the average of the first-year figures for total sales by salaries, bonuses costs, and all other operating expenses. Such analysis shows that BSC will break-even by the tenth month of operations.

Book VIII

Taking Care of Business

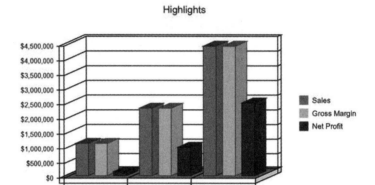

1.1 Mission

Business Solutions Consulting aims to offer comprehensive consulting services. BSC will focus on providing personal and specialized services to meet each client's specific needs.

1.2 Keys To Success

BSC's keys to success include:

1. A group of professionals with a broad range of specialty areas that complement each other.
2. A high level of experience in these specialty areas.
3. A team approach on most consulting projects.
4. Many business contacts among the consultant group.

Business Solutions Consulting

2.0 Company Summary

Business Solutions Consulting is a startup firm, which will focus on providing a wide range of business consulting services to other startups and companies in early stages of their operations. Business Solutions Consulting is a team of six Business Consultants. Each consultant specializes in a particular discipline, including finance, sales and marketing, technology, management, operations, and human resources.

2.1 Company Ownership

Business Solutions Consulting was registered in September, 2000 as an Oregon LLC, equally owned by Andrew B. Christiansen and David E. Fields.

3.0 Start-Up Summary

BSC's co-owners, Andrew B. Christiansen and David E. Fields, will each provide $50,000 that will cover the bulk of the start-up expenses. The rest of the required financing will come from the Small Business Administration (SBA) 10-year loan in the amount of $100,000. Combined, these funds will be sufficient to cover the company's expenses throughout the first year of operations, which is the most critical from the cash flow standpoint.

The following chart and table contain projected initial start-up cost data.

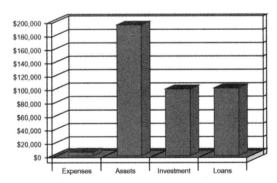

Book VIII

Taking
Care of
Business

Business Solutions Consulting

4.0 Service Description

BSC offers a list of services for business owners to choose from, depending on their particular business needs.

Start-up services include business plan preparation, marketing plan preparation, and financing search and procurement. Ongoing services include business plan updates, marketing plan updates, search and procurement of additional rounds of financing, management development, IT consulting services, e-commerce consulting services, operational advising, and human resources advising.

BSC is flexible, working with its clients in the fashion preferred by the client, be it on-site, remotely, or a combination of both. BSC typically works on a project in a team fashion to assist the client in all areas of the business simultaneously. This allows for all parties involved to be in sync in terms of understanding the interconnections of all functional areas of the business.

5.0 Market Analysis

BSC will have a focus on start-up businesses, preferably in the earlier stages of operation. Small and mid-sized businesses make up a sizable majority of U.S. and international markets. BSC prefers to establish a relationship with a younger operation and continue to nurture that relationship for the long term. The following chart and table show BSC's projected target markets and their growth for the first three years of this plan.

Market Analysis (Pie)

- Start-Up Companies
- 1-3 Year Old Companies
- 3 + Year Old Companies
- Other

Business Solutions Consulting

Table: Market Analysis

Market Analysis Potential Customers	Growth	2001	2002	2003	2004	2005	CAGR
Start-Up Companies	10%	1,900,000	2,090,000	2,299,000	2,528,900	2,781,790	10.00%
1-3 Year Old Companies	8%	900,000	972,000	1,049,760	1,133,741	1,224,440	8.00%
3 + Year Old Companies	6%	400,000	424,000	449,440	476,406	504,990	6.00%
Other	0%	0	0	0	0	0	0.00%
Total	8.96%	3,200,000	3,486,000	3,798,200	4,139,047	4,511,220	8.96%

5.1 Market Segmentation

Start-Ups

Start-up companies often are in need of expert advice and planning in initiating a successful start-up. It is believed that a majority of start-ups actually seek out consulting assistance. Those that do typically are searching for a comprehensive area of services.

1-3 Year Old Companies

Young companies, between 1 and 3 years old are less likely to be searching for expert business consulting services. Typically, they have already secured financing and have developed a satisfactory level of security. However, these businesses are still in the beginnings of their overall cycle and in most cases need the broad expertise of a team of expert consultants.

3 + Year-Old Companies

Established companies make up the final segment, and is significantly smaller than the start-up segment. The established company segment typically has a need for a less comprehensive range of services. These entities are in need of specialized services in one or two disciplines, e.g., operational planning or human resources.

5.2 Target Market Segment Strategy

Start-up companies are the target market of this firm. BSC intends to stay on the pulse of new business activity within the local area. Additionally, business contacts, referrals from among the group, and Internet marketing efforts will be made in pursuit of new clients.

5.3 Market Needs

Start-up company owners often lack the broad range of knowledge and expertise required to launch a new business. There is a serious need in the marketplace, and certainly a significant demand for, these types of start-up consulting services.

Book VIII

Taking Care of Business

Business Solutions Consulting

5.4 Service Business Analysis

The business consulting industry is very fragmented. Several large multi-national companies dominate the industry while many smaller (and often more specialized) firms occupy their market niches. Major management consulting companies, such as McKinsey, Bain, and Boston Consulting Group, have established their dominant position by providing services to the leading companies in various industries. Consulting practices of the major accounting firms (a.k.a. the Big Five) have established worldwide presence and sell their packaged services to companies of different sizes and industries. At the same time, numerous firms and individual business consultants prosper in the market niches that bigger players consider unprofitable to enter.

6.0 Strategy and Implementation

BSC intends to succeed by offering companies a comprehensive range of multi-cycle business planning solutions.

6.1 Competitive Edge

Our competitive edge is the team approach of consultants who are each focused in one or two business disciplines.

6.2 Sales Strategy

BSC intends to succeed by offering companies a comprehensive range of multi-cycle business planning solutions. The company will strive to optimize its billing hours. The following table outlines the sales forecast for the next three years.

Business Solutions Consulting

Sales by Year

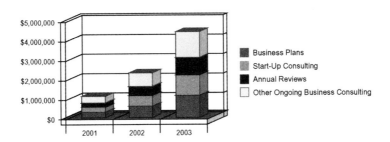

Legend:
- ▮ Business Plans
- ▨ Start-Up Consulting
- ▮ Annual Reviews
- ▢ Other Ongoing Business Consulting

Table: Sales Forecast

Sales Forecast			
Unit Sales	2001	2002	2003
Business Plans	191	397	763
Start-Up Consulting	175	364	699
Annual Reviews	223	464	890
Other Ongoing Business Consulting	223	464	890
Total Unit Sales	812	1,688	3,242
Unit Prices	2001	2002	2003
Business Plans	$1,500.00	$1,500.00	$1,500.00
Start-Up Consulting	$1,500.00	$1,500.00	$1,500.00
Annual Reviews	$1,000.00	$1,000.00	$1,000.00
Other Ongoing Business Consulting	$1,500.00	$1,500.00	$1,500.00
Sales			
Business Plans	$286,508	$595,937	$1,144,199
Start-Up Consulting	$262,633	$546,276	$1,048,850
Annual Reviews	$222,840	$463,507	$889,933
Other Ongoing Business Consulting	$334,260	$695,260	$1,334,899
Total Sales	$1,106,240	$2,300,980	$4,417,881
Direct Unit Costs	2001	2002	2003
Business Plans	$0.00	$0.00	$0.00
Start-Up Consulting	$0.00	$0.00	$0.00
Annual Reviews	$0.00	$0.00	$0.00
Other Ongoing Business Consulting	$0.00	$0.00	$0.00
Direct Cost of Sales	2001	2002	2003
Business Plans	$0	$0	$0
Start-Up Consulting	$0	$0	$0
Annual Reviews	$0	$0	$0
Other Ongoing Business Consulting	$0	$0	$0
Subtotal Direct Cost of Sales	$0	$0	$0

Book VIII

Taking Care of Business

Business Solutions Consulting

7.0 Management Team

Andrew B. Christiansen has extensive experience in business planning and finance, including CFO positions with ABC Conglomerate and DEF International. David E. Fields brings in experience in the area of marketing, advertising, and communications.

7.1 Personnel Plan

The following table illustrates the personnel plan for the next three years. No major changes in headcount are planned.

Table: Personnel

Personnel Plan	2001	2002	2003
Owner / Consultants	$600,000	$660,000	$726,000
Other	$0	$0	$0
Total People	6	7	8
Total Payroll	$600,000	$660,000	$726,000

Business Solutions Consulting

8.0 Financial Plan

BSC expects to raise $100,000 as its own capital, and to borrow $100,000 guaranteed by the SBA as a 10-year loan. This provides the bulk of the current financing required.

8.1 Break-even Analysis

BSC's Break-even Analysis is based on the average of the first-year figures for total sales by salaries, bonuses costs, and all other operating expenses. These are presented as per-unit revenue, per-unit cost, and fixed costs. These conservative assumptions make for a more accurate estimate of real risk. Such analysis shows that BSC will break-even by the tenth month of operations.

Break-even Analysis

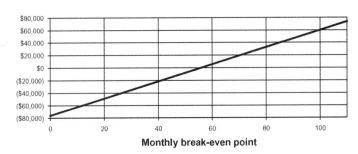

Monthly break-even point

Break-even point = where line intersects with 0

Table: **Break-even Analysis**

Break-even Analysis:	
Monthly Units Break-even	56
Monthly Revenue Break-even	$76,150
Assumptions:	
Average Per-Unit Revenue	$1,362.36
Average Per-Unit Variable Cost	$0.00
Estimated Monthly Fixed Cost	$76,150

Book VIII

Taking Care of Business

Business Solutions Consulting

8.2 Projected Profit and Loss

As the profit and loss table shows, BSC expects to continue its steady growth in profitability over the next three years of operations.

Table: Profit and Loss

Pro Forma Profit and Loss

	2001	2002	2003
Sales	$1,106,240	$2,300,980	$4,417,881
Direct Cost of Sales	$0	$0	$0
Other	$0	$0	$0
Total Cost of Sales	$0	$0	$0
Gross Margin	$1,106,240	$2,300,980	$4,417,881
Gross Margin %	100.00%	100.00%	100.00%
Expenses:			
Payroll	$600,000	$660,000	$726,000
Sales and Marketing and Other Expenses	$216,600	$227,430	$238,802
Depreciation	$6,000	$6,300	$6,615
Utilities	$1,200	$1,266	$1,336
Payroll Taxes	$90,000	$99,000	$108,900
Other	$0	$0	$0
Total Operating Expenses	$913,800	$993,996	$1,081,652
Profit Before Interest and Taxes	$192,440	$1,306,984	$3,336,229
Interest Expense	$10,000	$9,661	$8,948
Taxes Incurred	$45,236	$324,331	$845,684
Net Profit	$137,204	$972,992	$2,481,597
Net Profit/Sales	12.40%	42.29%	56.17%

Business Solutions Consulting

8.3 Projected Cash Flow

As the cash flow statement illustrates, BSC expects to maintain a steady rate of cash flow over the next three years of operations.

Cash

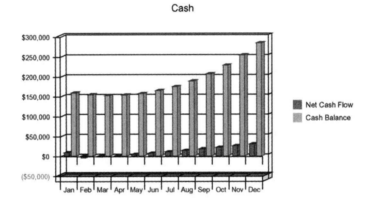

Net Cash Flow
Cash Balance

Book VIII

Taking Care of Business

Business Solutions Consulting

Table: Cash Flow

Pro Forma Cash Flow	2001	2002	2003
Cash Received			
Cash from Operations:			
Cash Sales	$1,106,240	$2,300,980	$4,417,881
Cash from Receivables	$0	$0	$0
Subtotal Cash from Operations	$1,106,240	$2,300,980	$4,417,881
Additional Cash Received			
Sales Tax, VAT, HST/GST Received	$0	$0	$0
New Current Borrowing	$0	$0	$0
New Other Liabilities (interest-free)	$0	$0	$0
New Long-term Liabilities	$0	$0	$0
Sales of Other Current Assets	$0	$0	$0
Sales of Long-term Assets	$0	$0	$0
New Investment Received	$0	$0	$0
Subtotal Cash Received	$1,106,240	$2,300,980	$4,417,881
Expenditures	2001	2002	2003
Expenditures from Operations:			
Cash Spending	$30,941	$60,769	$113,591
Payment of Accounts Payable	$904,859	$1,233,699	$1,767,875
Subtotal Spent on Operations	$935,800	$1,294,468	$1,881,466
Additional Cash Spent			
Sales Tax, VAT, HST/GST Paid Out	$0	$0	$0
Principal Repayment of Current Borrowing	$0	$0	$0
Other Liabilities Principal Repayment	$0	$0	$0
Long-term Liabilities Principal Repayment	$0	$6,777	$7,486
Purchase Other Current Assets	$0	$0	$0
Purchase Long-term Assets	$36,000	$45,000	$55,000
Dividends	$0	$0	$0
Subtotal Cash Spent	$971,800	$1,346,245	$1,943,952
Net Cash Flow	$134,440	$954,735	$2,473,929
Cash Balance	$284,440	$1,239,175	$3,713,104

8.4 Projected Balance Sheet

Following is a copy of the company's projected balance sheet.

Business Solutions Consulting

Table: Balance Sheet

Pro Forma Balance Sheet

Assets			
Current Assets	2001	2002	2003
Cash	$284,440	$1,239,175	$3,713,104
Other Current Assets	$20,000	$20,000	$20,000
Total Current Assets	$304,440	$1,259,175	$3,733,104
Long-term Assets			
Long-term Assets	$61,000	$106,000	$161,000
Accumulated Depreciation	$6,000	$12,300	$18,915
Total Long-term Assets	$55,000	$93,700	$142,085
Total Assets	$359,440	$1,352,875	$3,875,189
Liabilities and Capital			
Current Liabilities	2001	2002	2003
Accounts Payable	$28,236	$55,455	$103,658
Current Borrowing	$0	$0	$0
Other Current Liabilities	$0	$0	$0
Subtotal Current Liabilities	$28,236	$55,455	$103,658
Long-term Liabilities	$100,000	$93,223	$85,737
Total Liabilities	$128,236	$148,678	$189,395
Paid-in Capital	$99,500	$99,500	$99,500
Retained Earnings	($5,500)	$131,704	$1,104,696
Earnings	$137,204	$972,992	$2,481,597
Total Capital	$231,204	$1,204,196	$3,685,794
Total Liabilities and Capital	$359,440	$1,352,875	$3,875,189
Net Worth	$231,204	$1,204,196	$3,685,794

Book VIII

Taking Care of Business

Appendix

Appendix Table: General Assumptions

General Assumptions	Jan 1	Feb 2	Mar 3	Apr 4	May 5	Jun 6	Jul 7	Aug 8	Sep 9	Oct 10	Nov 11	Dec 12
Plan Month												
Current Interest Rate	10.00%	10.00%	10.00%	10.00%	10.00%	10.00%	10.00%	10.00%	10.00%	10.00%	10.00%	10.00%
Long-term Interest Rate	10.00%	10.00%	10.00%	10.00%	10.00%	10.00%	10.00%	10.00%	10.00%	10.00%	10.00%	10.00%
Tax Rate	30.00%	25.00%	25.00%	25.00%	25.00%	25.00%	25.00%	25.00%	25.00%	25.00%	25.00%	25.00%
Other	0	0	0	0	0	0	0	0	0	0	0	0

Appendix

Appendix Table: Profit and Loss

Pro Forma Profit and Loss

		Jan	Feb	Mar	Apr	May	Jun	Jul	Aug	Sep	Oct	Nov	Dec
Sales		$69,500	$72,975	$76,624	$80,455	$84,478	$88,702	$93,137	$97,793	$102,683	$107,817	$113,208	$118,889
Direct Cost of Sales		$0	$0	$0	$0	$0	$0	$0	$0	$0	$0	$0	$0
Other		$0	$0	$0	$0	$0	$0	$0	$0	$0	$0	$0	$0
Total Cost of Sales		$0	$0	$0	$0	$0	$0	$0	$0	$0	$0	$0	$0
Gross Margin		$69,500	$72,975	$76,624	$80,455	$84,478	$88,702	$93,137	$97,793	$102,683	$107,817	$113,208	$118,889
Gross Margin %		100.00%	100.00%	100.00%	100.00%	100.00%	100.00%	100.00%	100.00%	100.00%	100.00%	100.00%	100.00%
Expenses:													
Payroll		$50,000	$50,000	$50,000	$50,000	$50,000	$50,000	$50,000	$50,000	$50,000	$50,000	$50,000	$50,000
Sales and Marketing and Other Expenses		$18,050	$18,050	$18,050	$18,050	$18,050	$18,050	$18,050	$18,050	$18,050	$18,050	$18,050	$18,050
Depreciation	5%	$500	$500	$500	$500	$500	$500	$500	$500	$500	$500	$500	$500
Utilities	6%	$100	$100	$100	$100	$100	$100	$100	$100	$100	$100	$100	$100
Payroll Taxes	15%	$7,500	$7,500	$7,500	$7,500	$7,500	$7,500	$7,500	$7,500	$7,500	$7,500	$7,500	$7,500
Other		$0	$0	$0	$0	$0	$0	$0	$0	$0	$0	$0	$0
Total Operating Expenses		$76,150	$76,150	$76,150	$76,150	$76,150	$76,150	$76,150	$76,150	$76,150	$76,150	$76,150	$76,150
Profit Before Interest and Taxes		($6,650)	($3,175)	$474	$4,305	$8,328	$12,552	$16,987	$21,643	$26,533	$31,667	$37,058	$42,719
Interest Expense		$833	$833	$833	$833	$833	$833	$833	$833	$833	$833	$833	$833
Taxes Incurred		($2,245)	($1,002)	($90)	$868	$1,874	$2,930	$4,038	$5,203	$6,425	$7,708	$9,056	$10,471
Net Profit		($5,238)	($3,006)	($270)	$2,604	$5,621	$8,789	$12,115	$15,608	$19,275	$23,125	$27,169	$31,414
Net Profit/Sales		-7.54%	-4.12%	-0.35%	3.24%	6.65%	9.91%	13.01%	15.96%	18.77%	21.45%	24.00%	26.43%

Book VIII

Taking Care of Business

Appendix

Appendix Table: Cash Flow

Pro Forma Cash Flow		Jan	Feb	Mar	Apr	May	Jun	Jul	Aug	Sep	Oct	Nov	Dec
Cash Received													
Cash from Operations:													
Cash Sales		$69,500	$72,975	$76,624	$80,455	$84,478	$88,702	$93,137	$97,793	$102,683	$107,817	$113,208	$118,869
Cash from Receivables		$0	$0	$0	$0	$0	$0	$0	$0	$0	$0	$0	$0
Subtotal Cash from Operations		$69,500	$72,975	$76,624	$80,455	$84,478	$88,702	$93,137	$97,793	$102,683	$107,817	$113,208	$118,869
Additional Cash Received	0.00%												
Sales Tax, VAT, HST/GST Received		$0	$0	$0	$0	$0	$0	$0	$0	$0	$0	$0	$0
New Current Borrowing		$0	$0	$0	$0	$0	$0	$0	$0	$0	$0	$0	$0
New Other Liabilities (interest-free)		$0	$0	$0	$0	$0	$0	$0	$0	$0	$0	$0	$0
New Long-term Liabilities		$0	$0	$0	$0	$0	$0	$0	$0	$0	$0	$0	$0
Sales of Other Current Assets		$0	$0	$0	$0	$0	$0	$0	$0	$0	$0	$0	$0
Sales of Long-term Assets		$0	$0	$0	$0	$0	$0	$0	$0	$0	$0	$0	$0
New Investment Received		$0	$0	$0	$0	$0	$0	$0	$0	$0	$0	$0	$0
Subtotal Cash Received		$69,500	$72,975	$76,624	$80,455	$84,478	$88,702	$93,137	$97,793	$102,683	$107,817	$113,208	$118,869
Expenditures		Jan	Feb	Mar	Apr	May	Jun	Jul	Aug	Sep	Oct	Nov	Dec
Expenditures from Operations:													
Cash Spending		$2,011	$2,098	$2,189	$2,285	$2,386	$2,491	$2,602	$2,719	$2,841	$2,969	$3,104	$3,245
Payment of Accounts Payable		$56,729	$72,627	$73,410	$74,233	$75,096	$76,003	$76,965	$77,954	$79,004	$80,106	$81,263	$82,478
Subtotal Spent on Operations		$57,740	$74,725	$75,600	$76,518	$77,482	$78,494	$79,557	$80,673	$81,845	$83,075	$84,367	$85,724
Additional Cash Spent													
Sales Tax, VAT, HST/GST Paid Out		$0	$0	$0	$0	$0	$0	$0	$0	$0	$0	$0	$0
Principal Repayment of Current Borrowing		$0	$0	$0	$0	$0	$0	$0	$0	$0	$0	$0	$0
Other Liabilities Principal Repayment		$0	$0	$0	$0	$0	$0	$0	$0	$0	$0	$0	$0
Long-term Liabilities Principal Repayment		$0	$0	$0	$0	$0	$0	$0	$0	$0	$0	$0	$0
Purchase Other Current Assets		$0	$0	$0	$0	$0	$0	$0	$0	$0	$0	$0	$0
Purchase Long-term Assets		$0	$0	$0	$0	$0	$0	$0	$0	$0	$0	$0	$0
Dividends		$3,000	$3,000	$3,000	$3,000	$3,000	$3,000	$3,000	$3,000	$3,000	$3,000	$3,000	$3,000
Subtotal Cash Spent		$60,740	$77,725	$78,600	$79,518	$80,482	$81,494	$82,557	$83,673	$84,845	$86,075	$87,367	$88,724
Net Cash Flow		$8,760	($4,760)	($1,976)	$937	$3,996	$7,207	$10,580	$14,120	$17,838	$21,742	$25,841	$30,145
Cash Balance		$158,760	$154,009	$152,033	$152,970	$156,966	$164,173	$174,753	$188,873	$206,712	$228,454	$254,295	$284,440

Appendix

Appendix Table: Balance Sheet

Pro Forma Balance Sheet

	Starting Balances	Jan	Feb	Mar	Apr	May	Jun	Jul	Aug	Sep	Oct	Nov	Dec
Assets													
Current Assets													
Cash	$150,000	$158,760	$154,009	$152,033	$152,970	$156,966	$164,173	$174,753	$188,873	$206,712	$228,454	$254,295	$284,440
Other Current Assets	$20,000	$20,000	$20,000	$20,000	$20,000	$20,000	$20,000	$20,000	$20,000	$20,000	$20,000	$20,000	$20,000
Total Current Assets	$170,000	$178,760	$174,009	$172,033	$172,970	$176,966	$184,173	$194,753	$208,873	$226,712	$248,454	$274,295	$304,440
Long-term Assets													
Long-term Assets	$25,000	$28,000	$31,000	$34,000	$37,000	$40,000	$43,000	$46,000	$49,000	$52,000	$55,000	$58,000	$61,000
Accumulated Depreciation	$0	$500	$1,000	$1,500	$2,000	$2,500	$3,000	$3,500	$4,000	$4,500	$5,000	$5,500	$6,000
Total Long-term Assets	$25,000	$27,500	$30,000	$32,500	$35,000	$37,500	$40,000	$42,500	$45,000	$47,500	$50,000	$52,500	$55,000
Total Assets	$195,000	$206,260	$204,009	$204,533	$207,970	$214,466	$224,173	$237,253	$253,873	$274,212	$298,454	$326,795	$359,440
Liabilities and Capital													
Current Liabilities													
Accounts Payable	$1,000	$17,498	$18,254	$19,047	$19,881	$20,756	$21,674	$22,639	$23,652	$24,715	$25,832	$27,004	$28,236
Current Borrowing	$0	$0	$0	$0	$0	$0	$0	$0	$0	$0	$0	$0	$0
Other Current Liabilities	$0	$0	$0	$0	$0	$0	$0	$0	$0	$0	$0	$0	$0
Subtotal Current Liabilities	$1,000	$17,498	$18,254	$19,047	$19,881	$20,756	$21,674	$22,639	$23,652	$24,715	$25,832	$27,004	$28,236
Long-term Liabilities	$100,000	$100,000	$100,000	$100,000	$100,000	$100,000	$100,000	$100,000	$100,000	$100,000	$100,000	$100,000	$100,000
Total Liabilities	$101,000	$117,498	$118,254	$119,047	$119,881	$120,756	$121,674	$122,639	$123,652	$124,715	$125,832	$127,004	$128,236
Paid-in Capital	$99,500	$99,500	$99,500	$99,500	$99,500	$99,500	$99,500	$99,500	$99,500	$99,500	$99,500	$99,500	$99,500
Retained Earnings	($5,500)	($5,500)	($5,500)	($5,500)	($5,500)	($5,500)	($5,500)	($5,500)	($5,500)	($5,500)	($5,500)	($5,500)	($5,500)
Earnings	$0	($5,238)	($8,245)	($8,514)	($5,911)	($290)	$8,499	$20,614	$36,221	$55,496	$78,622	$105,790	$137,204
Total Capital	$94,000	$88,762	$85,755	$85,486	$88,089	$93,710	$102,499	$114,614	$130,221	$149,496	$172,622	$199,790	$231,204
Total Liabilities and Capital	$195,000	$206,260	$204,009	$204,533	$207,970	$214,466	$224,173	$237,253	$253,873	$274,212	$298,454	$326,795	$359,440
Net Worth	$94,000	$88,762	$85,755	$85,486	$88,089	$93,710	$102,499	$114,614	$130,221	$149,496	$172,622	$199,790	$231,204

Book VIII

Taking Care of Business

Index

• **C** •

• *N* •

FOR DUMMIES®

The easy way to get more done and have more fun

SONAL FINANCE & BUSINESS

1-894-41300-8

0-470-83320-3

Personal Finance For Canadians

1-894-41329-6

Also available:

Accounting For Dummies
(0-7645-5314-3)

Business Plans Kit For Dummies
(0-7645-5365-8)

Canadian Small Business Kit For Dummies
(1-894-41304-0)

Managing For Dummies
(0-7645-1771-6)

Mutual Funds For Canadians For Dummies
(0-470-83251-7)

QuickBooks All-in-One Desk Reference For Dummies
(0-7645-1963-8)

Resumes For Dummies
(0-7645-5471-9)

Starting an eBay Business For Dummies
(0-7645-1547-0)

Taxes For Canadians For Dummies 2003
(1-894-41338-5)

OME, GARDEN, FOOD & WINE

0-7645-5295-3

1-894-41337-7

0-7645-5250-3

Also available:

Bartending For Dummies
(0-7645-5051-9)

Christmas Cooking For Dummies
(0-7645-5407-7)

Cookies For Dummies
(0-7645-5390-9)

Diabetes Cookbook For Dummies
(0-7645-5230-9)

Grilling For Dummies
(0-7645-5076-4)

Home Maintenance For Dummies
(0-7645-5215-5)

Slow Cookers For Dummies
(0-7645-5240-6)

Wine For Dummies
(0-7645-5114-0)

NESS, SPORTS, HOBBIES & PETS

0-7645-5167-1

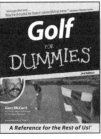

0-7645-5146-9

0-7645-5106-X

Also available:

Cats For Dummies
(0-7645-5275-9)

Chess For Dummies
(0-7645-5003-9)

Dog Training For Dummies
(0-7645-5286-4)

Knitting For Dummies
(0-7645-5395-X)

Labrador Retrievers For Dummies
(0-7645-5281-3)

Martial Arts For Dummies
(0-7645-5358-5)

Piano For Dummies
(0-7645-5105-1)

Pilates For Dummies
(0-7645-5397-6)

Power Yoga For Dummies
(0-7645-5342-9)

Puppies For Dummies
(0-7645-5255-4)

Rock Guitar For Dummies
(0-7645-5356-9)

Weight Training For Dummies
(0-7645-5168-X)

---

ilable wherever books are sold.
to www.dummies.com or call 1-800-567-4797 to order direct

FOR DUMMIES®

A world of resources to help you grow

TRAVEL

0-7645-5453-0

0-7645-5438-7

0-7645-5444-1

Also available:

America's National Parks For Dummies
(0-7645-5493-X)

Caribbean For Dummies
(0-7645-5445-X)

Cruise Vacations For Dummies 2003
(0-7645-5459-X)

Europe For Dummies
(0-7645-5456-5)

Ireland For Dummies
(0-7645-5455-7)

France For Dummies
(0-7645-6292-4)

Las Vegas For Dummies
(0-7645-5448-4)

London For Dummies
(0-7645-5416-6)

Mexico's Beach Resorts For Dummies
(0-7645-6262-2)

Paris For Dummies
(0-7645-5494-8)

RV Vacations For Dummies
(0-7645-5443-3)

EDUCATION & TEST PREPARATION

0-7645-5194-9

0-7645-5325-9

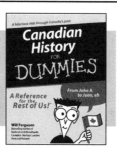
1-894-41319-9

Also available:

The ACT For Dummies
(0-7645-5474-3)

Chemistry For Dummies
(0-7645-5430-1)

English Grammar For Dummies
(0-7645-5322-4)

French For Dummies
(0-7645-5193-0)

GMAT For Dummies
(0-7645-5251-1)

Inglés Para Dummies
(0-7645-5427-1)

Italian For Dummies
(0-7645-5196-5)

Research Papers For Dumm
(0-7645-5426-3)

SAT I For Dummies
(0-7645-5472-7)

U.S. History For Dummies
(0-7645-5249-X)

World History For Dummie
(0-7645-5242-2)

HEALTH, SELF-HELP & SPIRITUALITY

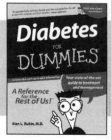
0-7645-5154-X

0-7645-5302-X

0-7645-5418-2

Also available:

The Bible For Dummies
(0-7645-5296-1)

Controlling Cholesterol For Dummies
(0-7645-5440-9)

Dating For Dummies
(0-7645-5072-1)

Dieting For Dummies
(0-7645-5126-4)

High Blood Pressure For Dummies
(0-7645-5424-7)

Judaism For Dummies
(0-7645-5299-6)

Menopause For Dummies
(0-7645-5458-1)

Nutrition For Dummies
(0-7645-5180-9)

Potty Training For Dummi
(0-7645-5417-4)

Pregnancy For Dummies
(0-7645-5074-8)

Rekindling Romance For Dummies
(0-7645-5303-8)

Religion For Dummies
(0-7645-5264-3)

Available wherever books are sold. Go to www.dummies.com or call 1-800-567-4797 to order direct

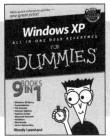
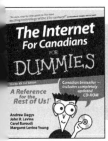